NEW TESTAMENT

CONTEMPORARY ENGLISH VERSION

NEW TESTAMENT

CONTEMPORARY ENGLISH VERSION

American Bible Society
New York

New Testament

Printed in the United States of America
CEV NT—105064
ABS-1993-65,000-165,000-W3

Translating the Contemporary English Version

Translation it is that opens the window, to let in the light; that breaks the shell, that we may eat the kernel; that puts aside the curtain, that we may look into the most holy place; that removes the cover of the well, that we may come by the water ("The Translators to the Reader." King James Version, 1611).

The Bible was written to be read! This means that a faithful translation of the Bible must be both *reliable* and *readable*. It must be a text that can be trusted and one that is suitable for both public and private reading, and also for memorizing.

The *Contemporary English New Testament* was translated with these goals in mind. Every attempt has been made to produce a text that is faithful to the *meaning* of the original and that can be read with ease and understanding by readers of all ages.

The translators of the *King James Version* had similar aims. According to the introduction that was published in the earliest editions of the KJV, the translators realized that a Hebrew or Greek word could not always be translated in the same way. They also knew that in order to make the *meaning* clear for their readers, they must often use a *form* that was very different from that of the original languages, but still true to the sacred text. That same translation principle has been followed in the CEV.

Like all reliable translations, the *Contemporary English New Testament* is made directly from the original Greek and is not an adaptation of any existing translation or translations. But not everyone who knows the biblical languages can do for today's readers what the KJV translators hoped to do for their own generation. Almost any scholar can produce a literal rendering of the original languages. But this is only the *first* step in the translation process. Two important questions must still be asked: "What do the words mean?" and "What is the most accurate and natural way to express this meaning in contemporary English?"

Not only was the Bible written to be read. It was written to be *understood*. But many readers fail to understand the meaning of a passage, because the translation itself keeps them from doing so. For example, "a kind of firstfruits of all he created" (James 1.18) may faithfully represent the *form* of the Greek text, but the *meaning* is certainly not clear, except for the reader who has special training in biblical backgrounds.

Traditional translations use words such as *justification, righteousness, redemption, reconciliation, propitiation, atonement, salvation, sanctification,* and *repentance.* All of these words are absent from the *Contemporary English Version.* One reason for this absence is that they are not used in everyday English. But there is an even more important reason: these are nouns, but they describe *actions* that God or people do. For example, the word *salvation* means "God saves people." *Repentance* is more difficult, because it refers to more than one event: Someone sinned and then turned from sin. In the *CEV,* each of these words may be translated in several different ways, depending on the special meaning they may have in a particular verse.

Many people are surprised to learn that one of the hardest words to translate is *grace!* The word is simple enough to pronounce, but it must always be explained. This is because in the New Testament *grace* means something far different from what it does in ordinary speech. The main problem is that the phrase "the grace of God" describes God in action, treating us much better than we deserve.

Acts 20.32 will show the difference between the way *grace* appears in traditional translations and how it is restructured by the *Contemporary English Version.* By following the form of the Greek text and using traditional language, the verse may be translated: "Now I commit you to God and to the word of his grace, which can build you up and give you an inheritance among all those who are sanctified."

"The word of his grace" is difficult for several reasons: (1) "word" means "message;" (2) "of" merely shows that there is some relation between "word" and "grace," but it does not tell what the actual relation is; and (3) "grace" is an event, not an object.

There are also other problems in the verse: (1) "build you up" is not contemporary English usage; (2) "inheritance" is used in the special biblical sense of "what belongs to God's people;" (3) "those who are sanctified" is a New Testament way of referring to God's people; and (4) in the Greek text the pronoun "which" refers to "word," rather than to "grace."

In the *Contemporary English Version* every word, phrase, and clause of the original was carefully studied by the translators. Then, with equal care, they tried to find the best way to translate the verse so it could be easily read and understood. As a result, the form is very different, but the meaning is both *accurate* and *clear;* "Now I place you in God's care. Remember the message about his great kindness! This message can help you and give you what belongs to you as God's people."

The *Contemporary English Version* New Testament has been translated directly from the Greek text published by the United Bible Societies (third edition, corrected, 1983). Drafts of the *Contemporary English Version* New Testament in its early stages were sent for review and comment to a number of biblical scholars, theologians, and educators representing a wide variety of denominations. In addition, drafts were sent for response to all English-speaking Bible Societies and more than forty UBS translation consultants around the world. Final approval of the text was given by the American Bible Society's Board of Trustees upon recommendation of its Translations Subcommittee.

At the back of this book is a *Word List* which explains a number of terms and phrases, along with some helpful *Maps*. The New Testament books are each preceded by an introduction (*About This Book*), and an outline of contents (*A Quick Look at This Book*). To help the reader, three kinds of notes are included: (1) notes that explain important differences in the Greek manuscripts, (2) notes that give another translation of the source text, and (3) notes that provide helpful information about Bible history and customs.

Contents

Matthew Tells the Good News 1
Mark Tells the Good News 57
Luke Tells the Good News 92
John Tells the Good News 150

The Acts of the Apostles 191

Paul's Letter to the Church in Rome 242
Paul's First Letter to the Church in Corinth 262
Paul's Second Letter to the Church in Corinth 281
Paul's Letter to the Churches in Galatia 294
Paul's Letter to the Church in Ephesus 301
Paul's Letter to the Church in Philippi 309
Paul's Letter to the Church in Colossae 315
Paul's First Letter to the Church in Thessalonica 320
Paul's Second Letter to the Church in Thessalonica 325
Paul's First Letter to Timothy 328
Paul's Second Letter to Timothy 334
Paul's Letter to Titus 339
Paul's Letter to Philemon 342

The Letter to the Hebrews 344
A Letter from James 360
Peter's First Letter 365
Peter's Second Letter 372
John's First Letter 376
John's Second Letter 382
John's Third Letter 383
A Letter from Jude 384

Revelation 387

Word List 415
Maps 421
Special Reader's Helps 425

About the New Testament

⟨≈⟩

In the first century A.D., Christians and Jews used the same Scriptures, which Christians later called the Old Testament. Both of these communities of faith usually used these Scriptures in a Greek translation (called the Septuagint) instead of in the original languages of Hebrew and Aramaic. This collection of sacred writings in Greek was the Bible of the early Christians. They found proof in these writings that Jesus is the Messiah and the Son of God, and they also found there how God wanted them to live.

Later in the first century, Christians started writing the books that would become the New Testament. These were the books about the life and teaching of Jesus (called Gospels), the letters of Paul and others, and the books of the Acts of the Apostles and Revelation. All of these were written in Greek, which was a language that people all over the Roman empire could understand. By the second century, these books were widely used by Christians for preaching, teaching, worshiping, and telling about their faith.

The writings of the New Testament are arranged in an order that gives the greatest value to the four books (Gospels) about Jesus, since they tell about his life and teaching, his miracles, his saving death on a cross, and his rising to life. These four Gospels (Matthew, Mark, Luke, and John) take up almost half of the New Testament, which is another reason why they are placed first.

The Acts of the Apostles follows the four Gospels. It actually continues the Gospel of Luke and shows the connection between the ministry of Jesus and the mission of the early church. Acts shows how the followers of Jesus answered the question of whether Gentiles could also become Christians.

The letters of Paul follow next, and they are arranged roughly in order of their length (from Romans to Philemon). Most of these letters were written to churches Paul had started, and in them he deals with problems that had come up. Paul's letters are then followed by a group of writings known as the "general letters," because they are mostly addressed to a general audience and were to be circulated to other followers. These letters are also arranged roughly in order of their length (From Hebrews to 3 John and Jude).

Revelation is the last book in the New Testament, and it was written to give hope and encouragement to Christians who were suffering because of their faith. It is also a prophecy and contains visions of how God will punish evil people and reward his faithful followers.

The New Testament is the world's most widely read book! More than 70 million copies are printed throughout the world each year, and the complete New Testament has been translated into more than seven hundred languages.

How can a book that is almost two thousand years old be in such demand and influence so many lives today? Why are people so interested in a young Jewish carpenter named Jesus, who lived his short life without going more than seventy miles from the small village where he was born? The New Testament is in demand because it tells the good news about Jesus Christ! And this good news is God's powerful way of saving *everyone* who has faith in Jesus. In the New Testament we learn that God is kind and that he loved the people of this world so much that he sent Jesus Christ into the world to save us all.

For these reasons, and many more, people keep coming to the New Testament for the light and power it gives for daily living. Jesus promised his followers that God's Spirit would always guide them to understand the message of the Scriptures. And so, in the New Testament we are not reading dead words from the past. Here we meet Jesus Christ, the living Word of God.

Matthew Tells the Good News

ABOUT THIS BOOK

The Sermon on the Mount (5.1—7.28), the Lord's Prayer (6.9–13), and the Golden Rule (7.12: "Treat others as you want them to treat you") are all in this book. It is perhaps the best known and the most quoted of all the books that have ever been written about Jesus. That is one reason why Matthew was placed first among the four books about Jesus called Gospels.

One of the most important ideas found here is that God expects his people to obey him, and this is what is meant by the Greek word that appears in many translations as *righteousness*. It is used seven times by Matthew, but only once by Luke, and not at all by Mark. So it is an important clue to much of what Matthew wants his readers to understand about the teaching of Jesus.

Jesus first uses this word at his own baptism, when he tells John the Baptist, "We must do all that God wants us to do" (3.15). Then, during his Sermon on the Mount, he speaks five more times of what God's people must do to obey him (5.6,10,20; 6.1,33). And finally, he reminds the chief priests and leaders of the people, "John the Baptist showed you how to do right" (21.32).

Matthew wanted to provide for the people of his time a record of Jesus' message and ministry. It is clear that the Old Testament Scriptures were very important to these people. And Matthew never fails to show when these texts point to the coming of Jesus as the Messiah sent from God. Matthew wrote this book to make sure Christians knew that their faith in Jesus as the Messiah was well anchored in the Old Testament Scriptures, and to help them grow in faith.

Matthew ends his story with the words of Jesus to his followers, which tell what they are to do after he leaves them:

I have been given all authority in heaven and on earth! Go to the people of all nations and make them my disciples. Baptize them in the name of the Father, the Son, and the Holy Spirit, and teach them to do everything I have told you. I will be with you always, even until the end of the world.

(28.18b–20)

A QUICK LOOK AT THIS BOOK

- The Ancestors and Birth of Jesus (1.1—2.23)
- The Message of John the Baptist (3.1–12)
- The Baptism and Temptation of Jesus (3.13—4.11)
- Jesus in Galilee (4.12—18.35)
- Jesus Goes from Galilee to Jerusalem (19.1—20.34)
- Jesus' Last Week: His Trial and Death (21.1—27.66)
- Jesus Is Alive (28.1–20)

The Ancestors of Jesus
(Luke 3.23–38)

1 Jesus Christ came from the family of King David and also from the family of Abraham. And this is a list of his ancestors. 2-6aFrom Abraham to King David, his ancestors were:

Abraham, Isaac, Jacob, Judah and his brothers (Judah's sons were Perez and Zerah, and their mother was Tamar), Hezron;

Ram, Amminadab, Nahshon, Salmon, Boaz (his mother was Rahab), Obed (his mother was Ruth), Jesse, and King David.

6b-11From David to the time of the exile in Babylonia, the ancestors of Jesus were:

David, Solomon (his mother had been Uriah's wife), Rehoboam, Abijah, Asa, Jehoshaphat, Jehoram;

Uzziah, Jotham, Ahaz, Hezekiah, Manasseh, Amon, Josiah, and Jehoiachin and his brothers.

12-16From the exile to the birth of Jesus, his ancestors were:

Jehoiachin, Shealtiel, Zerubbabel, Abiud, Eliakim, Azor, Zadok, Achim;

Eliud, Eleazer, Matthan, Jacob, and Joseph, the husband of Mary, the mother of Jesus, who is called the Messiah.

17There were fourteen generations from Abraham to David. There were also fourteen from David to the exile in Babylonia and fourteen more to the birth of the Messiah.

The Birth of Jesus
(Luke 2.1–7)

18This is how Jesus Christ was born. A young woman named Mary was engaged to Joseph from King David's family. But before they were married, she learned that she was going to have a baby by God's Holy Spirit. 19Joseph was a good man[a] and did not want to embarrass Mary in front of everyone. So he decided to quietly call off the wedding.

20While Joseph was thinking about this, an angel from the Lord came to him in a dream. The angel said, "Joseph, the baby that Mary will have is from the Holy Spirit. Go ahead and marry her. 21Then after her baby is born, name him Jesus,[b] because he will save his people from their sins."

22So God's promise came true, just as the prophet had said, 23"A virgin will have a baby boy, and he will be called Immanuel," which means "God is with us."

24After Joseph woke up, he and Mary were soon married, just as the Lord's angel had told him to do. 25But they did not live together before her baby was born. Then Joseph named him Jesus.

The Wise Men

2 When Jesus was born in the village of Bethlehem in Judea, Herod was king. During this time some wise men[c] from the east came to Jerusalem 2and said, "Where is the child born to be king of the Jews? We saw his star in the east[d] and have come to worship him."

3When King Herod heard about this, he was worried, and so was everyone else in Jerusalem. 4Herod brought together all the chief priests and the

---

[a]*good man*: Or "kind man," or "man who always did the right thing." [b]*name him Jesus*: In Hebrew the name "Jesus" means "the Lord saves." [c]*wise men*: People famous for studying the stars. [d]*his star in the east*: Or "his star rise."

teachers of the Law of Moses and asked them, "Where will the Messiah be born?"

5They told him, "He will be born in Bethlehem, just as the prophet wrote,

6'Bethlehem in the land
of Judea,
you are very important
among the towns of Judea.
From your town
will come a leader,
who will be like a shepherd
for my people Israel.' "

7Herod secretly called in the wise men and asked them when they had first seen the star. **8**He told them, "Go to Bethlehem and search carefully for the child. As soon as you find him, let me know. I want to go and worship him too."

9The wise men listened to what the king said and then left. And the star they had seen in the east went on ahead of them until it stopped over the place where the child was. **10**They were thrilled and excited to see the star.

11When the men went into the house and saw the child with Mary, his mother, they kneeled down and worshiped him. They took out their gifts of gold, frankincense, and myrrh*e* and gave them to him. **12**Later they were warned in a dream not to return to Herod, and they went back home by another road.

The Escape to Egypt

13After the wise men had gone, an angel from the Lord appeared to Joseph in a dream. The angel said, "Get up! Hurry and take the child and his mother to Egypt! Stay there until I tell you to return, because Herod is looking for the child and wants to kill him."

14That night Joseph got up and took his wife and the child to Egypt, **15**where they stayed until Herod died. So the Lord's promise came true, just as the prophet had said, "I called my son out of Egypt."

The Killing of the Children

16When Herod found out that the wise men from the east had tricked him, he was very angry. He gave orders for his men to kill all the boys who lived in or near Bethlehem and were two years old and younger.

17So the Lord's promise came true, just as the prophet Jeremiah had said,

18"In Ramah a voice was heard
crying and weeping loudly.
Rachel was mourning
for her children,
and she refused
to be comforted,
because they were dead."

The Return from Egypt

19After King Herod died, an angel from the Lord appeared in a dream to Joseph while he was still in Egypt. **20**The angel said, "Get up and take the child and his mother back to Israel. The people who wanted to kill him are now dead."

21Joseph got up and left with them for Israel. **22**But when he heard that Herod's son Archelaus was now ruler of Judea, he was afraid to go there. Then in a dream he was told to go to Galilee, **23**and they went to live there

---

e frankincense, and myrrh: Frankincense was a valuable powder that was burned to make a sweet smell. Myrrh was a valuable sweet-smelling powder often used in perfume.

in the town of Nazareth. So the Lord's promise came true, just as the prophet had said, "He will be called a Nazarene."[f]

The Preaching of John the Baptist
(Mark 1.1–8; Luke 3.1–18; John 1.19–28)

3 Years later John the Baptist started preaching in the desert of Judea. 2He said, "Turn back to God! The kingdom of heaven[g] will soon be here."[h]

3John was the one the prophet Isaiah was talking about, when he said,

"In the desert someone
　is shouting,
'Get the road ready
　for the Lord!
Make a straight path
　for him.' "

4John wore clothes made of camel's hair. He had a leather strap around his waist and ate grasshoppers and wild honey.

5From Jerusalem and all Judea and from the Jordan River Valley crowds of people went to John. 6They told how sorry they were for their sins, and he baptized them in the river.

7Many Pharisees and Sadducees also came to be baptized. But John said to them:

You bunch of snakes! Who warned you to run from the coming judgment? 8Do something to show that you have really given up your sins. 9And don't start telling yourselves that you belong to Abraham's family. I tell you that God can turn these stones into children for Abraham. 10An ax is ready to cut the trees down at their roots. Any tree that does not produce good fruit will be chopped down and thrown into a fire.

11I baptize you with water so that you will give up your sins.[i] But someone more powerful is going to come, and I am not good enough even to carry his sandals.[j] He will baptize you with the Holy Spirit and with fire. 12His threshing fork is in his hand, and he is ready to separate the wheat from the husks.[k] He will store the wheat in a barn and burn the husks in a fire that never goes out.

The Baptism of Jesus
(Mark 1.9–11; Luke 3.21, 22)

13Jesus left Galilee and went to the Jordan River to be baptized by John. 14But John kept objecting and said, "I ought to be baptized by you. Why have you come to me?"

15Jesus answered, "For now this is how it should be, because we must do all that God wants us to do." Then John agreed.

16So Jesus was baptized. And as soon as he came out of the water, the sky opened, and he saw the Spirit of

---

[f]*He will be called a Nazarene*: The prophet who said this is not known. [g]*kingdom of heaven*: In the Gospel of Matthew "kingdom of heaven" is used with the same meaning as "God's kingdom" in Mark and Luke. [h]*will soon be here*: Or "is already here." [i]*so that you will give up your sins*: Or "because you have given up your sins." [j]*carry his sandals*: This was one of the duties of a slave. [k]*His threshing fork is in his hand, and he is ready to separate the wheat from the husks*: After Jewish farmers had trampled out the grain, they used a large fork to pitch the grain and the husks into the air. Wind would blow away the light husks, and the grain would fall back to the ground, where it could be gathered up.

God coming down on him like a dove. [17]Then a voice from heaven said, "This is my own dear Son, and I am pleased with him."

Jesus and the Devil
(Mark 1.12, 13; Luke 4.1–13)

4 The Holy Spirit led Jesus into the desert, so that the devil could test him. [2]After Jesus went without eating[l] for forty days and nights, he was very hungry. [3]Then the devil came to him and said, "If you are God's Son, tell these stones to turn into bread."

[4]Jesus answered, "The Scriptures say:

'No one can live only on food.
People need every word
    that God has spoken.' "

[5]Next, the devil took Jesus to the holy city and had him stand on the highest part of the temple. [6]The devil said, "If you are God's Son, jump off. The Scriptures say:

'God will give his angels
    orders about you.
They will catch you
    in their arms,
and you will not hurt
    your feet on the stones.' "

[7]Jesus answered, "The Scriptures also say, 'Don't try to test the Lord your God!' "

[8]Finally, the devil took Jesus up on a very high mountain and showed him all the kingdoms on earth and their power. [9]The devil said to him, "I will give all this to you, if you will bow down and worship me."

[10]Jesus answered, "Go away Satan! The Scriptures say:

'Worship the Lord your God
    and serve only him.' "

[11]Then the devil left Jesus, and angels came to help him.

Jesus Begins His Work
(Mark 1.14, 15; Luke 4.14, 15)

[12]When Jesus heard that John had been put in prison, he went to Galilee. [13]But instead of staying in Nazareth, Jesus moved to Capernaum. This town was beside Lake Galilee in the territory of Zebulun and Naphtali.[m] [14]So God's promise came true, just as the prophet Isaiah had said,

[15]"Listen, lands of Zebulun
    and Naphtali,
lands along the road
to the sea and west
    of the Jordan!
Listen Galilee,
    land of the Gentiles!
[16]Although your people
    live in darkness,
they will see
    a bright light.
Although they live
    in the shadow of death,
a light will shine
    on them."

[17]Then Jesus started preaching, "Turn back to God! The kingdom of heaven will soon be here."[m]

Jesus Chooses Four Fishermen
(Mark 1.16–20; Luke 5.1–11)

[18]While Jesus was walking along the shore of Lake Galilee, he saw two

---

[l]*went without eating*: The Jewish people sometimes went without eating (also called "fasting") to show their love for God and to become better followers. [m]*Zebulun and Naphtali*: In Old Testament times these tribes were in northern Palestine, and in New Testament times many Gentiles lived where these tribes had once been. [n]*The kingdom of heaven will soon be here*: See the two notes at 3.2.

brothers. One was Simon, also known as Peter, and the other was Andrew. They were fishermen, and they were casting their net into the lake. 19Jesus said to them, "Come with me! I will teach you how to bring in people instead of fish." 20Right then the two brothers dropped their nets and went with him.

21Jesus walked on until he saw James and John, the sons of Zebedee. They were in a boat with their father, mending their nets. Jesus asked them to come with him too. 22Right away they left the boat and their father and went with Jesus.

Jesus Teaches, Preaches, and Heals
(Luke 6.17–19)

23Jesus went all over Galilee, teaching in the Jewish meeting places and preaching the good news about God's kingdom. He also healed every kind of disease and sickness. 24News about him spread all over Syria, and people with every kind of sickness or disease were brought to him. Some of them had a lot of demons in them, others were thought to be crazy,*o* and still others could not walk. But Jesus healed them all.

25Large crowds followed Jesus from Galilee and the region around the ten cities known as Decapolis.*p* They also came from Jerusalem, Judea, and from across the Jordan River.

The Sermon on the Mount

5 When Jesus saw the crowds, he went up on the side of a mountain and sat down.*q*

Blessings
(Luke 6.20–23)

Jesus' disciples gathered around him, 2and he taught them:
> 3God blesses those people
> 　who depend only on him.
> They belong to the kingdom
> 　of heaven!*r*
> 4God blesses those people
> 　who grieve.
> 　They will find comfort!
> 5God blesses those people
> 　who are humble.
> The earth will belong
> 　to them!
> 6God blesses those people
> who want to obey him*s*
> 　more than to eat or drink.
> They will be given
> 　what they want!
> 7God blesses those people
> 　who are merciful.
> They will be treated
> 　with mercy!
> 8God blesses those people
> 　whose hearts are pure.
> 　They will see him!
> 9God blesses those people
> 　who make peace.
> They will be called
> 　his children!

---

o thought to be crazy: In ancient times people with epilepsy were thought to be crazy. *p the ten cities known as Decapolis*: A group of ten cities east of Samaria and Galilee, where the people followed the Greek way of life. *q sat down*: Teachers in the ancient world, including Jewish teachers, usually sat down when they taught. *r They belong to the kingdom of heaven*: Or "The kingdom of heaven belongs to them." *s who want to obey him*: Or "who want to do right" or "who want everyone to be treated right."

10God blesses those people
who are treated badly
for doing right.
They belong to the kingdom
of heaven.*t*

11God will bless you when people insult you, mistreat you, and tell all kinds of evil lies about you because of me. 12Be happy and excited! You will have a great reward in heaven. People did these same things to the prophets who lived long ago.

Salt and Light
(Mark 9.50; Luke 14.34, 35)

13You are like salt for everyone on earth. But if salt no longer tastes like salt, how can it make food salty? All it is good for is to be thrown out and walked on.

14You are like light for the whole world. A city built on top of a hill cannot be hidden, 15and no one would light a lamp and put it under a clay pot. A lamp is placed on a lamp stand, where it can give light to everyone in the house. 16Make your light shine, so that others will see the good that you do and will praise your Father in heaven.

The Law of Moses

17Don't suppose that I came to do away with the Law and the Prophets.*u* I did not come to do away with them, but to give them their full meaning. 18Heaven and earth may disappear. But I prom-

ise you that not even a period or comma will ever disappear from the Law. Everything written in it must happen.

19If you reject even the least important command in the Law and teach others to do the same, you will be the least important person in the kingdom of heaven. But if you obey and teach others its commands, you will have an important place in the kingdom. 20You must obey God's commands better than the Pharisees and the teachers of the Law obey them. If you don't, I promise you that you will never get into the kingdom of heaven.

Anger

21You know that our ancestors were told, "Do not murder" and "A murderer must be brought to trial." 22But I promise you that if you are angry with someone,*v* you will have to stand trial. If you call someone a fool, you will be taken to court. And if you say that someone is worthless, you will be in danger of the fires of hell.

23So if you are about to place your gift on the altar and remember that someone is angry with you, 24leave your gift there in front of the altar. Make peace with that person, then come back and offer your gift to God.

25Before you are dragged into court, make friends with the person who has accused you of doing wrong. If you don't, you will be

---

*t*They belong to the kingdom of heaven: See the note at 5.3.   *u*the Law and the Prophets: The Jewish Scriptures, that is, the Old Testament.   *v*someone: In verses 22-24 the Greek text has "brother," which may refer to people in general or to other followers.

handed over to the judge and then to the officer who will put you in jail. 26I promise you that you will not get out until you have paid the last cent you owe.

Marriage

27You know the commandment which says, "Be faithful in marriage." 28But I tell you that if you look at another woman and want her, you are already unfaithful in your thoughts. 29If your right eye causes you to sin, poke it out and throw it away. It is better to lose one part of your body, than for your whole body to end up in hell. 30If your right hand causes you to sin, chop it off and throw it away! It is better to lose one part of your body, than for your whole body to be thrown into hell.

Divorce
(Matthew 19.9; Mark 10.11, 12; Luke 16.18)

31You have been taught that a man who divorces his wife must write out divorce papers for her.*w* 32But I tell you not to divorce your wife unless she has committed some terrible sexual sin.*x* If you divorce her, you will cause her to be unfaithful, just as any man who marries her is guilty of taking another man's wife.

Promises

33You know that our ancestors were told, "Don't use the Lord's name to make a promise unless you are going to keep it." 34But I tell you not to swear by anything when you make a promise! Heaven is God's throne, so don't swear by heaven. 35The earth is God's footstool, so don't swear by the earth. Jerusalem is the city of the great king, so don't swear by it. 36Don't swear by your own head. You cannot make one hair white or black. 37When you make a promise, say only "Yes" or "No." Anything else comes from the devil.

Revenge
(Luke 6.29, 30)

38You know that you have been taught, "An eye for an eye and a tooth for a tooth." 39But I tell you not to try to get even with a person who has done something to you. When someone slaps your right cheek,*y* turn and let that person slap your other cheek. 40If someone sues you for your shirt, give up your coat as well. 41If a soldier forces you to carry his pack one mile, carry it two miles.*z* 42When people ask you for something, give it to them. When they want to borrow money, loan it to them.

---

wwrite out divorce papers for her: Jewish men could divorce their wives, but the women could not divorce their husbands. The purpose of writing these papers was to make it harder for a man to divorce his wife. Before this law was made, all a man had to do was to send his wife away and say that she was no longer his wife. *xsome terrible sexual sin*: This probably refers to the laws about the wrong kinds of marriages that are forbidden in Leviticus or to some serious sexual sin. *yright cheek*: A slap on the right cheek was a bad insult. *ztwo miles*: A Roman soldier had the right to force a person to carry his pack as far as one mile.

Love
(Luke 6.27, 28, 32–36)

43You have heard people say, "Love your neighbors and hate your enemies." **44**But I tell you to love your enemies and pray for anyone who mistreats you. **45**Then you will be acting like your Father in heaven. He makes the sun rise on both good and bad people. And he sends rain for the ones who do right and for the ones who do wrong. **46**If you love only those people who love you, will God reward you for that? Even tax collectors*ᵃ* love their friends. **47**If you greet only your friends, what's so great about that? Don't even unbelievers do that? **48**But you must always act like your Father in heaven.

Giving

6 When you do good deeds, don't try to show off. If you do, you won't get a reward from your Father in heaven.
2When you give to the poor, don't blow a loud horn. That's what showoffs do in the meeting places and on the street corners, because they are always looking for praise. I promise you that they already have their reward. **3**When you give to the poor, don't let anyone know about it.*ᵇ* **4**Then your gift will be given in secret. Your Father knows what is done in secret, and he will reward you.

Prayer
(Luke 11.2–4)

5When you pray, don't be like those showoffs who love to stand up and pray in the meeting places and on the street corners. They do this just to look good. I promise you that they already have their reward.
6When you pray, go into a room alone and close the door. Pray to your Father in private. He knows what is done in private, and he will reward you.
7When you pray, don't talk on and on as people do who don't know God. They think God likes to hear long prayers. **8**Don't be like them. Your Father knows what you need before you ask.
9You should pray like this:
Our Father in heaven,
   help us to honor
      your name.
10Come and set up
   your kingdom,
so that everyone on earth
   will obey you,
as you are obeyed
   in heaven.
11Give us our food for today.*ᶜ*
12Forgive our sins,
   as we forgive others.*ᵈ*

ᵃtax collectors: These were usually Jewish people who paid the Romans for the right to collect taxes. They were hated by other Jews who thought of them as traitors to their country and to their religion. *ᵇdon't let anyone know about it*: The Greek text has, "Don't let your left hand know what your right hand is doing." *ᶜour food for today*: Or "the food that we need" or "our food for the coming day." *ᵈsins . . . others*: Or "what we owe . . . what others owe."

13Keep us from being tempted and protect us from evil.*e*

14If you forgive others for the wrongs they do to you, your Father in heaven will forgive you. 15But if you don't forgive others, your Father will not forgive your sins.

Worshiping God by Going without Eating

16When you go without eating,*f* don't try to look gloomy as those showoffs do when they go without eating. I promise you that they already have their reward. 17Instead, comb your hair and wash your face. 18Then others won't know that you are going without eating. But your Father sees what is done in private, and he will reward you.

Treasures in Heaven
(Luke 12.33, 34)

19Don't store up treasures on earth! Moths and rust can destroy them, and thieves can break in and steal them. 20Instead, store up your treasures in heaven, where moths and rust cannot destroy them, and thieves cannot break in and steal them. 21Your heart will always be where your treasure is.

Light
(Luke 11.34–36)

22Your eyes are like a window for your body. When they are good, you have all the light you need. 23But when your eyes are bad, everything is dark. If the light inside you is dark, you surely are in the dark.

Money
(Luke 16.13)

24You cannot be the slave of two masters! You will like one more than the other or be more loyal to one than the other. You cannot serve both God and money.

Worry
(Luke 12.22–31)

25I tell you not to worry about your life. Don't worry about having something to eat, drink, or wear. Isn't life more than food or clothing? 26Look at the birds in the sky! They don't plant or harvest. They don't even store grain in barns. Yet your Father in heaven takes care of them. Aren't you worth more than birds?

27Can worry make you live longer?*g* 28Why worry about clothes? Look how the wild flowers grow. They don't work hard to make their clothes. 29But I tell you that Solomon with all his wealth*h* was not as well clothed as one of them. 30God gives such beauty to everything that grows in the fields, even though it is here today and thrown into a fire tomorrow. He will surely do even

---

*e*evil: Or "the evil one," that is, the devil. Some manuscripts add, "The kingdom, the power, and the glory are yours forever. Amen." *f*without eating: See the note at 4.2. *g*live longer: Or "grow taller." *h*Solomon with all his wealth: The Jewish people thought that Solomon was the richest person who had ever lived.

more for you! Why do you have such little faith?

31Don't worry and ask yourselves, "Will we have anything to eat? Will we have anything to drink? Will we have any clothes to wear?" **32**Only people who don't know God are always worrying about such things. Your Father in heaven knows that you need all of these. **33**But more than anything else, put God's work first and do what he wants. Then all the other things will be yours as well.

34Don't worry about tomorrow. It will take care of itself. You have enough to worry about today.

Judging Others
(Luke 6.37, 38, 41, 42)

7 Don't condemn others, and God will not condemn you. **2**God will be as hard on you as you are on others! He will treat you exactly as you treat them.

3You can see the speck in your friend's eye, but you don't notice the log in your own eye. **4**How can you say, "My friend, let me take the speck out of your eye," when you don't see the log in your own eye? **5**You're nothing but show-offs! First, take the log out of your own eye. Then you can see how to take the speck out of your friend's eye.

6Don't give to dogs what belongs to God. They will only turn and attack you. Don't throw pearls down in front of pigs. They will trample all over them.

Ask, Search, Knock
(Luke 11.9–13)

7Ask, and you will receive. Search, and you will find. Knock, and the door will be opened for you. **8**Everyone who asks will receive. Everyone who searches will find. And the door will be opened for everyone who knocks. **9**Would any of you give your hungry child a stone, if the child asked for some bread? **10**Would you give your child a snake if the child asked for a fish? **11**As bad as you are, you still know how to give good gifts to your children. But your heavenly Father is even more ready to give good things to people who ask.

12Treat others as you want them to treat you. This is what the Law and the Prophets*i* are all about.

The Narrow Gate
(Luke 13.24)

13Go in through the narrow gate. The gate to destruction is wide, and the road that leads there is easy to follow. A lot of people go through that gate. **14**But the gate to life is very narrow. The road that leads there is so hard to follow that only a few people find it.

A Tree and Its Fruit
(Luke 6.43–45)

15Watch out for false prophets! They dress up like sheep, but inside they are wolves who have

ithe Law and the Prophets: See the note at 5.17.

come to attack you. 16You can tell what they are by what they do. No one picks grapes or figs from thorn bushes. 17A good tree produces good fruit, and a bad tree produces bad fruit. 18A good tree cannot produce bad fruit, and a bad tree cannot produce good fruit. 19Every tree that produces bad fruit will be chopped down and burned. 20You can tell who the false prophets are by their deeds.

A Warning
(Luke 13.26, 27)

21Not everyone who calls me their Lord will get into the kingdom of heaven. Only the ones who obey my Father in heaven will get in. 22On the day of judgment many will call me their Lord. They will say, "We preached in your name, and in your name we forced out demons and worked many miracles." 23But I will tell them, "I will have nothing to do with you! Get out of my sight, you evil people!"

Two Builders
(Luke 6.47–49)

24Anyone who hears and obeys these teachings of mine is like a wise person who built a house on solid rock. 25Rain poured down, rivers flooded, and winds beat against that house. But it did not fall, because it was built on solid rock.

26Anyone who hears my teachings and does not obey them is like a foolish person who built a house on sand. 27The rain poured down, the rivers flooded, and the winds blew and beat against that house. Finally, it fell with a crash.

28When Jesus finished speaking, the crowds were surprised at his teaching. 29He taught them like someone with authority, and not like their teachers of the Law of Moses.

Jesus Heals a Man
(Mark 1.40–45; Luke 5.12–16)

8 As Jesus came down the mountain, he was followed by large crowds. 2Suddenly a man with leprosy[j] came and kneeled in front of Jesus. He said, "Lord, you have the power to make me well, if only you wanted to."

3Jesus put his hand on the man and said, "I do want to! Now you are well." At once the man's leprosy disappeared. 4Jesus told him, "Don't tell anyone about this, but go and show the priest that you are well. Then take a gift to the temple just as Moses commanded, and everyone will know that you have been healed."[k]

Jesus Heals an Army Officer's Servant
(Luke 7.1–10; John 4.43–54)

5When Jesus was going into the town of Capernaum, an army officer

---

[j]*leprosy*: In biblical times the word "leprosy" was used for many different kinds of skin diseases.
[k]*everyone will know that you have been healed*: People with leprosy had to be examined by a priest and told that they were well (that is "clean") before they could once again live a normal life in the Jewish community. The gift that Moses commanded was the sacrifice of some lambs together with flour mixed with olive oil.

came up to him and said, 6"Lord, my servant is at home in such terrible pain that he can't even move."

7"I will go and heal him," Jesus replied.

8But the officer said, "Lord, I'm not good enough for you to come into my house. Just give the order, and my servant will get well. 9I have officers who give orders to me, and I have soldiers who take orders from me. I can say to one of them, 'Go!' and he goes. I can say to another, 'Come!' and he comes. I can say to my servant, 'Do this!' and he will do it."

10When Jesus heard this, he was so surprised that he turned and said to the crowd following him, "I tell you that in all of Israel I've never found anyone with this much faith! 11Many people will come from everywhere to enjoy the feast in the kingdom of heaven with Abraham, Isaac, and Jacob. 12But the ones who should have been in the kingdom will be thrown out into the dark. They will cry and grit their teeth in pain."

13Then Jesus said to the officer, "You may go home now. Your faith has made it happen."

Right then his servant was healed.

Jesus Heals Many People
(Mark 1.29–34; Luke 4.38–41)

14Jesus went to the home of Peter, where he found that Peter's mother-in-law was sick in bed with fever. 15He took her by the hand, and the fever left her. Then she got up and served Jesus a meal.

16That evening many people with demons in them were brought to Jesus. And with only a word he forced out the evil spirits and healed everyone who was sick. 17So God's promise came true, just as the prophet Isaiah had said,

"He healed our diseases
and made us well."

Some Who Wanted to Go
with Jesus
(Luke 9.57–62)

18When Jesus saw the crowd,*l* he went across Lake Galilee. 19A teacher of the Law of Moses came up to him and said, "Teacher, I'll go anywhere with you!"

20Jesus replied, "Foxes have dens, and birds have nests. But the Son of Man does not have a place to call his own."

21Another disciple said to Jesus, "Lord, let me wait till I bury my father."

22Jesus answered, "Come with me, and let the dead bury their dead." *m*

A Storm
(Mark 4.35–41; Luke 8.22–25)

23After Jesus left in a boat with his disciples, 24a terrible storm suddenly struck the lake, and waves started splashing into their boat.

Jesus was sound asleep, 25so the disciples went over to him and woke him up. They said, "Lord, save us! We're going to drown!"

26But Jesus replied, "Why are you so afraid? You surely don't have much faith." Then he got up and ordered the

---

*l*saw the crowd: Some manuscripts have "large crowd." Others have "large crowds." *m*let the dead bury their dead: For the Jewish people a proper burial of their dead was a very important duty. But Jesus teaches that following him is even more important.

wind and the waves to calm down. And
everything was calm.

27The men in the boat were
amazed and said, "Who is this? Even
the wind and the waves obey him."

Two Men with Demons in Them
(Mark 5.1–20; Luke 8.26–39)

28After Jesus had crossed the lake,
he came to shore near the town of Gadara[n] and started down the road. Two
men with demons in them came to him
from the tombs.[o] They were so fierce
that no one could travel that way.
29Suddenly they shouted, "Jesus, Son
of God, what do you want with us?
Have you come to punish us before our
time?"

30Not far from there a large herd
of pigs was feeding. 31So the demons
begged Jesus, "If you force us out,
please send us into those pigs!" 32Jesus
told them to go, and they went out of
the men and into the pigs. All at once
the pigs rushed down the steep bank
into the lake and drowned.

33The people taking care of the
pigs ran to the town and told everything, especially what had happened
to the two men. 34Everyone in town
came out to meet Jesus. When they
saw him, they begged him to leave
their part of the country.

Jesus Heals a Crippled Man
(Mark 2.1–12; Luke 5.17–26)

9 Jesus got into a boat and crossed
back over to the town where he
lived.[p] 2Some people soon brought to
him a crippled man lying on a mat.
When Jesus saw how much faith they
had, he said to the crippled man, "My
friend, don't worry! Your sins are forgiven."

3Some teachers of the Law of Moses said to themselves, "Jesus must
think he is God!"

4But Jesus knew what was in their
minds, and he said, "Why are you
thinking such evil things? 5Is it easier
for me to tell this crippled man that
his sins are forgiven or to tell him to
get up and walk? 6But I will show you
that the Son of Man has the right to
forgive sins here on earth." So Jesus
said to the man, "Get up! Pick up your
mat and go on home." 7The man got
up and went home. 8When the crowds
saw this, they were afraid[q] and praised
God for giving such authority to people.

Jesus Chooses Matthew
(Mark 2.13–17; Luke 5.27–32)

9As Jesus was leaving, he saw a
tax collector[r] named Matthew sitting
at the place for paying taxes. Jesus said
to him, "Come with me." Matthew got
up and went with him.

10Later, Jesus and his disciples
were having dinner at Matthew's
house.[s] Many tax collectors and other
sinners were also there. 11Some Pharisees asked Jesus' disciples, "Why does
your teacher eat with tax collectors and
other sinners?"

12Jesus heard them and answered,
"Healthy people don't need a doctor,
but sick people do. 13Go and learn what
the Scriptures mean when they say,
'Instead of offering sacrifices to me, I

---

[n]*Gadara*: Some manuscripts have "Gergasa." Others have "Gerasa."   [o]*tombs*: It was thought
that demons and evil spirits lived in tombs and in caves that were used for burying the dead.
[p]*where he lived*: Capernaum. See 4.13.   [q]*afraid*: Some manuscripts have "amazed."   [r]*tax
collector*: See the note at 5.46.   [s]*Matthew's house*: Or "Jesus' house."

want you to be merciful to others.' I
didn't come to invite good people to
be my followers. I came to invite sinners."

People Ask about Going
without Eating
(Mark 2.18–22; Luke 5.33–39)

14One day some followers of John
the Baptist came and asked Jesus,
"Why do we and the Pharisees often
go without eating,[t] while your disciples
never do?"

15Jesus answered:

The friends of a bridegroom
don't go without eating while he
is still with them. But the time
will come when he will be taken
from them. Then they will go
without eating.

16No one uses a new piece of
cloth to patch old clothes. The
patch would shrink and tear a
bigger hole.

17No one pours new wine into
old wineskins. The wine would
swell and burst the old skins.[u]
Then the wine would be lost, and
the skins would be ruined. New
wine must be put into new wineskins. Both the skins and the wine
will then be safe.

A Dead Girl and a Sick Woman
(Mark 5.21–43; Luke 8.40–56)

18While Jesus was still speaking,
a Jewish official came and kneeled in
front of him. The man said, "My
daughter has just now died! Please
come and place your hand on her.
Then she will live again."

19Jesus and his disciples got up
and went with the man.

20A woman who had been bleeding
for twelve years came up behind Jesus
and barely touched his clothes. 21She
had said to herself, "If I can just touch
his clothes, I will get well."

22Jesus turned. He saw the woman
and said, "Don't worry! You are now
well because of your faith." At that moment she was healed.

23When Jesus went into the home
of the Jewish official and saw the musicians and the crowd of mourners,[v] 24he
said, "Get out of here! The little girl
is not dead. She is just asleep." Everyone started laughing at Jesus. 25But after the crowd had been sent out of the
house, Jesus went to the girl's bedside.
He took her by the hand and helped
her up.

26News about this spread all over
that part of the country.

Jesus Heals Two Blind Men

27As Jesus was walking along, two
blind men began following him and
shouting, "Son of David,[w] have pity
on us!"

28After Jesus had gone indoors, the
two blind men came up to him. He
asked them, "Do you believe I can
make you well?"

"Yes, Lord," they answered.

---

[t]*without eating*: See the note at 4.2. [u]*swell and burst the old skins*: While the juice from
grapes was becoming wine, it would swell and stretch the skins in which it had been stored.
If the skins were old and stiff, they would burst. [v]*the crowd of mourners*: The Jewish people
often hired mourners for funerals. [w]*Son of David*: The Jewish people expected the Messiah
to be from the family of King David, and for this reason the Messiah was often called the
"Son of David."

29Jesus touched their eyes and said, "Because of your faith, you will be healed." 30They were able to see, and Jesus strictly warned them not to tell anyone about him. 31But they left and talked about him to everyone in that part of the country.

Jesus Heals a Man Who Could Not Talk

32As Jesus and his disciples were on their way, some people brought to him a man who could not talk because a demon was in him. 33After Jesus had forced the demon out, the man started talking. The crowds were so amazed that they began saying, "Nothing like this has ever happened in Israel!"

34But the Pharisees said, "The leader of the demons gives him the power to force out demons."

Jesus Has Pity on People

35Jesus went to every town and village. He taught in their meeting places and preached the good news about God's kingdom. Jesus also healed every kind of disease and sickness. 36When he saw the crowds, he felt sorry for them. They were confused and helpless, like sheep without a shepherd. 37He said to his disciples, "A large crop is in the fields, but there are only a few workers. 38Ask the Lord in charge of the harvest to send out workers to bring it in."

Jesus Chooses His Twelve Apostles
(Mark 3.13–19; Luke 6.12–16)

10 Jesus called together his twelve disciples. He gave them the power to force out evil spirits and to heal every kind of disease and sickness. 2The first of the twelve apostles was Simon, better known as Peter. His brother Andrew was an apostle, and so were James and John, the two sons of Zebedee. 3Philip, Bartholomew, Thomas, Matthew the tax collector,[x] James the son of Alphaeus, and Thaddaeus were also apostles. 4The others were Simon, known as the Eager One,[y] and Judas Iscariot,[z] who later betrayed Jesus.

Instructions for the Twelve Apostles
(Mark 6.7–13; Luke 9.1–6)

5Jesus sent out the twelve apostles with these instructions:

Stay away from the Gentiles and don't go to any Samaritan town. 6Go only to the people of Israel, because they are like a flock of lost sheep. 7As you go, announce that the kingdom of heaven will soon be here.[a] 8Heal the sick, raise the dead to life, heal people who have leprosy,[b] and force out demons. You received without paying, now give without being paid. 9Don't take along any gold, silver, or copper coins. 10And don't carry[c] a travel-

[x]*tax collector*: See the note at 5.46.   [y]*known as the Eager One*: The Greek text has "Cananaean," which probably comes from a Hebrew word meaning "zealous" (see Luke 6.15). "Zealot" was the name later given to the members of a Jewish group which resisted and fought against the Romans.   [z]*Iscariot*: This may mean "a man from Kerioth" (a place in Judea). But more probably it means "a man who was a liar" or "a man who was a betrayer." [a]*will soon be here*: Or "is already here."   [b]*leprosy*: See the note at 8.2.   [c]*Don't take along . . . don't carry*: Or "Don't accept . . . don't accept."

ing bag or an extra shirt or sandals or a walking stick.

Workers deserve their food.
11So when you go to a town or a village, find someone worthy enough to have you as their guest and stay with them until you leave. 12When you go to a home, give it your blessing of peace. 13If the home is deserving, let your blessing remain with them. But if the home is not deserving, take back your blessing of peace. 14If someone won't welcome you or listen to your message, leave their home or town. And shake the dust from your feet at them.*d* 15I promise you that the day of judgment will be easier for the towns of Sodom and Gomorrah*e* than for that town.

Warning about Trouble
(Mark 13.9–13; Luke 21.12–17)

16I am sending you like lambs into a pack of wolves. So be as wise as snakes and as innocent as doves. 17Watch out for people who will take you to court and have you beaten in their meeting places. 18Because of me, you will be dragged before rulers and kings to tell them and the Gentiles about your faith. 19But when someone arrests you, don't worry about what you will say or how you will say it. At that time you will be given the words to say. 20But you will not really be the one speaking. The Spirit from

your Father will tell you what to say.

21Brothers and sisters will betray one another and have each other put to death. Parents will betray their own children, and children will turn against their parents and have them killed. 22Everyone will hate you because of me. But if you remain faithful until the end, you will be saved. 23When people mistreat you in one town, hurry to another one. I promise you that before you have gone to all the towns of Israel, the Son of Man will come.

24Disciples are not better than their teacher, and slaves are not better than their master. 25It is enough for disciples to be like their teacher and for slaves to be like their master. If people call the head of the family Satan, what will they say about the rest of the family?

The One to Fear
(Luke 12.2–7)

26Don't be afraid of anyone! Everything that is hidden will be found out, and every secret will be known. 27Whatever I say to you in the dark, you must tell in the light. And you must announce from the housetops whatever I have whispered to you. 28Don't be afraid of people. They can kill you, but they cannot harm your soul. Instead, you should fear God who can destroy both your body and your soul in hell. 29Aren't two sparrows sold

---

d shake the dust from your feet at them: This was a way of showing rejection. See Acts 13.51.
e Sodom and Gomorrah: During the time of Abraham the Lord destroyed these towns because the people there were so evil.

for only a penny? But your Father knows when any one of them falls to the ground. 30Even the hairs on your head are counted. 31So don't be afraid! You are worth much more than many sparrows.

Telling Others about Christ
(Luke 12.8, 9)

32If you tell others that you belong to me, I will tell my Father in heaven that you are my followers. 33But if you reject me, I will tell my Father in heaven that you don't belong to me.

Not Peace, but Trouble
(Luke 12.51–53; 14.26, 27)

34Don't think that I came to bring peace to the earth! I came to bring trouble, not peace. 35I came to turn sons against their fathers, daughters against their mothers, and daughters-in-law against their mothers-in-law. 36Your worst enemies will be in your own family.

37If you love your father or mother or even your sons and daughters more than me, you are not fit to be my disciples. 38And unless you are willing to take up your cross and come with me, you are not fit to be my disciples. 39If you try to save your life, you will lose it. But if you give it up for me, you will surely find it.

Rewards
(Mark 9.41)

40Anyone who welcomes you welcomes me. And anyone who welcomes me also welcomes the one who sent me. 41Anyone who welcomes a prophet, just because that person is a prophet, will be given the same reward as a prophet. Anyone who welcomes a good person, just because that person is good, will be given the same reward as a good person. 42And anyone who gives one of my most humble followers a cup of cool water, just because that person is my follower, will surely be rewarded.

John the Baptist
(Luke 7.18–35)

11 After Jesus had finished instructing his twelve disciples, he left and began teaching and preaching in the towns.*f*

2John was in prison when he heard what Christ was doing. So John sent some of his followers 3to ask Jesus, "Are you the one we should be looking for? Or must we wait for someone else?"

4Jesus answered, "Go and tell John what you have heard and seen. 5The blind are now able to see, and the lame can walk. People with leprosy*g* are being healed, and the deaf can hear. The dead are raised to life, and the poor are hearing the good news. 6God will bless everyone who does not reject me because of what I do."

7As John's followers were going away, Jesus spoke to the crowds about John:

> What sort of person did you go out into the desert to see? Was

---

fthe towns: The Greek text has "their towns," which may refer to the towns of Galilee or to the towns where Jesus' disciples had lived.   *gleprosy*: See the note at 8.2.

he like tall grass blown about by the wind? 8What kind of man did you go out to see? Was he someone dressed in fine clothes? People who dress like that live in the king's palace. 9What did you really go out to see? Was he a prophet? He certainly was. I tell you that he was more than a prophet. 10In the Scriptures God says about him, "I am sending my messenger ahead of you to get things ready for you." 11I tell you that no one ever born on this earth is greater than John the Baptist. But whoever is least in the kingdom of heaven is greater than John.

12From the time of John the Baptist until now, violent people have been trying to take over the kingdom of heaven by force. 13All the Books of the Prophets and the Law of Moses*h* told what was going to happen up to the time of John. 14And if you believe them, John is Elijah, the prophet you are waiting for. 15If you have ears, pay attention!

16You people are like children sitting in the market and 17shouting to each other,
"We played the flute,
    but you would not dance!
We sang a funeral song,
    but you would not mourn!"
18John the Baptist did not go around eating and drinking, and you said, "That man has a demon in him!" 19But the Son of Man goes around eating and drinking, and you say, "That man eats and drinks too much! He is even a friend of tax collectors*i* and sinners." Yet Wisdom is shown to be right by what it does.

The Unbelieving Towns
(Luke 10.13–15)

20In the towns where Jesus had worked most of his miracles, the people refused to turn to God. So Jesus was upset with them and said:

21You people of Chorazin are in for trouble! You people of Bethsaida are in for trouble too! If the miracles that took place in your towns had happened in Tyre and Sidon, the people there would have turned to God long ago. They would have dressed in sackcloth and put ashes on their heads.*j* 22I tell you that on the day of judgment the people of Tyre and Sidon will get off easier than you will.

23People of Capernaum, do you think you will be honored in heaven? You will go down to hell! If the miracles that took place in your town had happened in Sodom, that town would still be standing. 24So I tell you that on the day of judgment the people of Sodom will get off easier than you.

Come to Me and Rest
(Luke 10.21, 22)

25At that moment Jesus said:
My Father, Lord of heaven and earth, I am grateful that you hid

---

h the Books of the Prophets and the Law of Moses: The Jewish Scriptures, that is, the Old Testament. *i tax collectors*: See the note at 5.46. *j sackcloth . . . ashes on their heads*: This was one way that people showed how sorry they were for their sins.

all this from wise and educated people and showed it to ordinary people. 26Yes, Father, that is what pleased you.

27My Father has given me everything, and he is the only one who knows the Son. The only one who truly knows the Father is the Son. But the Son wants to tell others about the Father, so that they can know him too.

28If you are tired from carrying heavy burdens, come to me and I will give you rest. 29Take the yoke*k* I give you. Put it on your shoulders and learn from me. I am gentle and humble, and you will find rest. 30This yoke is easy to bear, and this burden is light.

A Question about the Sabbath
(Mark 2.23–28; Luke 6.1–5)

12 One Sabbath Jesus and his disciples were walking through some wheat fields.*l* His disciples were hungry and began picking and eating grains of wheat. 2Some Pharisees said to Jesus, "Why are your disciples picking grain on the Sabbath? They are not supposed to do that!"

3Jesus answered:

You surely must have read what David did when he and his followers were hungry. 4He went into the house of God, and then they ate the sacred loaves of bread that only priests are supposed to eat. 5Haven't you read in the Law of Moses that the priests are allowed to work in the temple on the Sabbath? But no one says that they are guilty of breaking the law of the Sabbath. 6I tell you that there is something here greater than the temple. 7Don't you know what the Scriptures mean when they say, "Instead of offering sacrifices to me, I want you to be merciful to others?" If you knew what this means, you would not condemn these innocent disciples of mine. 8So the Son of Man is Lord over the Sabbath.

A Man with a Crippled Hand
(Mark 3.1–6; Luke 6.6–11)

9Jesus left and went into one of the Jewish meeting places, 10where there was a man whose hand was crippled. Some Pharisees wanted to accuse Jesus of doing something wrong, and they asked him, "Is it right to heal someone on the Sabbath?"

11Jesus answered, "If you had a sheep that fell into a ditch on the Sabbath, wouldn't you lift it out? 12People are worth much more than sheep, and so it is right to do good on the Sabbath." 13Then Jesus told the man, "Hold out your hand." The man did, and it became as healthy as the other one.

14The Pharisees left and started making plans to kill Jesus.

God's Chosen Servant

15When Jesus found out what was happening, he left there and large crowds followed him. He healed all of their sick, 16but warned them not to tell anyone about him. 17So God's

---

kyoke: Yokes were put on the necks of animals, so that they could pull a plow or wagon. A yoke was a symbol of obedience and hard work. *lwalking through some wheat fields*: It was the custom to let hungry travelers pick grains of wheat.

promise came true, just as Isaiah the prophet had said,

> 18"Here is my chosen servant!
> I love him,
>   and he pleases me.
> I will give him my Spirit,
>   and he will judge
>   the nations.
> 19He will not argue or shout
>   or be heard speaking
>   in the streets.
> 20He will not break off
>   a bent twig
>   or put out
>   a faintly burning flame
> until he makes justice
>   win the victory.
> 21All nations will place
>   their hope in him."

Jesus and the Ruler of the Demons
(Mark 3.20–30; Luke 11.14–23;12.10)

22Some people brought to Jesus a man who was blind and could not talk because he had a demon in him. Jesus cured the man, and then he was able to talk and see. 23The crowds were so amazed that they asked, "Could Jesus be the Son of David?"*m*

24When the Pharisees heard this, they said, "He forces out demons by the power of Beelzebul, the ruler of the demons!"

25Jesus knew what they were thinking, and he said to them:

Any kingdom where people fight each other will end up ruined. And a town or family that fights will soon destroy itself. 26So if Satan fights against himself, how can his kingdom last? 27If I use the power of Beelzebul to force out demons, whose power do your own followers use to force them out? Your followers are the ones who will judge you. 28But when I force out demons by the power of God's Spirit, it proves that God's kingdom has already come to you. 29How can anyone break into a strong man's house and steal his things, unless he first ties up the strong man? Then he can take everything.

30If you are not on my side, you are against me. If you don't gather in the harvest with me, you scatter it. 31-32I tell you that any sinful thing you do or say can be forgiven. Even if you speak against the Son of Man, you can be forgiven. But if you speak against the Holy Spirit, you can never be forgiven, either in this life or in the life to come.

A Tree and Its Fruit
(Luke 6.43–45)

33A good tree produces only good fruit, and a bad tree produces bad fruit. You can tell what a tree is like by the fruit it produces. 34You are a bunch of evil snakes, so how can you say anything good? Your words show what is in your hearts. 35Good people bring good things out of their hearts, but evil people bring evil things out of their hearts. 36I promise you that on the day of judgment, everyone will have to account for every careless word they have spoken. 37On that day they will be told that they are

---

m Could Jesus be the Son of David: Or "Does Jesus think he is the Son of David?" See the note at 9.27.

either innocent or guilty because of the things they have said.

A Sign from Heaven
(Mark 8.11, 12; Luke 11.29–32)

38Some Pharisees and teachers of the Law of Moses said, "Teacher, we want you to show us a sign from heaven."

39But Jesus replied:

You want a sign because you are evil and won't believe! But the only sign you will get is the sign of the prophet Jonah. **40**He was in the stomach of a big fish for three days and nights, just as the Son of Man will be deep in the earth for three days and nights. **41**On the day of judgment the people of Nineveh[n] will stand there with you and condemn you. They turned to God when Jonah preached, and yet here is something far greater than Jonah. **42**The Queen of the South[o] will also stand there with you and condemn you. She traveled a long way to hear Solomon's wisdom, and yet here is something much greater than Solomon.

Return of an Evil Spirit
(Luke 11.24–26)

43When an evil spirit leaves a person, it travels through the desert, looking for a place to rest. But when the demon doesn't find a place, **44**it says, "I will go back to the home I left." When it gets there and finds the place empty, clean, and fixed up, **45**it goes off and finds seven other evil spirits even worse than itself. They all come and make their home there, and the person ends up in worse shape than before. That's how it will be with you evil people of today.

Jesus' Mother and Brothers
(Mark 3.31–35; Luke 8.19–21)

46While Jesus was still speaking to the crowds, his mother and brothers came and stood outside because they wanted to talk with him. **47**Someone told Jesus, "Your mother and brothers are standing outside and want to talk with you."[p]

48Jesus answered, "Who is my mother and who are my brothers?" **49**Then he pointed to his disciples and said, "These are my mother and my brothers! **50**Anyone who obeys my Father in heaven is my brother or sister or mother."

A Story about a Farmer
(Mark 4.1–9; Luke 8.4–8)

13 That same day Jesus left the house and went out beside Lake Galilee, where he sat down to teach.[q] **2**Such large crowds gathered around him that he had to sit in a boat, while the people stood on the shore.

---

[n]*Nineveh*: During the time of Jonah this city was the capital of the Assyrian Empire, which was Israel's worst enemy. But Jonah was sent there to preach, so that the people would turn to the Lord and be saved. [o]*Queen of the South*: Sheba, probably a country in southern Arabia. [p]*with you*: Some manuscripts do not have verse 47. [q]*sat down to teach*: Teachers in the ancient world, including Jewish teachers, usually sat down when they taught.

3Then he taught them many things by using stories. He said:

A farmer went out to scatter seed in a field. 4While the farmer was scattering the seed, some of it fell along the road and was eaten by birds. 5Other seeds fell on thin, rocky ground and quickly started growing because the soil was not very deep. 6But when the sun came up, the plants were scorched and dried up, because they did not have enough roots. 7Some other seeds fell where thorn bushes grew up and choked the plants. 8But a few seeds did fall on good ground where the plants produced a hundred or sixty or thirty times as much as was scattered. 9If you have ears, pay attention!

Why Jesus Used Stories
(Mark 4.10–12; Luke 8.9, 10)

10Jesus' disciples came to him and asked, "Why do you use nothing but stories when you speak to the people?" 11Jesus answered:

I have explained the secrets about the kingdom of heaven to you, but not to others. 12Everyone who has something will be given more. But people who don't have anything will lose even what little they have. 13I use stories when I speak to them because when they look, they cannot see, and when they listen, they cannot hear or understand. 14So God's promise came true, just as the prophet Isaiah had said,

"These people will listen
and listen,
    but never understand.
They will look and look,
    but never see.
15All of them have
    stubborn minds!
Their ears are stopped up,
    and their eyes are covered.
They cannot see or hear
    or understand.
If they could,
they would turn to me,
    and I would heal them."

16But God has blessed you, because your eyes can see and your ears can hear! 17Many prophets and good people were eager to see what you see and to hear what you hear. But I tell you that they did not see or hear.

Jesus Explains the Story about the Farmer
(Mark 4.13–20; Luke 8.11–15)

18Now listen to the meaning of the story about the farmer:

19The seeds that fell along the road are the people who hear the message about the kingdom, but don't understand it. Then the evil one comes and snatches the message from their hearts. 20The seeds that fell on rocky ground are the people who gladly hear the message and accept it right away. 21But they don't have deep roots, and they don't last very long. As soon as life gets hard or the message gets them in trouble, they give up.

22The seeds that fell among the thorn bushes are also people who hear the message. But they start worrying about the needs of this life and are fooled by the desire to get rich. So the message gets choked out, and they never produce anything. 23The seeds that fell on good ground are the people who hear and understand the message. They produce as much as a hundred or sixty or thirty times what was planted.

Weeds among the Wheat

24Jesus then told them this story:

The kingdom of heaven is like what happened when a farmer scattered good seed in a field. 25But while everyone was sleeping, an enemy came and scattered weed seeds in the field and then left.

26When the plants came up and began to ripen, the farmer's servants could see the weeds. 27The servants came and asked, "Sir, didn't you scatter good seed in your field? Where did these weeds come from?"

28"An enemy did this," he replied.

His servants then asked, "Do you want us to go out and pull up the weeds?"

29"No!" he answered. "You might also pull up the wheat. 30Leave the weeds alone until harvest time. Then I'll tell my workers to gather the weeds and tie them up and burn them. But I'll have them store the wheat in my barn."

Stories about a Mustard Seed and Yeast
(Mark 4.30–32; Luke 13.18–21)

31Jesus told them another story:

The kingdom of heaven is like what happens when a farmer plants a mustard seed in a field. 32Although it is the smallest of all seeds, it grows larger than any garden plant and becomes a tree. Birds even come and nest on its branches.

33Jesus also said:

The kingdom of heaven is like what happens when a woman mixes a little yeast into three big batches of flour. Finally, all the dough rises.

The Reason for Teaching with Stories
(Mark 4.33, 34)

34Jesus used stories when he spoke to the people. In fact, he did not tell them anything without using stories. 35So God's promise came true, just as the prophet[r] had said,

"I will use stories
  to speak my message
and to explain things
  that have been hidden
since the creation
  of the world."

Jesus Explains the Story about the Weeds

36After Jesus left the crowd and went inside,[s] his disciples came to him and said, "Explain to us the story about the weeds in the wheat field."

37Jesus answered:

The one who scattered the good seed is the Son of Man. 38The field is the world, and the good seeds are the people who belong to the kingdom. The weed seeds are those who belong to the

---

[r]*the prophet*: Some manuscripts have "the prophet Isaiah."   [s]*went inside*: Or "went home."

evil one, 39and the one who scattered them is the devil. The harvest is the end of time, and angels are the ones who bring in the harvest.

40Weeds are gathered and burned. That's how it will be at the end of time. 41The Son of Man will send out his angels, and they will gather from his kingdom everyone who does wrong or causes others to sin. 42Then he will throw them into a flaming furnace, where people will cry and grit their teeth in pain. 43But everyone who has done right will shine like the sun in their Father's kingdom. If you have ears, pay attention!

A Hidden Treasure

44The kingdom of heaven is like what happens when someone finds treasure hidden in a field and buries it again. A person like that is happy and goes and sells everything in order to buy that field.

A Valuable Pearl

45The kingdom of heaven is like what happens when a shop owner is looking for fine pearls. 46After finding a very valuable one, the owner goes and sells everything in order to buy that pearl.

A Fish Net

47The kingdom of heaven is like what happens when a net is thrown into a lake and catches all kinds of fish. 48When the net is full, it is dragged to the shore, and the fishermen sit down to separate the fish. They keep the good ones, but throw the bad ones away. 49That's how it will be at the end of time. Angels will come and separate the evil people from the ones who have done right. 50Then those evil people will be thrown into a flaming furnace, where they will cry and grit their teeth in pain.

New and Old Treasures

51Jesus asked his disciples if they understood all these things. They said, "Yes, we do."

52So he told them, "Every student of the Scriptures who becomes a disciple in the kingdom of heaven is like someone who brings out new and old treasures from the storeroom."

The People of Nazareth Turn against Jesus
(Mark 6.1–6; Luke 4.16–30)

53When Jesus had finished telling these stories, he left 54and went to his hometown. He taught in their meeting place, and the people were so amazed that they asked, "Where does he get all this wisdom and the power to work these miracles? 55Isn't he the son of the carpenter? Isn't Mary his mother, and aren't James, Joseph, Simon, and Judas his brothers? 56Don't his sisters still live here in our town? How can he do all this?" 57So the people were very unhappy because of what he was doing.

But Jesus said, "Prophets are honored by everyone, except the people of their hometown and their own family." 58And because the people did not have any faith, Jesus did not work many miracles there.

The Death of John the Baptist
(Mark 6.14–29; Luke 9.7–9)

14 About this time Herod the ruler[t] heard the news about Jesus 2and told his officials, "This is John the Baptist! He has come back from death, and that's why he has the power to work these miracles."

3-4Herod had earlier arrested John and had him chained and put in prison. He did this because John had told him, "It isn't right for you to take Herodias, the wife of your brother Philip." 5Herod wanted to kill John. But the people thought John was a prophet, and Herod was afraid of what they might do.

6When Herod's birthday came, the daughter of Herodias danced for the guests. She pleased Herod 7so much that he swore to give her whatever she wanted. 8But the girl's mother told her to say, "Here on a platter I want the head of John the Baptist!"

9The king was sorry for what he had said. But he did not want to break the promise he had made in front of his guests. So he ordered a guard 10to go to the prison and cut off John's head. 11It was taken on a platter to the girl, and she gave it to her mother. 12John's followers took his body and buried it. Then they told Jesus what had happened.

Jesus Feeds Five Thousand
(Mark 6.30–44; Luke 9.10–17; John 6.1–14)

13After Jesus heard about John, he crossed Lake Galilee[u] to go to some place where he could be alone. But the crowds found out and followed him on foot from the towns. 14When Jesus got out of the boat, he saw the large crowd. He felt sorry for them and healed everyone who was sick.

15That evening the disciples came to Jesus and said, "This place is like a desert, and it is already late. Let the crowds leave, so they can go to the villages and buy some food."

16Jesus replied, "They don't have to leave. Why don't you give them something to eat?"

17But they said, "We have only five small loaves of bread[v] and two fish." 18Jesus asked his disciples to bring the food to him, 19and he told the crowd to sit down on the grass. Jesus took the five loaves and the two fish. He looked up toward heaven and blessed the food. Then he broke the bread and handed it to his disciples, and they gave it to the people.

20After everyone had eaten all they wanted, Jesus' disciples picked up twelve large baskets of leftovers. 21There were about five thousand men who ate, not counting the women and children.

Jesus Walks on the Water
(Mark 6.45–52; John 6.15–21)

22Right away Jesus made his disciples get into a boat and start back across the lake.[w] But he stayed until he had sent the crowds away. 23Then he went up on a mountain where he could be alone and pray. Later that evening, he was still there.

24By this time the boat was a long

---

[t]*Herod the ruler*: Herod Antipas, the son of Herod the Great (2.1).   [u]*crossed Lake Galilee*: To the east side.   [v]*small loaves of bread*: These would have been flat and round or in the shape of a bun.   [w]*back across the lake*: To the west side.

way from the shore. It was going against the wind and was being tossed around by the waves. 25A little while before morning, Jesus came walking on the water toward his disciples. 26When they saw him, they thought he was a ghost. They were terrified and started screaming.

27At once Jesus said to them, "Don't worry! I am Jesus. Don't be afraid."

28Peter replied, "Lord, if it is really you, tell me to come to you on the water."

29"Come on!" Jesus said. Peter then got out of the boat and started walking on the water toward him.

30But when Peter saw how strong the wind was, he was afraid and started sinking. "Lord, save me!" he shouted.

31Right away Jesus reached out his hand. He helped Peter up and said, "You surely don't have much faith. Why do you doubt?"

32When Jesus and Peter got into the boat, the wind died down. 33The men in the boat worshiped Jesus and said, "You really are the Son of God!"

Jesus Heals Sick People in Gennesaret
(Mark 6.53–56)

34Jesus and his disciples crossed the lake and came to shore near the town of Gennesaret. 35The people found out that he was there, and they sent word to everyone who lived in that part of the country. So they brought all the sick people to Jesus. 36They begged him just to let them touch his clothes, and everyone who did was healed.

The Teaching of the Ancestors
(Mark 7.1–13)

15 About this time some Pharisees and teachers of the Law of Moses came from Jerusalem. They asked Jesus, 2"Why don't your disciples obey what our ancestors taught us to do? They don't even wash their hands[x] before they eat."

3Jesus answered:

Why do you disobey God and follow your own teaching? 4Didn't God command you to respect your father and mother? Didn't he tell you to put to death all who curse their parents? 5But you let people get by without helping their parents when they should. You let them say that what they have has been offered to God.[y] 6Is this any way to show respect to your parents? You ignore God's commands in order to follow your own teaching. 7And you are nothing but showoffs! Isaiah the prophet was right when he wrote that God had said,

8"All of you praise me
  with your words,
but you never really
  think about me.
9It is useless for you
  to worship me,
when you teach rules
  made up by humans."

---

[x]*wash their hands*: The Jewish people had strict laws about washing their hands before eating, especially if they had been out in public. [y]*has been offered to God*: According to Jewish custom, when people said something was offered to God, it belonged to him and could not be used for anyone else, not even for their own parents.

What Really Makes People Unclean
(Mark 7.14–23)

10Jesus called the crowd together and said, "Pay attention and try to understand what I mean. 11The food that you put into your mouth doesn't make you unclean and unfit to worship God. The bad words that come out of your mouth are what make you unclean."

12Then his disciples came over to him and asked, "Do you know that you insulted the Pharisees by what you said?"

13Jesus answered, "Every plant that my Father in heaven did not plant will be pulled up by the roots. 14Stay away from those Pharisees! They are like blind people leading other blind people, and all of them will fall into a ditch."

15Peter replied, "What did you mean when you talked about the things that make people unclean?"

16Jesus then said:

Don't any of you know what I am talking about by now? 17Don't you know that the food you put into your mouth goes into your stomach and then out of your body? 18But the words that come out of your mouth come from your heart. And they are what make you unfit to worship God. 19Out of your heart come evil thoughts, murder, unfaithfulness in marriage, vulgar deeds, stealing, telling lies, and insulting others. 20These are what make you unclean. Eating without washing your hands will not make you unfit to worship God.

A Woman's Faith
(Mark 7.24–30)

21Jesus left and went to the territory near the cities of Tyre and Sidon. 22Suddenly a Canaanite woman[z] from there came out shouting, "Lord and Son of David,[a] have pity on me! My daughter is full of demons." 23Jesus did not say a word. But the woman kept following along and shouting, so his disciples came up and asked him to send her away.

24Jesus said, "I was sent only to the people of Israel! They are like a flock of lost sheep."

25The woman came closer. Then she kneeled down and begged, "Lord, please help me!"

26Jesus replied, "It isn't right to take food away from children and feed it to dogs."[b]

27"Lord, that's true," the woman said, "but even dogs get the crumbs that fall from their owner's table."

28Jesus answered, "Dear woman, you really do have a lot of faith, and you will be given what you want." At that moment her daughter was healed.

Jesus Heals Many People

29From there Jesus went along Lake Galilee. Then he climbed a hill and sat down. 30Large crowds came and brought many people who were crippled or blind or lame or unable to talk. They placed them, and many others, in front of Jesus, and he healed them all. 31Everyone was amazed at what they saw and heard. People who had never spoken could now speak. The lame were healed. The crippled

---

[z]*Canaanite woman*: This woman was not Jewish.　[a]*Son of David*: See the note at 9.27.　[b]*feed it to dogs*: The Jewish people sometimes referred to Gentiles as dogs.

could walk, and the blind were able to see. Everyone was praising the God of Israel.

Jesus Feeds Four Thousand
(Mark 8.1–10)

32Jesus called his disciples together and told them, "I feel sorry for these people. They have been with me for three days, and they don't have anything to eat. I don't want to send them away hungry. They might faint on their way home."

33His disciples said, "This place is like a desert. Where can we find enough food to feed such a crowd?"

34Jesus asked them how much food they had. They replied, "Seven small loaves of bread*c* and a few little fish."

35After Jesus had told the people to sit down, **36**he took the seven loaves of bread and the fish and gave thanks. He then broke them and handed them to his disciples, who passed them around to the crowds.

37Everyone ate all they wanted, and the leftovers filled seven large baskets.

38There were four thousand men who ate, not counting the women and children.

39After Jesus had sent the crowds away, he got into a boat and sailed across the lake. He came to shore near the town of Magadan.*d*

A Demand for a Sign from Heaven
(Mark 8.11–13; Luke 12.54–56)

16 The Pharisees and Sadducees came to Jesus and tried to test him by asking for a sign from heaven. **2**He told them:

If the sky is red in the evening, you say the weather will be good. **3**But if the sky is red and gloomy in the morning, you say it is going to rain. You can tell what the weather will be like by looking at the sky. But you don't understand what is happening now.*e* **4**You want a sign because you are evil and won't believe! But the only sign you will be given is what happened to Jonah.*f*

Then Jesus left.

The Yeast of the Pharisees and Sadducees
(Mark 8.14–21)

5The disciples had forgotten to bring any bread when they crossed the lake.*g* **6**Jesus then warned them, "Watch out! Guard against the yeast of the Pharisees and Sadducees."

7The disciples talked this over and said to each other, "He must be saying this because we didn't bring along any bread."

8Jesus knew what they were thinking and said:

You surely don't have much faith! Why are you talking about not having any bread? **9**Don't you understand? Have you forgotten about the five thousand people and all those baskets of leftovers from just five loaves of bread? **10**And what about the four thousand people and all those baskets

---

csmall loaves of bread: See the note at 14.17.   *dMagadan*: The location is unknown.   *eIf the sky is red . . . what is happening now*: The words of Jesus in verses 2 and 3 are not in some manuscripts.   *fwhat happened to Jonah*: Jonah was in the stomach of a big fish for three days and nights. See 12.40.   *gcrossed the lake*: To the east side.

of leftovers from only seven loaves of bread? 11Don't you know by now that I am not talking to you about bread? Watch out for the yeast of the Pharisees and Sadducees!

12Finally, the disciples understood that Jesus was not talking about the yeast used to make bread, but about the teaching of the Pharisees and Sadducees.

Who Is Jesus?
(Mark 8.27–30; Luke 9.18–21)

13When Jesus and his disciples were near the town of Caesarea Philippi, he asked them, "What do people say about the Son of Man?"

14The disciples answered, "Some people say you are John the Baptist or maybe Elijah^h or Jeremiah or some other prophet."

15Then Jesus asked them, "But who do you say I am?"

16Simon Peter spoke up, "You are the Messiah, the Son of the living God."

17Jesus told him:

Simon, son of Jonah, you are blessed! You didn't discover this on your own. It was shown to you by my Father in heaven. 18So I will call you Peter, which means "a rock." On this rock I will build my church, and death itself will not have any power over it. 19I will give you the keys to the kingdom of heaven, and God in heaven will allow whatever you allow on earth. But he will not allow anything that you don't allow.

20Jesus told his disciples not to tell anyone that he was the Messiah.

Jesus Speaks about His Suffering and Death
(Mark 8.31—9.1; Luke 9.22–27)

21From then on, Jesus began telling his disciples what would happen to him. He said, "I must go to Jerusalem. There the nation's leaders, the chief priests, and the teachers of the Law of Moses will make me suffer terribly. I will be killed, but three days later I will rise to life."

22Peter took Jesus aside and told him to stop talking like that. He said, "Lord, surely God won't let this happen to you!"

23Jesus turned to Peter and said, "Satan, get away from me! You're in my way because you think like everyone else and not like God."

24Then Jesus said to his disciples:

If any of you want to be my followers, you must forget about yourself. You must take up your cross and follow me. 25If you want to save your life,^{i} you will destroy it. But if you give up your life for me, you will find it. 26What will you gain, if you own the whole world but destroy yourself? What would you give to get back your soul?

27The Son of Man will soon come in the glory of his Father and with his angels to reward all people for what they have done. 28I promise you that some of those standing here will not die

---

^{h}Elijah: Many of the Jewish people expected the prophet Elijah to come and prepare the way for the Messiah. ^{i}life: In verses 25 and 26 the same Greek word is translated "life," "yourself," and "soul."

before they see the Son of Man coming with his kingdom.

The True Glory of Jesus
(Mark 9.2–13; Luke 9.28–36)

17 Six days later Jesus took Peter and the brothers James and John with him. They went up on a very high mountain where they could be alone. 2There in front of the disciples Jesus was completely changed. His face was shining like the sun, and his clothes became white as light.

3All at once Moses and Elijah were there talking with Jesus. 4So Peter said to him, "Lord, it is good for us to be here! Let us make three shelters, one for you, one for Moses, and one for Elijah."

5While Peter was still speaking, the shadow of a bright cloud passed over them. From the cloud a voice said, "This is my own dear Son, and I am pleased with him. Listen to what he says!" 6When the disciples heard the voice, they were so afraid that they fell flat on the ground. 7But Jesus came over and touched them. He said, "Get up and don't be afraid!" 8When they opened their eyes, they saw only Jesus.

9On their way down from the mountain, Jesus warned his disciples not to tell anyone what they had seen until after the Son of Man had been raised from death.

10The disciples asked Jesus, "Don't the teachers of the Law of Moses say that Elijah must come before the Messiah does?"

11Jesus told them, "Elijah certainly will come and get everything ready. 12In fact, he has already come.

But the people did not recognize him and treated him just as they wanted to. They will soon make the Son of Man suffer in the same way." 13Then the disciples understood that Jesus was talking to them about John the Baptist.

Jesus Heals a Boy
(Mark 9.14–29; Luke 9.37–43a)

14Jesus and his disciples returned to the crowd. A man kneeled in front of him 15and said, "Lord, have pity on my son! He has a bad case of epilepsy and often falls into a fire or into water. 16I brought him to your disciples, but none of them could heal him."

17Jesus said, "You people are too stubborn to have any faith! How much longer must I be with you? Why do I have to put up with you? Bring the boy here." 18Then Jesus spoke sternly to the demon. It went out of the boy, and right then he was healed.

19Later the disciples went to Jesus in private and asked him, "Why couldn't we force out the demon?"

20-21Jesus replied:

It is because you don't have enough faith! But I can promise you this. If you had faith no larger than a mustard seed, you could tell this mountain to move from here to there. And it would. Everything would be possible for you.*j*

Jesus Again Speaks about His Death
(Mark 9.30–32; Luke 9.43b–45)

22While Jesus and his disciples were going from place to place in

jfor you: Some manuscripts add, "But the only way to force out that kind of demon is by praying and going without eating."

Galilee, he told them, "The Son of Man will be handed over to people 23who will kill him. But three days later he will rise to life." All of this made the disciples very sad.

Paying the Temple Tax

24When Jesus and the others arrived in Capernaum, the collectors for the temple tax came to Peter and asked, "Does your teacher pay the temple tax?"

25"Yes, he does," Peter answered. After they had returned home, Jesus went up to Peter and asked him, "Simon, what do you think? Do the kings of this earth collect taxes and fees from their own people or from foreigners?"[k]

26Peter answered, "From foreigners."

Jesus replied, "Then their own people[l] don't have to pay. 27But we don't want to cause trouble. So go cast a line into the lake and pull out the first fish you hook. Open its mouth, and you will find a coin. Use it to pay your taxes and mine."

Who Is the Greatest?
(Mark 9.33–37; Luke 9.46–48)

18 About this time, the disciples came to Jesus and asked him who would be the greatest in the kingdom of heaven. 2Jesus called a child over and had the child stand near him. 3Then he said:

I promise you this. If you don't change and become like this child, you will never get into the kingdom of heaven. 4But if you are as humble as this child, you are the greatest in the kingdom of heaven. 5And when you welcome one of these children because of me, you welcome me.

Temptations to Sin
(Mark 9.42–48; Luke 17.1, 2)

6It will be terrible for people who cause even one of my little followers to sin. Those people would be better off thrown into the deepest part of the ocean with a heavy stone tied around the neck! 7The world is in for trouble because of the way it causes people to sin. There will always be something to cause people to sin, but anyone who does this will be in for trouble.

8If your hand or foot causes you to sin, chop it off and throw it away! You would be better off to go into life crippled or lame than to have two hands or two feet and be thrown into the fire that never goes out. 9If your eye causes you to sin, poke it out and get rid of it. You would be better off to go into life with only one eye than to have two eyes and be thrown into the fires of hell.

The Lost Sheep
(Luke 15.3–7)

10-11Don't be cruel to any of these little ones! I promise you that their angels are always with my Father in heaven.[m] 12Let me

---

[k]from their own people or from foreigners: Or "from their children or from others." [l]From foreigners . . . their own people: Or "From other people . . . their children." [m]in heaven: Some manuscripts add, "The Son of Man came to save people who are lost."

ask you this. What would you do if you had a hundred sheep and one of them wandered off? Wouldn't you leave the ninety-nine on the hillside and go look for the one that had wandered away? 13I am sure that finding it would make you happier than having the ninety-nine that never wandered off. 14That's how it is with your Father in heaven. He doesn't want any of these little ones to be lost.

When Someone Sins
(Luke 17.3)

15If one of my followers[n] sins against you, go and point out what was wrong. But do it in private, just between the two of you. If that person listens, you have won back a follower. 16But if that one refuses to listen, take along one or two others. The Scriptures teach that every complaint must be proven true by two or more witnesses. 17If the follower refuses to listen to them, report the matter to the church. Anyone who refuses to listen to the church must be treated like an unbeliever or a tax collector.[o]

Allowing and Not Allowing

18I promise you that God in heaven will allow whatever you allow on earth, but he will not allow anything you don't allow. 19I promise that when any two of you on earth agree about something you are praying for, my Father in heaven will do it for you. 20Whenever two or three of you come together in my name,[p] I am there with you.

An Official Who Refused to Forgive

21Peter came up to the Lord and asked, "How many times should I forgive someone[q] who does something wrong to me? Is seven times enough?" 22Jesus answered:

Not just seven times, but seventy-seven times![r] 23This story will show you what the kingdom of heaven is like:

One day a king decided to call in his officials and ask them to give an account of what they owed him. 24As he was doing this, one official was brought in who owed him fifty million silver coins. 25But he didn't have any money to pay what he owed. The king ordered him to be sold, along with his wife and children and all he owned, in order to pay the debt.

26The official got down on his knees and began begging, "Have pity on me, and I will pay you every cent I owe!" 27The king felt sorry for him and let him go free. He even told the official that he did not have to pay back the money.

28As the official was leaving, he happened to meet another official, who owed him a hundred

---

[n]*followers*: The Greek text has "brother," which is used here and elsewhere in this chapter to refer to a follower of Christ.   [o]*tax collector*: See the note at 5.46.   [p]*in my name*: Or "as my followers."   [q]*someone*: Or "a follower." See the note at 18.15.   [r]*seventy-seven times*: Or "seventy times seven." The large number means that one follower should never stop forgiving another.

silver coins. So he grabbed the man by the throat. He started choking him and said, "Pay me what you owe!"

29The man got down on his knees and began begging, "Have pity on me, and I will pay you back." 30But the first official refused to have pity. Instead, he went and had the other official put in jail until he could pay what he owed.

31When some other officials found out what had happened, they felt sorry for the man who had been put in jail. Then they told the king what had happened. 32The king called the first official back in and said, "You're an evil man! When you begged for mercy, I said you did not have to pay back a cent. 33Don't you think you should show pity to someone else, as I did to you?" 34The king was so angry that he ordered the official to be tortured until he could pay back everything he owed. 35That is how my Father in heaven will treat you, if you don't forgive each of my followers with all your heart.

Teaching about Divorce
(Mark 10.1–12)

19 When Jesus finished teaching, he left Galilee and went to the part of Judea that is east of the Jordan River. 2Large crowds followed him, and he healed their sick people.

3Some Pharisees wanted to test Jesus. They came up to him and asked, "Is it right for a man to divorce his wife for just any reason?"

4Jesus answered, "Don't you know that in the beginning the Creator made a man and a woman? 5That's why a man leaves his father and mother and gets married. He becomes like one person with his wife. 6Then they are no longer two people, but one. And no one should separate a couple that God has joined together."

7The Pharisees asked Jesus, "Why did Moses say that a man could write out divorce papers and send his wife away?"

8Jesus replied, "You are so heartless! That's why Moses allowed you to divorce your wife. But from the beginning God did not intend it to be that way. 9I say that if your wife has not committed some terrible sexual sin,s you must not divorce her to marry someone else. If you do, you are unfaithful."

10The disciples said, "If that's how it is between a man and a woman, it's better not to get married."

11Jesus told them, "Only those people who have been given the gift of staying single can accept this teaching. 12Some people are unable to marry because of birth defects or because of what someone has done to their bodies. Others stay single for the sake of the kingdom of heaven. Anyone who can accept this teaching should do so."

Jesus Blesses Little Children
(Mark 10.13–16; Luke 18.15–17)

13Some people brought their children to Jesus, so that he could place his hands on them and pray for them. His disciples told the people to stop bothering him. 14But Jesus said, "Let the children come to me, and don't try

---

ssome terrible sexual sin: See the note at 5.32.

to stop them! People who are like these children belong to God's kingdom."[t] [15]After Jesus had placed his hands on the children, he left.

A Rich Young Man
(Mark 10.17–31; Luke 18.18–30)

[16]A man came to Jesus and asked, "Teacher, what good thing must I do to have eternal life?"

[17]Jesus said to him, "Why do you ask me about what is good? Only God is good. If you want to have eternal life, you must obey his commandments."

[18]"Which ones?" the man asked.

Jesus answered, "Do not murder. Be faithful in marriage. Do not steal. Do not tell lies about others. [19]Respect your father and mother. And love others as much as you love yourself."

[20]The young man said, "I have obeyed all of these. What else must I do?"

[21]Jesus replied, "If you want to be perfect, go sell everything you own! Give the money to the poor, and you will have riches in heaven. Then come and be my follower." [22]When the young man heard this, he was sad, because he was very rich.

[23]Jesus said to his disciples, "It's terribly hard for rich people to get into the kingdom of heaven! [24]In fact, it's easier for a camel to go through the eye of a needle than for a rich person to get into God's kingdom."

[25]When the disciples heard this, they were greatly surprised and asked, "How can anyone ever be saved?"

[26]Jesus looked straight at them and said, "There are some things that people cannot do, but God can do anything."

[27]Peter replied, "Remember, we have left everything to be your followers! What will we get?"

[28]Jesus answered:

Yes, all of you have become my followers. And so in the future world, when the Son of Man sits on his glorious throne, I promise that you will sit on twelve thrones to judge the twelve tribes of Israel. [29]All who have given up home or brothers and sisters or father and mother or children or land for me will be given a hundred times as much. They will also have eternal life. [30]But many who are now first will be last, and many who are last will be first.

Workers in a Vineyard

20 As Jesus was telling what the kingdom of heaven would be like, he said:

Early one morning a man went out to hire some workers for his vineyard. [2]After he had agreed to pay them the usual amount for a day's work, he sent them off to his vineyard.

[3]About nine that morning, the man saw some other people standing in the market with nothing to do. [4]He said he would pay them what was fair, if they would work in his vineyard. [5]So they went.

At noon and again about three in the afternoon he returned to the market. And each time he made the same agreement with others who were loafing around with nothing to do.

---

[t]*People who are like these children belong to God's kingdom*: Or "God's kingdom belongs to people who are like these children."

6Finally, about five in the afternoon the man went back and found some others standing there. He asked them, "Why have you been standing here all day long doing nothing?"

7"Because no one has hired us," they answered. Then he told them to go work in his vineyard.

8That evening the owner of the vineyard told the man in charge of the workers to call them in and give them their money. He also told the man to begin with the ones who were hired last. 9When the workers arrived, the ones who had been hired at five in the afternoon were given a full day's pay.

10The workers who had been hired first thought they would be given more than the others. But when they were given the same, 11they began complaining to the owner of the vineyard. 12They said, "The ones who were hired last worked for only one hour. But you paid them the same that you did us. And we worked in the hot sun all day long!"

13The owner answered one of them, "Friend, I didn't cheat you. I paid you exactly what we agreed on. 14Take your money now and go! What business is it of yours if I want to pay them the same that I paid you? 15Don't I have the right to do what I want with my own money? Why should you be jealous, if I want to be generous?"

16Jesus then said, "So it is. Everyone who is now first will be last, and everyone who is last will be first."

Jesus Again Tells about His Death
(Mark 10.32–34; Luke 18.31–34)

17As Jesus was on his way to Jerusalem, he took his twelve disciples aside and told them in private:

18We are now on our way to Jerusalem, where the Son of Man will be handed over to the chief priests and the teachers of the Law of Moses. They will sentence him to death, 19and then they will hand him over to foreigners[u] who will make fun of him. They will beat him and nail him to a cross. But on the third day he will rise from death.

A Mother's Request
(Mark 10.35–45)

20The mother of James and John[v] came to Jesus with her two sons. She kneeled down and started begging him to do something for her. 21Jesus asked her what she wanted, and she said, "When you come into your kingdom, please let one of my sons sit at your right side and the other at your left."[w]

22Jesus answered, "Not one of you knows what you are asking. Are you able to drink from the cup[x] that I must soon drink from?"

James and John said, "Yes, we are!"

---

[u]foreigners: The Romans, who ruled Judea at this time. [v]mother of James and John: The Greek text has "mother of the sons of Zebedee." See 26.37. [w]right side . . . left: The most powerful people in a kingdom sat at the right and left side of the king. [x]drink from the cup: In the Scriptures a cup is sometimes used as a symbol of suffering. To "drink from the cup" is to suffer.

23Jesus replied, "You certainly will drink from my cup! But it is not for me to say who will sit at my right side and at my left. That is for my Father to say."

24When the ten other disciples heard this, they were angry with the two brothers. 25But Jesus called the disciples together and said:

You know that foreign rulers like to order their people around. And their great leaders have full power over everyone they rule. 26But don't act like them. If you want to be great, you must be the servant of all the others. 27And if you want to be first, you must be the slave of the rest. 28The Son of Man did not come to be a slave master, but a slave who will give his life to rescue*y* many people.

Jesus Heals Two Blind Men
(Mark 10.46–52; Luke 18.35–43)

29Jesus was followed by a large crowd as he and his disciples were leaving Jericho. 30Two blind men were sitting beside the road. And when they heard that Jesus was coming their way, they shouted, "Lord and Son of David,*z* have pity on us!"

31The crowd told them to be quiet, but they shouted even louder, "Lord and Son of David, have pity on us!"

32When Jesus heard them, he stopped and asked, "What do you want me to do for you?"

33They answered, "Lord, we want to see!"

34Jesus felt sorry for them and touched their eyes. Right away they could see, and they became his followers.

Jesus Enters Jerusalem
*(Mark 11.1–11; Luke 19.28–38;
John 12.12–19)*

21 When Jesus and his disciples came near to Jerusalem, he went to Bethphage on the Mount of Olives and sent two of them on ahead. 2He told them, "Go into the next village, where you will at once find a donkey and her colt. Untie the two donkeys and bring them to me. 3If anyone asks why you are doing that, just say, 'The Lord*a* needs them.' Right away he will let you have the donkeys."

4So God's promise came true, just as the prophet had said,

5"Announce to the people
        of Jerusalem:
'Your king is coming to you!
He is humble
        and rides on a donkey.
He comes on the colt
        of a donkey.'"

6The disciples left and did what Jesus had told them to do. 7They brought the donkey and its colt and laid some clothes on their backs. Then Jesus got on.

8Many people spread clothes in the road, while others put down branches*b* which they had cut from trees. 9Some people walked ahead of Jesus and others followed behind. They were all shouting,

---

y rescue: The Greek word often, though not always, means the payment of a price to free a slave or a prisoner. *z Son of David*: See the note at 9.27. *a The Lord*: Or "the master of the donkeys." *b spread clothes . . . put down branches*: This was one way that the Jewish people welcomed a famous person.

"Hooray[c] for the Son of David![d]
God bless the one who comes
in the name of the Lord.
Hooray for God
in heaven above!"

10When Jesus came to Jerusalem, everyone in the city was excited and asked, "Who can this be?"

11The crowd answered, "This is Jesus, the prophet from Nazareth in Galilee."

Jesus in the Temple
(Mark 11.15–19; Luke 19.45–48; John 2.13–22)

12Jesus went into the temple and chased out everyone who was selling or buying. He turned over the tables of the moneychangers and the benches of the ones who were selling doves. 13He told them, "The Scriptures say, 'My house should be called a place of worship.' But you have turned it into a place where robbers hide."

14Blind and lame people came to Jesus in the temple, and he healed them. 15But the chief priests and the teachers of the Law of Moses were angry when they saw his miracles and heard the children shouting praises to the Son of David.[d] 16The men said to Jesus, "Don't you hear what those children are saying?"

"Yes, I do!" Jesus answered. "Don't you know that the Scriptures say, 'Children and infants will sing praises'?" 17Then Jesus left the city and went out to the village of Bethany, where he spent the night.

Jesus Puts a Curse on a Fig Tree
(Mark 11.12–14, 20–24)

18When Jesus got up the next morning, he was hungry. He started out for the city, 19and along the way he saw a fig tree. But when he came to it, he found only leaves and no figs. So he told the tree, "You will never again grow any fruit!" Right then the fig tree dried up.

20The disciples were shocked when they saw how quickly the tree had dried up. 21But Jesus said to them, "If you have faith and don't doubt, I promise that you can do what I did to this tree. And you will be able to do even more. You can tell this mountain to get up and jump into the sea, and it will. 22If you have faith when you pray, you will be given whatever you ask for."

A Question about Jesus' Authority
(Mark 11.27–33; Luke 20.1–8)

23Jesus had gone into the temple and was teaching when the chief priests and the leaders of the people came up to him. They asked, "What right do you have to do these things? Who gave you this authority?"

24Jesus answered, "I have just one question to ask you. If you answer it, I will tell you where I got the right to do these things. 25Who gave John the right to baptize? Was it God in heaven or merely some human being?"

They thought it over and said to each other, "We can't say that God gave John this right. Jesus will ask us why we didn't believe John. 26On the other hand, these people think that

---

[c]Hooray: This translates a word that can mean "please save us." But it is most often used as a shout of praise to God.   [d]Son of David: See the note at 9.27.

John was a prophet, and we are afraid of what they might do to us. That's why we can't say that it was merely some human who gave John the right to baptize." 27So they told Jesus, "We don't know."

Jesus said, "Then I won't tell you who gave me the right to do what I do."

A Story about Two Sons

28Jesus said:

I will tell you a story about a man who had two sons. Then you can tell me what you think. The father went to the older son and said, "Go work in the vineyard today!" 29His son told him that he would not do it, but later he changed his mind and went. 30The man then told his younger son to go work in the vineyard. The boy said he would, but he didn't go. 31Which one of the sons obeyed his father?

"The older one," the chief priests and leaders answered.

Then Jesus told them:

You can be sure that tax collectors*e* and bad women will get into the kingdom of God before you ever will! 32When John the Baptist showed you how to do right, you would not believe him. But these evil people did believe. And even when you saw what they did, you still would not change your minds and believe.

Renters of a Vineyard
(Mark 12.1–12; Luke 20.9–19)

33Jesus told the chief priests and leaders to listen to this story:

A land owner once planted a vineyard. He built a wall around it and dug a pit to crush the grapes in. He also built a lookout tower. Then he rented out his vineyard and left the country.

34When it was harvest time, the owner sent some servants to get his share of the grapes. 35But the renters grabbed those servants. They beat up one, killed one, and stoned one of them to death. 36He then sent more servants than he did the first time. But the renters treated them in the same way.

37Finally, the owner sent his own son to the renters, because he thought they would respect him. 38But when they saw the man's son, they said, "Someday he will own the vineyard. Let's kill him! Then we can have it all for ourselves." 39So they grabbed him, threw him out of the vineyard, and killed him.

40Jesus asked, "When the owner of that vineyard comes, what do you suppose he will do to those renters?"

41The chief priests and leaders answered, "He will kill them in some horrible way. Then he will rent out his vineyard to people who will give him his share of grapes at harvest time."

42Jesus replied, "Surely you know that the Scriptures say,

'The stone that the builders
        tossed aside
is now the most important
        stone of all.
This is something
the Lord has done,
        and it is amazing to us.'

---

e tax collectors: See the note at 5.46.

43I tell you that God's kingdom will be taken from you and given to people who will do what he demands. 44Anyone who stumbles over this stone will be crushed, and anyone it falls on will be smashed to pieces."*f*

45When the chief priests and the Pharisees heard these stories, they knew that Jesus was talking about them. 46They looked for a way to kill him. But they were afraid to arrest Jesus, because the people thought he was a prophet.

The Great Banquet
(Luke 14.15–24)

22 Once again Jesus used stories to teach the people:

2The kingdom of heaven is like what happened when a king gave a wedding banquet for his son. 3The king sent some servants to tell the invited guests to come to the banquet, but the guests refused. 4He sent other servants to say to the guests, "The banquet is ready! My cattle and prize calves have all been prepared. Everything is ready. Come to the banquet!"

5But the guests did not pay any attention. Some of them left for their farms, and some went to their places of business. 6Others grabbed the servants, beat them up, and killed them.

7This made the king so furious that he sent an army to kill those murderers and burn down their city. 8Then he said to the servants, "It is time for the wedding banquet, and the invited guests don't deserve to come. 9Go out to the street corners and tell everyone you meet to come to the banquet." 10They went out on the streets and brought in everyone they could find, good and bad alike. And the banquet room was filled with guests.

11When the king went in to meet the guests, he found that one of them was not wearing the right kind of clothes for the wedding. 12The king asked, "Friend, why didn't you wear proper clothes for the wedding?" But the guest had no excuse. 13So the king gave orders for that person to be tied hand and foot and to be thrown outside into the dark. That's where people will cry and grit their teeth in pain. 14Many are invited, but only a few are chosen.

Paying Taxes
(Mark 12.13–17; Luke 20.20–26)

15The Pharisees got together and planned how they could trick Jesus into saying something wrong. 16They sent some of their followers and some of Herod's followers*g* to say to him, "Teacher, we know that you are honest. You teach the truth about what God wants people to do. And you treat everyone with the same respect, no matter who they are. 17Tell us what you think! Should we pay taxes to the Emperor or not?"

18Jesus knew their evil thoughts and said, "Why are you trying to test

---

f pieces: Verse 44 is not in some manuscripts.   *g Herod's followers*: People who were political followers of the family of Herod the Great (2.1) and his son Herod Antipas (14.1), and who wanted Herod to be king in Jerusalem.

me? You showoffs! 19Let me see one of the coins used for paying taxes." They brought him a silver coin, 20and he asked, "Whose picture and name are on it?"

21"The Emperor's," they answered.

Then Jesus told them, "Give the Emperor what belongs to him and give God what belongs to God." 22His answer surprised them so much that they walked away.

Life in the Future World
(Mark 12.18–27; Luke 20.27–40)

23The Sadducees did not believe that people would rise to life after death. So that same day some of the Sadducees came to Jesus and said:

24Teacher, Moses wrote that if a married man dies and has no children, his brother should marry the widow. Their first son would then be thought of as the son of the dead brother.

25Once there were seven brothers who lived here. The first one married, but died without having any children. So his wife was left to his brother. 26The same thing happened to the second and third brothers and finally to all seven of them. 27At last the woman died. 28When God raises people from death, whose wife will this woman be? She had been married to all seven brothers.

29Jesus answered:

You are completely wrong! You don't know what the Scriptures teach. And you don't know any-

thing about the power of God. 30When God raises people to life, they won't marry. They will be like the angels in heaven. 31And as for people being raised to life, God was speaking to you when he said, 32"I am the God worshiped by Abraham, Isaac, and Jacob."*h* He is not the God of the dead, but of the living.

33The crowds were surprised to hear what Jesus was teaching.

The Most Important Commandment
(Mark 12.28–34; Luke 10.25–28)

34After Jesus had made the Sadducees look foolish, the Pharisees heard about it and got together. 35One of them was an expert in the Jewish Law. So he tried to test Jesus by asking, 36"Teacher, what is the most important commandment in the Law?"

37Jesus answered:

Love the Lord your God with all your heart, soul, and mind. 38This is the first and most important commandment. 39The second most important commandment is like this one. And it is, "Love others as much as you love yourself." 40All the Law of Moses and the Books of the Prophets*i* are based on these two commandments.

About David's Son
(Mark 12.35–37; Luke 20.41–44)

41While the Pharisees were still there, Jesus asked them, 42"What do

---

hI am the God worshiped by Abraham, Isaac, and Jacob: Jesus argues that if God is worshiped by these three, they must still be alive, because he is the God of the living. *ithe Law of Moses and the Books of the Prophets*: The Jewish Scriptures, that is, the Old Testament.

you think about the Messiah? Whose family will he come from?"

They answered, "He will be a son of King David."[j]

43Jesus replied, "How then could the Spirit have David call the Messiah his Lord? David said,

44'The Lord said to my Lord:
    Sit at my right side[k]
until I make your enemies
    into a footstool for you.'

45If David called the Messiah his Lord, how can the Messiah be a son of King David?" 46No one was able to give Jesus an answer, and from that day on no one dared ask him any more questions.

Jesus Condemns the Pharisees and the Teachers of the Law of Moses
(Mark 12.38–40; Luke 11.37–52; 20.45–47)

23 Jesus said to the crowds and to his disciples:

2The Pharisees and the teachers of the Law are experts in the Law of Moses. 3So obey everything they teach you, but don't do as they do. After all, they say one thing and do something else.

4They pile heavy burdens on people's shoulders and won't lift a finger to help them. 5Everything they do is just to show off in front of others. They even make a big show of wearing Scripture verses on their foreheads and arms, and they wear big tassels[l] for everyone to see. 6They love the best seats at banquets and the front seats in the meeting places. 7And when they are in the market, they like to have people greet them as their teachers.

8But none of you should be called a teacher. You have only one teacher, and all of you are like brothers and sisters. 9Don't call anyone on earth your father. All of you have the same Father in heaven. 10None of you should be called the leader. The Messiah is your only leader. 11Whoever is the greatest should be the servant of the others. 12If you put yourself above others, you will be put down. But if you humble yourself, you will be honored.

13-14You Pharisees and teachers of the Law of Moses are in for trouble! You're nothing but showoffs. You lock people out of the kingdom of heaven. You won't go in yourselves, and you keep others from going in.[m]

15You Pharisees and teachers of the Law of Moses are in for trouble! You're nothing but showoffs. You travel over land and sea to win one follower. And when you have done so, you make that person twice as fit for hell as you are.

---

[j]son of King David: See the note at 9.27.   [k]right side: The place of power and honor.   [l]wearing Scripture verses on their foreheads and arms . . . tassels: As a sign of their love for the Lord and his teachings, the Jewish people had started wearing Scripture verses in small leather boxes. But the Pharisees tried to show off by making the boxes bigger than necessary. The Jewish people were also taught to wear tassels on the four corners of their robes to show their love for God.   [m]from going in: Some manuscripts add, "You Pharisees and teachers are in for trouble! And you're nothing but showoffs! You cheat widows out of their homes and then pray long prayers just to show off. So you will be punished most of all."

16You are in for trouble! You are supposed to lead others, but you are blind. You teach that it doesn't matter if a person swears by the temple. But you say that it does matter if someone swears by the gold in the temple. 17You blind fools! Which is greater, the gold or the temple that makes the gold sacred?

18You also teach that it doesn't matter if a person swears by the altar. But you say that it does matter if someone swears by the gift on the altar. 19Are you blind? Which is more important, the gift or the altar that makes the gift sacred? 20Anyone who swears by the altar also swears by everything on it. 21And anyone who swears by the temple also swears by God, who lives there. 22To swear by heaven is the same as swearing by God's throne and by the one who sits on that throne.

23You Pharisees and teachers are showoffs, and you're in for trouble! You give God a tenth of the spices from your garden, such as mint, dill, and cumin. Yet you neglect the more important matters of the Law, such as justice, mercy, and faithfulness. These are the important things you should have done, though you should not have left the others undone either. 24You blind leaders! You strain out a small fly but swallow a camel.

25You Pharisees and teachers are showoffs, and you're in for trouble! You wash the outside of your cups and dishes, while inside there is nothing but greed and selfishness. 26You blind Pharisee! First clean the inside of a cup, and then the outside will also be clean.

27You Pharisees and teachers are in for trouble! You're nothing but showoffs. You're like tombs that have been whitewashed.[n] On the outside they are beautiful, but inside they are full of bones and filth. 28That's what you are like. Outside you look good, but inside you are evil and only pretend to be good.

29You Pharisees and teachers are nothing but showoffs, and you're in for trouble! You build monuments for the prophets and decorate the tombs of good people. 30And you claim that you would not have taken part with your ancestors in killing the prophets. 31But you prove that you really are the relatives of the ones who killed the prophets. 32So keep on doing everything they did. 33You are nothing but snakes and the children of snakes! How can you escape going to hell?

34I will send prophets and wise people and experts in the Law of Moses to you. But you will kill them or nail them to a cross or beat them in your meeting places or chase them from town to town. 35That's why you will be held guilty for the murder of every good person, beginning with the good man Abel. This also

---

[n]whitewashed: Tombs were whitewashed to keep anyone from accidentally touching them. A person who touched a dead body or a tomb was considered unclean and could not worship with the rest of the Jewish people.

includes Barachiah's son Zechariah,[o] the man you murdered between the temple and the altar. 36I can promise that you people living today will be punished for all these things!

Jesus Loves Jerusalem
(Luke 13.34, 35)

37Jerusalem, Jerusalem! Your people have killed the prophets and have stoned the messengers who were sent to you. I have often wanted to gather your people, as a hen gathers her chicks under her wings. But you wouldn't let me. 38And now your temple will be deserted. 39You will not see me again until you say,

"Blessed is the one who comes in the name of the Lord."

The Temple Will Be Destroyed
(Mark 13.1, 2; Luke 21.5, 6)

24 After Jesus left the temple, his disciples came over and said, "Look at all these buildings!"

2Jesus replied, "Do you see these buildings? They will certainly all be torn down! Not one stone will be left in place."

Warning about Trouble
(Mark 13.3–13; Luke 21.7–19)

3Later, as Jesus was sitting on the Mount of Olives, his disciples came to him in private and asked, "When will this happen? What will be the sign of your coming and of the end of the world?"

4Jesus answered:

Don't let anyone fool you. 5Many will come and claim to be me. They will say that they are the Messiah, and they will fool many people.

6You will soon hear about wars and threats of wars, but don't be afraid. These things will have to happen first, but that is not the end. 7Nations and kingdoms will go to war against each other. People will starve to death, and in some places there will be earthquakes. 8But this is just the beginning of troubles.

9You will be arrested, punished, and even killed. Because of me, you will be hated by people of all nations. 10Many will give up and will betray and hate each other. 11Many false prophets will come and fool a lot of people. 12Evil will spread and cause many people to stop loving others. 13But if you keep on being faithful right to the end, you will be saved. 14When the good news about the kingdom has been preached all over the world and told to all nations, the end will come.

The Horrible Thing
(Mark 13.14–23; Luke 21.20–24)

15Someday you will see that "Horrible Thing" in the holy place, just as the prophet Daniel said. Everyone who reads this must try to understand! 16If you are living in Judea at that time, run to the mountains. 17If you are

[o]Zechariah: Genesis is the first book in the Jewish Scriptures, and it tells that Abel was the first person to be murdered. Second Chronicles is the last book in the Jewish Scriptures, and the last murder that it tells about is that of Zechariah.

on the roof[p] of your house, don't go inside to get anything. 18If you are out in the field, don't go back for your coat. 19It will be a terrible time for women who are expecting babies or nursing young children. 20And pray that you won't have to escape in winter or on a Sabbath.[q] 21This will be the worst time of suffering since the beginning of the world, and nothing this terrible will ever happen again. 22If God doesn't make the time shorter, no one will be left alive. But because of God's chosen ones, he will make the time shorter.

23Someone may say, "Here is the Messiah!" or "There he is!" But don't believe it. 24False messiahs and false prophets will come and work great miracles and signs. They will even try to fool God's chosen ones. 25But I have warned you ahead of time. 26If you are told that the Messiah is out in the desert, don't go there! And if you are told that he is in some secret place, don't believe it! 27The coming of the Son of Man will be like lightning that can be seen from east to west. 28Where there is a corpse, there will always be buzzards.[r]

When the Son of Man Appears
(Mark 13.24–27; Luke 21.25–28)

29Right after those days of suffering,
"The sun will become dark,
and the moon
    will no longer shine.
The stars will fall,
and the powers in the sky[s]
    will be shaken."
30Then a sign will appear in the sky. And there will be the Son of Man.[t] All nations on earth will weep when they see the Son of Man coming on the clouds of heaven with power and great glory. 31At the sound of a loud trumpet he will send his angels to bring his chosen ones together from all over the earth.

A Lesson from a Fig Tree
(Mark 13.28–31; Luke 21.29–33)

32Learn a lesson from a fig tree. When its branches sprout and start putting out leaves, you know that summer is near. 33So when you see all these things happening, you will know that the time has almost come.[u] 34I can promise you that some of the people living today will still be alive when all this happens.

---

[p]*roof*: In Palestine the houses usually had a flat roof. Stairs on the outside led up to the roof, which was made of beams and boards covered with packed earth.   [q]*in winter or on a Sabbath*: In Palestine the winters are cold and rainy and make travel difficult. The Jewish people were not allowed to travel much more than half a mile on the Sabbath. For these reasons it was hard for them to escape from their enemies in the winter or on a Sabbath.   [r]*Where there is a corpse, there will always be buzzards*: This saying may mean that when anything important happens, people soon know about it. Or the saying may mean that whenever something bad happens, curious people gather around and stare. But the word translated "buzzard" also means "eagle" and may refer to the Roman army, which had an eagle as its symbol.   [s]*the powers in the sky*: In ancient times people thought that the stars were spiritual powers. [t]*And there will be the Son of Man*: Or "And it will be the Son of Man."   [u]*the time has almost come*: Or "he (that is, the Son of Man) will soon be here."

35The sky and the earth won't last forever, but my words will.

No One Knows the Day or Time
(Mark 13.32–37; Luke 17.26–30, 34–36)

36No one knows the day or hour. The angels in heaven don't know, and the Son himself doesn't know.*v* Only the Father knows. 37When the Son of Man appears, things will be just as they were when Noah lived. 38People were eating, drinking, and getting married right up to the day that the flood came and Noah went into the big boat. 39They didn't know anything was happening until the flood came and swept them all away. That is how it will be when the Son of Man appears.

40Two men will be in the same field, but only one will be taken. The other will be left. 41Two women will be together grinding grain, but only one will be taken. The other will be left. 42So be on your guard! You don't know when your Lord will come. 43Homeowners never know when a thief is coming, and they are always on guard to keep one from breaking in. 44Always be ready! You don't know when the Son of Man will come.

Faithful and Unfaithful Servants
(Luke 12.35–48)

45Who are faithful and wise servants? Who are the ones the master will put in charge of giving the other servants their food supplies at the proper time? 46Servants are fortunate if their master comes and finds them doing their job. 47You may be sure that a servant who is always faithful will be put in charge of everything the master owns. 48But suppose one of the servants thinks that the master will not return until late. 49Suppose that evil servant starts beating all the other servants and eats and drinks with people who are drunk. 50If that happens, the master will surely come on a day and at a time when the servant least expects him. 51That servant will then be punished and thrown out with the ones who only pretended to serve their master. There they will cry and grit their teeth in pain.

A Story about Ten Girls

25 The kingdom of heaven is like what happened one night when ten girls took their oil lamps and went to a wedding to meet the groom.*w* 2Five of the girls were foolish and five were wise. 3The foolish ones took their lamps, but no extra oil. 4The ones who were wise took along extra oil for their lamps.

5The groom was late arriving, and the girls became drowsy and fell asleep. 6Then in the middle of the night someone shouted,

---

v and the Son himself doesn't know: These words are not in some manuscripts. *w to meet the groom*: Some manuscripts add "and the bride." It was the custom for the groom to go to the home of the bride's parents to get his bride. Young girls and other guests would then go with them to the home of the groom's parents, where the wedding feast would take place.

"Here's the groom! Come to meet him!"

7When the girls got up and started getting their lamps ready, 8the foolish ones said to the others, "Let us have some of your oil! Our lamps are going out."

9The girls who were wise answered, "There's not enough oil for all of us! Go and buy some for yourselves."

10While the foolish girls were on their way to get some oil, the groom arrived. The girls who were ready went into the wedding, and the doors were closed. 11Later the other girls returned and shouted, "Sir, sir! Open the door for us!"

12But the groom replied, "I don't even know you!"

13So, my disciples, always be ready! You don't know the day or the time when all this will happen.

A Story about Three Servants
(Luke 19.11–27)

14The kingdom is also like what happened when a man went away and put his three servants in charge of all he owned. 15The man knew what each servant could do. So he handed five thousand coins to the first servant, two thousand to the second, and one thousand to the third. Then he left the country.

16As soon as the man had gone, the servant with the five thousand coins used them to earn five thousand more. 17The servant who had two thousand coins did the same with his money and earned two thousand more. 18But the servant with one thousand coins dug a hole and hid his master's money in the ground.

19Some time later the master of those servants returned. He called them in and asked what they had done with his money. 20The servant who had been given five thousand coins brought them in with the five thousand that he had earned. He said, "Sir, you gave me five thousand coins, and I have earned five thousand more."

21"Wonderful!" his master replied. "You are a good and faithful servant. I left you in charge of only a little, but now I will put you in charge of much more. Come and share in my happiness!"

22Next, the servant who had been given two thousand coins came in and said, "Sir, you gave me two thousand coins, and I have earned two thousand more."

23"Wonderful!" his master replied. "You are a good and faithful servant. I left you in charge of only a little, but now I will put you in charge of much more. Come and share in my happiness!"

24The servant who had been given one thousand coins then came in and said, "Sir, I know that you are hard to get along with. You harvest what you don't plant and gather crops where you have not scattered seed. 25I was frightened and went out and hid your money in the ground. Here is every single coin!"

26The master of the servant told him, "You are lazy and good-for-nothing! You know that I harvest what I don't plant and gather crops where I have not scattered seed. 27You could have at least put my money in the bank, so that I could have earned interest on it."

28Then the master said, "Now your money will be taken away and given to the servant with ten thousand coins! 29Everyone who has something will be given more, and they will have more than enough. But everything will be taken from those who don't have anything. 30You are a worthless servant, and you will be thrown out into the dark where people will cry and grit their teeth in pain."

The Final Judgment

31When the Son of Man comes in his glory with all of his angels, he will sit on his royal throne. 32The people of all nations will be brought before him, and he will separate them, as shepherds separate their sheep from their goats.

33He will place the sheep on his right and the goats on his left. 34Then the king will say to those on his right, "My father has blessed you! Come and receive the kingdom that was prepared for you before the world was created. 35When I was hungry, you gave me something to eat, and when I was thirsty, you gave me something to drink. When I was a stranger, you welcomed me, 36and when I was naked, you gave me clothes to wear. When I was sick, you took care of me, and when I was in jail, you visited me."

37Then the ones who pleased the Lord will ask, "When did we give you something to eat or drink? 38When did we welcome you as a stranger or give you clothes to wear 39or visit you while you were sick or in jail?"

40The king will answer, "Whenever you did it for any of my people, no matter how unimportant they seemed, you did it for me."

41Then the king will say to those on his left, "Get away from me! You are under God's curse. Go into the everlasting fire prepared for the devil and his angels! 42I was hungry, but you did not give me anything to eat, and I was thirsty, but you did not give me anything to drink. 43I was a stranger, but you did not welcome me, and I was naked, but you did not give me any clothes to wear. I was sick and in jail, but you did not take care of me."

44Then the people will ask, "Lord, when did we fail to help you when you were hungry or thirsty or a stranger or naked or sick or in jail?"

45The king will say to them, "Whenever you failed to help any of my people, no matter how unimportant they seemed, you failed to do it for me."

46Then Jesus said, "Those people will be punished forever. But the ones who pleased God will have eternal life."

The Plot to Kill Jesus
(Mark 14.1, 2; Luke 22.1, 2; John 11.45–53)

26 When Jesus had finished teaching, he told his disci-

ples, 2"You know that two days from now will be Passover. That is when the Son of Man will be handed over to his enemies and nailed to a cross."

3At that time the chief priests and the nation's leaders were meeting at the home of Caiaphas the high priest. 4They planned how they could sneak around and have Jesus arrested and put to death. 5But they said, "We must not do it during Passover, because the people will riot."

At Bethany
(Mark 14.3–9; John 12.1–8)

6Jesus was in the town of Bethany, eating at the home of Simon, who had leprosy.ˣ 7A woman came in with a bottle of expensive perfume and poured it on Jesus' head. 8But when his disciples saw this, they became angry. They said, "Why such a waste? 9We could have sold this perfume for a lot of money and given it to the poor."

10Jesus knew what they were thinking, and he said:

Why are you bothering this woman? She has done a beautiful thing for me. 11You will always have the poor with you, but you will not always have me. 12She has poured perfume on my body to prepare it for burial.ʸ 13You may be sure that wherever the good news is told all over the world, people will remember what she has done. And they will tell others.

Judas and the Chief Priests
(Mark 14.10, 11; Luke 22.3–6)

14Judas Iscariotᶻ was one of the twelve disciples. He went to the chief priests 15and asked, "How much will you give me if I help you arrest Jesus?" They paid Judas thirty silver coins, 16and from then on he started looking for a good chance to betray Jesus.

Jesus Eats the Passover Meal with His Disciples
(Mark 14.12–21; Luke 22.7–13; John 13.21–30)

17On the first day of the Feast of Thin Bread, Jesus' disciples came to him and asked, "Where do you want us to prepare the Passover meal?"

18Jesus told them to go to a certain man in the city and tell him, "Our teacher says, 'My time has come! I want to eat the Passover meal with my disciples in your home.'" 19They did as Jesus told them and prepared the meal.

20-21When Jesus was eating with his twelve disciples that evening, he said, "One of you will surely hand me over to my enemies."

22The disciples were very sad, and each one said to Jesus, "Surely, Lord, you don't mean me!"

23He answered, "One of you men who has eaten with me from this dish will betray me. 24The Son of Man will die, as the Scriptures say. But it's going to be terrible for the one who betrays me! That man would be better off if he had never been born."

25Judas said, "Teacher, surely you don't mean me!"

ˣleprosy: See the note at 8.2. ʸpoured perfume on my body to prepare it for burial: The Jewish people taught that giving someone a proper burial was even more important than helping the poor. ᶻIscariot: See the note at 10.4.

"That's what you say!" Jesus replied. But later, Judas did betray him.

The Lord's Supper
(Mark 14.22–26; Luke 22.14–23;
1 Corinthians 11.23–25)

26During the meal Jesus took some bread in his hands. He blessed the bread and broke it. Then he gave it to his disciples and said, "Take this and eat it. This is my body."

27Jesus picked up a cup of wine and gave thanks to God. He then gave it to his disciples and said, "Take this and drink it. 28This is my blood, and with it God makes his agreement with you. It will be poured out, so that many people will have their sins forgiven. 29From now on I am not going to drink any wine, until I drink new wine with you in my Father's kingdom." 30Then they sang a hymn and went out to the Mount of Olives.

Peter's Promise
(Mark 14.27–31; Luke 22.31–34;
John 13.36–38)

31Jesus said to his disciples, "During this very night, all of you will reject me, as the Scriptures say,

'I will strike down
　　the shepherd,
　and the sheep
　　will be scattered.'

32But after I am raised to life, I will go to Galilee ahead of you."

33Peter spoke up, "Even if all the others reject you, I never will!"

34Jesus replied, "I promise you that before a rooster crows tonight, you will say three times that you don't know me." 35But Peter said, "Even if I have to die with you, I will never say I don't know you."

All the others said the same thing.

Jesus Prays
(Mark 14.32–42; Luke 22.39–46)

36Jesus went with his disciples to a place called Gethsemane. When they got there, he told them, "Sit here while I go over there and pray."

37Jesus took along Peter and the two brothers, James and John.*a* He was very sad and troubled, 38and he said to them, "I am so sad that I feel as if I am dying. Stay here and keep awake with me."

39Jesus walked on a little way. Then he kneeled with his face to the ground and prayed, "My Father, if it is possible, don't make me suffer by having me drink from this cup.*b* But do what you want, and not what I want."

40He came back and found his disciples sleeping. So he said to Peter, "Can't any of you stay awake with me for just one hour? 41Stay awake and pray that you will not be tested. You want to do what is right, but you are weak."

42Again Jesus went to pray and said, "My Father, if there is no other way, and I must suffer, I will still do what you want."

43Jesus came back and found them sleeping again. They simply could not keep their eyes open. 44He left them and prayed the same prayer once more. 45Finally, Jesus returned to his

---

athe two brothers, James and John: The Greek text has "the two sons of Zebedee." See 27.56.
bhaving me drink from this cup: In the Scriptures "to drink from a cup" sometimes means to suffer. See the note at 20.22.

disciples and said, "Are you still sleeping and resting?[c] The time has come for the Son of Man to be handed over to sinners. 46Get up! Let's go. The one who will betray me is already here."

Jesus Is Arrested
(Mark 14.43–50; Luke 22.47–53; John 18.3–12)

47Jesus was still speaking, when Judas the betrayer came up. He was one of the twelve disciples, and a large mob armed with swords and clubs was with him. They had been sent by the chief priests and the nation's leaders. 48Judas had told them ahead of time, "Arrest the man I greet with a kiss."[d]

49Judas walked right up to Jesus and said, "Hello, teacher." Then Judas kissed him.

50Jesus replied, "My friend, why are you here?"[e]

The men grabbed Jesus and arrested him. 51One of Jesus' followers pulled out a sword. He struck the servant of the high priest and cut off his ear.

52But Jesus told him, "Put your sword away. Anyone who lives by fighting will die by fighting. 53Don't you know that I could ask my Father, and right away he would send me more than twelve armies of angels? 54But then, how could the words of the Scriptures come true, which say that this must happen?"

55Jesus said to the mob, "Why do you come with swords and clubs to arrest me like a criminal? Day after day I sat and taught in the temple, and you didn't arrest me. 56But all this happened, so that what the prophets wrote would come true."

All of Jesus' disciples left him and ran away.

Jesus Is Questioned by the Jewish Council
(Mark 14.53–65; Luke 22.54, 55, 63–71; John 18.13, 14, 19–24)

57After Jesus had been arrested, he was led off to the house of Caiaphas the high priest. The nation's leaders and the teachers of the Law of Moses were meeting there. 58But Peter followed along at a distance and came to the courtyard of the high priest's palace. He went in and sat down with the guards to see what was going to happen.

59The chief priests and the whole council wanted to put Jesus to death. So they tried to find some people who would tell lies about him in court.[f] 60But they could not find any, even though many did come and tell lies. At last two men came forward 61and said, "This man claimed that he would tear down God's temple and build it again in three days."

62The high priest stood up and asked Jesus, "Why don't you say something in your own defense? Don't you hear the charges they are making against you?" 63But Jesus did not answer. So the high priest said, "With the living God looking on, you must tell the truth. Tell us, are you the Messiah, the Son of God?"[g]

---

[c]*Are you still sleeping and resting?*: Or "You may as well keep on sleeping and resting." [d]*the man I greet with a kiss*: It was the custom for people to greet each other with a kiss on the cheek. [e]*why are you here?*: Or "do what you came for." [f]*some people who would tell lies about him in court*: The Law of Moses taught that two witnesses were necessary before a person could be put to death. See verse 60. [g]*Son of God*: One of the titles used for the kings of Israel.

64"That is what you say!" Jesus answered. "But I tell all of you,

'Soon you will see
  the Son of Man
sitting at the right side^h
  of God All-Powerful
and coming on the clouds
  of heaven.' "

65The high priest then tore his robe and said, "This man claims to be God! We don't need any more witnesses! You have heard what he said. 66What do you think?"

They answered, "He is guilty and deserves to die!" 67Then they spit in his face and hit him with their fists. Others slapped him 68and said, "You think you are the Messiah! So tell us who hit you!"

Peter Says He Does Not Know Jesus
(Mark 14.66–72; Luke 22.56–62; John 18.15–18, 25–27)

69While Peter was sitting out in the courtyard, a servant girl came up to him and said, "You were with Jesus from Galilee."

70But in front of everyone Peter said, "That's not so! I don't know what you are talking about!"

71When Peter had gone out to the gate, another servant girl saw him and said to some people there, "This man was with Jesus from Nazareth."

72Again Peter denied it, and this time he swore, "I don't even know that man!"

73A little while later some people standing there walked over to Peter and said, "We know that you are one of them. We can tell it because you talk like someone from Galilee."

74Peter began to curse and swear, "I don't know that man!"

Right then a rooster crowed, 75and Peter remembered that Jesus had said, "Before a rooster crows, you will say three times that you don't know me." Then Peter went out and cried hard.

Jesus Is Taken to Pilate
(Mark 15.1; Luke 23.1, 2; John 18.28–32)

27 Early the next morning all the chief priests and the nation's leaders met and decided that Jesus should be put to death. 2They tied him up and led him away to Pilate the governor.

The Death of Judas
(Acts 1.18, 19)

3When Judas learned that Jesus had been sentenced to death, he was sorry for what he had done. He returned the thirty silver coins to the chief priests and leaders 4and said, "I have sinned by betraying a man who has never done anything wrong."

"So what? That's your problem," they replied. 5Judas threw the money into the temple and then went out and hanged himself.

6The chief priests picked up the money and said, "This money was paid to have a man killed. We can't put it in the temple treasury." 7Then they had a meeting and decided to buy a field that belonged to someone who made clay pots. They wanted to use it as a graveyard for foreigners. 8That is why people still call that place "Field of Blood." 9So the words of the prophet Jeremiah came true,

---

^h*right side*: See the note at 22.44.

"They took
    the thirty silver coins,
the price of a person
    among the people of Israel.
10They paid it
    for a potter's field,[i]
as the Lord
    had commanded me."

Pilate Questions Jesus
(Mark 15.2–5; Luke 23.3–5; John 18.33–38)

11Jesus was brought before Pilate the governor, who asked him, "Are you the King of the Jews?"

"Those are your words!" Jesus answered. 12And when the chief priests and leaders brought their charges against him, he did not say a thing.

13Pilate asked him, "Don't you hear what crimes they say you have done?" 14But Jesus did not say anything, and the governor was greatly amazed.

The Death Sentence
(Mark 15.6–15; Luke 23.13–26; John 18.39—19.16)

15During Passover the governor always freed a prisoner chosen by the people. 16At that time a well-known terrorist named Jesus Barabbas[j] was in jail. 17So when the crowd came together, Pilate asked them, "Which prisoner do you want me to set free? Do you want Jesus Barabbas or Jesus who is called the Messiah?" 18Pilate knew that the leaders had brought Jesus to him because they were jealous.

19While Pilate was judging the case, his wife sent him a message. It said, "Don't have anything to do with that innocent man. I have had nightmares because of him."

20But the chief priests and the leaders convinced the crowds to ask for Barabbas to be set free and for Jesus to be killed. 21Pilate asked the crowd again, "Which of these two men do you want me to set free?"

"Barabbas!" they replied.

22Pilate asked them, "What am I to do with Jesus, who is called the Messiah?"

They all yelled, "Nail him to a cross!"

23Pilate answered, "But what crime has he done?"

"Nail him to a cross!" they yelled even louder.

24Pilate saw that there was nothing he could do and that the people were starting to riot. So he took some water and washed his hands[k] in front of them and said, "I won't have anything to do with killing this man. You are the ones doing it!"

25Everyone answered, "We and our descendants will take the blame for his death!"

26Pilate set Barabbas free. Then he ordered his soldiers to beat Jesus with a whip and nail him to a cross.

Soldiers Make Fun of Jesus
(Mark 15.16–21; John 19.2, 3)

27The governor's soldiers led Jesus into the fortress[l] and brought together

---

[i]*a potter's field*: Perhaps a field owned by someone who made clay pots. But it may have been a field where potters came to get clay or to make pots or to throw away their broken pieces of pottery. [j]*Jesus Barabbas*: Here and in verse 17 many manuscripts have "Barabbas." [k]*washed his hands*: To show that he was innocent. [l]*fortress*: The place where the Roman governor stayed. It was probably at Herod's palace west of Jerusalem, though it may have been Fortress Antonio north of the temple, where the Roman troops were stationed.

the rest of the troops. 28They stripped off Jesus' clothes and put a scarlet robe*m* on him. 29They made a crown out of thorn branches and placed it on his head, and they put a stick in his right hand. The soldiers kneeled down and pretended to worship him. They made fun of him and shouted, "Hey, you king of the Jews!" 30Then they spit on him. They took the stick from him and beat him on the head with it.

Jesus Is Nailed to a Cross
(Mark 15.22–32; Luke 23.27–43;
John 19.17–27)

31When the soldiers had finished making fun of Jesus, they took off the robe. They put his own clothes back on him and led him off to be nailed to a cross. 32On the way they met a man from Cyrene named Simon, and they forced him to carry Jesus' cross.

33They came to a place named Golgotha, which means "Place of the Skull."*m* 34There they gave Jesus some wine mixed with a drug to ease the pain. But when Jesus tasted what it was, he refused to drink it.

35The soldiers nailed Jesus to a cross and gambled to see who would get his clothes. 36Then they sat down to guard him. 37Above his head they put a sign that told why he was nailed there. It read, "This is Jesus, the King of the Jews." 38The soldiers also nailed two criminals on crosses, one to the right of Jesus and the other to his left.

39People who passed by said terrible things about Jesus. They shook their heads and 40shouted, "So you're the one who claimed you could tear down the temple and build it again in three days! If you are God's Son, save yourself and come down from the cross!"

41The chief priests, the leaders, and the teachers of the Law of Moses also made fun of Jesus. They said, 42"He saved others, but he can't save himself. If he is the king of Israel, he should come down from the cross! Then we will believe him. 43He trusted God, so let God save him, if he wants to. He even said he was God's Son." 44The two criminals also said cruel things to Jesus.

The Death of Jesus
(Mark 15.33–41; Luke 23.44–49;
John 19.28–30)

45At noon the sky turned dark and stayed that way until three o'clock. 46Then about that time Jesus shouted, "Eli, Eli, lema sabachthani?"*o* which means, "My God, my God, why have you deserted me?"

47Some of the people standing there heard Jesus and said, "He's calling for Elijah."*p* 48One of them at once ran and grabbed a sponge. He soaked it in wine, then put it on a stick and held it up to Jesus.

49Others said, "Wait! Let's see if Elijah will come*q* and save him."

---

m scarlet robe: This was probably a Roman soldier's robe.   *n Place of the Skull*: The place was probably given this name because it was near a large rock in the shape of a human skull. *o Eli . . . sabachthani*: These words are in Aramaic, a language spoken in Palestine during the time of Jesus. *p Elijah*: In Aramaic the name "Elijah" sounds like "Eli," which means "my God."   *q Elijah will come*: Many of the Jewish people expected the prophet Elijah to come and prepare the way for the Messiah.

50Once again Jesus shouted, and then he died.

51At once the curtain in the temple[r] was torn in two from top to bottom. The earth shook, and rocks split apart. 52Graves opened, and many of God's people were raised to life. 53Then after Jesus had risen to life, they came out of their graves and went into the holy city, where many people saw them.

54The officer and the soldiers guarding Jesus felt the earthquake and saw everything else that happened. They were frightened and said, "This man really was God's Son!"

55Many women were looking on from a distance. They had come with Jesus from Galilee to be of help to him. 56Mary Magdalene, Mary the mother of James and Joseph, and the mother of James and John[s] were some of these women.

Jesus Is Buried
(Mark 15.42–47; Luke 23.50–56; John 19.38–42)

57That evening a rich disciple named Joseph from the town of Arimathea 58went and asked for Jesus' body. Pilate gave orders for it to be given to Joseph, 59who took the body and wrapped it in a clean linen cloth. 60Then Joseph put the body in his own tomb that had been cut into solid rock[t] and had never been used. He rolled a big stone against the entrance to the tomb and went away.

61All this time Mary Magdalene and the other Mary were sitting across from the tomb.

62On the next day, which was a Sabbath, the chief priests and the Pharisees went together to Pilate. 63They said, "Sir, we remember what that liar said while he was still alive. He claimed that in three days he would come back from death. 64So please order the tomb to be carefully guarded for three days. If you don't, his disciples may come and steal his body. They will tell the people that he has been raised to life, and this last lie will be worse than the first one."[u]

65Pilate said to them, "All right, take some of your soldiers and guard the tomb as well as you know how." 66So they sealed it tight and placed soldiers there to guard it.

Jesus Is Alive
(Mark 16.1–8; Luke 24.1–12; John 20.1–10)

28 The Sabbath was over, and it was almost daybreak on Sunday when Mary Magdalene and the other Mary went to see the tomb. 2Suddenly a strong earthquake struck, and the Lord's angel came down from heaven. He rolled away the stone and sat on it. 3The angel looked as bright as lightning, and his clothes were white as snow. 4The guards shook from fear and fell down, as though they were dead.

5The angel said to the women, "Don't be afraid! I know you are looking for Jesus, who was nailed to a cross.

---

[r]curtain in the temple: There were two curtains in the temple. One was at the entrance, and the other separated the holy place from the most holy place that the Jewish people thought of as God's home on earth. The second curtain is probably the one that is meant. [s]of James and John: The Greek text has "of Zebedee's sons." See 26.37. [t]tomb . . . solid rock: Some of the Jewish people buried their dead in rooms carved into solid rock. A heavy stone was rolled against the entrance. [u]the first one: Probably the belief that Jesus is the Messiah.

⁶He is not here! God has raised him to life, just as Jesus said he would. Come, see the place where his body was lying. ⁷Now hurry! Tell his disciples that he has been raised to life and is on his way to Galilee. Go there, and you will see him. That is what I came to tell you."

⁸The women were frightened and yet very happy, as they hurried from the tomb and ran to tell his disciples. ⁹Suddenly Jesus met them and greeted them. They went near to him, held on to his feet, and worshiped him. ¹⁰Jesus said to them, "Don't be afraid! Tell my followers to go to Galilee. They will see me there."

Report of the Guard

¹¹While the women were on their way, some soldiers who had been guarding the tomb went into the city. They told the chief priests everything that had happened. ¹²So the chief priests met with the leaders and decided to bribe the soldiers with a lot of money. ¹³They said to the soldiers, "Tell everyone that Jesus' disciples came during the night and stole his body while you were asleep. ¹⁴If the governor*ᵛ* hears about this, we will talk to him. You won't have anything to worry about." ¹⁵The soldiers took the money and did what they were told. The Jewish people still tell each other this story.

What Jesus' Followers Must Do
(Mark 16.14–18; Luke 24.36–49; John 20.19–23; Acts 1.6–8)

¹⁶Jesus' eleven disciples went to a mountain in Galilee, where Jesus had told them to meet him. ¹⁷They saw him and worshiped him, but some of them doubted.

¹⁸Jesus came to them and said:

I have been given all authority in heaven and on earth! ¹⁹Go to the people of all nations and make them my disciples. Baptize them in the name of the Father, the Son, and the Holy Spirit, ²⁰and teach them to do everything I have told you. I will be with you always, even until the end of the world.

ᵛgovernor: Pontius Pilate.

Mark Tells
the Good News

≈≫≪≈

ABOUT THIS BOOK

This is the shortest of the four New Testament books that tell about the life and teachings of Jesus, but it is also the most action-packed. From the very beginning of his ministry, Jesus worked mighty wonders. After choosing four followers (1.16–20), he immediately performed many miracles of healing. Among those healed were a man with an evil spirit in him (1.21–28), Simon's mother-in-law (1.30,31), crowds of sick people (1.32–34), and a man with leprosy (1.40–45). Over and over Mark tells how Jesus healed people, but always in such a way as to show that he did these miracles by the power of God.

The religious leaders refused to accept Jesus. This led to conflicts (2.2—3.6) that finally made them start looking for a way to kill him (11.18). But the demons saw the power of Jesus, and they knew that he was the Son of God, although Jesus would not let them tell anyone.

This book is full of miracles that amazed the crowds and Jesus' followers. But, according to Mark, the most powerful miracle of Jesus is his suffering and death. The first person to understand this miracle was the Roman soldier who saw Jesus die on the cross and said, "This man really was the Son of God!" (15.39).

This Gospel is widely thought to be the first one written. The many explanations of Aramaic words and Jewish customs in Mark suggest that Mark wrote to Gentile or non-Jewish Christians. He wants to tell about Jesus and to encourage readers to believe in the power of Jesus to rescue them from sickness, demons, and death. He also wants to remind them that the new life of faith is not an easy life, and that they must follow Jesus by serving others and being ready to suffer as he did.

The first followers of Jesus to discover the empty tomb were three women, and the angel told them:

> Don't be alarmed! You are looking for Jesus from Nazareth, who was nailed to a cross. God has raised him to life, and he is not here. (16.6)

A QUICK LOOK AT THIS BOOK

- The Message of John the Baptist (1.1–8)
- The Baptism and Temptation of Jesus (1.9–13)
- Jesus in Galilee (1.14—9.50)
- Jesus Goes from Galilee to Jerusalem (10.1–52)
- Jesus' Last Week: His Trial and Death (11.1—15.47)
- Jesus Is Alive (16.1–8)
- Jesus Appears to His Followers (16.9–20)

The Preaching of John the Baptist
(Matthew 3.1–12; Luke 3.1–18; John 1.19–28)

1 This is the good news about Jesus Christ, the Son of God.[a] 2It began just as God had said in the book written by Isaiah the prophet,

"I am sending my messenger
to get the way ready
for you.
3In the desert
someone is shouting,
'Get the road ready
for the Lord!
Make a straight path
for him.' "

4So John the Baptist showed up in the desert and told everyone, "Turn back to God and be baptized! Then your sins will be forgiven."

5From all Judea and Jerusalem crowds of people went to John. They told how sorry they were for their sins, and he baptized them in the Jordan River.

6John wore clothes made of camel's hair. He had a leather strap around his waist and ate grasshoppers and wild honey.

7John also told the people, "Someone more powerful is going to come. And I am not good enough even to stoop down and untie his sandals.[b] 8I baptize you with water, but he will baptize you with the Holy Spirit!"

The Baptism of Jesus
(Matthew 3.13–17; Luke 3.21, 22)

9About that time Jesus came from Nazareth in Galilee, and John baptized him in the Jordan River. 10As soon as Jesus came out of the water, he saw the sky open and the Holy Spirit coming down to him like a dove. 11A voice from heaven said, "You are my own dear Son, and I am pleased with you."

Jesus and Satan
(Matthew 4.1–11; Luke 4.1–13)

12Right away God's Spirit made Jesus go into the desert. 13He stayed there for forty days while Satan tested him. Jesus was with the wild animals, but angels took care of him.

Jesus Begins His Work
(Matthew 4.12–17; Luke 4.14, 15)

14After John was arrested, Jesus went to Galilee and told the good news that comes from God.[c] 15He said, "The time has come! God's kingdom will soon be here.[d] Turn back to God and believe the good news!"

Jesus Chooses Four Fishermen
(Matthew 4.18–22; Luke 5.1–11)

16As Jesus was walking along the shore of Lake Galilee, he saw Simon and his brother Andrew. They were fishermen and were casting their nets into the lake. 17Jesus said to them, "Come with me! I will teach you how to bring in people instead of fish." 18Right then the two brothers dropped their nets and went with him.

19Jesus walked on and soon saw James and John, the sons of Zebedee. They were in a boat, mending their nets. 20At once Jesus asked them to come with him. They left their father

---

[a]*the Son of God*: These words are not in some manuscripts. [b]*untie his sandals*: This was the duty of a slave. [c]*that comes from God*: Or "that is about God." [d]*will soon be here*: Or "is already here."

in the boat with the hired workers and went with him.

A Man with an Evil Spirit
(Luke 4.31–37)

21Jesus and his disciples went to the town of Capernaum. Then on the next Sabbath he went into the Jewish meeting place and started teaching. 22Everyone was amazed at his teaching. He taught with authority, and not like the teachers of the Law of Moses. 23Suddenly a man with an evil spirit*e* in him entered the meeting place and yelled, 24"Jesus from Nazareth, what do you want with us? Have you come to destroy us? I know who you are! You are God's Holy One."

25Jesus told the evil spirit, "Be quiet and come out of the man!" 26The spirit shook him. Then it gave a loud shout and left.

27Everyone was completely surprised and kept saying to each other, "What is this? It must be some new kind of powerful teaching! Even the evil spirits obey him." 28News about Jesus quickly spread all over that part of Galilee.

Jesus Heals Many People
(Matthew 8.14–17; Luke 4.38–41)

29As soon as Jesus left the meeting place with James and John, they went home with Simon and Andrew. 30When they got there, Jesus was told that Simon's mother-in-law was sick in bed with fever. 31Jesus went to her. He took hold of her hand and helped her up. The fever left her, and she served them a meal.

32That evening after sunset,*f* all who were sick or had demons in them were brought to Jesus. 33In fact, the whole town gathered around the door of the house. 34Jesus healed all kinds of terrible diseases and forced out a lot of demons. But the demons knew who he was, and he did not let them speak.

35Very early the next morning Jesus got up and went to a place where he could be alone and pray. 36Simon and the others started looking for him. 37And when they found him, they said, "Everyone is looking for you!"

38Jesus replied, "We must go to the nearby towns, so that I can tell the good news to those people. This is why I have come." 39Then Jesus went to Jewish meeting places everywhere in Galilee, where he preached and forced out demons.

Jesus Heals a Man
(Matthew 8.1–4; Luke 5.12–16)

40A man with leprosy*g* came to Jesus and kneeled down.*h* He begged, "You have the power to make me well, if only you wanted to."

41Jesus felt sorry for*i* the man. So he put his hand on him and said, "I want to! Now you are well." 42At once the man's leprosy disappeared, and he was well.

43After Jesus strictly warned the man, he sent him on his way. 44He said, "Don't tell anyone about this. Just

---

eevil spirit: A Jewish person who had an evil spirit was considered "unclean" and was not allowed to eat or worship with other Jewish people. *fafter sunset*: The Sabbath was over, and a new day began at sunset. *gleprosy*: In biblical times the word "leprosy" was used for many different kinds of skin diseases. *hand kneeled down*: These words are not in some manuscripts. *ifelt sorry for*: Some manuscripts have "was angry with."

go and show the priest that you are well. Then take a gift to the temple as Moses commanded, and everyone will know that you have been healed."[j]

45The man talked about it so much and told so many people, that Jesus could no longer go openly into a town. He had to stay away from the towns, but people still came to him from everywhere.

Jesus Heals a Crippled Man
(Matthew 9.1–8; Luke 5.17–26)

2 Jesus went back to Capernaum, and a few days later people heard that he was at home.[k] **2**Then so many of them came to the house that there was not even standing room left in front of the door.

Jesus was still teaching **3**when four people came up, carrying a crippled man on a mat. **4**But because of the crowd, they could not get him to Jesus. So they made a hole in the roof[l] above him and let the man down in front of everyone.

5When Jesus saw how much faith they had, he said to the crippled man, "My friend, your sins are forgiven."

6Some of the teachers of the Law of Moses were sitting there. They started wondering, **7**"Why would he say such a thing? He must think he is God! Only God can forgive sins."

8Right away Jesus knew what they were thinking, and he said to them,

"Why are you thinking such things? **9**Is it easier for me to tell this crippled man that his sins are forgiven or to tell him to get up and pick up his mat and go on home? **10**I will show you that the Son of Man has the right to forgive sins here on earth." So Jesus said to the man, **11**"Get up! Pick up your mat and go on home."

12The man got right up. He picked up his mat and went out while everyone watched in amazement. They praised God and said, "We have never seen anything like this!"

Jesus Chooses Levi
(Matthew 9.9–13; Luke 5.27–32)

13Once again Jesus went to the shore of Lake Galilee. A large crowd gathered around him, and he taught them. **14**As he walked along, he saw Levi, the son of Alphaeus. Levi was sitting at the place for paying taxes, and Jesus said to him, "Come with me!" So he got up and went with Jesus.

15Later, Jesus and his disciples were having dinner at Levi's house.[m] Many tax collectors[n] and other sinners had become followers of Jesus, and they were also guests at the dinner.

16Some of the teachers of the Law of Moses were Pharisees, and they saw that Jesus was eating with sinners and tax collectors. So they asked his disciples, "Why does he eat with tax collectors and sinners?"

---

[j]*everyone will know that you have been healed*: People with leprosy had to be examined by a priest and told that they were well (that is "clean") before they could once again live a normal life in the Jewish community. The gift that Moses commanded was the sacrifice of some lambs together with flour mixed with olive oil. [k]*at home*: Or "in the house" (perhaps Simon Peter's home). [l]*roof*: In Palestine the houses usually had a flat roof. Stairs on the outside led up to the roof that was made of beams and boards covered with packed earth. [m]*Levi's house*: Or "Jesus' house." [n]*tax collectors*: These were usually Jewish people who paid the Romans for the right to collect taxes. They were hated by other Jews who thought of them as traitors to their country and to their religion.

17Jesus heard them and answered, "Healthy people don't need a doctor, but sick people do. I didn't come to invite good people to be my followers. I came to invite sinners."

People Ask about Going without Eating
(Matthew 9.14–17; Luke 5.33–39)

18The followers of John the Baptist and the Pharisees often went without eating.*⁰* Some people came and asked Jesus, "Why do the followers of John and those of the Pharisees often go without eating, while your disciples never do?"

19Jesus answered:

The friends of a bridegroom don't go without eating while he is still with them. 20But the time will come when he will be taken from them. Then they will go without eating.

21No one patches old clothes by sewing on a piece of new cloth. The new piece would shrink and tear a bigger hole.

22No one pours new wine into old wineskins. The wine would swell and burst the old skins.*ᵖ* Then the wine would be lost, and the skins would be ruined. New wine must be put into new wineskins.

A Question about the Sabbath
(Matthew 12.1–8; Luke 6.1–5)

23One Sabbath Jesus and his disciples were walking through some wheat fields. His disciples were picking grains of wheat as they went along.*q* 24Some Pharisees asked Jesus, "Why are your disciples picking grain on the Sabbath? They are not supposed to do that!"

25Jesus answered, "Haven't you read what David did when he and his followers were hungry and in need? 26It was during the time of Abiathar the high priest. David went into the house of God and ate the sacred loaves of bread that only priests are allowed to eat. He also gave some to his followers."

27Jesus finished by saying, "People were not made for the good of the Sabbath. The Sabbath was made for the good of people. 28So the Son of Man is Lord over the Sabbath."

A Man with a Crippled Hand
(Matthew 12.9–14; Luke 6.6–11)

3 The next time that Jesus went into the meeting place, a man with a crippled hand was there. 2The Pharisees*ʳ* wanted to accuse Jesus of doing something wrong, and they kept watching to see if Jesus would heal him on the Sabbath.

3Jesus told the man to stand up where everyone could see him. 4Then he asked, "On the Sabbath should we do good deeds or evil deeds? Should we save someone's life or destroy it?" But no one said a word.

5Jesus was angry as he looked around at the people. Yet he felt sorry

---

⁰without eating: The Jewish people sometimes went without eating (also called "fasting") to show their love for God and to become better followers.   *ᵖswell and burst the old skins*: While the juice from grapes was becoming wine, it would swell and stretch the skins in which it had been stored. If the skins were old and stiff, they would burst.   *qwent along*: It was the custom to let hungry travelers pick grains of wheat.   *ʳPharisees*: The Greek text has "they," but see verse 6.

for them because they were so stubborn. Then he told the man, "Stretch out your hand." He did, and his bad hand was healed.

6The Pharisees left. And right away they started making plans with Herod's followers[s] to kill Jesus.

Large Crowds Come to Jesus

7Jesus led his disciples down to the shore of the lake. Large crowds followed him from Galilee, Judea, 8and Jerusalem. People came from Idumea, as well as other places east of the Jordan River. They also came from the region around the cities of Tyre and Sidon. All of these crowds came because they had heard what Jesus was doing. 9He even had to tell his disciples to get a boat ready to keep him from being crushed by the crowds.

10After Jesus had healed many people, all the other sick people begged him to let them touch him. 11And whenever any evil spirits saw Jesus, they would fall to the ground and shout, "You are the Son of God!" 12But Jesus warned the spirits not to tell who he was.

Jesus Chooses His Twelve Apostles
(Matthew 10.1–4; Luke 6.12–16)

13Jesus decided to ask some of his disciples to go up on a mountain with him, and they went. 14Then he chose twelve of them to be his apostles,[t] so that they could be with him. He also wanted to send them out to preach 15and to force out demons. 16Simon was one of the twelve, and Jesus named him Peter. 17There were also James and John, the two sons of Zebedee. Jesus called them Boanerges, which means "Thunderbolts." 18Andrew, Philip, Bartholomew, Matthew, Thomas, James son of Alphaeus, and Thaddaeus were also apostles. The others were Simon, known as the Eager One,[u] 19and Judas Iscariot,[v] who later betrayed Jesus.

Jesus and the Ruler of Demons
(Matthew 12.22–32; Luke 11.14–23; 12.10)

20Jesus went back home,[w] and once again such a large crowd gathered that there was no chance even to eat. 21When Jesus' family heard what he was doing, they thought he was crazy and went to get him under control.

22Some teachers of the Law of Moses came from Jerusalem and said, "This man is under the power of Beelzebul, the ruler of demons! He is even forcing out demons with the help of Beelzebul."

23Jesus told the people to gather around him. Then he spoke to them in riddles and said:

How can Satan force himself out? 24A nation whose people fight each other won't last very

---

[s]Herod's followers: People who were political followers of the family of Herod the Great and his son Herod Antipas.   [t]to be his apostles: These words are not in some manuscripts.   [u]known as the Eager One: The Greek text has "Cananaean," which probably comes from a Hebrew word meaning "zealous" (see Luke 6.15). "Zealot" was the name later given to the members of a Jewish group which resisted and fought against the Romans.   [v]Iscariot: This may mean "a man from Kerioth" (a place in Judea). But more probably it means "a man who was a liar" or "a man who was a betrayer."   [w]went back home: Or "entered a house" (perhaps the home of Simon Peter).

long. 25And a family that fights won't last long either. 26So if Satan fights against himself, that will be the end of him.

27How can anyone break into the house of a strong man and steal his things, unless he first ties up the strong man? Then he can take everything.

28I promise you that any of the sinful things you say or do can be forgiven, no matter how terrible those things are. 29But if you speak against the Holy Spirit, you can never be forgiven. That sin will be held against you forever. 30Jesus said this because the people were saying that he had an evil spirit in him.

Jesus' Mother and Brothers
(Matthew 12.46–50; Luke 8.19–21)

31Jesus' mother and brothers came and stood outside. Then they sent someone with a message for him to come out to them. 32The crowd that was sitting around Jesus told him, "Your mother and your brothers and sisters*x* are outside and want to see you."

33Jesus asked, "Who is my mother and who are my brothers?" 34Then he looked at the people sitting around him and said, "Here are my mother and my brothers. 35Anyone who obeys God is my brother or sister or mother."

A Story about a Farmer
(Matthew 13.1–9; Luke 8.4–8)

4 The next time Jesus taught beside Lake Galilee, a big crowd gathered. It was so large that he had to sit in a boat out on the lake, while the people stood on the shore. 2He used stories to teach them many things, and this is part of what he taught:

3Now listen! A farmer went out to scatter seed in a field. 4While the farmer was scattering the seed, some of it fell along the road and was eaten by birds. 5Other seeds fell on thin, rocky ground and quickly started growing because the soil was not very deep. 6But when the sun came up, the plants were scorched and dried up, because they did not have enough roots. 7Some other seeds fell where thorn bushes grew up and choked out the plants. So they did not produce any grain. 8But a few seeds did fall on good ground where the plants grew and produced thirty or sixty or even a hundred times as much as was scattered.

9Then Jesus said, "If you have ears, pay attention."

Why Jesus Used Stories
(Matthew 13.10–17; Luke 8.9, 10)

10When Jesus was alone with the twelve apostles and some others, they asked him about these stories. 11He answered:

I have explained the secrets about God's kingdom to you, but for others I can use only stories. 12The reason is,

"These people will look
    and look, but never see.
They will listen and listen,
    but never understand.
If they did,
    they would turn to God,
and he
    would forgive them."

---

x and sisters: These words are not in some manuscripts.

Jesus Explains the Story about the Farmer
(Matthew 13.18–23; Luke 8.11–15)

13Jesus told them:

If you don't understand this story, you won't understand any others. 14What the farmer is spreading is really the message about the kingdom. 15The seeds that fell along the road are the people who hear the message. But Satan soon comes and snatches it away from them. 16The seeds that fell on rocky ground are the people who gladly hear the message and accept it right away. 17But they don't have any roots, and they don't last very long. As soon as life gets hard or the message gets them in trouble, they give up.

18The seeds that fell among the thorn bushes are also people who hear the message. 19But they start worrying about the needs of this life. They are fooled by the desire to get rich and to have all kinds of other things. So the message gets choked out, and they never produce anything. 20The seeds that fell on good ground are the people who hear and welcome the message. They produce thirty or sixty or even a hundred times as much as was planted.

Light
(Luke 8.16–18)

21Jesus also said:

You don't light a lamp and put it under a clay pot or under a bed. Don't you put a lamp on a lampstand? 22There is nothing hidden that will not be made public. There is no secret that will not be well known. 23If you have ears, pay attention!

24Listen carefully to what you hear! The way you treat others will be the way you will be treated. 25Everyone who has something will be given more. But people who don't have anything will lose what little they have.

Another Story about Seeds

26Again Jesus said:

God's kingdom is like what happens when a farmer scatters seed in a field. 27The farmer sleeps at night and is up and around during the day. Yet the seeds keep sprouting and growing, and he doesn't understand how. 28It is the ground that makes the seeds sprout and grow into plants that produce grain. 29Then when harvest season comes and the grain is ripe, the farmer cuts it with a sickle.*y*

A Mustard Seed
(Matthew 13.31, 32; Luke 13.18, 19)

30Finally, Jesus said:

What is God's kingdom like? What story can I use to explain it? 31It is like what happens when a mustard seed is planted in the ground. It is the smallest seed in all the world. 32But once it is planted, it grows larger than any garden plant. It even puts out branches that are big enough for birds to nest in its shade.

---

y sickle: A knife with a long curved blade, used to cut grain and other crops.

The Reason for Teaching with Stories
(Matthew 13.34, 35)

33Jesus used many other stories when he spoke to the people, and he taught them as much as they could understand. 34He did not tell them anything without using stories. But when he was alone with his disciples, he explained everything to them.

A Storm
(Matthew 8.23–27; Luke 8.22–25)

35That evening Jesus said to his disciples, "Let's cross to the east side." 36So they left the crowd, and his disciples started across the lake with him in the boat. Some other boats followed along. 37Suddenly a windstorm struck the lake. Waves started splashing into the boat, and it was about to sink.

38Jesus was in the back of the boat with his head on a pillow, and he was asleep. His disciples woke him and said, "Teacher, don't you care that we're about to drown?"

39Jesus got up and ordered the wind and the waves to be quiet. The wind stopped, and everything was calm.

40Jesus asked his disciples, "Why were you afraid? Don't you have any faith?"

41Now they were more afraid than ever and said to each other, "Who is this? Even the wind and the waves obey him!"

A Man with Evil Spirits
(Matthew 8.28–34; Luke 8.26–39)

5 Jesus and his disciples crossed Lake Galilee and came to shore near the town of Gerasa.z 2When he was getting out of the boat, a man with an evil spirit quickly ran to him 3from the graveyarda where he had been living. No one was able to tie the man up anymore, not even with a chain. 4He had often been put in chains and leg irons, but he broke the chains and smashed the leg irons. No one could control him. 5Night and day he was in the graveyard or on the hills, yelling and cutting himself with stones.

6When the man saw Jesus in the distance, he ran up to him and kneeled down. 7He shouted, "Jesus, Son of God in heaven, what do you want with me? Promise me in God's name that you won't torture me!" 8The man said this because Jesus had already told the evil spirit to come out of him.

9Jesus asked him, "What is your name?"

The man answered, "My name is Lots, because I have 'lots' of evil spirits." 10He then begged Jesus not to send them away.

11Over on the hillside a large herd of pigs was feeding. 12So the evil spirits begged Jesus, "Send us into those pigs! Let us go into them." 13Jesus let them go, and they went out of the man and into the pigs. The whole herd of about two thousand pigs rushed down the steep bank into the lake and drowned.

14The men taking care of the pigs ran to the town and the farms to spread the news. Then the people came out to see what had happened. 15When they came to Jesus, they saw the man who had once been full of demons. He was sitting there with his clothes on and in his right mind, and they were terrified.

---

zGerasa: Some manuscripts have "Gadara," and others have "Gergesa."   agraveyard: It was thought that demons and evil spirits lived in graveyards.

16Everyone who had seen what had happened told about the man and the pigs. 17Then the people started begging Jesus to leave their part of the country.

18When Jesus was getting into the boat, the man begged to go with him. 19But Jesus would not let him. Instead, he said, "Go home to your family and tell them how much the Lord has done for you and how good he has been to you."

20The man went away into the region near the ten cities known as Decapolis[b] and began telling everyone how much Jesus had done for him. Everyone who heard what happened was amazed.

A Dying Girl and a Sick Woman
(Matthew 9.18–26; Luke 8.40–56)

21Once again Jesus got into the boat and crossed Lake Galilee.[c] Then as he stood on the shore, a large crowd gathered around him. 22The person in charge of the Jewish meeting place was also there. His name was Jairus, and when he saw Jesus, he went over to him. He kneeled at Jesus' feet 23and started begging him for help. He said, "My daughter is about to die! Please come and touch her, so she will get well and live." 24Jesus went with Jairus. Many people followed along and kept crowding around.

25In the crowd was a woman who had been bleeding for twelve years. 26She had gone to many doctors, and they had not done anything except cause her a lot of pain. She had paid them all the money she had. But instead of getting better, she only got worse.

27The woman had heard about Jesus, so she came up behind him in the crowd and barely touched his clothes. 28She had said to herself, "If I can just touch his clothes, I will get well." 29As soon as she touched them, her bleeding stopped, and she knew she was well.

30At that moment Jesus felt power go out from him. He turned to the crowd and asked, "Who touched my clothes?"

31His disciples said to him, "Look at all these people crowding around you! How can you ask who touched you?" 32But Jesus turned to see who had touched him.

33The woman knew what had happened to her. She came shaking with fear and kneeled down in front of Jesus. Then she told him the whole story.

34Jesus said to the woman, "You are now well because of your faith. May God give you peace! You are healed, and you will no longer be in pain."

35While Jesus was still speaking, some men came from Jairus' home and said, "Your daughter has died! Why bother the teacher anymore?"

36Jesus heard[d] what they said, and he said to Jairus, "Don't worry. Just have faith!"

37Jesus did not let anyone go with him except Peter and the two brothers, James and John. 38They went home with Jairus and saw the people crying and making a lot of noise.[e] 39Then

---

[b]the ten cities known as Decapolis: A group of ten cities east of Samaria and Galilee, where the people followed the Greek way of life.   [c]crossed Lake Galilee: To the west side.   [d]heard: Or "ignored."   [e]crying and making a lot of noise: The Jewish people often hired mourners for funerals.

Jesus went inside and said to them, "Why are you crying and carrying on like this? The child is not dead. She is just asleep." 40But the people laughed at him.

After Jesus had sent them all out of the house, he took the girl's father and mother and his three disciples and went to where she was. 41-42He took the twelve-year-old girl by the hand and said, "Talitha, koum!"*f* which means, "Little girl, get up!" The girl got right up and started walking around.

Everyone was greatly surprised. 43But Jesus ordered them not to tell anyone what had happened. Then he said, "Give her something to eat."

The People of Nazareth Turn against Jesus
(Matthew 13.53–58; Luke 4.16–30)

6 Jesus left and returned to his home-town*g* with his disciples. 2The next Sabbath he taught in the Jewish meeting place. Many of the people who heard him were amazed and asked, "How can he do all this? Where did he get such wisdom and the power to work these miracles? 3Isn't he the car-penter,*h* the son of Mary? Aren't James, Joseph, Judas, and Simon his brothers? Don't his sisters still live here in our town?" The people were very unhappy because of what he was doing.

4But Jesus said, "Prophets are hon-ored by everyone, except the people of their hometown and their relatives and their own family." 5Jesus could not work any miracles there, except to heal a few sick people by placing his hands on them. 6He was surprised that the people did not have any faith.

Instructions for the Twelve Apostles
(Matthew 10.5–15; Luke 9.1–6)

Jesus taught in every town and vil-lage. 7Then he called together his twelve apostles and sent them out two by two with power over evil spirits. 8He told them, "You may take along a walk-ing stick. But don't carry food or a trav-eling bag or any money. 9It's all right to wear sandals, but don't take along a change of clothes. 10When you are welcomed into a home, stay there until you leave that town. 11If any place won't welcome you or listen to your message, leave and shake the dust from your feet*i* as a warning to them."

12The apostles left and started tell-ing everyone to turn to God. 13They forced out many demons and healed a lot of sick people by putting olive oil*j* on them.

The Death of John the Baptist
(Matthew 14.1–12; Luke 9.7–9)

14Jesus became so well-known that Herod the ruler*k* heard about him. Some people thought he was John the Baptist, who had come back to life with the power to work miracles. 15Others

---

*f*Talitha, koum: These words are in Aramaic, a language spoken in Palestine during the time of Jesus. *g*hometown: Nazareth. *h*carpenter: The Greek word may also mean someone who builds or works with stone or brick. *i*shake the dust from your feet: This was a way of showing rejection. *j*olive oil: The Jewish people used olive oil as a way of healing people. Sometimes olive oil is a symbol for healing by means of a miracle (see James 5.14). *k*Herod the ruler: Herod Antipas, the son of Herod the Great.

thought he was Elijah[l] or some other prophet who had lived long ago. 16But when Herod heard about Jesus, he said, "This must be John! I had his head cut off, and now he has come back to life."

17-18Herod had earlier married Herodias, the wife of his brother Philip. But John had told him, "It isn't right for you to take your brother's wife!" So, in order to please Herodias, Herod arrested John and put him in prison.

19Herodias had a grudge against John and wanted to kill him. But she could not do it 20because Herod was afraid of John and protected him. He knew that John was a good and holy man. Even though Herod was confused by what John said,[m] he was glad to listen to him. And he often did.

21Finally, Herodias got her chance when Herod gave a great birthday celebration for himself and invited his officials, his army officers, and the leaders of Galilee. 22The daughter of Herodias[n] came in and danced for Herod and his guests. She pleased them so much that Herod said, "Ask for anything, and it's yours! 23I swear that I will give you as much as half of my kingdom, if you want it."

24The girl left and asked her mother, "What do you think I should ask for?"

Her mother answered, "The head of John the Baptist!"

25The girl hurried back and told Herod, "Right now on a platter I want the head of John the Baptist!"

26The king was very sorry for what he had said. But he did not want to break the promise he had made in front of his guests. 27At once he ordered a guard to cut off John's head there in prison. 28The guard put the head on a platter and took it to the girl. Then she gave it to her mother.

29When John's followers learned that he had been killed, they took his body and put it in a tomb.

Jesus Feeds Five Thousand
(Matthew 14.13–21; Luke 9.10–17;
John 6.1–14)

30After the apostles returned to Jesus,[o] they told him everything they had done and taught. 31But so many people were coming and going that Jesus and the apostles did not even have a chance to eat. Then Jesus said, "Let's go to a place[p] where we can be alone and get some rest." 32They left in a boat for a place where they could be alone. 33But many people saw them leave and figured out where they were going. So people from every town ran on ahead and got there first.

34When Jesus got out of the boat, he saw the large crowd that was like sheep without a shepherd. He felt sorry for the people and started teaching them many things.

35That evening the disciples came to Jesus and said, "This place is like a desert, and it is already late. 36Let the crowds leave, so they can go to the farms and villages near here and buy something to eat."

---

[l]*Elijah*: Many of the Jewish people expected the prophet Elijah to come and prepare the way for the Messiah.   [m]*was confused by what John said*: Some manuscripts have "did many things because of what John said."   [n]*Herodias*: Some manuscripts have "Herod."   [o]*the apostles returned to Jesus*: From the mission on which he had sent them (see 6.7,12,13).   [p]*a place*: This was probably northeast of Lake Galilee (see verse 45).

37Jesus replied, "You give them something to eat."

But they asked him, "Don't you know that it would take almost a year's wages[q] to buy all of these people something to eat?"

38Then Jesus said, "How much bread do you have? Go and see!"

They found out and answered, "We have five small loaves of bread[r] and two fish." **39**Jesus told his disciples to have the people sit down on the green grass. **40**They sat down in groups of a hundred and groups of fifty.

41Jesus took the five loaves and the two fish. He looked up toward heaven and blessed the food. Then he broke the bread and handed it to his disciples to give to the people. He also divided the two fish, so that everyone could have some.

42After everyone had eaten all they wanted, **43**Jesus' disciples picked up twelve large baskets of leftover bread and fish.

44There were five thousand men who ate the food.

Jesus Walks on the Water
(Matthew 14.22–33; John 6.15–21)

45Right away Jesus made his disciples get into the boat and start back across to Bethsaida. But he stayed until he had sent the crowds away. **46**Then he told them goodby and went up on the side of a mountain to pray.

47Later that evening he was still there by himself, and the boat was somewhere in the middle of the lake. **48**He could see that the disciples were struggling hard, because they were rowing against the wind. Not long before morning, Jesus came toward them. He was walking on the water and was about to pass the boat.

49When the disciples saw Jesus walking on the water, they thought he was a ghost, and they started screaming. **50**All of them saw him and were terrified. But at that same time he said, "Don't worry! I am Jesus. Don't be afraid." **51**He then got into the boat with them, and the wind died down. The disciples were completely confused. **52**Their minds were closed, and they could not understand the true meaning of the loaves of bread.

Jesus Heals Sick People in Gennesaret
(Matthew 14.34–36)

53Jesus and his disciples crossed the lake and brought the boat to shore near the town of Gennesaret. **54**As soon as they got out of the boat, the people recognized Jesus. **55**So they ran all over that part of the country to bring their sick people to him on mats. They brought them to him each time they heard where he was. **56**In every village or farm or market place where Jesus went, the people brought their sick to him. They begged him to let them just touch his clothes, and everyone who did was healed.

The Teaching of the Ancestors
(Matthew 15.1–9)

7 Some Pharisees and several teachers of the Law of Moses from Jerusalem came and gathered around

---

[q]*almost a year's wages*: The Greek text has "two hundred silver coins." Each coin was the average day's wage for a worker. [r]*small loaves of bread*: These would have been flat and round or in the shape of a bun.

Jesus. [2]They noticed that some of his disciples ate without first washing their hands.[s]

[3]The Pharisees and all other Jewish people obey the teachings of their ancestors. They always wash their hands in the proper way[t] before eating. [4]None of them will eat anything they buy in the market until it is washed. They also follow a lot of other teachings, such as washing cups, pitchers, and bowls.[u]

[5]The Pharisees and teachers asked Jesus, "Why don't your disciples obey what our ancestors taught us to do? Why do they eat without washing their hands?"

[6]Jesus replied:

You are nothing but showoffs! The prophet Isaiah was right when he wrote that God had said,

"All of you praise me
   with your words,
but you never really
   think about me.
[7]It is useless for you
   to worship me,
when you teach rules
   made up by humans."

[8]You disobey God's commands in order to obey what humans have taught. [9]You are good at rejecting God's commands so that you can follow your own teachings! [10]Didn't Moses command you to respect your father and mother? Didn't he tell you to put to death all who curse their par-

ents? [11]But you let people get by without helping their parents when they should. You let them say that what they own has been offered to God.[v] [12]You won't let those people help their parents. [13]And you ignore God's commands in order to follow your own teaching. You do a lot of other things that are just as bad.

What Really Makes People Unclean
(Matthew 15.10–20)

[14]Jesus called the crowd together again and said, "Pay attention and try to understand what I mean. [15-16]The food that you put into your mouth does not make you unclean and unfit to worship God. The bad words that come out of your mouth are what make you unclean."[w]

[17]After Jesus and his disciples had left the crowd and had gone into the house, they asked him what these sayings meant. [18]He answered, "Don't you know what I am talking about by now? Surely you know that the food you put into your mouth cannot make you unclean. [19]It does not go into your heart, but into your stomach, and then out of your body." By saying this, Jesus meant that all foods were fit to eat.

[20]Then Jesus said:

What comes from your heart
is what makes you unclean.
[21]Out of your heart come evil

---

[s]*without first washing their hands*: The Jewish people had strict laws about washing their hands before eating, especially if they had been out in public. [t]*in the proper way*: The Greek text has "with the fist," but the exact meaning is not clear. It could mean "to the wrist" or "to the elbow." [u]*bowls*: Some manuscripts add "and sleeping mats." [v]*has been offered to God*: According to Jewish custom, when anything was offered to God, it could not be used for anyone else, not even for a person's parents. [w]*unclean*: Some manuscripts add, "If you have ears, pay attention."

thoughts, vulgar deeds, stealing, murder, 22unfaithfulness in marriage, greed, meanness, deceit, indecency, envy, insults, pride, and foolishness. 23All of these come from your heart, and they are what make you unfit to worship God.

A Woman's Faith
(Matthew 15.21–28)

24Jesus left and went to the region near the city of Tyre, where he stayed in someone's home. He did not want people to know he was there, but they found out anyway. 25A woman whose daughter had an evil spirit in her heard where Jesus was. And right away she came and kneeled down at his feet. 26The woman was Greek and had been born in the part of Syria known as Phoenicia. She begged Jesus to force the demon out of her daughter. 27But Jesus said, "The children must first be fed! It isn't right to take away their food and feed it to dogs."*x*

28The woman replied, "Lord, even dogs eat the crumbs that children drop from the table."

29Jesus answered, "That's true! You may go now. The demon has left your daughter." 30When the woman got back home, she found her child lying on the bed. The demon had gone.

Jesus Heals a Man Who Was Deaf and Could Hardly Talk

31Jesus left the region around Tyre and went by way of Sidon toward Lake Galilee. He went through the land near the ten cities known as Decapolis.*y* 32Some people brought to him a man who was deaf and could hardly talk. They begged Jesus just to touch him.

33After Jesus had taken him aside from the crowd, he stuck his fingers in the man's ears. Then he spit and put it on the man's tongue. 34Jesus looked up toward heaven, and with a groan he said, "Effatha!"*z* which means "Open up!" 35At once the man could hear, and he had no more trouble talking clearly.

36Jesus told the people not to say anything about what he had done. But the more he told them, the more they talked about it. 37They were completely amazed and said, "Everything he does is good! He even heals people who cannot hear or talk."

Jesus Feeds Four Thousand
(Matthew 15.32–39)

8 One day another large crowd gathered around Jesus. They had not brought along anything to eat. So Jesus called his disciples together and said, 2"I feel sorry for these people. They have been with me for three days, and they don't have anything to eat. 3Some of them live a long way from here. If I send them away hungry, they might faint on their way home."

4The disciples said, "This place is like a desert. Where can we find enough food to feed such a crowd?"

5Jesus asked them how much food they had. They replied, "Seven small loaves of bread."*a*

6After Jesus told the crowd to sit down, he took the seven loaves and

---

xfeed it to dogs: The Jewish people often referred to Gentiles as dogs.   *ythe ten cities known as Decapolis*: See the note at 5.20.   *zEffatha*: This word is in Aramaic, a language spoken in Palestine during the time of Jesus.   *asmall loaves of bread*: See the note at 6.38.

blessed them. He then broke the loaves and handed them to his disciples, who passed them out to the crowd. 7They also had a few little fish, and after Jesus had blessed these, he told the disciples to pass them around.

8-9The crowd of about four thousand people ate all they wanted, and the leftovers filled seven large baskets.

As soon as Jesus had sent the people away, 10he got into the boat with the disciples and crossed to the territory near Dalmanutha.*b*

A Sign from Heaven
(Matthew 16.1–4)

11The Pharisees came out and started an argument with Jesus. They wanted to test him by asking for a sign from heaven. 12Jesus groaned and said, "Why are you always looking for a sign? I can promise you that you will not be given one!" 13Then he left them. He again got into a boat and crossed over to the other side of the lake.

The Yeast of the Pharisees and of Herod
(Matthew 16.5–12)

14The disciples had forgotten to bring any bread, and they had only one loaf with them in the boat. 15Jesus warned them, "Watch out! Guard against the yeast of the Pharisees and of Herod."*c*

16The disciples talked this over and said to each other, "He must be saying this because we don't have any bread."

17Jesus knew what they were thinking and asked, "Why are you talking about not having any bread? Don't you understand? Are your minds still closed? 18Are your eyes blind and your ears deaf? Don't you remember 19how many baskets of leftovers you picked up when I fed those five thousand people with only five small loaves of bread?"

"Yes," the disciples answered. "There were twelve baskets."

20Jesus then asked, "And how many baskets of leftovers did you pick up when I broke seven small loaves of bread for those four thousand people?"

"Seven," they answered.

21"Don't you know what I am talking about by now?" Jesus asked.

Jesus Heals a Blind Man at Bethsaida

22As Jesus and his disciples were going into Bethsaida, some people brought a blind man to him and begged him to touch the man. 23Jesus took him by the hand and led him out of the village, where he spit into the man's eyes. He placed his hands on the blind man and asked him if he could see anything. 24The man looked up and said, "I see people, but they look like trees walking around."

25Once again Jesus placed his hands on the man's eyes, and this time the man stared. His eyes were healed, and he saw everything clearly. 26Jesus said to the man, "You may return home now, but don't go into the village."

Who Is Jesus?
(Matthew 16.13–20; Luke 9.18–21)

27Jesus and his disciples went to the villages near the town of Caesarea

---

*b*Dalmanutha: The place is unknown.   *c*Herod: Herod Antipas, the son of Herod the Great.

Philippi. As they were walking along, he asked them, "What do people say about me?"

28The disciples answered, "Some say you are John the Baptist or maybe Elijah.[d] Others say you are one of the prophets."

29Then Jesus asked them, "But who do you say I am?"

"You are the Messiah!" Peter replied.

30Jesus warned the disciples not to tell anyone about him.

Jesus Speaks about His Suffering and Death
(Matthew 16.21–28; Luke 9.22–27)

31Jesus began telling his disciples what would happen to him. He said, "The nation's leaders, the chief priests, and the teachers of the Law of Moses will make the Son of Man suffer terribly. He will be rejected and killed, but three days later he will rise to life." 32Then Jesus explained clearly what he meant.

Peter took Jesus aside and told him to stop talking like that. 33But when Jesus turned and saw the disciples, he corrected Peter. He said to him, "Satan, get away from me! You are thinking like everyone else and not like God."

34Jesus then told the crowd and the disciples to come closer, and he said:

If any of you want to be my followers, you must forget about yourself. You must take up your cross and follow me. 35If you want to save your life,[e] you will destroy it. But if you give up your life for me and for the good news,

you will save it. 36What will you gain, if you own the whole world but destroy yourself? 37What could you give to get back your soul?

38Don't be ashamed of me and my message among these unfaithful and sinful people! If you are, the Son of Man will be ashamed of you when he comes in the glory of his Father with the holy angels.

9 I promise you that some of the people standing here will not die before they see God's kingdom come with power.

The True Glory of Jesus
(Matthew 17.1–13; Luke 9.28–36)

2Six days later Jesus took Peter, James, and John with him. They went up on a high mountain, where they could be alone. There in front of the disciples, Jesus was completely changed. 3And his clothes became much whiter than any bleach on earth could make them. 4Then Moses and Elijah were there talking with Jesus.

5Peter said to Jesus, "Teacher it is good for us to be here! Let us make three shelters, one for you, one for Moses, and one for Elijah." 6But Peter and the others were terribly frightened, and he did not know what he was talking about.

7The shadow of a cloud passed over and covered them. From the cloud a voice said, "This is my Son, and I love him. Listen to what he says!" 8At once the disciples looked around, but they saw only Jesus.

9As Jesus and his disciples were

---

[d]*Elijah*: See the note at 6.15.   [e]*life*: In verses 35-37 the same Greek word is translated "life," "yourself," and "soul."

coming down the mountain, he told them not to say a word about what they had seen, until the Son of Man had been raised from death. 10So they kept it to themselves. But they wondered what he meant by the words "raised from death."

11The disciples asked Jesus, "Don't the teachers of the Law of Moses say that Elijah must come before the Messiah does?"

12Jesus answered:

Elijah certainly will come*f* to get everything ready. But don't the Scriptures also say that the Son of Man must suffer terribly and be rejected? 13I promise you that Elijah has already come. And people treated him just as they wanted to, as the Scriptures say they would.

Jesus Heals a Boy
(Matthew 17.14–20; Luke 9.37–43a)

14When Jesus and his three disciples came back down, they saw a large crowd around the other disciples. The teachers of the Law of Moses were arguing with them.

15The crowd was really surprised to see Jesus, and everyone hurried over to greet him.

16Jesus asked, "What are you arguing about?"

17Someone from the crowd answered, "Teacher, I brought my son to you. A demon keeps him from talking. 18Whenever the demon attacks my son, it throws him to the ground and makes him foam at the mouth and grit his teeth in pain. Then he becomes stiff. I asked your disciples to force out the demon, but they couldn't do it."

19Jesus said, "You people don't have any faith! How much longer must I be with you? Why do I have to put up with you? Bring the boy to me."

20They brought the boy, and as soon as the demon saw Jesus, it made the boy shake all over. He fell down and began rolling on the ground and foaming at the mouth.

21Jesus asked the boy's father, "How long has he been like this?"

The man answered, "Ever since he was a child. 22The demon has often tried to kill him by throwing him into a fire or into water. Please have pity and help us if you can!"

23Jesus replied, "Why do you say 'if you can'? Anything is possible for someone who has faith!"

24Right away the boy's father shouted, "I do have faith! Please help me to have even more."

25When Jesus saw that a crowd was gathering fast, he spoke sternly to the evil spirit that had kept the boy from speaking or hearing. He said, "I order you to come out of the boy! Don't ever bother him again."

26The spirit screamed and made the boy shake all over. Then it went out of him. The boy looked dead, and almost everyone said he was. 27But Jesus took hold of his hand and helped him stand up.

28After Jesus and the disciples had gone back home and were alone, they asked him, "Why couldn't we force out that demon?"

29Jesus answered, "Only prayer can force out that kind of demon."

---

f Elijah certainly will come: See the note at 6.15.

Jesus Again Speaks about His Death
(Matthew 17.22, 23; Luke 9.43b–45)

30Jesus left with his disciples and started through Galilee. He did not want anyone to know about it, **31**because he was teaching the disciples that the Son of Man would be handed over to people who would kill him. But three days later he would rise to life. **32**The disciples did not understand what Jesus meant, and they were afraid to ask.

Who Is the Greatest?
(Matthew 18.1–5; Luke 9.46–48)

33Jesus and his disciples went to his home in Capernaum. After they were inside the house, Jesus asked them, "What were you arguing about along the way?" **34**They had been arguing about which one of them was the greatest, and so they did not answer. **35**After Jesus sat down and told the twelve disciples to gather around him, he said, "If you want the place of honor, you must become a slave and serve others!"

36Then Jesus had a child stand near him. He put his arm around the child and said, **37**"When you welcome even a child because of me, you welcome me. And when you welcome me, you welcome the one who sent me."

For or against Jesus
(Luke 9.49, 50)

38John said, "Teacher, we saw a man using your name to force demons out of people. But he was not one of us, and we told him to stop."

39Jesus said to his disciples:

Don't stop him! No one who works miracles in my name will soon turn and say something bad about me. **40**Anyone who is not against us is for us. **41**And anyone who gives you a cup of water in my name, just because you belong to me, will surely be rewarded.

Temptations to Sin
(Matthew 18.6–9; Luke 17.1, 2)

42It will be terrible for people who cause even one of my little followers to sin. Those people would be better off thrown into the ocean with a heavy stone tied around the neck. **43-44**So if your hand causes you to sin, cut it off! You would be better off to go into life crippled than to have two hands and be thrown into the fires of hell that never go out.[h] **45-46**If your foot causes you to sin, chop it off. You would be better off to go into life lame than to have two feet and be thrown into hell.[i] **47**If your eye causes you to sin, get rid of it. You would be better off to go into God's kingdom with only one eye than to have two eyes and be thrown into hell. **48**The worms there never die, and the fire never stops burning.

49Everyone must be salted with fire.[j]

---

[h]*never go out*: Some manuscripts add, "The worms there never die, and the fire never stops burning." [i]*thrown into hell*: Some manuscripts add, "The worms there never die, and the fire never stops burning." [j]*salted with fire*: Some manuscripts add "and every sacrifice will be seasoned with salt." The verse may mean that Christ's followers must suffer because of their faith.

⁵⁰Salt is good. But if it no longer tastes like salt, how can it be made salty again? Have salt among you and live at peace with each other.ᵏ

Teaching about Divorce
(Matthew 19.1–12; Luke 16.18)

10 After Jesus left, he went to Judea and then on to the other side of the Jordan River. Once again large crowds came to him, and as usual, he taught them.

²Some Pharisees wanted to test Jesus. So they came up to him and asked if it was right for a man to divorce his wife. ³Jesus asked them, "What does the Law of Moses say about that?"

⁴They answered, "Moses allows a man to write out divorce papers and send his wife away."

⁵Jesus replied, "Moses gave you this law because you are so heartless. ⁶But in the beginning God made a man and a woman. ⁷That's why a man leaves his father and mother and gets married. ⁸He becomes like one person with his wife. Then they are no longer two people, but one. ⁹And no one should separate a couple that God has joined together."

¹⁰When Jesus and his disciples were back in the house, they asked him about what he had said. ¹¹He told them, "A man who divorces his wife and marries someone else is unfaithful to his wife. ¹²A woman who divorces her husbandˡ and marries again is also unfaithful."

Jesus Blesses Little Children
(Matthew 19.13–15; Luke 18.15–17)

¹³Some people brought their children to Jesus so that he could bless them by placing his hands on them. But his disciples told the people to stop bothering him.

¹⁴When Jesus saw this, he became angry and said, "Let the children come to me! Don't try to stop them. People who are like these little children belong to the kingdom of God.ᵐ ¹⁵I promise you that you cannot get into God's kingdom, unless you accept it the way a child does." ¹⁶Then Jesus took the children in his arms and blessed them by placing his hands on them.

A Rich Man
(Matthew 19.16–30; Luke 18.18–30)

¹⁷As Jesus was walking down a road, a man ran up to him. He kneeled down, and asked, "Good teacher, what can I do to have eternal life?"

¹⁸Jesus replied, "Why do you call me good? Only God is good. ¹⁹You know the commandments. 'Do not murder. Be faithful in marriage. Do not steal. Do not tell lies about others. Do not cheat. Respect your father and mother.' "

²⁰The man answered, "Teacher, I have obeyed all these commandments since I was a young man."

ᵏ*Have salt among you and live at peace with each other*: This may mean that when Christ's followers have to suffer because of their faith, they must still try to live at peace with each other. ˡ*A woman who divorces her husband*: Roman law let a woman divorce her husband, but Jewish law did not let a woman do this. ᵐ*People who are like these little children belong to the kingdom of God*: Or "The kingdom of God belongs to people who are like these little children."

21Jesus looked closely at the man. He liked him and said, "There's one thing you still need to do. Go sell everything you own. Give the money to the poor, and you will have riches in heaven. Then come with me."

22When the man heard Jesus say this, he went away gloomy and sad because he was very rich.

23Jesus looked around and said to his disciples, "It's hard for rich people to get into God's kingdom!" 24The disciples were shocked to hear this. So Jesus told them again, "It's terribly hard[n] to get into God's kingdom! 25In fact, it's easier for a camel to go through the eye of a needle than for a rich person to get into God's kingdom."

26Jesus' disciples were even more amazed. They asked each other, "How can anyone ever be saved?"

27Jesus looked at them and said, "There are some things that people cannot do, but God can do anything."

28Peter replied, "Remember, we left everything to be your followers!" 29Jesus told him:

You can be sure that anyone who gives up home or brothers or sisters or mother or father or children or land for me and for the good news 30will be rewarded. In this world they will be given a hundred times as many houses and brothers and sisters and mothers and children and pieces of land, though they will also be mistreated. And in the world to come, they will have eternal life. 31But many who are now first will be last, and many who are now last will be first.

Jesus Again Tells about His Death
(Matthew 20.17–19; Luke 18.31–34)

32The disciples were confused as Jesus led them toward Jerusalem, and his other followers were afraid. Once again Jesus took the twelve disciples aside and told them what was going to happen to him. He said:

33We are now on our way to Jerusalem where the Son of Man will be handed over to the chief priests and the teachers of the Law of Moses. They will sentence him to death and hand him over to foreigners,[o] 34who will make fun of him and spit on him. They will beat him and kill him. But three days later he will rise to life.

The Request of James and John
(Matthew 20.20–28)

35James and John, the sons of Zebedee, came up to Jesus and asked, "Teacher, will you do us a favor?"

36Jesus asked them what they wanted, 37and they answered, "When you come into your glory, please let one of us sit at your right side and the other at your left."[p]

38Jesus told them, "You don't really know what you're asking! Are you able to drink from the cup[q] that I must soon drink from or be baptized as I must be baptized?"[r]

[n]*hard*: Some manuscripts add "for people who trust in their wealth." Others add "for the rich." [o]*foreigners*: The Romans who ruled Judea at this time. [p]*right side . . . left*: The most powerful people in a kingdom sat at the right and left side of the king. [q]*drink from the cup*: In the Scriptures a "cup" is sometimes used as a symbol of suffering. To "drink from the cup" would be to suffer. [r]*as I must be baptized*: Baptism is used with the same meaning that "cup" has in this verse.

39"Yes, we are!" James and John answered.

Then Jesus replied, "You certainly will drink from the cup from which I must drink. And you will be baptized just as I must! 40But it is not for me to say who will sit at my right side and at my left. That is for God to decide."

41When the ten other disciples heard this, they were angry with James and John. 42But Jesus called the disciples together and said:

You know that those foreigners who call themselves kings like to order their people around. And their great leaders have full power over the people they rule. 43But don't act like them. If you want to be great, you must be the servant of all the others. 44And if you want to be first, you must be everyone's slave. 45The Son of Man did not come to be a slave master, but a slave who will give his life to rescue*r* many people.

Jesus Heals Blind Bartimaeus
(Matthew 20.29–34; Luke 18.35–43)

46Jesus and his disciples went to Jericho. And as they were leaving, they were followed by a large crowd. A blind beggar by the name of Bartimaeus son of Timaeus was sitting beside the road. 47When he heard that it was Jesus from Nazareth, he shouted, "Jesus, Son of David,*s* have pity on me!" 48Many people told the man to stop, but he shouted even louder, "Son of David, have pity on me!"

49Jesus stopped and said, "Call him over!"

They called out to the blind man and said, "Don't be afraid! Come on! He is calling for you." 50The man threw off his coat as he jumped up and ran to Jesus.

51Jesus asked, "What do you want me to do for you?"

The blind man answered, "Master,*t* I want to see!"

52Jesus told him, "You may go. Your eyes are healed because of your faith."

Right away the man could see, and he went down the road with Jesus.

Jesus Enters Jerusalem
*(Matthew 21.1–11; Luke 19.28–40;
John 12.12–19)*

11 Jesus and his disciples reached Bethphage and Bethany near the Mount of Olives. When they were getting close to Jerusalem, Jesus sent two of them on ahead. 2He told them, "Go into the next village. As soon as you enter it, you will find a young donkey that has never been ridden. Untie the donkey and bring it here. 3If anyone asks why you are doing that, say, 'The Lord*u* needs it and will soon bring it back.' "

4The disciples left and found the donkey tied near a door that faced the street. While they were untying it, 5some of the people standing there asked, "Why are you untying the donkey?" 6They told them what Jesus had said, and the people let them take it.

---

*s*rescue: The Greek word often, though not always, means the payment of a price to free a slave or a prisoner. *t*Son of David: The Jewish people expected the Messiah to be from the family of King David, and for this reason the Messiah was often called the "Son of David." *u*Master: A Hebrew word that may also mean "Teacher." *v*The Lord: Or "The master of the donkey."

7The disciples led the donkey to Jesus. They put some of their clothes on its back, and Jesus got on. 8Many people spread clothes on the road, while others went to cut branches from the fields.*w*

9In front of Jesus and behind him, people went along shouting,

"Hooray!*x*
God bless the one who comes
    in the name of the Lord!
10God bless
the coming kingdom
    of our ancestor David.
Hooray for God
    in heaven above!"

11After Jesus had gone to Jerusalem, he went into the temple and looked around at everything. But since it was already late in the day, he went back to Bethany with the twelve disciples.

Jesus Puts a Curse on a Fig Tree
(Matthew 21.18, 19)

12When Jesus and his disciples left Bethany the next morning, he was hungry. 13From a distance Jesus saw a fig tree covered with leaves, and he went to see if there were any figs on the tree. But there were not any, because it was not the season for figs. 14So Jesus said to the tree, "Never again will anyone eat fruit from this tree!" The disciples heard him say this.

Jesus in the Temple
(Matthew 21.12–17; Luke 19.45–48; John 2.13–22)

15After Jesus and his disciples reached Jerusalem, he went into the temple and began chasing out everyone who was selling and buying. He turned over the tables of the money-changers and the benches of those who were selling doves. 16Jesus would not let anyone carry things through the temple. 17Then he taught the people and said, "The Scriptures say, 'My house should be called a place of worship for all nations.' But you have made it a place where robbers hide!"

18The chief priests and the teachers of the Law of Moses heard what Jesus said, and they started looking for a way to kill him. They were afraid of him, because the crowds were completely amazed at his teaching.

19That evening Jesus and the disciples went outside the city.

A Lesson from the Fig Tree
(Matthew 21.20–22)

20As the disciples walked past the fig tree the next morning, they noticed that it was completely dried up, roots and all. 21Peter remembered what Jesus had said to the tree. Then Peter said, "Teacher, look! The tree you put a curse on has dried up."

22Jesus told his disciples:

Have faith in God! 23If you have faith in God and don't doubt, you can tell this mountain to get up and jump into the sea, and it will. 24Everything you ask for in prayer will be yours, if you only have faith.

25-26Whenever you stand up to pray, you must forgive what others have done to you. Then

---

wspread . . . branches from the fields: This was one way that the Jewish people welcomed a famous person. *xHooray*: This translates a word that can mean "please save us." But it is most often used as a shout of praise to God.

your Father in heaven will forgive
your sins.*y*

A Question about Jesus' Authority
(Matthew 21.23–27; Luke 20.1–8)

27Jesus and his disciples returned
to Jerusalem. And as he was walking
through the temple, the chief priests,
the nation's leaders, and the teachers
of the Law of Moses came over to him.
28They asked, "What right do you have
to do these things? Who gave you this
authority?"

29Jesus answered, "I have just one
question to ask you. If you answer it,
I will tell you where I got the right to
do these things. 30Who gave John the
right to baptize? Was it God in heaven
or merely some human being?"

31They thought it over and said to
each other, "We can't say that God
gave John this right. Jesus will ask us
why we didn't believe John. 32On the
other hand, these people think that
John was a prophet. So we can't say
that it was merely some human who
gave John the right to baptize."

They were afraid of the crowd
33and told Jesus, "We don't know."

Jesus replied, "Then I won't tell
you who gave me the right to do
what I do."

Renters of a Vineyard
(Matthew 21.33–46; Luke 20.9–19)

12 This is one of the stories Jesus
used when he spoke to the
people:

A farmer once planted a vineyard. He built a wall around it and
dug a pit to crush the grapes in.

He also built a lookout tower.
Then he rented out his vineyard
and left the country.

2When it was harvest time, he
sent a servant to get his share of
the grapes. 3The renters grabbed
the servant. They beat him up
and sent him away without a
thing.

4The owner sent another servant, but the renters beat him on
the head and insulted him terribly. 5Then the man sent another
servant, and they killed him. He
kept sending servant after servant. They beat some of them and
killed others.

6The owner had a son he loved
very much. Finally, he sent his
son to the renters because he
thought they would respect him.
7But they said to themselves,
"Someday he will own this vineyard. Let's kill him! That way we
can have it all for ourselves." 8So
they grabbed the owner's son and
killed him. Then they threw his
body out of the vineyard.

9Jesus asked, "What do you think
the owner of the vineyard will do? I'll
tell you what he will do. He will come
and kill those renters and let someone
else have his vineyard. 10Surely you
know that the Scriptures say,

'The stone that the builders
tossed aside
is now the most important
stone of all.
11This is something
the Lord has done,
and it is amazing to us.' "

12The leaders knew that Jesus was
really talking about them, and they

---

y your sins: Some manuscripts add, "But if you do not forgive others, God will not forgive
you."

wanted to arrest him. But because they were afraid of the crowd, they let him alone and left.

Paying Taxes
(*Matthew 22.15–22; Luke 20.20–26*)

13The Pharisees got together with Herod's followers.[z] Then they sent some men to trick Jesus into saying something wrong. 14They went to him and said, "Teacher, we know that you are honest. You treat everyone with the same respect, no matter who they are. And you teach the truth about what God wants people to do. Tell us, should we pay taxes to the Emperor or not?"

15Jesus knew what they were up to, and he said, "Why are you trying to test me? Show me a coin!"

16They brought him a silver coin, and he asked, "Whose picture and name are on it?"

"The Emperor's," they answered.

17Then Jesus told them, "Give the Emperor what belongs to him and give God what belongs to God." The men were amazed at Jesus.

Life in the Future World
(*Matthew 22.23–33; Luke 20.27–40*)

18The Sadducees did not believe that people would rise to life after death. So some of them came to Jesus and said:

19Teacher, Moses wrote that if a married man dies and has no children, his brother should marry the widow. Their first son would then be thought of as the son of the dead brother. 20There were once seven brothers. The first one married, but died without having any children. 21The second brother married his brother's widow, and he also died without having children. The same thing happened to the third brother, 22and finally to all seven brothers. At last the woman died. 23When God raises people from death, whose wife will this woman be? After all, she had been married to all seven brothers.

24Jesus answered:

You are completely wrong! You don't know what the Scriptures teach. And you don't know anything about the power of God. 25When God raises people to life, they won't marry. They will be like the angels in heaven. 26You surely know about people being raised to life. You know that in the story about Moses and the burning bush, God said, "I am the God worshiped by Abraham, Isaac, and Jacob."[a] 27He is not the God of the dead, but of the living. You Sadducees are all wrong.

The Most Important Commandment
(*Matthew 22.34–40; Luke 10.25–28*)

28One of the teachers of the Law of Moses came up while Jesus and the Sadducees were arguing. When he heard Jesus give a good answer, he

---

[z]*Herod's followers*: People who were political followers of the family of Herod the Great and his son Herod Antipas. [a]*"I am the God worshiped by Abraham, Isaac, and Jacob"*: Jesus argues that if God is worshiped by these three, they must still be alive, because he is the God of the living.

asked him, "What is the most important commandment?"

29Jesus answered, "The most important one says: 'People of Israel, you have only one Lord and God. 30You must love him with all your heart, soul, mind, and strength.' 31The second most important commandment says: 'Love others as much as you love yourself.' No other commandment is more important than these."

32The man replied, "Teacher, you are certainly right to say there is only one God. 33It is also true that we must love God with all our heart, mind, and strength, and that we must love others as much as we love ourselves. These commandments are more important than all the sacrifices and offerings that we could possibly make."

34When Jesus saw that the man had given a sensible answer, he told him, "You are not far from God's kingdom." After this, no one dared ask Jesus any more questions.

About David's Son
(Matthew 22.41–46; Luke 20.41–44)

35As Jesus was teaching in the temple, he said, "How can the teachers of the Law of Moses say that the Messiah will come from the family of King David? 36The Holy Spirit had David say,

'The Lord said to my Lord:
Sit at my right side[b]
until I make your enemies
into a footstool for you.'

37If David called the Messiah his Lord, how can the Messiah be his son?"[c]

The large crowd enjoyed listening to Jesus teach.

Jesus Condemns the Pharisees and the Teachers of the Law of Moses
(Matthew 23.1–36; Luke 20.45–47)

38As Jesus was teaching, he said:
Guard against the teachers of the Law of Moses! They love to walk around in long robes and be greeted in the market. 39They like the front seats in the meeting places and the best seats at banquets. 40But they cheat widows out of their homes and pray long prayers just to show off. They will be punished most of all.

A Widow's Offering
(Luke 21.1–4)

41Jesus was sitting in the temple near the offering box and watching people put in their gifts. He noticed that many rich people were giving a lot of money. 42Finally, a poor widow came up and put in two coins that were worth only a few pennies. 43Jesus told his disciples to gather around him. Then he said:
I tell you that this poor widow has put in more than all the others. 44Everyone else gave what they didn't need. But she is very poor and gave everything she had. Now she doesn't have a cent to live on.

The Temple Will Be Destroyed
(Matthew 24.1, 2; Luke 21.5, 6)

13 As Jesus was leaving the temple, one of his disciples said to him, "Teacher, look at these beautiful stones and wonderful buildings!"

2Jesus replied, "Do you see these

---

[b]*right side*: The place of power and honor.   [c]*David . . . his son*: See the note at 10.47.

huge buildings? They will certainly be torn down! Not one stone will be left in place."

Warning about Trouble
(Matthew 24.3–14; Luke 21.7–19)

3Later, as Jesus was sitting on the Mount of Olives across from the temple, Peter, James, John, and Andrew came to him in private. **4**They asked, "When will these things happen? What will be the sign that they are about to take place?"

5Jesus answered:

Watch out and don't let anyone fool you! **6**Many will come and claim to be me. They will use my name and fool many people.

7When you hear about wars and threats of wars, don't be afraid. These things will have to happen first, but that is not the end. **8**Nations and kingdoms will go to war against each other. There will be earthquakes in many places, and people will starve to death. But this is just the beginning of troubles.

9Be on your guard! You will be taken to courts and beaten with whips in their meeting places. And because of me, you will have to stand before rulers and kings to tell about your faith. **10**But before the end comes, the good news must be preached to all nations.

11When you are arrested, don't worry about what you will say. You will be given the right words when the time comes. But you will not really be the ones speak-ing. Your words will come from the Holy Spirit.

12Brothers and sisters will betray each other and have each other put to death. Parents will betray their own children, and children will turn against their parents and have them killed. **13**Everyone will hate you because of me. But if you keep on being faithful right to the end, you will be saved.

The Horrible Thing
(Matthew 24.15–21; Luke 21.20–24)

14Someday you will see that "Horrible Thing" where it should not be.*d* Everyone who reads this must try to understand! If you are living in Judea at that time, run to the mountains. **15**If you are on the roof *e* of your house, don't go inside to get anything. **16**If you are out in the field, don't go back for your coat. **17**It will be an awful time for women who are expecting babies or nursing young children. **18**Pray that it won't happen in winter.*f* **19**This will be the worst time of suffering since God created the world, and nothing this terrible will ever happen again. **20**If the Lord doesn't make the time shorter, no one will be left alive. But because of his chosen and special ones, he will make the time shorter.

21If someone should say, "Here is the Messiah!" or "There he is!" don't believe it. **22**False messiahs and false prophets will come and work miracles and

---

d where it should not be: Probably the holy place in the temple.   *e roof*: See the note at 2.4.
f in winter: In Palestine the winters are cold and rainy and make travel difficult.

signs. They will even try to fool God's chosen ones. 23But be on your guard! That's why I am telling you these things now.

When the Son of Man Appears
(Matthew 24.29–31; Luke 21.25–28)

24In those days, right after that time of suffering,

"The sun will become dark,
and the moon
     will no longer shine.
25The stars will fall,
     and the powers in the sky^g
     will be shaken."

26Then the Son of Man will be seen coming in the clouds with great power and glory. 27He will send his angels to gather his chosen ones from all over the earth.

A Lesson from a Fig Tree
(Matthew 24.32–35; Luke 21.29–33)

28Learn a lesson from a fig tree. When its branches sprout and start putting out leaves, you know summer is near. 29So when you see all these things happening, you will know that the time has almost come.^h 30You can be sure that some of the people living today will still be alive when all this happens. 31The sky and the earth will not last forever, but my words will.

No One Knows the Day or Time
(Matthew 24.36–44)

32No one knows the day or the time. The angels in heaven don't know, and the Son himself doesn't know. Only the Father knows. 33So watch out and be ready! You don't know when the time will come. 34It is like what happens when a man goes away for a while and places his servants in charge of everything. He tells each of them what to do, and he orders the watchmen to be on their guard. 35So be on your guard! You don't know when the master of the house will come back. It could be in the evening or at midnight or before dawn or in the morning. 36But if he comes suddenly, don't let him find you asleep. 37I tell everyone just what I have told you. Be on your guard!

A Plot to Kill Jesus
*(Matthew 26.1–5; Luke 22.1, 2;
John 11.45–53)*

14 It was now two days before Passover and the Feast of Thin Bread. The chief priests and the teachers of the Law of Moses were planning how they could sneak around and have Jesus arrested and put to death. 2They were saying, "We must not do it during the feast, because the people will riot."

At Bethany
(Matthew 26.6–13; John 12.1–8)

3Jesus was eating in Bethany at the home of Simon, who once had leprosy,ⁱ when a woman came in with a very expensive bottle of sweet-smelling perfume.^j After breaking it open, she

---

^g*the powers in the sky*: In ancient times people thought that the stars were spiritual powers. ^h*the time has almost come*: Or "he (that is, the Son of Man) will soon be here." ⁱ*leprosy*: In biblical times the word "leprosy" was used for many different skin diseases. ^j*sweet-smelling perfume*: The Greek text has "perfume made of pure spikenard," a plant used to make perfume.

poured the perfume on Jesus' head.
⁴This made some of the guests angry,
and they said, "Why such a waste?
⁵We could have sold this perfume for
more than three hundred silver coins
and given the money to the poor!" So
they started saying cruel things to the
woman.

⁶But Jesus said:

Leave her alone! Why are you
bothering her? She has done a
beautiful thing for me. ⁷You will
always have the poor with you.
And whenever you want to, you
can give to them. But you will not
always have me here with you.
⁸She has done all she could by
pouring perfume on my body to
prepare it for burial. ⁹You may
be sure that wherever the good
news is told all over the world,
people will remember what she
has done. And they will tell
others.

Judas and the Chief Priests
(Matthew 26.14–16; Luke 22.3–6)

¹⁰Judas Iscariot^k was one of the
twelve disciples. He went to the chief
priests and offered to help them arrest
Jesus. ¹¹They were glad to hear this,
and they promised to pay him. So Judas
started looking for a good chance to betray Jesus.

Jesus Eats with His Disciples
(Matthew 26.17–25; Luke 22.7–14, 21–23;
John 13.21–30)

¹²It was the first day of the Feast
of Thin Bread, and the Passover lambs
were being killed. Jesus' disciples

asked him, "Where do you want us to
prepare the Passover meal?"

¹³Jesus said to two of the disciples,
"Go into the city, where you will meet
a man carrying a jar of water.^l Follow
him, ¹⁴and when he goes into a house,
say to the owner, 'Our teacher wants
to know if you have a room where he
can eat the Passover meal with his disciples.' ¹⁵The owner will take you upstairs and show you a large room fur-
nished and ready for you to use.
Prepare the meal there."

¹⁶The two disciples went into the
city and found everything just as Jesus
had told them. So they prepared the
Passover meal.

¹⁷⁻¹⁸While Jesus and the twelve
disciples were eating together that evening, he said, "The one who will betray
me is now eating with me."

¹⁹This made the disciples sad, and
one after another they said to Jesus,
"Surely you don't mean me!"

²⁰He answered, "It is one of you
twelve men who is eating from this
dish with me. ²¹The Son of Man will
die, just as the Scriptures say. But it
is going to be terrible for the one who
betrays me. That man would be better
off if he had never been born."

The Lord's Supper
(Matthew 26.26–30; Luke 22.14–23;
1 Corinthians 11.23–25)

²²During the meal Jesus took some
bread in his hands. He blessed the
bread and broke it. Then he gave it to
his disciples and said, "Take this. It is
my body."

²³Jesus picked up a cup of wine
and gave thanks to God. He then gave

---

^k*Iscariot*: See the note at 3.19. ^l*a man carrying a jar of water*: A male slave carrying water
could mean that the family was rich.

it to his disciples and said, "Drink it!"
So they all drank some. 24Then he said,
"This is my blood, which is poured out
for many people, and with it God
makes his agreement. 25From now on
I will not drink any wine, until I drink
new wine in God's kingdom." 26Then
they sang a hymn and went out to the
Mount of Olives.

Peter's Promise
(Matthew 26.31–35; Luke 22.31–34;
John 13.36–38)

27Jesus said to his disciples, "All
of you will reject me, as the Scriptures say,

'I will strike down
    the shepherd,
and the sheep
    will be scattered.'
28But after I am raised to life, I will
go ahead of you to Galilee."

29Peter spoke up, "Even if all the
others reject you, I never will!"

30Jesus replied, "This very night before a rooster crows twice, you will say
three times that you don't know me."

31But Peter was so sure of himself
that he said, "Even if I have to die with
you, I will never say that I don't
know you!"

All the others said the same thing.

Jesus Prays
(Matthew 26.36–46; Luke 22.39–46)

32Jesus went with his disciples to
a place called Gethsemane, and he told
them, "Sit here while I pray."

33Jesus took along Peter, James,
and John. He was sad and troubled and
34told them, "I am so sad that I feel

as if I am dying. Stay here and keep
awake with me."

35-36Jesus walked on a little way.
Then he kneeled down on the ground
and prayed, "Father,*m* if it is possible,
don't let this happen to me! Father, you
can do anything. Don't make me suffer
by having me drink from this cup.*n*
But do what you want, and not what I
want."

37When Jesus came back and
found the disciples sleeping, he said
to Simon Peter, "Are you asleep? Can't
you stay awake for just one hour?
38Stay awake and pray that you will
not be tested. You want to do what is
right, but you are weak."

39Jesus went back and prayed the
same prayer. 40But when he returned
to the disciples, he found them sleeping again. They simply could not keep
their eyes open, and they did not know
what to say.

41When Jesus returned to the disciples the third time, he said, "Are you
still sleeping and resting?*o* Enough of
that! The time has come for the Son
of Man to be handed over to sinners.
42Get up! Let's go. The one who will
betray me is already here."

Jesus Is Arrested
(Matthew 26.47–56; Luke 22.47–53;
John 18.3–12)

43Jesus was still speaking, when
Judas the betrayer came up. He was
one of the twelve disciples, and a mob
of men armed with swords and clubs
were with him. They had been sent by
the chief priests, the nation's leaders,
and the teachers of the Law of Moses.
44Judas had told them ahead of time,

---

m Father: The Greek text has "Abba," which is an Aramaic word meaning "father."   *n by having*
me drink from this cup: See the note at 10.38.   *o Are you still sleeping and resting?* : Or "You
may as well keep on sleeping and resting."

"Arrest the man I greet with a kiss.*p* Tie him up tight and lead him away."

45Judas walked right up to Jesus and said, "Teacher!" Then Judas kissed him, **46**and the men grabbed Jesus and arrested him.

47Someone standing there pulled out a sword. He struck the servant of the high priest and cut off his ear.

48Jesus said to the mob, "Why do you come with swords and clubs to arrest me like a criminal? **49**Day after day I was with you and taught in the temple, and you didn't arrest me. But what the Scriptures say must come true."

50All of Jesus' disciples ran off and left him. **51**One of them was a young man who was wearing only a linen cloth. And when the men grabbed him, **52**he left the cloth behind and ran away naked.

Jesus Is Questioned by the Jewish Council
(Matthew 26.57–68; Luke 22.54, 55, 63–71; John 18.13, 14, 19–24)

53Jesus was led off to the high priest. Then the chief priests, the nation's leaders, and the teachers of the Law of Moses all met together. **54**Peter had followed at a distance. And when he reached the courtyard of the high priest's house, he sat down with the guards to warm himself beside a fire.

55The chief priests and the whole council tried to find someone to accuse Jesus of a crime, so they could put him to death. But they could not find anyone to accuse him. **56**Many people did tell lies against Jesus, but they did not agree on what they said. **57**Finally, some men stood up and lied about him. They said, **58**"We heard him say he would tear down this temple that we built. He also claimed that in three days he would build another one without any help." **59**But even then they did not agree on what they said.

60The high priest stood up in the council and asked Jesus, "Why don't you say something in your own defense? Don't you hear the charges they are making against you?" **61**But Jesus kept quiet and did not say a word. The high priest asked him another question, "Are you the Messiah, the Son of the glorious God?"*q*

62"Yes, I am!" Jesus answered.

"Soon you will see
the Son of Man
sitting at the right side*r*
of God All-Powerful,
and coming with the clouds
of heaven."

63At once the high priest ripped his robe apart and shouted, "Why do we need more witnesses? **64**You heard him claim to be God! What is your decision?" They all agreed that he should be put to death.

65Some of the people started spitting on Jesus. They blindfolded him, hit him with their fists, and said, "Tell us who hit you!" Then the guards took charge of Jesus and beat him.

Peter Says He Does Not Know Jesus
(Matthew 26.69–75; Luke 22.56–62; John 18.15–18, 25–27)

66While Peter was still in the courtyard, a servant girl of the high priest came up **67**and saw Peter warming himself by the fire. She stared at him and said, "You were with Jesus from Nazareth!"

*p*greet with a kiss: It was the custom for people to greet each other with a kiss on the cheek.
*q*Son of the glorious God: "Son of God" was one of the titles used for the kings of Israel.
*r*right side: See the note at 12.36.

68Peter replied, "That's not true! I don't know what you're talking about. I don't have any idea what you mean." He went out to the gate, and a rooster crowed.*r*

69The servant girl saw Peter again and said to the people standing there, "This man is one of them!"

70"No, I'm not!" Peter replied.

A little while later some of the people said to Peter, "You certainly are one of them. You're a Galilean!"

71This time Peter began to curse and swear, "I don't even know the man you're talking about!"

72Right away the rooster crowed a second time. Then Peter remembered that Jesus had told him, "Before a rooster crows twice, you will say three times that you don't know me." So Peter started crying.

Pilate Questions Jesus
(Matthew 27.1, 2, 11–14; Luke 23.1–5; John 18.28–38)

15 Early the next morning the chief priests, the nation's leaders, and the teachers of the Law of Moses met together with the whole Jewish council. They tied up Jesus and led him off to Pilate.

2He asked Jesus, "Are you the king of the Jews?"

"Those are your words," Jesus answered.

3The chief priests brought many charges against Jesus. **4**Then Pilate questioned him again, "Don't you have anything to say? Don't you hear what crimes they say you have done?" **5**But Jesus did not answer, and Pilate was amazed.

The Death Sentence
(Matthew 27.15–26; Luke 23.13–25; John 18.39—19.16)

6During Passover, Pilate always freed one prisoner chosen by the people. **7**And at that time there was a prisoner named Barabbas. He and some others had been arrested for murder during a riot. **8**The Jewish people now came and asked Pilate to set a prisoner free, just as he usually did.

9Pilate asked them, "Do you want me to free the king of the Jews?" **10**Pilate knew that the chief priests had brought Jesus to him because they were jealous.

11But the chief priests told the crowd to ask Pilate to free Barabbas. **12**Then Pilate asked the crowd, "What do you want me to do with this man you say is*s* the king of the Jews?"

13They yelled, "Nail him to a cross!"

14Pilate asked, "But what crime has he done?"

"Nail him to a cross!" they yelled even louder.

15Pilate wanted to please the crowd. So he set Barabbas free. Then he ordered his soldiers to beat Jesus with a whip and nail him to a cross.

Soldiers Make Fun of Jesus
(Matthew 27.27–30; John 19.2, 3)

16The soldiers led Jesus inside the courtyard of the fortress*t* and called together the rest of the troops. **17**They put a purple robe*u* on him, and on his

---

s a rooster crowed: These words are not in some manuscripts. *t this man you say is*: These words are not in some manuscripts. *u fortress*: The place where the Roman governor stayed. It was probably at Herod's palace west of Jerusalem, though it may have been Fortress Antonio, north of the temple, where the Roman troops were stationed. *v purple robe*: This was probably a Roman soldier's robe.

head they placed a crown that they had made out of thorn branches. 18They made fun of Jesus and shouted, "Hey, you king of the Jews!" 19Then they beat him on the head with a stick. They spit on him and kneeled down and pretended to worship him.

20When the soldiers had finished making fun of Jesus, they took off the purple robe. They put his own clothes back on him and led him off to be nailed to a cross. 21Simon from Cyrene happened to be coming in from a farm, and they forced him to carry Jesus' cross. Simon was the father of Alexander and Rufus.

Jesus Is Nailed to a Cross
(*Matthew 27.31–44; Luke 23.27–43; John 19.17–27*)

22The soldiers took Jesus to Golgotha, which means "Place of a Skull."*w* 23There they gave him some wine mixed with a drug to ease the pain, but he refused to drink it.

24They nailed Jesus to a cross and gambled to see who would get his clothes. 25It was about nine o'clock in the morning when they nailed him to the cross. 26On it was a sign that told why he was nailed there. It read, "This is the King of the Jews." 27-28The soldiers also nailed two criminals on crosses, one to the right of Jesus and the other to his left.*x*

29People who passed by said terrible things about Jesus. They shook their heads and shouted, "Ha! So you're the one who claimed you could tear down the temple and build it again in three days. 30Save yourself and come down from the cross!"

31The chief priests and the teachers of the Law of Moses also made fun of Jesus. They said to each other, "He saved others, but he can't save himself. 32If he is the Messiah, the king of Israel, let him come down from the cross! Then we will see and believe." The two criminals also said cruel things to Jesus.

The Death of Jesus
(*Matthew 27.45–56; Luke 23.44–49; John 19.28–30*)

33About noon the sky turned dark and stayed that way until around three o'clock. 34Then about that time Jesus shouted, "Eloi, Eloi, lema sabachthani?"*y* which means, "My God, my God, why have you deserted me?"

35Some of the people standing there heard Jesus and said, "He is calling for Elijah."*z* 36One of them ran and grabbed a sponge. After he had soaked it in wine, he put it on a stick and held it up to Jesus. He said, "Let's wait and see if Elijah will come*a* and take him down!" 37Jesus shouted and then died.

38At once the curtain in the temple*b* tore in two from top to bottom.

---

w"*Place of a Skull*": The place was probably given this name because it was near a large rock in the shape of a human skull.   *xleft*: Some manuscripts add, "So the Scriptures came true which say, 'He was accused of being a criminal.'"   *yEloi . . . sabachthani*: These words are in Aramaic, a language spoken in Palestine during the time of Jesus.   *zElijah*: The name "Elijah" sounds something like "Eloi," which means "my God."   *asee if Elijah will come*: See the note at 6.15.   *bcurtain in the temple*: There were two curtains in the temple. One was at the entrance, and the other separated the holy place from the most holy place that the Jewish people thought of as God's home on earth. The second curtain is probably the one which is meant.

39A Roman army officer was standing in front of Jesus. When the officer saw how Jesus died, he said, "This man really was the Son of God!"

40-41 Some women were looking on from a distance. They had come with Jesus to Jerusalem. But even before this they had been his followers and had helped him while he was in Galilee. Mary Magdalene and Mary the mother of the younger James and of Joseph were two of these women. Salome was also one of them.

Jesus Is Buried
(Matthew 27.57–61; Luke 23.50–56; John 19.38–42)

42It was now the evening before the Sabbath, and the Jewish people were getting ready for that sacred day. **43**A man named Joseph from Arimathea was brave enough to ask Pilate for the body of Jesus. Joseph was a highly respected member of the Jewish council, and he was also waiting for God's kingdom to come.

44Pilate was surprised to hear that Jesus was already dead, and he called in the army officer to find out if Jesus had been dead very long. **45**After the officer told him, Pilate let Joseph have Jesus' body.

46Joseph bought a linen cloth and took the body down from the cross. He had it wrapped in the cloth, and he put it in a tomb that had been cut into solid rock. Then he rolled a big stone against the entrance to the tomb.

47Mary Magdalene and Mary the mother of Joseph were watching and saw where the body was placed.

Jesus Is Alive
(Matthew 28.1–8; Luke 24.1–12; John 20.1–10)

16 After the Sabbath, Mary Magdalene, Salome, and Mary the mother of James bought some spices to put on Jesus' body. **2**Very early on Sunday morning, just as the sun was coming up, they went to the tomb. **3**On their way, they were asking one another, "Who will roll the stone away from the entrance for us?" **4**But when they looked, they saw that the stone had already been rolled away. And it was a huge stone!

5The women went into the tomb, and on the right side they saw a young man in a white robe sitting there. They were alarmed.

6The man said, "Don't be alarmed! You are looking for Jesus from Nazareth, who was nailed to a cross. God has raised him to life, and he is not here. You can see the place where they put his body. **7**Now go and tell his disciples, and especially Peter, that he will go ahead of you to Galilee. You will see him there, just as he told you."

8When the women ran from the tomb, they were confused and shaking all over. They were too afraid to tell anyone what had happened.

Jesus Appears to Mary Magdalene[b]
(Matthew 28.9, 10; John 20.11–18)

9Very early on the first day of the week, after Jesus had risen to life, he appeared to Mary Magdalene. Earlier he had forced seven demons out of her. **10**She left and told his friends, who were crying and mourning. **11**Even

---

[c]*Jesus Appears to Mary Magdalene*: Mark 16.9-20 is not in some manuscripts.

though they heard that Jesus was alive and that Mary had seen him, they would not believe it.

Jesus Appears to Two Disciples
(Luke 24.13–35)

12Later, Jesus appeared in another form to two disciples, as they were on their way out of the city. 13But when these disciples told what had happened, the others would not believe.

What Jesus' Followers Must Do
(Matthew 28.16–20; Luke 24.36–49; John 20.19–23; Acts 1.6–8)

14Afterwards, Jesus appeared to his eleven disciples as they were eating. He scolded them because they were too stubborn to believe the ones who had seen him after he had been raised to life. 15Then he told them:

Go and preach the good news to everyone in the world. 16Anyone who believes me and is baptized will be saved. But anyone who refuses to believe me will be condemned. 17Everyone who believes me will be able to do wonderful things. By using my name they will force out demons, and they will speak new languages. 18They will handle snakes and will drink poison and not be hurt. They will also heal sick people by placing their hands on them.

Jesus Returns to Heaven
(Luke 24.50–53; Acts 1.9–11)

19After the Lord Jesus had said these things to the disciples, he was taken back up to heaven where he sat down at the right side^d of God. 20Then the disciples left and preached everywhere. The Lord was with them, and the miracles they worked proved that their message was true.

ANOTHER OLD ENDING TO MARK'S GOSPEL^e

9-10The women quickly told Peter and his friends what had happened. Later, Jesus sent the disciples to the east and to the west with his sacred and everlasting message of how people can be saved forever.

---

^{d}*right side*: See the note at 12.36. ^{e}*Another Old Ending to Mark's Gospel*: Some manuscripts and early translations have both this shorter ending and the longer one (verses 9-20).

Luke Tells
the Good News

ABOUT THIS BOOK

God's love is for everyone! Jesus came into the world to be the Savior of all people! These are two of the main thoughts in this book. Several of the best known stories that Jesus used for teaching about God's love are found only in Luke's Gospel: The Good Samaritan (10.25–37), A Lost Sheep (15.1–7), and A Lost Son (15.11–32). Only Luke tells how Jesus visited in the home of a hated tax collector (19.1–10) and promised life in paradise to a dying criminal (23.39–43).

Luke mentions God's Spirit more than any of the other New Testament writers. For example, the power of the Spirit was with John the Baptist from the time he was born (1.15). And the angel promised Mary, "The Holy Spirit will come down to you . . . So your child will be called the holy Son of God" (1.35). Jesus followed the Spirit (4.1, 14, 18; 10.21) and taught that the Spirit is God's greatest gift (11.13).

Luke shows how important prayer was to Jesus. Jesus prayed often: after being baptized (3.21), before choosing the disciples (6.12), before asking his disciples who they thought he was (9.18), and before giving up his life on the cross (23.34,46). From Luke we learn of three stories that Jesus told to teach about prayer (11.5–9; 18.1–8, 9–14).

An important part of Luke's story is the way in which he shows the concern of Jesus for the poor: the good news is preached to them (4.18; 7.22), they receive God's blessings (6.20), they are invited to the great feast (14.13, 21), the poor man Lazarus is taken to heaven by angels (16.20,22), and Jesus commands his disciples to sell what they have and give the money to the poor (12.33).

To make sure that readers would understand that Jesus was raised physically from death, Luke reports that the risen Jesus ate a piece of fish (24.42, 43). There could be no mistake about the risen Jesus: he was not a ghost. His being raised from death was real and not someone's imagination. Luke also wrote another book—the Acts of the Apostles—to show what happened to Jesus' followers after he was raised from death and taken up to heaven. No other Gospel has a second volume that continues the story.

Luke closes this first book that he wrote by telling that Jesus returned to heaven. But right before Jesus leaves, he tells his disciples:

The Scriptures say that the Messiah must suffer, then three days later he will rise from death. They also say that all people of every nation must be told in my name to turn to God, in order to be forgiven. So beginning in Jerusalem, you must tell everything that has happened.   (24.46–48)

A QUICK LOOK AT THIS BOOK

- Why Luke Wrote this Book(1.1–4)
- The Births of John the Baptist and Jesus (1.5—2.52)

- The Message of John the Baptist (3.1–20)
- The Baptism and Temptation of Jesus (3.21—4.13)
- Jesus' Ministry in Galilee (4.14—9.50)
- Jesus Goes from Galilee to Jerusalem (9.51—19.27)
- Jesus' Last Week: His Trial and Death (19.28—23.56)
- Jesus Is Alive (24.1–12)
- Jesus Appears. He Is Taken to Heaven (24.13–53)

1 Many people have tried to tell the story of what God has done among us. ²They wrote what we had been told by the ones who were there in the beginning and saw what happened. ³So I made a careful study^a of everything and then decided to write and tell you exactly what took place. Honorable Theophilus, ⁴I have done this to let you know if what you have heard is true.

An Angel Tells about the Birth of John

⁵When Herod was king of Judea, there was a priest by the name of Zechariah from the priestly group of Abijah. His wife Elizabeth was from the family of Aaron.^b ⁶Both of them were good people and pleased the Lord God by obeying all that he had commanded. ⁷But they did not have children. Elizabeth could not have any, and both Zechariah and Elizabeth were already old.

⁸One day Zechariah's group of priests were on duty, and he was serving God as a priest. ⁹According to the custom of the priests, he had been chosen to go into the Lord's temple that day and to burn incense,^c ¹⁰while the people stood outside praying.

¹¹All at once an angel from the Lord came and appeared to Zechariah at the right side of the altar. ¹²Zechariah was confused and afraid when he saw the angel. ¹³But the angel told him:

Don't be afraid, Zechariah! God has heard your prayers. Your wife Elizabeth will have a son, and you must name him John. ¹⁴His birth will make you very happy, and many people will be glad. ¹⁵Your son will be a great servant of the Lord. He must never drink wine or beer, and the power of the Holy Spirit will be with him from the time he is born.

¹⁶John will lead many people in Israel to turn back to the Lord their God. ¹⁷He will go ahead of the Lord with the same power and spirit that Elijah^d had. And because of John, parents will be more thoughtful of their children. And people who now disobey God will begin to think as they ought to. That is how John will get people ready for the Lord.

¹⁸Zechariah said to the angel, "How will I know this is going to happen? My wife and I are both very old." ¹⁹The angel answered, "I am Gabriel, God's servant, and I was sent to

^a*a careful study*: Or "a study from the beginning." ^b*Abijah . . . Aaron*: The Jewish priests were divided into two groups, and one of these groups was named after Abijah. Each group served in the temple once a year for two weeks at a time. Aaron, the brother of Moses, was the first priest. ^c*burn incense*: This was done twice a day, once in the morning and again in the late afternoon. ^d*Elijah*: The prophet Elijah was known for his power to work miracles.

tell you this good news. 20You have not believed what I have said. So you will not be able to say a thing until all this happens. But everything will take place when it is supposed to."

21The crowd was waiting for Zechariah and kept wondering why he was staying so long in the temple. 22When he did come out, he could not speak, and they knew he had seen a vision. He motioned to them with his hands, but did not say a thing.

23When Zechariah's time of service in the temple was over, he went home. 24Soon after that, his wife was expecting a baby, and for five months she did not leave the house. She said to herself, 25"What the Lord has done for me will keep people from looking down on me."*e*

An Angel Tells about the Birth of Jesus

26One month later God sent the angel Gabriel to the town of Nazareth in Galilee 27with a message for a virgin named Mary. She was engaged to Joseph from the family of King David. 28The angel greeted Mary and said, "You are truly blessed! The Lord is with you."

29Mary was confused by the angel's words and wondered what they meant. 30Then the angel told Mary, "Don't be afraid! God is pleased with you, 31and you will have a son. His name will be Jesus. 32He will be great and will be called the Son of God Most High. The Lord God will make him king, as his ancestor David was. 33He will rule the people of Israel forever, and his kingdom will never end."

34Mary asked the angel, "How can this happen? I am not married!"

35The angel answered, "The Holy Spirit will come down to you, and God's power will come over you. So your child will be called the holy Son of God. 36Your relative Elizabeth is also going to have a son, even though she is old. No one thought she could ever have a baby, but in three months she will have a son. 37Nothing is impossible for God!"

38Mary said, "I am the Lord's servant! Let it happen as you have said." And the angel left her.

Mary Visits Elizabeth

39A short time later Mary hurried to a town in the hill country of Judea. 40She went into Zechariah's home, where she greeted Elizabeth. 41When Elizabeth heard Mary's greeting, her baby moved within her.

The Holy Spirit came upon Elizabeth. 42Then in a loud voice she said to Mary:

God has blessed you more than any other woman! He has also blessed the child you will have. 43Why should the mother of my Lord come to me? 44As soon as I heard your greeting, my baby became happy and moved within me. 45The Lord has blessed you because you believed that he will keep his promise.

Mary's Song of Praise

46Mary said:
47With all my heart
    I praise the Lord,

---

e keep people from looking down on me: When a married woman could not have children, it was thought that the Lord was punishing her.

and I am glad
    because of God my Savior.
48He cares for me,
    his humble servant.
From now on,
all people will say
    God has blessed me.
49God All-Powerful has done
great things for me,
    and his name is holy.
50He always shows mercy
to everyone
    who worships him.
51The Lord has used
    his powerful arm
to scatter those
    who are proud.
52He drags strong rulers
    from their thrones
and puts humble people
    in places of power.
53He gives the hungry
    good things to eat,
and he sends the rich away
with nothing
    in their hands.
54He helps his servant Israel
and is always merciful
    to his people.
55He made this promise
    to our ancestors,
to Abraham and his family
    forever!
56Mary stayed with Elizabeth about three months. Then she went back home.

The Birth of John the Baptist

57When Elizabeth's son was born, 58her neighbors and relatives heard how kind the Lord had been to her, and they too were glad.

59Eight days later they did for the child what the Law of Moses commands.*f* They were going to name him Zechariah, after his father. 60But Elizabeth said, "No! His name is John."

61The people argued, "No one in your family has ever been named John." 62So they motioned to Zechariah to find out what he wanted to name his son.

63Zechariah asked for a writing tablet. Then he wrote, "His name is John." Everyone was amazed. 64Right away Zechariah started speaking and praising God.

65All the neighbors were frightened because of what had happened, and everywhere in the hill country people kept talking about these things. 66Everyone who heard about this wondered what this child would grow up to be. They knew that the Lord was with him.

Zechariah Praises the Lord

67The Holy Spirit came upon Zechariah, and he began to speak:
68Praise the Lord,
    the God of Israel!
He has come
    to save his people.
69Our God has given us
    a mighty Savior*g*
from the family
    of David his servant.
70Long ago the Lord promised
by the words
    of his holy prophets

---

fwhat the Law of Moses commands: This refers to circumcision. It is the cutting off of skin from the private part of Jewish boys eight days after birth to show that they belong to the Lord. See Word List: **Circumcise**. *9a mighty Savior*: The Greek text has "a horn of salvation." In the Scriptures animal horns are often a symbol of great strength.

71to save us from our enemies
and from everyone
who hates us.
72God said he would be kind
to our people and keep
his sacred promise.
73He told our ancestor Abraham
74that he would rescue us
from our enemies.
Then we could serve him
without fear,
75by being holy and good
as long as we live.

76You, my son, will be called
a prophet of God
in heaven above.
You will go ahead of the Lord
to get everything ready
for him.
77You will tell his people
that they can be saved
when their sins
are forgiven.
78God's love and kindness
will shine upon us
like the sun that rises
in the sky.*h*
79On us who live
in the dark shadow
of death
this light will shine
to guide us
into a life of peace.
80As John grew up, God's Spirit
gave him great power. John lived in
the desert until the time he was sent
to the people of Israel.

The Birth of Jesus
(Matthew 1.18–25)

2 About that time Emperor Augustus gave orders for the names of all the people to be listed in record books.*i* 2These first records were made when Quirinius was governor of Syria.*j*

3Everyone had to go to their own hometown to be listed. 4So Joseph had to leave Nazareth in Galilee and go to Bethlehem in Judea. Long ago Bethlehem had been King David's hometown, and Joseph went there because he was from David's family.

5Mary was engaged to Joseph and traveled with him to Bethlehem. She was soon going to have a baby, 6and while they were there, 7she gave birth to her first-born*k* son. She dressed him in baby clothes*l* and laid him in a feed box, because there was no room for them in the inn.

The Shepherds

8That night in the fields near Bethlehem some shepherds were guarding their sheep. 9All at once an angel came down to them from the Lord, and the brightness of the Lord's glory flashed around them. The shepherds were frightened. 10But the angel said, "Don't be afraid! I have good news for you, which will make everyone happy. 11This very day in King David's hometown a Savior was born for you. He is Christ the Lord. 12You will know who

---

*h*like the sun that rises in the sky: Or "like the Messiah coming from heaven." *i*names . . . listed in record books: This was done so that everyone could be made to pay taxes to the Emperor. *j*Quirinius was governor of Syria: It is known that Quirinius made a record of the people in A.D. 6 or 7. But the exact date of the record taking that Luke mentions is not known. *k*first-born: The Jewish people said that the first-born son in each of their families belonged to the Lord. *l*dressed him in baby clothes: The Greek text has "wrapped him in wide strips of cloth," which was how young babies were dressed.

he is, because you will find him dressed in baby clothes and lying in a feed box."

13Suddenly many other angels came down from heaven and joined in praising God. They said:

14"Praise God in heaven!
Peace on earth to everyone
    who pleases God."

15After the angels had left and gone back to heaven, the shepherds said to each other, "Let's go to Bethlehem and see what the Lord has told us about." 16They hurried off and found Mary and Joseph, and they saw the baby lying in the feed box.

17When the shepherds saw Jesus, they told his parents what the angel had said about him. 18Everyone listened and was surprised. 19But Mary kept thinking about all this and wondering what it meant.

20As the shepherds returned to their sheep, they were praising God and saying wonderful things about him. Everything they had seen and heard was just as the angel had said.

21Eight days later Jesus' parents did for him what the Law of Moses commands.m And they named him Jesus, just as the angel had told Mary when he promised she would have a baby.

Simeon Praises the Lord

22The time came for Mary and Joseph to do what the Law of Moses says a mother is supposed to do after her baby is born.n

They took Jesus to the temple in Jerusalem and presented him to the Lord, 23just as the Law of the Lord says, "Each first-borno baby boy belongs to the Lord." 24The Law of the Lord also says that parents have to offer a sacrifice, giving at least a pair of doves or two young pigeons. So that is what Mary and Joseph did.

25At this time a man named Simeon was living in Jerusalem. Simeon was a good man. He loved God and was waiting for God to save the people of Israel. God's Spirit came to him 26and told him that he would not die until he had seen Christ the Lord.

27When Mary and Joseph brought Jesus to the temple to do what the Law of Moses says should be done for a new baby, the Spirit told Simeon to go into the temple. 28Simeon took the baby Jesus in his arms and praised God,

29"Lord, I am your servant,
    and now I can die in peace,
  because you have kept
    your promise to me.
30With my own eyes I have seen
    what you have done
      to save your people,
31and foreign nations
    will also see this.
32Your mighty power is a light
    for all nations,
  and it will bring honor
    to your people Israel."

33Jesus' parents were surprised at what Simeon had said. 34Then he blessed them and told Mary, "This child of yours will cause many people in Israel to fall and others to stand. The child will be like a warning sign. Many people will reject him, 35and you,

---

mwhat the Law of Moses commands: See the note at 1.59. nafter her baby is born: After a Jewish mother gave birth to a son, she was considered "unclean" and had to stay home until he was circumcised (see the note at 1.59). Then she had to stay home for another 33 days, before offering a sacrifice to the Lord. ofirst-born: See the note at 2.7.

Mary, will suffer as though you had been stabbed by a dagger. But all this will show what people are really thinking."

Anna Speaks about the Child Jesus

36The prophet Anna was also there in the temple. She was the daughter of Phanuel from the tribe of Asher, and she was very old. In her youth she had been married for seven years, but her husband died. 37And now she was eighty-four years old.[p] Night and day she served God in the temple by praying and often going without eating.[q]

38At that time Anna came in and praised God. She spoke about the child Jesus to everyone who hoped for Jerusalem to be set free.

The Return to Nazareth

39After Joseph and Mary had done everything that the Law of the Lord commands, they returned home to Nazareth in Galilee. 40The child Jesus grew. He became strong and wise, and God blessed him.

The Boy Jesus in the Temple

41Every year Jesus' parents went to Jerusalem for Passover. 42And when Jesus was twelve years old, they all went there as usual for the celebration. 43After Passover his parents left, but they did not know that Jesus had stayed on in the city. 44They thought he was traveling with some other peo-

ple, and they went a whole day before they started looking for him. 45When they could not find him with their relatives and friends, they went back to Jerusalem and started looking for him there.

46Three days later they found Jesus sitting in the temple, listening to the teachers and asking them questions. 47Everyone who heard him was surprised at how much he knew and at the answers he gave.

48When his parents found him, they were amazed. His mother said, "Son, why have you done this to us? Your father and I have been very worried, and we have been searching for you!"

49Jesus answered, "Why did you have to look for me? Didn't you know that I would be in my Father's house?"[r] 50But they did not understand what he meant.

51Jesus went back to Nazareth with his parents and obeyed them. His mother kept on thinking about all that had happened.

52Jesus became wise, and he grew strong. God was pleased with him and so were the people.

The Preaching of John the Baptist
(Matthew 3.1–12; Mark 1.1–8; John 1.19–28)

3 For fifteen years[s] Emperor Tiberius had ruled that part of the world. Pontius Pilate was governor of Judea, and Herod[t] was the ruler of Galilee. Herod's brother, Philip, was the

---

[p]And now she was eighty-four years old: Or "And now she had been a widow for eighty-four years." [q]without eating: The Jewish people sometimes went without eating (also called "fasting") to show their love for God and to become better followers. [r]in my Father's house: Or "doing my Father's work." [s]For fifteen years: This was either A.D. 28 or 29, and Jesus was about thirty years old (see 3.23). [t]Herod: Herod Antipas, the son of Herod the Great.

ruler in the countries of Iturea and Trachonitis, and Lysanias was the ruler of Abilene. 2Annas and Caiaphas were the Jewish high priests.*u*

At that time God spoke to Zechariah's son John, who was living in the desert. 3So John went along the Jordan Valley, telling the people, "Turn back to God and be baptized! Then your sins will be forgiven." 4Isaiah the prophet wrote about John when he said,

"In the desert
   someone is shouting,
'Get the road ready
      for the Lord!
Make a straight path
      for him.
 5Fill up every valley
   and level every mountain
      and hill.
Straighten the crooked paths
   and smooth out
      the rough roads.
 6Then everyone will see
      the saving power of God.' "

7Crowds of people came out to be baptized, but John said to them, "You bunch of snakes! Who warned you to run from the coming judgment? 8Do something to show that you really have given up your sins. Don't start saying that you belong to Abraham's family. God can turn these stones into children for Abraham.*v* 9An ax is ready to cut the trees down at their roots. Any tree that does not produce good fruit will be cut down and thrown into a fire."

10The crowds asked John, "What should we do?"

11John told them, "If you have two coats, give one to someone who doesn't have any. If you have food, share it with someone else."

12When tax collectors*w* came to be baptized, they asked John, "Teacher, what should we do?"

13John told them, "Don't make people pay more than they owe."

14Some soldiers asked him, "And what about us? What do we have to do?"

John told them, "Don't force people to pay money to make you leave them alone. Be satisfied with your pay."

15Everyone became excited and wondered, "Could John be the Messiah?"

16John said, "I am just baptizing with water. But someone more powerful is going to come, and I am not good enough even to untie his sandals.*x* He will baptize you with the Holy Spirit and with fire. 17His threshing fork*y* is in his hand, and he is ready to separate the wheat from the husks. He will store the wheat in his barn and burn the husks with a fire that never goes out."

18In many different ways John preached the good news to the people. 19But to Herod the ruler, he said, "It was wrong for you to take Herodias, your brother's wife." John also said that

---

uAnnas and Caiaphas . . . high priests: Annas was high priest from A.D. 6 until 15. His son-in-law Caiaphas was high priest from A.D. 18 until 37. *vchildren for Abraham*: The Jewish people thought they were God's chosen people because of God's promises to their ancestor Abraham. *wtax collectors*: These were usually Jewish people who paid the Romans for the right to collect taxes. They were hated by other Jews who thought of them as traitors to their country and to their religion. *xuntie his sandals*: This was the duty of a slave. *ythreshing fork*: After Jewish farmers had trampled out the grain, they used a large fork to pitch the grain and the husks into the air. Wind would blow away the light husks, and the grain would fall back to the ground, where it could be gathered up.

Herod had done many other bad things. 20Finally, Herod put John in jail, and this was the worst thing he had done.

The Baptism of Jesus
(Matthew 3.13–17; Mark 1.9–11)

21After everyone else had been baptized, Jesus himself was baptized. Then as he prayed, the sky opened up, 22and the Holy Spirit came down upon him in the form of a dove. A voice from heaven said, "You are my own dear Son, and I am pleased with you."

The Ancestors of Jesus
(Matthew 1.1–17)

23When Jesus began to preach, he was about thirty years old. Everyone thought he was the son of Joseph. But his family went back through Heli, 24Matthat, Levi, Melchi, Jannai, Joseph, 25Mattathias, Amos, Nahum, Esli, Naggai, 26Maath, Mattathias, Semein, Josech, Joda;

27Joanan, Rhesa, Zerubbabel, Shealtiel, Neri, 28Melchi, Addi, Cosam, Elmadam, Er, 29Joshua, Eliezer, Jorim, Matthat, Levi;

30Simeon, Judah, Joseph, Jonam, Eliakim, 31Melea, Menna, Mattatha, Nathan, David, 32Jesse, Obed, Boaz, Salmon, Nahshon;

33Amminadab, Admin, Arni, Hezron, Perez, Judah, 34Jacob, Isaac, Abraham, Terah, Nahor, 35Serug, Reu, Peleg, Eber, Shelah;

36Cainan, Arphaxad, Shem, Noah, Lamech, 37Methuselah, Enoch, Jared, Mahalaleel, Kenan, 38Enosh, and Seth. The family of Jesus went all the way back to Adam and then to God.

Jesus and the Devil
(Matthew 4.1–11; Mark 1.12, 13)

4 When Jesus returned from the Jordan River, the power of the Holy Spirit was with him, and the Spirit led him into the desert. 2For forty days Jesus was tested by the devil, and during that time he went without eating.z When it was all over, he was hungry.

3The devil said to Jesus, "If you are God's Son, tell this stone to turn into bread."

4Jesus answered, "The Scriptures say, 'No one can live only on food.'"

5Then the devil led Jesus up to a high place and quickly showed him all the nations on earth. 6The devil said, "I will give all this power and glory to you. It has been given to me, and I can give it to anyone I want to. 7Just worship me, and you can have it all."

8Jesus answered, "The Scriptures say:

'Worship the Lord your God
   and serve only him!'"

9Finally, the devil took Jesus to Jerusalem and had him stand on top of the temple. The devil said, "If you are God's Son, jump off. 10-11The Scriptures say:

'God will tell his angels
   to take care of you.
They will catch you
   in their arms,
and you will not hurt
   your feet on the stones.'"

12Jesus answered, "The Scriptures also say, 'Don't try to test the Lord your God!'"

13After the devil had finished test-

---

z*went without eating*: See the note at 2.37.

ing Jesus in every way possible, he left him for a while.

Jesus Begins His Work
(Matthew 4.12–17; Mark 1.14, 15)

14Jesus returned to Galilee with the power of the Spirit. News about him spread everywhere. 15He taught in the Jewish meeting places, and everyone praised him.

The People of Nazareth Turn against Jesus
(Matthew 13.53–58; Mark 6.1–6)

16Jesus went back to Nazareth, where he had been brought up, and as usual he went to the meeting place on the Sabbath. When he stood up to read from the Scriptures, 17he was given the book of Isaiah the prophet. He opened it and read,
18"The Lord's Spirit
    has come to me,
because he has chosen me
to tell the good news
    to the poor.
The Lord has sent me
to announce freedom
    for prisoners,
to give sight to the blind,
to free everyone
    who suffers,
19and to say, 'This is the year
    the Lord has chosen.'"
20Jesus closed the book, then handed it back to the man in charge and sat down. Everyone in the meeting place looked straight at Jesus. 21Then Jesus said to them, "What you have just heard me read has come true today."
22All the people started talking about Jesus and were amazed at the wonderful things he said. They kept on asking, "Isn't he Joseph's son?"
23Jesus answered:
You will certainly want to tell me this saying, "Doctor, first make yourself well." You will tell me to do the same things here in my own hometown that you heard I did in Capernaum. 24But you can be sure that no prophets are liked by the people of their own hometown.
25Once during the time of Elijah there was no rain for three and a half years, and people everywhere were starving. There were many widows in Israel, 26but Elijah was sent only to a widow in the town of Zarephath near the city of Sidon. 27During the time of the prophet Elisha, many men in Israel had leprosy.*a* But no one was healed, except Naaman who lived in Syria.
28When the people in the meeting place heard Jesus say this, they became so angry 29that they got up and threw him out of town. They dragged him to the edge of the cliff on which the town was built, because they wanted to throw him down from there. 30But Jesus slipped through the crowd and got away.

A Man with an Evil Spirit
(Mark 1.21–28)

31Jesus went to the town of Capernaum in Galilee and taught the people on the Sabbath. 32His teaching amazed them because he spoke with power. 33There in the Jewish meeting place was a man with an evil spirit.

---

a leprosy: In biblical times the word "leprosy" was used for many different kinds of skin diseases.

He yelled out, 34"Hey, Jesus of Nazareth, what do you want with us? Are you here to get rid of us? I know who you are! You are God's Holy One."

35Jesus ordered the evil spirit to be quiet and come out. The demon threw the man to the ground in front of everyone and left without harming him.

36They all were amazed and kept saying to each other, "What kind of teaching is this? He has power to order evil spirits out of people!" 37News about Jesus spread all over that part of the country.

Jesus Heals Many People
(Matthew 8.14–17; Mark 1.29–34)

38Jesus left the meeting place and went to Simon's home. When Jesus got there, he was told that Simon's mother-in-law was sick with a high fever. 39So Jesus went over to her and ordered the fever to go away. Right then she was able to get up and serve them.

40After the sun had set, people with all kinds of diseases were brought to Jesus. He put his hands on each one of them and healed them. 41Demons went out of many people and shouted, "You are the Son of God!" But Jesus ordered the demons not to speak because they knew he was the Messiah.

42The next morning Jesus went out to a place where he could be alone, and crowds came looking for him. When they found him, they tried to stop him from leaving. 43But Jesus said, "People in other towns must hear the good news about God's kingdom. That's why I was sent." 44So he kept on preaching in the Jewish meeting places in Judea.*b*

Jesus Chooses His First Disciples
(Matthew 4.18–22; Mark 1.16–20)

5 Jesus was standing on the shore of Lake Gennesaret,*x* teaching the people as they crowded around him to hear God's message. 2Near the shore he saw two boats left there by some fishermen who had gone to wash their nets. 3Jesus got into the boat that belonged to Simon and asked him to row it out a little way from the shore. Then Jesus sat down*c* in the boat to teach the crowd.

4When Jesus had finished speaking, he told Simon, "Row the boat out into the deep water and let your nets down to catch some fish."

5"Master," Simon answered, "we have worked hard all night long and have not caught a thing. But if you tell me to, I will let the nets down." 6They did it and caught so many fish that their nets began ripping apart. 7Then they signaled for their partners in the other boat to come and help them. The men came, and together they filled the two boats so full that they both began to sink.

8When Simon Peter saw this happen, he kneeled down in front of Jesus and said, "Lord, don't come near me! I am a sinner." 9Peter and everyone with him were completely surprised at all the fish they had caught. 10His partners James and John, the sons of Zebedee, were surprised too.

Jesus told Simon, "Don't be afraid! From now on you will bring in people instead of fish." 11The men pulled their

---

*b*Judea: Some manuscripts have "Galilee."   *x*Lake Gennesaret: Another name for Lake Galilee.
*c*sat down: Teachers in the ancient world, including Jewish teachers, usually sat down when they taught.

boats up on the shore. Then they left everything and went with Jesus.

Jesus Heals a Man
(Matthew 8.1–4; Mark 1.40–45)

12Jesus came to a town where there was a man who had leprosy.*d* When the man saw Jesus, he kneeled down to the ground in front of Jesus and begged, "Lord, you have the power to make me well, if only you wanted to."

13Jesus put his hand on him and said, "I do want to! Now you are well." At once the man's leprosy disappeared. 14Jesus told him, "Don't tell anyone about this, but go and show yourself to the priest. Then take a gift to the temple, just as Moses commanded, and everyone will know that you have been healed."*e*

15News about Jesus kept spreading. Large crowds came to listen to him teach and to be healed of their diseases. 16But Jesus would often go to some place where he could be alone and pray.

Jesus Heals a Crippled Man
(Matthew 9.1–8; Mark 2.1–12)

17One day some Pharisees and experts in the Law of Moses sat listening to Jesus teach. They had come from every village in Galilee and Judea and from Jerusalem.

God had given Jesus the power to heal the sick, 18and some people came carrying a crippled man on a mat. They tried to take him inside the house and put him in front of Jesus. 19But because of the crowd, they could not get him to Jesus. So they went up on the roof,*f* where they removed some tiles and let the mat down in the middle of the room.

20When Jesus saw how much faith they had, he said to the crippled man, "My friend, your sins are forgiven."

21The Pharisees and the experts began arguing, "Jesus must think he is God! Only God can forgive sins."

22Jesus knew what they were thinking, and he said, "Why are you thinking that? 23Is it easier for me to tell this crippled man that his sins are forgiven or to tell him to get up and walk? 24But now you will see that the Son of Man has the right to forgive sins here on earth." Jesus then said to the man, "Get up! Pick up your mat and walk home."

25At once the man stood up in front of everyone. He picked up his mat and went home, giving thanks to God. 26Everyone was amazed and praised God. What they saw surprised them, and they said, "We have seen a great miracle today!"

Jesus Chooses Levi
(Matthew 9.9–13; Mark 2.13–17)

27Later, Jesus went out and saw a tax collector*g* named Levi sitting at the

---

dleprosy: See the note at 4.27.   *everyone will know that you have been healed*: People with leprosy had to be examined by a priest and told that they were well (that is "clean") before they could once again live a normal life in the Jewish community. The gift that Moses commanded was the sacrifice of some lambs together with flour mixed with olive oil.   *froof*: In Palestine the houses usually had a flat roof. Stairs on the outside led up to the roof, which was made of beams and boards covered with packed earth. Luke says that the roof was made of (clay) tiles, which were also used for making roofs in New Testament times.   *gtax collector*: See the note at 3.12.

place for paying taxes. Jesus said to him, "Come with me." 28Levi left everything and went with Jesus.

29In his home Levi gave a big dinner for Jesus. Many tax collectors and other guests were also there.

30The Pharisees and some of their teachers of the Law of Moses grumbled to Jesus' disciples, "Why do you eat and drink with those tax collectors and other sinners?"

31Jesus answered, "Healthy people don't need a doctor, but sick people do. 32I didn't come to invite good people to turn to God. I came to invite sinners."

People Ask about Going without Eating
(Matthew 9.14–17; Mark 2.18–22)

33Some people said to Jesus, "John's followers often pray and go without eating,*ʰ* and so do the followers of the Pharisees. But your disciples never go without eating or drinking."

34Jesus told them, "The friends of a bridegroom don't go without eating while he is still with them. 35But the time will come when he will be taken from them. Then they will go without eating."

36Jesus then told them these sayings:

No one uses a new piece of cloth to patch old clothes. The patch would shrink and make the hole even bigger.

37No one pours new wine into old wineskins. The new wine would swell and burst the old skins.*ⁱ* Then the wine would be lost, and the skins would be ruined. 38New wine must be put only into new wineskins.

39No one wants new wine after drinking old wine. They say, "The old wine is better."

A Question about the Sabbath
(Matthew 12.1–8; Mark 2.23–28)

6 One Sabbath when Jesus and his disciples were walking through some wheat fields,*ʲ* the disciples picked some wheat. They rubbed the husks off with their hands and started eating the grain.

2Some Pharisees said, "Why are you picking grain on the Sabbath? You're not supposed to do that!"

3Jesus answered, "You surely have read what David did when he and his followers were hungry. 4He went into the house of God and took the sacred loaves of bread that only priests were supposed to eat. He not only ate some himself, but even gave some to his followers."

5Jesus finished by saying, "The Son of Man is Lord over the Sabbath."

A Man with a Crippled Hand
(Matthew 12.9–14; Mark 3.1–6)

6On another Sabbath*ᵏ* Jesus was teaching in a Jewish meeting place, and a man with a crippled right hand was there. 7Some Pharisees and teachers of the Law of Moses kept watching Jesus to see if he would heal the man. They did this because they wanted to

---

ʰwithout eating: See the note at 2.37.   *ⁱswell and burst the old skins*: While the juice from grapes was becoming wine, it would swell and stretch the skins in which it had been stored. If the skins were old and stiff, they would burst.   *ʲwalking through some wheat fields*: It was the custom to let hungry travelers pick grains of wheat.   *ᵏOn another Sabbath*: Some manuscripts have a reading which may mean "the Sabbath after the next."

accuse Jesus of doing something wrong.

8Jesus knew what they were thinking. So he told the man to stand up where everyone could see him. And the man stood up. **9**Then Jesus asked the people, "On the Sabbath should we do good deeds or evil deeds? Should we save someone's life or destroy it?"

10After he had looked around at everyone, he told the man, "Stretch out your hand." He did, and his bad hand became completely well.

11The teachers and the Pharisees were furious and started saying to each other, "What can we do about Jesus?"

Jesus Chooses His Twelve Apostles
(Matthew 10.1–4; Mark 3.13–19)

12About that time Jesus went off to a mountain to pray, and he spent the whole night there. **13**The next morning he called his disciples together and chose twelve of them to be his apostles. **14**One was Simon, and Jesus named him Peter. Another was Andrew, Peter's brother. There were also James, John, Philip, Bartholomew, **15**Matthew, Thomas, and James the son of Alphaeus. The rest of the apostles were Simon, known as the Eager One,*l* **16**Jude, who was the son of James, and Judas Iscariot,*m* who later betrayed Jesus.

Jesus Teaches, Preaches, and Heals
(Matthew 4.23–25)

17Jesus and his apostles went down from the mountain and came to some flat, level ground. Many other disciples were there to meet him. Large crowds of people from all over Judea, Jerusalem, and the coastal cities of Tyre and Sidon were there too. **18**These people had come to listen to Jesus and to be healed of their diseases. All who were troubled by evil spirits were also healed. **19**Everyone was trying to touch Jesus, because power was going out from him and healing them all.

Blessings and Troubles
(Matthew 5.1–12)

20Jesus looked at his disciples and said:

> God will bless you people
> who are poor.
> His kingdom belongs
> to you!
> **21**God will bless
> you hungry people.
> You will have plenty
> to eat!
> God will bless you people
> who are crying.
> You will laugh!

22God will bless you when others hate you and won't have anything to do with you. God will bless you when people insult you and say cruel things about you, all because you are a follower of the Son of Man! **23**Long ago your own people did these same things to the prophets. So when this happens to you, be happy and jump for joy! You will have a great reward in heaven.

> **24**But you rich people
> are in for trouble.

---

l known as the Eager One: The word "eager" translates the Greek word "zealot," which was a name later given to the members of a Jewish group that resisted and fought against the Romans. *m Iscariot*: This may mean "a man from Kerioth" (a place in Judea). But more probably it means "a man who was a liar" or "a man who was a betrayer."

You have already had
an easy life!
25You well-fed people
are in for trouble.
You will go hungry!
You people
who are laughing now
are in for trouble.
You are going to cry
and weep!
26You are in for trouble when
everyone says good things about
you. That is what your own people said about those prophets who
told lies.

Love for Enemies
(Matthew 5.38–48; 7.12a)

27This is what I say to all who
will listen to me:

Love your enemies, and be
good to everyone who hates you.
28Ask God to bless anyone who
curses you, and pray for everyone
who is cruel to you. 29If someone
slaps you on one cheek, don't stop
that person from slapping you on
the other cheek. If someone
wants to take your coat, don't try
to keep back your shirt. 30Give to
everyone who asks and don't ask
people to return what they have
taken from you. 31Treat others
just as you want to be treated.

32If you love only someone
who loves you, will God praise
you for that? Even sinners love
people who love them. 33If you
are kind only to someone who is
kind to you, will God be pleased
with you for that? Even sinners
are kind to people who are kind
to them. 34If you lend money only

to someone you think will pay you
back, will God be pleased with
you for that? Even sinners lend
to sinners because they think
they will get it all back.

35But love your enemies and
be good to them. Lend without
expecting to be paid back.[n] Then
you will get a great reward, and
you will be the true children of
God in heaven. He is good even
to people who are unthankful and
cruel. 36Have pity on others, just
as your Father has pity on you.

Judging Others
(Matthew 7.1–5)

37Jesus said:

Don't judge others, and God
will not judge you. Don't be hard
on others, and God will not be
hard on you. Forgive others, and
God will forgive you. 38If you give
to others, you will be given a full
amount in return. It will be
packed down, shaken together,
and spilling over into your lap.
The way you treat others is the
way you will be treated.

39Jesus also used some sayings as
he spoke to the people. He said:

Can one blind person lead another blind person? Won't they
both fall into a ditch? 40Are stu-
dents better than their teacher?
But when they are fully trained,
they will be like their teacher.

41You can see the speck in
your friend's eye. But you don't
notice the log in your own eye.
42How can you say, "My friend,
let me take the speck out of your
eye," when you don't see the log

---

[n]*without expecting to be paid back*: Some manuscripts have "without giving up on anyone."

in your own eye? You showoffs! First, get the log out of your own eye. Then you can see how to take the speck out of your friend's eye.

A Tree and Its Fruit
(Matthew 7.17–20; 12.34b, 35)

43A good tree cannot produce bad fruit, and a bad tree cannot produce good fruit. 44You can tell what a tree is like by the fruit it produces. You cannot pick figs or grapes from thorn bushes. 45Good people do good things because of the good in their hearts. Bad people do bad things because of the evil in their hearts. Your words show what is in your hearts.

Two Builders
(Matthew 7.24–27)

46Why do you keep on saying that I am your Lord, when you refuse to do what I say? 47Anyone who comes and listens to me and obeys me 48is like someone who dug down deep and built a house on solid rock. When the flood came and the river rushed against the house, it was built so well that it didn't even shake. 49But anyone who hears what I say and doesn't obey me is like someone whose house was not built on solid rock. As soon as the river rushed against that house, it was smashed to pieces!

Jesus Heals an Army Officer's Servant
(Matthew 8.5–13; John 4.43–54)

7 After Jesus had finished teaching the people, he went to Capernaum. 2In that town an army officer's servant was sick and about to die. The officer liked this servant very much. 3And when he heard about Jesus, he sent some Jewish leaders to ask him to come and heal the servant.

4The leaders went to Jesus and begged him to do something. They said, "This man deserves your help! 5He loves our nation and even built us a meeting place." 6So Jesus went with them.

When Jesus was not far from the house, the officer sent some friends to tell him, "Lord, don't go to any trouble for me! I am not good enough for you to come into my house. 7And I am certainly not worthy to come to you. Just say the word, and my servant will get well. 8I have officers who give orders to me, and I have soldiers who take orders from me. I can say to one of them, 'Go!' and he goes. I can say to another, 'Come!' and he comes. I can say to my servant, 'Do this!' and he will do it."

9When Jesus heard this, he was so surprised that he turned and said to the crowd following him, "In all of Israel I've never found anyone with this much faith!"

10The officer's friends returned and found the servant well.

A Widow's Son

11Soon Jesus and his disciples were on their way to the town of Nain, and a big crowd was going along with them. 12As they came near the gate of the town, they saw people carrying out the body of a widow's only son. Many people from the town were walking along with her. 13When the Lord saw the woman, he felt sorry for her and said, "Don't cry!"

14Jesus went over and touched the stretcher on which the people were carrying the dead boy. They stopped, and Jesus said, "Young man, get up!" 15The boy sat up and began to speak. Jesus then gave him back to his mother.

16Everyone was frightened and praised God. They said, "A great prophet is here with us! God has come to his people."

17News about Jesus spread all over Judea and everywhere else in that part of the country.

John the Baptist
(Matthew 11.1–19)

18-19John's followers told John everything that was being said about Jesus. So he sent two of them to ask the Lord, "Are you the one we should be looking for? Or must we wait for someone else?"

20When these messengers came to Jesus, they said, "John the Baptist sent us to ask, 'Are you the one we should be looking for? Or are we supposed to wait for someone else?'"

21At that time Jesus was healing many people who were sick or in pain or were troubled by evil spirits, and he was giving sight to a lot of blind people. 22Jesus said to the messengers sent by John, "Go and tell John what you have seen and heard. Blind people are now able to see, and the lame can walk. People who have leprosy*o* are being healed, and the deaf can now hear. The dead are raised to life, and the poor are hearing the good news. 23God will bless everyone who does not reject me because of what I do."

24After John's messengers had gone, Jesus began speaking to the crowds about John:

What kind of person did you go out to the desert to see? Was he like tall grass blown about by the wind? 25What kind of man did you really go out to see? Was he someone dressed in fine clothes? People who wear expensive clothes and live in luxury are in the king's palace. 26What then did you go out to see? Was he a prophet? He certainly was! I tell you that he was more than a prophet. 27In the Scriptures, God calls John his messenger and says, "I am sending my messenger ahead of you to get things ready for you." 28No one ever born on this earth is greater than John. But whoever is least important in God's kingdom is greater than John.

29Everyone had been listening to John. Even the tax collectors*p* had obeyed God and had done what was right by letting John baptize them. 30But the Pharisees and the experts in the Law of Moses refused to obey God and be baptized by John.

31Jesus went on to say:

What are you people like? What kind of people are you? 32You are like children sitting in the market and shouting to each other,

"We played the flute,
    but you would not dance!
We sang a funeral song,
    but you would not cry!"

33John the Baptist did not go around eating and drinking, and

---

oleprosy: See the note at 4.27. *Ptax collectors*: See the note at 3.12.

you said, "John has a demon in him!" 34But because the Son of Man goes around eating and drinking, you say, "Jesus eats and drinks too much! He is even a friend of tax collectors and sinners." 35Yet Wisdom is shown to be right by what its followers do.

Simon the Pharisee

36A Pharisee invited Jesus to have dinner with him. So Jesus went to the Pharisee's home and got ready to eat.*q* 37When a sinful woman in that town found out that Jesus was there, she bought an expensive bottle of perfume. 38Then she came and stood behind Jesus. She cried and started washing his feet with her tears and drying them with her hair. The woman kissed his feet and poured the perfume on them.

39The Pharisee who had invited Jesus saw this and said to himself, "If this man really were a prophet, he would know what kind of woman is touching him! He would know that she is a sinner."

40Jesus said to the Pharisee, "Simon, I have something to say to you."

"Teacher, what is it?" Simon replied.

41Jesus told him, "Two people were in debt to a moneylender. One of them owed him five hundred silver coins, and the other owed him fifty. 42Since neither of them could pay him

back, the moneylender said that they didn't have to pay him anything. Which one of them will like him more?"

43Simon answered, "I suppose it would be the one who had owed more and didn't have to pay it back."

"You are right," Jesus said.

44He turned toward the woman and said to Simon, "Have you noticed this woman? When I came into your home, you didn't give me any water so I could wash my feet. But she has washed my feet with her tears and dried them with her hair. 45You didn't greet me with a kiss, but from the time I came in, she has not stopped kissing my feet. 46You didn't even pour olive oil on my head,*r* but she has poured expensive perfume on my feet. 47So I tell you that all her sins are forgiven, and that is why she has shown great love. But anyone who has been forgiven only a little will show only a little love."

48Then Jesus said to the woman, "Your sins are forgiven."

49Some other guests started saying to one another, "Who is this who dares to forgive sins?"

50But Jesus told the woman, "Because of your faith, you are now saved.*s* May God give you peace!"

Women Who Helped Jesus

8 Soon after this, Jesus was going through towns and villages, telling

---

*q*got ready to eat: On special occasions the Jewish people often followed the Greek and Roman custom of lying down on their left side and leaning on their left elbow, while eating with their right hand. This is how the woman could come up behind Jesus and wash his feet (see verse 38). *r*washed my feet . . . greet me with a kiss . . . pour olive oil on my head: Guests in a home were usually offered water so they could wash their feet, because most people either went barefoot or wore sandals and would come in the house with very dusty feet. Guests were also greeted with a kiss on the cheek, and special ones often had sweet-smelling olive oil poured on their head. *s*saved: Or "healed." The Greek word may have either meaning.

the good news about God's kingdom. His twelve apostles were with him, 2and so were some women who had been healed of evil spirits and all sorts of diseases. One of the women was Mary Magdalene,*t* who once had seven demons in her. 3Joanna, Susanna, and many others had also used what they owned to help Jesus*u* and his disciples. Joanna's husband Chuza was one of Herod's officials.*v*

A Story about a Farmer
(Matthew 13.1–9; Mark 4.1–9)

4When a large crowd from several towns had gathered around Jesus, he told them this story:

5A farmer went out to scatter seed in a field. While the farmer was doing it, some of the seeds fell along the road and were stepped on or eaten by birds. 6Other seeds fell on rocky ground and started growing. But the plants did not have enough water and soon dried up. 7Some other seeds fell where thorn bushes grew up and choked the plants. 8The rest of the seeds fell on good ground where they grew and produced a hundred times as many seeds.

When Jesus had finished speaking, he said, "If you have ears, pay attention!"

Why Jesus Used Stories
(Matthew 13.10–17; Mark 4.10–12)

9Jesus' disciples asked him what the story meant. 10So he answered:

I have explained the secrets about God's kingdom to you, but for others I can only use stories. These people look, but they don't see, and they hear, but they don't understand.

Jesus Explains the Story about the Farmer
(Matthew 13.18–23; Mark 4.13–20)

11This is what the story means: The seed is God's message, 12and the seeds that fell along the road are the people who hear the message. But the devil comes and snatches the message out of their hearts, so that they will not believe and be saved. 13The seeds that fell on rocky ground are the people who gladly hear the message and accept it. But they don't have deep roots, and they believe only for a little while. As soon as life gets hard, they give up. 14The seeds that fell among the thorn bushes are also people who hear the message. But they are so eager for riches and pleasures that they never produce anything. 15Those seeds that fell on good ground are the people who listen to the message and keep it in good and honest hearts. They last and produce a harvest.

Light
(Mark 4.21–25)

16No one lights a lamp and puts it under a bowl or under a

---

tMagdalene: Meaning "from Magdala," a small town on the western shore of Lake Galilee. There is no hint that she is the sinful woman in 7.36-50. *uused what they owned to help Jesus*: Women often helped Jewish teachers by giving them money. *vHerod's officials*: Herod Antipas, the son of Herod the Great.

bed. A lamp is always put on a lampstand, so that people who come into a house will see the light. 17There is nothing hidden that will not be found. There is no secret that will not be well known. 18Pay attention to how you listen! Everyone who has something will be given more, but people who have nothing will lose what little they think they have.

Jesus' Mother and Brothers
(Matthew 12.46–50; Mark 3.31–35)

19Jesus' mother and brothers went to see him, but because of the crowd they could not get near him. 20Someone told Jesus, "Your mother and brothers are standing outside and want to see you."

21Jesus answered, "My mother and my brothers are those people who hear and obey God's message."

A Storm
(Matthew 8.23–27; Mark 4.35–41)

22One day Jesus and his disciples got into a boat, and he said, "Let's cross the lake."*w* They started out, 23and while they were sailing across, he went to sleep.

Suddenly a windstorm struck the lake, and the boat started sinking. They were in danger. 24So they went to Jesus and woke him up, "Master, Master! We are about to drown!"

Jesus got up and ordered the wind and waves to stop. They obeyed, and everything was calm. 25Then Jesus asked the disciples, "Don't you have any faith?"

But they were frightened and amazed. They said to each other, "Who is this? He can give orders to the wind and the waves, and they obey him!"

A Man with Demons in Him
(Matthew 8.28–34; Mark 5.1–20)

26Jesus and his disciples sailed across Lake Galilee and came to shore near the town of Gerasa.*x* 27As Jesus was getting out of the boat, he was met by a man from that town. The man had demons in him. He had gone naked for a long time and no longer lived in a house, but in the graveyard.*y*

28The man saw Jesus and screamed. He kneeled down in front of him and shouted, "Jesus, Son of God in heaven, what do you want with me? I beg you not to torture me!" 29He said this because Jesus had already told the evil spirit to go out of him.

The man had often been attacked by the demon. And even though he had been bound with chains and leg irons and kept under guard, he smashed whatever bound him. Then the demon would force him out into lonely places.

30Jesus asked the man, "What is your name?"

He answered, "My name is Lots." He said this because there were 'lots' of demons in him. 31They begged Jesus not to send them to the deep pit,*z* where they would be punished.

32On a hillside not far from there a large herd of pigs was feeding. So the demons begged Jesus to let them

---

w cross the lake: To the eastern shore of Lake Galilee, where most of the people were not Jewish. *x Gerasa*: Some manuscripts have "Gergesa." *y graveyard*: It was thought that demons and evil spirits lived in graveyards. *z deep pit*: The place where evil spirits are kept and punished.

go into the pigs, and Jesus let them go. 33Then the demons left the man and went into the pigs. The whole herd rushed down the steep bank into the lake and drowned.

34When the men taking care of the pigs saw this, they ran to spread the news in the town and on the farms. 35The people went out to see what had happened, and when they came to Jesus, they also found the man. The demons had gone out of him, and he was sitting there at the feet of Jesus. He had clothes on and was in his right mind. But the people were terrified.

36Then all who had seen the man healed told about it. 37Everyone from around Gerasa*a* begged Jesus to leave, because they were so frightened.

When Jesus got into the boat to start back, 38the man who had been healed begged to go with him. But Jesus sent him off and said, 39"Go back home and tell everyone how much God has done for you." The man then went all over town, telling everything that Jesus had done for him.

A Dying Girl and a Sick Woman
(*Matthew 9.18–26; Mark 5.21–43*)

40Everyone had been waiting for Jesus, and when he came back, a crowd was there to welcome him. 41Just then the man in charge of the Jewish meeting place came and kneeled down in front of Jesus. His name was Jairus, and he begged Jesus to come to his home 42because his twelve-year-old child was dying. She was his only daughter.

While Jesus was on his way, people were crowding all around him. 43In the crowd was a woman who had been bleeding for twelve years. She had spent everything she had on doctors,*b* but none of them could make her well.

44As soon as she came up behind Jesus and barely touched his clothes, her bleeding stopped.

45"Who touched me?" Jesus asked.

While everyone was denying it, Peter said, "Master, people are crowding all around and pushing you from every side."*c*

46But Jesus answered, "Someone touched me, because I felt power going out from me." 47The woman knew that she could not hide, so she came trembling and kneeled down in front of Jesus. She told everyone why she had touched him and that she had been healed right away.

48Jesus said to the woman, "You are now well because of your faith. May God give you peace!"

49While Jesus was speaking, someone came from Jairus' home and said, "Your daughter has died! Why bother the teacher anymore?"

50When Jesus heard this, he told Jairus, "Don't worry! Have faith, and your daughter will get well."

51Jesus went into the house, but he did not let anyone else go with him, except Peter, John, James, and the girl's father and mother. 52Everyone was crying and weeping for the girl. But Jesus said, "The child is not dead. She is just asleep." 53The people laughed at him because they knew she was dead.

54Jesus took hold of the girl's hand

---

aGerasa: See the note at 8.26. *bShe had spent everything she had on doctors*: Some manuscripts do not have these words. *cfrom every side*: Some manuscripts add "and you ask, 'Who touched me?'"

and said, "Child, get up!" 55She came back to life and got right up. Jesus told them to give her something to eat. 56Her parents were surprised, but Jesus ordered them not to tell anyone what had happened.

Instructions for the Twelve Apostles
(Matthew 10.5–15; Mark 6.7–13)

9 Jesus called together his twelve apostles and gave them complete power over all demons and diseases. 2Then he sent them to tell about God's kingdom and to heal the sick. 3He told them, "Don't take anything with you! Don't take a walking stick or a traveling bag or food or money or even a change of clothes. 4When you are welcomed into a home, stay there until you leave that town. 5If people won't welcome you, leave the town and shake the dust from your feet*d* as a warning to them."

6The apostles left and went from village to village, telling the good news and healing people everywhere.

Herod Is Worried
(Matthew 14.1–12; Mark 6.14–29)

7Herod*e* the ruler heard about all that was happening, and he was worried. Some people were saying that John the Baptist had come back to life. 8Others were saying that Elijah had come*f* or that one of the prophets from long ago had come back to life. 9But Herod said, "I had John's head cut off! Who is this I hear so much about?" Herod was eager to meet Jesus.

Jesus Feeds Five Thousand
(Matthew 14.13–21; Mark 6.30–44; John 6.1–14)

10The apostles came back and told Jesus everything they had done. He then took them with him to the village of Bethsaida, where they could be alone. 11But a lot of people found out about this and followed him. Jesus welcomed them. He spoke to them about God's kingdom and healed everyone who was sick.

12Late in the afternoon the twelve apostles came to Jesus and said, "Send the crowd to the villages and farms around here. They need to find a place to stay and something to eat. There is nothing in this place. It is like a desert!"

13Jesus answered, "You give them something to eat."

But they replied, "We have only five small loaves of bread*g* and two fish. If we are going to feed all these people, we will have to go and buy food." 14There were about five thousand men in the crowd.

Jesus said to his disciples, "Have the people sit in groups of fifty." 15They did this, and all the people sat down. 16Jesus took the five loaves and the two fish. He looked up toward heaven and blessed the food. Then he broke the bread and fish and handed them to his disciples to give to the people.

17Everyone ate all they wanted.

---

d shake the dust from your feet: This was a way of showing rejection. *e Herod*: Herod Antipas, the son of Herod the Great. *f Elijah had come*: Many of the Jewish people expected the prophet Elijah to come and prepare the way for the Messiah. *g small loaves of bread*: These would have been flat and round or in the shape of a bun.

What was left over filled twelve baskets.

Who Is Jesus?
(Matthew 16.13–19; Mark 8.27–29)

18When Jesus was alone praying, his disciples came to him, and he asked them, "What do people say about me?"

19They answered, "Some say that you are John the Baptist or Elijah[h] or a prophet from long ago who has come back to life."

20Jesus then asked them, "But who do you say I am?"

Peter answered, "You are the Messiah sent from God."

21Jesus strictly warned his disciples not to tell anyone what had happened.

Jesus Speaks about His Suffering and Death
(Matthew 16.20–28; Mark 8.30—9.1)

22Jesus told his disciples, "The nation's leaders, the chief priests, and the teachers of the Law of Moses will make the Son of Man suffer terribly. They will reject him and kill him, but three days later he will rise to life."

23Then Jesus said to all the people: If any of you want to be my followers, you must forget about yourself. You must take up your cross each day and follow me. 24If you want to save your life,[i] you will destroy it. But if you give up your life for me, you will save it. 25What will you gain, if you own the whole world but destroy yourself or waste your life? 26If you

are ashamed of me and my message, the Son of Man will be ashamed of you when he comes in his glory and in the glory of his Father and the holy angels. 27You can be sure that some of the people standing here will not die before they see God's kingdom.

The True Glory of Jesus
(Matthew 17.1–8; Mark 9.2–8)

28About eight days later Jesus took Peter, John, and James with him and went up on a mountain to pray. 29While he was praying, his face changed, and his clothes became shining white. 30Suddenly Moses and Elijah were there speaking with him. 31They appeared in heavenly glory and talked about all that Jesus' death[j] in Jerusalem would mean.

32Peter and the other two disciples had been sound asleep. All at once they woke up and saw how glorious Jesus was. They also saw the two men who were with him.

33Moses and Elijah were about to leave, when Peter said to Jesus, "Master, it is good for us to be here! Let us make three shelters, one for you, one for Moses, and one for Elijah." But Peter did not know what he was talking about.

34While Peter was still speaking, a shadow from a cloud passed over them, and they were frightened as the cloud covered them. 35From the cloud a voice spoke, "This is my chosen Son. Listen to what he says!"

36After the voice had spoken, Pe-

---

[h]*Elijah*: See the note at 9.8. [i]*life*: In verses 24,25 a Greek word which often means "soul" is translated "life" and "yourself." [j]*Jesus' death*: In Greek this is "his departure," which probably includes his rising to life and his return to heaven.

ter, John, and James saw only Jesus. For some time they kept quiet and did not say anything about what they had seen.

Jesus Heals a Boy
(Matthew 17.14–18; Mark 9.14–27)

37The next day Jesus and his three disciples came down from the mountain and were met by a large crowd. 38Just then someone in the crowd shouted, "Teacher, please do something for my son! He is my only child! 39A demon often attacks him and makes him scream. It shakes him until he foams at the mouth, and it won't leave him until it has completely worn the boy out. 40I begged your disciples to force out the demon, but they couldn't do it."

41Jesus said to them, "You people are stubborn and don't have any faith! How much longer must I be with you? Why do I have to put up with you?"

Then Jesus said to the man, "Bring your son to me." 42While the boy was being brought, the demon attacked him and made him shake all over. Jesus ordered the demon to stop. Then he healed the boy and gave him back to his father. 43Everyone was amazed at God's great power.

Jesus Again Speaks about His Death
(Matthew 17.22, 23; Mark 9.30–32)

While everyone was still amazed at what Jesus was doing, he said to his disciples, 44"Pay close attention to what I am telling you! The Son of Man will be handed over to his ene-

mies." 45But the disciples did not know what he meant. The meaning was hidden from them. They could not understand it, and they were afraid to ask.

Who Is the Greatest?
(Matthew 18.1–5; Mark 9.33–37)

46Jesus' disciples were arguing about which one of them was the greatest. 47Jesus knew what they were thinking, and he had a child stand there beside him. 48Then he said to his disciples, "When you welcome even a child because of me, you welcome me. And when you welcome me, you welcome the one who sent me. Whichever one of you is the most humble is the greatest."

For or against Jesus
(Mark 9.38–40)

49John said, "Master, we saw a man using your name to force demons out of people. But we told him to stop, because he is not one of us."

50"Don't stop him!" Jesus said. "Anyone who is not against you is for you."

A Samaritan Village Refuses to Receive Jesus

51Not long before it was time for Jesus to be taken up to heaven, he made up his mind to go to Jerusalem. 52He sent some messengers on ahead to a Samaritan village to get things ready for him. 53But he was on his way to Jerusalem, so the people there refused to welcome him. 54When the disciples James and John saw what was happening, they asked, "Lord, do you want us to call down fire from heaven to destroy these people?"[k]

55But Jesus turned and corrected them for what they had said.[l] 56Then they all went on to another village.

Three People Who Wanted To Be Followers
(Matthew 8.19–22)

57Along the way someone said to Jesus, "I'll go anywhere with you!"

58Jesus said, "Foxes have dens, and birds have nests, but the Son of Man doesn't have a place to call his own."

59Jesus told someone else to come with him. But the man said, "Lord, let me wait until I bury my father."[m]

60Jesus answered, "Let the dead take care of the dead, while you go and tell about God's kingdom."

61Then someone said to Jesus, "I want to go with you, Lord, but first let me go back and take care of things at home."

62Jesus answered, "Anyone who starts plowing and keeps looking back isn't worth a thing in God's kingdom!"

The Work of the Seventy-two Followers

10 Later the Lord chose seventy-two[n] other followers and sent them out two by two to every town and village where he was about to go. 2He said to them:

A large crop is in the fields, but there are only a few workers. Ask the Lord in charge of the harvest to send out workers to bring it in. 3Now go, but remember, I am sending you like lambs into a pack of wolves. 4Don't take along a moneybag or a traveling bag or sandals. And don't waste time greeting people on the road.[o] 5As soon as you enter a home, say, "God bless this home with peace." 6If the people living there are peace-loving, your prayer for peace will bless them. But if they are not peace-loving, your prayer will return to you. 7Stay with the same family, eating and drinking whatever they give you, because workers are worth what they earn. Don't move around from house to house.

8If the people of a town welcome you, eat whatever they offer you. 9Heal their sick and say, "God's kingdom will soon be here!"[p]

10But if the people of a town refuse to welcome you, go out into the street and say, 11"We are shaking the dust from our feet[q] as a warning to you. You can be

---

[k]to destroy these people: Some manuscripts add "as Elijah did." [l]what they had said: Some manuscripts add, "and said, 'Don't you know what spirit you belong to? The Son of Man did not come to destroy people's lives, but to save them.'" [m]bury my father: The Jewish people taught that giving someone a proper burial was even more important than helping the poor. [n]seventy-two: Some manuscripts have "seventy." According to the book of Genesis, there were seventy nations on earth. But the ancient Greek translation of the Old Testament has "seventy-two" in place of "seventy." Jesus probably chose this number of followers to show that his message was for everyone in the world. [o]waste time greeting people on the road: In those days a polite greeting could take a long time. [p]will soon be here: Or "is already here." [q]shaking the dust from our feet: This was a way of showing rejection.

sure that God's kingdom will soon be here!"[r] [12]I tell you that on the day of judgment the people of Sodom will get off easier than the people of that town!

The Unbelieving Towns
(Matthew 11.20–24)

[13]You people of Chorazin are in for trouble! You people of Bethsaida are also in for trouble! If the miracles that took place in your towns had happened in Tyre and Sidon, the people there would have turned to God long ago. They would have dressed in sackcloth and put ashes on their heads.[s] [14]On the day of judgment the people of Tyre and Sidon will get off easier than you will. [15]People of Capernaum, do you think you will be honored in heaven? Well, you will go down to hell!

[16]My followers, whoever listens to you is listening to me. Anyone who says "No" to you is saying "No" to me. And anyone who says "No" to me is really saying "No" to the one who sent me.

The Return of the Seventy-two

[17]When the seventy-two[t] followers returned, they were excited and said, "Lord, even the demons obeyed when we spoke in your name!"

[18]Jesus told them:

I saw Satan fall from heaven like a flash of lightning. [19]I have given you the power to trample on snakes and scorpions and to defeat the power of your enemy Satan. Nothing can harm you. [20]But don't be happy because evil spirits obey you. Be happy that your names are written in heaven!

Jesus Thanks His Father
(Matthew 11.25–27; 13.16, 17)

[21]At that same time Jesus felt the joy that comes from the Holy Spirit,[u] and he said:

My Father, Lord of heaven and earth, I am grateful that you hid all this from wise and educated people and showed it to ordinary people. Yes, Father, that is what pleased you.

[22]My Father has given me everything, and he is the only one who knows the Son. The only one who really knows the Father is the Son. But the Son wants to tell others about the Father, so that they can know him too.

[23]Jesus then turned to his disciples and said to them in private, "You are really blessed to see what you see! [24]Many prophets and kings were eager to see what you see and to hear what you hear. But I tell you that they did not see or hear."

The Good Samaritan

[25]An expert in the Law of Moses stood up and asked Jesus a question to see what he would say. "Teacher," he asked, "what must I do to have eternal life?"

---

[r]*will soon be here*: Or "is already here." [s]*dressed in sackcloth . . . ashes on their heads*: This was one way that people showed how sorry they were for their sins. [t]*seventy-two*: See the note at 10.1. [u]*the Holy Spirit*: Some manuscripts have "his spirit."

26Jesus answered, "What is written in the Scriptures? How do you understand them?"

27The man replied, "The Scriptures say, 'Love the Lord your God with all your heart, soul, strength, and mind.' They also say, 'Love your neighbors as much as you love yourself.' "

28Jesus said, "You have given the right answer. If you do this, you will have eternal life."

29But the man wanted to show that he knew what he was talking about. So he asked Jesus, "Who are my neighbors?"

30Jesus replied:

As a man was going down from Jerusalem to Jericho, robbers attacked him and grabbed everything he had. They beat him up and ran off, leaving him half dead.

31A priest happened to be going down the same road. But when he saw the man, he walked by on the other side. 32Later a temple helper*w* came to the same place. But when he saw the man who had been beaten up, he also went by on the other side.

33A man from Samaria then came traveling along that road. When he saw the man, he felt sorry for him 34and went over to him. He treated his wounds with olive oil and wine*x* and bandaged them. Then he put him on his own donkey and took him to an inn, where he took care of him. 35The next morning he gave the innkeeper two silver coins and

said, "Please take care of the man. If you spend more than this on him, I will pay you when I return."

36Then Jesus asked, "Which one of these three people was a real neighbor to the man who was beaten up by robbers?"

37The teacher answered, "The one who showed pity."

Jesus said, "Go and do the same!"

Martha and Mary

38The Lord and his disciples were traveling along and came to a village. When they got there, a woman named Martha welcomed him into her home. 39She had a sister named Mary, who sat down in front of the Lord and was listening to what he said. 40Martha was worried about all that had to be done. Finally, she went to Jesus and said, "Lord, doesn't it bother you that my sister has left me to do all the work by myself? Tell her to come and help me!"

41The Lord answered, "Martha, Martha! You are worried and upset about so many things, 42but only one thing is necessary. Mary has chosen what is best, and it will not be taken away from her."

Prayer
(Matthew 6.9–13; 7.7–11)

11 When Jesus had finished praying, one of his disciples said to him, "Lord, teach us to pray, just as John taught his followers to pray."

---

w temple helper: A man from the tribe of Levi, whose job it was to work around the temple.
x olive oil and wine: In New Testament times these were used as medicine. Sometimes olive oil is a symbol for healing by means of a miracle (James 5.14).

2So Jesus told them, "Pray in this way:

'Father, help us
　　to honor your name.
Come and set up
　　your kingdom.
　3Give us each day
　　the food we need.*y*
　4Forgive our sins,
　　as we forgive everyone
　　　who has done wrong to us.
And keep us
　　from being tempted.' "

5Then Jesus went on to say:

Suppose one of you goes to a friend in the middle of the night and says, "Let me borrow three loaves of bread. **6**A friend of mine has dropped in, and I don't have a thing for him to eat." **7**And suppose your friend answers, "Don't bother me! The door is bolted, and my children and I are in bed. I cannot get up to give you something."

8He may not get up and give you the bread, just because you are his friend. But he will get up and give you as much as you need, simply because you are not ashamed to keep on asking.

9So I tell you to ask and you will receive, search and you will find, knock and the door will be opened for you. **10**Everyone who asks will receive, everyone who searches will find, and the door will be opened for everyone who knocks. **11**Which one of you fathers would give your hungry child a snake if the child asked for a fish? **12**Which one of you would give your child a scorpion if the child asked for an egg? **13**As bad as you are, you still know how to give good gifts to your children. But your heavenly Father is even more ready to give the Holy Spirit to anyone who asks.

Jesus and the Ruler of Demons
(Matthew 12.22–30; Mark 3.20–27)

14Jesus forced a demon out of a man who could not talk. After the demon had gone out, the man started speaking, and the crowds were amazed. **15**But some people said, "He forces out demons by the power of Beelzebul, the ruler of the demons!"

16Others wanted to put Jesus to the test. So they asked him to show them a sign from God. **17**Jesus knew what they were thinking, and he said:

A kingdom where people fight each other will end up in ruin. And a family that fights will break up. **18**If Satan fights against himself, how can his kingdom last? Yet you say that I force out demons by the power of Beelzebul. **19**If I use his power to force out demons, whose power do your own followers use to force them out? They are the ones who will judge you. **20**But if I use God's power to force out demons, it proves that God's kingdom has already come to you.

21When a strong man arms himself and guards his home, everything he owns is safe. **22**But if a stronger man comes and defeats him, he will carry off the weapons in which the strong man trusted. Then he will divide with others what he has taken. **23**If you are not on my side, you are

---

y the food we need: Or "food for today" or "food for the coming day."

against me. If you don't gather in the crop with me, you scatter it.

Return of an Evil Spirit
(Matthew 12.43–45)

24When an evil spirit leaves a person, it travels through the desert, looking for a place to rest. But when it doesn't find a place, it says, "I will go back to the home I left." 25When it gets there and finds the place clean and fixed up, 26it goes off and finds seven other evil spirits even worse than itself. They all come and make their home there, and that person ends up in worse shape than before.

Being Really Blessed

27While Jesus was still talking, a woman in the crowd spoke up, "The woman who gave birth to you and nursed you is blessed!"

28Jesus replied, "That's true, but the people who are really blessed are the ones who hear and obey God's message!"ᶻ

A Sign from God
(Matthew 12.38–42; Mark 8.12)

29As crowds were gathering around Jesus, he said:

You people of today are evil! You keep looking for a sign from God. But what happened to Jonahᵃ is the only sign you will be given. 30Just as Jonah was a sign to the people of Nineveh, the Son of Man will be a sign to the people of today. 31When the judgment comes, the Queen of the Southᵇ will stand there with you and condemn you. She traveled a long way to hear Solomon's wisdom, and yet here is something far greater than Solomon. 32The people of Nineveh will also stand there with you and condemn you. They turned to God when Jonah preached, and yet here is something far greater than Jonah.

Light
(Matthew 5.15; 6.22, 23)

33No one lights a lamp and then hides it or puts it under a clay pot. A lamp is put on a lampstand, so that everyone who comes into the house can see the light. 34Your eyes are the lamp for your body. When your eyes are good, you have all the light you need. But when your eyes are bad, everything is dark. 35So be sure that your light is not darkness. 36If you have light, and nothing is dark, then light will be everywhere, as when a lamp shines brightly on you.

Jesus Condemns the Pharisees and Teachers of the Law of Moses
(Matthew 23.1–36; Mark 12.38–40; Luke 20.45–47)

37When Jesus finished speaking, a Pharisee invited him home for a

---

ᶻ*"That's true, but the people who are really blessed . . . message"*: Or " 'That's not true, the people who are blessed . . . message.' " ᵃ*what happened to Jonah*: Jonah was in the stomach of a big fish for three days and nights. See Matthew 12.40. ᵇ*Queen of the South*: Sheba, probably a country in southern Arabia.

meal. Jesus went and sat down to eat.[b] 38The Pharisee was surprised that he did not wash his hands[c] before eating. 39So the Lord said to him:

You Pharisees clean the outside of cups and dishes, but on the inside you are greedy and evil. 40You fools! Didn't God make both the outside and the inside?[d] 41If you would only give what you have to the poor, everything you do would please God.

42You Pharisees are in for trouble! You give God a tenth of the spices from your gardens, such as mint and rue. But you cheat people, and you don't love God. You should be fair and kind to others and still give a tenth to God.

43You Pharisees are in for trouble! You love the front seats in the meeting places, and you like to be greeted with honor in the market. 44But you are in for trouble! You are like unmarked graves[e] that people walk on without even knowing it.

45A teacher of the Law of Moses spoke up, "Teacher, you said cruel things about us."

46Jesus replied:

You teachers are also in for trouble! You load people down with heavy burdens, but you won't lift a finger to help them carry the loads. 47Yes, you are really in for trouble. You build monuments to honor the prophets your own people murdered long ago. 48You must think that was the right thing for your people to do, or else you would not have built monuments for the prophets they murdered.

49Because of your evil deeds, the Wisdom of God said, "I will send prophets and apostles to you. But you will murder some and mistreat others." 50You people living today will be punished for all the prophets who have been murdered since the beginning of the world. 51This includes every prophet from the time of Abel to the time of Zechariah,[f] who was murdered between the altar and the temple. You people will certainly be punished for all of this.

52You teachers of the Law of Moses are really in for trouble! You carry the keys to the door of knowledge about God. But you never go in, and you keep others from going in.

53Jesus was about to leave, but the teachers and the Pharisees wanted to get even with him. They tried to make him say what he thought about other things, 54so that they could catch him saying something wrong.

---

[b]sat down to eat: See the note at 7.36. [c]did not wash his hands: The Jewish people had strict laws about washing their hands before eating, especially if they had been out in public. [d]Didn't God make both the outside and the inside?: Or "Doesn't the person who washes the outside always wash the inside too?" [e]unmarked graves: Tombs were whitewashed to keep anyone from accidentally touching them. A person who touched a dead body or a tomb was considered unclean and could not worship with other Jewish people. [f]from the time of Abel . . . Zechariah: Genesis is the first book in the Jewish Scriptures, and it tells that Abel was the first person to be murdered. Second Chronicles is the last book in the Jewish Scriptures, and the last murder that it tells about is that of Zechariah.

Warnings

12 As thousands of people crowded around Jesus and were stepping on each other, he told his disciples:

Be sure to guard against the dishonest teaching[h] of the Pharisees! It is their way of fooling people. 2Everything that is hidden will be found out, and every secret will be known. 3Whatever you say in the dark will be heard when it is day. Whatever you whisper in a closed room will be shouted from the housetops.

The One to Fear
(Matthew 10.28–31)

4My friends, don't be afraid of people. They can kill you, but after that, there is nothing else they can do. 5God is the one you must fear. Not only can he take your life, but he can throw you into hell. God is certainly the one you should fear!

6Five sparrows are sold for just two pennies, but God does not forget a one of them. 7Even the hairs on your head are counted. So don't be afraid! You are worth much more than many sparrows.

Telling Others about Christ
(Matthew 10.32, 33; 12.32; 10.19, 20)

8If you tell others that you belong to me, the Son of Man will tell God's angels that you are my followers. 9But if you reject me, you will be rejected in front of them. 10If you speak against the Son of Man, you can be forgiven, but if you speak against the Holy Spirit, you cannot be forgiven.

11When you are brought to trial in the Jewish meeting places or before rulers or officials, don't worry about how you will defend yourselves or what you will say. 12At that time the Holy Spirit will tell you what to say.

A Rich Fool

13A man in a crowd said to Jesus, "Teacher, tell my brother to give me my share of what our father left us when he died."

14Jesus answered, "Who gave me the right to settle arguments between you and your brother?"

15Then he said to the crowd, "Don't be greedy! Owning a lot of things won't make your life safe."

16So Jesus told them this story:

A rich man's farm produced a big crop, 17and he said to himself, "What can I do? I don't have a place large enough to store everything."

18Later, he said, "Now I know what I'll do. I'll tear down my barns and build bigger ones, where I can store all my grain and other goods. 19Then I'll say to myself, 'You have stored up enough good things to last for years to come. Live it up! Eat, drink, and enjoy yourself.' "

20But God said to him, "You fool! Tonight you will die. Then

---

[h]dishonest teaching: The Greek text has "yeast," which is used here of a teaching that is not true. See Matthew 16.6,12.

who will get what you have stored up?"

21"This is what happens to people who store up everything for themselves, but are poor in the sight of God."

Worry
(Matthew 6.25–34)

22Jesus said to his disciples:

I tell you not to worry about your life! Don't worry about having something to eat or wear. 23Life is more than food or clothing. 24Look at the crows! They don't plant or harvest, and they don't have storehouses or barns. But God takes care of them. You are much more important than any birds. 25Can worry make you live longer?*i* 26If you don't have power over small things, why worry about everything else?

27Look how the wild flowers grow! They don't work hard to make their clothes. But I tell you that Solomon with all his wealth*j* was not as well clothed as one of these flowers. 28God gives such beauty to everything that grows in the fields, even though it is here today and thrown into a fire tomorrow. Won't he do even more for you? You have such little faith!

29Don't keep worrying about having something to eat or drink. 30Only people who don't know God are always worrying about such things. Your Father knows what you need. 31But put God's

work first, and these things will be yours as well.

Treasures in Heaven
(Matthew 6.19–21)

32My little group of disciples, don't be afraid! Your Father wants to give you the kingdom. 33Sell what you have and give the money to the poor. Make yourselves moneybags that never wear out. Make your treasure safe in heaven, where thieves cannot steal it and moths cannot destroy it. 34Your heart will always be where your treasure is.

Faithful and Unfaithful Servants
(Matthew 24.45–51)

35Be ready and keep your lamps burning just 36like those servants who wait up for their master to return from a wedding feast. As soon as he comes and knocks, they open the door for him. 37Servants are fortunate if their master finds them awake and ready when he comes! I promise you that he will get ready and have his servants sit down so he can serve them. 38Those servants are really fortunate if their master finds them ready, even though he comes late at night or early in the morning. 39You would surely not let a thief break into your home, if you knew when the thief was coming. 40So always be ready! You don't know when the Son of Man will come.

---

i live longer: Or "grow taller." *j Solomon with all his wealth*: The Jewish people thought that Solomon was the richest person who had ever lived.

41Peter asked Jesus, "Did you say this just for us or for everyone?"

42The Lord answered:

Who are faithful and wise servants? Who are the ones the master will put in charge of giving the other servants their food supplies at the proper time? 43Servants are fortunate if their master comes and finds them doing their job. 44A servant who is always faithful will surely be put in charge of everything the master owns.

45But suppose one of the servants thinks that the master will not return until late. Suppose that servant starts beating all the other servants and eats and drinks and gets drunk. 46If that happens, the master will surely come on a day and at a time when the servant least expects him. That servant will then be punished and thrown out with the servants who cannot be trusted.

47If servants are not ready or willing to do what their master wants them to do, they will be beaten hard. 48But servants who don't know what their master wants them to do will not be beaten so hard for doing wrong. If God has been generous with you, he will expect you to serve him well. But if he has been more than generous, he will expect you to serve him even better.

Not Peace, but Trouble
(Matthew 10.34–36)

49I came to set fire to the earth, and I surely wish it were already on fire! 50I am going to be put to a hard test. And I will have to suffer a lot of pain until it is over. 51Do you think that I came to bring peace to earth? No indeed! I came to make people choose sides. 52A family of five will be divided, with two of them against the other three. 53Fathers and sons will turn against one another, and mothers and daughters will do the same. Mothers-in-law and daughters-in-law will also turn against each other.

Knowing What to Do
(Matthew 16.2, 3; 5.25, 26)

54Jesus said to all the people:

As soon as you see a cloud coming up in the west, you say, "It's going to rain," and it does. 55When the south wind blows, you say, "It's going to get hot," and it does. 56Are you trying to fool someone? You can predict the weather by looking at the earth and sky, but you don't really know what's going on right now. 57Why don't you understand the right thing to do? 58When someone accuses you of something, try to settle things before you are taken to court. If you don't, you will be dragged before the judge. Then the judge will hand you over to the jailer, and you will be locked up. 59You won't get out until you have paid the last cent you owe.

Turn Back to God

13 About this same time Jesus was told that Pilate had given orders for some people from Galilee to be killed while they were offering sacrifices. 2Jesus replied:

Do you think that these people were worse sinners than everyone else in Galilee just because of what happened to them? 3Not at all! But you can be sure that if you don't turn back to God, every one of you will also be killed. 4What about those eighteen people who died when the tower in Siloam fell on them? Do you think they were worse than everyone else in Jerusalem? 5Not at all! But you can be sure that if you don't turn back to God, every one of you will also die.

A Story about a Fig Tree

6Jesus then told them this story:
A man had a fig tree growing in his vineyard. One day he went out to pick some figs, but he didn't find any. 7So he said to the gardener, "For three years I have come looking for figs on this tree, and I haven't found any yet. Chop it down! Why should it take up space?"

8The gardener answered, "Master, leave it for another year. I'll dig around it and put some manure on it to make it grow. 9Maybe it will have figs on it next year. If it doesn't, you can have it cut down."

Healing a Woman on the Sabbath

10One Sabbath Jesus was teaching in a Jewish meeting place, 11and a woman was there who had been crippled by an evil spirit for eighteen years. She was completely bent over and could not straighten up. 12When Jesus saw the woman, he called her over and said, "You are now well." 13He placed his hands on her, and right away she stood up straight and praised God.

14The man in charge of the meeting place was angry because Jesus had healed someone on the Sabbath. So he said to the people, "Each week has six days when we can work. Come and be healed on one of those days, but not on the Sabbath."

15The Lord replied, "Are you trying to fool someone? Won't any one of you untie your ox or donkey and lead it out to drink on a Sabbath? 16This woman belongs to the family of Abraham, but Satan has kept her bound for eighteen years. Isn't it right to set her free on the Sabbath?" 17Jesus' words made all his enemies ashamed. But everyone else in the crowd was happy about the wonderful things he was doing.

A Mustard Seed and Yeast
(Matthew 13.31–33; Mark 4.30–32)

18Jesus said, "What is God's kingdom like? What can I compare it with? 19It is like what happens when someone plants a mustard seed in a garden. The seed grows as big as a tree, and birds nest in its branches."

20Then Jesus said, "What can I compare God's kingdom with? 21It is like what happens when a woman mixes yeast into three batches of flour. Finally, all the dough rises."

The Narrow Door
(Matthew 7.13, 14, 21–23)

22As Jesus was on his way to Jerusalem, he taught the people in the towns and villages. 23Someone asked him, "Lord, are only a few people going to be saved?"

Jesus answered:

24Do all you can to go in by the narrow door! A lot of people will try to get in, but will not be able to. 25Once the owner of the house gets up and locks the door, you will be left standing outside. You will knock on the door and say, "Sir, open the door for us!"

But the owner will answer, "I don't know a thing about you!" 26Then you will start saying, "We dined with you, and you taught in our streets."

27But he will say, "I really don't know who you are! Get away from me, all you evil people!"

28Then when you have been thrown outside, you will weep and grit your teeth because you will see Abraham and Isaac and all the prophets in God's kingdom. 29People will come from all directions and sit down to feast in God's kingdom. 30There the ones who are now least important will be the most important, and those who are now most important will be least important.

Jesus and Herod

31At that time some Pharisees came to Jesus and said, "You had better get away from here! Herod[j] wants to kill you."

32Jesus said to them:

Go tell that fox, "I am going to force out demons and heal people today and tomorrow, and three days later I'll be through." 33But I am going on my way today and tomorrow and the next day. After all, Jerusalem is the place where prophets are killed.

Jesus Loves Jerusalem
(Matthew 23.37–39)

34Jerusalem, Jerusalem! Your people have killed the prophets and have stoned the messengers who were sent to you. I have often wanted to gather your people, as a hen gathers her chicks under her wings. But you wouldn't let me. 35Now your temple will be deserted. You will not see me again until the time when you say,

"Blessed is the one who comes in the name of the Lord."

Jesus Heals a Sick Man

14 One Sabbath Jesus was having dinner in the home of an important Pharisee, and everyone was carefully watching Jesus. 2All of a sudden a man with swollen legs stood up in front of him. 3Jesus turned and asked the Pharisees and the teachers of the Law of Moses, "Is it right to heal on the Sabbath?" 4But they did not say a word.

Jesus took hold of the man. Then he healed him and sent him away. 5Afterwards, Jesus asked the people, "If your son or ox falls into a well, wouldn't you pull him out right away, even on the Sabbath?" 6There was nothing they could say.

How To Be a Guest

7Jesus saw how the guests had tried to take the best seats. So he told them:

8When you are invited to a wedding feast, don't sit in the best

---

[j] *Herod*: Herod Antipas, the son of Herod the Great.

place. Someone more important may have been invited. 9Then the one who invited you will come and say, "Give your place to this other guest!" You will be embarrassed and will have to sit in the worst place.

10When you are invited to be a guest, go and sit in the worst place. Then the one who invited you may come and say, "My friend, take a better seat!" You will then be honored in front of all the other guests. 11If you put yourself above others, you will be put down. But if you humble yourself, you will be honored.

12Then Jesus said to the man who had invited him:

When you give a dinner or a banquet, don't invite your friends and family and relatives and rich neighbors. If you do, they will invite you in return, and you will be paid back. 13When you give a feast, invite the poor, the crippled, the lame, and the blind. 14They cannot pay you back. But God will bless you and reward you when his people rise from death.

The Great Banquet
(Matthew 22.1–10)

15After Jesus had finished speaking, one of the guests said, "The greatest blessing of all is to be at the banquet in God's kingdom!"

16Jesus told him:

A man once gave a great banquet and invited a lot of guests. 17When the banquet was ready, he sent a servant to tell the guests, "Everything is ready! Please come."

18One guest after another started making excuses. The first one said, "I bought some land, and I've got to look it over. Please excuse me."

19Another guest said, "I bought five teams of oxen, and I need to try them out. Please excuse me."

20Still another guest said, "I have just gotten married, and I can't be there."

21The servant told his master what happened, and the master became so angry that he said, "Go as fast as you can to every street and alley in town! Bring in everyone who is poor or crippled or blind or lame."

22When the servant returned, he said, "Master, I've done what you told me, and there is still plenty room for more people."

23His master then told him, "Go out along the back roads and fence rows and make people come in, so that my house will be full. 24Not one of the guests I first invited will get even a bite of my food!"

Being a Disciple
(Matthew 10.37, 38)

25Large crowds were walking along with Jesus, when he turned and said:

26You cannot be my disciple, unless you love me more than you love your father and mother, your wife and children, and your brothers and sisters. You cannot come with me unless you love me more than you love your own life.

27You cannot be my disciple unless you carry your own cross and come with me.

28Suppose one of you wants to build a tower. What is the first thing you will do? Won't you sit down and figure out how much it will cost and if you have enough money to pay for it? 29Otherwise, you will start building the tower, but not be able to finish. Then everyone who sees what is happening will laugh at you. 30They will say, "You started building, but could not finish the job."

31What will a king do if he has only ten thousand soldiers to defend himself against a king who is about to attack him with twenty thousand soldiers? Before he goes out to battle, won't he first sit down and decide if he can win? 32If he thinks he won't be able to defend himself, he will send messengers and ask for peace while the other king is still a long way off. 33So then, you cannot be my disciple unless you give away everything you own.

Salt and Light
(Matthew 5.13; Mark 9.50)

34Salt is good, but if it no longer tastes like salt, how can it be made to taste salty again? 35It is no longer good for the soil or even for the manure pile. People simply throw it out. If you have ears, pay attention!

One Sheep
(Matthew 18.12–14)

15 Tax collectors*l* and sinners were all crowding around to listen to Jesus. 2So the Pharisees and the teachers of the Law of Moses started grumbling, "This man is friendly with sinners. He even eats with them."

3Then Jesus told them this story:
4If any of you has a hundred sheep, and one of them gets lost, what will you do? Won't you leave the ninety-nine in the field and go look for the lost sheep until you find it? 5And when you find it, you will be so glad that you will put it on your shoulder 6and carry it home. Then you will call in your friends and neighbors and say, "Let's celebrate! I've found my lost sheep."

7Jesus said, "In the same way there is more happiness in heaven because of one sinner who turns to God than over ninety-nine good people who don't need to."

One Coin

8Jesus told the people another story:
What will a woman do if she has ten silver coins and loses one of them? Won't she light a lamp, sweep the floor, and look carefully until she finds it? 9Then she will call in her friends and neighbors and say, "Let's celebrate! I've found the coin I lost."

10Jesus said, "In the same way God's angels are happy when even one person turns to him."

Two Sons

11Jesus also told them another story:
Once a man had two sons. 12The younger son said to his father, "Give me my share of the

---

*l*Tax collectors: See the note at 3.12.

property." So the father divided his property between his two sons.

¹³Not long after that, the younger son packed up everything he owned and left for a foreign country, where he wasted all his money in wild living. ¹⁴He had spent everything, when a bad famine spread through that whole land. Soon he had nothing to eat.

¹⁵He went to work for a man in that country, and the man sent him out to take care of his pigs.ᵐ ¹⁶He would have been glad to eat what the pigs were eating,ⁿ but no one gave him a thing.

¹⁷Finally, he came to his senses and said, "My father's workers have plenty to eat, and here I am, starving to death! ¹⁸I will leave and go to my father and say to him, 'Father, I have sinned against God in heaven and against you. ¹⁹I am no longer good enough to be called your son. Treat me like one of your workers.' "

²⁰The younger son got up and started back to his father. But when he was still a long way off, his father saw him and felt sorry for him. He ran to his son and hugged and kissed him.

²¹The son said, "Father, I have sinned against God in heaven and against you. I am no longer good enough to be called your son."

²²But his father said to the servants, "Hurry and bring the best clothes and put them on him. Give him a ring for his finger and sandalsᵒ for his feet. ²³Get the best calf and prepare it, so we can eat and celebrate. ²⁴This son of mine was dead, but has now come back to life. He was lost and has now been found." And they began to celebrate.

²⁵The older son had been out in the field. But when he came near the house, he heard the music and dancing. ²⁶So he called one of the servants over and asked, "What's going on here?"

²⁷The servant answered, "Your brother has come home safe and sound, and your father ordered us to kill the best calf." ²⁸The older brother got so mad that he would not even go into the house.

His father came out and begged him to go in. ²⁹But he said to his father, "For years I have worked for you like a slave and have always obeyed you. But you have never even given me a little goat, so that I could give a dinner for my friends. ³⁰This other son of yours wasted your money on bad women. And now that he has come home, you ordered the best calf to be killed for a feast."

³¹His father replied, "My son, you are always with me, and

ᵐ*pigs*: The Jewish religion taught that pigs were not fit to eat or even to touch. A Jewish man would have felt terribly insulted if he had to feed pigs, much less eat with them. ⁿ*what the pigs were eating*: The Greek text has "(bean) pods," which came from a tree in Palestine. These were used to feed animals. Poor people sometimes ate them too. ᵒ*ring . . . sandals*: These show that the young man's father fully accepted him as his son. A ring was a sign of high position in the family. Sandals showed that he was a son instead of a slave, since slaves did not usually wear sandals.

everything I have is yours. 32But we should be glad and celebrate! Your brother was dead, but he is now alive. He was lost and has now been found."

A Dishonest Manager

16 Jesus said to his disciples: A rich man once had a manager to take care of his business. But he was told that his manager was wasting money. 2So the rich man called him in and said, "What is this I hear about you? Tell me what you have done! You are no longer going to work for me."

3The manager said to himself, "What shall I do now that my master is going to fire me? I can't dig ditches, and I'm ashamed to beg. 4I know what I'll do, so that people will welcome me into their homes after I've lost my job."

5Then one by one he called in the people who were in debt to his master. He asked the first one, "How much do you owe my master?"

6"A hundred barrels of olive oil," the man answered.

So the manager said, "Take your bill and sit down and quickly write 'fifty'."

7The manager asked someone else who was in debt to his master, "How much do you owe?"

"A thousand bushels*o* of wheat," the man replied.

The manager said, "Take your bill and write 'eight hundred'."

8The master praised his dishonest manager for looking out for himself so well. That's how it is! The people of this world look out for themselves better than the people who belong to the light.

9My disciples, I tell you to use wicked wealth to make friends for yourselves. Then when it is gone, you will be welcomed into an eternal home. 10Anyone who can be trusted in little matters can also be trusted in important matters. But anyone who is dishonest in little matters will be dishonest in important matters. 11If you cannot be trusted with this wicked wealth, who will trust you with true wealth? 12And if you cannot be trusted with what belongs to someone else, who will give you something that will be your own? 13You cannot be the slave of two masters. You will like one more than the other or be more loyal to one than to the other. You cannot serve God and money.

Some Sayings of Jesus
(Matthew 11.12, 13; 5.31, 32; Mark 10.11, 12)

14The Pharisees really loved money. So when they heard what Jesus said, they made fun of him. 15But Jesus told them:

You are always making yourselves look good, but God sees what is in your heart. The things that most people think are important are worthless as far as God is concerned.

---

oA thousand bushels: The Greek text has "A hundred measures," and each measure is about ten or twelve bushels.

16Until the time of John the Baptist, people had to obey the Law of Moses and the Books of the Prophets.*q* But since God's kingdom has been preached, everyone is trying hard to get in. 17Heaven and earth will disappear before the smallest letter of the Law does.

18It is a terrible sin*r* for a man to divorce his wife and marry another woman. It is also a terrible sin for a man to marry a divorced woman.

Lazarus and the Rich Man

19There was once a rich man who wore expensive clothes and every day ate the best food. 20But a poor beggar named Lazarus was brought to the gate of the rich man's house. 21He was happy just to eat the scraps that fell from the rich man's table. His body was covered with sores, and dogs kept coming up to lick them. 22The poor man died, and angels took him to the place of honor next to Abraham.*s*

The rich man also died and was buried. 23He went to hell*t* and was suffering terribly. When he looked up and saw Abraham far off and Lazarus at his side, 24he said to Abraham, "Have pity on me! Send Lazarus to dip his finger in water and touch my tongue. I'm suffering terribly in this fire."

25Abraham answered, "My friend, remember that while you lived, you had everything good, and Lazarus had everything bad. Now he is happy, and you are in pain. 26And besides, there is a deep ditch between us, and no one from either side can cross over."

27But the rich man said, "Abraham, then please send Lazarus to my father's home. 28Let him warn my five brothers, so they won't come to this horrible place."

29Abraham answered, "Your brothers can read what Moses and the prophets*u* wrote. They should pay attention to that."

30Then the rich man said, "No, that's not enough! If only someone from the dead would go to them, they would listen and turn to God."

31So Abraham said, "If they won't pay attention to Moses and the prophets, they won't listen even to someone who comes back from the dead."

Faith and Service
(Matthew 18.6, 7, 21, 22; Mark 9.42)

17 Jesus said to his disciples: There will always be something that causes people to sin. But anyone who causes them

---

q the Law of Moses and the Books of the Prophets: The Jewish Scriptures, that is, the Old Testament. *r a terrible sin*: The Greek text uses a word that means the sin of being unfaithful in marriage. *s the place of honor next to Abraham*: The Jewish people thought that heaven would be a banquet that God would give for them. Abraham would be the most important person there, and the guest of honor would sit next to him. *t hell*: The Greek text has "hades," which the Jewish people often thought of as the place where the dead wait for the final judgment. *u Moses and the prophets*: The Jewish Scriptures, that is, the Old Testament.

to sin is in for trouble. A person who causes even one of my little followers to sin ²would be better off thrown into the ocean with a heavy stone tied around the neck. ³So be careful what you do.

Correct any followers*v* of mine who sin, and forgive the ones who say they are sorry. ⁴Even if one of them mistreats you seven times in one day and says, "I am sorry," you should still forgive that person.

⁵The apostles said to the Lord, "Make our faith stronger!"

⁶Jesus replied:

If you had faith no bigger than a tiny mustard seed, you could tell this mulberry tree to pull itself up, roots and all, and to plant itself in the ocean. And it would!

⁷If your servant comes in from plowing or from taking care of the sheep, would you say, "Welcome! Come on in and have something to eat?" ⁸No, you wouldn't say that. You would say, "Fix me something to eat. Get ready to serve me, so I can have my meal. Then later on you can eat and drink." ⁹Servants don't deserve special thanks for doing what they are supposed to do. ¹⁰And that's how it should be with you. When you've done all you should, then say, "We are merely servants, and we have simply done our duty."

Ten Men with Leprosy

¹¹On his way to Jerusalem, Jesus went along the border between Sa-

maria and Galilee. ¹²As he was going into a village, ten men with leprosy*w* came toward him. They stood at a distance ¹³and shouted, "Jesus, Master, have pity on us!"

¹⁴Jesus looked at them and said, "Go show yourselves to the priests."*x*

On their way they were healed. ¹⁵When one of them discovered that he was healed, he came back, shouting praises to God. ¹⁶He bowed down at the feet of Jesus and thanked him. The man was from the country of Samaria.

¹⁷Jesus asked, "Weren't ten men healed? Where are the other nine? ¹⁸Why was this foreigner the only one who came back to thank God?" ¹⁹Then Jesus told the man, "You may get up and go. Your faith has made you well."

God's Kingdom
(Matthew 24.23–28, 37–41)

²⁰Some Pharisees asked Jesus when God's kingdom would come. He answered, "God's kingdom is not something you can see. ²¹There is no use saying, 'Look! Here it is' or 'Look! There it is.' God's kingdom is here with you."*y*

²²Jesus said to his disciples:

The time will come when you will long to see one of the days of the Son of Man, but you will not. ²³When people say to you, "Look there," or "Look here," don't go looking for him. ²⁴The day of the Son of Man will be like lightning flashing across the sky. ²⁵But first he must suffer terribly and be rejected by the people of

---

*v*followers: The Greek text has "brothers," which is often used in the New Testament for followers of Jesus. *w*leprosy: See the note at 4.27. *x*show yourselves to the priests: See the note at 5.14. *y*here with you: Or "in your hearts."

today. 26When the Son of Man comes, things will be just as they were when Noah lived. 27People were eating, drinking, and getting married right up to the day when Noah went into the big boat. Then the flood came and drowned everyone on earth.

28When Lot^z lived, people were also eating and drinking. They were buying, selling, planting, and building. 29But on the very day Lot left Sodom, fiery flames poured down from the sky and killed everyone. 30The same will happen on the day when the Son of Man appears.

31At that time no one on a rooftop^a should go down into the house to get anything. No one in a field should go back to the house for anything. 32Remember what happened to Lot's wife.^b

33People who try to save their lives will lose them, and those who lose their lives will save them. 34On that night two people will be sleeping in the same bed, but only one will be taken. The other will be left. 35-36Two women will be together grinding wheat, but only one will be taken. The other will be left.^c

37Then Jesus' disciples spoke up, "But where will this happen, Lord?" Jesus said, "Where there is a corpse, there will always be buzzards."^d

A Widow and a Judge

18 Jesus told his disciples a story about how they should keep on praying and never give up:

2In a town there was once a judge who didn't fear God or care about people. 3In that same town there was a widow who kept going to the judge and saying, "Make sure that I get fair treatment in court."

4For a while the judge refused to do anything. Finally, he said to himself, "Even though I don't fear God or care about people, 5I will help this widow because she keeps on bothering me. If I don't help her, she will wear me out."

6The Lord said:

Think about what that crooked judge said. 7Won't God protect his chosen ones who pray to him day and night? Won't he be concerned for them? 8He will surely hurry and help them. But when the Son of Man comes, will he find on this earth anyone with faith?

A Pharisee and a Tax Collector

9Jesus told a story to some people who thought they were better than

---

^zNoah . . . Lot: When God destroyed the earth by a flood, he saved Noah and his family. And when God destroyed the cities of Sodom and Gomorrah and the evil people who lived there, he rescued Lot and his family.   ^arooftop: See the note at 5.19.   ^bwhat happened to Lot's wife: She turned to a block of salt when she disobeyed God.   ^cwill be left: Some manuscripts add, "Two men will be in the same field, but only one will be taken. The other will be left."   ^dWhere there is a corpse, there will always be buzzards: This saying may mean that when anything important happens, people soon know about it. Or the saying may mean that whenever something bad happens, curious people gather around and stare. But the word translated "buzzard" also means "eagle" and may refer to the Roman army, which had an eagle as its symbol.

others and who looked down on everyone else:

¹⁰Two men went into the temple to pray.ᵉ One was a Pharisee and the other a tax collector.ᶠ ¹¹The Pharisee stood over by himself and prayed,ᵍ "God, I thank you that I am not greedy, dishonest, and unfaithful in marriage like other people. And I am really glad that I am not like that tax collector over there. ¹²I go without eatingʰ for two days a week, and I give you one tenth of all I earn."

¹³The tax collector stood off at a distance and did not think he was good enough even to look up toward heaven. He was so sorry for what he had done that he pounded his chest and prayed, "God, have pity on me! I am such a sinner."

¹⁴Then Jesus said, "When the two men went home, it was the tax collector and not the Pharisee who was pleasing to God. If you put yourself above others, you will be put down. But if you humble yourself, you will be honored."

Jesus Blesses Little Children
(Matthew 19.13–15; Mark 10.13–16)

¹⁵Some people brought their little children for Jesus to bless. But when his disciples saw them doing this, they told the people to stop bothering him. ¹⁶So Jesus called the children over to him and said, "Let the children come to me! Don't try to stop them. People who are like these children belong to God's kingdom.ⁱ ¹⁷You will never get into God's kingdom unless you enter it like a child!"

A Rich and Important Man
(Matthew 19.16–30; Mark 10.17–31)

¹⁸An important man asked Jesus, "Good Teacher, what must I do to have eternal life?"

¹⁹Jesus said, "Why do you call me good? Only God is good. ²⁰You know the commandments: 'Be faithful in marriage. Do not murder. Do not steal. Do not tell lies about others. Respect your father and mother.'"

²¹He told Jesus, "I have obeyed all these commandments since I was a young man."

²²When Jesus heard this, he said, "There is one thing you still need to do. Go and sell everything you own! Give the money to the poor, and you will have riches in heaven. Then come and be my follower." ²³When the man heard this, he was sad, because he was very rich.

²⁴Jesus saw how sad the man was. So he said, "It's terribly hard for rich people to get into God's kingdom! ²⁵In fact, it's easier for a camel to go through the eye of a needle than for a rich person to get into God's kingdom."

²⁶When the people heard this, they asked, "How can anyone ever be saved?"

²⁷Jesus replied, "There are some things that people cannot do, but God can do anything."

ᵉ*into the temple to pray*: Jewish people usually prayed there early in the morning and late in the afternoon. ᶠ*tax collector*: See the note at 3.12. ᵍ*stood over by himself and prayed*: Some manuscripts have "stood up and prayed to himself." ʰ*without eating*: See the note at 2.37. ⁱ*People who are like these children belong to God's kingdom*: Or "God's kingdom belongs to people who are like these children."

28Peter said, "Remember, we left everything to be your followers!"

29Jesus answered, "You can be sure that anyone who gives up home or wife or brothers or family or children because of God's kingdom **30**will be given much more in this life. And in the future world they will have eternal life."

Jesus Again Tells about His Death
(*Matthew 20.17–19; Mark 10.32–34*)

31Jesus took the twelve apostles aside and said:

We are now on our way to Jerusalem. Everything that the prophets wrote about the Son of Man will happen there. **32**He will be handed over to foreigners,[j] who will make fun of him, mistreat him, and spit on him. **33**They will beat him and kill him, but three days later he will rise to life.

34The apostles did not understand what Jesus was talking about. They could not understand, because the meaning of what he said was hidden from them.

Jesus Heals a Blind Beggar
(*Matthew 20.29–34; Mark 10.46–52*)

35When Jesus was coming close to Jericho, a blind man sat begging beside the road. **36**The man heard the crowd walking by and asked what was happening. **37**Some people told him that Jesus from Nazareth was passing by. **38**So the blind man shouted, "Jesus, Son of David,[k] have pity on me!" **39**The people who were going along with

Jesus told the man to be quiet. But he shouted even louder, "Son of David, have pity on me!"

40Jesus stopped and told some people to bring the blind man over to him. When the blind man was getting near, Jesus asked, **41**"What do you want me to do for you?"

"Lord, I want to see!" he answered.

42Jesus replied, "Look and you will see! Your eyes are healed because of your faith." **43**Right away the man could see, and he went with Jesus and started thanking God. When the crowds saw what happened, they praised God.

Zacchaeus

19 Jesus was going through Jericho, **2**where a man named Zacchaeus lived. He was in charge of collecting taxes[l] and was very rich. **3-4**Jesus was heading his way, and Zacchaeus wanted to see what he was like. But Zacchaeus was a short man and could not see over the crowd. So he ran ahead and climbed up into a sycamore tree.

5When Jesus got there, he looked up and said, "Zacchaeus, hurry down! I want to stay with you today." **6**Zacchaeus hurried down and gladly welcomed Jesus.

7Everyone who saw this started grumbling, "This man Zacchaeus is a sinner! And Jesus is going home to eat with him."

8Later that day Zacchaeus stood up and said to the Lord, "I will give half of my property to the poor. And I will

---

[j]*foreigners*: The Romans, who ruled Judea at this time. [k]*Son of David*: The Jewish people expected the Messiah to be from the family of King David, and for this reason the Messiah was often called the "Son of David." [l]*in charge of collecting taxes*: See the note at 3.12.

now pay back four times as much[m] to everyone I have ever cheated."

9Jesus said to Zacchaeus, "Today you and your family have been saved,[n] because you are a true son of Abraham.[o] 10The Son of Man came to look for and to save people who are lost."

A Story about Ten Servants
(Matthew 25.14–30)

11The people were still listening to Jesus as he was getting close to Jerusalem. Many of them thought that God's kingdom would soon appear, 12and Jesus told them this story:

A prince once went to a foreign country to be crowned king and then to return. 13But before leaving, he called in ten servants and gave each of them some money. He told them, "Use this to earn more money until I get back."

14But the people of his country hated him, and they sent messengers to the foreign country to say, "We don't want this man to be our king."

15After the prince had been made king, he returned and called in his servants. He asked them how much they had earned with the money they had been given.

16The first servant came and said, "Sir, with the money you gave me I have earned ten times as much."

17"That's fine, my good servant!" the king said. "Since you have shown that you can be trusted with a small amount, you will be given ten cities to rule."

18The second one came and said, "Sir, with the money you gave me, I have earned five times as much."

19The king said, "You will be given five cities."

20Another servant came and said, "Sir, here is your money. I kept it safe in a handkerchief. 21You are a hard man, and I was afraid of you. You take what is not yours, and you harvest crops you didn't plant."

22"You worthless servant!" the king told him. "You have condemned yourself by what you have just said. You knew that I am a hard man, taking what is not mine and harvesting what I've not planted. 23Why didn't you put my money in the bank? On my return, I could have had the money together with interest."

24Then he said to some other servants standing there, "Take the money away from him and give it to the servant who earned ten times as much."

25But they said, "Sir, he already has ten times as much!"

26The king replied, "Those who have something will be given more. But everything will be taken away from those who don't have anything. 27Now bring me the enemies who didn't want me to be their king. Kill them while I watch!"

---

[m]pay back four times as much: Both Jewish and Roman law said that a person must pay back four times the amount that was taken. [n]saved: Zacchaeus was Jewish, but it is only now that he is rescued from sin and placed under God's care. [o]son of Abraham: As used in this verse, the words mean that Zacchaeus is truly one of God's special people.

Jesus Enters Jerusalem
(Matthew 21.1–11; Mark 11.1–11;
John 12.12–19)

28When Jesus had finished saying all this, he went on toward Jerusalem. **29**As he was getting near to Bethphage and Bethany on the Mount of Olives, he sent two of his disciples on ahead. **30**He told them, "Go into the next village, where you will find a young donkey that has never been ridden. Untie the donkey and bring it here. **31**If anyone asks why you are doing that, just say, 'The Lord^p needs it.'"

32They went off and found everything just as Jesus had said. **33**While they were untying the donkey, its owners asked, "Why are you doing that?"

34They answered, "The Lord^p needs it."

35Then they led the donkey to Jesus. They put some of their clothes on its back and helped Jesus get on. **36**And as he rode along, the people spread clothes on the road^q in front of him. **37**When Jesus was starting down the Mount of Olives, his large crowd of disciples were happy and praised God because of all the miracles they had seen. **38**They shouted,

"Blessed is the king who comes
in the name of the Lord!
Peace in heaven
and glory to God."

39Some Pharisees in the crowd said to Jesus, "Teacher, make your disciples stop shouting!"

40But Jesus answered, "If they keep quiet, these stones will start shouting."

41When Jesus came closer and could see Jerusalem, he cried **42**and said:

It is too bad that today your people don't know what will bring them peace! Now it is hidden from them. **43**Jerusalem, the time will come when your enemies will build walls around you to attack you. Armies will surround you and close in on you from every side. **44**They will level you to the ground and kill your people. Not one stone in your buildings will be left on top of another. This will happen because you did not see that God had come to save you.^r

Jesus in the Temple
(Matthew 21.12–17; Mark 11.15–19;
John 2.13–22)

45When Jesus entered the temple, he started chasing out the people who were selling things. **46**He told them, "The Scriptures say, 'My house should be a place of worship.' But you have made it a place where robbers hide!"

47Each day Jesus kept on teaching in the temple. So the chief priests, the teachers of the Law of Moses, and some other important people tried to have him killed. **48**But they could not find a way to do it, because everyone else was eager to listen to him.

A Question about Jesus' Authority
(Matthew 21.23–27; Mark 11.27–33)

20 One day Jesus was teaching in the temple and telling the good

---

^p*The Lord*: Or "The master of the donkey." ^q*spread clothes on the road*: This was one way that the Jewish people welcomed a famous person. ^r*that God had come to save you*: The Jewish people looked for the time when God would come and rescue them from their enemies. But when Jesus came, many of them refused to obey him.

news. So the chief priests, the teachers, and the nation's leaders 2asked him, "What right do you have to do these things? Who gave you this authority?"

3Jesus replied, "I want to ask you a question. 4Who gave John the right to baptize? Was it God in heaven or merely some human being?"

5They talked this over and said to each other, "We can't say that God gave John this right. Jesus will ask us why we didn't believe John. 6And we can't say that it was merely some human who gave John the right to baptize. The crowd will stone us to death, because they think John was a prophet."

7So they told Jesus, "We don't know who gave John the right to baptize."

8Jesus replied, "Then I won't tell you who gave me the right to do what I do."

Renters of a Vineyard
(Matthew 21.33–46; Mark 12.1–12)

9Jesus told the people this story:
A man once planted a vineyard and rented it out. Then he left the country for a long time. 10When it was time to harvest the crop, he sent a servant to ask the renters for his share of the grapes. But they beat up the servant and sent him away without anything. 11So the owner sent another servant. The renters also beat him up. They insulted him terribly and sent him away without a thing. 12The owner sent a third servant. He was also beaten terribly and thrown out of the vineyard.

13The owner then said to himself, "What am I going to do? I know what. I'll send my son, the one I love so much. They will surely respect him!"

14When the renters saw the owner's son, they said to one another, "Someday he will own the vineyard. Let's kill him! Then we can have it all for ourselves." 15So they threw him out of the vineyard and killed him.

Jesus asked, "What do you think the owner of the vineyard will do? 16I'll tell you what he will do! He will come and kill those renters and let someone else have his vineyard."

When the people heard this, they said, "This must never happen!"

17But Jesus looked straight at them and said, "Then what do the Scriptures mean when they say, 'The stone that the builders tossed aside is now the most important stone of all'? 18Anyone who stumbles over this stone will get hurt, and anyone it falls on will be smashed to pieces."

19The chief priests and the teachers of the Law of Moses knew that Jesus was talking about them when he was telling this story. They wanted to arrest him right then, but they were afraid of the people.

Paying Taxes
(Matthew 22.15–22; Mark 12.13–17)

20Jesus' enemies kept watching him closely, because they wanted to hand him over to the Roman governor. So they sent some men who pretended to be good. But they were really spies trying to catch Jesus saying something wrong. 21The spies said to him, "Teacher, we know that you teach the truth about what God wants people to do. And you treat everyone with the

same respect, no matter who they are.
22Tell us, should we pay taxes to the
Emperor or not?"

23Jesus knew that they were trying
to trick him. So he told them, 24"Show
me a coin." Then he asked, "Whose
picture and name are on it?"

"The Emperor's," they answered.

25Then he told them, "Give the
Emperor what belongs to him and give
God what belongs to God." 26Jesus' enemies could not catch him saying anything wrong there in front of the people. They were amazed at his answer
and kept quiet.

Life in the Future World
(*Matthew 22.23–33; Mark 12.18–27*)

27The Sadducees did not believe
that people would rise to life after
death. So some of them came to Jesus
28and said:

Teacher, Moses wrote that if a
married man dies and has no
children, his brother should
marry the widow. Their first son
would then be thought of as the
son of the dead brother.

29There were once seven
brothers. The first one married,
but died without having any children. 30The second one married
his brother's widow, and he also
died without having any children.
31The same thing happened to
the third one. Finally, all seven
brothers married that woman and
died without having any children.
32At last the woman died.
33When God raises people from

death, whose wife will this
woman be? All seven brothers
had married her.

34Jesus answered:

The people in this world get
married. 35But in the future
world no one who is worthy to rise
from death will either marry 36or
die. They will be like the angels
and will be God's children, because they have been raised to
life.

37In the story about the burning bush, Moses clearly shows
that people will live again. He
said, "The Lord is the God worshiped by Abraham, Isaac, and
Jacob."*s* 38So the Lord is not the
God of the dead, but of the living.
This means that everyone is alive
as far as God is concerned.

39Some of the teachers of the Law
of Moses said, "Teacher, you have
given a good answer!" 40From then on,
no one dared to ask Jesus any questions.

About David's Son
(*Matthew 22.41–46; Mark 12.35–37*)

41Jesus asked, "Why do people say
that the Messiah will be the son of King
David?*t* 42In the book of Psalms, David
himself says,

'The Lord said to my Lord,
Sit at my right side*u*
43until I make your enemies
into a footstool for you.'
44David spoke of the Messiah as his
Lord, so how can the Messiah be his
son?"

---

s"The Lord is the God worshiped by Abraham, Isaac, and Jacob": Jesus argues that if God is
worshiped by these three, they must be alive, because he is the God of the living. *t the son
of King David*: See the note at 18.38. *u right side*: The place of power and honor.

Jesus and the Teachers of the Law of Moses

*(Matthew 23.1–36; Mark 12.38–40;
Luke 11.37–54)*

45While everyone was listening to Jesus, he said to his disciples:

46Guard against the teachers of the Law of Moses! They love to walk around in long robes, and they like to be greeted in the market. They want the front seats in the meeting places and the best seats at banquets. 47But they cheat widows out of their homes and then pray long prayers just to show off. These teachers will be punished most of all.

A Widow's Offering

(Mark 12.41–44)

21 Jesus looked up and saw some rich people tossing their gifts into the offering box. 2He also saw a poor widow putting in two pennies. 3And he said, "I tell you that this poor woman has put in more than all the others. 4Everyone else gave what they didn't need. But she is very poor and gave everything she had."

The Temple Will Be Destroyed

(Matthew 24.1, 2; Mark 13.1, 2)

5Some people were talking about the beautiful stones used to build the temple and about the gifts that had been placed in it. Jesus said, 6"Do you see these stones? The time is coming when not one of them will be left in place. They will all be knocked down."

Warning about Trouble

(Matthew 24.3–14; Mark 13.3–13)

7Some people asked, "Teacher, when will all this happen? How can we know when these things are about to take place?"

8Jesus replied:

Don't be fooled by all those who will come and claim to be me. They will say, "I am Christ!" and "Now is the time!" But don't follow them. 9When you hear about wars and riots, don't be afraid. These things will have to happen first, but that is not the end.

10Nations will go to war against one another, and kingdoms will attack each other. 11There will be great earthquakes, and in many places people will starve to death and suffer terrible diseases. All sorts of frightening things will be seen in the sky.

12Before all this happens, you will be arrested and punished. You will be tried in the Jewish meeting places and put in jail. Because of me you will be placed on trial before kings and governors. 13But this will be your chance to tell about your faith.

14Don't worry about what you will say to defend yourselves. 15I will give you the wisdom to know what to say. None of your enemies will be able to oppose you or to say that you are wrong. 16You will be betrayed by your own parents, brothers, family, and friends. Some of you will even be killed. 17Because of me you will be hated by everyone. 18But don't worry!*v* 19You will be saved by being faithful to me.

vBut don't worry: The Greek text has "Not a hair of your head will be lost," which means, "There's no need to worry."

Jerusalem Will Be Destroyed
(Matthew 24.15–21; Mark 13.14–19)

20When you see Jerusalem surrounded by soldiers, you will know that it will soon be destroyed. 21If you are living in Judea at that time, run to the mountains. If you are in the city, leave it. And if you are out in the country, don't go back into the city. 22This time of punishment is what is written about in the Scriptures. 23It will be an awful time for women who are expecting babies or nursing young children! Everywhere in the land people will suffer horribly and be punished. 24Some of them will be killed by swords. Others will be carried off to foreign countries. Jerusalem will be overrun by foreign nations until their time comes to an end.

When the Son of Man Appears
(Matthew 24.29–31; Mark 13.24–27)

25Strange things will happen to the sun, moon, and stars. The nations on earth will be afraid of the roaring sea and tides, and they won't know what to do. 26People will be so frightened that they will faint because of what is happening to the world. Every power in the sky will be shaken.*w* 27Then the Son of Man will be seen, coming in a cloud with great power and glory. 28When all of this starts happening, stand up straight and be brave. You will soon be set free.

A Lesson from a Fig Tree
(Matthew 24.32–35; Mark 13.28–31)

29Then Jesus told them a story:

When you see a fig tree or any other tree 30putting out leaves, you know that summer will soon come. 31So, when you see these things happening, you know that God's kingdom will soon be here. 32You can be sure that some of the people living today will still be alive when all of this takes place. 33The sky and the earth won't last forever, but my words will.

A Warning

34Don't spend all of your time thinking about eating or drinking or worrying about life. If you do, the final day will suddenly catch you 35like a trap. That day will surprise everyone on earth. 36Watch out and keep praying that you can escape all that is going to happen and that the Son of Man will be pleased with you.

37Jesus taught in the temple each day, and he spent each night on the Mount of Olives. 38Everyone got up early and came to the temple to hear him teach.

A Plot to Kill Jesus
(Matthew 26.1–5, 14, 16; Mark 14.1, 2, 10, 11; John 11.45–53)

22 The Feast of Thin Bread, also called Passover, was near. 2The chief priests and the teachers of the Law of Moses were looking for a way to get rid of Jesus, because they were

---

w Every power in the sky will be shaken: In ancient times people thought that the stars were spiritual powers.

afraid of what the people might do.
³Then Satan entered the heart of Judas
Iscariot,ˣ who was one of the twelve
apostles.

⁴Judas went to talk with the chief
priests and the officers of the temple
police about how he could help them
arrest Jesus. ⁵They were very pleased
and offered to pay Judas some money.
⁶He agreed and started looking for a
good chance to betray Jesus when the
crowds were not around.

Jesus Eats with His Disciples
(Matthew 26.17–25; Mark 14.12–21;
John 13.21–30)

⁷The day had come for the Feast
of Thin Bread, and it was time to kill
the Passover lambs. ⁸So Jesus said to
Peter and John, "Go and prepare the
Passover meal for us to eat."

⁹But they asked, "Where do you
want us to prepare it?"

¹⁰Jesus told them, "As you go into
the city, you will meet a man carrying
a jar of water.ʸ Follow him into the
house ¹¹and say to the owner, 'Our
teacher wants to know where he can
eat the Passover meal with his disciples.' ¹²The owner will take you upstairs and show you a large room
ready for you to use. Prepare the meal
there."

¹³Peter and John left. They found
everything just as Jesus had told them,
and they prepared the Passover meal.

The Lord's Supper
(Matthew 26.26–30; Mark 14.22–26;
1 Corinthians 11.23–25)

¹⁴When the time came for Jesus
and the apostles to eat, ¹⁵he said to
them, "I have very much wanted to eat
this Passover meal with you before I
suffer. ¹⁶I tell you that I will not eat
another Passover meal until it is finally
eaten in God's kingdom."

¹⁷Jesus took a cup of wine in his
hands and gave thanks to God. Then
he told the apostles, "Take this wine
and share it with each other. ¹⁸I tell
you that I will not drink any more wine
until God's kingdom comes."

¹⁹Jesus took some bread in his
hands and gave thanks for it. He broke
the bread and handed it to his apostles.
Then he said, "This is my body, which
is given for you. Eat this as a way of
remembering me!"

²⁰After the meal he took another
cup of wine in his hands. Then he said,
"This is my blood. It is poured out for
you, and with it God makes his new
agreement. ²¹The one who will betray
me is here at the table with me! ²²The
Son of Man will die in the way that
has been decided for him, but it
will be terrible for the one who betrays him!"

²³Then the apostles started arguing about who would ever do such a
thing.

An Argument about Greatness

²⁴The apostles got into an argument about which one of them was the
greatest. ²⁵So Jesus told them:

Foreign kings order their people around, and powerful rulers
call themselves everyone's
friends.ᶻ ²⁶But don't be like them.
The most important one of you
should be like the least important,
and your leader should be like a

ˣ*Iscariot*: See the note at 6.16.   ʸ*a man carrying a jar of water*: A male slave carrying water
would probably mean that the family was rich.   ᶻ*everyone's friends*: This translates a Greek
word that rulers sometimes used as a title for themselves or for special friends.

servant. **27**Who do people think is the greatest, a person who is served or one who serves? Isn't it the one who is served? But I have been with you as a servant.

28You have stayed with me in all my troubles. **29**So I will give you the right to rule as kings, just as my Father has given me the right to rule as a king. **30**You will eat and drink with me in my kingdom, and you will each sit on a throne to judge the twelve tribes of Israel.

Jesus' Disciples Will Be Tested
(Matthew 26.31–35; Mark 14.27–31; John 13.36–38)

31Jesus said, "Simon, listen to me! Satan has demanded the right to test each one of you, as a farmer does when he separates wheat from the husks.*a* **32**But Simon, I have prayed that your faith will be strong. And when you have come back to me, help the others."

33Peter said, "Lord, I am ready to go with you to jail and even to die with you."

34Jesus replied, "Peter, I tell you that before a rooster crows tomorrow morning, you will say three times that you don't know me."

Moneybags, Traveling Bags, and Swords

35Jesus asked his disciples, "When I sent you out without a moneybag or a traveling bag or sandals, did you need anything?"

"No!" they answered.

36Jesus told them, "But now, if you have a moneybag, take it with you. Also take a traveling bag, and if you don't have a sword,*b* sell some of your clothes and buy one. **37**Do this because the Scriptures say, 'He was considered a criminal.' This was written about me, and it will soon come true."

38The disciples said, "Lord, here are two swords!"

"Enough of that!" Jesus replied.

Jesus Prays
(Matthew 26.36–46; Mark 14.32–42)

39Jesus went out to the Mount of Olives, as he often did, and his disciples went with him. **40**When they got there, he told them, "Pray that you will not be tested."

41Jesus walked on a little way before he kneeled down and prayed, **42**"Father, if you will, please don't make me suffer by having me drink from this cup.*c* But do what you want, and not what I want."

43Then an angel from heaven came to help him. **44**Jesus was in great pain and prayed so sincerely that his sweat fell to the ground like drops of blood.*d*

45Jesus got up from praying and went over to his disciples. They were asleep and worn out from being so sad. **46**He said to them, "Why are you asleep? Wake up and pray that you will not be tested."

---

aseparates wheat from the husks: See the note at 3.17. *bmoneybag . . . traveling bag . . . sword*: These were things that someone would take on a dangerous journey. Jesus was telling his disciples to be ready for anything that might happen. They seem to have understood what he meant (see 22.49-51). *chaving me drink from this cup*: In the Scriptures "to drink from a cup" sometimes means to suffer. *dThen an angel . . . like drops of blood*: Verses 43,44 are not in some manuscripts.

Jesus Is Arrested

(Matthew 26.47–56; Mark 14.43–50;
John 18.3–11)

47While Jesus was still speaking, a crowd came up. It was led by Judas, one of the twelve apostles. He went over to Jesus and greeted him with a kiss.*e*

48Jesus asked Judas, "Are you betraying the Son of Man with a kiss?"

49When Jesus' disciples saw what was about to happen, they asked, "Lord, should we attack them with a sword?" **50**One of the disciples even struck at the high priest's servant with his sword and cut off the servant's right ear.

51"Enough of that!" Jesus said. Then he touched the servant's ear and healed it.

52Jesus spoke to the chief priests, the temple police, and the leaders who had come to arrest him. He said, "Why do you come out with swords and clubs and treat me like a criminal? **53**I was with you everyday in the temple, and you didn't arrest me. But this is your time, and darkness*f* is in control."

Peter Says He Does Not Know Jesus

(Matthew 26.57, 58, 67–75; Mark 14.53,
54, 66–72; John 18.12–18, 25–27)

54Jesus was arrested and led away to the house of the high priest, while Peter followed at a distance. **55**Some people built a fire in the middle of the courtyard and were sitting around it. Peter sat there with them, **56**and a servant girl saw him. Then after she had looked at him carefully, she said, "This man was with Jesus!"

57Peter said, "Woman, I don't even know that man!"

58A little later someone else saw Peter and said, "You surely are one of them!"

"No, I'm not!" Peter replied.

59About an hour later another man insisted, "This man must have been with Jesus. They both come from Galilee."

60Peter replied, "I don't know what you are talking about!" Right then, while Peter was still speaking, a rooster crowed.

61The Lord turned and looked at Peter. And Peter remembered that the Lord had said, "Before a rooster crows tomorrow morning, you will say three times that you don't know me." **62**Then Peter went out and cried hard.

63The men who were guarding Jesus made fun of him and beat him. **64**They put a blindfold on him and said, "Tell us who struck you!" **65**They kept on insulting Jesus in many other ways.

Jesus Is Questioned by the Jewish Council

(Matthew 26.59–66; Mark 14.55–64;
John 18.19–24)

66At daybreak the nation's leaders, the chief priests, and the teachers of the Law of Moses got together and brought Jesus before their council. **67**They said, "Tell us! Are you the Messiah?"

Jesus replied, "If I said so, you wouldn't believe me. **68**And if I asked you a question, you wouldn't answer. **69**But from now on, the Son of Man will be seated at the right side of God All-Powerful."

---

e greeted him with a kiss: It was the custom for people to greet each other with a kiss on the cheek.　*f darkness*. Darkness stands for the power of the devil.

70Then they asked, "Are you the Son of God?"*g*

Jesus answered, "You say I am!"*h*

71They replied, "Why do we need more witnesses? He said it himself!"

Pilate Questions Jesus
(Matthew 27.1, 2, 11–14; Mark 15.1–5; John 18.28–38)

23 Everyone in the council got up and led Jesus off to Pilate. **2**They started accusing him and said, "We caught this man trying to get our people to riot and to stop paying taxes to the Emperor. He also claims that he is the Messiah, our king."

3Pilate asked Jesus, "Are you the king of the Jews?"

"Those are your words," Jesus answered.

4Pilate told the chief priests and the crowd, "I don't find him guilty of anything."

5But they all kept on saying, "He has been teaching and causing trouble all over Judea. He started in Galilee and has now come all the way here."

Jesus Is Brought before Herod

6When Pilate heard this, he asked, "Is this man from Galilee?" **7**After Pilate learned that Jesus came from the region ruled by Herod,*i* he sent him to Herod, who was in Jerusalem at that time.

8For a long time Herod had wanted to see Jesus and was very happy because he finally had this chance. He had heard many things about Jesus and hoped to see him work a miracle. **9**Herod asked him a lot of ques-

tions, but Jesus did not answer. **10**Then the chief priests and the teachers of the Law of Moses stood up and accused him of all kinds of bad things.

11Herod and his soldiers made fun of Jesus and insulted him. They put a fine robe on him and sent him back to Pilate. **12**That same day Herod and Pilate became friends, even though they had been enemies before this.

The Death Sentence
(Matthew 27.15–26; Mark 15.6–15; John 18.39—19.16)

13Pilate called together the chief priests, the leaders, and the people. **14**He told them, "You brought Jesus to me and said he was a troublemaker. But I have questioned him here in front of you, and I have not found him guilty of anything that you say he has done. **15**Herod didn't find him guilty either and sent him back. This man doesn't deserve to be put to death! **16-17**I will just have him beaten with a whip and set free."*j*

18But the whole crowd shouted, "Kill Jesus! Give us Barabbas!" **19**Now Barabbas was in jail because he had started a riot in the city and had murdered someone.

20Pilate wanted to set Jesus free, so he spoke again to the crowds. **21**But they kept shouting, "Nail him to a cross! Nail him to a cross!"

22Pilate spoke to them a third time, "But what crime has he done? I have not found him guilty of anything for which he should be put to death. I will have him beaten with a whip and set free."

g Son of God: This was one of the titles used for the kings of Israel. *h You say I am:* Or "That's what you say." *i Herod:* Herod Antipas, the son of Herod the Great. *j set free:* Some manuscripts add, "Pilate said this, because at every Passover he was supposed to set one prisoner free for the Jewish people."

23The people kept on shouting as loud as they could for Jesus to be put to death. 24Finally, Pilate gave in. 25He freed the man who was in jail for rioting and murder, because he was the one the crowd wanted to be set free. Then Pilate handed Jesus over for them to do what they wanted with him.

Jesus Is Nailed to a Cross
(Matthew 27.31–44; Mark 15.21–32; John 19.17–27)

26As Jesus was being led away, some soldiers grabbed hold of a man from Cyrene named Simon. He was coming in from the fields, but they put the cross on him and made him carry it behind Jesus.

27A large crowd was following Jesus, and in the crowd a lot of women were crying and weeping for him. 28Jesus turned to the women and said:

Women of Jerusalem, don't cry for me! Cry for yourselves and for your children. 29Someday people will say, "Women who never had children are really fortunate!" 30At that time everyone will say to the mountains, "Fall on us!" They will say to the hills, "Hide us!" 31If this can happen when the wood is green, what do you think will happen when it is dry?*k*

32Two criminals were led out to be put to death with Jesus. 33When the soldiers came to the place called "The Skull,"*l* they nailed Jesus to a cross. They also nailed the two criminals to crosses, one on each side of Jesus.

34-35Jesus said, "Father, forgive these people! They don't know what they're doing."*m*

While the crowd stood there watching Jesus, the soldiers gambled for his clothes. The leaders insulted him by saying, "He saved others. Now he should save himself, if he really is God's chosen Messiah!"

36The soldiers made fun of Jesus and brought him some wine. 37They said, "If you are the king of the Jews, save yourself!"

38Above him was a sign that said, "This is the King of the Jews."

39One of the criminals hanging there also insulted Jesus by saying, "Aren't you the Messiah? Save yourself and save us!"

40But the other criminal told the first one off, "Don't you fear God? Aren't you getting the same punishment as this man? 41We got what was coming to us, but he didn't do anything wrong." 42Then he said to Jesus, "Remember me when you come into power!"

43Jesus replied, "I promise that today you will be with me in paradise."*m*

The Death of Jesus
(Matthew 27.45–56; Mark 15.33–41; John 19.28–30)

44Around noon the sky turned dark and stayed that way until the middle

---

*k*If this can happen when the wood is green, what do you think will happen when it is dry?: This saying probably means, "If this can happen to an innocent person, what do you think will happen to one who is guilty?" *l*"The Skull": The place was probably given this name because it was near a large rock in the shape of a human skull. *m*Jesus said, "Father, forgive these people! They don't know what they're doing.": These words are not in some manuscripts. *n*paradise: In the Greek translation of the Old Testament, this word is used for the Garden of Eden. In New Testament times it was sometimes used for the place where God's people are happy and at rest, as they wait for the final judgment.

of the afternoon. 45The sun stopped shining, and the curtain in the temple^o split down the middle. 46Jesus shouted, "Father, I put myself in your hands!" Then he died.

47When the Roman officer saw what had happened, he praised God and said, "Jesus must really have been a good man!"

48A crowd had gathered to see the terrible sight. After they saw it, they felt brokenhearted and went home. 49All of Jesus' close friends and the women who had come with him from Galilee stood at a distance and watched.

Jesus Is Buried
(Matthew 27.57–61; Mark 15.42–47; John 19.38–42)

50-51There was a man named Joseph, who was from Arimathea in Judea. Joseph was a good and honest man, and he was eager for God's kingdom to come. He was also a member of the Jewish council, but he did not agree with what they had decided. 52Joseph went to Pilate and asked for Jesus' body. 53He took the body down from the cross and wrapped it in fine cloth. Then he put it in a tomb that had been cut out of solid rock and had never been used. 54It was Friday, and the Sabbath was about to begin.^p

55The women who had come with Jesus from Galilee followed Joseph and watched how Jesus' body was placed in the tomb. 56Then they went to prepare some sweet-smelling spices for his burial. But on the Sabbath they rested, as the Law of Moses commands.

Jesus Is Alive
(Matthew 28.1–10; Mark 16.1–8; John 20.1–10)

24 Very early on Sunday morning the women went to the tomb, carrying the spices that they had prepared. 2When they found the stone rolled away from the entrance, 3they went in. But they did not find the body of the Lord^q Jesus, 4and they did not know what to think.

Suddenly two men in shining white clothes stood beside them. 5The women were afraid and bowed to the ground. But the men said, "Why are you looking in the place of the dead for someone who is alive? 6Jesus is not here! He has been raised from death. Remember that while he was still in Galilee, he told you, 7'The Son of Man will be handed over to sinners who will nail him to a cross. But three days later he will rise to life.' " 8Then they remembered what Jesus had said.

9-10Mary Magdalene, Joanna, Mary the mother of James, and some other women were the ones who had gone to the tomb. When they returned, they told the eleven apostles and the others what had happened. 11The apostles thought it was all nonsense, and they would not believe.

12But Peter ran to the tomb. And when he stooped down and looked in, he saw only the burial clothes. Then

---

^o*curtain in the temple*: There were two curtains in the temple. One was at the entrance, and the other separated the holy place from the most holy place that the Jewish people thought of as God's home on earth. The second curtain is probably the one which is meant. ^p*the Sabbath was about to begin*: The Sabbath begins at sunset on Friday. ^q*the Lord*: These words are not in some manuscripts.

he returned, wondering what had happened.*ʳ*

Jesus Appears to Two Disciples
(Mark 16.12, 13)

¹³That same day two of Jesus' disciples were going to the village of Emmaus, which was about seven miles from Jerusalem. ¹⁴As they were talking and thinking about what had happened, ¹⁵Jesus came near and started walking along beside them. ¹⁶But they did not know who he was.

¹⁷Jesus asked them, "What were you talking about as you walked along?"

The two of them stood there looking sad and gloomy. ¹⁸Then the one named Cleopas asked Jesus, "Are you the only person from Jerusalem who didn't know what was happening there these last few days?"

¹⁹"What do you mean?" Jesus asked.

They answered:

Those things that happened to Jesus from Nazareth. By what he did and said he showed that he was a powerful prophet, who pleased God and all the people. ²⁰Then the chief priests and our leaders had him arrested and sentenced to die on a cross. ²¹We had hoped that he would be the one to set Israel free! But it has already been three days since all this happened.

²²Some women in our group surprised us. They had gone to the tomb early in the morning, ²³but did not find the body of Jesus. They came back, saying that they had seen a vision of angels who told them that he is alive. ²⁴Some men from our group went to the tomb and found it just as the women had said. But they didn't see Jesus either.

²⁵Then Jesus asked the two disciples, "Why can't you understand? How can you be so slow to believe all that the prophets said? ²⁶Didn't you know that the Messiah would have to suffer before he was given his glory?" ²⁷Jesus then explained everything written about himself in the Scriptures, beginning with the Law of Moses and the Books of the Prophets.*ˢ*

²⁸When the two of them came near the village where they were going, Jesus seemed to be going farther. ²⁹They begged him, "Stay with us! It's already late, and the sun is going down." So Jesus went into the house to stay with them.

³⁰After Jesus sat down to eat, he took some bread. He blessed it and broke it. Then he gave it to them. ³¹At once they knew who he was, but he disappeared. ³²They said to each other, "When he talked with us along the road and explained the Scriptures to us, didn't it warm our hearts?" ³³So they got right up and returned to Jerusalem.

The two disciples found the eleven apostles and the others gathered together. ³⁴And they learned from the group that the Lord was really alive and had appeared to Peter. ³⁵Then the disciples from Emmaus told what happened on the road and how they knew he was the Lord when he broke the bread.

ʳwhat had happened: Verse 12 is not in some manuscripts.   *ˢthe Law of Moses and the Books of the Prophets*: The Jewish Scriptures, that is, the Old Testament.

What Jesus' Followers Must Do
*(Matthew 28.16–20; Mark 16.14–18;
John 20.19–23; Acts 1.6–8)*

36While Jesus' disciples were talking about what had happened, Jesus appeared to them and said, "May God give you peace!" 37They were frightened and terrified because they thought they were seeing a ghost.

38But Jesus said, "Why are you so frightened? Why do you doubt? 39Look at my hands and my feet and see who I am! Touch me and find out for yourselves. Ghosts don't have flesh and bones as you see I have."

40After Jesus said this, he showed them his hands and his feet. 41The disciples were so glad and amazed that they could not believe it. Jesus then asked them, "Do you have something to eat?" 42They gave him a piece of baked fish. 43He took it and ate it as they watched.

44Jesus said to them, "While I was still with you, I told you that everything written about me in the Law of Moses, the Books of the Prophets, and in the Psalms*t* had to happen."

45Then he helped them understand the Scriptures. 46He told them:

The Scriptures say that the Messiah must suffer, then three days later he will rise from death. 47They also say that all people of every nation must be told in my name to turn to God, in order to be forgiven. So beginning in Jerusalem, 48you must tell everything that has happened. 49I will send you the one my Father has promised,*u* but you must stay in the city until you are given power from heaven.

Jesus Returns to Heaven
(Mark 16.19, 20; Acts 1.9–11)

50Jesus led his disciples out to Bethany, where he raised his hands and blessed them. 51As he was doing this, he left and was taken up to heaven.*v* 52After his disciples had worshiped him,*w* they returned to Jerusalem and were very happy. 53They spent their time in the temple, praising God.

---

t Psalms: The Jewish Scriptures were made up of three parts: (1) the Law of Moses, (2) the Books of the Prophets, (3) and the Writings, which included the Psalms. Sometimes the Scriptures were just called the Law or the Law (of Moses) and the Books of the Prophets. *u the one my Father has promised*: Jesus means the Holy Spirit. *v and was taken up to heaven*: These words are not in some manuscripts. *w After his disciples had worshiped him*: These words are not in some manuscripts.

John Tells
the Good News

ABOUT THIS BOOK

Who is Jesus Christ? John answers this question in the first chapter of his Gospel. Using the words of an early Christian hymn, he calls Jesus the "Word" by which God created everything and by which he gave life to everyone (1.3,4). He shows how John the Baptist announced Jesus' coming, "Here is the Lamb of God who takes away the sin of the world" (1.29). When Philip met Jesus he knew Jesus was "the one that Moses and the Prophets wrote about" (1.45). And, in the words of Nathanael, Jesus is "the Son of God and the King of Israel" (1.49).

In John's Gospel we learn a lot about who Jesus is by observing what he said and did when he was with other people. These include a Samaritan woman who received Jesus' offer of life-giving water, a woman who had been caught in sin, his friend Lazarus who was brought back to life by Jesus, and his follower Thomas who doubted that Jesus was raised from death. Jesus also refers to himself as "I am", a phrase which translates the most holy name for God in the Hebrew Scriptures. He uses this name for himself when he makes his claim to be the life-giving bread, the light of the world, the good shepherd, and the true vine.

Jesus performs seven miracles that are more than miracles. Each of them is a "sign" that tells us something about Jesus as the Son of God. For example, by healing a lame man (5.1–8), Jesus shows that he is just like his Father, who never stops working (5.17). This sign also teaches that the Son does only what he sees his Father doing (5.19), and that like the Father "the Son gives life to anyone he wants to" (5.21).

The way John tells the story of Jesus is quite different from the other three gospels. Here, Jesus has long conversations with people about who he is and what God sent him to do. In these conversations he teaches many important things—for example, that he is the way, the truth and the life.

Why did John write? John himself tells us, "So that you will put your faith in Jesus as the Messiah and the Son of God" (20.31). How is this possible? Jesus answers that question in his words to Nicodemus:

God loved the people of this world so much that he gave his only Son, so that everyone who has faith in him will have eternal life and never die. (3.16)

A QUICK LOOK AT THIS BOOK

- A Hymn in Praise of the Word (1.1–18)
- The Message of John the Baptist (1.19–34)
- Jesus Chooses His First Disciples (1.35–51)
- Jesus' Seven Special Miracles (2.1—12.50)
- Jesus' Last Week: His Trial and Death (13.1—19.42)
- Jesus Is Alive (20.1–10)
- Jesus Appears to His Disciples (20.11—21.25)

The Word of Life

1 In the beginning was the one
who is called the Word.
The Word was with God
and was truly God.
2 From the very beginning
the Word was with God.

3 And with this Word,
God created all things.
Nothing was made
without the Word.
Everything that was created
4   received its life from him,
and his life gave light
to everyone.
5 The light keeps shining
in the dark,
and darkness has never
put it out.*a*
6 God sent a man named John,
7 who came to tell
about the light
and to lead all people
to have faith.
8 John wasn't that light.
He came only to tell
about the light.

9 The true light that shines
on everyone
was coming into the world.
10 The Word was in the world,
but no one knew him,
though God had made the world
with his Word.
11 He came into his own world,
but his own nation
did not welcome him.
12 Yet some people accepted him
and put their faith in him.
So he gave them the right
to be the children of God.

13 They were not God's children
by nature or because
of any human desires.
God himself was the one
who made them
his children.

14 The Word became
a human being
and lived here with us.
We saw his true glory,
the glory of the only Son
of the Father.
From him all the kindness
and all the truth of God
have come down to us.

15 John spoke about him and
shouted, "This is the one I told you
would come! He is greater than I am,
because he was alive before I was
born."

16 Because of all that the Son is,
we have been given one blessing after
another.*b* 17 The Law was given by Moses, but Jesus Christ brought us undeserved kindness and truth. 18 No one
has ever seen God. The only Son, who
is truly God and is closest to the Father,
has shown us what God is like.

John the Baptist Tells about Jesus
(Matthew 3.1–12; Mark 1.1–8;
Luke 3.15–17)

19-20 The Jewish leaders in Jerusalem sent priests and temple helpers to
ask John who he was. He told them
plainly, "I am not the Messiah."
21 Then when they asked him if he
were Elijah, he said, "No, I am not!"
And when they asked if he were the
Prophet,*c* he also said "No!"
22 Finally, they said, "Who are you

---

a put it out: Or "understood it." *b one blessing after another*: Or "one blessing in place of
another." *c the Prophet*: Many of the Jewish people expected God to send them a prophet
who would be like Moses, but with even greater power. See Deuteronomy 18.15, 18.

then? We have to give an answer to the ones who sent us. Tell us who you are!"

23John answered in the words of the prophet Isaiah, "I am only someone shouting in the desert, 'Get the road ready for the Lord!' "

24Some Pharisees had also been sent to John. **25**They asked him, "Why are you baptizing people, if you are not the Messiah or Elijah or the Prophet?"

26John told them, "I use water to baptize people. But here with you is someone you don't know. **27**Even though I came first, I am not good enough to untie his sandals." **28**John said this as he was baptizing east of the Jordan River in Bethany.[d]

The Lamb of God

29The next day John saw Jesus coming toward him and said:

Here is the Lamb of God who takes away the sin of the world! **30**He is the one I told you about when I said, "Someone else will come. He is greater than I am, because he was alive before I was born." **31**I didn't know who he was. But I came to baptize you with water, so that everyone in Israel would see him.

32I was there and saw the Spirit come down on him like a dove from heaven. And the Spirit stayed on him. **33**Before this I didn't know who he was. But the one who sent me to baptize with water had told me, "You will see the Spirit come down and stay on someone. Then you will know that he is the one who will baptize

with the Holy Spirit." **34**I saw this happen, and I tell you that he is the Son of God.

The First Disciples of Jesus

35The next day John was there again, and two of his followers were with him. **36**When he saw Jesus walking by, he said, "Here is the Lamb of God!" **37**John's two followers heard him, and they went with Jesus.

38When Jesus turned and saw them, he asked, "What do you want?"

They answered, "Rabbi, where do you live?" The Hebrew word "Rabbi" means "Teacher."

39Jesus replied, "Come and see!" It was already about four o'clock in the afternoon when they went with him and saw where he lived. So they stayed on for the rest of the day.

40One of the two men who had heard John and had gone with Jesus was Andrew, the brother of Simon Peter. **41**The first thing Andrew did was to find his brother and tell him, "We have found the Messiah!" The Hebrew word "Messiah" means the same as the Greek word "Christ."

42Andrew brought his brother to Jesus. And when Jesus saw him, he said, "Simon son of John, you will be called Cephas." This name can be translated as "Peter."[e]

Jesus Chooses Philip and Nathanael

43-44 The next day Jesus decided to go to Galilee. There he met Philip, who was from Bethsaida, the home-

---

[d]*Bethany*: An unknown village east of the Jordan with the same name as the village near Jerusalem. [e]*Peter*: The Aramaic name "Cephas" and the Greek name "Peter" each mean "rock."

town of Andrew and Peter. Jesus said to Philip, "Come with me."

45Philip then found Nathanael and said, "We have found the one that Moses and the Prophets[f] wrote about. He is Jesus, the son of Joseph from Nazareth."

46Nathanael asked, "Can anything good come from Nazareth?"

Philip answered, "Come and see."

47When Jesus saw Nathanael coming toward him, he said, "Here is a true descendant of our ancestor Israel. And he is not deceitful."[g]

48"How do you know me?" Nathanael asked.

Jesus answered, "Before Philip called you, I saw you under the fig tree."

49Nathanael said, "Rabbi, you are the Son of God and the King of Israel!"

50Jesus answered, "Did you believe me just because I said that I saw you under the fig tree? You will see something even greater. **51**I tell you for certain that you will see heaven open and God's angels going up and coming down on the Son of Man."[h]

Jesus at a Wedding in Cana

2 Three days later Mary, the mother of Jesus, was at a wedding feast in the village of Cana in Galilee. **2**Jesus and his disciples had also been invited and were there.

3When the wine was all gone, Mary said to Jesus, "They don't have any more wine."

4Jesus replied, "Mother, my time has not yet come![i] You must not tell me what to do."

5Mary then said to the servants, "Do whatever Jesus tells you to do."

6At the feast there were six stone water jars that were used by the people for washing themselves in the way that their religion said they must. Each jar held about twenty or thirty gallons. **7**Jesus told the servants to fill them to the top with water. Then after the jars had been filled, **8**he said, "Now take some water and give it to the man in charge of the feast."

The servants did as Jesus told them, **9**and the man in charge drank some of the water that had now turned into wine. He did not know where the wine had come from, but the servants did. He called the bridegroom over **10**and said, "The best wine is always served first. Then after the guests have had plenty, the other wine is served. But you have kept the best until last!"

11This was Jesus' first miracle,[j] and he did it in the village of Cana in Galilee. There Jesus showed his glory, and his disciples put their faith in him. **12**After this, he went with his mother, his brothers, and his disciples to the town of Capernaum, where they stayed for a few days.

---

[f]*Moses and the Prophets*: The Jewish Scriptures, that is, the Old Testament. [g]*Israel . . . not deceitful*: Israel (meaning "a man who wrestled with God" or "a prince of God") was the name that the Lord gave to Jacob (meaning "cheater" or "deceiver"), the famous ancestor of the Jewish people. [h]*going up and coming down on the Son of Man*: When Jacob (see the note at verse 47) was running from his brother Esau, he had a dream in which he saw angels going up and down on a ladder from earth to heaven. See Genesis 32.22-32. [i]*my time has not yet come!*: The time when the true glory of Jesus would be seen, and he would be recognized as God's Son. See 12.23. [j]*miracle*: The Greek text has "sign." In the Gospel of John the word "sign" is used for the miracle itself and as a way of pointing to Jesus as the Son of God.

Jesus in the Temple
(Matthew 21.12, 13; Mark 11.15–17;
Luke 19.45, 46)

13Not long before the Jewish festival of Passover, Jesus went to Jerusalem. 14There he found people selling cattle, sheep, and doves in the temple. He also saw moneychangers sitting at their tables. 15So he took some rope and made a whip. Then he chased everyone out of the temple, together with their sheep and cattle. He turned over the tables of the moneychangers and scattered their coins.

16Jesus said to the people who had been selling doves, "Get those doves out of here! Don't make my Father's house a marketplace."

17The disciples then remembered that the Scriptures say, "My love for your house burns in me like a fire."

18The Jewish leaders asked Jesus, "What miracle*j* will you work to show us why you have done this?"

19"Destroy this temple," Jesus answered, "and in three days I will build it again!"

20The leaders replied, "It took forty-six years to build this temple. What makes you think you can rebuild it in three days?"

21But Jesus was talking about his body as a temple. 22And when he was raised from death, his disciples remembered what he had told them. Then they believed the Scriptures and the words of Jesus.

Jesus Knows What People Are Like

23In Jerusalem during Passover many people put their faith in Jesus, because they saw him work miracles.*j*

24But Jesus knew what was in their hearts, and he would not let them have power over him. 25No one had to tell him what people were like. He already knew.

Jesus and Nicodemus

3 There was a man named Nicodemus who was a Pharisee and a Jewish leader. 2One night he went to Jesus and said, "Sir, we know that God has sent you to teach us. You could not work these miracles, unless God were with you."

3Jesus replied, "I tell you for certain that you must be born from above*k* before you can see God's kingdom!"

4Nicodemus asked, "How can a grown man ever be born a second time?"

5Jesus answered:

I tell you for certain that before you can get into God's kingdom, you must be born not only by water, but by the Spirit. 6Humans give life to their children. Yet only God's Spirit can change you into a child of God. 7Don't be surprised when I say that you must be born from above. 8Only God's Spirit gives new life. The Spirit is like the wind that blows wherever it wants to. You can hear the wind, but you don't know where it comes from or where it is going.

9"How can this be?" Nicodemus asked.

10Jesus replied:

How can you be a teacher of Israel and not know these things? 11I tell you for certain that we know what we are talking about because we have seen it our-

---

jmiracle(s): See the note at 2.11.   *kfrom above*: Or "in a new way." The same Greek word is used in verses 7, 31.

selves. But none of you will accept what we say. [12]If you don't believe when I talk to you about things on earth, how can you possibly believe if I talk to you about things in heaven?

[13]No one has gone up to heaven except the Son of Man, who came down from there. [14]And the Son of Man must be lifted up, just as that metal snake was lifted up by Moses in the desert.[l] [15]Then everyone who has faith in the Son of Man will have eternal life.

[16]God loved the people of this world so much that he gave his only Son, so that everyone who has faith in him will have eternal life and never die. [17]God did not send his Son into the world to condemn its people. He sent him to save them! [18]No one who has faith in God's Son will be condemned. But everyone who does not have faith in him has already been condemned for not having faith in God's only Son.

[19]The light has come into the world, and people who do evil things are judged guilty because they love the dark more than the light. [20]People who do evil hate the light and won't come to the light, because it clearly shows what they have done. [21]But everyone who lives by the truth will come to the light, because they want others to know that God is really the one doing what they do.

Jesus and John the Baptist

[22]Later, Jesus and his disciples went to Judea, where he stayed with them for a while and was baptizing people.

[23-24]John had not yet been put in jail. He was at Aenon near Salim, where there was a lot of water, and people were coming there for John to baptize them.

[25]John's followers got into an argument with a Jewish man[m] about a ceremony of washing.[n] [26]They went to John and said, "Rabbi, you spoke about a man when you were with him east of the Jordan. He is now baptizing people, and everyone is going to him."

[27]John replied:

No one can do anything unless God in heaven allows it. [28]Surely you remember how I told you that I am not the Messiah. I am only the one sent ahead of him.

[29]At a wedding the groom is the one who gets married. The best man is glad just to be there and to hear the groom's voice. That's why I am so glad. [30]Jesus must become more important, while I become less important.

The One Who Comes from Heaven

[31]God's Son comes from heaven and is above all others.

---

[l]*just as that metal snake was lifted up by Moses in the desert*: When the Lord punished the people of Israel by sending snakes to bite them, he told Moses to hold a metal snake up on a pole. Everyone who looked at the snake was cured of the snake bites. See Numbers 21.4-9. [m]*a Jewish man*: Some manuscripts have "some Jewish men." [n]*about a ceremony of washing*: The Jewish people had many rules about washing themselves and their dishes, in order to make themselves fit to worship God.

Everyone who comes from the earth belongs to the earth and speaks about earthly things. The one who comes from heaven is above all others. 32He speaks about what he has seen and heard, and yet no one believes him. 33But everyone who does believe him has shown that God is truthful. 34The Son was sent to speak God's message, and he has been given the full power of God's Spirit.

35The Father loves the Son and has given him everything. 36Everyone who has faith in the Son has eternal life. But no one who rejects him will ever share in that life, and God will be angry with them forever.

4 Jesus knew that the Pharisees had heard that he was winning and baptizing more followers than John was. 2But Jesus' disciples were really the ones doing the baptizing, and not Jesus himself.

Jesus and the Samaritan Woman

3Jesus left Judea and started for Galilee again. 4This time he had to go through Samaria, 5and on his way he came to the town of Sychar. It was near the field that Jacob had long ago given to his son Joseph. 6-8The well that Jacob had dug was still there, and Jesus sat down beside it because he was tired from traveling. It was noon, and after Jesus' disciples had gone into town to buy some food, a Samaritan woman came to draw water from the well.

Jesus asked her, "Would you please give me a drink of water?"

9"You are a Jew," she replied, "and I am a Samaritan woman. How can you ask me for a drink of water when Jews and Samaritans won't have anything to do with each other?"*o*

10Jesus answered, "You don't know what God wants to give you, and you don't know who is asking you for a drink. If you did, you would ask him for the water that gives life."

11"Sir," the woman said, "you don't even have a bucket, and the well is deep. Where are you going to get this life-giving water? 12Our ancestor Jacob dug this well for us, and his family and animals got water from it. Are you greater than Jacob?"

13Jesus answered, "Everyone who drinks this water will get thirsty again. 14But no one who drinks the water I give will ever be thirsty again. The water I give is like a flowing fountain that gives eternal life."

15The woman replied, "Sir, please give me a drink of that water! Then I won't get thirsty and have to come to this well again."

16Jesus told her, "Go and bring your husband."

17-18The woman answered, "I don't have a husband."

"That's right," Jesus replied, "you're telling the truth. You don't have a husband. You have already been married five times, and the man you are now living with is not your husband."

19The woman said, "Sir, I can see that you are a prophet. 20My ancestors

*o*won't have anything to do with each other: Or "won't use the same cups." The Samaritans lived in the land between Judea and Galilee. They worshiped God differently from the Jews and did not get along with them.

worshiped on this mountain,[p] but you Jews say Jerusalem is the only place to worship."

21Jesus said to her:

Believe me, the time is coming when you won't worship God either on this mountain or in Jerusalem. 22You Samaritans don't really know the one you worship. But we Jews do know the God we worship, and by using us God will save the world. 23But a time is coming, and it is already here! Even now the true worshipers are being led by the Spirit to worship the Father according to the truth. These are the ones the Father is seeking to worship him. 24God is Spirit, and those who worship God must be led by the Spirit to worship him according to the truth.

25The woman said, "I know that the Messiah will come. He is the one we call Christ. When he comes, he will explain everything to us."

26"I am that one," Jesus told her, "and I am speaking to you now."

27The disciples returned about this time and were surprised to find Jesus talking with a woman. But none of them asked him what he wanted or why he was talking with her.

28The woman left her water jar and ran back into town. She said to the people, 29"Come and see a man who told me everything I have ever done! Could he be the Messiah?" 30Everyone in town went out to see Jesus.

31While this was happening, Jesus' disciples were saying to him, "Teacher, please eat something."

32But Jesus told them, "I have food that you don't know anything about."

33His disciples started asking each other, "Has someone brought him something to eat?"

34Jesus said:

My food is to do what God wants! He is the one who sent me, and I must finish the work that he gave me to do. 35You may say that there are still four months until harvest time. But I tell you to look, and you will see that the fields are ripe and ready to harvest.

36Even now the harvest workers are receiving their reward by gathering a harvest that brings eternal life. Then everyone who planted the seed and everyone who harvests the crop will celebrate together. 37So the saying proves true, "Some plant the seed, and others harvest the crop." 38I am sending you to harvest crops in fields where others have done all the hard work.

39A lot of Samaritans in that town put their faith in Jesus because the woman had said, "This man told me everything I have ever done." 40They came and asked him to stay in their town, and he stayed on for two days.

41Many more Samaritans put their faith in Jesus because of what they heard him say. 42They told the woman, "We no longer have faith in Jesus just because of what you told us. We have heard him ourselves, and we are certain that he is the Savior of the world!"

Jesus Heals an Official's Son
(Matthew 8.5–13; Luke 7.1–10)

43-44Jesus had said, "Prophets are honored everywhere, except in their

[p]*this mountain*: Mount Gerizim, near the city of Shechem.

own country." Then two days later he left ⁴⁵and went to Galilee. The people there welcomed him, because they had gone to the festival in Jerusalem and had seen everything he had done.

⁴⁶While Jesus was in Galilee, he returned to the village of Cana, where he had turned the water into wine. There was an official in Capernaum whose son was sick. ⁴⁷And when the man heard that Jesus had come from Judea, he went and begged him to keep his son from dying.

⁴⁸Jesus told the official, "You won't have faith unless you see miracles and wonders!"

⁴⁹The man replied, "Lord, please come before my son dies!"

⁵⁰Jesus then said, "Your son will live. Go on home to him." The man believed Jesus and started back home.

⁵¹Some of the official's servants met him along the road and told him, "Your son is better!" ⁵²He asked them when the boy got better, and they answered, "The fever left him yesterday at one o'clock."

⁵³The boy's father realized that at one o'clock the day before Jesus had told him, "Your son will live!" So the man and everyone in his family put their faith in Jesus.

⁵⁴This was the second miracle*q* that Jesus worked after he left Judea and went to Galilee.

Jesus Heals a Sick Man

5 Later, Jesus went to Jerusalem for another Jewish festival.*r* ²In the city near the sheep gate was a pool with five porches, and its name in Hebrew was Bethzatha.*s*

³⁻⁴Many sick, blind, lame, and crippled people were lying close to the pool.*t*

⁵Beside the pool was a man who had been sick for thirty-eight years. ⁶When Jesus saw the man and realized that he had been crippled for a long time, he asked him, "Do you want to be healed?"

⁷The man answered, "Lord, I don't have anyone to put me in the pool when the water is stirred up. I try to get in, but someone else always gets there first."

⁸Jesus told him, "Pick up your mat and walk!" ⁹Right then the man was healed. He picked up his mat and started walking around. The day on which this happened was a Sabbath.

¹⁰When the Jewish leaders saw the man carrying his mat, they said to him, "This is the Sabbath! No one is allowed to carry a mat on the Sabbath."

¹¹But he replied, "The man who healed me told me to pick up my mat and walk."

¹²They asked him, "Who is this man that told you to pick up your mat and walk?" ¹³But he did not know who Jesus was, and Jesus had left because of the crowd.

¹⁴Later, Jesus met the man in the temple and told him, "You are now well. But don't sin anymore or something worse might happen to you." ¹⁵The man left and told the leaders

---

q miracle: See the note at 2.11. *r another Jewish festival*: Either the Festival of Shelters or Passover. *s Bethzatha*: Some manuscripts have "Bethesda" and others have "Bethsaida." *t pool*: Some manuscripts add, "They were waiting for the water to be stirred, because an angel from the Lord would sometimes come down and stir it. The first person to get into the pool after that would be healed."

that Jesus was the one who had healed him. 16They started making a lot of trouble for Jesus because he did things like this on the Sabbath.

17But Jesus said, "My Father has never stopped working, and that is why I keep on working." 18Now the leaders wanted to kill Jesus for two reasons. First, he had broken the law of the Sabbath. But even worse, he had said that God was his Father, which made him equal with God.

The Son's Authority

19Jesus told the people:

I tell you for certain that the Son cannot do anything on his own. He can do only what he sees the Father doing, and he does exactly what he sees the Father do. 20The Father loves the Son and has shown him everything he does. The Father will show him even greater things, and you will be amazed. 21Just as the Father raises the dead and gives life, so the Son gives life to anyone he wants to.

22The Father doesn't judge anyone, but he has made his Son the judge of everyone. 23The Father wants all people to honor the Son as much as they honor him. When anyone refuses to honor the Son, that is the same as refusing to honor the Father who sent him. 24I tell you for certain that everyone who hears my message and has faith in the one who sent me has eternal life and will never be condemned. They have already gone from death to life.

25I tell you for certain that the time will come, and it is already here, when all of the dead will

hear the voice of the Son of God. And those who listen to it will live! 26The Father has the power to give life, and he has given that same power to the Son. 27And he has given his Son the right to judge everyone, because he is the Son of Man.

28Don't be surprised! The time will come when all of the dead will hear the voice of the Son of Man, 29and they will come out of their graves. Everyone who has done good things will rise to life, but everyone who has done evil things will rise and be condemned.

30I cannot do anything on my own. The Father sent me, and he is the one who told me how to judge. I judge with fairness, because I obey him, and I don't just try to please myself.

Witnesses to Jesus

31If I speak for myself, there is no way to prove I am telling the truth. 32But there is someone else who speaks for me, and I know what he says is true. 33You sent messengers to John, and he told them the truth. 34I don't depend on what people say about me, but I tell you these things so that you may be saved. 35John was a lamp that gave a lot of light, and you were glad to enjoy his light for a while.

36But something more important than John speaks for me. I mean the things that the Father has given me to do! All of these speak for me and say that the Father sent me.

37The Father who sent me also

speaks for me, but you have never heard his voice or seen him face to face. 38You have not believed his message, because you refused to have faith in the one he sent.

39You search the Scriptures, because you think you will find eternal life in them. The Scriptures tell about me, 40but you refuse to come to me for eternal life.

41I don't care about human praise, 42but I do know that none of you love God. 43I have come with my Father's authority, and you have not welcomed me. But you will welcome people who come on their own. 44How could you possibly believe? You like to have your friends praise you, and you don't care about praise that the only God can give!

45Don't think that I will be the one to accuse you to the Father. You have put your hope in Moses, yet he is the very one who will accuse you. 46Moses wrote about me, and if you had believed Moses, you would have believed me. 47But if you don't believe what Moses wrote, how can you believe what I say?

Feeding Five Thousand
(*Matthew 14.13–21; Mark 6.30–44; Luke 9.10–17*)

6 Jesus crossed Lake Galilee, which was also known as Lake Tiberias. 2A large crowd had seen him work miracles to heal the sick, and those people went with him. 3-4It was almost time for the Jewish festival of Passover, and Jesus went up on a mountain with his disciples and sat down.*u*

5When Jesus saw the large crowd coming toward him, he asked Philip, "Where will we get enough food to feed all these people?" 6He said this to test Philip, since he already knew what he was going to do.

7Philip answered, "Don't you know that it would take almost a year's wages*v* just to buy only a little bread for each of these people?"

8Andrew, the brother of Simon Peter, was one of the disciples. He spoke up and said, 9"There is a boy here who has five small loaves*w* of barley bread and two fish. But what good is that with all these people?"

10The ground was covered with grass, and Jesus told his disciples to have everyone sit down. About five thousand men were in the crowd. 11Jesus took the bread in his hands and gave thanks to God. Then he passed the bread to the people, and he did the same with the fish, until everyone had plenty to eat.

12The people ate all they wanted, and Jesus told his disciples to gather up the leftovers, so that nothing would be wasted. 13The disciples gathered them up and filled twelve large baskets with what was left over from the five barley loaves.

14After the people had seen Jesus work this miracle,*x* they began saying, "This must be the Prophet*y* who is to come into the world!" 15Jesus realized that they would try to force him to be

---

u sat down: Possibly to teach. Teachers in the ancient world, including Jewish teachers, usually sat down to teach. *v almost a year's wages*: The Greek text has "two hundred silver coins." Each coin was worth the average day's wages for a worker. *w small loaves*: These would have been flat and round or in the shape of a bun. *x miracle*: See the note at 2.11. *y the Prophet*: See the note at 1.21.

their king. So he went up on a mountain, where he could be alone.

Jesus Walks on the Water
(Matthew 14.22–27; Mark 6.45–52)

16That evening Jesus' disciples went down to the lake. **17**They got into a boat and started across for Capernaum. Later that evening Jesus had still not come to them, **18**and a strong wind was making the water rough.

19When the disciples had rowed for three or four miles, they saw Jesus walking on the water. He kept coming closer to the boat, and they were terrified. **20**But he said, "I am Jesus!*z* Don't be afraid!" **21**The disciples wanted to take him into the boat, but suddenly the boat reached the shore where they were headed.

The Bread That Gives Life

22The people who had stayed on the east side of the lake knew that only one boat had been there. They also knew that Jesus had not left in it with his disciples. But the next day **23**some boats from Tiberias sailed near the place where the crowd had eaten the bread for which the Lord had given thanks. **24**They saw that Jesus and his disciples had left. Then they got into the boats and went to Capernaum to look for Jesus. **25**They found him on the west side of the lake and asked, "Rabbi, when did you get here?"

26Jesus answered, "I tell you for certain that you are not looking for me because you saw the miracles,*a* but be-cause you ate all the food you wanted. **27**Don't work for food that spoils. Work for food that gives eternal life. The Son of Man will give you this food, because God the Father has given him the right to do so."

28"What exactly does God want us to do?" the people asked.

29Jesus answered, "God wants you to have faith in the one he sent."

30They replied, "What miracle will you work, so that we can have faith in you? What will you do? **31**For example, when our ancestors were in the desert, they were given manna*b* to eat. It happened just as the Scriptures say, 'God gave them bread from heaven to eat.' "

32Jesus then told them, "I tell you for certain that Moses was not the one who gave you bread from heaven. My Father is the one who gives you the true bread from heaven. **33**And the bread that God gives is the one who came down from heaven to give life to the world."

34The people said, "Lord, give us this bread and don't ever stop!"

35Jesus replied:

I am the bread that gives life! No one who comes to me will ever be hungry. No one who has faith in me will ever be thirsty. **36**I have told you already that you have seen me and still do not have faith in me. **37**Everything and everyone that the Father has given me will come to me, and I won't turn any of them away.

38I didn't come from heaven to do what I want! I came to do

---

z I am Jesus: The Greek text has "I am." See the note at 8.24. *a miracles*: The Greek text has "signs" here and "sign" in verse 30. See the note at 2.11. *b manna*: When the people of Israel were wandering through the desert, the Lord gave them a special kind of food to eat. It tasted like a wafer and was called "manna," which in Hebrew means, "What is this?"

what the Father wants me to do. He sent me, [39]and he wants to make certain that none of the ones he has given me will be lost. Instead, he wants me to raise them to life on the last day.[c] [40]My Father wants everyone who sees the Son to have faith in him and to have eternal life. Then I will raise them to life on the last day.

[41]The people started grumbling because Jesus had said he was the bread that had come down from heaven. [42]They were asking each other, "Isn't he Jesus, the son of Joseph? Don't we know his father and mother? How can he say that he has come down from heaven?"

[43]Jesus told them:

Stop grumbling! [44]No one can come to me, unless the Father who sent me makes them want to come. But if they do come, I will raise them to life on the last day. [45]One of the prophets wrote, "God will teach all of them." And so everyone who listens to the Father and learns from him will come to me.

[46]The only one who has seen the Father is the one who has come from him. No one else has ever seen the Father. [47]I tell you for certain that everyone who has faith in me has eternal life.

[48]I am the bread that gives life! [49]Your ancestors ate manna[d] in the desert, and later they died. [50]But the bread from heaven has come down, so that no one who eats it will ever die. [51]I am that bread from heaven! Everyone who eats it will live forever. My flesh is the life-giving bread that I give to the people of this world.

[52]They started arguing with each other and asked, "How can he give us his flesh to eat?"

[53]Jesus answered:

I tell you for certain that you won't live unless you eat the flesh and drink the blood of the Son of Man. [54]But if you do eat my flesh and drink my blood, you will have eternal life, and I will raise you to life on the last day. [55]My flesh is the true food, and my blood is the true drink. [56]If you eat my flesh and drink my blood, you are one with me, and I am one with you.

[57]The living Father sent me, and I have life because of him. Now everyone who eats my flesh will live because of me. [58]The bread that comes down from heaven is not like what your ancestors ate. They died, but whoever eats this bread will live forever.

[59]Jesus was teaching in a Jewish place of worship in Capernaum when he said these things.

The Words of Eternal Life

[60]Many of Jesus' disciples heard him and said, "This is too hard for anyone to understand."

[61]Jesus knew that his disciples were grumbling. So he asked, "Does this bother you? [62]What if you should see the Son of Man go up to heaven where he came from? [63]The Spirit is the one who gives life! Human strength can do nothing. The words that I have spoken to you are from that

---

[c]*the last day*: When God will judge all people.   [d]*manna*: See the note at 6.31.

life-giving Spirit. 64But some of you refuse to have faith in me." Jesus said this, because from the beginning he knew who would have faith in him. He also knew which one would betray him.

65Then Jesus said, "You cannot come to me, unless the Father makes you want to come. That is why I have told these things to all of you."

66Because of what Jesus said, many of his disciples turned their backs on him and stopped following him. 67Jesus then asked his twelve disciples if they were going to leave him. 68Simon Peter answered, "Lord, there is no one else that we can go to! Your words give eternal life. 69We have faith in you, and we are sure that you are God's Holy One."

70Jesus told his disciples, "I chose all twelve of you, but one of you is a demon!" 71Jesus was talking about Judas, the son of Simon Iscariot.*e* He would later betray Jesus, even though he was one of the twelve disciples.

Jesus' Brothers Don't Have Faith in Him

7 Jesus decided to leave Judea and to start going through Galilee because the Jewish leaders wanted to kill him. 2It was almost time for the Festival of Shelters, 3and Jesus' brothers said to him, "Why don't you go to Judea? Then your disciples can see what you are doing. 4No one does anything in secret, if they want others to know about them. So let the world know what you are doing!" 5Even Jesus' own brothers had not yet become his followers.

6Jesus answered, "My time hasn't yet come,*f* but your time is always here. 7The people of this world cannot hate you. They hate me, because I tell them that they do evil things. 8Go on to the festival. My time hasn't yet come, and I am not going." 9Jesus said this and stayed on in Galilee.

Jesus at the Festival of Shelters

10After Jesus' brothers had gone to the festival, he decided to go, and he went secretly, without telling anyone. 11During the festival the Jewish leaders looked for Jesus and asked, "Where is he?" 12The crowds even got into an argument about him. Some were saying, "Jesus is a good man," while others were saying, "He is lying to everyone." 13But the people were afraid of their leaders, and none of them talked in public about him.

14When the festival was about half over, Jesus stood up and started teaching in the temple. 15The leaders were surprised and said, "How does this man know so much? He has never been taught!"

16Jesus replied:

I am not teaching something that I thought up. What I teach comes from the one who sent me. 17If you really want to obey God, you will know if what I teach comes from God or from me. 18If I wanted to bring honor to myself, I would speak for myself. But I want to honor the one who sent me. That is why I tell the truth and not a lie. 19Didn't Moses give you the Law? Yet none of you

---

e Iscariot: See the note at 12.4.   *f My time hasn't yet come*: See the note at 2.4.

obey it! So why do you want to kill me?

20The crowd replied, "You're crazy! What makes you think someone wants to kill you?"

21Jesus answered:

I worked one miracle,[g] and it amazed you. **22**Moses commanded you to circumcise your sons. But it wasn't really Moses who gave you this command. It was your ancestors, and even on the Sabbath you circumcise your sons **23**in order to obey the Law of Moses. Why are you angry with me for making someone completely well on the Sabbath? **24**Don't judge by appearances. Judge by what is right.

25Some of the people from Jerusalem were saying, "Isn't this the man they want to kill? **26**Yet here he is, speaking for everyone to hear. And no one is arguing with him. Do you suppose the authorities know that he is the Messiah? **27**But how could that be? No one knows where the Messiah will come from, but we know where this man comes from."

28As Jesus was teaching in the temple, he shouted, "Do you really think you know me and where I came from? I didn't come on my own! The one who sent me is truthful, and you don't know him. **29**But I know the one who sent me, because I came from him."

30Some of the people wanted to arrest Jesus right then. But no one even laid a hand on him, because his time had not yet come.[h] **31**A lot of people in the crowd put their faith in him and said, "When the Messiah comes, he surely won't perform more miracles[i] than this man has done!"

Officers Sent to Arrest Jesus

32When the Pharisees heard the crowd arguing about Jesus, they got together with the chief priests and sent some temple police to arrest him. **33**But Jesus told them, "I will be with you a little while longer, and then I will return to the one who sent me. **34**You will look for me, but you won't find me. You cannot go where I am going."

35The Jewish leaders asked each other, "Where can he go to keep us from finding him? Is he going to some foreign country where our people live? Is he going there to teach the Greeks?[j] **36**What did he mean by saying that we will look for him, but won't find him? Why can't we go where he is going?"

Streams of Life-Giving Water

37On the last and most important day of the festival, Jesus stood up and shouted, "If you are thirsty, come to me and drink! **38**Have faith in me, and you will have life-giving water flowing from deep inside you, just as the Scriptures say." **39**Jesus was talking about the Holy Spirit, who would be given to everyone that had faith in him. The Spirit had not yet been given to anyone, since Jesus had not yet been given his full glory.[k]

---

[g]*one miracle*: The healing of the lame man (5.1-18). See the note at 2.11. [h]*his time had not yet come*: See the note at 2.4. [i]*miracles*: See the note at 2.11. [j]*Greeks*: Perhaps Gentiles or Jews who followed Greek customs. [k]*had not yet been given his full glory*: In the Gospel of John, Jesus is given his full glory both when he is nailed to the cross and when he is raised from death to sit beside his Father in heaven.

The People Take Sides

40When the crowd heard Jesus say this, some of them said, "He must be the Prophet!"*l* **41**Others said, "He is the Messiah!" Others even said, "Can the Messiah come from Galilee? **42**The Scriptures say that the Messiah will come from the family of King David. Doesn't this mean that he will be born in David's hometown of Bethlehem?" **43**The people started taking sides against each other because of Jesus. **44**Some of them wanted to arrest him, but no one laid a hand on him.

The Jewish Leaders Refuse to Have Faith in Jesus

45When the temple police returned to the chief priests and Pharisees, they were asked, "Why didn't you bring Jesus here?"

46They answered, "No one has ever spoken like that man!"

47The Pharisees said to them, "Have you also been fooled? **48**Not one of the chief priests or the Pharisees has faith in him. **49**And these people who don't know the Law are under God's curse anyway."

50Nicodemus was there at the time. He was the same one who had earlier come to see Jesus.*m* Nicodemus was a member of the Jewish council and said, **51**"Our Law doesn't let us condemn people before we hear what they have to say. We cannot judge them before we know what they have done."

52Then they said, "Nicodemus, you must be from Galilee! Read the Scriptures, and you will find that no prophet is to come from Galilee."

A Woman Caught in Sin

8 **53**Everyone else went home, **1**but Jesus walked out to the Mount of Olives. **2**Then early the next morning he went to the temple. The people came to him, and he sat down*n* and started teaching them.

3The Pharisees and the teachers of the Law of Moses brought in a woman who had been caught in bed with a man who was not her husband. They made her stand in the middle of the crowd. **4**Then they said, "Teacher, this woman was caught sleeping with a man who is not her husband. **5**The Law of Moses teaches that a woman like this should be stoned to death! What do you say?"

6They asked Jesus this question, because they wanted to test him and bring some charge against him. But Jesus simply bent over and started writing on the ground with his finger.

7They kept on asking Jesus about the woman. Finally, he stood up and said, "If any of you have never sinned, then go ahead and throw the first stone at her!" **8**Once again he bent over and began writing on the ground. **9**The people left one by one, beginning with the oldest one in the crowd. Finally, Jesus and the woman were there alone.

10Jesus stood up and asked her, "Where is everyone? Isn't there anyone left to accuse you?"

11"No sir," the woman answered. Then Jesus told her, "I am not

---

*l*the Prophet: See the note at 1.21. *m*who had earlier come to see Jesus: See 3.1-21. *n*sat down: See the note at 6.3-4.

going to accuse you either. You may go now, but don't sin anymore."[o]

Jesus Is the Light for the World

12Once again Jesus spoke to the people. This time he said, "I am the light for the world! Follow me, and you won't be walking in the dark. You will have the light that gives life."

13The Pharisees objected, "You are the only one speaking for yourself, and what you say isn't true!"

14Jesus replied:

Even if I do speak for myself, what I say is true! I know where I came from and where I am going. But you don't know where I am from or where I am going. 15You judge in the same way that everyone else does, but I don't judge anyone. 16If I did judge, I would judge fairly, because I would not be doing it alone. The Father who sent me is here with me. 17Your Law requires two witnesses to prove that something is true. 18I am one of my witnesses, and the Father who sent me is the other one.

19"Where is your Father?" they asked Jesus.

"You don't know me or my Father!" Jesus answered. "If you knew me, you would know my Father."

20Jesus said this while he was still teaching in the place where the temple treasures were stored. But no one arrested him, because his time had not yet come.[p]

You Cannot Go Where I Am Going

21Jesus also told them, "I am going away, and you will look for me. But you cannot go where I am going, and you will die with your sins unforgiven."

22The Jewish leaders asked, "Does he intend to kill himself? Is that what he means by saying we cannot go where he is going?"

23Jesus answered, "You are from below, but I am from above. You belong to this world, but I don't. 24That is why I said you will die with your sins unforgiven. If you don't have faith in me for who I am,[q] you will die, and your sins will not be forgiven."

25"Who are you?" they asked Jesus.

Jesus answered, "I am exactly who I told you at the beginning. 26I have a lot more to say about you, especially about all the evil you have done. The one who sent me is truthful, and I tell the people of this world only what I have heard from him."

27No one understood that Jesus was talking to them about the Father.

28Jesus went on to say, "When you have lifted up the Son of Man,[r] you will know who I am. You will also know that I don't do anything on my own. I say only what my Father taught me. 29The one who sent me is with me. I always do what pleases him, and he will never leave me."

30After Jesus said this, many of the people put their faith in him.

---

[o]*don't sin anymore*: Verses 1-11 are not in some manuscripts. In other manuscripts these verses are placed after 7.36 or after 21.25 or after Luke 21.38, with some differences in the text. [p]*his time had not yet come*: See the note at 2.4. [q]*I am*: For the Jewish people the most holy name of God is "Yahweh," which may be translated "I am." In the Gospel of John "I am" is sometimes used by Jesus to show that he is that one. [r]*lifted up the Son of Man*: See the note at 7.39.

The Truth Will Set You Free

31Jesus told the people who had faith in him, "If you keep on obeying what I have said, you truly are my disciples. 32You will know the truth, and the truth will set you free."

33They answered, "We are Abraham's children! We have never been anyone's slaves. How can you say we will be set free?"

34Jesus replied:

I tell you for certain that anyone who sins is a slave of sin! 35And slaves don't stay in the family forever, though the Son will always remain in the family. 36If the Son gives you freedom, you are free! 37I know that you are from Abraham's family. Yet you want to kill me, because my message is not really in your hearts. 38I am telling you what my Father has shown me, just as you are doing what your father has taught you.

Your Father Is the Devil

39The people said to Jesus, "Abraham is our father!"

Jesus replied, "If you were Abraham's children, you would do what Abraham did. 40Instead, you want to kill me for telling you the truth that God gave me. Abraham never did anything like that. 41But you are doing exactly what your father does."

"Don't accuse us of having someone else as our father!" they said. "We just have one father, and he is God."

42Jesus answered:

If God were your Father, you would love me, because I came from God and only from him. He sent me. I did not come on my own. 43Why can't you understand what I am talking about? Can't you stand to hear what I am saying? 44Your father is the devil, and you do exactly what he wants. He has always been a murderer and a liar. There is nothing truthful about him. He speaks on his own, and everything he says is a lie. Not only is he a liar himself, but he is also the father of all lies.

45Everything I have told you is true, and you still refuse to have faith in me. 46Can any of you accuse me of sin? If you cannot, why won't you have faith in me? After all, I am telling you the truth. 47Anyone who belongs to God will listen to his message. But you refuse to listen, because you don't belong to God.

Jesus and Abraham

48The people told Jesus, "We were right to say that you are a Samaritan[s] and that you have a demon in you!"

49Jesus answered, "I don't have a demon in me. I honor my Father, and you refuse to honor me. 50I don't want honor for myself. But there is one who wants me to be honored, and he is also the one who judges. 51I tell you for certain that if you obey my words, you will never die."

52Then the people said, "Now we are sure that you have a demon. Abraham is dead, and so are the prophets. How can you say that no one who obeys your words will ever die? 53Are you greater than our father Abraham? He

[s]*Samaritan*: See 4.9 and the note there.

died, and so did the prophets. Who do you think you are?"

⁵⁴Jesus replied, "If I honored myself, it would mean nothing. My Father is the one who honors me. You claim that he is your God, ⁵⁵even though you don't really know him. If I said I didn't know him, I would be a liar, just like all of you. But I know him, and I do what he says. ⁵⁶Your father Abraham was really glad to see me."

⁵⁷"You are not even fifty years old!" they said. "How could you have seen Abraham?"

⁵⁸Jesus answered, "I tell you for certain that even before Abraham was, I was, and I am."ᵗ ⁵⁹The people picked up stones to kill Jesus, but he hid and left the temple.

Jesus Heals a Man Born Blind

9 As Jesus walked along, he saw a man who had been blind since birth. ²Jesus' disciples asked, "Teacher, why was this man born blind? Was it because he or his parents sinned?"

³"No, it wasn't!" Jesus answered. "But because of this, you will see God work a miracle for him. ⁴As long as it is day, we must do what the one who sent me wants me to do. When night comes, no one can work. ⁵While I am in the world, I am the light for the world."

⁶After Jesus said this, he spit on the ground. He made some mud and smeared it on the man's eyes. ⁷Then he said, "Go and wash off the mud in Siloam Pool." The man went and washed in Siloam, which means "One Who Is Sent." When he had washed off the mud, he could see.

⁸The man's neighbors and the people who had seen him begging wondered if he really could be the same man. ⁹Some of them said he was the same beggar, while others said he only looked like him. But he told them, "I am that man."

¹⁰"Then how can you see?" they asked.

¹¹He answered, "Someone named Jesus made some mud and smeared it on my eyes. He told me to go and wash it off in Siloam Pool. When I did, I could see."

¹²"Where is he now?" they asked. "I don't know," he answered.

The Pharisees Try to Find Out What Happened

¹³⁻¹⁴The day when Jesus made the mud and healed the man was a Sabbath. So the people took the man to the Pharisees. ¹⁵They asked him how he was able to see, and he answered, "Jesus made some mud and smeared it on my eyes. Then after I washed off the mud, I could see."

¹⁶Some of the Pharisees said, "This man Jesus does not come from God. If he did, he would not break the law of the Sabbath."

Others asked, "How could someone who is a sinner work such a miracle?"ᵘ

Since the Pharisees could not agree among themselves, ¹⁷they asked the man, "What do you say about this one who healed your eyes?"

"He is a prophet!" the man told them.

¹⁸But the Jewish leaders would not believe that the man had once been blind. They sent for his parents ¹⁹and asked them, "Is this the son that you

---

ᵗI am: See the note at 8.24.   ᵘmiracle: See the note at 2.11.

said was born blind? How can he now see?"

20The man's parents answered, "We are certain that he is our son, and we know that he was born blind. **21**But we don't know how he got his sight or who gave it to him. Ask him! He is old enough to speak for himself."

22-23 The man's parents said this because they were afraid of the Jewish leaders. The leaders had already agreed that no one was to have anything to do with anyone who said Jesus was the Messiah.

24The leaders called the man back and said, "Swear by God to tell the truth! We know that Jesus is a sinner."

25The man replied, "I don't know if he is a sinner or not. All I know is that I used to be blind, but now I can see!"

26"What did he do to you?" the Jewish leaders asked. "How did he heal your eyes?"

27The man answered, "I have already told you once, and you refused to listen. Why do you want me to tell you again? Do you also want to become his disciples?"

28The leaders insulted the man and said, "You are his follower! We are followers of Moses. **29**We are sure that God spoke to Moses, but we don't even know where Jesus comes from."

30The man replied, "How strange! He healed my eyes, and yet you don't know where he comes from. **31**We know that God listens only to people who love and obey him. God doesn't listen to sinners. **32**And this is the first time in history that anyone has ever given sight to someone born blind. **33**Jesus could not do anything unless he came from God."

34The leaders told the man, "You have been a sinner since the day you were born! Do you think you can teach us anything?" Then they said, "You can never come back into any of our meeting places!"

35When Jesus heard what had happened, he went and found the man. Then Jesus asked, "Do you have faith in the Son of Man?"

36He replied, "Sir, if you will tell me who he is, I will put my faith in him."

37"You have already seen him," Jesus answered, "and right now he is talking with you."

38The man said, "Lord, I put my faith in you!" Then he worshiped Jesus.

39Jesus told him, "I came to judge the people of this world. I am here to give sight to the blind and to make blind everyone who sees."

40When the Pharisees heard Jesus say this, they asked, "Are we blind?"

41Jesus answered, "If you were blind, you would not be guilty. But now that you claim to see, you will keep on being guilty."

A Story about Sheep

10 Jesus said:
I tell you for certain that only thieves and robbers climb over the fence instead of going in through the gate to the sheep pen. **2-3**But the gatekeeper opens the gate for the shepherd, and he goes in through it. The sheep know their shepherd's voice. He calls each of them by name and leads them out.

4When he has led out all of his sheep, he walks in front of them, and they follow, because they know his voice. **5**The sheep will not follow strangers. They don't recognize a stranger's voice, and they run away.

6Jesus told the people this story. But they did not understand what he was talking about.

Jesus Is the Good Shepherd

7Jesus said:

I tell you for certain that I am the gate for the sheep. 8Everyone who came before me was a thief or a robber, and the sheep did not listen to any of them. 9I am the gate. All who come in through me will be saved. Through me they will come and go and find pasture.

10A thief comes only to rob, kill, and destroy. I came so that everyone would have life, and have it in its fullest. 11I am the good shepherd, and the good shepherd gives up his life for his sheep. 12Hired workers are not like the shepherd. They don't own the sheep, and when they see a wolf coming, they run off and leave the sheep. Then the wolf attacks and scatters the flock. 13Hired workers run away because they don't care about the sheep.

14I am the good shepherd. I know my sheep, and they know me. 15Just as the Father knows me, I know the Father, and I give up my life for my sheep. 16I have other sheep that are not in this sheep pen. I must bring them together too, when they hear my voice. Then there will be one flock of sheep and one shepherd.

17The Father loves me, be-cause I give up my life, so that I may receive it back again. 18No one takes my life from me. I give it up willingly! I have the power to give it up and the power to receive it back again, just as my Father commanded me to do.

19The Jews took sides because of what Jesus had told them. 20Many of them said, "He has a demon in him! He is crazy! Why listen to him?"

21But others said, "How could anyone with a demon in him say these things? No one like that could give sight to a blind person!"

Jesus Is Rejected

22That winter Jesus was in Jerusalem for the Temple Festival. 23One day he was walking in that part of the temple known as Solomon's Porch,*v* 24and the people gathered all around him. They said, "How long are you going to keep us guessing? If you are the Messiah, tell us plainly!"

25Jesus answered:

I have told you, and you re-fused to believe me. The things I do by my Father's authority show who I am. 26But since you are not my sheep, you don't believe me. 27My sheep know my voice, and I know them. They follow me, 28and I give them eternal life, so that they will never be lost. No one can snatch them out of my hand. 29My Father gave them to me, and he is greater than all others.*w* No one can snatch them from his hands, 30and I am one with the Father.

31Once again the Jewish leaders picked up stones in order to kill Jesus.

---

v Solomon's Porch: A public place with tall columns along the east side of the temple.   *w he is greater than all others*: Some manuscripts have "they are greater than all others."

32But he said, "I have shown you many good things that my Father sent me to do. Which one are you going to stone me for?"

33They answered, "We are not stoning you because of any good thing you did. We are stoning you because you did a terrible thing. You are just a man, and here you are claiming to be God!"

34Jesus replied:

In your Scriptures doesn't God say, "You are gods?" 35The Scriptures cannot be destroyed, and God spoke to those people and called them gods. 36So why do you accuse me of a terrible sin for saying that I am the Son of God? After all, it is the Father who prepared me for this work. He is also the one who sent me into the world. 37If I don't do as my Father does, you should not believe me. 38But if I do what my Father does, you should believe because of that, even if you don't have faith in me. Then you will know for certain that the Father is one with me, and I am one with the Father.

39Again they wanted to arrest Jesus. But he escaped 40and crossed the Jordan to the place where John had earlier been baptizing. While Jesus was there, 41many people came to him. They were saying, "John didn't work any miracles, but everything he said about Jesus is true." 42A lot of those people also put their faith in Jesus.

The Death of Lazarus

11 1-2 A man by the name of Lazarus was sick in the village of Bethany. He had two sisters, Mary and Martha. This was the same Mary who later poured perfume on the Lord's head and wiped his feet with her hair. 3The sisters sent a message to the Lord and told him that his good friend Lazarus was sick.

4When Jesus heard this, he said, "His sickness won't end in death. It will bring glory to God and his Son."

5Jesus loved Martha and her sister and brother. 6But he stayed where he was for two more days. 7Then he said to his disciples, "Now we'll go back to Judea."

8"Teacher," they said, "the people there want to stone you to death! Why do you want to go back?"

9Jesus answered, "Aren't there twelve hours in each day? If you walk during the day, you will have light from the sun, and you won't stumble. 10But if you walk during the night, you will stumble, because there isn't any light inside you." 11Then he told them, "Our friend Lazarus is asleep, and I am going there to wake him up."

12They replied, "Lord, if he is asleep, he will get better." 13Jesus really meant that Lazarus was dead, but they thought he was talking only about sleep.

14Then Jesus told them plainly, "Lazarus is dead! 15I am glad that I wasn't there, because now you will have a chance to put your faith in me. Let's go to him."

16Thomas, whose nickname was "Twin," said to the other disciples, "Come on. Let's go so we can die with him."

Jesus Brings Lazarus to Life

17When Jesus got to Bethany, he found that Lazarus had already been in the tomb four days. 18Bethany was only about two miles from Jerusalem, 19and many people had come from the city to comfort Martha and

Mary because their brother had died.

20When Martha heard that Jesus had arrived, she went out to meet him, but Mary stayed in the house. **21**Martha said to Jesus, "Lord, if you had been here, my brother would not have died. **22**Yet even now I know that God will do anything you ask."

23Jesus told her, "Your brother will live again!"

24Martha answered, "I know that he will be raised to life on the last day,[x] when all the dead are raised."

25Jesus then said, "I am the one who raises the dead to life! Everyone who has faith in me will live, even if they die. **26**And everyone who lives because of faith in me will never die. Do you believe this?"

27"Yes, Lord!" she replied. "I believe that you are Christ, the Son of God. You are the one we hoped would come into the world."

28After Martha said this, she went and privately said to her sister Mary, "The Teacher is here, and he wants to see you." **29**As soon as Mary heard this, she got up and went out to Jesus. **30**He was still outside the village where Martha had gone to meet him. **31**Many people had come to comfort Mary, and when they saw her quickly leave the house, they thought she was going out to the tomb to cry. So they followed her.

32Mary went to where Jesus was. Then as soon as she saw him, she kneeled at his feet and said, "Lord, if you had been here, my brother would not have died."

33When Jesus saw that Mary and the people with her were crying, he was terribly upset **34**and asked, "Where have you put his body?"

They replied, "Lord, come and you will see."

35Jesus started crying, **36**and the people said, "See how much he loved Lazarus."

37Some of them said, "He gives sight to the blind. Why couldn't he have kept Lazarus from dying?"

38Jesus was still terribly upset. So he went to the tomb, which was a cave with a stone rolled against the entrance. **39**Then he told the people to roll the stone away. But Martha said, "Lord, you know that Lazarus has been dead four days, and there will be a bad smell."

40Jesus replied, "Didn't I tell you that if you had faith, you would see the glory of God?"

41After the stone had been rolled aside, Jesus looked up toward heaven and prayed, "Father, I thank you for answering my prayer. **42**I know that you always answer my prayers. But I said this, so that the people here would believe that you sent me."

43When Jesus had finished praying, he shouted, "Lazarus, come out!" **44**The man who had been dead came out. His hands and feet were wrapped with strips of burial cloth, and a cloth covered his face.

Jesus then told the people, "Untie him and let him go."

The Plot to Kill Jesus
(*Matthew 26.1–5; Mark 14.1, 2;*
Luke 22.1, 2)

45Many of the people who had come to visit Mary saw the things that Jesus did, and they put their faith in him. **46**Others went to the Pharisees

---

[x]*the last day*: When God will judge all people.

and told what Jesus had done. ⁴⁷Then the chief priests and the Pharisees called the council together and said, "What should we do? This man is working a lot of miracles.ʸ ⁴⁸If we don't stop him now, everyone will put their faith in him. Then the Romans will come and destroy our temple and our nation."ᶻ

⁴⁹One of the council members was Caiaphas, who was also high priest that year. He spoke up and said, "You people don't have any sense at all! ⁵⁰Don't you know it is better for one person to die for the people than for the whole nation to be destroyed?" ⁵¹Caiaphas did not say this on his own. As high priest that year, he was prophesying that Jesus would die for the nation. ⁵²Yet Jesus would not die just for the Jewish nation. He would die to bring together all of God's scattered people. ⁵³From that day on, the council started making plans to put Jesus to death.

⁵⁴Because of this plot against him, Jesus stopped going around in public. He went to the town of Ephraim, which was near the desert, and he stayed there with his disciples.

⁵⁵It was almost time for Passover. Many of the Jewish people who lived out in the country had come to Jerusalem to get themselves readyᵃ for the festival. ⁵⁶They looked around for Jesus. Then when they were in the temple, they asked each other, "You don't think he will come here for Passover, do you?"

⁵⁷The chief priests and the Pharisees told the people to let them know if any of them saw Jesus. That is how they hoped to arrest him.

At Bethany
(Matthew 26.6–13; Mark 14.3–9)

12 Six days before Passover Jesus went back to Bethany, where he had raised Lazarus from death. ²A meal had been prepared for Jesus. Martha was doing the serving, and Lazarus himself was there.

³Mary took a very expensive bottle of perfumeᵇ and poured it on Jesus' feet. She wiped them with her hair, and the sweet smell of the perfume filled the house.

⁴A disciple named Judas Iscariotᶜ was there. He was the one who was going to betray Jesus, and he asked, ⁵"Why wasn't this perfume sold for three hundred silver coins and the money given to the poor?" ⁶Judas did not really care about the poor. He asked this because he carried the moneybag and sometimes would steal from it.

⁷Jesus replied, "Leave her alone! She has kept this perfume for the day of my burial. ⁸You will always have the poor with you, but you won't always have me."

A Plot to Kill Lazarus

⁹A lot of people came when they heard that Jesus was there. They also

---

ʸmiracles: See the note at 2.11. ᶻdestroy our temple and our nation: The Jewish leaders were afraid that Jesus would lead his followers to rebel against Rome and that the Roman army would then destroy their nation. ᵃget themselves ready: The Jewish people had to do certain things to prepare themselves to worship God. ᵇvery expensive bottle of perfume: The Greek text has "expensive perfume made of pure spikenard," a plant used to make perfume. ᶜIscariot: This may mean "a man from Kerioth" (a place in Judea). But more probably it means "a man who was a liar" or "a man who was a betrayer."

wanted to see Lazarus, because Jesus had raised him from death. 10So the chief priests made plans to kill Lazarus. 11He was the reason that many of the Jewish people were turning from them and putting their faith in Jesus.

Jesus Enters Jerusalem
(Matthew 21.1–11; Mark 11.1–11; Luke 19.28–40)

12The next day a large crowd was in Jerusalem for Passover. When they heard that Jesus was coming for the festival, 13they took palm branches and went out to greet him.*d* They shouted,

"Hooray!*e*
God bless the one who comes
    in the name of the Lord!
God bless the King
    of Israel!"

14Jesus found a donkey and rode on it, just as the Scriptures say,

15"People of Jerusalem,
    don't be afraid!
Your King is now coming,
    and he is riding
    on a donkey."

16At first, Jesus' disciples did not understand. But after he had been given his glory,*f* they remembered all this. Everything had happened exactly as the Scriptures said it would.

17-18A crowd had come to meet Jesus because they had seen him call Lazarus out of the tomb. They kept talking about him and this miracle.*g* 19But the Pharisees said to each other, "There is nothing that can be done! Everyone in the world is following Jesus."

Some Greeks Want to Meet Jesus

20Some Greeks*h* had gone to Jerusalem to worship during Passover. 21Philip from Bethsaida in Galilee was there too. So they went to him and said, "Sir, we would like to meet Jesus." 22Philip told Andrew. Then the two of them went to Jesus and told him.

The Son of Man Must Be Lifted Up

23Jesus said:

The time has come for the Son of Man to be given his glory.*i* 24I tell you for certain that a grain of wheat that falls on the ground will never be more than one grain unless it dies. But if it dies, it will produce lots of wheat. 25If you love your life, you will lose it. If you give it up in this world, you will be given eternal life. 26If you serve me, you must go with me. My servants will be with me wherever I am. If you serve me, my Father will honor you.

27Now I am deeply troubled, and I don't know what to say. But I must not ask my Father to keep me from this time of suffering. In fact, I came into the world to suffer. 28So Father, bring glory to yourself.

A voice from heaven then said, "I have already brought glory to myself, and I will do it again!" 29When the crowd heard the voice, some of them thought it was thunder. Others thought an angel had spoken to Jesus. 30Then Jesus told the crowd, "That

---

dtook palm branches and went out to greet him: This was one way that the Jewish people welcomed a famous person. *eHooray*: This translates a word that can mean "please save us." But it is most often used as a shout of praise to God. *fhad been given his glory*: See the note at 7.39. *gmiracle*: See the note at 2.11. *hGreeks*: Perhaps Gentiles who worshiped with the Jews. See the note at 7.35. *ibe given his glory*: See the note at 7.39.

voice spoke to help you, not me. 31This world's people are now being judged, and the ruler of this world*j* is already being thrown out! 32If I am lifted up above the earth, I will make everyone want to come to me." 33Jesus was talking about the way he would be put to death.

34The crowd said to Jesus, "The Scriptures teach that the Messiah will live forever. How can you say that the Son of Man must be lifted up? Who is this Son of Man?"

35Jesus answered, "The light will be with you for only a little longer. Walk in the light while you can. Then you won't be caught walking blindly in the dark. 36Have faith in the light while it is with you, and you will be children of the light."

The People Refuse to Have Faith in Jesus

After Jesus had said these things, he left and went into hiding. 37He had worked a lot of miracles*k* among the people, but they were still not willing to have faith in him. 38This happened so that what the prophet Isaiah had said would come true,

"Lord, who has believed
our message?
And who has seen
your mighty strength?"
39The people could not have faith in Jesus, because Isaiah had also said,
40"The Lord has blinded
the eyes of the people,
and he has made
the people stubborn.

He did this so that they
could not see
or understand,
and so that they
would not turn to the Lord
and be healed."
41Isaiah said this, because he saw the glory of Jesus and spoke about him.*l* 42Even then, many of the leaders put their faith in Jesus, but they did not tell anyone about it. The Pharisees had already given orders for the people not to have anything to do with anyone who had faith in Jesus. 43And besides, the leaders liked praise from others more than they liked praise from God.

Jesus Came to Save the World

44In a loud voice Jesus said:
Everyone who has faith in me also has faith in the one who sent me. 45And everyone who has seen me has seen the one who sent me. 46I am the light that has come into the world. No one who has faith in me will stay in the dark.

47I am not the one who will judge those who refuse to obey my teachings. I came to save the people of this world, not to be their judge. 48But everyone who rejects me and my teachings will be judged on the last day*m* by what I have said. 49I don't speak on my own. I say only what the Father who sent me has told me to say. 50I know that his commands will bring eternal life. That is why I tell you exactly what the Father has told me.

jworld: In the Gospel of John "world" sometimes refers to the people who live in this world and to the evil forces that control their lives. *kmiracles*: See the note at 2.11. *lhe saw the glory of Jesus and spoke about him*: Or "he saw the glory of God and spoke about Jesus." *mthe last day*: When God will judge all people.

Jesus Washes the Feet of His Disciples

13 It was before Passover, and Jesus knew that the time had come for him to leave this world and to return to the Father. He had always loved his followers in this world, and he loved them to the very end.

2Even before the evening meal started, the devil had made Judas, the son of Simon Iscariot,[n] decide to betray Jesus.

3Jesus knew that he had come from God and would go back to God. He also knew that the Father had given him complete power. **4**So during the meal Jesus got up, removed his outer garment, and wrapped a towel around his waist. **5**He put some water into a large bowl. Then he began washing his disciples' feet and drying them with the towel he was wearing.

6But when he came to Simon Peter, that disciple asked, "Lord, are you going to wash my feet?"

7Jesus answered, "You don't really know what I am doing, but later you will understand."

8"You will never wash my feet!" Peter replied.

"If I don't wash you," Jesus told him, "you don't really belong to me."

9Peter said, "Lord, don't wash just my feet. Wash my hands and my head."

10Jesus answered, "People who have bathed and are clean all over need to wash just their feet. And you, my disciples, are clean, except for one of you." **11**Jesus knew who would betray him. That is why he said, "except for one of you."

12After Jesus had washed his disciples' feet and had put his outer garment back on, he sat down again.[o] Then he said:

Do you understand what I have done? **13**You call me your teacher and Lord, and you should, because that is who I am. **14**And if your Lord and teacher has washed your feet, you should do the same for each other. **15**I have set the example, and you should do for each other exactly what I have done for you. **16**I tell you for certain that servants are not greater than their master, and messengers are not greater than the one who sent them. **17**You know these things, and God will bless you, if you do them.

18I am not talking about all of you. I know the ones I have chosen. But what the Scriptures say must come true. And they say, "The man who ate with me has turned against me!" **19**I am telling you this before it all happens. Then when it does happen, you will believe who I am.[p] **20**I tell you for certain that anyone who welcomes my messengers also welcomes me, and anyone who welcomes me welcomes the one who sent me.

Jesus Tells What Will Happen to Him
(Matthew 26.20–25; Mark 14.17–21; Luke 22.21–23)

21After Jesus had said these things, he was deeply troubled and told his disciples, "I tell you for certain that

---

[n]*Iscariot*: See the note at 12.4. [o]*sat down again*: On special occasions the Jewish people followed the Greek and Roman custom of lying down on their left side and leaning on their left elbow, while eating with their right hand. [p]*I am*: See the note at 8.24.

one of you will betray me." 22They were confused about what he meant. And they just stared at each other.

23Jesus' favorite disciple was sitting next to him at the meal, 24and Simon motioned for that disciple to find out which one Jesus meant. 25So the disciple leaned toward Jesus and asked, "Lord, which one of us are you talking about?"

26Jesus answered, "I will dip this piece of bread in the sauce and give it to the one I was talking about."

Then Jesus dipped the bread and gave it to Judas, the son of Simon Iscariot.q 27Right then Satan took control of Judas.

Jesus said, "Judas, go quickly and do what you have to do." 28No one at the meal understood what Jesus meant. 29But because Judas was in charge of the money, some of them thought that Jesus had told him to buy something they needed for the festival. Others thought that Jesus had told him to give some money to the poor. 30Judas took the piece of bread and went out.

It was already night.

The New Command

31After Judas had gone, Jesus said:
Now the Son of Man will be given glory, and he will bring glory to God. 32Then, after God is given glory because of him, God will bring glory to him, and God will do it very soon.

33My children, I will be with you for a little while longer. Then you will look for me, but you won't find me. I tell you just as I told the people, "You cannot go where I am going." 34But I am giving you a new command. You must love each other, just as I have loved you. 35If you love each other, everyone will know that you are my disciples.

Peter's Promise
(Matthew 26.31–35; Mark 14.27–31; Luke 22.31–34)

36Simon Peter asked, "Lord, where are you going?"

Jesus answered, "You can't go with me now, but later on you will."

37Peter asked, "Lord, why can't I go with you now? I would die for you!"

38"Would you really die for me?" Jesus asked. "I tell you for certain that before a rooster crows, you will say three times that you don't even know me."

Jesus Is the Way to the Father

14 Jesus said to his disciples, "Don't be worried! Have faith in God and have faith in me.r 2There are many rooms in my Father's house. I wouldn't tell you this, unless it was true. I am going there to prepare a place for each of you. 3After I have done this, I will come back and take you with me. Then we will be together. 4You know the way to where I am going."

5Thomas said, "Lord, we don't even know where you are going! How can we know the way?"

6"I am the way, the truth, and the life!" Jesus answered. "Without me, no one can go to the Father. 7If you had

---

qIscariot: See the note at 12.4.   rHave faith in God and have faith in me: Or "You have faith in God, so have faith in me."

known me, you would have known the Father. But from now on, you do know him, and you have seen him."

8Philip said, "Lord, show us the Father. That is all we need."

9Jesus replied:

Philip, I have been with you for a long time. Don't you know who I am? If you have seen me, you have seen the Father. How can you ask me to show you the Father? 10Don't you believe that I am one with the Father and that the Father is one with me? What I say is not said on my own. The Father who lives in me does these things.

11Have faith in me when I say that the Father is one with me and that I am one with the Father. Or else have faith in me simply because of the things I do. 12I tell you for certain that if you have faith in me, you will do the same things that I am doing. You will do even greater things, now that I am going back to the Father. 13Ask me, and I will do whatever you ask. This way the Son will bring honor to the Father. 14I will do whatever you ask me to do.

The Holy Spirit Is Promised

15Jesus said to his disciples:

If you love me, you will do as I command. 16Then I will ask the Father to send you the Holy Spirit who will help*s* you and always be with you. 17The Spirit will show you what is true. The people of this world cannot accept the Spirit, because they don't see or know him. But you know the Spirit, who is with you and will keep on living in you.

18I won't leave you like orphans. I will come back to you. 19In a little while the people of this world won't be able to see me, but you will see me. And because I live, you will live. 20Then you will know that I am one with the Father. You will know that you are one with me, and I am one with you. 21If you love me, you will do what I have said, and my Father will love you. I will also love you and show you what I am like.

22The other Judas, not Judas Iscariot,*t* then spoke up and asked, "Lord, what do you mean by saying that you will show us what you are like, but you will not show the people of this world?"

23Jesus replied:

If anyone loves me, they will obey me. Then my Father will love them, and we will come to them and live in them. 24But anyone who doesn't love me, won't obey me. What they have heard me say doesn't really come from me, but from the Father who sent me.

25I have told you these things while I am still with you. 26But the Holy Spirit will come and help*u* you, because the Father will send the Spirit to take my place. The Spirit will teach you everything and will remind you of what I said while I was with you.

27I give you peace, the kind of

---

*s*help: The Greek word may mean "comfort," "encourage," or "defend." *t*Iscariot: See the note at 12.4. *u*help: See the note at verse 16.

peace that only I can give. It is not like the peace that this world can give. So don't be worried or afraid.

28You have already heard me say that I am going and that I will also come back to you. If you really love me, you should be glad that I am going back to the Father, because he is greater than I am.

29I am telling you this before I leave, so that when it does happen, you will have faith in me. **30**I cannot speak with you much longer, because the ruler of this world is coming. But he has no power over me. **31**I obey my Father, so that everyone in the world might know that I love him.

It is time for us to go now.

Jesus Is the True Vine

15 Jesus said to his disciples: I am the true vine, and my Father is the gardener. **2**He cuts away every branch of mine that does not produce fruit. But he trims clean every branch that does produce fruit, so that it will produce even more fruit. **3**You are already clean because of what I have said to you.

4Stay joined to me, and I will stay joined to you. Just as a branch cannot produce fruit unless it stays joined to the vine, you cannot produce fruit unless you stay joined to me. **5**I am the vine, and you are the branches. If you stay joined to me, and I stay joined to you, then you will pro-

duce lots of fruit. But you cannot do anything without me. **6**If you don't stay joined to me, you will be thrown away. You will be like dry branches that are gathered up and burned in a fire.

7Stay joined to me and let my teachings become part of you. Then you can pray for whatever you want, and your prayer will be answered. **8**When you become fruitful disciples of mine, my Father will be honored. **9**I have loved you, just as my Father has loved me. So make sure that I keep on loving you. **10**If you obey me, I will keep loving you, just as my Father keeps loving me, because I have obeyed him.

11I have told you this to make you as completely happy as I am. **12**Now I tell you to love each other, as I have loved you. **13**The greatest way to show love for friends is to die for them. **14**And you are my friends, if you obey me. **15**Servants don't know what their master is doing, and so I don't speak to you as my servants. I speak to you as my friends, and I have told you everything that my Father has told me.

16You did not choose me. I chose you and sent you out to produce fruit, the kind of fruit that will last. Then my Father will give you whatever you ask for in my name.^{v} **17**So I command you to love each other.

The World's Hatred

18If the people of this world^w hate you, just remember that they

---

^{v}*in my name*: Or "because you are my followers." ^{w}*world*: See the note at 12.31.

hated me first. ¹⁹If you belonged to the world, its people would love you. But you don't belong to the world. I have chosen you to leave the world behind, and that is why its people hate you. ²⁰Remember how I told you that servants are not greater than their master. So if people mistreat me, they will mistreat you. If they do what I say, they will do what you say.

²¹People will do to you exactly what they did to me. They will do it because you belong to me, and they don't know the one who sent me. ²²If I had not come and spoken to them, they would not be guilty of sin. But now they have no excuse for their sin.

²³Everyone who hates me also hates my Father. ²⁴I have done things that no one else has ever done. If they had not seen me do these things, they would not be guilty. But they did see me do these things, and they still hate me and my Father too. ²⁵That is why the Scriptures are true when they say, "People hated me for no reason."

²⁶I will send you the Spirit who comes from the Father and shows what is true. The Spirit will help[x] you and will tell you about me. ²⁷Then you will also tell others about me, because you have been with me from the beginning.

16 I am telling you this to keep you from being afraid. ²You will be chased out of the Jewish meeting places. The time will come when people will kill you and think they are doing

God a favor. ³They will do all these things because they don't know either the Father or me. ⁴I am saying this to you now, so that when the time comes, you will remember what I have said.

The Work of the Holy Spirit

I was with you at the first, and so I didn't tell you these things. ⁵But now I am going back to the Father who sent me, and none of you asks me where I am going. ⁶You are very sad from hearing all of this. ⁷But I tell you that I am going to do what is best for you. That is why I am going away. The Holy Spirit cannot come to help[x] you until I leave. But after I am gone, I will send the Spirit to you.

⁸The Spirit will come and show the people of this world the truth about sin and God's justice and the judgment. ⁹The Spirit will show them that they are wrong about sin, because they didn't have faith in me. ¹⁰They are wrong about God's justice, because I am going to the Father, and you won't see me again. ¹¹And they are wrong about the judgment, because God has already judged the ruler of this world.

¹²I have much more to say to you, but right now it would be more than you could understand. ¹³The Spirit shows what is true and will come and guide you into the full truth. The Spirit does not speak on his own. He will tell you

---

[x]*help*: See the note at 14.16.

only what he has heard from me, and he will let you know what is going to happen. 14The Spirit will bring glory to me by taking my message and telling it to you. 15Everything that the Father has is mine. That is why I have said that the Spirit takes my message and tells it to you.

Sorrow Will Turn into Joy

16Jesus told his disciples, "You will see me for a little while, and then for a little while you won't see me."

17They said to each other, "What does Jesus mean by saying that we will see him for a little while, and then we won't see him for a little while? What does he mean by saying that he is going to the Father? 18What is this 'little while' that he is talking about? We don't know what he means."

19Jesus knew that they had some questions, so he said:

You are wondering what I meant when I said that you will see me for a little while, and then in a little while you won't see me. 20I tell you for certain that you will cry and be sad, but the world will be happy. You will be sad, but later you will be happy.

21When a woman is about to give birth, she is in great pain. But after it is all over, she forgets the pain and is happy, because she has brought a child into the world. 22You are now very sad. But later I will see you, and you will be so happy that no one will be able to change the way you feel. 23When that time comes, you won't have to ask me about

anything. I tell you for certain that the Father will give you whatever you ask for in my name. 24You have not asked for anything in this way before, but now you must ask in my name.*y* Then it will be given to you, so that you will be completely happy.

25I have used examples to explain to you what I have been talking about. But the time will come when I will speak to you plainly about the Father and will no longer use examples like these. 26You will ask the Father in my name,*z* and I won't have to ask him for you. 27God the Father loves you because you love me, and you believe that I have come from him. 28I came from the Father into the world, but I am leaving the world and returning to the Father.

29The disciples said, "Now you are speaking plainly to us! You are not using examples. 30At last we know that you understand everything, and we don't have any more questions. Now we believe that you truly have come from God."

31Jesus replied:

Do you really believe me? 32The time will come and is already here when all of you will be scattered. Each of you will go back home and leave me by myself. But the Father will be with me, and I won't be alone. 33I have told you this, so that you might have peace in your hearts because of me. While you are in the world, you will have to suffer. But cheer up! I have defeated the world.*a*

---

y in my name . . . in my name: Or "as my disciples . . . as my disciples."   *z in my name*: Or "because you are my followers."   *a world*: See the note at 12.31.

Jesus Prays

17 After Jesus had finished speaking to his disciples, he looked up toward heaven and prayed:

Father, the time has come for you to bring glory to your Son, in order that he may bring glory to you. 2And you gave him power over all people, so that he would give eternal life to everyone you give him. 3Eternal life is to know you, the only true God, and to know Jesus Christ, the one you sent. 4I have brought glory to you here on earth by doing everything you gave me to do. 5Now, Father, give me back the glory that I had with you before the world was created.

6You have given me some followers from this world, and I have shown them what you are like. They were yours, but you gave them to me, and they have obeyed you. 7They know that you gave me everything I have. 8I told my followers what you told me, and they accepted it. They know that I came from you, and they believe that you are the one who sent me. 9I am praying for them, but not for those who belong to this world.*a* My followers belong to you, and I am praying for them. 10All that I have is yours, and all that you have is mine, and they will bring glory to me.

11Holy Father, I am no longer in the world. I am coming to you, but my followers are still in the world. So keep them safe by the power of the name that you have given me. Then they will be one with each other, just as you and I are one. 12While I was with them, I kept them safe by the power you have given me. I guarded them, and not one of them was lost, except the one who had to be lost. This happened so that what the Scriptures say would come true.

13Father, I am on my way to you. But I say these things while I am still in the world, so that my followers will have the same complete joy that I do. 14I have told them your message. But the people of this world hate them, because they don't belong to this world, just as I don't.

15Father, I don't ask you to take my followers out of the world, but keep them safe from the evil one. 16They don't belong to this world, and neither do I. 17Your word is the truth. So let this truth make them completely yours. 18I am sending them into the world, just as you sent me. 19I have given myself completely for their sake, so that they may belong completely to the truth.

20Father, I am not praying just for these followers. I am also praying for everyone else who will have faith because of what my followers will say about me. 21I want all of them to be one with each other, just as I am one with you and you are one with me. I also want them to be one with us. Then the people of this world will believe that you sent me.

22I have honored my followers in the same way that you honored me, in order that they may be one

---

a world: See the note at 12.31.

with each other, just as we are one. 23I am one with them, and you are one with me, so that they may become completely one. Then this world's people will know that you sent me. They will know that you love my followers as much as you love me.

24Father, I want everyone you have given me to be with me, wherever I am. Then they will see the glory that you have given me, because you loved me before the world was created. 25Good Father, the people of this world don't know you. But I know you, and my followers know that you sent me. 26I told them what you are like, and I will tell them even more. Then the love that you have for me will become part of them, and I will be one with them.

Jesus Is Betrayed and Arrested
(Matthew 26.47–56; Mark 14.43–50;
Luke 22.47–53)

18 When Jesus had finished praying, he and his disciples crossed the Kidron Valley and went into a garden.*b* 2Jesus had often met there with his disciples, and Judas knew where the place was.

3-5Judas had promised to betray Jesus. So he went to the garden with some Roman soldiers and temple police, who had been sent by the chief priests and the Pharisees. They carried torches, lanterns, and weapons. Jesus already knew everything

that was going to happen, but he asked, "Who are you looking for?"

They answered, "We are looking for Jesus from Nazareth!"

Jesus told them, "I am Jesus!"*c* 6At once they all backed away and fell to the ground.

7Jesus again asked, "Who are you looking for?"

"We are looking for Jesus from Nazareth," they answered.

8This time Jesus replied, "I have already told you that I am Jesus. If I am the one you are looking for, let these others go. 9Then everything will happen, just as the Scriptures say, 'I did not lose anyone you gave me.' "

10Simon Peter had brought along a sword. He now pulled it out and struck at the servant of the high priest. The servant's name was Malchus, and Peter cut off his right ear. 11Jesus told Peter, "Put your sword away. I must drink from the cup*d* that the Father has given me."

Jesus Is Brought to Annas
(Matthew 26.57, 58; Mark 14.53, 54;
Luke 22.54)

12The Roman officer and his men, together with the temple police, arrested Jesus and tied him up. 13They took him first to Annas, who was the father-in-law of Caiaphas, the high priest that year. 14This was the same Caiaphas who had told the Jewish leaders, "It is better if one person dies for the people."

bgarden: The Greek word is usually translated "garden," but probably referred to an olive orchard. *cI am Jesus*: The Greek text has "I am." See the note at 8.24. *ddrink from the cup*: In the Scriptures a cup is sometimes used as a symbol of suffering. To "drink from the cup" is to suffer.

Peter Says He Does Not Know Jesus
(Matthew 26.69, 70; Mark 14.66–68; Luke 22.55–57)

15Simon Peter and another disciple followed Jesus. That disciple knew the high priest, and he followed Jesus into the courtyard of the high priest's house. 16Peter stayed outside near the gate. But the other disciple came back out and spoke to the girl at the gate. She let Peter go in, 17but asked him, "Aren't you one of that man's followers?"

"No, I am not!" Peter answered.

18It was cold, and the servants and temple police had made a charcoal fire. They were warming themselves around it, when Peter went over and stood near the fire to warm himself.

Jesus Is Questioned by the High Priest
(Matthew 26.59–66; Mark 14.55–64; Luke 22.66–71)

19The high priest questioned Jesus about his followers and his teaching. 20But Jesus told him, "I have spoken freely in front of everyone. And I have always taught in our meeting places and in the temple, where all of our people come together. I have not said anything in secret. 21Why are you questioning me? Why don't you ask the people who heard me? They know what I have said."

22As soon as Jesus said this, one of the temple police hit him and said, "That's no way to talk to the high priest!"

23Jesus answered, "If I have done something wrong, say so. But if not, why did you hit me?" 24Jesus was still tied up, and Annas sent him to Caiaphas the high priest.

Peter Again Denies that He Knows Jesus
(Matthew 26.71–75; Mark 14.69–72; Luke 22.58–62)

25While Simon Peter was standing there warming himself, someone asked him, "Aren't you one of Jesus' followers?"

Again Peter denied it and said, "No, I am not!"

26One of the high priest's servants was there. He was a relative of the servant whose ear Peter had cut off, and he asked, "Didn't I see you in the garden with that man?"

27Once more Peter denied it, and right then a rooster crowed.

Jesus Is Tried by Pilate
(Matthew 27.1, 2, 11–14; Mark 15.1–5; Luke 23.1–5)

28It was early in the morning when Jesus was taken from Caiaphas to the building where the Roman governor stayed. But the Jewish crowd waited outside. Any of them who had gone inside would have become unclean and would not be allowed to eat the Passover meal.*e*

29Pilate came out and asked, "What charges are you bringing against this man?"

30They answered, "He is a crimi-

---

*e*would have become unclean and would not be allowed to eat the Passover meal: Jewish people who came in close contact with foreigners right before Passover were not allowed to eat the Passover meal.

nal! That's why we brought him to you."

31Pilate told them, "Take him and judge him by your own laws."

The crowd replied, "We are not allowed to put anyone to death." **32**And so what Jesus said about his death*f* would soon come true.

33Pilate then went back inside. He called Jesus over and asked, "Are you the king of the Jews?"

34Jesus answered, "Are you asking this on your own or did someone tell you about me?"

35"You know I'm not a Jew!" Pilate said. "Your own people and the chief priests brought you to me. What have you done?"

36Jesus answered, "My kingdom does not belong to this world. If it did, my followers would have fought to keep the Jewish leaders from handing me over to you. No, my kingdom does not belong to this world."

37"So you are a king," Pilate replied.

"You are saying that I am a king," Jesus told him. "I was born into this world to tell about the truth. And everyone who belongs to the truth knows my voice."

38Pilate asked Jesus, "What is truth?"

Jesus Is Sentenced to Death
(Matthew 27.15–31; Mark 15.6–20;
Luke 23.13–25)

Pilate went back out to the Jewish crowd and said, "I don't find this man guilty of anything! **39**And since I usually set a prisoner free for you at Passover, would you like for me to set free the king of the Jews?"

40They all shouted, "No, not him! We want Barabbas." Now Barabbas was a terrorist.*g*

19 Pilate gave orders for Jesus to be beaten with a whip. **2**The soldiers made a crown out of thorn branches and put it on Jesus. Then they put a purple robe on him. **3**They came up to him and said, "Hey, you king of the Jews!" They also hit him with their fists.

4Once again Pilate went out to the crowd. This time he said, "I will have Jesus brought out to you again. Then you can see for yourselves that I have not found him guilty."

5Jesus came out, wearing the crown of thorns and the purple robe. Pilate said, "Here is the man!"*h*

6When the chief priests and the temple police saw him, they yelled, "Nail him to a cross! Nail him to a cross!"

Pilate told them, "You take him and nail him to a cross! I don't find him guilty of anything."

7The crowd replied, "He claimed to be the Son of God! Our Jewish law says that he must be put to death."

8When Pilate heard this, he was terrified. **9**He went back inside and asked Jesus, "Where are you from?" But Jesus did not answer.

10"Why won't you answer my question?" Pilate asked. "Don't you

---

fabout his death: Jesus had said that he would die by being "lifted up," which meant that he would die on a cross. The Romans killed criminals by nailing them on a cross, but they did not let the Jews kill anyone in this way.   *gterrorist*: Someone who stirred up trouble against the Romans in the hope of gaining freedom for the Jewish people.   *h"Here is the man!"*: Or "Look at the man!"

know that I have the power to let you go free or to nail you to a cross?"

11Jesus replied, "If God had not given you the power, you couldn't do anything at all to me. But the one who handed me over to you did something even worse."

12Then Pilate wanted to set Jesus free. But the Jewish crowd again yelled, "If you set this man free, you are no friend of the Emperor! Anyone who claims to be a king is an enemy of the Emperor."

13When Pilate heard this, he brought Jesus out. Then he sat down on the judge's bench at the place known as "The Stone Pavement." In Aramaic this pavement is called "Gabbatha." 14It was about noon on the day before Passover, and Pilate said to the crowd, "Look at your king!"

15"Kill him! Kill him!" they yelled. "Nail him to a cross!"

"So you want me to nail your king to a cross?" Pilate asked.

The chief priests replied, "The Emperor is our king!" 16Then Pilate handed Jesus over to be nailed to a cross.

Jesus Is Nailed to a Cross
(Matthew 27.32–44; Mark 15.21–32; Luke 23.26–43)

Jesus was taken away, 17and he carried his cross to a place known as "The Skull."[i] In Aramaic this place is called "Golgotha." 18There Jesus was nailed to the cross, and on each side of him a man was also nailed to a cross.

19Pilate ordered the charge against Jesus to be written on a board and put above the cross. It read, "Jesus of Nazareth, King of the Jews." 20The words were written in Hebrew, Latin, and Greek.

The place where Jesus was taken was not far from the city, and many of the Jewish people read the charge against him. 21So the chief priests went to Pilate and said, "Why did you write that he is King of the Jews? You should have written, 'He claimed to be King of the Jews.'"

22But Pilate told them, "What is written will not be changed!"

23After the soldiers had nailed Jesus to the cross, they divided up his clothes into four parts, one for each of them. But his outer garment was made from a single piece of cloth, and it did not have any seams. 24The soldiers said to each other, "Let's not rip it apart. We'll gamble to see who gets it." This happened so that the Scriptures would come true, which say,

"They divided up my clothes
  and gambled
    for my garments."

The soldiers then did what they had decided.

25Jesus' mother stood beside his cross with her sister and Mary the wife of Clopas. Mary Magdalene was standing there too.[j] 26When Jesus saw his mother and his favorite disciple with

---

[i]"The Skull": The place was probably given this name because it was near a large rock in the shape of a human skull. [j]Jesus' mother stood beside his cross with her sister and Mary the wife of Clopas. Mary Magdalene was standing there too: The Greek text may also be understood to include only three women ("Jesus' mother stood beside the cross with her sister, Mary the mother of Clopas. Mary Magdalene was standing there too.") or merely two women ("Jesus' mother was standing there with her sister Mary of Clopas, that is Mary Magdalene."). "Of Clopas" may mean "daughter of" or "mother of."

her, he said to his mother, "This man is now your son." 27Then he said to the disciple, "She is now your mother." From then on, that disciple took her into his own home.

The Death of Jesus
(Matthew 27.45–56; Mark 15.33–41; Luke 23.44–49)

28Jesus knew that he had now finished his work. And in order to make the Scriptures come true, he said, "I am thirsty!" 29A jar of cheap wine was there. Someone then soaked a sponge with the wine and held it up to Jesus' mouth on the stem of a hyssop plant. 30After Jesus drank the wine, he said, "Everything is done!" He bowed his head and died.

A Spear Is Stuck in Jesus' Side

31The next day would be both a Sabbath and the Passover. It was a special day for the Jewish people,[k] and they did not want the bodies to stay on the crosses during that day. So they asked Pilate to break the men's legs[l] and take their bodies down. 32The soldiers first broke the legs of the other two men who were nailed there. 33But when they came to Jesus, they saw that he was already dead, and they did not break his legs.

34One of the soldiers stuck his spear into Jesus' side, and blood and water came out. 35We know this is true, because it was told by someone who saw it happen. Now you can have faith too. 36All this happened so that

the Scriptures would come true, which say, "No bone of his body will be broken" 37and, "They will see the one in whose side they stuck a spear."

Jesus Is Buried
(Matthew 27.57–61; Mark 15.42–47; Luke 23.50–56)

38Joseph from Arimathea was one of Jesus' disciples. He had kept it secret though, because he was afraid of the Jewish leaders. But now he asked Pilate to let him have Jesus' body. Pilate gave him permission, and Joseph took it down from the cross.

39Nicodemus also came with about seventy-five pounds of spices made from myrrh and aloes. This was the same Nicodemus who had visited Jesus one night.[m] 40The two men wrapped the body in a linen cloth, together with the spices, which was how the Jewish people buried their dead. 41In the place where Jesus had been nailed to a cross, there was a garden with a tomb that had never been used. 42The tomb was nearby, and since it was the time to prepare for the Sabbath, they were in a hurry to put Jesus' body there.

Jesus Is Alive
(Matthew 28.1–10; Mark 16.1–8; Luke 24.1–12)

20 On Sunday morning while it was still dark, Mary Magdalene went to the tomb and saw that the stone had been rolled away from the entrance. 2She ran to Simon Peter and

---

[k]*a special day for the Jewish people*: Passover could be any day of the week. But according to the Gospel of John, Passover was on a Sabbath in the year that Jesus was nailed to a cross. [l]*break the men's legs*: This was the way that the Romans sometimes speeded up the death of a person who had been nailed to a cross. [m]*Nicodemus who had visited Jesus one night*: See 3.1-21.

to Jesus' favorite disciple and said, "They have taken the Lord from the tomb! We don't know where they have put him."

³Peter and the other disciple started for the tomb. ⁴They ran side by side, until the other disciple ran faster than Peter and got there first. ⁵He bent over and saw the strips of linen cloth lying inside the tomb, but he did not go in.

⁶When Simon Peter got there, he went into the tomb and saw the strips of cloth. ⁷He also saw the piece of cloth that had been used to cover Jesus' face. It was rolled up and in a place by itself. ⁸The disciple who got there first then went into the tomb, and when he saw it, he believed. ⁹At that time Peter and the other disciple did not know that the Scriptures said Jesus would rise to life. ¹⁰So the two of them went back to the other disciples.

Jesus Appears to Mary Magdalene
(Mark 16.9–11)

¹¹Mary Magdalene stood crying outside the tomb. She was still weeping, when she stooped down ¹²and saw two angels inside. They were dressed in white and were sitting where Jesus' body had been. One was at the head and the other was at the foot. ¹³The angels asked Mary, "Why are you crying?"

She answered, "They have taken away my Lord's body! I don't know where they have put him."

¹⁴As soon as Mary said this, she turned around and saw Jesus standing there. But she did not know who he was. ¹⁵Jesus asked her, "Why are you crying? Who are you looking for?"

She thought he was the gardener and said, "Sir, if you have taken his body away, please tell me, so I can go and get him."

¹⁶Then Jesus said to her, "Mary!"

She turned and said to him, "Rabboni." The Aramaic word "Rabboni" means "Teacher."

¹⁷Jesus told her, "Don't hold on to me! I have not yet gone to the Father. But tell my disciples that I am going to the one who is my Father and my God, as well as your Father and your God." ¹⁸Mary Magdalene then went and told the disciples that she had seen the Lord. She also told them what he had said to her.

Jesus Appears to His Disciples
(Matthew 28.16–20; Mark 16.14–18; Luke 24.36–49)

¹⁹The disciples were afraid of the Jewish leaders, and on the evening of that same Sunday they locked themselves in a room. Suddenly, Jesus appeared in the middle of the group. He greeted them ²⁰and showed them his hands and his side. When the disciples saw the Lord, they became very happy.

²¹After Jesus had greeted them again, he said, "I am sending you, just as the Father has sent me." ²²Then he breathed on them and said, "Receive the Holy Spirit. ²³If you forgive anyone's sins, they will be forgiven. But if you don't forgive their sins, they will not be forgiven."

Jesus and Thomas

²⁴Although Thomas the Twin was one of the twelve disciples, he was not with the others when Jesus appeared to them. ²⁵So they told him, "We have seen the Lord!"

But Thomas said, "First, I must see

the nail scars in his hands and touch them with my finger. I must put my hand where the spear went into his side. I won't believe unless I do this!"

26A week later the disciples were together again. This time Thomas was with them. Jesus came in while the doors were still locked and stood in the middle of the group. He greeted his disciples **27**and said to Thomas, "Put your finger here and look at my hands! Put your hand into my side. Stop doubting and have faith!"

28Thomas replied, "You are my Lord and my God!"

29Jesus said, "Thomas, do you have faith because you have seen me? The people who have faith in me without seeing me are the ones who are really blessed!"

Why John Wrote His Book

30Jesus worked many other miracles[n] for his disciples, and not all of them are written in this book. **31**But these are written so that you will put your faith in Jesus as the Messiah and the Son of God. If you have faith in[o] him, you will have true life.

Jesus Appears to Seven Disciples

21 Jesus later appeared to his disciples along the shore of Lake Tiberias. **2**Simon Peter, Thomas the Twin, Nathanael from Cana in Galilee, and the two sons of Zebedee,[p] were there, together with two other disciples. **3**Simon Peter said, "I'm going fishing!"

The others said, "We'll go with you." They went out in their boat. But they didn't catch a thing that night.

4Early the next morning Jesus stood on the shore, but the disciples did not realize who he was. **5**Jesus shouted, "Friends, have you caught anything?"

"No!" they answered.

6So he told them, "Let your net down on the right side of your boat, and you will catch some fish."

They did, and the net was so full of fish that they could not drag it up into the boat.

7Jesus' favorite disciple told Peter, "It's the Lord!" When Simon heard that it was the Lord, he put on the clothes that he had taken off while he was working. Then he jumped into the water. **8**The boat was only about a hundred yards from shore. So the other disciples stayed in the boat and dragged in the net full of fish.

9When the disciples got out of the boat, they saw some bread and a charcoal fire with fish on it. **10**Jesus told his disciples, "Bring some of the fish you just caught." **11**Simon Peter got back into the boat and dragged the net to shore. In it were one hundred fifty-three large fish, but still the net did not rip.

12Jesus said, "Come and eat!" But none of the disciples dared ask who he was. They knew he was the Lord. **13**Jesus took the bread in his hands and gave some of it to his disciples. He did the same with the fish. **14**This was the third time that Jesus appeared to his disciples after he was raised from death.

---

[n]*miracles*: See the note at 2.11. [o]*put your faith in . . . have faith in*: Some manuscripts have "keep on having faith in . . . keep on having faith in." [p]*the two sons of Zebedee*: James and John.

Jesus and Peter

15When Jesus and his disciples had finished eating, he asked, "Simon son of John, do you love me more than the others do?"*q*

Simon Peter answered, "Yes, Lord, you know I do!"

"Then feed my lambs," Jesus said.

16Jesus asked a second time, "Simon son of John, do you love me?"

Peter answered, "Yes, Lord, you know I love you!"

"Then take care of my sheep," Jesus told him.

17Jesus asked a third time, "Simon son of John, do you love me?"

Peter was hurt because Jesus had asked him three times if he loved him. So he told Jesus, "Lord, you know everything. You know I love you."

Jesus replied, "Feed my sheep. **18**I tell you for certain that when you were a young man, you dressed yourself and went wherever you wanted to go. But when you are old, you will hold out your hands. Then others will wrap your belt around you and lead you where you don't want to go."

19Jesus said this to tell how Peter would die and bring honor to God. Then he said to Peter, "Follow me!"

Jesus and His Favorite Disciple

20Peter turned and saw Jesus' favorite disciple following them. He was the same one who had sat next to Jesus at the meal and had asked, "Lord, who is going to betray you?" **21**When Peter saw that disciple, he asked Jesus, "Lord, what about him?"

22Jesus answered, "What is it to you, if I want him to live until I return? You must follow me." **23**So the rumor spread among the other disciples that this disciple would not die. But Jesus did not say he would not die. He simply said, "What is it to you, if I want him to live until I return?"

24This disciple is the one who told all of this. He wrote it, and we know he is telling the truth.

25Jesus did many other things. If they were all written in books, I don't suppose there would be room enough in the whole world for all the books.

---

q more than the others do?: Or "more than you love these things?"

The Acts of the Apostles

ABOUT THIS BOOK

This is the second book written by Luke. His first one is commonly known as the Gospel of Luke. In it he told "all that Jesus did and taught from the very first until he was taken up to heaven" (1.1,2). In this book Luke continues the story by describing some of the struggles the disciples faced as they tried to obey the command of Jesus: "You will tell everyone about me in Jerusalem, in all Judea, in Samaria, and everywhere in the world" (1.8).

So many different countries are mentioned in Acts that the book may seem to have been written only to tell about the spread of the Christian message. But that is only part of the story. After Jesus was taken up to heaven, one of the big problems for his followers was deciding who could belong to God's people. And since Jesus and his first followers were Jews, it was only natural for many of them to think that his message was only for Jews. But in Acts the Spirit is always present to show that Jesus came to save both Jews and Gentiles, and that God wants followers from every nation and race to be part of his people.

The first conflict between Christians and Jews took place when some of the Jewish religious leaders rejected the message about Jesus (4.1–31; 7.1–59). But the most serious problems for the early church happened because the disciples at first failed to understand that anyone could become a follower of Jesus without first becoming a Jew. This began to change when Philip dared to take the message to the Samaritans (8.7–25), and when Peter went to the home of Cornelius, a captain in the Roman army (10.1–48).

Finally, Peter reported to the church in Jerusalem (11.1–18) and a meeting was held there (15.3–35) to discuss the question of who could become followers of Christ. Before the meeting was over, everyone agreed that the Spirit of God was leading them to reach out to Gentiles as well as Jews with the good news of Jesus.

The one who did the most for the spread of the faith was a man named Paul, and much of the book tells about his preaching among the Gentiles. Finally, he took the message to Rome, the world's most important city at that time (28.16–31). One of Luke's main reasons for writing was to show that nothing could keep the Christian message from spreading everywhere:

> For two years Paul stayed in a rented house and welcomed everyone who came to see him. He bravely preached about God's kingdom and taught about the Lord Jesus Christ, and no one tried to stop him.
>
> (28.30,31)

A QUICK LOOK AT THIS BOOK

- Telling the Good News in Jerusalem (1.1—8.3)
- The Good News in Judea and Samaria (8.4—12.25)
- Paul's First Journey to Tell the Good News (13.1—14.28)
- An Important Decision in Jerusalem (15.1–35)
- Paul's Second Journey to Tell the Good News (15.36—18.22)
- Paul's Third Journey to Tell the Good News (18.23—21.16)
- Paul's Arrest in Jerusalem (21.17—23.22)
- Paul Is Taken to Caesarea (23.23—26.32)
- Paul Is Taken to Rome (27.1—28.31)

1 Theophilus, I first wrote to you[a] about all that Jesus did and taught from the very first ²until he was taken up to heaven. But before he was taken up, he gave orders to the apostles he had chosen with the help of the Holy Spirit.

³For forty days after Jesus had suffered and died, he proved in many ways that he had been raised from death. He appeared to his apostles and spoke to them about God's kingdom. ⁴While he was still with them, he said:

Don't leave Jerusalem yet. Wait here for the Father to give you the Holy Spirit, just as I told you he has promised to do. ⁵John baptized with water, but in a few days you will be baptized with the Holy Spirit.

Jesus Is Taken to Heaven

⁶While the apostles were still with Jesus, they asked him, "Lord, are you now going to give Israel its own king again?"[b]

⁷Jesus said to them, "You don't need to know the time of those events that only the Father controls. ⁸But the Holy Spirit will come upon you and give you power. Then you will tell everyone about me in Jerusalem, in all Judea, in Samaria, and everywhere in the world." ⁹After Jesus had said this and while they were watching, he was taken up into a cloud. They could not see him, ¹⁰but as he went up, they kept looking up into the sky.

Suddenly two men dressed in white clothes were standing there beside them. ¹¹They said, "Why are you men from Galilee standing here and looking up into the sky? Jesus has been taken to heaven. But he will come back in the same way that you have seen him go."

Someone to Take the Place of Judas

¹²⁻¹³The Mount of Olives was about half a mile from Jerusalem. The apostles who had gone there were Peter, John, James, Andrew, Philip, Thomas, Bartholomew, Matthew, James the son of Alphaeus, Simon, known as the Eager One,[c] and Judas the son of James.

After the apostles returned to the

---

[a]*I first wrote to you*: The Gospel of Luke. [b]*are you now going to give Israel its own king again?*: Or "Are you now going to rule Israel as its king?" [c]*known as the Eager One*: The Greek text has "Cananaean," which probably comes from a Hebrew word meaning "zealous" (see Luke 6.15). "Zealot" was the name later given to the members of a Jewish group which resisted and fought against the Romans.

city, they went upstairs to the room where they had been staying.

14The apostles often met together and prayed with a single purpose in mind.[d] The women and Mary the mother of Jesus would meet with them, and so would his brothers. **15**One day there were about a hundred and twenty of the Lord's followers meeting together, and Peter stood up to speak to them. **16-17**He said:

My friends, long ago by the power of the Holy Spirit, David said something about Judas, and what he said has now happened. Judas was one of us and had worked with us, but he brought the mob to arrest Jesus. **18**Then Judas bought some land with the money he was given for doing that evil thing. He fell headfirst into the field. His body burst open, and all his insides came out. **19**When the people of Jerusalem found out about this, they called the place Akeldama, which in the local language means "Field of Blood."

20In the book of Psalms David said,

"Leave his house empty,
and don't let anyone
live there."

It also says,

"Let someone else
have his job."

21-22 So we need someone else to help us tell others that Jesus has been raised from death. He must also be one of the men who was with us from the very begin-ning. He must have been with us from the time the Lord Jesus was baptized by John until the day he was taken to heaven.

23Two men were suggested: One of them was Joseph Barsabbas, known as Justus, and the other was Matthias. **24**Then they all prayed, "Lord, you know what everyone is like! Show us the one you have chosen **25**to be an apostle and to serve in place of Judas, who got what he deserved." **26**They drew names, and Matthias was chosen to join the group of the eleven apostles.

The Coming of the Holy Spirit

2 On the day of Pentecost[e] all the Lord's followers were together in one place. **2**Suddenly there was a noise from heaven like the sound of a mighty wind! It filled the house where they were meeting. **3**Then they saw what looked like fiery tongues moving in all directions, and a tongue came and settled on each person there. **4**The Holy Spirit took control of everyone, and they began speaking whatever languages the Spirit let them speak.

5Many religious Jews from every country in the world were living in Jerusalem. **6**And when they heard this noise, a crowd gathered. But they were surprised, because they were hearing everything in their own languages. **7**They were excited and amazed, and said:

Don't all these who are speaking come from Galilee? **8**Then why do we hear them speaking our very own languages? **9**Some

---

[d]*met together and prayed with a single purpose in mind*: Or "met together in a special place for prayer." [e]*Pentecost*: A Jewish festival that came fifty days after Passover and celebrated the wheat harvest. Jews later celebrated Pentecost as the time when they were given the Law of Moses.

of us are from Parthia, Media, and Elam. Others are from Mesopotamia, Judea, Cappadocia, Pontus, Asia, 10Phrygia, Pamphylia, Egypt, parts of Libya near Cyrene, Rome, 11-12Crete, and Arabia. Some of us were born Jews, and others of us have chosen to be Jews. Yet we all hear them using our own languages to tell the wonderful things God has done.

Everyone was excited and confused. Some of them even kept asking each other, "What does all this mean?" 13Others made fun of the Lord's followers and said, "They are drunk."

Peter Speaks to the Crowd

14Peter stood with the eleven apostles and spoke in a loud and clear voice to the crowd:

Friends and everyone else living in Jerusalem, listen carefully to what I have to say! 15You are wrong to think that these people are drunk. After all, it is only nine o'clock in the morning. 16But this is what God had the prophet Joel say,

17"When the last days come,
I will give my Spirit
to everyone.
Your sons and daughters
will prophesy.
Your young men
will see visions,
and your old men
will have dreams.
18In those days I will give
my Spirit to my servants,
both men and women,
and they will prophesy.

19I will work miracles
in the sky above

and wonders
on the earth below.
There will be blood and fire
and clouds of smoke.
20The sun will turn dark,
and the moon
will be as red as blood
before the great
and wonderful day
of the Lord appears.
21Then the Lord
will save everyone
who asks for his help."

22Now, listen to what I have to say about Jesus from Nazareth. God proved that he sent Jesus to you by having him work miracles, wonders, and signs. All of you know this. 23God had already planned and decided that Jesus would be handed over to you. So you took him and had evil men put him to death on a cross. 24But God set him free from death and raised him to life. Death could not hold him in its power. 25What David said are really the words of Jesus,

"I always see the Lord
near me,
and I will not be afraid
with him at my right side.
26Because of this,
my heart will be glad,
my words will be joyful,
and I will live in hope.
27The Lord won't leave me
in the grave.
I am his holy one,
and he won't let
my body decay.
28He has shown me
the path to life,
and he makes me glad
by being near me."

29My friends, it is right for me

to speak to you about our ancestor David. He died and was buried, and his tomb is still here. 30But David was a prophet, and he knew that God had made a promise he would not break. He had told David that someone from his own family would someday be king.

31David knew this would happen, and so he told us that Christ would be raised to life. He said that God would not leave him in the grave or let his body decay. 32All of us can tell you that God has raised Jesus to life!

33Jesus was taken up to sit at the right side*f* of God, and he was given the Holy Spirit, just as the Father had promised. Jesus is also the one who has given the Spirit to us, and that is what you are now seeing and hearing.

34David didn't go up to heaven. So he wasn't talking about himself when he said, "The Lord told my Lord to sit at his right side, 35until he made my Lord's enemies into a footstool for him." 36Everyone in Israel should then know for certain that God has made Jesus both Lord and Christ, even though you put him to death on a cross.

37When the people heard this, they were very upset. They asked Peter and the other apostles, "Friends, what shall we do?"

38Peter said, "Turn back to God! Be baptized in the name of Jesus Christ, so that your sins will be for-given. Then you will be given the Holy Spirit. 39This promise is for you and your children. It is for everyone our Lord God will choose, no matter where they live."

40Peter told them many other things as well. Then he said, "I beg you to save yourselves from what will happen to all these evil people." 41On that day about three thousand believed his message and were baptized. 42They spent their time learning from the apostles, and they were like family to each other. They also broke bread*g* and prayed together.

Life among the Lord's Followers

43Everyone was amazed by the many miracles and wonders that the apostles worked. 44All the Lord's followers often met together, and they shared everything they had. 45They would sell their property and possessions and give the money to whoever needed it. 46Day after day they met together in the temple. They broke bread*g* together in different homes and shared their food happily and freely, 47while praising God. Everyone liked them, and each day the Lord added to their group others who were being saved.

Peter and John Heal a Lame Man

3 The time of prayer*h* was about three o'clock in the afternoon, and Peter and John were going into the temple. 2A man who had been born

---

f right side: The place of honor and power. *g broke bread*: They ate together and celebrated the Lord's Supper. *h The time of prayer*: Many of the Jewish people prayed in their homes at regular times each day (see Daniel 6.11), and on special occasions they prayed in the temple.

lame was being carried to the temple door. Each day he was placed beside this door, known as the Beautiful Gate. He sat there and begged from the people who were going in.

³The man saw Peter and John entering the temple, and he asked them for money. ⁴But they looked straight at him and said, "Look up at us!"

⁵The man stared at them and thought he was going to get something. ⁶But Peter said, "I don't have any silver or gold! But I will give you what I do have. In the name of Jesus Christ from Nazareth, get up and start walking." ⁷Peter then took him by the right hand and helped him up.

At once the man's feet and ankles became strong, ⁸and he jumped up and started walking. He went with Peter and John into the temple, walking and jumping and praising God. ⁹Everyone saw him walking around and praising God. ¹⁰They knew that he was the beggar who had been lying beside the Beautiful Gate, and they were completely surprised. They could not imagine what had happened to the man.

Peter Speaks in the Temple

¹¹While the man kept holding on to Peter and John, the whole crowd ran to them in amazement at the place known as Solomon's Porch.[i] ¹²Peter saw that a crowd had gathered, and he said:

Friends, why are you surprised at what has happened? Why are you staring at us? Do you think we have some power of our own? Do you think we were able to make this man walk because we are so religious? ¹³The God that Abraham, Isaac, Jacob, and our other ancestors worshiped has brought honor to his Servant[j] Jesus. He is the one you betrayed. You turned against him when he was being tried by Pilate, even though Pilate wanted to set him free.

¹⁴You rejected Jesus, who was holy and good. You asked for a murderer to be set free, ¹⁵and you killed the one who leads people to life. But God raised him from death, and all of us can tell you what he has done. ¹⁶You see this man, and you know him. He put his faith in the name of Jesus and was made strong. Faith in Jesus made this man completely well while everyone was watching.

¹⁷My friends, I am sure that you and your leaders didn't know what you were doing. ¹⁸But God had his prophets tell that his Messiah would suffer, and now he has kept that promise. ¹⁹So turn to God! Give up your sins, and you will be forgiven. ²⁰Then that time will come when the Lord will give you fresh strength. He will send you Jesus, his chosen Messiah. ²¹But Jesus must stay in heaven until God makes all things new, just as his holy prophets promised long ago.

²²Moses said, "The Lord your God will choose one of your own people to be a prophet, just as he chose me. Listen to everything he tells you. ²³No one who disobeys that prophet will be one of God's people any longer."

---

[i]*Solomon's Porch*: A public place with tall columns along the east side of the temple.   [j]*Servant*: Or "Son."

24Samuel and all the other prophets who came later also spoke about what is now happening. 25You are really the ones God told his prophets to speak to. And you were given the promise that God made to your ancestors. He said to Abraham, "All nations on earth will be blessed because of someone from your family." 26God sent his chosen Son[k] to you first, because God wanted to bless you and make each one of you turn away from your sins.

Peter and John Are Brought in Front of the Council

4 The apostles were still talking to the people, when some priests, the captain of the temple guard, and some Sadducees arrived. 2These men were angry because the apostles were teaching the people that the dead would be raised from death, just as Jesus had been raised from death. 3By now it was already late in the afternoon, and they arrested Peter and John and put them in jail for the night. 4But a lot of people who had heard the message believed it. So by now there were about five thousand followers of the Lord.

5The next morning the leaders, the elders, and the teachers of the Law of Moses met in Jerusalem. 6The high priest Annas was there, as well as Caiaphas, John, Alexander, and other members of the high priest's family. 7They brought in Peter and John and made them stand in the middle while they questioned them. They asked, "By what power and in whose name have you done this?"

8Peter was filled with the Holy Spirit and told the nation's leaders and the elders:

9You are questioning us today about a kind deed in which a crippled man was healed. 10But there is something we must tell you and everyone else in Israel. This man is standing here completely well because of the power of Jesus Christ from Nazareth. You put Jesus to death on a cross, but God raised him to life. 11He is the stone that you builders thought was worthless, and now he is the most important stone of all. 12Only Jesus has the power to save! His name is the only one in all the world that can save anyone.

13The officials were amazed to see how brave Peter and John were, and they knew that these two apostles were only ordinary men and not well educated. The officials were certain that these men had been with Jesus. 14But they could not deny what had happened. The man who had been healed was standing there with the apostles.

15The officials commanded them to leave the council room. Then the officials said to each other, 16"What can we do with these men? Everyone in Jerusalem knows about this miracle, and we cannot say it didn't happen. 17But to keep this thing from spreading, we will warn them never again to speak to anyone about the name of Jesus." 18So they called the two apostles back in and told them that they must never, for any reason, teach anything about the name of Jesus.

19Peter and John answered, "Do you think God wants us to obey you or to obey him? 20We cannot keep quiet about what we have seen and heard."

[k] Son: Or "Servant."

21-22 The officials could not find any reason to punish Peter and John. So they threatened them and let them go. The man who was healed by this miracle was more than forty years old, and everyone was praising God for what had happened.

Peter and Others Pray for Courage

23As soon as Peter and John had been set free, they went back and told the others everything that the chief priests and the leaders had said to them. **24**When the rest of the Lord's followers heard this, they prayed together and said:

Master, you created heaven and earth, the sea, and everything in them. **25**And by the Holy Spirit you spoke to our ancestor David. He was your servant, and you told him to say:

"Why are all the Gentiles
    so furious?
Why do people
    make foolish plans?
26The kings of earth
    prepare for war,
and the rulers
    join together
against the Lord
    and his Messiah."

27Here in Jerusalem, Herod[l] and Pontius Pilate got together with the Gentiles and the people of Israel. Then they turned against your holy Servant[m] Jesus, your chosen Messiah. **28**They did what you in your power and wisdom had already decided would happen. **29**Lord, listen to their threats!

We are your servants. So make us brave enough to speak your message. **30**Show your mighty power, as we heal people and work miracles and wonders in the name of your holy Servant[m] Jesus.

31After they had prayed, the meeting place shook. They were all filled with the Holy Spirit and bravely spoke God's message.

Sharing Possessions

32The group of followers all felt the same way about everything. None of them claimed that their belongings were their own, and they shared everything they had with each other. **33**In a powerful way the apostles told everyone that the Lord Jesus was now alive. God greatly blessed his followers,[n] **34**and no one went in need of anything. Everyone who owned land or houses would sell them and bring the money **35**to the apostles. Then they would give the money to anyone who needed it.

36-37 Joseph was one of the followers who had sold a piece of property and brought the money to the apostles. He was a Levite from Cyprus, and the apostles called him Barnabas, which means, "one who encourages others."

Peter Condemns Ananias and Sapphira

5 Ananias and his wife Sapphira also sold a piece of property. **2**But they agreed to cheat and keep some of the money for themselves.

So when Ananias took the rest of

---

[l]*Herod*: Herod Antipas, the son of Herod the Great.   [m]*Servant*: See the note at 3.13.
[n]*God greatly blessed his followers*: Or "Everyone highly respected his followers."

the money to the apostles, 3Peter said, "Why has Satan made you keep back some of the money from the sale of the property? Why have you lied to the Holy Spirit? 4The property was yours before you sold it, and even after you sold it, the money was still yours. What made you do such a thing? You didn't lie to people. You lied to God!"

5As soon as Ananias heard this, he dropped dead, and everyone who heard about it was frightened. 6Some young men came in and wrapped up his body. Then they took it out and buried it.

7Three hours later Sapphira came in, but she did not know what had happened to her husband. 8Peter asked her, "Tell me, did you sell the property for this amount?"

"Yes," she answered, "that's the amount."

9Then Peter said, "Why did the two of you agree to test the Lord's Spirit? The men who buried Ananias are by the door, and they will carry you out!" 10At once she fell at Peter's feet and died.

When the young men came back in, they found Sapphira lying there dead. So they carried her out and buried her beside her husband. 11All the church members were afraid, and so was everyone else who heard what had happened.

Peter's Unusual Power

12The apostles worked many miracles and wonders among the people. All of the Lord's followers often met in the part of the temple known as Solomon's Porch.*o* 13No one outside their group dared join them, even though everyone liked them very much.

14Many men and women started having faith in the Lord. 15Then sick people were brought out to the road and placed on cots and mats. It was hoped that Peter would walk by, and his shadow would fall on them and heal them. 16A lot of people living in the towns near Jerusalem brought those who were sick or troubled by evil spirits, and they were all healed.

The Jewish Leaders Make Trouble for the Apostles

17The high priest and all the other Sadducees who were with him became jealous. 18They arrested the apostles and put them in the city jail. 19But that night an angel from the Lord opened the doors of the jail and led the apostles out. The angel said, 20"Go to the temple and tell the people everything about this new life." 21So they went into the temple before sunrise and started teaching.

The high priest and his men called together their council, which included all of Israel's leaders. Then they ordered the apostles to be brought to them from the jail. 22The servants who were sent to the jail did not find the apostles. They returned and said, 23"We found the jail locked tight and the guards standing at the doors. But when we opened the doors and went in, we didn't find anyone there." 24The captain of the temple guard and the chief priests listened to their report, but they did not know what to think about it.

25Just then someone came in and said, "Right now those men you put

---

oSolomon's Porch: See the note at 3.11.

in jail are in the temple, teaching the people!" 26The captain of the temple police went with some of his servants and brought the apostles back. But they did not use force. They were afraid that the people might start throwing stones at them.

27When the apostles were brought before the council, the high priest said to them, 28"We told you plainly not to teach in the name of Jesus. But look what you have done! You have been teaching all over Jerusalem, and you are trying to blame us for his death."

29Peter and the apostles replied:
We don't obey people. We obey God. 30You killed Jesus by nailing him to a cross. But the God our ancestors worshiped raised him to life 31and made him our Leader and Savior. Then God gave him a place at his right side,*p* so that the people of Israel would turn back to him and be forgiven. 32We are here to tell you about all this, and so is the Holy Spirit, who is God's gift to everyone who obeys God.

33When the council members heard this, they became so angry that they wanted to kill the apostles. 34But one of them was the Pharisee Gamaliel, a highly respected teacher. He ordered the apostles to be taken out of the room for a little while. 35Then he said to the council:

Men of Israel, be careful what you do with these two men. 36Not long ago Theudas claimed to be someone important, and about four hundred men joined him. But he was killed. All his follow-

ers were scattered, and that was the end of that.

37Later, when the people of our nation were being counted, Judas from Galilee showed up. A lot of people followed him, but he was killed, and all his followers were scattered.

38So I advise you to stay away from these men. Leave them alone. If what they are planning is something of their own doing, it will fail. 39But if God is behind it, you cannot stop it anyway, unless you want to fight against God.

The council members agreed with what he said, 40and they called the apostles back in. They had them beaten with a whip and warned them not to speak in the name of Jesus. Then they let them go.

41The apostles left the council and were happy, because God had considered them worthy to suffer for the sake of Jesus. 42Every day they spent time in the temple and in one home after another. They never stopped teaching and telling the good news that Jesus is the Messiah.

Seven Leaders for the Church

6 A lot of people were now becoming followers of the Lord. But some of the ones who spoke Greek started complaining about the ones who spoke Aramaic. They complained that the Greek-speaking widows were not given their share when the food supplies were handed out each day.

2The twelve apostles called the whole group of followers together and said, "We should not give up preaching

p right side: See the note at 2.33.

God's message in order to serve at tables.[q] [3]My friends, choose seven men
who are respected and wise and filled
with God's Spirit. We will put them in
charge of these things. [4]We can spend
our time praying and serving God by
preaching."

[5]This suggestion pleased everyone, and they began by choosing Stephen. He had great faith and was filled
with the Holy Spirit. Then they chose
Philip, Prochorus, Nicanor, Timon,
Parmenas, and also Nicolaus, who worshiped with the Jewish people[r] in Antioch. [6]These men were brought to the
apostles. Then the apostles prayed and
placed their hands on the men to show
that they had been chosen to do this
work. [7]God's message spread, and
many more people in Jerusalem became followers. Even a large number
of priests put their faith in the Lord.

Stephen Is Arrested

[8]God gave Stephen the power to
work great miracles and wonders
among the people. [9]But some Jews
from Cyrene and Alexandria were
members of a group who called themselves "Free Men."[s] They started arguing with Stephen. Some others from
Cilicia and Asia also argued with him.
[10]But they were no match for Stephen,
who spoke with the great wisdom that
the Spirit gave him. [11]So they talked
some men into saying, "We heard Stephen say terrible things against Moses
and God!"

[12]They turned the people and their
leaders and the teachers of the Law
of Moses against Stephen. Then they
all grabbed Stephen and dragged him
in front of the council.

[13]Some men agreed to tell lies
about Stephen, and they said, "This
man keeps on saying terrible things
about this holy temple and the Law of
Moses. [14]We have heard him claim
that Jesus from Nazareth will destroy
this place and change the customs that
Moses gave us." [15]Then all the council
members stared at Stephen. They saw
that his face looked like the face of an
angel.

Stephen's Speech

7 The high priest asked Stephen,
"Are they telling the truth about
you?"

[2]Stephen answered:

Friends, listen to me. Our glorious God appeared to our ancestor Abraham while he was still in
Mesopotamia, before he had
moved to Haran. [3]God told him,
"Leave your country and your relatives and go to a land that I will
show you." [4]Then Abraham left
the land of the Chaldeans and
settled in Haran.

After his father died, Abraham
came and settled in this land
where you now live. [5]God didn't
give him any part of it, not even
a square foot. But God did promise to give it to him and his family
forever, even though Abraham
didn't have any children. [6]God

---

[q]*to serve at tables*: This may mean either that they were in charge of handing out food to the
widows or that they were in charge of the money, since the Greek word "table" may also
mean "bank." [r]*worshiped with the Jewish people*: This translates the Greek word "proselyte"
that means a Gentile who had accepted the Jewish religion. [s]*"Free Men"*: A group of Jewish
men who had once been slaves, but had been freed.

said that Abraham's descendants would live for a while in a foreign land. There they would be slaves and would be mistreated four hundred years. 7But he also said, "I will punish the nation that makes them slaves. Then later they will come and worship me in this place."

8God said to Abraham, "Every son in each family must be circumcised to show that you have kept your agreement with me." So when Isaac was eight days old, Abraham circumcised him. Later, Isaac circumcised his son Jacob, and Jacob circumcised his twelve sons. 9These men were our ancestors.

Joseph was also one of our famous ancestors. His brothers were jealous of him and sold him as a slave to be taken to Egypt. But God was with him 10and rescued him from all his troubles. God made him so wise that the Egyptian king Pharaoh thought highly of him. Pharaoh even made Joseph governor over Egypt and put him in charge of everything he owned.

11Everywhere in Egypt and Canaan the grain crops failed. There was terrible suffering, and our ancestors could not find enough to eat. 12But when Jacob heard that there was grain in Egypt, he sent our ancestors there for the first time. 13It was on their second trip that Joseph told his brothers who he was, and Pharaoh learned about Joseph's family.

14Joseph sent for his father and his relatives. In all, there were seventy-five of them. 15His father went to Egypt and died there, just as our ancestors did. 16Later their bodies were taken back to Shechem and placed in the tomb that Abraham had bought from the sons of Hamor.

17Finally, the time came for God to do what he had promised Abraham. By then the number of our people in Egypt had greatly increased. 18Another king was ruling Egypt, and he didn't know anything about Joseph. 19He tricked our ancestors and was cruel to them. He even made them leave their babies outside, so they would die.

20During this time Moses was born. He was a very beautiful child, and for three months his parents took care of him in their home. 21Then when they were forced to leave him outside, the king's daughter found him and raised him as her own son. 22Moses was given the best education in Egypt. He was a strong man and a powerful speaker.

23When Moses was forty years old, he wanted to help the Israelites because they were his own people. 24One day he saw an Egyptian mistreating one of them. So he rescued the man and killed the Egyptian. 25Moses thought the rest of his people would realize that God was going to use him to set them free. But they didn't understand.

26The next day Moses saw two of his own people fighting, and he tried to make them stop. He said, "Men, you are both Israelites. Why are you so cruel to each other?"

27But the man who had started

the fight pushed Moses aside and asked, "Who made you our ruler and judge? 28Are you going to kill me, just as you killed that Egyptian yesterday?" 29When Moses heard this, he ran away to live in the country of Midian. His two sons were born there.

30Forty years later, an angel appeared to Moses from a burning bush in the desert near Mount Sinai. 31Moses was surprised by what he saw. He went closer to get a better look, and the Lord said, 32"I am the God who was worshiped by your ancestors, Abraham, Isaac, and Jacob." Moses started shaking all over and didn't dare to look at the bush.

33The Lord said to him, "Take off your sandals. The place where you are standing is holy. 34With my own eyes I have seen the suffering of my people in Egypt. I have heard their groans and have come down to rescue them. Now I am sending you back to Egypt."

35This was the same Moses that the people rejected by saying, "Who made you our leader and judge?" God's angel had spoken to Moses from the bush. And God had even sent the angel to help Moses rescue the people and be their leader.

36In Egypt and at the Red Sea and in the desert, Moses rescued the people by working miracles and wonders for forty years. 37Moses is the one who told the people of Israel, "God will choose one of your people to be a prophet, just as he chose me." 38Moses brought our people together in the desert, and the angel spoke to him on Mount Sinai. There he

was given these life-giving words to pass on to us. 39But our ancestors refused to obey Moses. They rejected him and wanted to go back to Egypt.

40The people said to Aaron, "Make some gods to lead us! Moses led us out of Egypt, but we don't know what's happened to him now." 41Then they made an idol in the shape of a calf. They offered sacrifices to the idol and were pleased with what they had done.

42God turned his back on his people and left them. Then they worshiped the stars in the sky, just as it says in the Book of the Prophets, "People of Israel, you didn't offer sacrifices and offerings to me during those forty years in the desert. 43Instead, you carried the tent where the god Molech is worshiped, and you took along the star of your god Rephan. You made those idols and worshiped them. So now I will have you carried off beyond Babylonia."

44The tent where our ancestors worshiped God was with them in the desert. This was the same tent that God had commanded Moses to make. And it was made like the model that Moses had seen. 45Later it was given to our ancestors, and they took it with them when they went with Joshua. They carried the tent along as they took over the land from those people that God had chased out for them. Our ancestors used this tent until the time of King David. 46He pleased God and asked him if he could build a house of worship for the people[t] of Israel. 47And it was finally King Solomon who built a house for God.[u]

48But the Most High God does not live in houses made by humans. It is just as the prophet said, when he spoke for the Lord,

49"Heaven is my throne,
and the earth
is my footstool.
What kind of house
will you build for me?
In what place will I rest?
50   I have made everything."

51You stubborn and hardheaded people! You are always fighting against the Holy Spirit, just as your ancestors did. 52Is there one prophet that your ancestors didn't mistreat? They killed the prophets who told about the coming of the One Who Obeys God.[v] And now you have turned against him and killed him. 53Angels gave you God's Law, but you still don't obey it.

Stephen Is Stoned to Death

54When the council members heard Stephen's speech, they were angry and furious. 55But Stephen was filled with the Holy Spirit. He looked toward heaven, where he saw our glorious God and Jesus standing at his right side.[w] 56Then Stephen said, "I see heaven open and the Son of Man standing at the right side of God!"

57The council members shouted and covered their ears. At once they all attacked Stephen 58and dragged him out of the city. Then they started throwing stones at him. The men who had brought charges against him put their coats at the feet of a young man named Saul.[x]

59As Stephen was being stoned to death, he called out, "Lord Jesus, please welcome me!" 60He kneeled down and shouted, "Lord, don't blame them for what they have done." Then he died.

8 1-2Saul approved the stoning of Stephen. Some faithful followers of the Lord buried Stephen and mourned very much for him.

Saul Makes Trouble for the Church

At that time the church in Jerusalem suffered terribly. All of the Lord's followers, except the apostles, were scattered everywhere in Judea and Samaria. 3Saul started making a lot of trouble for the church. He went from house to house, arresting men and women and putting them in jail.

The Good News Is Preached in Samaria

4The Lord's followers who had been scattered went from place to place, telling the good news. 5Philip went to the town of Samaria and told the people about Christ. 6They crowded around Philip because they were eager to hear what he was saying and to see him work miracles. 7Many people with evil spirits were healed, and the spirits went out of them with a shout. A lot of crippled and lame people were also healed. 8Everyone in that

---

[t] the people: Some manuscripts have "God." [u] God: Or "the people." [v] One Who Obeys God: That is, Jesus. [w] standing at his right side: The "right side" is the place of honor and power. "Standing" may mean that Jesus is welcoming Stephen (see verse 59). [x] Saul: Better known as Paul, who became a famous follower of Jesus.

city was very glad because of what was happening.

⁹For some time a man named Simon had lived in the city of Samaria and had amazed the people. He practiced witchcraft and claimed to be somebody great. ¹⁰Everyone, rich and poor, crowded around him. They said, "This man is the power of God called 'The Great Power.'"

¹¹For a long time Simon had used witchcraft to amaze the people, and they kept crowding around him. ¹²But when they believed what Philip was saying about God's kingdom and about the name of Jesus Christ, they were all baptized. ¹³Even Simon believed and was baptized. He stayed close to Philip, because he marveled at all the miracles and wonders.

¹⁴When the apostles in Jerusalem heard that some people in Samaria had accepted God's message, they sent Peter and John. ¹⁵When the two apostles arrived, they prayed that the people would be given the Holy Spirit. ¹⁶Before this, the Holy Spirit had not been given to anyone in Samaria though some of them had been baptized in the name of the Lord Jesus. ¹⁷Peter and John then placed their hands on everyone who had faith in the Lord, and they were given the Holy Spirit.

¹⁸Simon noticed that the Spirit was given only when the apostles placed their hands on the people. So he brought money ¹⁹and said to Peter and John, "Let me have this power too! Then anyone I place my hands on will also be given the Holy Spirit."

²⁰Peter said to him, "You and your money will both end up in hell if you think you can buy God's gift! ²¹You don't have any part in this, and God sees that your heart is not right. ²²Get rid of these evil thoughts and ask God to forgive you. ²³I can see that you are jealous and bound by your evil ways."

²⁴Simon said, "Please pray to the Lord, so that what you said won't happen to me."

²⁵After Peter and John had preached about the Lord, they returned to Jerusalem. On their way they told the good news in many villages of Samaria.

Philip and an Ethiopian Official

²⁶The Lord's angel said to Philip, "Go south*y* along the desert road that leads from Jerusalem to Gaza."*z* ²⁷So Philip left.

An important Ethiopian official happened to be going along that road in his chariot. He was the chief treasurer for Candace, the Queen of Ethiopia. The official had gone to Jerusalem to worship ²⁸and was now on his way home. He was sitting in his chariot, reading the book of the prophet Isaiah.

²⁹The Spirit told Philip to catch up with the chariot. ³⁰Philip ran up close and heard the man reading aloud from the book of Isaiah. Philip asked him, "Do you understand what you are reading?"

³¹The official answered, "How can I understand unless someone helps me?" He then invited Philip to come up and sit beside him.

³²The man was reading the passage that said,

"He was led like a sheep
        on its way to be killed.

---

y Go south: Or "About noon go." *z the desert road that leads from Jerusalem to Gaza*: Or "the road that leads from Jerusalem to Gaza in the desert."

He was silent as a lamb,
whose wool
   is being cut off,
and he did not say
   a word.
33He was treated like a nobody
and did not receive
   a fair trial.
How can he have children,
if his life
   is snatched away?"

34The official said to Philip, "Tell me, was the prophet talking about himself or about someone else?" 35So Philip began at this place in the Scriptures and explained the good news about Jesus.

36-37As they were going along the road, they came to a place where there was some water. The official said, "Look! Here is some water. Why can't I be baptized?"*a* 38He ordered the chariot to stop. Then they both went down into the water, and Philip baptized him.

39After they had come out of the water, the Lord's Spirit took Philip away. The official never saw him again, but he was very happy as he went on his way.

40Philip later appeared in Azotus. He went from town to town, all the way to Caesarea, telling people about Jesus.

Saul Becomes a Follower of the Lord
(*Acts 22.6–16; 26.12–18*)

9 Saul kept on threatening to kill the Lord's followers. He even went to the high priest 2and asked for letters to the Jewish leaders in Damascus. He did this because he wanted to arrest and take to Jerusalem any man or woman who.had accepted the Lord's Way.*b* 3When Saul had almost reached Damascus, a bright light from heaven suddenly flashed around him. 4He fell to the ground and heard a voice that said, "Saul! Saul! Why are you so cruel to me?"

5"Who are you?" Saul asked.

"I am Jesus," the. Lord answered. "I am the one you are so cruel to. 6Now get up and go into the city, where you will be told what to do."

7The men with Saul stood there speechless. They had heard the voice, but they had not seen anyone. 8Saul got up from the ground, and when he opened his eyes, he could not see a thing. Someone then led him by the hand to Damascus, 9and for three days he was blind and did not eat or drink.

10A follower named Ananias lived in Damascus, and the Lord spoke to him in a vision. Ananias answered, "Lord, here I am."

11The Lord said to him, "Get up and go to the house of Judas on Straight Street. When you get there, you will find a man named Saul from the city of Tarsus. Saul is praying, 12and he has seen a vision. He saw a man named Ananias coming to him and putting his hands on him, so that he could see again."

13Ananias replied, "Lord, a lot of people have told me about the terrible things this man has done to your followers in Jerusalem. 14Now the chief

---

aWhy can't I be baptized: Some manuscripts add, "Philip replied, 'You can, if you believe with all your heart.' The official answered, 'I believe that Jesus Christ is the Son of God.' "
baccepted the Lord's Way: In the book of Acts, this means to become a follower of the Lord Jesus.

priests have given him the power to come here and arrest anyone who worships in your name."

¹⁵The Lord said to Ananias, "Go! I have chosen him to tell foreigners, kings, and the people of Israel about me. ¹⁶I will show him how much he must suffer for worshiping in my name."

¹⁷Ananias left and went into the house where Saul was staying. Ananias placed his hands on him and said, "Saul, the Lord Jesus has sent me. He is the same one who appeared to you along the road. He wants you to be able to see and to be filled with the Holy Spirit."

¹⁸Suddenly something like fish scales fell from Saul's eyes, and he could see. He got up and was baptized. ¹⁹Then he ate and felt much better.

Saul Preaches in Damascus

For several days Saul stayed with the Lord's followers in Damascus. ²⁰Soon he went to the Jewish meeting places and started telling people that Jesus is the Son of God. ²¹Everyone who heard Saul was amazed and said, "Isn't this the man who caused so much trouble for those people in Jerusalem who worship in the name of Jesus? Didn't he come here to arrest them and take them to the chief priests?"

²²Saul preached with such power that he completely confused the Jewish people in Damascus, as he tried to show them that Jesus is the Messiah.

²³Later some of them made plans to kill Saul, ²⁴but he found out about it. He learned that they were guarding the gates of the city day and night in order to kill him. ²⁵Then one night his followers let him down over the city wall in a large basket.

Saul in Jerusalem

²⁶When Saul arrived in Jerusalem, he tried to join the followers. But they were all afraid of him, because they did not believe he was a true follower. ²⁷Then Barnabas helped him by taking him to the apostles. He explained how on the road to Damascus, Saul had seen the Lord and how the Lord had spoken to Saul. Barnabas also said that when Saul was in Damascus, he had spoken bravely in the name of Jesus.

²⁸Saul moved about freely with the followers in Jerusalem and told everyone about the Lord. ²⁹He was always arguing with the Jews who spoke Greek, and so they tried to kill him. ³⁰But the followers found out about this and took Saul to Caesarea. From there they sent him to the city of Tarsus.

³¹The church in Judea, Galilee, and Samaria now had a time of peace and kept on worshiping the Lord. The church became stronger, as the Holy Spirit encouraged it and helped it grow.

Peter Heals Aeneas

³²While Peter was traveling from place to place, he visited the Lord's followers who lived in the town of Lydda. ³³There he met a man named Aeneas, who for eight years had been sick in bed and could not move. ³⁴Peter said to Aeneas, "Jesus Christ has healed you! Get up and make up your bed."ᶜ Right away he stood up.

³⁵Many people in the towns of Lydda and Sharon saw Aeneas and became followers of the Lord.

ᶜ*and make up your bed*: Or "and fix something to eat."

Peter Brings Dorcas Back to Life

36In Joppa there was a follower named Tabitha. Her Greek name was Dorcas, which means "deer." She was always doing good things for people and had given much to the poor. **37**But she got sick and died, and her body was washed and placed in an upstairs room. **38**Joppa was not far from Lydda, and the followers heard that Peter was there. They sent two men to say to him, "Please come with us as quickly as you can!" **39**Right away Peter went with them.

The men took Peter upstairs into the room. Many widows were there crying. They showed him the coats and clothes that Dorcas had made while she was still alive.

40After Peter had sent everyone out of the room, he kneeled down and prayed. Then he turned to the body of Dorcas and said, "Tabitha, get up!" The woman opened her eyes, and when she saw Peter, she sat up. **41**He took her by the hand and helped her to her feet.

Peter called in the widows and the other followers and showed them that Dorcas had been raised from death. **42**Everyone in Joppa heard what had happened, and many of them put their faith in the Lord. **43**Peter stayed on for a while in Joppa in the house of a man named Simon, who made leather.

Peter and Cornelius

10 In Caesarea there was a man named Cornelius, who was the captain of a group of soldiers called "The Italian Unit." **2**Cornelius was a very religious man. He worshiped God, and so did everyone else who lived in his house. He had given a lot of money to the poor and was always praying to God.

3One afternoon at about three o'clock,*d* Cornelius had a vision. He saw an angel from God coming to him and calling him by name. **4**Cornelius was surprised and stared at the angel. Then he asked, "What is this all about?"

The angel answered, "God has heard your prayers and knows about your gifts to the poor. **5**Now send some men to Joppa for a man named Simon Peter. **6**He is visiting with Simon the leather maker, who lives in a house near the sea." **7**After saying this, the angel left.

Cornelius called in two of his servants and one of his soldiers who worshiped God. **8**He explained everything to them and sent them off to Joppa.

9The next day about noon these men were coming near to Joppa. Peter went up on the roof*e* of the house to pray **10**and became very hungry. While the food was being prepared, he fell sound asleep and had a vision. **11**He saw heaven open, and something came down like a huge sheet held up by its four corners. **12**In it were all kinds of animals, snakes, and birds. **13**A voice said to him, "Peter, get up! Kill these and eat them."

14But Peter said, "Lord, I can't do that! I've never eaten anything that is unclean and not fit to eat."*f*

15The voice spoke to him again,

---

*d*at about three o'clock: Probably while he was praying. See 3.1 and the note there. *e*roof: In Palestine the houses usually had a flat roof. Stairs on the outside led up to the roof, which was made of beams and boards covered with packed earth. *f*unclean and not fit to eat: The Law of Moses taught that some foods were not fit to eat.

"When God says that something can be used for food, don't say it isn't fit to eat."

16This happened three times before the sheet was suddenly taken back to heaven.

17Peter was still wondering what all of this meant, when the men sent by Cornelius came and stood at the gate. They had found their way to Simon's house 18and were asking if Simon Peter was staying there.

19While Peter was still thinking about the vision, the Holy Spirit said to him, "Three*g* men are here looking for you. 20Hurry down and go with them. Don't worry, I sent them."

21Peter went down and said to the men, "I am the one you are looking for. Why have you come?"

22They answered, "Captain Cornelius sent us. He is a good man and worships God. All the Jewish people like him. One of God's holy angels told Cornelius to send for you, so he could hear what you have to say." 23Peter invited them to spend the night.

The next morning Peter and some of the Lord's followers in Joppa left with the men who had come from Cornelius. 24The next day they all arrived in Caesarea where Cornelius was waiting for them. He had also invited his relatives and close friends.

25When Peter arrived, Cornelius greeted him. Then he kneeled at Peter's feet and started worshiping him. 26But Peter took hold of him and said, "Stand up! I am nothing more than a human."

27As Peter entered the house, he was still talking with Cornelius. Many people were there, 28and Peter said to them, "You know that we Jews are not allowed to have anything to do with other people. But God has shown me that he doesn't think anyone is unclean or unfit. 29I agreed to come here, but I want to know why you sent for me."

30Cornelius answered:

Four days ago at about three o'clock in the afternoon I was praying at home. Suddenly a man in bright clothes stood in front of me. 31He said, "Cornelius, God has heard your prayers, and he knows about your gifts to the poor. 32Now send to Joppa for Simon Peter. He is visiting in the home of Simon the leather maker, who lives near the sea."

33I sent for you right away, and you have been good enough to come. All of us are here in the presence of the Lord God, so that we can hear what he has to say. 34Peter then said:

Now I am certain that God treats all people alike. 35God is pleased with everyone who worships him and does right, no matter what nation they come from. 36This is the same message that God gave to the people of Israel, when he sent Jesus Christ, the Lord of all, to offer peace to them.

37You surely know what happened*h* everywhere in Judea. It all began in Galilee after John had told everyone to be baptized. 38God gave the Holy Spirit and power to Jesus from Nazareth. He was with Jesus, as he went around doing good and healing everyone who was under the power of the devil. 39We all saw

---

gThree: Some manuscripts have "two;" one manuscript has "some."   *hwhat happened*: Or "the message that went."

what Jesus did both in Israel and in the city of Jerusalem.

Jesus was put to death on a cross. 40But three days later, God raised him to life and let him be seen. 41Not everyone saw him. He was seen only by us, who ate and drank with him after he was raised from death. We were the ones God chose to tell others about him.

42God told us to announce clearly to the people that Jesus is the one he has chosen to judge the living and the dead. 43Every one of the prophets has said that all who have faith in Jesus will have their sins forgiven in his name.

44While Peter was still speaking, the Holy Spirit took control of everyone who was listening. 45Some Jewish followers of the Lord had come with Peter, and they were surprised that the Holy Spirit had been given to Gentiles. 46Now they were hearing Gentiles speaking unknown languages and praising God.

Peter said, 47"These Gentiles have been given the Holy Spirit, just as we have! I am certain that no one would dare stop us from baptizing them." 48Peter ordered them to be baptized in the name of Jesus Christ, and they asked him to stay on for a few days.

Peter Reports to the Church in Jerusalem

11 The apostles and the followers in Judea heard that Gentiles had accepted God's message. 2So when Peter came to Jerusalem, some of the Jewish leaders started arguing with him. They wanted Gentile followers to be circumcised, and 3they said, "You stayed in the homes of Gentiles, and you even ate with them!"

4Then Peter told them exactly what had happened:

5I was in the town of Joppa and was praying when I fell sound asleep and had a vision. I saw heaven open, and something like a huge sheet held by its four corners came down to me. 6When I looked in it, I saw animals, wild beasts, snakes, and birds. 7I heard a voice saying to me, "Peter, get up! Kill these and eat them."

8But I said, "Lord, I can't do that! I've never taken a bite of anything that is unclean and not fit to eat."i

9The voice from heaven spoke to me again, "When God says that something can be used for food, don't say it isn't fit to eat." 10This happened three times before it was all taken back into heaven.

11Suddenly three men from Caesarea stood in front of the house where I was staying. 12The Holy Spirit told me to go with them and not to worry. Then six of the Lord's followers went with me to the home of a man 13who told us that an angel had appeared to him. The angel had ordered him to send to Joppa for someone named Simon Peter. 14Then Peter would tell him how he and everyone in his house could be saved.

15After I started speaking, the Holy Spirit was given to them, just as the Spirit had been given

---

iunclean and not fit to eat: See the note at 10.14.

to us at the beginning. 16I remembered that the Lord had said, "John baptized with water, but you will be baptized with the Holy Spirit." 17God gave those Gentiles the same gift that he gave us when we put our faith in the Lord Jesus Christ. So how could I have gone against God?

18When the Jewish leaders heard Peter say this, they stopped arguing and started praising God. They said, "God has now let Gentiles turn to him, and he has given life to them!"

The Church in Antioch

19Some of the Lord's followers had been scattered because of the terrible trouble that started when Stephen was killed. They went as far as Phoenicia, Cyprus, and Antioch, but they told the message only to the Jews.

20Some of the followers from Cyprus and Cyrene went to Antioch and started telling Gentiles*j* the good news about the Lord Jesus. 21The Lord's power was with them, and many people turned to the Lord and put their faith in him. 22News of what was happening reached the church in Jerusalem. Then they sent Barnabas to Antioch.

23When Barnabas got there and saw what God had been kind enough to do for them, he was very glad. So he begged them to remain faithful to the Lord with all their hearts. 24Barnabas was a good man of great faith, and he was filled with the Holy Spirit.

Many more people turned to the Lord.

25Barnabas went to Tarsus to look for Saul. 26He found Saul and brought him to Antioch, where they met with the church for a whole year and taught many of its people. There in Antioch the Lord's followers were first called Christians.

27During this time some prophets from Jerusalem came to Antioch. 28One of them was Agabus. Then with the help of the Spirit, he told that there would be a terrible famine everywhere in the world. And it happened when Claudius was Emperor.*k* 29The followers in Antioch decided to send whatever help they could to the followers in Judea. 30So they had Barnabas and Saul take their gifts to the church leaders in Jerusalem.

Herod Causes Trouble for the Church

12 At that time King Herod*l* caused terrible suffering for some members of the church. 2He ordered soldiers to cut off the head of James, the brother of John. 3When Herod saw that this pleased the Jewish people, he had Peter arrested during the Feast of Thin Bread. 4He put Peter in jail and ordered four squads of soldiers to guard him. Herod planned to put him on trial in public after the feast.

5While Peter was being kept in jail, the church never stopped praying to God for him.

---

jGentiles: This translates a Greek word that may mean "people who speak Greek" or "people who live as Greeks do." Here the word seems to mean "people who are not Jews." Some manuscripts have "Greeks," which also seems to mean "people who are not Jews." *kwhen Claudius was Emperor*: A.D. 41-54. *lHerod*: Herod Agrippa I, the grandson of Herod the Great.

Peter Is Rescued

6The night before Peter was to be put on trial, he was asleep and bound by two chains. A soldier was guarding him on each side, and two other soldiers were guarding the entrance to the jail. **7**Suddenly an angel from the Lord appeared, and light flashed around in the cell. The angel poked Peter in the side and woke him up. Then he said, "Quick! Get up!"

The chains fell off his hands, **8**and the angel said, "Get dressed and put on your sandals." Peter did what he was told. Then the angel said, "Now put on your coat and follow me." **9**Peter left with the angel, but he thought everything was only a dream. **10**They went past the two groups of soldiers, and when they came to the iron gate to the city, it opened by itself. They went out and were going along the street, when all at once the angel disappeared.

11Peter now realized what had happened, and he said, "I am certain that the Lord sent his angel to rescue me from Herod and from everything the Jewish leaders planned to do to me." **12**Then Peter went to the house of Mary the mother of John whose other name was Mark. Many of the Lord's followers had come together there and were praying.

13Peter knocked on the gate, and a servant named Rhoda came to the door. **14**When she heard Peter's voice, she was too excited to open the gate. She ran back into the house and said that Peter was standing there.

15Everyone told her, "You are crazy!" But she kept saying that it was Peter. Then they said, "It must be his angel."*m* **16**But Peter kept on knocking, until finally they opened the gate. They saw him and were completely amazed.

17Peter motioned for them to keep quiet. Then he told how the Lord had led him out of jail. He also said, "Tell James and the others what has happened." After that, he left and went somewhere else.

18The next morning the soldiers who had been on guard were terribly worried and wondered what had happened to Peter. **19**Herod ordered his own soldiers to search for him, but they could not find him. Then he questioned the guards and had them put to death. After this, Herod left Judea to stay in Caesarea for a while.

Herod Dies

20Herod and the people of Tyre and Sidon were very angry with each other. But their country got its food supply from the region that he ruled. So a group of them went to see Blastus, who was one of Herod's high officials. They convinced Blastus that they wanted to make peace between their cities and Herod, **21**and a day was set for them to meet with him.

Herod came dressed in his royal robes. He sat down on his throne and made a speech. **22**The people shouted, "You speak more like a god than a man!" **23**At once an angel from the Lord struck him down because he took the honor that belonged to God. Later, Herod was eaten by worms and died.

24God's message kept spreading. **25**And after Barnabas and Saul had done the work they were sent to do, they went back to Jerusalem*n* with John, whose other name was Mark.

---

m his angel: Probably meaning "his guardian angel."   *n went back to Jerusalem*: Some manuscripts have "left Jerusalem," and others have "went to Antioch."

Barnabas and Saul Are Chosen and Sent

13 The church at Antioch had several prophets and teachers. They were Barnabas, Simeon, also called Niger, Lucius from Cyrene, Manaen, who was Herod's[o] close friend, and Saul. 2While they were worshiping the Lord and going without eating,[p] the Holy Spirit told them, "Appoint Barnabas and Saul to do the work for which I have chosen them." 3Everyone prayed and went without eating for a while longer. Next, they placed their hands on Barnabas and Saul to show that they had been appointed to do this work. Then everyone sent them on their way.

Barnabas and Saul in Cyprus

4After Barnabas and Saul had been sent by the Holy Spirit, they went to Seleucia. From there they sailed to the island of Cyprus. 5They arrived at Salamis and began to preach God's message in the Jewish meeting places. They also had John[q] as a helper.

6They went all the way to the city of Paphos on the other end of the island, where they met a Jewish man named Bar-Jesus. He practiced witchcraft and was a false prophet. 7He also worked for Sergius Paulus, who was very smart and was the governor of the island. Sergius Paulus wanted to hear God's message, and he sent for Barnabas and Saul. 8But Bar-Jesus, whose other name was Elymas, was against

them. He even tried to keep the governor from having faith in the Lord.

9Then Saul, better known as Paul, was filled with the Holy Spirit. He looked straight at Elymas 10and said, "You son of the devil! You are a liar, a crook, and an enemy of everything that is right. When will you stop speaking against the true ways of the Lord? 11The Lord is going to punish you by making you completely blind for a while."

Suddenly the man's eyes were covered by a dark mist, and he went around trying to get someone to lead him by the hand. 12When the governor saw what had happened, he was amazed at this teaching about the Lord. So he put his faith in the Lord.

Paul and Barnabas in Antioch of Pisidia

13Paul and the others left Paphos and sailed to Perga in Pamphylia. But John[q] left them and went back to Jerusalem. 14The rest of them went on from Perga to Antioch in Pisidia. Then on the Sabbath they went to the Jewish meeting place and sat down.

15After the reading of the Law and the Prophets,[r] the leaders sent someone over to tell Paul and Barnabas, "Friends, if you have anything to say that will help the people, please say it."

16Paul got up. He motioned with his hand and said:

People of Israel, and everyone else who worships God, listen!

[o]*Herod's*: Herod Antipas, the son of Herod the Great. [p]*going without eating*: The Jews often went without eating as a way of showing how much they loved God. This is also called "fasting." [q]*John*: Whose other name was Mark (12.12, 25). [r]*the Law and the Prophets*: The Jewish Scriptures, that is, the Old Testament.

17The God of Israel chose our ancestors, and he let our people prosper while they were living in Egypt. Then with his mighty power he led them out, 18and for about forty years he took care of[s] them in the desert. 19He destroyed seven nations in the land of Canaan and gave their land to our people. 20All this happened in about 450 years.

Then God gave our people judges until the time of the prophet Samuel, 21but the people demanded a king. So for forty years God gave them King Saul, the son of Kish from the tribe of Benjamin. 22Later, God removed Saul and let David rule in his place. God said about him, "David the son of Jesse is the kind of person who pleases me most! He does everything I want him to do."

23God promised that someone from David's family would come to save the people of Israel, and Jesus is that one. 24But before Jesus came, John was telling everyone in Israel to turn back to God and be baptized. 25Then, when John's work was almost done, he said, "Who do you people think I am? Do you think I am the Promised One? He will come later, and I am not good enough to untie his sandals."

26Now listen, you descendants of Abraham! Pay attention, all of you Gentiles who are here to worship God! Listen to this message about how to be saved, because it is for everyone. 27The people of Jerusalem and their leaders didn't realize who Jesus was. And they didn't understand the words of the prophets that they read each Sabbath. So they condemned Jesus just as the prophets had said.

28-29They did exactly what the Scriptures said they would. Even though they couldn't find any reason to put Jesus to death, they still asked Pilate to have him killed.

After Jesus had been put to death, he was taken down from the cross[t] and put in a tomb. 30But God raised him from death! 31Then for many days Jesus appeared to his followers who had gone with him from Galilee to Jerusalem. Now they are telling our people about him.

32God made a promise to our ancestors. And we are here to tell you the good news 33that he has kept this promise to us. It is just as the second Psalm says about Jesus,

"You are my son because today
I have become
     your Father."

34God raised Jesus from death and will never let his body decay. It is just as God said,

"I will make to you
the same holy promise
     that I made to David."

35And in another psalm it says, "God will never let the body of his Holy One decay."

36When David was alive, he obeyed God. Then after he died, he was buried in the family grave,

---

[s]*took care of*: Some manuscripts have "put up with."   [t]*cross*: This translates a Greek word that means "wood," "pole," or "tree."

and his body decayed. 37But God raised Jesus from death, and his body did not decay.

38My friends, the message is that Jesus can forgive your sins! The Law of Moses could not set you free from all your sins. 39But everyone who has faith in Jesus is set free. 40Make sure that what the prophets have said doesn't happen to you. They said,

41"Look, you people
who make fun of God!
Be amazed
and disappear.
I will do something today
that you won't believe,
even if someone
tells you about it!"

42As Paul and Barnabas were leaving the meeting, the people begged them to say more about these same things on the next Sabbath. 43After the service, many Jews and a lot of Gentiles who worshiped God went with them. Paul and Barnabas begged them all to remain faithful to God, who had been so kind to them.

44The next Sabbath almost everyone in town came to hear the message about the Lord.u 45When the Jewish people saw the crowds, they were very jealous. They insulted Paul and spoke against everything he said.

46But Paul and Barnabas bravely said:

We had to tell God's message to you before we told it to anyone else. But you rejected the message! This proves that you don't deserve eternal life. Now we are going to the Gentiles. 47The Lord has given us this command,
"I have placed you here
as a light
for the Gentiles.
You are to take
the saving power of God
to people everywhere
on earth."

48This message made the Gentiles glad, and they praised what they had heard about the Lord.u Everyone who had been chosen for eternal life then put their faith in the Lord.

49The message about the Lord spread all over that region. 50But the Jewish leaders went to some of the important men in the town and to some respected women who were religious. They turned them against Paul and Barnabas and started making trouble for them. They even chased them out of that part of the country.

51Paul and Barnabas shook the dust from that place off their feetv and went on to the city of Iconium.

52But the Lord's followers in Antioch were very happy and were filled with the Holy Spirit.

Paul and Barnabas in Iconium

14 Paul and Barnabas spoke in the Jewish meeting place in Iconium, just as they had done at Antioch, and many Jews and Gentilesw put their faith in the Lord. 2But the Jews who did not have faith in him made the other Gentiles angry and turned them against the Lord's followers.

3Paul and Barnabas stayed there

---

uthe Lord: Some manuscripts have "God." vshook the dust from that place off their feet: This was a way of showing rejection. wGentiles: The Greek text has "Greeks," which probably means people who were not Jews. But it may mean Gentiles who worshiped with the Jews.

for a while, having faith in the Lord and bravely speaking his message. The Lord gave them the power to work miracles and wonders, and he showed that their message about his great kindness was true.

4The people of Iconium did not know what to think. Some of them believed the Jewish group, and others believed the apostles. 5Finally, some Gentiles and Jews, together with their leaders, decided to make trouble for Paul and Barnabas and to kill them by throwing stones at them.

6-7But when the two apostles found out what was happening, they escaped to the region of Lycaonia. They preached the good news there in the towns of Lystra and Derbe and in the nearby countryside.

Paul and Barnabas in Lystra

8In Lystra there was a man who had been born with crippled feet and had never been able to walk. 9The man was listening to Paul speak, when Paul saw that he had faith in Jesus and could be healed. So he looked straight at the man 10and shouted, "Stand up!" The man jumped up and started walking around.

11When the crowd saw what Paul had done, they yelled out in the language of Lycaonia, "The gods have turned into humans and have come down to us!" 12They gave Barnabas the name Zeus, and they gave Paul the name Hermes,ˣ because he did the talking.

13The temple of Zeus was near the entrance to the city. Its priest and the crowds wanted to offer a sacrifice to Barnabas and Paul. So the priest brought some bulls and flowers to the city gates. 14When the two apostles found out about this, they tore their clothes in horror and ran to the crowd, shouting:

15Why are you doing this? We are humans just like you. Please give up all this foolishness. Turn to the living God, who made the sky, the earth, the sea, and everything in them. 16In times past, God let each nation go its own way. 17But he showed that he was there by the good things he did. God sends rain from heaven and makes your crops grow. He gives food to you and makes your hearts glad.

18Even after Paul and Barnabas had said all this, they could hardly keep the people from offering a sacrifice to them.

19Some Jewish leaders from Antioch and Iconium came and turned the crowds against Paul. They hit him with stones and dragged him out of the city, thinking he was dead. 20But when the Lord's followers gathered around Paul, he stood up and went back into the city. The next day he and Barnabas went to Derbe.

Paul and Barnabas Return to Antioch in Syria

21Paul and Barnabas preached the good news in Derbe and won some people to the Lord. Then they went back to Lystra, Iconium, and Antioch in Pisidia. 22They encouraged the followers and begged them to remain faithful. They told them, "We have to suffer a

ˣHermes: The Greeks thought of Hermes as the messenger of the other gods, especially of Zeus, their chief god.

lot before we can get into God's kingdom." 23Paul and Barnabas chose some of those who had faith in the Lord to be leaders for each of the churches. Then they went without eating[y] and prayed that the Lord would take good care of these leaders.

24Paul and Barnabas went on through Pisidia to Pamphylia, 25where they preached in the town of Perga. Then they went down to Attalia 26and sailed to Antioch in Syria. It was there that they had been placed in God's care for the work they had now completed.[z]

27After arriving in Antioch, they called the church together. They told the people what God had helped them do and how he had made it possible for the Gentiles to believe. 28Then they stayed there with the followers for a long time.

15 Some people came from Judea and started teaching the Lord's followers that they could not be saved, unless they were circumcised as Moses had taught. 2This caused trouble, and Paul and Barnabas argued with them about this teaching. So it was decided to send Paul and Barnabas and a few others to Jerusalem to discuss this problem with the apostles and the church leaders.

The Church Leaders Meet in Jerusalem

3The men who were sent by the church went through Phoenicia and Samaria and told how the Gentiles had turned to God. This news made the Lord's followers very happy. 4When the men arrived in Jerusalem, they were welcomed by all the church, including the apostles and the leaders. They told them everything that God had helped them do. 5But some Pharisees had become followers of the Lord. They stood up and said, "Gentiles who have faith in the Lord must be circumcised and told to obey the Law of Moses."

6The apostles and church leaders met to discuss this problem about Gentiles. 7They had talked it over for a long time, when Peter got up and said:

My friends, you know that God decided long ago to let me be the one from your group to preach the good news to the Gentiles. God did this so that they would hear and obey him. 8He knows what is in everyone's heart. And he showed that he had chosen the Gentiles, when he gave them the Holy Spirit, just as he had given his Spirit to us. 9God treated them in the same way that he treated us. They put their faith in him, and he made their hearts pure.

10Now why are you trying to make God angry by placing a heavy burden on these followers? This burden was too heavy for us or our ancestors. 11But our Lord Jesus was kind to us Jews, and we are saved by faith in him, just as the Gentiles are.

12Everyone kept quiet and listened as Barnabas and Paul told how God had given them the power to work a lot of miracles and wonders for the Gentiles.

13After they had finished speaking, James[a] said:

---

[y]went without eating: See the note at 13.2.   [z]the work they had now completed: See 13.1-3.
[a]James: The Lord's brother.

My friends, listen to me! [14]Simon Peter[b] has told how God first came to the Gentiles and made some of them his own people. [15]This agrees with what the prophets wrote,

[16]"I, the Lord, will return
    and rebuild
        David's fallen house.
I will build it from its ruins
    and set it up again.
[17]Then other nations
    will turn to me
        and be my chosen ones.
I, the Lord, say this.
[18]   I promised it long ago."

[19]And so, my friends, I don't think we should place burdens on the Gentiles who are turning to God. [20]We should simply write and tell them not to eat anything that has been offered to idols. They should be told not to eat the meat of any animal that has been strangled or that still has blood in it. They must also not commit any terrible sexual sins.[c]

[21]We must remember that the Law of Moses has been preached in city after city for many years, and every Sabbath it is read when we Jews meet.

A Letter to Gentiles Who Had Faith in the Lord

[22]The apostles, the leaders, and all the church members decided to send some men to Antioch along with Paul and Barnabas. They chose Silas and Judas Barsabbas,[d] who were two leaders of the Lord's followers. [23]They wrote a letter that said:

We apostles and leaders send friendly greetings to all of you Gentiles who are followers of the Lord in Antioch, Syria, and Cilicia.

[24]We have heard that some people from here have terribly upset you by what they said. But we did not send them! [25]So we met together and decided to choose some men and to send them to you along with our good friends Barnabas and Paul. [26]These men have risked their lives for our Lord Jesus Christ. [27]We are also sending Judas and Silas, who will tell you in person the same things that we are writing.

[28]The Holy Spirit has shown us that we should not place any extra burden on you. [29]But you should not eat anything offered to idols. You should not eat any meat that still has the blood in it or any meat of any animal that has been strangled. You must also not commit any terrible sexual sins. If you follow these instructions, you will do well.

We send our best wishes.

[30]The four men left Jerusalem and went to Antioch. Then they called all the church members together and gave them the letter. [31]When the letter was read, it made everyone glad and gave them lots of encouragement. [32]Judas

---

[b]*Simon Peter*: The Greek text has "Simeon," which is another form of the name "Simon." The apostle Peter is meant.   [c]*not commit any terrible sexual sins*: This probably refers to the laws about the wrong kind of marriages that are forbidden in Leviticus 18.6-18 or to some serious sexual sin.   [d]*Judas Barsabbas*: He may have been a brother of Joseph Barsabbas (see 1.23), but the name "Barsabbas" was often used by the Jewish people.

and Silas were prophets, and they spoke a long time, encouraging and helping the Lord's followers.

33The men from Jerusalem stayed on in Antioch for a while. And when they left to return to the ones who had sent them, the followers wished them well. **34-35**But Silas, Paul, and Barnabas stayed on in Antioch, where they and many others taught and preached about the Lord.*e*

Paul and Barnabas Go Their Separate Ways

36Sometime later Paul said to Barnabas, "Let's go back and visit the Lord's followers in all the cities where we preached his message. Then we will know how they are doing." **37**Barnabas wanted to take along John, whose other name was Mark. **38**But Paul did not want to, because Mark had left them in Pamphylia and had stopped working with them.

39Paul and Barnabas argued, then each of them went his own way. Barnabas took Mark and sailed to Cyprus, **40**but Paul took Silas and left after the followers had placed them in God's care. **41**They traveled through Syria and Cilicia, encouraging the churches.

Timothy Works with Paul and Silas

16 Paul and Silas went back to Derbe and Lystra, where there was a follower named Timothy. His mother was also a follower. She was Jewish, and his father was Greek. **2**The Lord's followers in Lystra and Iconium

said good things about Timothy, **3**and Paul wanted him to go with them. But Paul first had him circumcised, because all the Jewish people around there knew that Timothy's father was Greek.*f*

4As Paul and the others went from city to city, they told the followers what the apostles and leaders in Jerusalem had decided, and they urged them to follow these instructions. **5**The churches became stronger in their faith, and each day more people put their faith in the Lord.

Paul's Vision in Troas

6Paul and his friends went through Phrygia and Galatia, but the Holy Spirit would not let them preach in Asia. **7**After they arrived in Mysia, they tried to go into Bithynia, but the Spirit of Jesus would not let them. **8**So they went on through Mysia until they came to Troas.

9During the night, Paul had a vision of someone from Macedonia who was standing there and begging him, "Come over to Macedonia and help us!" **10**After Paul had seen the vision, we began looking for a way to go to Macedonia. We were sure that God had called us to preach the good news there.

Lydia Becomes a Follower of the Lord

11We sailed from Troas and went straight to Samothrace. The next day we arrived in Neapolis. **12**From there we went to Philippi, which is a Roman

---

*e*Verse 34, which says that Silas decided to stay on in Antioch, is not in some manuscripts.
f had him circumcised . . . Timothy's father was Greek: Timothy would not have been acceptable to the Jews unless he had been circumcised, and Greeks did not circumcise their sons.

colony in the first district of Macedonia.[g]

We spent several days in Philippi. 13Then on the Sabbath we went outside the city gate to a place by the river, where we thought there would be a Jewish meeting place for prayer. We sat down and talked with the women who came. 14One of them was Lydia, who was from the city of Thyatira and sold expensive purple cloth. She was a worshiper of the Lord God, and he made her willing to accept what Paul was saying. 15Then after she and her family were baptized, she kept on begging us, "If you think I really do have faith in the Lord, come stay in my home." Finally, we accepted her invitation.

Paul and Silas Are Put in Jail

16One day on our way to the place of prayer, we were met by a slave girl. She had a spirit in her that gave her the power to tell the future. By doing this she made a lot of money for her owners. 17The girl followed Paul and the rest of us and kept yelling, "These men are servants of the Most High God! They are telling you how to be saved."

18This went on for several days. Finally, Paul got so upset that he turned and said to the spirit, "In the name of Jesus Christ, I order you to leave this girl alone!" At once the evil spirit left her.

19When the girl's owners realized that they had lost all chances for making more money, they grabbed Paul and Silas and dragged them into court. 20They told the officials, "These Jews are upsetting our city! 21They are telling us to do things we Romans are not allowed to do."

22The crowd joined in the attack on Paul and Silas. Then the officials tore the clothes off the two men and ordered them to be beaten with a whip. 23After they had been badly beaten, they were put in jail, and the jailer was told to guard them carefully. 24The jailer did as he was told. He put them deep inside the jail and chained their feet to heavy blocks of wood.

25About midnight Paul and Silas were praying and singing praises to God, while the other prisoners listened. 26Suddenly a strong earthquake shook the jail to its foundations. The doors opened, and the chains fell from all the prisoners.

27When the jailer woke up and saw that the doors were open, he thought that the prisoners had escaped. He pulled out his sword and was about to kill himself. 28But Paul shouted, "Don't harm yourself! No one has escaped."

29The jailer asked for a torch and went into the jail. He was shaking all over as he kneeled down in front of Paul and Silas. 30After he had led them out of the jail, he asked, "What must I do to be saved?"

31They replied, "Have faith in the Lord Jesus and you will be saved! This is also true for everyone who lives in your home."

32Then Paul and Silas told him and everyone else in his house about the Lord. 33While it was still night, the jailer took them to a place where he could wash their cuts and bruises. Then he and everyone in his home

---

[g]*in the first district of Macedonia*: Some manuscripts have "and the leading city of Macedonia."

were baptized. 34They were very glad that they had put their faith in God. After this, the jailer took Paul and Silas to his home and gave them something to eat.

35The next morning the officials sent some police with orders for the jailer to let Paul and Silas go. 36The jailer told Paul, "The officials have ordered me to set you free. Now you can leave in peace."

37But Paul told the police, "We are Roman citizens,*h* and the Roman officials had us beaten in public without giving us a trial. They threw us into jail. Now do they think they can secretly send us away? No, they cannot! They will have to come here themselves and let us out."

38When the police told the officials that Paul and Silas were Roman citizens, the officials were afraid. 39So they came and apologized. They led them out of the jail and asked them to please leave town. 40But Paul and Silas went straight to the home of Lydia, where they saw the Lord's followers and encouraged them. Then they left.

Trouble in Thessalonica

17 After Paul and his friends had traveled through Amphipolis and Apollonia, they went on to Thessalonica. A Jewish meeting place was in that city. 2So as usual, Paul went there to worship, and on three Sabbaths he spoke to the people. He used the Scriptures 3to show them that the Messiah had to suffer, but that he would rise from death. Paul also told them that Jesus is the Messiah he was preaching about. 4Some of the Jews believed

what Paul had said, and they became followers with Paul and Silas. Some Gentiles*i* and many important women also believed the message.

5The Jewish leaders were jealous and got some worthless bums who hung around the marketplace to start a riot in the city. They wanted to drag Paul and Silas out to the mob, and so they went straight to Jason's home. 6But when they did not find them there, they dragged out Jason and some of the Lord's followers. They took them to the city authorities and shouted, "Paul and Silas have been upsetting things everywhere. Now they have come here, 7and Jason has welcomed them into his home. All of them break the laws of the Roman Emperor by claiming that someone named Jesus is king."

8The officials and all the people were upset when they heard this. 9So they made Jason and the other followers pay bail before they would let them go.

People in Berea Welcome the Message

10That same night the Lord's followers sent Paul and Silas on to Berea, and after they arrived, they went to the Jewish meeting place. 11The people in Berea were much nicer than those in Thessalonica, and they gladly accepted the message. Day after day they studied the Scriptures to see if these things were true. 12Many of them put their faith in the Lord, including some important Greek women and several men.

13When the Jewish leaders in Thessalonica heard that Paul had been

---

h Roman citizens: Only a small number of the people living in the Roman Empire were citizens, and they had special rights and privileges. *i Gentiles*: See the note at 14.1.

preaching God's message in Berea, they went there and caused trouble by turning the crowds against Paul.

14Right away the followers sent Paul down to the coast, but Silas and Timothy stayed in Thessalonica. **15**Some men went with Paul as far as Athens. They returned with instructions for Silas and Timothy to join him as soon as possible.

Paul in Athens

16While Paul was waiting in Athens, he was upset to see all the idols in the city. **17**He went to the Jewish meeting place to speak to the Jews and to anyone who worshiped with them. Day after day he also spoke to everyone he met in the market. **18**Some of them were Epicureans*j* and some were Stoics,*k* and they started arguing with him.

People were asking, "What is this know-it-all trying to say?"

Some even said, "Paul must be preaching about foreign gods! That's what he means when he talks about Jesus and about people rising from death."*l*

19They brought Paul before a council called the Areopagus, and said, "Tell us what your new teaching is all about. **20**We have heard you say some strange things, and we want to know what it means."

21More than anything else the people of Athens and the foreigners living there loved to hear and to talk about anything new. **22**So Paul stood up in front of the council and said:

People of Athens, I see that you are very religious. **23**As I was going through your city and looking at the things you worship, I found an altar with the words, "To an Unknown God." You worship this God, but you don't really know him. So I want to tell you about him. **24**This God made the world and everything in it. He is Lord of heaven and earth, and he doesn't live in temples built by human hands. **25**He doesn't need help from anyone. He gives life, breath, and everything else to all people. **26**From one person God made all nations who live on earth, and he decided when and where every nation would be.

27God has done all this, so that we will look for him and reach out and find him. He is not far from any of us, **28**and he gives us the power to live, to move, and to be who we are. "We are his children," just as some of your poets have said.

29Since we are God's children, we must not think that he is like an idol made out of gold or silver or stone. He is not like anything that humans have thought up and made. **30**In the past God forgave all this because people did not know what they were doing. But now he says that everyone everywhere must turn to him. **31**He has set a day when he will judge all the world's people with fairness. And he has chosen the man Jesus to do the judging for him.

---

jEpicureans: People who followed the teaching of a man named Epicurus, who taught that happiness should be the main goal in life. *kStoics*: Followers of a man named Zeno, who taught that people should learn self-control and be guided by their consciences. *lpeople rising from death*: Or "a goddess named 'Rising from Death.' "

God has given proof of this to all of us by raising Jesus from death.

32As soon as the people heard Paul say that a man had been raised from death, some of them started laughing. Others said, "We'll hear you talk about this some other time." **33**When Paul left the council meeting, **34**some of the men put their faith in the Lord and went with Paul. One of them was a council member named Dionysius. A woman named Damaris and several others also put their faith in the Lord.

Paul in Corinth

18 Paul left Athens and went to Corinth, **2**where he met Aquila, a Jewish man from Pontus. Not long before this, Aquila had come from Italy with his wife Priscilla, because Emperor Claudius had ordered all the Jewish people to leave Rome.*ᵐ* Paul went to see Aquila and Priscilla **3**and found out that they were tent makers. Paul was a tent maker too. So he stayed with them, and they worked together.

4Every Sabbath Paul went to the Jewish meeting place. He spoke to Jews and Gentiles*ⁿ* and tried to win them over. **5**But after Silas and Timothy came from Macedonia, he spent all his time preaching to the Jews about Jesus the Messiah. **6**Finally, they turned against him and insulted him. So he shook the dust from his clothes*ᵒ* and told them, "Whatever happens to you will be your own fault! I am not to blame. From now on I am going to preach to the Gentiles."

7Paul then moved into the house of a man named Titius Justus, who worshiped God and lived next door to the Jewish meeting place. **8**Crispus was the leader of the meeting place. He and everyone in his family put their faith in the Lord. Many others in Corinth also heard the message, and all the people who had faith in the Lord were baptized.

9One night Paul had a vision, and in it the Lord said, "Don't be afraid to keep on preaching. Don't stop! **10**I am with you, and you won't be harmed. Many people in this city belong to me." **11**Paul stayed on in Corinth for a year and a half, teaching God's message to the people.

12While Gallio was governor of Achaia, some of the Jewish leaders got together and grabbed Paul. They brought him into court **13**and said, "This man is trying to make our people worship God in a way that is against our Law!"

14Even before Paul could speak, Gallio said, "If you were charging this man with a crime or some other wrong, I would have to listen to you. **15**But since this concerns only words, names, and your own law, you will have to take care of it. I refuse to judge such matters." **16**Then he sent them all out of the court. **17**The crowd grabbed Sosthenes, the Jewish leader, and beat him up in front of the court. But none of this mattered to Gallio.

Paul Returns to Antioch in Syria

18After Paul had stayed for a while with the Lord's followers in Corinth,

---

ᵐEmperor Claudius had ordered all the Jewish people to leave Rome: Probably A.D. 49, though it may have been A.D. 41.   *ⁿGentiles*: Here the word is "Greeks." But see the note at 14.1.
ᵒshook the dust from his clothes: This means the same as shaking dust from the feet. See the note at 13.51.

he told them good-by and sailed on to Syria with Aquila and Priscilla. But before he left, he had his head shaved[p] at Cenchreae because he had made a promise to God.

19The three of them arrived in Ephesus, where Paul left Priscilla and Aquila. He then went into the Jewish meeting place to talk with the people there. 20They asked him to stay longer, but he refused. 21He told them good-by and said, "If God lets me, I will come back."

22Paul sailed to Caesarea, where he greeted the church. Then he went on to Antioch. 23After staying there for a while, he left and visited several places in Galatia and Phrygia. He helped all the followers there to become stronger in their faith.

Apollos in Ephesus

24A Jewish man named Apollos came to Ephesus. Apollos had been born in the city of Alexandria. He was a very good speaker and knew a lot about the Scriptures. 25He also knew much about the Lord's Way,[q] and he spoke about it with great excitement. What he taught about Jesus was right, but all he knew was John's message about baptism.

26Apollos started speaking bravely in the Jewish meeting place. But when Priscilla and Aquila heard him, they took him to their home and helped him understand God's Way even better.

27Apollos decided to travel through Achaia. So the Lord's followers wrote letters and encouraged the followers there to welcome him. After Apollos arrived in Achaia, he was a great help to everyone who had put their faith in the Lord Jesus because of God's kindness. 28He got into fierce arguments with the Jewish people, and in public he used the Scriptures to prove that Jesus is the Messiah.

Paul in Ephesus

19 While Apollos was in Corinth, Paul traveled across the hill country to Ephesus, where he met some of the Lord's followers. 2He asked them, "When you put your faith in Jesus, were you given the Holy Spirit?"

"No!" they answered. "We have never even heard of the Holy Spirit."

3"Then why were you baptized?" Paul asked.

They answered, "Because of what John taught."[r]

4Paul replied, "John baptized people so that they would turn to God. But he also told them that someone else was coming, and that they should put their faith in him. Jesus is the one that John was talking about." 5After the people heard Paul say this, they were baptized in the name of the Lord Jesus. 6Then Paul placed his hands on them. The Holy Spirit was given to them, and they spoke unknown languages and prophesied. 7There were about twelve men in this group.

8For three months Paul went to the Jewish meeting place and talked bravely with the Jewish people about

---

[p]he had his head shaved: Paul had promised to be a "Nazarite" for a while. This meant that for the time of the promise, he could not cut his hair or drink wine. When the time was over, he would have to cut his hair and offer a sacrifice to God. [q]the Lord's Way: See the note at 9.2. [r]Then why were you baptized? . . . Because of what John taught: Or "In whose name were you baptized? . . . We were baptized in John's name."

God's kingdom. He tried to win them over, 9but some of them were stubborn and refused to believe. In front of everyone they said terrible things about God's Way. Paul left and took the followers with him to the lecture hall of Tyrannus. He spoke there every day 10for two years, until every Jew and Gentile[s] in Asia had heard the Lord's message.

The Sons of Sceva

11God gave Paul the power to work great miracles. 12People even took handkerchiefs and aprons that had touched Paul's body, and they carried them to everyone who was sick. All of the sick people were healed, and the evil spirits went out.

13Some Jewish men started going around trying to force out evil spirits by using the name of the Lord Jesus. They said to the spirits, "Come out in the name of that same Jesus that Paul preaches about!"

14Seven sons of a Jewish high priest named Sceva were doing this, 15when an evil spirit said to them, "I know Jesus! And I have heard about Paul. But who are you?" 16Then the man with the evil spirit jumped on them and beat them up. They ran out of the house, naked and bruised.

17All the Jews and Gentiles[s] in Ephesus heard about this. They were so frightened that they praised the name of the Lord Jesus. 18Many who were followers now started telling everyone about the evil things they had been doing. 19Some who had been practicing witchcraft even brought their books and burned them in public. These books were worth about fifty thousand silver coins. 20So the Lord's message spread and became even more powerful.

The Riot in Ephesus

21After all of this had happened, Paul decided[t] to visit Macedonia and Achaia on his way to Jerusalem. Paul had said, "From there I will go on to Rome." 22So he sent his two helpers, Timothy and Erastus, to Macedonia. But he stayed on in Asia for a while.

23At that time there was serious trouble because of the Lord's Way.[u] 24A silversmith named Demetrius had a business that made silver models of the temple of the goddess Artemis. Those who worked for him earned a lot of money. 25Demetrius brought together everyone who was in the same business and said:

Friends, you know that we make a good living at this. 26But you have surely seen and heard how this man Paul is upsetting a lot of people, not only in Ephesus, but almost everywhere in Asia. He claims that the gods we humans make are not really gods at all. 27Everyone will start saying terrible things about our business. They will stop respecting the temple of the goddess Artemis, who is worshiped in Asia and all over the world. Our great goddess will be forgotten!

28When the workers heard this, they got angry and started shouting, "Great is Artemis, the goddess of the

---

[s]*Gentile(s)*: The text has "Greek(s)" (see the note at 14.1).   [t]*Paul decided*: Or "Paul was led by the Holy Spirit."   [u]*the Lord's Way*: See the note at 9.2.

Ephesians!" 29Soon the whole city was in a riot, and some men grabbed Gaius and Aristarchus, who had come from Macedonia with Paul. Then everyone in the crowd rushed to the place where the town meetings were held.

30Paul wanted to go out and speak to the people, but the Lord's followers would not let him. 31A few of the local officials were friendly to Paul, and they sent someone to warn him not to go.

32Some of the people in the meeting were shouting one thing, and others were shouting something else. Everyone was completely confused, and most of them did not even know why they were there.

33Several of the Jewish leaders pushed a man named Alexander to the front of the crowd and started telling him what to say. He motioned with his hand and tried to explain what was going on. 34But when the crowd saw that he was Jewish, they all shouted for two hours, "Great is Artemis, the goddess of the Ephesians!"

35Finally, a town official made the crowd be quiet. Then he said:

People of Ephesus, who in the world does not know that our city is the center for worshiping the great goddess Artemis? Who does not know that her image which fell from heaven is right here? 36No one can deny this, and so you should calm down and not do anything foolish. 37You have brought men in here who have not robbed temples or spoken against our goddess.

38If Demetrius and his workers have a case against these men, we have courts and judges.

Let them take their complaints there. 39But if you want to do more than that, the matter will have to be brought before the city council. 40We could easily be accused of starting a riot today. There is no excuse for it! We cannot even give a reason for this uproar.

41After saying this, he told the people to leave.

Paul Goes through Macedonia and Greece

20 When the riot was over, Paul sent for the followers and encouraged them. He then told them good-by and left for Macedonia. 2As he traveled from place to place, he encouraged the followers with many messages. Finally, he went to Greece*ᵘ* 3and stayed there for three months.

Paul was about to sail to Syria. But some of the Jewish leaders plotted against him, so he decided to return by way of Macedonia. 4With him were Sopater, son of Pyrrhus from Berea, and Aristarchus and Secundus from Thessalonica. Gaius from Derbe was also with him, and so were Timothy and the two Asians, Tychicus and Trophimus. 5They went on ahead to Troas and waited for us there. 6After the Feast of Thin Bread, we sailed from Philippi. Five days later we met them in Troas and stayed there for a week.

Paul's Last Visit to Troas

7On the first day of the week*ʷ* we met to worship and to break bread to-

---

ᵘGreece: Probably Corinth. *ᵛOn the first day of the week*: Since the Jewish day began at sunset, the meeting would have begun in the evening.

gether.[x] Paul spoke to the people until midnight because he was leaving the next morning. [8]In the upstairs room where we were meeting, there were a lot of lamps. [9]A young man by the name of Eutychus was sitting on a window sill. While Paul was speaking, the young man got very sleepy. Finally, he went to sleep and fell three floors all the way down to the ground. When they picked him up, he was dead.

[10]Paul went down and bent over Eutychus. He took him in his arms and said, "Don't worry! He's alive." [11]After Paul had gone back upstairs, he broke bread, and ate with us. He then spoke until dawn and left. [12]Then the followers took the young man home alive and were very happy.

The Voyage from Troas to Miletus

[13]Paul decided to travel by land to Assos. The rest of us went on ahead by ship, and we were to take him aboard there. [14]When he met us in Assos, he came aboard, and we sailed on to Mitylene. [15]The next day we came to a place near Chios, and the following day we reached Samos. The day after that we sailed to Miletus. [16]Paul had decided to sail on past Ephesus, because he did not want to spend too much time in Asia. He was in a hurry and wanted to be in Jerusalem in time for Pentecost.[y]

Paul Says Good-by to the Church Leaders of Ephesus

[17]From Miletus Paul sent a message for the church leaders at Ephesus to come and meet with him. [18]When they got there, he said:

You know everything I did during the time I was with you when I first came to Asia. [19]Some of the Jews plotted against me and caused me a lot of sorrow and trouble. But I served the Lord and was humble. [20]When I preached in public or taught in your homes, I didn't hold back from telling anything that would help you. [21]I told Jews and Gentiles to turn to God and have faith in our Lord Jesus.

[22]I don't know what will happen to me in Jerusalem, but I must obey God's Spirit and go there. [23]In every city that I visit, the Holy Spirit tells me I will be put in jail and will be in trouble in Jerusalem. [24]But I don't care what happens to me, as long as I finish the work that the Lord Jesus gave me to do. And that work is to tell the good news about God's great kindness.

[25]I have gone from place to place, preaching to you about God's kingdom, but now I know that none of you will ever see me again. [26]I tell you today that I am no longer responsible for any of you! [27]I have told you everything that God wants you to know. [28]Look after yourselves and everyone the Holy Spirit has placed in your care. Be like shepherds to God's church. It is the flock that he bought with the blood of his own Son.[z] [29]I know that after I am gone,

---

[x]*break bread together*: See the note at 2.42. [y]*in time for Pentecost*: The Jewish people liked to be in Jerusalem for this festival. See the note at 2.1. [z]*the blood of his own Son*: Or "his own blood."

others will come like fierce wolves to attack you. 30Some of your own people will tell lies to win over the Lord's followers. 31Be on your guard! Remember how day and night for three years I kept warning you with tears in my eyes.

32I now place you in God's care. Remember the message about his great kindness! This message can help you and give you what belongs to you as God's people. 33I have never wanted anyone's money or clothes. 34You know how I have worked with my own hands to make a living for myself and my friends. 35By everything I did, I showed how you should work to help everyone who is weak. Remember that our Lord Jesus said, "More blessings come from giving than from receiving."

36After Paul had finished speaking, he kneeled down with all of them and prayed. 37Everyone cried and hugged and kissed him. 38They were especially sad because Paul had told them, "You will never see me again."

Then they went with him to the ship.

Paul Goes to Jerusalem

21 After saying good-by, we sailed straight to Cos. The next day we reached Rhodes and from there sailed on to Patara. 2We found a ship going to Phoenicia, so we got on board and sailed off.

3We came within sight of Cyprus and then sailed south of it on to the port of Tyre in Syria. The ship was going to unload its cargo there. 4We looked up the Lord's followers and stayed with them for a week. The Holy Spirit had told them to warn Paul not to go on to Jerusalem. 5But when the week was over, we started on our way again. All the men, together with their wives and children, walked with us from the town to the seashore. We kneeled on the beach and prayed. 6Then after saying good-by to each other, we got into the ship, and they went back home.

7We sailed from Tyre to Ptolemais, where we greeted the followers and stayed with them for a day. 8The next day we went to Caesarea and stayed with Philip, the preacher. He was one of the seven men who helped the apostles, 9and he had four unmarried[a] daughters who prophesied.

10We had been in Caesarea for several days, when the prophet Agabus came to us from Judea. 11He took Paul's belt, and with it he tied up his own hands and feet. Then he told us, "The Holy Spirit says that some of the Jewish leaders in Jerusalem will tie up the man who owns this belt. They will also hand him over to the Gentiles." 12After Agabus said this, we and the followers living there begged Paul not to go to Jerusalem.

13But Paul answered, "Why are you crying and breaking my heart? I am not only willing to be put in jail for the Lord Jesus. I am even willing to die for him in Jerusalem!"

14Since we could not get Paul to change his mind, we gave up and said, "Lord, please make us willing to do what you want."

15Then we got ready to go to Jerusalem. 16Some of the followers from

_____
[a]unmarried: Or "virgin."

Caesarea went with us and took us to
stay in the home of Mnason. He was
from Cyprus and had been a follower
from the beginning.

Paul Visits James

17When we arrived in Jerusalem,
the Lord's followers gladly welcomed
us. 18Paul went with us to see James[b]
the next day, and all the church leaders
were present. 19Paul greeted them and
told how God had used him to help the
Gentiles. 20Everyone who heard this
praised God and said to Paul:

My friend, you can see how
many tens of thousands of the
Jewish people have become followers! And all of them are eager
to obey the Law of Moses. 21But
they have been told that you are
teaching those who live among
the Gentiles to disobey this Law.
They claim that you are telling
them not to circumcise their sons
or to follow Jewish customs.

22What should we do now that
our people have heard that you
are here? 23Please do what we
ask, because four of our men have
made special promises to God.
24Join with them and prepare
yourself for the ceremony that
goes with the promises. Pay the
cost for their heads to be shaved.
Then everyone will learn that the
reports about you are not true.
They will know that you do obey
the Law of Moses.

25Some while ago we told the
Gentile followers what we think
they should do. We instructed
them not to eat anything offered
to idols. They were told not to eat

any meat with blood still in it or
the meat of an animal that has
been strangled. They were also
told not to commit any terrible
sexual sins.[c]

26The next day Paul took the four
men with him and got himself ready
at the same time they did. Then he
went into the temple and told when
the final ceremony would take place
and when an offering would be made
for each of them.

Paul Is Arrested

27When the period of seven days
for the ceremony was almost over,
some of the Jewish people from Asia
saw Paul in the temple. They got a
large crowd together and started attacking him. 28They were shouting,
"Friends, help us! This man goes
around everywhere, saying bad things
about our nation and about the Law
of Moses and about this temple. He has
even brought shame to this holy temple by bringing in Gentiles." 29Some
of them thought that Paul had brought
Trophimus from Ephesus into the temple, because they had seen them together in the city.

30The whole city was in an uproar,
and the people turned into a mob. They
grabbed Paul and dragged him out of
the temple. Then suddenly the doors
were shut. 31The people were about to
kill Paul when the Roman army commander heard that all Jerusalem was
starting to riot. 32So he quickly took
some soldiers and officers and ran to
where the crowd had gathered.

As soon as the mob saw the commander and soldiers, they stopped
beating Paul. 33The army commander

---

[a]James: The Lord's brother. [b]not to commit any terrible sexual sins: See the note at 15.20.

went over and arrested him and had him bound with two chains. Then he tried to find out who Paul was and what he had done. 34Part of the crowd shouted one thing, and part of them shouted something else. But they were making so much noise that the commander could not find out a thing. Then he ordered Paul to be taken into the fortress. 35As they reached the steps, the crowd became so wild that the soldiers had to lift Paul up and carry him. 36The crowd followed and kept shouting, "Kill him! Kill him!"

Paul Speaks to the Crowd

37When Paul was about to be taken into the fortress, he asked the commander, "Can I say something to you?"

"How do you know Greek?" the commander asked. 38"Aren't you that Egyptian who started a riot not long ago and led four thousand terrorists into the desert?"

39"No!" Paul replied. "I am a Jew from Tarsus, an important city in Cilicia. Please let me speak to the crowd."

40The commander told him he could speak, so Paul stood on the steps and motioned to the people. When they were quiet, he spoke to them in Aramaic:

22 "My friends and leaders of our nation, listen as I explain what happened!" 2When the crowd heard Paul speak to them in Aramaic, they became even quieter. Then Paul said:

3I am a Jew, born and raised in the city of Tarsus in Cilicia. I was a student of Gamaliel and was taught to follow every single law of our ancestors. In fact, I was just as eager to obey God as any of you are today.

4I made trouble for everyone who followed the Lord's Way,*d* and I even had some of them killed. I had others arrested and put in jail. I didn't care if they were men or women. 5The high priest and all the council members can tell you that this is true. They even gave me letters to the Jewish leaders in Damascus, so that I could arrest people there and bring them to Jerusalem to be punished.

6One day about noon I was getting close to Damascus, when a bright light from heaven suddenly flashed around. 7I fell to the ground and heard a voice asking me, "Saul, Saul, why are you so cruel to me?"

8"Who are you?" I answered.

The Lord replied, "I am Jesus from Nazareth! I am the one you are so cruel to." 9The men who were traveling with me saw the light, but did not hear the voice.

10I asked, "Lord, what do you want me to do?"

Then he told me, "Get up and go to Damascus. When you get there, you will be told what to do." 11The light had been so bright that I couldn't see. And the other men had to lead me by the hand to Damascus.

12In that city there was a man named Ananias, who faithfully obeyed the Law of Moses and was well liked by all the Jewish people living there. 13He came to me and said, "Saul, my friend, you can now see again!"

dfollowed the Lord's Way: See the note at 9.2.

At once I could see. 14Then Ananias told me, "The God that our ancestors worshiped has chosen you to know what he wants done. He has chosen you to see the One Who Obeys God *e* and to hear his voice. 15You must tell everyone what you have seen and heard. 16What are you waiting for? Get up! Be baptized, and wash away your sins by praying to the Lord."

17After this I returned to Jerusalem and went to the temple to pray. There I had a vision 18of the Lord who said to me, "Hurry and leave Jerusalem! The people will not listen to what you say about me."

19I replied, "Lord, they know that in many of our meeting places I arrested and beat people who had faith in you. 20Stephen was killed because he spoke for you, and I stood there and cheered them on. I even guarded the clothes of the men who murdered him."

21But the Lord told me to go, and he promised to send me far away to the Gentiles.

22The crowd listened until Paul said this. Then they started shouting, "Get rid of this man! He doesn't deserve to live." 23They kept shouting. They waved their clothes around and threw dust into the air.

Paul and the Roman Army Commander

24The Roman commander ordered Paul to be taken into the fortress and beaten with a whip. He did this to find out why the people were screaming at Paul.

25While the soldiers were tying Paul up to be beaten, he asked the officer standing there, "Is it legal to beat a Roman citizen before he has been tried in court?"

26When the officer heard this, he went to the commander and said, "What are you doing? This man is a Roman citizen!"

27The commander went to Paul and asked, "Tell me, are you a Roman citizen?"

"Yes," Paul answered.

28The commander then said, "I paid a lot of money to become a Roman citizen."*f*

But Paul replied, "I was born a Roman citizen."

29The men who were about to beat and question Paul quickly backed off. And the commander himself was frightened when he realized that he had put a Roman citizen in chains.

Paul Is Tried by the Council

30The next day the commander wanted to know the real reason why the Jewish leaders had brought charges against Paul. So he had Paul's chains removed, and he ordered the chief priests and the whole council to meet. Then he had Paul led in and made him stand in front of them.

23 Paul looked straight at the council members and said, "My friends, to this day I have served God with a clear conscience!"

2Then Ananias the high priest ordered the men standing beside Paul to hit him on the mouth. 3Paul turned

---

*d*One Who Obeys God: That is, Jesus.   *e*Roman citizen: See the note at 16.37.

to the high priest and said, "You white-washed wall!*g* God will hit you. You sit there to judge me by the Law of Moses. But at the same time you order men to break the Law by hitting me."

4The men standing beside Paul asked, "Don't you know you are insulting God's high priest?"

5Paul replied, "Oh! I didn't know he was the high priest. The Scriptures do tell us not to speak evil about a leader of our people."

6When Paul saw that some of the council members were Sadducees and others were Pharisees, he shouted, "My friends, I am a Pharisee and the son of a Pharisee. I am on trial simply because I believe that the dead will be raised to life."

7As soon as Paul said this, the Pharisees and the Sadducees got into a big argument, and the council members started taking sides. 8The Sadducees do not believe in angels or spirits or that the dead will rise to life. But the Pharisees believe in all of these, 9and so there was a lot of shouting. Some of the teachers of the Law of Moses were Pharisees. Finally, they became angry and said, "We don't find anything wrong with this man. Maybe a spirit or an angel really did speak to him."

10The argument became fierce, and the commander was afraid that Paul would be pulled apart. So he ordered the soldiers to go in and rescue Paul. Then they took him back into the fortress.

11That night the Lord stood beside Paul and said, "Don't worry! Just as you have told others about me in Jeru-salem, you must also tell about me in Rome."

A Plot to Kill Paul

12-13The next morning more than forty Jewish men got together and vowed that they would not eat or drink anything until they had killed Paul. 14Then some of them went to the chief priests and the nation's leaders and said, "We have promised God that we would not eat a thing until we have killed Paul. 15You and everyone in the council must go to the commander and pretend that you want to find out more about the charges against Paul. Ask for him to be brought before your court. Meanwhile, we will be waiting to kill him before he gets there."

16When Paul's nephew heard about the plot, he went to the fortress and told Paul about it. 17So Paul said to one of the army officers, "Take this young man to the commander. He has something to tell him."

18The officer took the young man to the commander and said, "The prisoner named Paul asked me to bring this young man to you, because he has something to tell you."

19The commander took the young man aside and asked him in private, "What do you want to tell me?"

20He answered, "Some men are planning to ask you to bring Paul down to the Jewish council tomorrow. They will claim that they want to find out more about him. 21But please don't do what they say. More than forty men are going to attack Paul. They have made a vow not to eat or drink anything until they have killed him. Even now

gwhitewashed wall: Someone who pretends to be good, but really isn't.

they are waiting to hear what you decide."

²²The commander sent the young man away after saying to him, "Don't let anyone know that you told me this."

Paul Is Sent to Felix the Governor

²³The commander called in two of his officers and told them, "By nine o'clock tonight have two hundred soldiers ready to go to Caesarea. Take along seventy men on horseback and two hundred foot soldiers with spears. ²⁴Get a horse ready for Paul and make sure that he gets safely through to Felix the governor."

²⁵The commander wrote a letter that said:

²⁶Greetings from Claudius Lysias to the Honorable Governor Felix:

²⁷Some Jews grabbed this man and were about to kill him. But when I found out that he was a Roman citizen, I took some soldiers and rescued him.

²⁸I wanted to find out what they had against him. So I brought him before their council ²⁹and learned that the charges concern only their Jewish laws. This man is not guilty of anything for which he should die or even be put in jail.

³⁰As soon as I learned that there was a plot against him, I sent him to you and told their leaders to bring charges against him in your court.

³¹The soldiers obeyed the commander's orders, and that same night they took Paul to the city of Antipatris. ³²The next day the foot soldiers returned to the fortress and let the soldiers on horseback take him the rest of the way. ³³When they came to Caesarea, they gave the letter to the governor and handed Paul over to him.

³⁴The governor read the letter. Then he asked Paul and found out that he was from Cilicia. ³⁵The governor said, "I will listen to your case as soon as the people come to bring their charges against you." After saying this, he gave orders for Paul to be kept as a prisoner in Herod's palace.[h]

Paul Is Accused in the Court of Felix

24 Five days later Ananias the high priest, together with the Jewish leaders and a lawyer named Tertullus, went to the governor to present their case against Paul. ²So Paul was called in, and Tertullus stated the case against him:[i]

Honorable Felix, you have brought our people a long period of peace, and because of your concern our nation is much better off. ³All of us are always grateful for what you have done. ⁴I don't want to bother you, but please be patient with us and listen to me for just a few minutes.

⁵This man has been found to be a real pest and troublemaker for Jews all over the world. He is also a leader of a group called Nazarenes. ⁶⁻⁸When he tried to disgrace the temple, we arrested

---

[h]Herod's palace: The palace built by Herod the Great and used by the Roman governors of Palestine. [i]Paul was called in, and Tertullus stated the case against him: Or "Tertullus was called in and stated the case against Paul."

him.[j] If you question him, you will find out for yourself that all our charges are true.

9The Jewish crowd spoke up and agreed with what Tertullus had said.

Paul Defends Himself

10The governor motioned for Paul to speak, and he began:

I know that you have judged the people of our nation for many years, and I am glad to defend myself in your court.

11It was no more than twelve days ago that I went to worship in Jerusalem. You can find this out easily enough. 12Never once did the Jews find me arguing with anyone in the temple. I didn't cause trouble in the Jewish meeting places or in the city itself. 13There is no way that they can prove these charges that they are now bringing against me.

14I admit that the Jewish leaders think that the Lord's Way[k] which I follow is based on wrong beliefs. But I still worship the same God that my ancestors worshiped. And I believe everything written in the Law of Moses and in the Prophets.[l] 15I am just as sure as these people are that God will raise from death everyone who is good or evil. 16And because I am sure, I try my best to have a clear conscience in whatever I do for God or for people.

17After being away for several years, I returned here to bring gifts for the poor people of my nation and to offer sacrifices. 18This is what I was doing when I was found going through a ceremony in the temple. I was not with a crowd, and there was no uproar. 19Some Jews from Asia were there at that time, and if they have anything to say against me, they should be here now. 20Or ask the ones who are here. They can tell you that they didn't find me guilty of anything when I was tried by their own council. 21The only charge they can bring against me is what I shouted out in court, when I said, "I am on trial today because I believe that the dead will be raised to life!"

22Felix knew a lot about the Lord's Way.[m] But he brought the trial to an end and said, "I will make my decision after Lysias the commander arrives." 23He then ordered the army officer to keep Paul under guard, but not to lock him up or to stop his friends from helping him.

Paul Is Kept under Guard

24Several days later Felix and his wife Drusilla, who was Jewish, went to the place where Paul was kept under guard. They sent for Paul and listened while he spoke to them about having faith in Christ Jesus. 25But Felix was frightened when Paul started talking to them about doing right, about self-

---

[i]*we arrested him*: Some manuscripts add, "We wanted to judge him by our own laws. But Lysias the commander took him away from us by force. Then Lysias ordered us to bring our charges against this man in your court." [j]*the Lord's Way*: See the note at 9.2. [k]*Law of Moses . . . the Prophets*: The Jewish Scriptures, that is, the Old Testament. [l]*the Lord's Way*: See the note at 9.2.

control, and about the coming judgment. So he said to Paul, "That's enough for now. You may go. But when I have time I will send for you." 26After this, Felix often sent for Paul and talked with him, because he hoped that Paul would offer him a bribe.

27Two years later Porcius Festus became governor in place of Felix. But since Felix wanted to do the Jewish leaders a favor, he kept Paul in jail.

Paul Asks To Be Tried by the Roman Emperor

25 Three days after Festus had become governor, he went from Caesarea to Jerusalem. 2There the chief priests and the Jewish leaders told him about their charges against Paul. They also asked Festus 3if he would be willing to bring Paul to Jerusalem. They begged him to do this because they were planning to attack and kill Paul on the way. 4But Festus told them, "Paul will be kept in Caesarea, and I am soon going there myself. 5If he has done anything wrong, let your leaders go with me and bring charges against him there."

6Festus stayed in Jerusalem for eight or ten more days before going to Caesarea. Then the next day he took his place as judge and had Paul brought into court. 7As soon as Paul came in, the Jewish leaders from Jerusalem crowded around him and said he was guilty of many serious crimes. But they could not prove anything. 8Then Paul spoke in his own defense, "I have not broken the Law of my people. And I have not done anything against either the temple or the Emperor."

9Festus wanted to please the Jewish leaders. So he asked Paul, "Are you willing to go to Jerusalem and be tried by me on these charges?"

10Paul replied, "I am on trial in the Emperor's court, and that's where I should be tried. You know very well that I have not done anything to harm the Jewish nation. 11If I had done something deserving death, I would not ask to escape the death penalty. But I am not guilty of any of these crimes, and no one has the right to hand me over to these Jews. I now ask to be tried by the Emperor himself."

12After Festus had talked this over with members of his council, he told Paul, "You have asked to be tried by the Emperor, and to the Emperor you will go!"

Paul Speaks to Agrippa and Bernice

13A few days later King Agrippa and Bernice came to Caesarea to visit Festus. 14They had been there for several days, when Festus told the king about the charges against Paul. He said:

Felix left a man here in jail, 15and when I went to Jerusalem, the chief priests and the Jewish leaders came and asked me to find him guilty. 16I told them that it is not the Roman custom to hand a man over to people who are bringing charges against him. He must first have the chance to meet them face to face and to defend himself against their charges.

17So when they came here with me, I wasted no time. On the very next day I took my place on the judge's bench and ordered him to be brought in. 18But when the men stood up to make their charges against him, they did not accuse him of any of the crimes that I thought they would. 19Instead, they argued with him about some of their Jewish beliefs and about a dead man named Jesus, who Paul said was alive.

20Since I did not know how to find out the truth about all this, I asked Paul if he would be willing to go to Jerusalem and be put on trial there. 21But Paul asked to be kept in jail until the Emperor could decide his case. So I ordered him to be kept here until I could send him to the Emperor.

22Then Agrippa said to Festus, "I would also like to hear what this man has to say."

Festus answered, "You can hear him tomorrow."

23The next day Agrippa and Bernice made a big show as they came into the meeting room. High ranking army officers and leading citizens of the town were also there. Festus then ordered Paul to be brought in 24and said:

King Agrippa and other guests, look at this man! Every Jew from Jerusalem and Caesarea has come to me, demanding for him to be put to death. 25I have not found him guilty of any crime deserving death. But because he has asked to be judged by the Emperor, I have decided to send him to Rome.

26I have to write some facts about this man to the Emperor. So I have brought him before all of you, but especially before you, King Agrippa. After we have talked about his case, I will then have something to write. 27It makes no sense to send a prisoner to the Emperor without stating the charges against him.

Paul's Defense before Agrippa

26 Agrippa told Paul, "You may now speak for yourself."

Paul stretched out his hand and said:

2King Agrippa, I am glad for this chance to defend myself before you today on all these charges that my own people have brought against me. 3You know a lot about our Jewish customs and the beliefs that divide us. So I ask you to listen patiently to me.

4-5All the Jews have known me since I was a child. They know what kind of life I have lived in my own country and in Jerusalem. If they were willing, they could tell you that I was a Pharisee, a member of a group that is more strict than any other. 6Now I am on trial because I believe the promise that God made to our people long ago.

7Day and night our twelve tribes have earnestly served God, waiting for his promised blessings. King Agrippa, because of this hope, the Jewish leaders have brought charges against me. 8Why should any of you doubt that God raises the dead to life?

9I once thought that I should do everything I could to oppose Jesus from Nazareth. 10I did this first in Jerusalem, and with the authority of the chief priests I put many of God's people in jail. I even voted for them to be killed. 11I often had them punished in our meeting places, and I tried to make them give up their faith. In fact, I was so angry with them, that I went looking for them in foreign cities.

12King Agrippa, one day I was on my way to Damascus with the authority and permission of the chief priests. 13About noon I saw a light brighter than the sun. It flashed from heaven on me and on everyone traveling with me. 14We all fell to the ground. Then I heard a voice say to me in Aramaic, "Saul, Saul, why are you so cruel to me? It's foolish to fight against me!"

15"Who are you?" I asked.

Then the Lord answered, "I am Jesus! I am the one you are so cruel to. 16Now stand up. I have appeared to you, because I have chosen you to be my servant. You are to tell others what you have learned about me and what I will show you later."

17The Lord also said, "I will protect you from the Jews and from the Gentiles that I am sending you to. 18I want you to open their eyes, so that they will turn from darkness to light and from the power of Satan to God. Then their sins will be forgiven, and by faith in me they will become part of God's holy people."

19King Agrippa, I obeyed this vision from heaven. 20First I preached to the people in Damascus, and then I went to Jerusalem and all over Judea. Finally, I went to the Gentiles and said, "Stop sinning and turn to God! Then prove what you have done by the way you live."

21That is why the Jews grabbed me in the temple and tried to kill me. 22But all this time God has helped me, and I have preached both to the rich and to the poor. I have told them only what the prophets and Moses said would happen. 23I told them how the Messiah would suffer and be the first to be raised from death, so that he could bring light to his own people and to the Gentiles.

24Before Paul finished defending himself, Festus shouted, "Paul, you're crazy! Too much learning has driven you out of your mind."

25But Paul replied, "Honorable Festus, I am not crazy. What I am saying is true, and it makes sense. 26None of these things happened off in a corner somewhere. I am sure that King Agrippa knows what I am talking about. That's why I can speak so plainly to him."

27Then Paul said to Agrippa, "Do you believe what the prophets said? I know you do."

28Agrippa asked Paul, "In such a short time do you think you can talk me into being a Christian?"

29Paul answered, "Whether it takes a short time or a long time, I wish you and everyone else who hears me today would become just like me! Except, of course, for these chains."

30Then King Agrippa, Governor Festus, Bernice, and everyone who was with them got up. 31But before they left, they said, "This man is not guilty of anything. He doesn't deserve to die or to be put in jail."

32Agrippa told Festus, "Paul could have been set free, if he had not asked to be tried by the Roman Emperor."

Paul Is Taken to Rome

27 When it was time for us to sail to Rome, Captain Julius from the Emperor's special troops was put

in charge of Paul and the other prisoners. 2We went aboard a ship from Adramyttium that was about to sail to some ports along the coast of Asia. Aristarchus from Thessalonica in Macedonia sailed on the ship with us.

3The next day we came to shore at Sidon. Captain Julius was very kind to Paul. He even let him visit his friends, so they could give him whatever he needed. 4When we left Sidon, the winds were blowing against us, and we sailed close to the island of Cyprus to be safe from the wind. 5Then we sailed south of Cilicia and Pamphylia until we came to the port of Myra in Lycia. 6There the army captain found a ship from Alexandria that was going to Italy. So he ordered us to board that ship.

7We sailed along slowly for several days and had a hard time reaching Cnidus. The wind would not let us go any farther in that direction, so we sailed past Cape Salmone, where the island of Crete would protect us from the wind. 8We went slowly along the coast and finally reached a place called Fair Havens, not far from the town of Lasea.

9By now we had already lost a lot of time, and sailing was no longer safe. In fact, even the Day of Atonement[n] was past. 10Then Paul spoke to the crew of the ship, "Men, listen to me! If we sail now, our ship and its cargo will be badly damaged, and many lives will be lost." 11But Julius listened to the captain of the ship and its owner, rather than to Paul.

12The harbor at Fair Havens was not a good place to spend the winter. Because of this, almost everyone agreed that we should at least try to sail along the coast of Crete as far as Phoenix. It had a harbor that opened toward the southwest and northwest,[o] and we could spend the winter there.

The Storm at Sea

13When a gentle wind from the south started blowing, the men thought it was a good time to do what they had planned. So they pulled up the anchor, and we sailed along the coast of Crete. 14But soon a strong wind called "The Northeaster" blew against us from the island. 15The wind struck the ship, and we could not sail against it. So we let the wind carry the ship.

16We went along the island of Cauda on the side that was protected from the wind. We had a hard time holding the lifeboat in place, 17but finally we got it where it belonged. Then the sailors wrapped ropes around the ship to hold it together. They lowered the sail and let the ship drift along, because they were afraid it might hit the sandbanks in the gulf of Syrtis.

18The storm was so fierce that the next day they threw some of the ship's cargo overboard. 19Then on the third day, with their bare hands they threw overboard some of the ship's gear. 20For several days we could not see either the sun or the stars. A strong wind kept blowing, and we finally gave up all hope of being saved.

21Since none of us had eaten anything for a long time, Paul stood up and told the men:

---

[n]Day of Atonement: This Jewish festival took place near the end of September. The sailing season was dangerous after the middle of September, and it was stopped completely between the middle of November and the middle of March. [o]southwest and northwest: Or "northeast and southeast."

You should have listened to me! If you had stayed on in Crete, you would not have had this damage and loss. 22But now I beg you to cheer up, because you will be safe. Only the ship will be lost. 23I belong to God, and I worship him. Last night he sent an angel 24to tell me, "Paul, don't be afraid! You will stand trial before the Emperor. And because of you, God will save the lives of everyone on the ship." 25Cheer up! I am sure that God will do exactly what he promised. 26But we will first be shipwrecked on some island.

27For fourteen days and nights we had been blown around over the Mediterranean Sea. But about midnight the sailors realized that we were getting near land. 28They measured and found that the water was about one hundred and twenty feet deep. A little later they measured again and found it was only about ninety feet. 29The sailors were afraid that we might hit some rocks, and they let down four anchors from the back of the ship. Then they prayed for daylight.

30The sailors wanted to escape from the ship. So they lowered the lifeboat into the water, pretending that they were letting down an anchor from the front of the ship. 31But Paul said to Captain Julius and the soldiers, "If the sailors don't stay on the ship, you won't have any chance to save your lives." 32The soldiers then cut the ropes that held the lifeboat and let it fall into the sea.

33Just before daylight Paul begged the people to eat something. He told them, "For fourteen days you have been so worried that you haven't eaten a thing. 34I beg you to eat something. Your lives depend on it. Do this and not one of you will be hurt."

35After Paul had said this, he took a piece of bread and gave thanks to God. Then in front of everyone, he broke the bread and ate some. 36They all felt encouraged, and each of them ate something. 37There were 276 people on the ship, 38and after everyone had eaten, they threw the cargo of wheat into the sea to make the ship lighter.

The Shipwreck

39Morning came, and the ship's crew saw a coast that they did not recognize. But they did see a cove with a beach. So they decided to try to run the ship aground on the beach. 40They cut the anchors loose and let them sink into the sea. At the same time they untied the ropes that were holding the rudders. Next, they raised the sail at the front of the ship and let the wind carry the ship toward the beach. 41But it ran aground on a sandbank. The front of the ship stuck firmly in the sand, and the rear was being smashed by the force of the waves.

42The soldiers decided to kill the prisoners to keep them from swimming away and escaping. 43But Captain Julius wanted to save Paul's life, and he did not let the soldiers do what they had planned. Instead, he ordered everyone who could swim to dive into the water and head for shore. 44Then he told the others to hold on to planks of wood or parts of the ship. At last, everyone safely reached shore.

On the Island of Malta

28 When we came ashore, we learned that the island was

called Malta. 2The local people were very friendly, and they welcomed us by building a fire, because it was rainy and cold.

3After Paul had gathered some wood and had put it on the fire, the heat caused a snake to crawl out, and it bit him on the hand. 4When the local people saw the snake hanging from Paul's hand, they said to each other, "This man must be a murderer! He didn't drown in the sea, but the goddess of justice will kill him anyway."

5Paul shook the snake off into the fire and was not harmed. 6The people kept thinking that Paul would either swell up or suddenly drop dead. They watched him for a long time, and when nothing happened to him, they changed their minds and said, "This man is a god."

7The governor of the island was named Publius, and he owned some of the land around there. Publius was very friendly and welcomed us into his home for three days. 8His father was in bed, sick with fever and stomach trouble, and Paul went to visit him. Paul healed the man by praying and placing his hands on him.

9After this happened, everyone on the island brought their sick people to Paul, and they were all healed. 10The people were very respectful to us, and when we sailed, they gave us everything we needed.

From Malta to Rome

11Three months later we sailed in a ship that had been docked at Malta for the winter. The ship was from Alex-andria in Egypt and was known as "The Twin Gods."*p* 12We arrived in Syracuse and stayed for three days. 13From there we sailed to Rhegium. The next day a south wind began to blow, and two days later we arrived in Puteoli. 14There we found some of the Lord's followers, who begged us to stay with them. A week later we left for the city of Rome.

15Some of the followers in Rome heard about us and came to meet us at the Market of Appius and at the Three Inns. When Paul saw them, he thanked God and was encouraged.

Paul in Rome

16We arrived in Rome, and Paul was allowed to live in a house by himself with a soldier to guard him.

17Three days after we got there, Paul called together some of the Jewish leaders and said:

My friends, I have never done anything to hurt our people, and I have never gone against the customs of our ancestors. But in Jerusalem I was handed over as a prisoner to the Romans. 18They looked into the charges against me and wanted to release me. They found that I had not done anything deserving death. 19The Jewish leaders disagreed, so I asked to be tried by the Emperor. But I don't have anything to say against my own nation. 20I am bound by these chains because of what we people of Israel hope for. That's why I have called you here to talk about this hope of ours.

---

p known as "The Twin Gods": Or "carried on its bow a wooden carving of the Twin Gods." These gods were Castor and Pollux, two of the favorite gods among sailors.

21The Jewish leaders replied, "No one from Judea has written us a letter about you. And not one of them has come here to report on you or to say anything against you. 22But we would like to hear what you have to say. We understand that people everywhere are against this new group."

23They agreed on a time to meet with Paul, and many of them came to his house. From early morning until late in the afternoon, Paul talked to them about God's kingdom. He used the Law of Moses and the Books of the Prophets[q] to try to win them over to Jesus.

24Some of the Jewish leaders agreed with what Paul said, but others did not. 25Since they could not agree among themselves, they started leaving. But Paul said, "The Holy Spirit said the right thing when he sent Isaiah the prophet 26to tell our ancestors,

'Go to these people
    and tell them:
You will listen and listen,
    but never understand.
You will look and look,
    but never see.
27All of you
    have stubborn hearts.
Your ears are stopped up,
    and your eyes are covered.
You cannot see or hear
    or understand.
If you could,
you would turn to me,
    and I would heal you.' "

28-29Paul said, "You may be sure that God wants to save the Gentiles! And they will listen."[r]

30For two years Paul stayed in a rented house and welcomed everyone who came to see him. 31He bravely preached about God's kingdom and taught about the Lord Jesus Christ, and no one tried to stop him.

---

[q]*Law of Moses and the Books of the Prophets*: The Jewish Bible, that is, the Old Testament.
[r]*And they will listen*: Some manuscripts add, "After Paul said this, the people left, but they got into a fierce argument among themselves."

Paul's Letter
to the Church in Rome

ABOUT THIS LETTER

Paul wrote this letter to introduce himself and his message to the church at Rome. He had never been to this important city, although he knew the names of many Christians there and hoped to visit them soon (15.22—16.21). Paul tells them that he is an apostle, chosen to preach the good news (1.1). And the message he proclaims "is God's powerful way of saving all people who have faith, whether they are Jews or Gentiles" (1.16).

Paul reminds his readers, "All of us have sinned and fallen short of God's glory" (3.23). But how can we be made acceptable to God? This is the main question that Paul answers in this letter. He begins by showing how everyone has failed to do what God requires. The Jews have not obeyed the Law of Moses, and the Gentiles have refused even to think about God, although God has spoken to them in many different ways (1.18—3.20).

Now we see how God does make us acceptable to him . . . God treats everyone alike. He accepts people only because they have faith in Jesus Christ . . . God treats us much better than we deserve. And because of Jesus Christ, he freely accepts us and sets us free from our sins.

(3.21, 22, 24)

God gave Jesus to die for our sins, and he raised him to life, so that we would be made acceptable to God. *(4.25)*

A QUICK LOOK AT THIS LETTER

- Paul and His Message of Good News (1.1–17)
- Everyone Is Guilty (1.18—3.20)
- God's Way of Accepting People (3.21—4.25)
- A New Life for God's People (5.1—8.39)
- What about the People of Israel? (9.1—11.36)
- How to Live the New Life of Love (12.1—15.13)
- Paul's Plans and Personal Greetings (15.14—16.27)

---

1 From Paul, a servant of Christ Jesus.

God chose me to be an apostle, and he appointed me to preach the good news [2]that he promised long ago by what his prophets said in the holy Scriptures. [3-4]This good news is about his Son, our Lord Jesus Christ! As a human, he was from the family of David. But the Holy Spirit[a] proved that Jesus is the powerful Son of God,[b] because he was raised from death.

5Jesus was kind to me and chose me to be an apostle,[c] so that people of all nations would obey and have faith. 6You are some of those people chosen by Jesus Christ.

7This letter is to all of you in Rome. God loves you and has chosen you to be his very own people.

I pray that God our Father and our Lord Jesus Christ will be kind to you and will bless you with peace!

A Prayer of Thanks

8First, I thank God in the name of Jesus Christ for all of you. I do this because people everywhere in the world are talking about your faith. 9God has seen how I never stop praying for you, while I serve him with all my heart and tell the good news about his Son.

10In all my prayers, I ask God to make it possible for me to visit you. 11I want to see you and share with you the same blessings that God's Spirit has given me. Then you will grow stronger in your faith. 12What I am saying is that we can encourage each other by the faith that is ours.

13My friends, I want you to know that I have often planned to come for a visit. But something has always kept me from doing it. I want to win followers to Christ in Rome, as I have done in many other places. 14-15It doesn't matter if people are civilized and educated or if they are uncivilized and uneducated. I must tell the good news to everyone. That's why I am eager to visit all of you in Rome.

The Power of the Good News

16I am proud of the good news! It is God's powerful way of saving all people who have faith, whether they are Jews or Gentiles. 17The good news tells how God accepts everyone who has faith, but only those who have faith.[d] It is just as the Scriptures say, "The people God accepts because of their faith will live."[e]

Everyone Is Guilty

18From heaven God shows how angry he is with all the wicked and evil things that sinful people do to crush the truth. 19They know everything that can be known about God, because God has shown it all to them. 20God's eternal power and character cannot be seen. But from the beginning of creation, God has shown what these are like by all he has made. That's why those people don't have any excuse. 21They know about God, but they don't honor him or even thank him. Their thoughts are useless, and their stupid minds are in the dark. 22They claim to be wise, but they are fools. 23They don't worship the glorious and eternal God. Instead, they worship idols that are made to look like humans who cannot live forever, and like birds, animals, and reptiles.

---

[a]the Holy Spirit: Or "his own spirit of holiness." [b]proved that Jesus is the powerful Son of God: Or "proved in a powerful way that Jesus is the Son of God." [c]Jesus was kind to me and chose me to be an apostle: Or "Jesus was kind to us and chose us to be his apostles." [d]but only those who have faith: Or "and faith is all that matters." [e]The people God accepts because of their faith will live: Or "The people God accepts will live because of their faith."

24So God let these people go their own way. They did what they wanted to do, and their filthy thoughts made them do shameful things with their bodies. 25They gave up the truth about God for a lie, and they worshiped God's creation instead of God, who will be praised forever. Amen.

26God let them follow their own evil desires. Women no longer wanted to have sex in a natural way, and they did things with each other that were not natural. 27Men behaved in the same way. They stopped wanting to have sex with women and had strong desires for sex with other men. They did shameful things with each other, and what has happened to them is punishment for their foolish deeds.

28Since these people refused even to think about God, he let their useless minds rule over them. That's why they do all sorts of indecent things. 29They are evil, wicked, and greedy, as well as mean in every possible way. They want what others have, and they murder, argue, cheat, and are hard to get along with. They gossip, 30say cruel things about others, and hate God. They are proud, conceited, and boastful, always thinking up new ways to do evil.

These people don't respect their parents. 31They are stupid, unreliable, and don't have any love or pity for others. 32They know God has said that anyone who acts this way deserves to die. But they keep on doing evil things, and they even encourage others to do them.

God's Judgment Is Fair

2 Some of you accuse others of doing wrong. But there is no excuse for what you do. When you judge others, you condemn yourselves, because you are guilty of doing the very same things. 2We know that God is right to judge everyone who behaves in this way. 3Do you really think God won't punish you, when you behave exactly like the people you accuse? 4You surely don't think much of God's wonderful goodness or of his patience and willingness to put up with you. Don't you know that the reason God is good to you is because he wants you to turn to him?

5But you are stubborn and refuse to turn to God. So you are making things even worse for yourselves on that day when he will show how angry he is and will judge the world with fairness. 6God will reward each of us for what we have done. 7He will give eternal life to everyone who has patiently done what is good in the hope of receiving glory, honor, and life that lasts forever. 8But he will show how angry and furious he can be with every selfish person who rejects the truth and wants to do evil. 9All who are wicked will be punished with trouble and suffering. It doesn't matter if they are Jews or Gentiles. 10But all who do right will be rewarded with glory, honor, and peace, whether they are Jews or Gentiles. 11God doesn't have any favorites!

12Those people who don't know about God's Law will still be punished for what they do wrong. And the Law will be used to judge everyone who knows what it says. 13God accepts those who obey his Law, but not those who simply hear it.

14Some people naturally obey the Law's commands, even though they don't have the Law. 15This proves that the conscience is like a law written in the human heart. And it will show whether we are forgiven or condemned, 16when God has Jesus Christ judge everyone's secret thoughts, just as my message says.

The Jews and the Law

17Some of you call yourselves Jews. You trust in the Law and take pride in God. 18By reading the Scriptures you learn how God wants you to behave, and you discover what is right. 19You are sure that you are a guide for the blind and a light for all who are in the dark. 20And since there is knowledge and truth in God's Law, you think you can instruct fools and teach young people.

21But how can you teach others when you refuse to learn? You preach that it is wrong to steal. But do you steal? 22You say people should be faithful in marriage. But are you faithful? You hate idols, yet you rob their temples. 23You take pride in the Law, but you disobey the Law and bring shame to God. 24It is just as the Scriptures tell us, "You have made foreigners say insulting things about God."

25Being circumcised is worthwhile, if you obey the Law. But if you don't obey the Law, you are no better off than people who are not circumcised. 26In fact, if they obey the Law, they are as good as anyone who is circumcised. 27So everyone who obeys the Law, but has never been circumcised, will condemn you. Even though you are circumcised and have the Law, you still don't obey its teachings.

28Just because you live like a Jew and are circumcised does not make you a real Jew. 29To be a real Jew you must obey the Law. True circumcision is something that happens deep in your heart, not something done to your body. And besides, you should want praise from God and not from humans.

3 What good is it to be a Jew? What good is it to be circumcised? 2It is good in a lot of ways! First of all, God's messages were spoken to the Jews. 3It is true that some Jews did not believe the message. But does this mean that God cannot be trusted, just because they did not have faith? 4No, indeed! God tells the truth, even if everyone else is a liar. The Scriptures say about God,

"Your words
    will be proven true,
and in court
    you will win your case."

5If our evil deeds show how right God is, then what can we say? Is it wrong for God to become angry and punish us? What a foolish thing to ask. 6But the answer is, "No." Otherwise, how could God judge the world? 7Since your lies bring great honor to God by showing how truthful he is, you may ask why God still says you are a sinner. 8You might as well say, "Let's do something evil, so that something good will come of it!" Some people even claim that we are saying this. But God is fair and will judge them as well.

No One Is Good

9What does all this mean? Does it mean that we Jews are better off*f* than the Gentiles? No, it doesn't! Jews, as well as Gentiles, are ruled by sin, just as I have said. 10The Scriptures tell us,

"No one is acceptable to God!
11Not one of them understands
    or even searches for God.

f better off: Or "worse off."

¹²They have all turned away
and are worthless.
There is not one person
who does right.
¹³Their words are like
an open pit,
and their tongues are good
only for telling lies.
Each word is as deadly
as the fangs of a snake,
¹⁴and they say nothing
but bitter curses.
¹⁵These people quickly
become violent.
¹⁶Wherever they go,
they leave ruin
and destruction.
¹⁷They don't know how
to live in peace.
¹⁸   They don't even fear God."

¹⁹We know that everything in the Law was written for those who are under its power. The Law says these things to stop anyone from making excuses and to let God show that the whole world is guilty. ²⁰God does not accept people simply because they obey the Law. No, indeed! All the Law does is to point out our sin.

God's Way of Accepting People

²¹Now we see how God does make us acceptable to him. The Law and the Prophets⁹ tell how we become acceptable, and it isn't by obeying the Law of Moses. ²²God treats everyone alike. He accepts people only because they have faith in Jesus Christ. ²³All of us have sinned and fallen short of God's glory. ²⁴But God treats us much better than

we deserve.ʰ And because of Jesus Christ, he freely accepts us and sets us free from our sins. ²⁵⁻²⁶God sent Christ to be our sacrifice. Christ offered his life's blood, so that by faith in him we could come to God. And God did this to show that in the past he was right to be patient and forgive sinners. This also shows that God is right when he accepts people who have faith in Jesus.

²⁷What is left for us to brag about? Not a thing! Is it because we obeyed some law? No! It is because of faith. ²⁸We see that people are acceptable to God because they have faith, and not because they obey the Law. ²⁹Does God belong only to the Jews? Isn't he also the God of the Gentiles? Yes, he is! ³⁰There is only one God, and he accepts Gentiles as well as Jews, simply because of their faith. ³¹Do we destroy the Law by our faith? Not at all! We make it even more powerful.

The Example of Abraham

4 Well then, what can we say about our ancestor Abraham? ²If he became acceptable to God because of what he did, then he would have something to brag about. But he would never be able to brag about it to God. ³The Scriptures say, "God accepted Abraham because Abraham had faith in him."

⁴Money paid to workers isn't a gift. It is something they earn by working. ⁵But you cannot make God accept you because of something you do. God ac-

---

⁹*The Law and the Prophets*: The Jewish Scriptures, that is, the Old Testament. ʰ*treats us much better than we deserve*: The Greek word *charis*, traditionally rendered "grace," is translated here and other places in the CEV to express the overwhelming kindness of God.

cepts sinners only because they have faith in him. 6In the Scriptures David talks about the blessings that come to people who are acceptable to God, even though they don't do anything to deserve these blessings. David says,

7"God blesses people
whose sins are forgiven
and whose evil deeds
are forgotten.
8The Lord blesses people
whose sins are erased
from his book."

9Are these blessings meant for circumcised people or for those who are not circumcised? Well, the Scriptures say that God accepted Abraham because Abraham had faith in him. 10But when did this happen? Was it before or after Abraham was circumcised? Of course, it was before.

11Abraham let himself be circumcised to show that he had been accepted because of his faith even before he was circumcised. This makes Abraham the father of all who are acceptable to God because of their faith, even though they are not circumcised. 12This also makes Abraham the father of everyone who is circumcised and has faith in God, as Abraham did before he was circumcised.

The Promise Is for All Who Have Faith

13God promised Abraham and his descendants that he would give them the world. This promise was not made because Abraham had obeyed the Law, but because his faith in God made him acceptable. 14If Abraham and his descendants were given this promise because they had obeyed the Law, then faith would mean nothing, and the promise would be worthless.

15God becomes angry when his law is broken. But where there isn't a Law, it cannot be broken. 16Everything depends on having faith in God, so that God can keep his promise because he is kind. This promise is not only for Abraham's descendants who have the Law. It is for all who are Abraham's descendants because they have faith, just as he did. Abraham is the ancestor of us all. 17The Scriptures say that Abraham would become the ancestor of many nations. This promise was made to Abraham because he had faith in God, who raises the dead to life and creates new things.

18God promised Abraham a lot of descendants. And when it all seemed hopeless, Abraham still had faith in God and became the ancestor of many nations. 19Abraham's faith never became weak, not even when he was nearly a hundred years old. He knew that he was almost dead and that his wife Sarah could not have children. 20But Abraham never doubted or questioned God's promise. His faith made him strong, and he gave all the credit to God.

21Abraham was certain that God could do what he had promised. 22So God accepted him, 23just as we read in the Scriptures. But these words were not written only for Abraham. 24They were written for us, since we will also be accepted because of our faith in God, who raised our Lord Jesus to life. 25God gave Jesus to die for our sins, and he raised him to life, so that we would be made acceptable to God.

What It Means To Be Acceptable To God

5 By faith we have been made acceptable to God. And now, because

of our Lord Jesus Christ, we live at peace[i] with God. 2Christ has also introduced us[j] to God's undeserved kindness on which we take our stand. So we are happy, as we look forward to sharing in the glory of God. 3But that's not all! We gladly suffer,[k] because we know that suffering helps us to endure. 4And endurance builds character, which gives us a hope 5that will never disappoint us. All of this happens because God has given us the Holy Spirit, who fills our hearts with his love.

6Christ died for us at a time when we were helpless and sinful. 7No one is really willing to die for an honest person, though someone might be willing to die for a truly good person. 8But God showed how much he loved us by having Christ die for us, even though we were sinful.

9But there is more! Now that God has accepted us because Christ sacrificed his life's blood, we will also be kept safe from God's anger. 10Even when we were God's enemies, he made peace with us, because his Son died for us. Yet something even greater than friendship is ours. Now that we are at peace with God, we will be saved by his Son's life. 11And in addition to everything else, we are happy because God sent our Lord Jesus Christ to make peace with us.

Adam and Christ

12Adam sinned, and that sin brought death into the world. Now everyone has sinned, and so everyone must die. 13Sin was in the world before the Law came. But no record of sin was kept, because there was no Law. 14Yet death still had power over all who lived from the time of Adam to the time of Moses. This happened, though not everyone disobeyed a direct command from God, as Adam did.

In some ways Adam is like Christ who came later. 15But the gift that God was kind enough to give was very different from Adam's sin. That one sin brought death to many others. Yet in an even greater way, Jesus Christ alone brought God's gift of kindness to many people.

16There is a lot of difference between Adam's sin and God's gift. That one sin led to punishment. But God's gift made it possible for us to be acceptable to him, even though we have sinned many times. 17Death ruled like a king because Adam had sinned. But that cannot compare with what Jesus Christ has done. God has been so kind to us, and he has accepted us because of Jesus. And so we will live and rule like kings.

18Everyone was going to be punished because Adam sinned. But because of the good thing that Christ has done, God accepts us and gives us the gift of life. 19Adam disobeyed God and caused many others to be sinners. But Jesus obeyed him and will make many people acceptable to God.

20The Law came, so that the full power of sin could be seen. Yet where sin was powerful, God's kindness was even more powerful. 21Sin ruled by means of death. But God's kindness now rules, and God has accepted us because of Jesus Christ our Lord. This means that we will have eternal life.

---

[i]*we live at peace*: Some manuscripts have "let us live at peace."   [j]*introduced us*: Some manuscripts add "by faith."   [k]*We gladly suffer*: Or "Let us gladly suffer."

Dead to Sin but Alive because of Christ

6 What should we say? Should we keep on sinning, so that God's kindness will show up even better? 2No, we should not! If we are dead to sin, how can we go on sinning? 3Don't you know that all who share in Christ Jesus by being baptized also share in his death? 4When we were baptized, we died and were buried with Christ. We were baptized, so that we would live a new life, as Christ was raised to life by the glory of God the Father.

5If we shared in Jesus' death by being baptized, we will surely be raised to life with him. 6We know that the persons we used to be were nailed to the cross with Jesus. This was done, so that our sinful bodies would no longer be the slaves of sin. 7We know that sin does not have power over dead people.

8As surely as we died with Christ, we believe we will also live with him. 9We know that death no longer has any power over Christ. He died and was raised to life, never again to die. 10When Christ died, he died for sin once and for all. But now he is alive, and he lives only for God. 11In the same way, you must think of yourselves as dead to the power of sin. But Christ Jesus has given life to you, and you live for God.

12Don't let sin rule your body. After all, your body is bound to die, so don't obey its desires 13or let any part of it become a slave of evil. Give yourselves to God, as people who have been raised from death to life. Make every part of your body a slave that pleases God. 14Don't let sin keep ruling your lives. You are ruled by God's kindness and not by the Law.

Slaves Who Do What Pleases God

15What does all this mean? Does it mean we are free to sin, because we are ruled by God's kindness and not by the Law? Certainly not! 16Don't you know that you are slaves of anyone you obey? You can be slaves of sin and die, or you can be obedient slaves of God and be acceptable to him. 17You used to be slaves of sin. But I thank God that with all your heart you obeyed the teaching you received from me. 18Now you are set free from sin and are slaves who please God.

19I am using these everyday examples, because in some ways you are still weak. You used to let the different parts of your body be slaves of your evil thoughts. But now you must make every part of your body serve God, so that you will belong completely to him.

20When you were slaves of sin, you didn't have to please God. 21But what good did you receive from the things you did? All you have to show for them is your shame, and they lead to death. 22Now you have been set free from sin, and you are God's slaves. This will make you holy and will lead you to eternal life. 23Sin pays off with death. But God's gift is eternal life given by Jesus Christ our Lord.

An Example from Marriage

7 My friends, you surely understand enough about law to know that laws only have power over people who are alive. 2For example, the Law says that a man's wife must remain his wife as long as he lives. But once her husband is dead, she is free 3to marry someone else. However, if she goes off with another man while her husband is still alive, she is said to be unfaithful.

4That is how it is with you, my friends. You are now part of the body of Christ and are dead to the power of the Law. You are free to belong to Christ, who was raised to life so that we could serve God. 5When we thought only of ourselves, the Law made us have sinful desires. It made every part of our bodies into slaves who are doomed to die. 6But the Law no longer rules over us. We are like dead people, and it cannot have any power over us. Now we can serve God in a new way by obeying his Spirit, and not in the old way by obeying the written Law.

The Battle with Sin

7Does this mean that the Law is sinful? Certainly not! But if it had not been for the Law, I would not have known what sin is really like. For example, I would not have known what it means to want something that belongs to someone else, unless the Law had told me not to do that. 8It was sin that used this command as a way of making me have all kinds of desires. But without the Law, sin is dead.

9Before I knew about the Law, I was alive. But as soon as I heard that command, sin came to life, 10and I died. The very command that was supposed to bring life to me, instead brought death. 11Sin used this command to trick me, and because of it I died. 12Still, the Law and its commands are holy and correct and good.

13Am I saying that something good caused my death? Certainly not! It was sin that killed me by using something good. Now we can see how terrible and evil sin really is. 14We know that the Law is spiritual. But I am merely a human, and I have been sold as a slave to sin. 15In fact, I don't understand why I act the way I do. I don't do what I know is right. I do the things I hate. 16Although I don't do what I know is right, I agree that the Law is good. 17So I am not the one doing these evil things. The sin that lives in me is what does them.

18I know that my selfish desires won't let me do anything that is good. Even when I want to do right, I cannot. 19Instead of doing what I know is right, I do wrong. 20And so, if I don't do what I know is right, I am no longer the one doing these evil things. The sin that lives in me is what does them.

21The Law has shown me that something in me keeps me from doing what I know is right. 22With my whole heart I agree with the Law of God. 23But in every part of me I discover something fighting against my mind, and it makes me a prisoner of sin that controls everything I do. 24What a miserable person I am. Who will rescue me from this body that is doomed to die? 25Thank God! Jesus Christ will rescue me.*l*

So with my mind I serve the Law of God, although my selfish desires make me serve the law of sin.

Living by the Power of God's Spirit

8 If you belong to Christ Jesus, you won't be punished. 2The Holy Spirit will give you life that comes from Christ Jesus and will set you*m* free from sin and death. 3The Law of Moses cannot do this, because our selfish desires make the Law weak. But God set you free when he sent his own Son to

*l*me: Or "us."   *m*you: Some manuscripts have "me."

be like us sinners and to be a sacrifice for our sin. God used Christ's body to condemn sin. 4He did this, so that we would do what the Law commands by obeying the Spirit instead of our own desires.

5People who are ruled by their desires think only of themselves. Everyone who is ruled by the Holy Spirit thinks about spiritual things. 6If our minds are ruled by our desires, we will die. But if our minds are ruled by the Spirit, we will have life and peace. 7Our desires fight against God, because they do not and cannot obey God's laws. 8If we follow our desires, we cannot please God.

9You are no longer ruled by your desires, but by God's Spirit, who lives in you. People who don't have the Spirit of Christ in them don't belong to him. 10But Christ lives in you. So you are alive because God has accepted you, even though your bodies must die because of your sins. 11Yet God raised Jesus to life! God's Spirit now lives in you, and he will raise you to life by his Spirit.

12My dear friends, we must not live to satisfy our desires. 13If you do, you will die. But you will live, if by the help of God's Spirit you say "No" to your desires. 14Only those people who are led by God's Spirit are his children. 15God's Spirit doesn't make us slaves who are afraid of him. Instead, we become his children and call him our Father.*n* 16God's Spirit makes us sure that we are his children. 17His Spirit lets us know that together with Christ we will be given what God has

promised. We will also share in the glory of Christ, because we have suffered with him.

A Wonderful Future for God's People

18I am sure that what we are suffering now cannot compare with the glory that will be shown to us. 19In fact, all creation is eagerly waiting for God to show who his children are. 20Meanwhile, creation is confused, but not because it wants to be confused. God made it this way in the hope 21that creation would be set free from decay and would share in the glorious freedom of his children. 22We know that all creation is still groaning and is in pain, like a woman about to give birth.

23The Spirit makes us sure about what we will be in the future. But now we groan silently, while we wait for God to show that we are his children.*o* This means that our bodies will also be set free. 24And this hope is what saves us. But if we already have what we hope for, there is no need to keep on hoping. 25However, we hope for something we have not yet seen, and we patiently wait for it.

26In certain ways we are weak, but the Spirit is here to help us. For example, when we don't know what to pray for, the Spirit prays for us in ways that cannot be put into words. 27All of our thoughts are known to God. He can understand what is in the mind of the Spirit, as the Spirit prays for God's people. 28We know that God is always at work for the good of everyone who

---

*n*our Father: The Greek text uses the Aramaic word "Abba" (meaning "father"), which shows the close relation between the children and their father. *o*to show that we are his children: These words are not in some manuscripts. The translation of the remainder of the verse would then read, "while we wait for God to set our bodies free."

loves him.*p* They are the ones God has chosen for his purpose, 29and he has always known who his chosen ones would be. He had decided to let them become like his own Son, so that his Son would be the first of many children. 30God then accepted the people he had already decided to choose, and he has shared his glory with them.

God's Love

31What can we say about all this? If God is on our side, can anyone be against us? 32God did not keep back his own Son, but he gave him for us. If God did this, won't he freely give us everything else? 33If God says his chosen ones are acceptable to him, can anyone bring charges against them? 34Or can anyone condemn them? No indeed! Christ died and was raised to life, and now he is at God's right side,*q* speaking to him for us. 35Can anything separate us from the love of Christ? Can trouble, suffering, and hard times, or hunger and nakedness, or danger and death? 36It is exactly as the Scriptures say,

"For you we face death
     all day long.
We are like sheep
     on their way
          to the butcher."

37In everything we have won more than a victory because of Christ who loves us. 38I am sure that nothing can separate us from God's love—not life or death, not angels or spirits, not the present or the future, 39and not powers above or powers below. Nothing in all creation can separate us from God's love for us in Christ Jesus our Lord!

God's Choice of Israel

9 I am a follower of Christ, and the Holy Spirit is a witness to my conscience. So I tell the truth and I am not lying when I say 2my heart is broken and I am in great sorrow. 3I would gladly be placed under God's curse and be separated from Christ for the good of my own Jewish people. 4They are the descendants of Israel, and they are also God's chosen people. God showed them his glory. He made agreements with them and gave them his Law. The temple is theirs and so are the promises that God made to them. 5They have those famous ancestors, who were also the ancestors of Jesus Christ. I pray that God, who rules over all, will be praised forever!*r* Amen.

6It cannot be said that God broke his promise. After all, not all of the people of Israel are the true people of God. 7-8In fact, when God made the promise to Abraham, he meant only Abraham's descendants by his son Isaac. God was talking only about Isaac when he promised 9Sarah, "At this time next year I will return, and you will already have a son."

10Don't forget what happened to the twin sons of Isaac and Rebecca. 11-12Even before they were born or had done anything good or bad, the Lord told Rebecca that her older son would

---

pGod is always at work for the good of everyone who loves him: Or "All things work for the good of everyone who loves God" or "God's Spirit always works for the good of everyone who loves God." *qright side*: The place of power and honor. *rChrist. I pray that God, who rules over all, will be praised forever*: Or "Christ, who rules over all. I pray that God will be praised forever" or "Christ. And I pray that Christ, who is God and rules over all, will be praised forever."

serve the younger one. The Lord said this to show that he makes his own choices and that it was not because of anything either of them had done. 13That's why the Scriptures say that the Lord liked Jacob more than Esau.

14Are we saying that God is unfair? Certainly not! 15The Lord told Moses that he has pity and mercy on anyone he wants to. 16Everything then depends on God's mercy and not on what people want or do. 17In the Scriptures the Lord says to Pharaoh, "I let you become king, so that I could show you my power and be praised by all people on earth." 18Everything depends on what God decides to do, and he can either have pity on people or make them stubborn.

God's Anger and Mercy

19Someone may ask, "How can God blame us, if he makes us behave in the way he wants us to?" 20But, my friend, I ask, "Who do you think you are to question God? Does the clay have the right to ask the potter why he shaped it the way he did? 21Doesn't a potter have the right to make a fancy bowl and a plain bowl out of the same lump of clay?"

22God wanted to show his anger and reveal his power against everyone who deserved to be destroyed. But instead, he patiently put up with them. 23He did this by showing how glorious he is when he has pity on the people he has chosen to share in his glory. 24Whether Jews or Gentiles, we are those chosen ones, 25just as the Lord says in the book of Hosea,

"Although they are not
    my people,
I will make them
    my people.
I will treat with love
those nations
    that have never been loved.
26Once they were told,
    'You are not my people.'
But in that very place
they will be called
    children of the living God."
27And this is what the prophet Isaiah said about the people of Israel,
"The people of Israel
    are as many
as the grains of sand
    along the beach.
But only a few who are left
    will be saved.
28The Lord will be quick
    and sure to do on earth
what he has warned
    he will do."
29Isaiah also said,
"If the Lord All-Powerful
    had not spared some
    of our descendants,
we would have been destroyed
like the cities of Sodom
    and Gomorrah."[s]

Israel and the Good News

30What does all of this mean? It means that the Gentiles were not trying to be acceptable to God, but they found that he would accept them if they had faith. 31It also means that the people of Israel were not acceptable to God. And why not? It was because they were trying[t] to be acceptable by

---

[s]*Sodom and Gomorrah*: During the time of Abraham the Lord destroyed these two cities because their people were so sinful.   [t]*because they were trying*: Or "while they were trying" or "even though they were trying."

obeying the Law [32]instead of by having faith in God. The people of Israel fell over the stone that makes people stumble, [33]just as God says in the Scriptures,

"Look! I am placing in Zion
a stone to make people
stumble and fall.
But those who have faith
in that one will never
be disappointed."

10 Dear friends, my greatest wish and my prayer to God is for the people of Israel to be saved. [2]I know they love God, but they don't understand [3]what makes people acceptable to him. So they refuse to trust God, and they try to be acceptable by obeying the Law. [4]But Christ makes the Law no longer necessary[u] for those who become acceptable to God by faith.

Anyone Can Be Saved

[5]Moses said that a person could become acceptable to God by obeying the Law. He did this when he wrote, "If you want to live, you must do all that the Law commands."

[6]But people whose faith makes them acceptable to God will never ask, "Who will go up to heaven to bring Christ down?" [7]Neither will they ask, "Who will go down into the world of the dead to raise him to life?"

[8]All who are acceptable because of their faith simply say, "The message is as near as your mouth or your heart." And this is the same message we preach about faith. [9]So you will be saved, if you honestly say, "Jesus is Lord," and if you believe with all your heart that God raised him from death. [10]God will accept you and save you, if you truly believe this and tell it to others.

[11]The Scriptures say that no one who has faith will be disappointed, [12]no matter if that person is a Jew or a Gentile. There is only one Lord, and he is generous to everyone who asks for his help. [13]All who call out to the Lord will be saved.

[14]But how can people ask the Lord to save them, if they have never had faith in him? How can they hear about him unless someone tells them? [15]And how can anyone tell them without being sent by the Lord? The Scriptures say it is a beautiful sight to see even the feet of someone coming to preach the good news. [16]Yet not everyone has believed the message. For example, the prophet Isaiah asked, "Lord, has anyone believed what we said?"

[17]No one can have faith without hearing the message about Christ. [18]But am I saying that the people of Israel did not hear? No, I am not! The Scriptures say,

"The message was told
everywhere on earth.
It was announced
all over the world."

[19]Did the people of Israel understand or not? Moses answered this question when he told that the Lord had said,

"I will make Israel jealous
of people
who are a nation
of nobodies.
I will make them angry
at people
who don't understand
a thing."

---

[u]*But Christ makes the Law no longer necessary*: Or "But Christ gives the full meaning to the Law."

20Isaiah was fearless enough to tell that the Lord had said,

"I was found by people
who were not looking
for me.
I appeared to the ones
who were not asking
about me."

21And Isaiah said about the people of Israel,

"All day long the Lord
has reached out
to people who are stubborn
and refuse to obey."

God Has Not Rejected His People

11 Am I saying that God has turned his back on his people? Certainly not! I am one of the people of Israel, and I myself am a descendant of Abraham from the tribe of Benjamin. 2God did not turn his back on his chosen people. Don't you remember reading in the Scriptures how Elijah complained to God about the people of Israel? 3He said, "Lord, they killed your prophets and destroyed your altars. I am the only one left, and now they want to kill me."

4But the Lord told Elijah, "I still have seven thousand followers who have not worshiped Baal." 5It is the same way now. God was kind to the people of Israel, and so a few of them are still his followers. 6This happened because of God's undeserved kindness and not because of anything they have done. It could not have happened except for God's kindness.

7This means that only a chosen few of the people of Israel found what all of them were searching for. And the rest of them were stubborn, 8just as the Scriptures say,

"God made them so stupid
that their eyes are blind,
and their ears
are still deaf."
9Then David said,
"Turn their meals
into bait for a trap,
so that they will stumble
and be given
what they deserve.
10Blindfold their eyes!
Don't let them see.
Bend their backs
beneath a burden
that will never be lifted."

Gentiles Will Be Saved

11Do I mean that the people of Israel fell, never to get up again? Certainly not! Their failure made it possible for the Gentiles to be saved, and this will make the people of Israel jealous. 12But if the rest of the world's people were helped so much by Israel's sin and loss, they will be helped even more by Israel's full return.

13I am now speaking to you Gentiles, and as long as I am an apostle to you, I will take pride in my work. 14I hope in this way to make some of my own people jealous enough to be saved. 15When Israel rejected God,[a] the rest of the people in the world were able to turn to him. So when God makes friends with Israel, it will be like bringing the dead back to life. 16If part of a batch of dough is made holy by being offered to God, then all of the dough is holy. If the roots of a tree are holy, the rest of the tree is holy too.

17You Gentiles are like branches of a wild olive tree that were made to be part of a cultivated olive tree. You have taken the place of some branches that were cut away from it. And

[a]When Israel rejected God: Or "When Israel was rejected."

because of this, you enjoy the blessings that come from being part of that cultivated tree. 18But don't think you are better than the branches that were cut away. Just remember that you are not supporting the roots of that tree. Its roots are supporting you.

19Maybe you think those branches were cut away, so that you could be put in their place. 20That's true enough. But they were cut away because they did not have faith, and you are where you are because you do have faith. So don't be proud, but be afraid. 21If God cut away those natural branches, couldn't he do the same to you?

22Now you see both how kind and how hard God can be. He was hard on those who fell, but he was kind to you. And he will keep on being kind to you, if you keep on trusting in his kindness. Otherwise, you will be cut away too.

23If those other branches will start having faith, they will be made a part of that tree again. God has the power to put them back. 24After all, it was not natural for branches to be cut from a wild olive tree and to be made part of a cultivated olive tree. So it is much more likely that God will join the natural branches back to the cultivated olive tree.

The People of Israel Will Be Brought Back

25My friends, I don't want you Gentiles to be too proud of yourselves. So I will explain the mystery of what has happened to the people of Israel. Some of them have become stubborn, and they will stay like that until the complete number of you Gentiles has come in. 26In this way all of Israel will be saved, as the Scriptures say,

"From Zion someone will come
    to rescue us.
Then Jacob's descendants
    will stop being evil.
27This is what the Lord
    has promised to do
when he forgives
    their sins."

28The people of Israel are treated as God's enemies, so that the good news can come to you Gentiles. But they are still the chosen ones, and God loves them because of their famous ancestors. 29God does not take back the gifts he has given or forget about the people he has chosen.

30At one time you Gentiles rejected God. But now Israel has rejected God, and you have been shown mercy. 31And because of the mercy shown to you, they will also be shown mercy. 32All people have disobeyed God, and that's why he treats them as prisoners. But he does this, so that he can have mercy on all of them.

33Who can measure the wealth and wisdom and knowledge of God? Who can understand his decisions or explain what he does?
34"Has anyone known
    the thoughts of the Lord
        or given him advice?
35Has anyone loaned
    something to the Lord
        that must be repaid?"
36Everything comes from the Lord. All things were made because of him and will return to him. Praise the Lord forever! Amen.

Christ Brings New Life

12 Dear friends, God is good. So I beg you to offer your bodies to him as a living sacrifice, pure and pleasing. That's the most sensible way

to serve God. 2Don't be like the people of this world, but let God change the way you think. Then you will know how to do everything that is good and pleasing to him.

3I realize how kind God has been to me, and so I tell each of you not to think you are better than you really are. Use good sense and measure yourself by the amount of faith God has given you. 4A body is made up of many parts, and each of them has its own use. 5That's how it is with us. There are many of us, but we each are part of the body of Christ, as well as part of one another.

6God has also given each of us different gifts to use. If we can prophesy, we should do it according to the amount of faith we have. 7If we can serve others, we should serve. If we can teach, we should teach. 8If we can encourage others, we should encourage them. If we can give, we should be generous. If we are leaders, we should do our best. If we are good to others, we should do it cheerfully.

Rules for Christian Living

9Be sincere in your love for others. Hate everything that is evil and hold tight to everything that is good. 10Love each other as brothers and sisters and honor others more than you do yourself. 11Never give up. Eagerly follow the Holy Spirit and serve the Lord. 12Let your hope make you glad. Be patient in time of trouble and never stop praying. 13Take care of God's needy people and welcome strangers into your home. *

14Ask God to bless everyone who mistreats you. Ask him to bless them and not to curse them. 15When others are happy, be happy with them, and when they are sad, be sad. 16Be friendly with everyone. Don't be proud and feel that you are smarter than others. Make friends with ordinary people.^{v} 17Don't mistreat someone who has mistreated you. But try to earn the respect of others, 18and do your best to live at peace with everyone.

19Dear friends, don't try to get even. Let God take revenge. In the Scriptures the Lord says,

"I am the one to take revenge
    and pay them back."
20The Scriptures also say,
"If your enemies are hungry,
        give them something to eat.
And if they are thirsty,
give them something
    to drink.
This will be the same
as piling burning coals
    on their heads."
21Don't let evil defeat you, but defeat evil with good.

Obey Rulers

13 Obey the rulers who have authority over you. Only God can give authority to anyone, and he puts these rulers in their places of power. 2People who oppose the authorities are opposing what God has done, and they will be punished. 3Rulers are a threat to evil people, not to good people. There is no need to be afraid of the authorities. Just do right, and they will praise you for it. 4After all, they are God's servants, and it is their duty to help you.

---

^{b}*Make friends with ordinary people*: Or "Do ordinary jobs."

If you do something wrong, you ought to be afraid, because these rulers have the right to punish you. They are God's servants who punish criminals to show how angry God is. 5But you should obey the rulers because you know it is the right thing to do, and not just because of God's anger.

6You must also pay your taxes. The authorities are God's servants, and it is their duty to take care of these matters. 7Pay all that you owe, whether it is taxes and fees or respect and honor.

Love

8Let love be your only debt! If you love others, you have done all that the Law demands. 9In the Law there are many commands, such as, "Be faithful in marriage. Do not murder. Do not steal. Do not want what belongs to others." But all of these are summed up in the command that says, "Love others as much as you love yourself." 10No one who loves others will harm them. So love is all that the Law demands.

The Day When Christ Returns

11You know what sort of times we live in, and so you should live properly. It is time to wake up. You know that the day when we will be saved is nearer now than when we first put our faith in the Lord. 12Night is almost over, and day will soon appear. We must stop behaving as people do in the dark and be ready to live in the light. 13So behave properly, as people do in the day. Don't go to wild parties or get drunk or be vulgar or indecent. Don't quarrel or be jealous. 14Let the Lord Jesus Christ be as near to you as the clothes you wear. Then you won't try to satisfy your selfish desires.

Don't Criticize Others

14 Welcome all the Lord's followers, even those whose faith is weak. Don't criticize them for having beliefs that are different from yours. 2Some think it is all right to eat anything, while those whose faith is weak will eat only vegetables. 3But you should not criticize others for eating or for not eating. After all, God welcomes everyone. 4What right do you have to criticize someone else's servants? Only their Lord can decide if they are doing right, and the Lord will make sure that they do right.

5Some of the Lord's followers think one day is more important than another. Others think all days are the same. But each of you should make up your own mind. 6Any followers who count one day more important than another day do it to honor their Lord. And any followers who eat meat give thanks to God, just like the ones who don't eat meat.

7Whether we live or die, it must be for God, rather than for ourselves. 8Whether we live or die, it must be for the Lord. Alive or dead, we still belong to the Lord. 9This is because Christ died and rose to life, so that he would be the Lord of the dead and of the living. 10Why do you criticize other followers of the Lord? Why do you look down on them? The day is coming when God will judge all of us. 11In the Scriptures God says,

"I swear by my very life
that everyone will kneel down
and praise my name!"

12And so, each of us must give an account to God for what we do.

Don't Cause Problems for Others

13We must stop judging others. We must also make up our minds not to upset anyone's faith. 14The Lord Jesus has made it clear to me that God considers all foods fit to eat. But if you think some foods are unfit to eat, then for you they are not fit.

15If you are hurting others by the foods you eat, you are not guided by love. Don't let your appetite destroy someone Christ died for. 16Don't let your right to eat bring shame to Christ. 17God's kingdom is not about eating and drinking. It is about pleasing God, about living in peace, and about true happiness. All this comes from the Holy Spirit. 18If you serve Christ in this way, you will please God and be respected by people. 19We should try*w* to live at peace and help each other have a strong faith.

20Don't let your appetite destroy what God has done. All foods are fit to eat, but it is wrong to cause problems for others by what you eat. 21It is best not to eat meat or drink wine or do anything else that causes problems for other followers of the Lord. 22What you believe about these things should be kept between you and God. You are fortunate, if your actions don't make you have doubts. 23But if you do have doubts about what you eat, you are going against your beliefs. And you know that is wrong, because anything you do against your beliefs is sin.

Please Others and Not Yourself

15 If our faith is strong, we should be patient with the Lord's followers whose faith is weak. We should try to please them instead of ourselves.

2We should think of their good and try to help them by doing what pleases them. 3Even Christ did not try to please himself. But as the Scriptures say, "The people who insulted you also insulted me." 4And the Scriptures were written to teach and encourage us by giving us hope. 5God is the one who makes us patient and cheerful. I pray that he will help you live at peace with each other, as you follow Christ. 6Then all of you together will praise God, the Father of our Lord Jesus Christ.

The Good News Is for Jews and Gentiles

7Honor God by accepting each other, as Christ has accepted you. 8I tell you that Christ came as a servant of the Jews to show that God has kept the promises he made to their famous ancestors. Christ also came, 9so that the Gentiles would praise God for being kind to them. It is just as the Scriptures say,

"I will tell the nations
about you,
and I will sing praises
to your name."

10The Scriptures also say to the Gentiles, "Come and celebrate with God's people."

11Again the Scriptures say,
"Praise the Lord,
all you Gentiles.
All you nations, come
and worship him."

12Isaiah says,
"Someone from David's family
will come to power.
He will rule the nations,
and they will put their hope
in him."

---

wWe should try: Some manuscripts have "We try."

13I pray that God, who gives hope, will bless you with complete happiness and peace because of your faith. And may the power of the Holy Spirit fill you with hope.

Paul's Work as a Missionary

14My friends, I am sure that you are very good and that you have all the knowledge you need to teach each other. 15But I have spoken to you plainly and have tried to remind you of some things. God was so kind to me! 16He chose me to be a servant of Christ Jesus for the Gentiles and to do the work of a priest in the service of his good news. God did this so that the Holy Spirit could make the Gentiles into a holy offering, pleasing to him.

17Because of Christ Jesus, I can take pride in my service for God. 18In fact, all I will talk about is how Christ let me speak and work, so that the Gentiles would obey him. 19Indeed, I will tell how Christ worked miracles and wonders by the power of the Holy Spirit. I have preached the good news about him all the way from Jerusalem to Illyricum. 20But I have always tried to preach where people have never heard about Christ. I am like a builder who doesn't build on anyone else's foundation. 21It is just as the Scriptures say,

> "All who have not
> been told about him
> will see him,
> and those who have not
> heard about him
> will understand."

Paul's Plan to Visit Rome

22My work has always kept me from coming to see you. 23Now there is nothing left for me to do in this part of the world, and for years I have wanted to visit you. 24So I plan to stop off on my way to Spain. Then after a short, but refreshing, visit with you, I hope you will quickly send me on.

25-26I am now on my way to Jerusalem to deliver the money that the Lord's followers in Macedonia and Achaia collected for God's needy people. 27This is something they really wanted to do. But sharing their money with the Jews was also like paying back a debt, because the Jews had already shared their spiritual blessings with the Gentiles. 28After I have safely delivered this money, I will visit you and then go on to Spain. 29And when I do arrive in Rome, I know it will be with the full blessings of Christ.

30My friends, by the power of the Lord Jesus Christ and by the love that comes from the Holy Spirit, I beg you to pray sincerely with me and for me. 31Pray that God will protect me from the unbelievers in Judea, and that his people in Jerusalem will be pleased with what I am doing. 32Ask God to let me come to you and have a pleasant and refreshing visit. 33I pray that God, who gives peace, will be with all of you. Amen.

Personal Greetings

16 I have good things to say about Phoebe, who is a leader in the church at Cenchreae. 2Welcome her in a way that is proper for someone who has faith in the Lord and is one of God's own people. Help her in any way you can. After all, she has proved to be a

respected leader for many others, including me.

3Give my greetings to Priscilla and Aquila. They have not only served Christ Jesus together with me, 4but they have even risked their lives for me. I am grateful for them and so are all the Gentile churches. 5Greet the church that meets in their home.

Greet my dear friend Epaenetus, who was the first person in Asia to have faith in Christ.

6Greet Mary, who has worked so hard for you.

7Greet my relatives*x* Andronicus and Junias, who were in jail with me. They are highly respected by the apostles and were followers of Christ before I was.

8Greet Ampliatus, my dear friend whose faith is in the Lord.

9Greet Urbanus, who serves Christ along with us.

Greet my dear friend Stachys.

10Greet Apelles, a faithful servant of Christ.

Greet Aristobulus and his family.

11Greet Herodion, who is a relative*x* of mine.

Greet Narcissus and the others in his family, who have faith in the Lord.

12Greet Tryphaena and Tryphosa, who work hard for the Lord.

Greet my dear friend Persis. She also works hard for the Lord.

13Greet Rufus, that special servant of the Lord, and greet his mother, who has been like a mother to me.

14Greet Asyncritus, Phlegon, Hermes, Patrobas, and Hermas, as well as our friends who are with them.

15Greet Philologus, Julia, Nereus and his sister, and Olympas, and all of God's people who are with them.

16Be sure to give each other a warm greeting.

All of Christ's churches greet you.

17My friends, I beg you to watch out for anyone who causes trouble and divides the church by refusing to do what all of you were taught. Stay away from them! 18They want to serve themselves and not Christ the Lord. Their flattery and fancy talk fool people who don't know any better. 19I am glad that everyone knows how well you obey the Lord. But still, I want you to understand what is good and not have anything to do with evil. 20Then God, who gives peace, will soon crush Satan under your feet. I pray that our Lord Jesus will be kind to you.

21Timothy, who works with me, sends his greetings, and so do my relatives,*x* Lucius, Jason, and Sosipater.

22I, Tertius, also send my greetings. I am a follower of the Lord, and I wrote this letter.*y*

23-24Gaius welcomes me and the whole church into his home, and he sends his greetings.

Erastus, the city treasurer, and our dear friend Quartus send their greetings too.*z*

Paul's Closing Prayer

25Praise God! He can make you strong by means of my good news, which is the message about*a* Jesus Christ. For ages and ages this message was kept secret, 26but now at last it

---

xrelative(s): Or "Jewish friend(s)." *yI wrote this letter*: Paul probably dictated this letter to Tertius. *zsend their greetings too*: Some manuscripts add, "I pray that our Lord Jesus Christ will always be kind to you. Amen." *aabout*: Or "from."

has been told. The eternal God commanded his prophets to write about the good news, so that all nations would obey and have faith. ²⁷And now, because of Jesus Christ, we can praise the only wise God forever! Amen.ᵃ

ᵃ*Amen*: Some manuscripts have verses 25-27 after 14.23. Others have the verses here and after 14.23, and one manuscript has them after 15.33.

Paul's First Letter to the Church in Corinth

ABOUT THIS LETTER

A lthough this letter is called the First Letter to the Corinthians, it is not really the first one that Paul wrote to this church. We know this because he mentions in this letter that he had written one before (5.9). The Christians in Corinth had also written to him (7.1), and part of First Corinthians contains Paul's answers to questions they had asked.

Corinth is a large port city in southern Greece. Paul began his work there in a Jewish meeting place, but he had to move next door to the home of a Gentile who had become a follower of Jesus (Act 18.1–17). Most of the followers in Corinth were poor people (1 Corinthians 1.26–29), though some of them were wealthy (1 Corinthians 11.18–21), and one was even the city treasurer (Romans 16.23). While he was in Corinth, Paul worked as a tentmaker to earn a living (Acts 18.3; 1 Corinthians 4.12; 9.1–18).

Paul was especially concerned about the way the Corinthian Christians were always arguing and dividing themselves into groups (1.10—4.21) and about the way they treated one another (5.1—6.20). These are two of Paul's main concerns as he writes this letter. But he also wants to answer the questions they asked him about marriage (7.1–40) and food offered to idols (8.1–13). Paul encourages them to worship God the right way (10.1—14.40) and to be firm in their belief that God has given them victory over death (15.1–58).

Love, Paul tells them, is even more important than faith or hope. All of the problems in the church could be solved, if all the members would love one another, as Christians should:

> *Love is kind and patient,*
> *never jealous, boastful,*
>   *proud, or rude.*
> *Love rejoices in the truth,*
>   *but not in evil.*

> *Love is always supportive,*
> *loyal, hopeful,*
>   *and trusting.*
> *Love never fails!*
>   *(13.4, 5a, 6–8)*

A QUICK LOOK AT THIS LETTER

- Paul's Greeting and Prayer (1.1–9)
- A Call for Unity (1.10—4.21)
- Problems in Relationships (5.1—7.40)
- Honoring God Instead of Idols (8.1—11.1)
- Guidance for Worship and Church Life (11.2—14.40)
- Christ's Victory Over Death (15.1–58)
- An Offering for the Poor (16.1–4)
- Paul's Travel Plans (16.5–12)
- Personal Concerns and Greetings (16.13–24)

1 From Paul, chosen by God to be an apostle of Christ Jesus, and from Sosthenes, who is also a follower.

2To God's church in Corinth. Christ Jesus chose you to be his very own people, and you worship in his name, as we and all others do who call him Lord.

3My prayer is that God our Father and the Lord Jesus Christ will be kind to you and will bless you with peace!

4I never stop thanking my God for being kind enough to give you Christ Jesus, **5**who helps you speak and understand so well. **6**Now you are certain that everything we told you about our Lord Christ Jesus is true. **7**You are not missing out on any blessings, as you wait for him to return. **8**And until the day Christ does return, he will keep you completely innocent. **9**God can be trusted, and he chose you to be partners with his Son, our Lord Jesus Christ.

Taking Sides

10My dear friends, as a follower of our Lord Jesus Christ, I beg you to get along with each other. Don't take sides. Always try to agree in what you think. **11**Several people from Chloe's family*a* have already reported to me that you keep arguing with each other. **12**They have said that some of you claim to follow me, while others claim to follow Apollos or Peter*b* or Christ.

13Has Christ been divided up? Was I nailed to a cross for you? Were you baptized in my name? **14**I thank God*c* that I didn't baptize any of you except Crispus and Gaius. **15**Not one of you can say that you were baptized in my name. **16**I did baptize the family*d* of Stephanas, but I don't remember if I baptized anyone else. **17**Christ did not send me to baptize. He sent me to tell the good news without using big words that would make the cross of Christ lose its power.

Christ Is God's Power and Wisdom

18The message about the cross doesn't make any sense to lost people. But for those of us who are being

---

*a*family: Family members and possibly slaves and others who may have lived in the house. *b*Peter: The Greek text has "Cephas," which is an Aramaic name meaning "rock." Peter is the Greek name with the same meaning. *c*I thank God: Some manuscripts have "I thank my God." *d*family: See the note at 1.11.

saved, it is God's power at work. 19As God says in the Scriptures,

"I will destroy the wisdom
of all who claim
    to be wise.
I will confuse those
who think they know
    so much."

20What happened to those wise people? What happened to those experts in the Scriptures? What happened to the ones who think they have all the answers? Didn't God show that the wisdom of this world is foolish? 21God was wise and decided not to let the people of this world use their wisdom to learn about him.

Instead, God chose to save only those who believe the foolish message we preach. 22Jews ask for miracles, and Greeks want something that sounds wise. 23But we preach that Christ was nailed to a cross. Most Jews have problems with this, and most Gentiles think it is foolish. 24Our message is God's power and wisdom for the Jews and the Greeks that he has chosen. 25Even when God is foolish, he is wiser than everyone else, and even when God is weak, he is stronger than everyone else.

26My dear friends, remember what you were when God chose you. The people of this world didn't think that many of you were wise. Only a few of you were in places of power, and not many of you came from important families. 27But God chose the foolish things of this world to put the wise to shame. He chose the weak things of this world to put the powerful to shame.

28What the world thinks is worthless, useless, and nothing at all is what God has used to destroy what the world considers important. 29God did all this to keep anyone from bragging to him. 30You are God's children. He sent Christ Jesus to save us and to make us wise, acceptable, and holy. 31So if you want to brag, do what the Scriptures say and brag about the Lord.

Telling about Christ and the Cross

2 Friends, when I came and told you the mystery*e* that God had shared with us, I didn't use big words or try to sound wise. 2In fact, while I was with you, I made up my mind to speak only about Jesus Christ, who had been nailed to a cross.

3At first, I was weak and trembling with fear. 4When I talked with you or preached, I didn't try to prove anything by sounding wise. I simply let God's Spirit show his power. 5That way you would have faith because of God's power and not because of human wisdom.

6We do use wisdom when speaking to people who are mature in their faith. But it is not the wisdom of this world or of its rulers, who will soon disappear. 7We speak of God's hidden and mysterious wisdom that God decided to use for our glory long before the world began. 8The rulers of this world didn't know anything about this wisdom. If they had known about it, they would not have nailed the glorious Lord to a cross. 9But it is just as the Scriptures say,

---

e mystery: Some manuscripts have "testimony."

"What God has planned
   for people who love him
is more than eyes have seen
   or ears have heard.
It has never even
   entered our minds!"

10God's Spirit has shown you everything. His Spirit finds out everything, even what is deep in the mind of God. **11**You are the only one who knows what is in your own mind, and God's Spirit is the only one who knows what is in God's mind. **12**But God has given us his Spirit. That's why we don't think the same way that the people of this world think. That's also why we can recognize the blessings that God has given us.

13Every word we speak was taught to us by God's Spirit, not by human wisdom. And this same Spirit helps us teach spiritual things to spiritual people.*f* **14**That's why only someone who has God's Spirit can understand spiritual blessings. Anyone who does not have God's Spirit thinks these blessings are foolish. **15**People who are guided by the Spirit can make all kinds of judgments, but they cannot be judged by others. **16**The Scriptures ask,
"Has anyone ever known
   the thoughts of the Lord
   or given him advice?"
But we understand what Christ is thinking.*g*

Working Together for God

3 My friends, you are acting like the people of this world. That's why I could not speak to you as spiritual peo-

ple. You are like babies as far as your faith in Christ is concerned. **2**So I had to treat you like babies and feed you milk. You could not take solid food, and you still cannot, **3**because you are not yet spiritual. You are jealous and argue with each other. This proves that you are not spiritual and that you are acting like the people of this world.

4Some of you say that you follow me, and others claim to follow Apollos. Isn't that how ordinary people behave? **5**Apollos and I are merely servants who helped you to have faith. It was the Lord who made it all happen. **6**I planted the seeds, Apollos watered them, but God made them sprout and grow. **7**What matters is not those who planted or watered, but God who made the plants grow. **8**The one who plants is just as important as the one who waters. Each one will be paid for what they do. **9**Apollos and I work together for God, and you are God's garden and God's building.

Only One Foundation

10God was kind and let me become an expert builder. I laid a foundation on which others have built. But we must each be careful how we build, **11**because Christ is the only foundation. **12-13**Whatever we build on that foundation will be tested by fire on the day of judgment. Then everyone will find out if we have used gold, silver, and precious stones, or wood, hay, and straw. **14**We will be rewarded if our building is left standing. **15**But if it is destroyed by the fire, we will lose

---

f teach spiritual things to spiritual people: Or "compare spiritual things with spiritual things."
g we understand what Christ is thinking: Or "we think as Christ does."

everything. Yet we ourselves will be saved, like someone escaping from flames.

16All of you surely know that you are God's temple and that his Spirit lives in you. 17Together you are God's holy temple, and God will destroy anyone who destroys his temple.

18Don't fool yourselves! If any of you think you are wise in the things of this world, you will have to become foolish before you can be truly wise. 19This is because God considers the wisdom of this world to be foolish. It is just as the Scriptures say, "God catches the wise when they try to outsmart him." 20The Scriptures also say, "The Lord knows that the plans made by wise people are useless." 21-22So stop bragging about what anyone has done. Paul and Apollos and Peter*h* all belong to you. In fact, everything is yours, including the world, life, death, the present, and the future. Everything belongs to you, 23and you belong to Christ, and Christ belongs to God.

The Work of the Apostles

4 Think of us as servants of Christ who have been given the work of explaining God's mysterious ways. 2And since our first duty is to be faithful to the one we work for, 3it doesn't matter to me if I am judged by you or even by a court of law. In fact, I don't judge myself. 4I don't know of anything against me, but that doesn't prove that I am right. The Lord is my judge. 5So don't judge anyone until the Lord comes. He will show what is hidden in the dark and what is in everyone's

heart. Then God will be the one who praises each of us.

6Friends, I have used Apollos and myself as examples to teach you the meaning of the saying, "Follow the rules." I want you to stop saying that one of us is better than the other. 7What is so special about you? What do you have that you were not given? And if it was given to you, how can you brag? 8Are you already satisfied? Are you now rich? Have you become kings while we are still nobodies? I wish you were kings. Then we could have a share in your kingdom.

9It seems to me that God has put us apostles in the worst possible place. We are like prisoners on their way to death. Angels and the people of this world just laugh at us. 10Because of Christ we are thought of as fools, but Christ has made you wise. We are weak and hated, but you are powerful and respected. 11Even today we go hungry and thirsty and don't have anything to wear except rags. We are mistreated and don't have a place to live. 12We work hard with our own hands, and when people abuse us, we wish them well. When we suffer, we are patient. 13When someone curses us, we answer with kind words. Until now we are thought of as nothing more than the trash and garbage of this world.

14I am not writing to embarrass you. I want to help you, just as parents help their own dear children. 15Ten thousand people may teach you about Christ, but I am your only father. You became my children when I told you about Christ Jesus, 16and I want you to be like me. 17That's why I sent Timothy to you. I love him like a son, and he is a faithful servant of the Lord.

h Peter: See the note at 1.12.

Timothy will tell you what I do to follow Christ and how it agrees with what I always teach about Christ in every church.

18Some of you think I am not coming for a visit, and so you are bragging. 19But if the Lord lets me come, I will soon be there. Then I will find out if the ones who are doing all this bragging really have any power. 20God's kingdom is not just a lot of words. It is power. 21What do you want me to do when I arrive? Do you want me to be hard on you or to be kind and gentle?

Immoral Followers

5 I have heard terrible things about some of you. In fact, you are behaving worse than the Gentiles. A man is even sleeping with his own stepmother.*i* 2You are proud, when you ought to feel bad enough to chase away anyone who acts like that.

3-4I am with you only in my thoughts. But in the name of our Lord Jesus I have already judged this man, as though I were with you in person. So when you meet together and the power of the Lord Jesus is with you, I will be there too. 5You must then hand that man over to Satan. His body will be destroyed, but his spirit will be saved when the Lord Jesus returns.

6Stop being proud! Don't you know how a little yeast can spread through the whole batch of dough? 7Get rid of the old yeast! Then you will be like fresh bread made without yeast, and that is what you are. Our Passover lamb is Christ, who has already been sacrificed. 8So don't celebrate the festival by being evil and sinful, which is like serving bread made with yeast. Be pure and truthful and celebrate by using bread made without yeast.

9In my other letter*j* I told you not to have anything to do with immoral people. 10But I wasn't talking about the people of this world. You would have to leave this world to get away from everyone who is immoral or greedy or who cheats or worships idols. 11I was talking about your own people who are immoral or greedy or worship idols or curse others or get drunk or cheat. Don't even eat with them! 12Why should I judge outsiders? Aren't we supposed to judge only church members? 13God judges everyone else. The Scriptures say, "Chase away any of your own people who are evil."

Taking Each Other to Court

6 When one of you has a complaint against another, do you take your complaint to a court of sinners? Or do you take it to God's people? 2Don't you know that God's people will judge the world? And if you are going to judge the world, can't you settle small problems? 3Don't you know that we will judge angels? And if that is so, we can surely judge everyday matters. 4Why do you take everyday complaints to judges who are not respected by the church? 5I say this to your shame. Aren't any of you wise enough to act as a judge between one follower and another? 6Why should one of you take another to be tried by unbelievers?

7When one of you takes another

---

i is even sleeping with his own stepmother: Or "has even married his own stepmother."
j other letter: An unknown letter that Paul wrote to the Christians at Corinth before he wrote this one.

to court, all of you lose. It would be better to let yourselves be cheated and robbed. 8But instead, you cheat and rob other followers.

9Don't you know that evil people won't have a share in the blessings of God's kingdom? Don't fool yourselves! No one who is immoral or worships idols or is unfaithful in marriage or is a pervert or behaves like a homosexual 10will share in God's kingdom. Neither will any thief or greedy person or drunkard or anyone who curses and cheats others. 11Some of you used to be like that. But now the name of our Lord Jesus Christ and the power of God's Spirit have washed you and made you holy and acceptable to God.

Honor God with Your Body

12Some of you say, "We can do anything we want to." But I tell you that not everything is good for us. So I refuse to let anything have power over me. 13You also say, "Food is meant for our bodies, and our bodies are meant for food." But I tell you that God will destroy them both. We are not supposed to do indecent things with our bodies. We are to use them for the Lord who is in charge of our bodies. 14God will raise us from death by the same power that he used when he raised our Lord to life.

15Don't you know that your bodies are part of the body of Christ? Is it right for me to join part of the body of Christ to an immoral woman? No, it isn't! 16Don't you know that a man who does that becomes part of her body? The Scriptures say, "The two of them will be like one person." 17But anyone who is joined to the Lord is one in spirit with him.

18Don't be immoral in matters of sex. That is a sin against your own body in a way that no other sin is. 19Surely you know that your body is a temple where the Holy Spirit lives. The Spirit is in you and is a gift from God. You are no longer your own. 20God paid a great price for you. So use your body to honor God.

Questions about Marriage

7 Now I will answer the questions that you asked in your letter. You asked, "Is it best for people not to marry?"*k* 2Well, having your own husband or wife should keep you from doing something immoral. 3Husbands and wives should be fair with each other about having sex. 4A wife belongs to her husband instead of to herself, and a husband belongs to his wife instead of to himself. 5So don't refuse sex to each other, unless you agree not to have sex for a little while, in order to spend time in prayer. Then Satan won't be able to tempt you because of your lack of self-control. 6In my opinion that is what should be done, though I don't know of anything the Lord said about this matter. 7I wish that all of you were like me, but God has given different gifts to each of us.

8Here is my advice for people who have never been married and for widows. You should stay single, just as I am. 9But if you don't have enough self-control, then go ahead and get married. After all, it is better to marry than to burn with desire.*l*

10I instruct married couples to stay

---

kpeople not to marry: Or "married couples not to have sex."   *lwith desire*: Or "in the flames of hell."

together, and this is exactly what the Lord himself taught. A wife who leaves her husband [11]should either stay single or go back to her husband. And a husband should not leave his wife.

[12]I don't know of anything else the Lord said about marriage. All I can do is to give you my own advice. If your wife is not a follower of the Lord, but is willing to stay with you, don't divorce her. [13]If your husband is not a follower, but is willing to stay with you, don't divorce him. [14]Your husband or wife who is not a follower is made holy by having you as a mate. This also makes your children holy and keeps them from being unclean in God's sight.

[15]If your husband or wife is not a follower of the Lord and decides to divorce you, then you should agree to it. You are no longer bound to that person. After all, God chose you and wants you to live at peace. [16]And besides, how do you know if you will be able to save your husband or wife who is not a follower?

Obeying the Lord at All Times

[17]In every church I tell the people to stay as they were when the Lord Jesus chose them and God called them to be his own. Now I say the same thing to you. [18]If you are already circumcised, don't try to change it. If you are not circumcised, don't get circumcised. [19]Being circumcised or uncircumcised is not really what matters. The important thing is to obey God's commands. [20]So don't try to change what you were when God chose you.

[21]Are you a slave? Don't let that bother you. But if you can win your freedom, you should. [22]When the Lord chooses slaves, they become his free people. And when he chooses free people, they become slaves of Christ. [23]God paid a great price for you. So don't become slaves of anyone else. [24]Stay what you were when God chose you.

Unmarried People

[25]I don't know of anything that the Lord said about widows or people who have never been married.[m] But I will tell you what I think. And you can trust me, because the Lord has treated me with kindness. [26]We are now going through hard times, and I think it is best for you to stay as you are. [27]If you are married, stay married. If you are not married, don't try to get married. [28]It isn't wrong to marry, even if you have never been married before. But those who marry will have a lot of trouble, and I want to protect you from that.

[29]My friends, what I mean is that the Lord will soon come,[n] and it won't matter if you are married or not. [30]It will be all the same if you are crying or laughing, or if you are buying or are completely broke. [31]It won't make any difference how much good you are getting from this world or how much you like it. This world as we know it is now passing away.

[32]I want all of you to be free from worry. An unmarried man worries about how to please the Lord. [33]But a married man has more worries. He must worry about the things of this world, because he wants to please his

---

[m]*people who have never been married*: Or "virgins." [n]*the Lord will soon come*: Or "There's not much time left" or "The time for decision comes quickly."

wife. 34So he is pulled in two directions. Unmarried women and women who have never been married° worry only about pleasing the Lord, and they keep their bodies and minds pure. But a married woman worries about the things of this world, because she wants to please her husband. 35What I am saying is for your own good. I want to help you to live right and to love the Lord above all else.

36But suppose you are engaged to someone old enough to be married, and you want her so much that all you can think about is getting married. Then go ahead and marry.ᴾ There is nothing wrong with that. 37But it is better to have self-control and to make up your mind not to marry. 38It is perfectly all right to marry, but it is better not to get married at all.

39A wife should stay married to her husband until he dies. Then she is free to marry again, but only to a man who is a follower of the Lord. 40However, I think I am obeying God's Spirit when I say she would be happier to stay single.

Food Offered to Idols

8 In your letter you asked me about food offered to idols. All of us know something about this subject. But knowledge makes us proud of ourselves, while love makes us helpful to others. 2In fact, people who think they know so much don't know anything at all. 3But God has no doubts about who loves him.

4Even though food is offered to idols, we know that none of the idols in this world are alive. After all, there is only one God. 5Many things in heaven and on earth are called gods and lords, but none of them really are gods or lords. 6We have only one God, and he is the Father. He created everything, and we live for him. Jesus Christ is our only Lord. Everything was made by him, and by him life was given to us.

7Not everyone knows these things. In fact, many people have grown up with the belief that idols have life in them. So when they eat meat offered to idols, they are bothered by a weak conscience. 8But food doesn't bring us any closer to God. We are no worse off if we don't eat, and we are no better off if we do.

9Don't cause problems for someone with a weak conscience, just because you have the right to eat anything. 10You know all this, and so it doesn't bother you to eat in the temple of an idol. But suppose a person with a weak conscience sees you and decides to eat food that has been offered to idols. 11Then what you know has destroyed someone Christ died for. 12When you sin by hurting a follower with a weak conscience, you sin against Christ. 13So if I hurt one of the Lord's followers by what I eat, I will never eat meat as long as I live.

°women who have never been married: Or "virgins." ᴾBut suppose you are engaged . . . go ahead and marry: Verses 36-38 may also be translated: 36"If you feel that you are not treating your grown daughter right by keeping her from getting married, then let her marry. You won't be doing anything wrong. 37But it is better to have self-control and make up your mind not to let your daughter get married. 38It is all right for you to let her marry. But it is better if you don't let her marry at all."

The Rights of an Apostle

9 I am free. I am an apostle. I have seen the Lord Jesus and have led you to have faith in him. 2Others may think that I am not an apostle, but you are proof that I am an apostle to you.

3When people question me, I tell them 4that Barnabas and I have the right to our food and drink. 5We each have the right to marry one of the Lord's followers and to take her along with us, just as the other apostles and the Lord's brothers and Peter*q* do. 6Are we the only ones who have to support ourselves by working at another job? 7Do soldiers pay their own salaries? Don't people who raise grapes eat some of what they grow? Don't shepherds get milk from their own goats?

8-9I am not saying this on my own authority. The Law of Moses tells us not to muzzle an ox when it is grinding grain. But was God concerned only about an ox? 10No, he wasn't! He was talking about us. This was written in the Scriptures so that all who plow and all who grind the grain will look forward to sharing in the harvest.

11When we told the message to you, it was like planting spiritual seed. So we have the right to accept material things as our harvest from you. 12If others have the right to do this, we have an even greater right. But we haven't used this right of ours. We are willing to put up with anything to keep from causing trouble for the message about Christ.

13Don't you know that people who work in the temple make their living from what is brought to the temple? Don't you know that a person who serves at the altar is given part of what

is offered? 14In the same way, the Lord wants everyone who preaches the good news to make a living from preaching this message.

15But I have never used these privileges of mine, and I am not writing this because I want to start now. I would rather die than have someone rob me of the right to take pride in this. 16I don't have any reason to brag about preaching the good news. Preaching is something God told me to do, and if I don't do it, I am doomed. 17If I preach because I want to, I will be paid. But even if I don't want to, it is still something that God has sent me to do. 18What pay am I given? It is the chance to preach the good news free of charge and not to use the privileges that are mine because I am a preacher.

19I am not anyone's slave. But I have become a slave to everyone, so that I can win as many people as possible. 20When I am with the Jews, I live like a Jew to win Jews. They are ruled by the Law of Moses, and I am not. But I live by the Law to win them. 21And when I am with people who are not ruled by the Law, I forget about the Law to win them. Of course, I never really forget about the law of God. In fact, I am ruled by the law of Christ. 22When I am with people whose faith is weak, I live as they do to win them. I do everything I can to win everyone I possibly can. 23I do all this for the good news, because I want to share in its blessings.

A Race and a Fight

24You know that many runners enter a race, and only one of them wins

---

qPeter: See the note at 1.12.

the prize. So run to win! 25Athletes work hard to win a crown that cannot last, but we do it for a crown that will last forever. 26I don't run without a goal. And I don't box by beating my fists in the air. 27I keep my body under control and make it my slave, so I won't lose out after telling the good news to others.

Don't Worship Idols

10 Friends, I want to remind you that all of our ancestors walked under the cloud and went through the sea. 2This was like being baptized and becoming followers of Moses. 3All of them also ate the same spiritual food 4and drank the same spiritual drink, which flowed from the spiritual rock that followed them. That rock was Christ. 5But most of them did not please God. So they died, and their bodies were scattered all over the desert.

6What happened to them is a warning to keep us from wanting to do the same evil things. 7They worshiped idols, just as the Scriptures say, "The people sat down to eat and drink. Then they got up to dance around." So don't worship idols. 8Some of those people did shameful things, and in a single day about twenty-three thousand of them died. Don't do shameful things as they did. 9And don't try to test Christ,ʳ as some of them did and were later bitten by poisonous snakes. 10Don't even grumble, as some of them did and were killed by the destroying angel. 11These things happened to them as a warning to us. All this was written in the Scriptures to teach us who live in these last days.

12Even if you think you can stand

up to temptation, be careful not to fall. 13You are tempted in the same way that everyone else is tempted. But God can be trusted not to let you be tempted too much, and he will show you how to escape from your temptations.

14My friends, you must keep away from idols. 15I am speaking to you as people who have enough sense to know what I am talking about. 16When we drink from the cup that we ask God to bless, isn't that sharing in the blood of Christ? When we eat the bread that we break, isn't that sharing in the body of Christ? 17By sharing in the same loaf of bread, we become one body, even though there are many of us.

18Aren't the people of Israel sharing in the worship when they gather around the altar and eat the sacrifices offered there? 19Am I saying that either the idols or the food sacrificed to them is anything at all? 20No, I am not! That food is really sacrificed to demons and not to God. I don't want you to have anything to do with demons. 21You cannot drink from the cup of demons and still drink from the Lord's cup. You cannot eat at the table of demons and still eat at the Lord's table. 22We would make the Lord jealous if we did that. And we are not stronger than the Lord.

Always Honor God

23Some of you say, "We can do whatever we want to!" But I tell you that not everything we do is good or helpful. 24We should think about others and not about ourselves. 25However, when you buy meat in the market, go ahead and eat it. Keep your conscience clear by not asking where the meat came from. 26The Scriptures

---

ʳChrist: Some manuscripts have "the Lord."

say, "The earth and everything in it belong to the Lord."

27If an unbeliever invites you to dinner, and you want to go, then go. Eat whatever you are served. Don't cause a problem for someone's conscience by asking where the food came from. 28-29But if you are told that it has been sacrificed to idols, don't cause a problem by eating it. I don't mean a problem for yourself, but for the one who told you. Why should my freedom be limited by someone else's conscience? 30If I give thanks for what I eat, why should anyone accuse me of doing wrong?

31When you eat or drink or do anything else, always do it to honor God. 32Don't cause problems for Jews or Greeks or anyone else who belongs to God's church. 33I always try to please others instead of myself, in the hope that many of them will be saved. 1You must follow my example, as I follow the example of Christ.

Rules for Worship

2I am proud of you, because you always remember me and obey the teachings I gave you. 3Now I want you to know that Christ is the head over all men, and a man is the head over a woman. But God is the head over Christ. 4This means that any man who prays or prophesies with something on his head brings shame to his head.

5But any woman who prays or prophesies without something on her head brings shame to her head. In fact,

she may as well shave her head.^s 6A woman should wear something on her head. It is a disgrace for a woman to shave her head or cut her hair. But if she refuses to wear something on her head, let her cut off her hair.

7Men were created to be like God and to bring honor to God. This means that a man should not wear anything on his head. Women were created to bring honor to men. 8It was the woman who was made from a man, and not the man who was made from a woman. 9He was not created for her. She was created for him. 10And so, because of this, and also because of the angels, a woman ought to wear something on her head. This will show that she is under someone's authority.

11As far as the Lord is concerned, men and women need each other. 12It is true that the first woman came from a man, but all other men have been given birth by women. Yet God is the one who created everything. 13Ask yourselves if it is proper for a woman to pray without something on her head. 14Isn't it unnatural and disgraceful for men to have long hair? 15But long hair is a beautiful way for a woman to cover her head. 16This is how things are done in all of God's churches,^t and that's why none of you should argue about what I have said.

Rules for the Lord's Supper

17Your worship services do you more harm than good. I am certainly not going to praise you for this. 18I am told that you can't get along with each

---

^s*she may as well shave her head*: A woman's hair was a mark of beauty, and it was shameful for a woman to cut her hair short or to shave her head, so that she looked like a man.   ^t*This is how things are done in all of God's churches*: Or "There is no set rule for this in any of God's churches."

other when you worship, and I am sure that some of what I have heard is true. [19]You are bound to argue with each other, but it is easy to see which of you have God's approval.

[20]When you meet together, you don't really celebrate the Lord's Supper. [21]You even start eating before everyone gets to the meeting, and some of you go hungry, while others get drunk. [22]Don't you have homes where you can eat and drink? Do you hate God's church? Do you want to embarrass people who don't have anything? What can I say to you? I certainly cannot praise you.

The Lord's Supper
(*Matthew* 26.26–29; *Mark* 14.22–25; *Luke* 22.14–20)

[23]I have already told you what the Lord Jesus did on the night he was betrayed. And it came from the Lord himself.

He took some bread in his hands. [24]Then after he had given thanks, he broke it and said, "This is my body, which is given for you. Eat this and remember me."

[25]After the meal, Jesus took a cup of wine in his hands and said, "This is my blood, and with it God makes his new agreement with you. Drink this and remember me."

[26]The Lord meant that when you eat this bread and drink from this cup, you tell about his death until he comes. [27]But if you eat the bread and drink the wine in a way that is not worthy of the Lord, you sin against his body and blood. [28]That's why you must examine the way you eat and drink. [29]If you fail to understand that you are

the body of the Lord, you will condemn yourselves by the way you eat and drink. [30]That's why many of you are sick and weak and why a lot of others have died. [31]If we carefully judge ourselves, we won't be punished. [32]But when the Lord judges and punishes us, he does it to keep us from being condemned with the rest of the world.

[33]My dear friends, you should wait until everyone gets there before you start eating. [34]If you really are hungry, you can eat at home. Then you won't condemn yourselves when you meet together.

After I arrive, I will instruct you about the other matters.

Spiritual Gifts

12 My friends, you asked me about spiritual gifts. [2]I want you to remember that before you became followers of the Lord, you were led in all the wrong ways by idols that cannot even talk. [3]Now I want you to know that if you are led by God's Spirit, you will say that Jesus is Lord, and you will never curse Jesus.

[4]There are different kinds of spiritual gifts, but they all come from the same Spirit. [5]There are different ways to serve the same Lord, [6]and we can each do different things. Yet the same God works in all of us and helps us in everything we do.

[7]The Spirit has given each of us a special way of serving others. [8]Some of us can speak with wisdom, while others can speak with knowledge, but these gifts come from the same Spirit. [9]To others the Spirit has given great faith or the power to heal the sick [10]or the power to work mighty miracles. Some of us are prophets, and some of us recognize when God's Spirit

is present.*a* Others can speak different kinds of languages, and still others can tell what these languages mean. 11But it is the Spirit who does all this and decides which gifts to give to each of us.

One Body with Many Parts

12The body of Christ has many different parts, just as any other body does. 13Some of us are Jews, and others are Gentiles. Some of us are slaves, and others are free. But God's Spirit baptized each of us and made us part of the body of Christ. Now we each drink from that same Spirit.*u*

14Our bodies don't have just one part. They have many parts. 15Suppose a foot says, "I'm not a hand, and so I'm not part of the body." Wouldn't the foot still belong to the body? 16Or suppose an ear says, "I'm not an eye, and so I'm not part of the body." Wouldn't the ear still belong to the body? 17If our bodies were only an eye, we couldn't hear a thing. And if they were only an ear, we couldn't smell a thing. 18But God has put all parts of our body together in the way that he decided is best.

19A body is not really a body, unless there is more than one part. 20It takes many parts to make a single body. 21That's why the eyes cannot say they don't need the hands. That's also why the head cannot say it doesn't need the feet. 22In fact, we cannot get along without the parts of the body that seem to be the weakest. 23We take special care to dress up some parts of our bod-

ies. We are modest about our personal parts, 24but we don't have to be modest about other parts.

God put our bodies together in such a way that even the parts that seem the least important are valuable. 25He did this to make all parts of the body work together smoothly, with each part caring about the others. 26If one part of our body hurts, we hurt all over. If one part of our body is honored, the whole body will be happy.

27Together you are the body of Christ. Each one of you is part of his body. 28First, God chose some people to be apostles and prophets and teachers for the church. But he also chose some to work miracles or heal the sick or help others or be leaders or speak different kinds of languages. 29Not everyone is an apostle. Not everyone is a prophet. Not everyone is a teacher. Not everyone can work miracles. 30Not everyone can heal the sick. Not everyone can speak different kinds of languages. Not everyone can tell what these languages mean. 31I want you to desire the best gifts.*v* So I will show you a much better way.

Love

13 What if I could speak
all languages of humans
    and of angels?
If I did not love others,
    I would be nothing more
than a noisy gong
    or a clanging cymbal.
2What if I could prophesy

---

a and some of us . . present: Or "and some of us recognize the difference between God's Spirit and other spirits." *u Some of us are Jews . . . that same Spirit*: Verse 13 may also be translated, "God's Spirit is inside each of us, and all around us as well. So it doesn't matter that some of us are Jews and others are Gentiles and that some are slaves and others are free. Together we are one body." *v I want you to desire the best gifts*: Or "You desire the best gifts."

and understand all secrets
and all knowledge?
And what if I had faith
that moved mountains?
I would be nothing,
unless I loved others.
3What if I gave away all
that I owned
and let myself
be burned alive?*w*
I would gain nothing,
unless I loved others.
4Love is kind and patient,
never jealous, boastful,
proud, or 5rude.
Love isn't selfish
or quick tempered.
It doesn't keep a record
of wrongs that others do.
6Love rejoices in the truth,
but not in evil.
7Love is always supportive,
loyal, hopeful,
and trusting.
8Love never fails!

Everyone who prophesies
will stop,
and unknown languages
will no longer
be spoken.
All that we know
will be forgotten.
9We don't know everything,
and our prophecies
are not complete.
10But what is perfect
will someday appear,
and what is not perfect
will then disappear.

11When we were children,
we thought and reasoned
as children do.

But when we grew up,
we quit our childish ways.
12Now all we can see of God
is like a cloudy picture
in a mirror.
Later we will see him
face to face.
We don't know everything,
but then we will,
just as God completely
understands us.
13For now there are faith,
hope, and love.
But of these three,
the greatest is love.

Speaking Unknown Languages and Prophesying

14 Love should be your guide. Be eager to have the gifts that come from the Holy Spirit, especially the gift of prophecy. 2If you speak languages that others don't know, God will understand what you are saying, though no one else will know what you mean. You will be talking about mysteries that only the Spirit understands. 3But when you prophesy, you will be understood, and others will be helped. They will be encouraged and made to feel better.

4By speaking languages that others don't know, you help only yourself. But by prophesying you help everyone in the church. 5I am glad for you to speak unknown languages, although I had rather for you to prophesy. In fact, prophesying does much more good than speaking unknown languages, unless someone can help the church by explaining what you mean.

6My friends, what good would it do, if I came and spoke unknown lan-

wand let myself be burned alive: Some manuscripts have "so that I could brag."

guages to you and didn't explain what I meant? How would I help you, unless I told you what God had shown me or gave you some knowledge or prophecy or teaching? 7If all musical instruments sounded alike, how would you know the difference between a flute and a harp? 8If a bugle call isn't clear, how would you know to get ready for battle?

9That's how it is when you speak unknown languages. If no one can understand what you are talking about, you will only be talking to the wind. 10There are many different languages in this world, and all of them make sense. 11But if I don't understand the language that someone is using, we will be like foreigners to each other. 12If you really want spiritual gifts, choose the ones that will be most helpful to the church.

13When we speak languages that others don't know, we should pray for the power to explain what we mean. 14For example, if I use an unknown language in my prayers, my spirit prays but my mind is useless. 15Then what should I do? There are times when I should pray with my spirit, and times when I should pray with my mind. Sometimes I should sing with my spirit, and at other times I should sing with my mind.

16Suppose some strangers are in your worship service, when you are praising God with your spirit. If they don't understand you, how will they know to say, "Amen"? 17You may be worshiping God in a wonderful way, but no one else will be helped. 18I thank God that I speak unknown languages more than any of you. 19But words that make sense can help the church. That's why in church I had rather speak five words that make sense than to speak ten thousand

words in a language that others don't know.

20My friends, stop thinking like children. Think like mature people and be as innocent as tiny babies. 21In the Scriptures the Lord says,

"I will use strangers
who speak unknown languages
to talk to my people.
They will speak to them
in foreign languages,
but still my people
won't listen to me."

22Languages that others don't know may mean something to unbelievers, but not to the Lord's followers. Prophecy, on the other hand, is for followers, not for unbelievers. 23Suppose everyone in your worship service started speaking unknown languages, and some outsiders or some unbelievers come in. Won't they think you are crazy? 24But suppose all of you are prophesying when those unbelievers and outsiders come in. They will realize that they are sinners, and they will want to change their ways because of what you are saying. 25They will tell what is hidden in their hearts. Then they will kneel down and say to God, "We are certain that you are with these people."

Worship Must Be Orderly

26My friends, when you meet to worship, you must do everything for the good of everyone there. That's how it should be when someone sings or teaches or tells what God has said or speaks an unknown language or explains what the language means. 27No more than two or three of you should speak unknown languages during the meeting. You must take turns, and someone should always be there to explain what you mean. 28If no one can explain, you must keep silent in church and speak only to yourself and to God.

29Two or three persons may prophesy, and everyone else must listen carefully. 30If someone sitting there receives a message from God, the speaker must stop and let the other person speak. 31Let only one person speak at a time, then all of you will learn something and be encouraged. 32A prophet should be willing to stop and let someone else speak. 33God wants everything to be done peacefully and in order.

When God's people meet in church, 34the women must not be allowed to speak. They must keep quiet and listen, as the Law of Moses teaches. 35If there is something they want to know, they can ask their husbands when they get home. It is disgraceful for women to speak in church. 36God's message did not start with you people, and you are not the only ones it has reached.

37If you think of yourself as a prophet or a spiritual person, you will know that I am writing only what the Lord has commanded. 38So don't pay attention to anyone who ignores what I am writing.

39My friends, be eager to prophesy and don't stop anyone from speaking languages that others don't know. 40But do everything properly and in order.

Christ Was Raised to Life

15 My friends, I want you to remember the message that I preached and that you believed and trusted. 2You will be saved by this message, if you hold firmly to it. But if you don't, your faith was all for nothing.

3I told you the most important part of the message, and you believed it. That part is:

Christ died for our sins,
    as the Scriptures say.
4He was buried,
    and three days later
he was raised to life,
    as the Scriptures say.
5Christ appeared to Peter,[x]
    then to the twelve.
6After this, he appeared
to more than five hundred
    other followers.
Most of them are still alive,
    but some have died.
7He also appeared to James,
    and then to all
    of the apostles.

8Finally, he appeared to me, even though I am like someone who was born at the wrong time.[y]

9I am the least important of all the apostles. In fact, I caused so much trouble for God's church that I don't even deserve to be called an apostle. 10But God was kind! He made me what I am, and his kindness was not wasted. I worked much harder than any of the other apostles, although it was really God's kindness at work and not me. 11But it doesn't matter if I preached or if they preached. All of you believed the message just the same.

God's People Will Be Raised to Life

12If we preach that Christ was raised from death, how can some of you

---

[x]*Peter*: See the note at 1.12.   [y]*who was born at the wrong time*: The meaning of these words in Greek is not clear.

say that the dead will not be raised to life? 13If they won't be raised to life, Christ himself was not raised to life. 14And if Christ was not raised to life, our message is worthless, and so is your faith. 15If the dead won't be raised to life, we have told lies about God by saying that he raised Christ to life, when he really did not.

16So if the dead won't be raised to life, Christ was not raised to life. 17Unless Christ was raised to life, your faith is useless, and you are still living in your sins. 18And those people who died after putting their faith in him are completely lost. 19If our hope in Christ is good only for this life, we are worse off than anyone else.

20But Christ has been raised to life! And he makes us certain that others will also be raised to life. 21Just as we will die because of Adam, we will be raised to life because of Christ. 22Adam brought death to all of us, and Christ will bring life to all of us. 23But we must each wait our turn. Christ was the first to be raised to life, and his people will be raised to life when he returns. 24Then after Christ has destroyed all powers and forces, the end will come, and he will give the kingdom to God the Father.

25Christ will rule until he puts all his enemies under his power, 26and the last enemy he destroys will be death. 27When the Scriptures say that he will put everything under his power, they don't include God. It was God who put everything under the power of Christ. 28After everything is under the power of God's Son, he will put himself under the power of God, who put everything under his Son's power. Then God will mean everything to everyone.

29If the dead are not going to be raised to life, what will people do who are being baptized for them? Why are they being baptized for those dead people? 30And why do we always risk our lives 31and face death every day? The pride that I have in you because of Christ Jesus our Lord is what makes me say this. 32What do you think I gained by fighting wild animals in Ephesus? If the dead are not raised to life,

"Let's eat and drink.
Tomorrow we die."

33Don't fool yourselves. Bad friends will destroy you. 34Be sensible and stop sinning. You should be embarrassed that some people still don't know about God.

What Our Bodies Will Be Like

35Some of you have asked, "How will the dead be raised to life? What kind of bodies will they have?" 36Don't be foolish. A seed must die before it can sprout from the ground. 37Wheat seeds and all other seeds look different from the sprouts that come up. 38This is because God gives everything the kind of body he wants it to have. 39People, animals, birds, and fish are each made of flesh, but none of them are alike. 40Everything in the heavens has a body, and so does everything on earth. But each one is very different from all the others. 41The sun is not like the moon, the moon is not like the stars, and each star is different.

42That's how it will be when our bodies are raised to life. These bodies will die, but the bodies that are raised will live forever. 43These ugly and weak bodies will become beautiful and strong. 44As surely as there are physical bodies, there are spiritual bodies.

And our physical bodies will be changed into spiritual bodies.

45The first man was named Adam, and the Scriptures tell us that he was a living person. But Jesus, who may be called the last Adam, is a life-giving spirit. **46**We see that the one with a spiritual body did not come first. He came after the one who had a physical body. **47**The first man was made from the dust of the earth, but the second man came from heaven. **48**Everyone on earth has a body like the body of the one who was made from the dust of the earth. And everyone in heaven has a body like the body of the one who came from heaven. **49**Just as we are like the one who was made out of earth, we will be like the one who came from heaven.

50My friends, I want you to know that our bodies of flesh and blood will decay. This means that they cannot share in God's kingdom, which lasts forever. **51**I will explain a mystery to you. Not every one of us will die, but we will all be changed. **52**It will happen suddenly, quicker than the blink of an eye. At the sound of the last trumpet the dead will be raised. We will all be changed, so that we will never die again. **53**Our dead and decaying bodies will be changed into bodies that won't die or decay. **54**The bodies we now have are weak and can die. But they will be changed into bodies that are eternal. Then the Scriptures will come true,

"Death has lost the battle!
55Where is its victory?
Where is its sting?"
56Sin is what gives death its sting, and the Law is the power behind sin. **57**But thank God for letting our Lord Jesus Christ give us the victory!

58My dear friends, stand firm and don't be shaken. Always keep busy working for the Lord. You know that everything you do for him is worthwhile.

A Collection for God's People

16 When you collect money for God's people, I want you to do exactly what I told the churches in Galatia to do. **2**That is, each Sunday each of you must put aside part of what you have earned. If you do this, you won't have to take up a collection when I come. **3**Choose some followers to take the money to Jerusalem. I will send them on with the money and with letters which show that you approve of them. **4**If you think I should go along, they can go with me.

Paul's Travel Plans

5After I have gone through Macedonia, I hope to see you **6**and visit with you for a while. I may even stay all winter, so that you can help me on my way to wherever I will be going next. **7**If the Lord lets me, I would rather come later for a longer visit than to stop off now for only a short visit. **8**I will stay in Ephesus until Pentecost, **9**because there is a wonderful opportunity for me to do some work here. But there are also many people who are against me.

10When Timothy arrives, give him a friendly welcome. He is doing the Lord's work, just as I am. **11**Don't let anyone mistreat him. I am looking for him to return to me together with the other followers. So when he leaves, send him off with your blessings.

12I have tried hard to get our friend Apollos to visit you with the other followers. He doesn't want to come just now, but he will come when he can.

Personal Concerns and Greetings

13Keep alert. Be firm in your faith. Stay brave and strong. 14Show love in everything you do.

15You know that Stephanas and his family were the first in Achaia to have faith in the Lord. They have done all they can for God's people. My friends, I ask you 16to obey leaders like them and to do the same for all others who work hard with you.

17I was glad to see Stephanas and Fortunatus and Achaicus. Having them here was like having you. 18They made me feel much better, just as they made you feel better. You should appreciate people like them.

19Greetings from the churches in Asia.

Aquila and Priscilla, together with the church that meets in their house, send greetings in the name of the Lord.

20All of the Lord's followers send their greetings.

Give each other a warm greeting.

21I am signing this letter myself: PAUL.

22I pray that God will put a curse on everyone who does not love the Lord. And may the Lord come soon.

23I pray that the Lord Jesus will be kind to you.

24I love everyone who belongs to Christ Jesus. Amen.

Paul's Second Letter to the Church in Corinth

≈≈◁▷≈≈

ABOUT THIS LETTER

In the beginning of this letter Paul answers the concerns of the Christians in Corinth who accused him of not living up to his promise to visit them. Paul had changed his mind for a good reason. He had stayed away from Corinth so that he would not seem to be too hard and demanding (1.23). He also wanted to see if they would follow his instructions about forgiving and comforting people who had sinned (2.5–11).

Paul reminds the Corinthians that God is generous and wants them to be just as generous in their giving to help God's people in Jerusalem and Judea (8.1—9.15).

Paul is a servant of God's new agreement (3.1–17). He is faithful in trying to bring people to God, even if it means terrible suffering for himself (4.1—6.13; 10.1—12.10). And what has God done to make it possible for us to come to him?

God has done it all! He sent Christ to make peace between himself and us, and he has given us the work of making peace between himself and others.

What we mean is that God was in Christ, offering peace and forgiveness to the people of this world. And he has given us the work of sharing his message about peace.   *(5.18,19)*

A QUICK LOOK AT THIS LETTER

- Paul Gives Thanks to God (1.1–11)
- The Work of an Apostle for God's People (1.12—2.17)
- Guided by the Love of Christ (3.1—7.16)
- Gifts for the Poor (8.1—9.15)
- Paul Is a True Apostle (10.1—13.10)
- Final Greetings (13.11–13)

1 From Paul, chosen by God to be an apostle of Jesus Christ, and from Timothy, who is also a follower.

To God's church in Corinth and to all of God's people in Achaia.

²I pray that God our Father and the Lord Jesus Christ will be kind to you and will bless you with peace!

Paul Gives Thanks

³Praise God, the Father of our Lord Jesus Christ! The Father is a merciful God, who always gives us comfort. ⁴He comforts us when we are in trouble, so that we can share that same comfort with others in trouble. ⁵We share in the terrible sufferings of Christ, but also in the wonderful comfort he gives. ⁶We suffer in the hope that you will be comforted and saved. And because we are comforted, you will also be comforted, as you patiently endure suffering like ours. ⁷You never disappoint us. You suffered as much as we did, and we know that you will be comforted as we were.

⁸My friends, I want you to know what a hard time we had in Asia. Our sufferings were so horrible and so unbearable that death seemed certain. ⁹In fact, we felt sure that we were going to die. But this made us stop trusting in ourselves and start trusting God, who raises the dead to life. ¹⁰God saved us from the threat of death,ᵃ and we are sure that he will do it again and again. ¹¹Please help us by praying for us. Then many people will give thanks for the blessings we receive in answer to all these prayers.

Paul's Change of Plans

¹²We can be proud of our clear conscience. We have always lived honestly and sincerely, especially when we were with you. And we were guided by God's kindness instead of by the wisdom of this world. ¹³I am not writing anything you cannot read and understand. I hope you will understand it completely, ¹⁴just as you already partly understand us. Then when our Lord Jesus returns, you can be as proud of us as we are of you.

¹⁵I was so sure of your pride in us that I had planned to visit you first of all. In this way you would have the blessing of two visits from me. ¹⁶Once on my way to Macedonia and again on my return from there. Then you could send me on to Judea. ¹⁷Do you think I couldn't make up my mind about what to do? Or do I seem like someone who says "Yes" or "No" simply to please others? ¹⁸God can be trusted, and so can I, when I say that our answer to you has always been "Yes" and never "No." ¹⁹This is because Jesus Christ the Son of God is always "Yes" and never "No." And he is the one that

---

ᵃ*the threat of death*: Some manuscripts have "many threats of death."

Silas,[b] Timothy, and I told you about. 20Christ says "Yes" to all of God's promises. That's why we have Christ to say "Amen"[c] for us to the glory of God. 21And so God makes it possible for you and us to stand firmly together with Christ. God is also the one who chose us 22and put his Spirit in our hearts to show that we belong only to him.

23God is my witness that I stayed away from Corinth, just to keep from being hard on you. 24We are not bosses who tell you what to believe. We are working with you to make you glad, because your faith is strong.

2 I have decided not to make my next visit with you so painful. 2If I make you feel bad, who would be left to cheer me up, except the people I had made to feel bad? 3The reason I want to be happy is to make you happy. I wrote as I did because I didn't want to visit you and be made to feel bad, when you should make me feel happy. 4At the time I wrote, I was suffering terribly. My eyes were full of tears, and my heart was broken. But I didn't want to make you feel bad. I only wanted to let you know how much I cared for you.

Forgiveness

5I don't want to be hard on you. But if one of you has made someone feel bad, I am not really the one who has been made to feel bad. Some of you are the ones. 6Most of you have already pointed out the wrong that person did, and that is punishment enough for what was done. 7When people sin, you should for-

give and comfort them, so they won't give up in despair. 8You should make them sure of your love for them.

9I also wrote because I wanted to test you and find out if you would follow my instructions. 10I will forgive anyone you forgive. Yes, for your sake and with Christ as my witness, I have forgiven whatever needed to be forgiven. 11I have done this to keep Satan from getting the better of us. We all know what goes on in his mind.

12When I went to Troas to preach the good news about Christ, I found that the Lord had already prepared the way. 13But I was worried when I didn't find my friend Titus there. So I left the other followers and went on to Macedonia.

14I am grateful that God always makes it possible for Christ to lead us to victory. God also helps us spread the knowledge about Christ everywhere, and this knowledge is like the smell of perfume. 15-16In fact, God thinks of us as a perfume that brings Christ to everyone. For people who are being saved, this perfume has a sweet smell and leads them to a better life. But for people who are lost, it has a bad smell and leads them to a horrible death.

No one really has what it takes to do this work. 17A lot of people try to get rich from preaching God's message. But we are God's sincere messengers, and by the power of Christ we speak our message with God as our witness.

God's New Agreement

3 Are we once again bragging about ourselves? Do we need letters to

---

[b]*Silas*: The Greek text has "Silvanus," which is another form of the name Silas.   [c]*Amen*: The word "amen" is used here with the meaning of "yes."

you or from you to tell others about us? Some people do need letters that tell about them. 2But you are our letter, and you are in our*d* hearts for everyone to read and understand. 3You are like a letter written by Christ and delivered by us. But you are not written with pen and ink or on tablets made of stone. You are written in our hearts by the Spirit of the living God.

4We are sure about all this. Christ makes us sure in the very presence of God. 5We don't have the right to claim that we have done anything on our own. God gives us what it takes to do all that we do. 6He makes us worthy to be the servants of his new agreement that comes from the Holy Spirit and not from a written Law. After all, the Law brings death, but the Spirit brings life.

7The Law of Moses brought only the promise of death, even though it was carved on stones and given in a wonderful way. Still the Law made Moses' face shine so brightly that the people of Israel could not look at it, even though it was a fading glory. 8So won't the agreement that the Spirit brings to us be even more wonderful? 9If something that brings the death sentence is glorious, won't something that makes us acceptable to God be even more glorious? 10In fact, the new agreement is so wonderful that the Law is no longer glorious at all. 11The Law was given with a glory that faded away. But the glory of the new agreement is much greater, because it will never fade away.

12This wonderful hope makes us feel like speaking freely. 13We are not like Moses. His face was shining, but he covered it to keep the people of Is-

rael from seeing the brightness fade away. 14The people were stubborn, and something still keeps them from seeing the truth when the Law is read. Only Christ can take away the covering that keeps them from seeing.

15When the Law of Moses is read, the people of Israel have their minds covered over 16with a covering that is removed only for those who turn to the Lord. 17The Lord and the Spirit are one and the same, and the Lord's Spirit sets us free. 18So our faces are not covered. They show the bright glory of the Lord, as the Lord's Spirit makes us more and more like our glorious Lord.

Treasure in Clay Jars

4 God has been kind enough to trust us with this work. That's why we never give up. 2We don't do shameful things that must be kept secret. And we don't try to fool anyone or twist God's message around. God is our witness that we speak only the truth, so others will be sure that we can be trusted. 3If there is anything hidden about our message, it is hidden only to someone who is lost.

4The god who rules this world has blinded the minds of unbelievers. They cannot see the light, which is the good news about our glorious Christ, who shows what God is like. 5We are not preaching about ourselves. Our message is that Jesus Christ is Lord. He also sent us to be your servants. 6The Scriptures say, "God commanded light to shine in the dark." Now God is shining in our hearts to let you know that his glory is seen in Jesus Christ.

7We are like clay jars in which this treasure is stored. The real power

---

dour: Some manuscripts have "your."

comes from God and not from us. 8We often suffer, but we are never crushed. Even when we don't know what to do, we never give up. 9In times of trouble, God is with us, and when we are knocked down, we get up again. 10-11We face death every day because of Jesus. Our bodies show what his death was like, so that his life can also be seen in us. 12This means that death is working in us, but life is working in you.

13In the Scriptures it says, "I spoke because I had faith." We have that same kind of faith. So we speak 14because we know that God raised Jesus Christ to life. And just as God raised Jesus, he will also raise us to life. Then he will bring us into his presence together with you. 15All of this has been done for you, so that more and more people will know how kind God is and will praise and honor him.

want to live in that heavenly home. 3We want to put it on like clothes and not be naked.

4These tents we now live in are like a heavy burden, and we groan. But we don't do this just because we want to leave these bodies that will die. It is because we want to change them for bodies that will never die. 5God is the one who makes all of this possible. He has given us his Spirit to make us certain that he will do it. 6So always be cheerful!

As long as we are in these bodies, we are away from the Lord. 7But we live by faith, not by what we see. 8We should be cheerful, because we would rather leave these bodies and be at home with the Lord. 9But whether we are at home with the Lord or away from him, we still try our best to please him. 10After all, Christ will judge each of us for the good or the bad that we do while living in these bodies.

Faith in the Lord

16We never give up. Our bodies are gradually dying, but we ourselves are being made stronger each day. 17These little troubles are getting us ready for an eternal glory that will make all our troubles seem like nothing. 18Things that are seen don't last forever, but things that are not seen are eternal. That's why we keep our minds on the things that cannot be seen.

5 Our bodies are like tents that we live in here on earth. But when these tents are destroyed, we know that God will give each of us a place to live. These homes will not be buildings that someone has made, but they are in heaven and will last forever. 2While we are here on earth, we sigh because we

Bringing People to God

11We know what it means to respect the Lord, and we encourage everyone to turn to him. God himself knows what we are like, and I hope you also know what kind of people we are. 12We are not trying once more to brag about ourselves. But we want you to be proud of us, when you are with those who are not sincere and brag about what others think of them.

13If we seem out of our minds, it is between God and us. But if we are in our right minds, it is for your good. 14We are ruled by Christ's love for us. We are certain that if one person died for everyone else, then all of us have died. 15And Christ did die for all of us. He died so we would no longer live for ourselves, but for the one who died and was raised to life for us.

16We are careful not to judge people by what they seem to be, though we once judged Christ in that way. 17Anyone who belongs to Christ is a new person. The past is forgotten, and everything is new. 18God has done it all! He sent Christ to make peace between himself and us, and he has given us the work of making peace between himself and others.

19What we mean is that God was in Christ, offering peace and forgiveness to the people of this world. And he has given us the work of sharing his message about peace. 20We were sent to speak for Christ, and God is begging you to listen to our message. We speak for Christ and sincerely ask you to make peace with God. 21Christ never sinned! But God treated him as a sinner, so that Christ could make us acceptable to God.

6 We work together with God, and we beg you to make good use of God's kindness to you. 2In the Scriptures God says,

"When the time came,
I listened to you,
and when you needed help,
I came to save you."

That time has come. This is the day for you to be saved.

3We don't want anyone to find fault with our work, and so we try hard not to cause problems. 4But in everything and in every way we show that we truly are God's servants. We have always been patient, though we have had a lot of trouble, suffering, and hard times. 5We have been beaten, put in jail, and hurt in riots. We have worked hard and have gone without sleep or food. 6But we have kept ourselves pure and have been understanding, patient, and kind. The Holy Spirit has been with us, and our love has been real. 7We have spoken the truth, and God's power has worked in us. In all our struggles we have said and done only what is right.

8Whether we were honored or dishonored or praised or cursed, we always told the truth about ourselves. But some people said we did not. 9We are unknown to others, but well known to you. We seem to be dying, and yet we are still alive. We have been punished, but never killed, 10and we are always happy, even in times of suffering. Although we are poor, we have made many people rich. And though we own nothing, everything is ours.

11Friends in Corinth, we are telling the truth when we say that there is room in our hearts for you. 12We are not holding back on our love for you, but you are holding back on your love for us. 13I speak to you as I would speak to my own children. Please make room in your hearts for us.

The Temple of the Living God

14Stay away from people who are not followers of the Lord! Can someone who is good get along with someone who is evil? Are light and darkness the same? 15Is Christ a friend of Satan?*e* Can people who follow the Lord have anything in common with those who don't? 16Do idols belong in the temple of God? We are the temple of the living God, as God himself says,

---

*e*Satan: The Greek text has "Beliar," which is another form of the Hebrew word "Belial," meaning "wicked" or "useless." The Jewish people sometimes used this as a name for Satan.

"I will live with these people
and walk among them.
I will be their God,
and they will be
my people."
17The Lord also says,
"Leave them and stay away!
Don't touch anything
that is not clean.
Then I will welcome you
18   and be your Father.
You will be my sons
and my daughters,
as surely as I am God,
the all-powerful."

7 My friends, God has made us these promises. So we should stay away from everything that keeps our bodies and spirits from being clean. We should honor God and try to be completely like him.

The Church Makes Paul Happy

2Make a place for us in your hearts! We haven't mistreated anyone or hurt anyone. We haven't cheated anyone. 3I am not saying this to be hard on you. But, as I have said before, you will always be in our thoughts, whether we live or die. 4I trust you completely.f I am always proud of you, and I am greatly encouraged. In all my trouble I am still very happy.

5After we came to Macedonia, we didn't have any chance to rest. We were faced with all kinds of problems. We were troubled by enemies and troubled by fears. 6But God cheers up people in need, and that is what he did when he sent Titus to us. 7Of course, we were glad to see Titus, but what really made us glad is the way you cheered him up. He told how sorry you were and how concerned you were about me. And this made me even happier.

8I don't feel bad anymore, even though my letter g hurt your feelings. I did feel bad at first, but I don't now. I know that the letter hurt you for a while. 9Now I am happy, but not because I hurt your feelings. It is because God used your hurt feelings to make you turn back to him, and none of you were harmed by us. 10When God makes you feel sorry enough to turn to him and be saved, you don't have anything to feel bad about. But when this world makes you feel sorry, it can cause your death.

11Just look what God has done by making you feel sorry! You sincerely want to prove that you are innocent. You are angry. You are shocked. You are eager to see that justice is done. You have proved that you were completely right in this matter. 12When I wrote you, it wasn't to accuse the one who was wrong or to take up for the one who was hurt. I wrote, so that God would show you how much you do care for us. 13And we were greatly encouraged.

Although we were encouraged, we felt even better when we saw how happy Titus was, because you had shown that he had nothing to worry about. 14We had told him how much we thought of you, and you did not disappoint us. Just as we have always told you the truth, so everything we told him about you has also proved to be true. 15Titus loves all of you very much, especially when he remembers

---

fI trust you completely: Or "I have always spoken the truth to you" or "I can speak freely to you."   gmy letter: There is no copy of this letter that Paul wrote to the church at Corinth.

how you obeyed him and how you trembled with fear when you welcomed him. 16It makes me really glad to know that I can depend on you.

Generous Giving

8 My friends, we want you to know that the churches in Macedonia[h] have shown others how kind God is. 2Although they were going through hard times and were very poor, they were glad to give generously. 3They gave as much as they could afford and even more, simply because they wanted to. 4They even asked and begged us to let them have the joy of giving their money for God's people. 5And they did more than we had hoped. They gave themselves first to the Lord and then to us, just as God wanted them to do.

6Titus was the one who got you started doing this good thing, so we begged him to have you finish what you had begun. 7You do everything better than anyone else. You have stronger faith. You speak better and know more. You are eager to give, and you love us better.[i] Now you must give more generously than anyone else.

8I am not ordering you to do this. I am simply testing how real your love is by comparing it with the concern that others have shown. 9You know that our Lord Jesus Christ was kind enough to give up all his riches and become poor, so that you could become rich.

10A year ago you were the first ones to give, and you gave because you wanted to. So listen to my advice. 11I think you should finish what you started. If you give according to what you have, you will prove that you are as eager to give as you were to think about giving. 12It doesn't matter how much you have. What matters is how much you are willing to give from what you have.

13I am not trying to make life easier for others by making life harder for you. But it is only fair 14for you to share with them when you have so much, and they have so little. Later, when they have more than enough, and you are in need, they can share with you. Then everyone will have a fair share, 15just as the Scriptures say,

"Those who gathered
too much
        had nothing left.
Those who gathered
only a little
        had all they needed."

Titus and His Friends

16I am grateful that God made Titus care as much about you as we do. 17When we begged Titus to visit you, he said he would. He wanted to because he cared so much for you. 18With Titus we are also sending one of the Lord's followers who is well known in every church for spreading the good news. 19The churches chose this follower to travel with us while we carry this gift that will bring praise to the Lord and show how much we hope to help. 20We don't want anyone to find fault with the way we handle your generous gift. 21But we want to do what

---

[h]*churches in Macedonia*: The churches that Paul had started in Philippi and Thessalonica. The church in Berea is probably also meant. [i]*you love us better*: Some manuscripts have "we love you better."

pleases the Lord and what people think is right.

22We are also sending someone else with Titus and the other follower. We approve of this man. In fact, he has already shown us many times that he wants to help. And now he wants to help even more than ever, because he trusts you so much. 23Titus is my partner, who works with me to serve you. The other two followers are sent by the churches, and they bring honor to Christ. 24Treat them in such a way that the churches will see your love and will know why we bragged about you.

The Money for God's People

9 I don't need to write you about the money you plan to give for God's people. 2I know how eager you are to give. And I have proudly told the Lord's followers in Macedonia that you people in Achaia have been ready for a whole year. Now your desire to give has made them want to give. 3That's why I am sending Titus and the two others to you. I want you to be ready, just as I promised. This will prove that we were not wrong to brag about you.

4Some followers from Macedonia may come with me, and I want them to find that you have the money ready. If you don't, I would be embarrassed for trusting you to do this. But you would be embarrassed even more. 5So I have decided to ask Titus and the others to spend some time with you before I arrive. This way they can arrange to collect the money you have promised. Then you will have the chance to give because you want to, and not because you feel forced to.

6Remember this saying,

"A few seeds make

a small harvest,
but a lot of seeds make
a big harvest."

7Each of you must make up your own mind about how much to give. But don't feel sorry that you must give and don't feel that you are forced to give. God loves people who love to give. 8God can bless you with everything you need, and you will always have more than enough to do all kinds of good things for others. 9The Scriptures say,

"God freely gives his gifts
to the poor,
and always does right."

10God gives seed to farmers and provides everyone with food. He will increase what you have, so that you can give even more to those in need. 11You will be blessed in every way, and you will be able to keep on being generous. Then many people will thank God when we deliver your gift.

12What you are doing is much more than a service that supplies God's people with what they need. It is something that will make many others thank God. 13The way in which you have proved yourselves by this service will bring honor and praise to God. You believed the message about Christ, and you obeyed it by sharing generously with God's people and with everyone else. 14Now they are praying for you and want to see you, because God used you to bless them so very much. 15Thank God for his gift that is too wonderful for words!

Paul Defends His Work for Christ

10 Do you think I am a coward when I am with you and brave when I am far away? Well, I ask you to listen, because Christ himself was humble and gentle. 2Some people have

said that we act like the people of this world. So when I arrive, I expect I will have to be firm and forceful in what I say to them. Please don't make me treat you that way. 3We live in this world, but we don't act like its people 4or fight our battles with the weapons of this world. Instead, we use God's power that can destroy fortresses. We destroy arguments 5and every bit of pride that keeps anyone from knowing God. We capture people's thoughts and make them obey Christ. 6And when you completely obey him, we will punish anyone who refuses to obey.

7You judge by appearances.*j* If any of you think you are the only ones who belong to Christ, then think again. We belong to Christ as much as you do. 8Maybe I brag a little too much about the authority that the Lord gave me to help you and not to hurt you. Yet I am not embarrassed to brag. 9And I am not trying to scare you with my letters. 10Some of you are saying, "Paul's letters are harsh and powerful. But in person, he is a weakling and has nothing worth saying." 11Those people had better understand that when I am with you, I will do exactly what I say in my letters.

12We won't dare compare ourselves with those who think so much of themselves. But they are foolish to compare themselves with themselves. 13We won't brag about something we don't have a right to brag about. We will only brag about the work that God has sent us to do, and you are part of that work. 14We are not bragging more than we should. After all, we did bring the message about Christ to you.

15We don't brag about what others have done, as if we had done those things ourselves. But I hope that as you become stronger in your faith, we will be able to reach many more of the people around you.*k* That has always been our goal. 16Then we will be able to preach the good news in other lands where we cannot take credit for work someone else has already done. 17The Scriptures say, "If you want to brag, then brag about the Lord." 18You may brag about yourself, but the only approval that counts is the Lord's approval.

Paul and the False Apostles

11 Please put up with a little of my foolishness. 2I am as concerned about you as God is. You were like a virgin bride I had chosen only for Christ. 3But now I fear that you will be tricked, just as Eve was tricked by that lying snake. I am afraid that you might stop thinking about Christ in an honest and sincere way. 4We told you about Jesus, and you received the Holy Spirit and accepted our message. But you let some people tell you about another Jesus. Now you are ready to receive another spirit and accept a different message. 5I think I am as good as any of those super apostles. 6I may not speak as well as they do, but I know as much. And this has already been made perfectly clear to you.

7Was it wrong for me to lower myself and honor you by preaching God's message free of charge? 8I robbed other churches by taking money from them

---

j You judge by appearances: Or "Take a close look at yourselves."   *k we will be able to reach many more of the people around you*: Or "you will praise us even more because of our work among you."

to serve you. 9Even when I was in need, I still didn't bother you. In fact, some of the Lord's followers from Macedonia brought me what I needed. I have not been a burden to you in the past, and I will never be a burden. 10As surely as I speak the truth about Christ, no one in Achaia can stop me from bragging about this. 11And it isn't because I don't love you. God himself knows how much I do love you.

12I plan to go on doing just what I have always done. Then those people won't be able to brag about doing the same things we are doing. 13Anyway, they are no more than false apostles and dishonest workers. They only pretend to be apostles of Christ. 14And it is no wonder. Even Satan tries to make himself look like an angel of light. 15So why does it seem strange for Satan's servants to pretend to do what is right? Someday they will get exactly what they deserve.

Paul's Sufferings for Christ

16I don't want any of you to think that I am a fool. But if you do, then let me be a fool and brag a little. 17When I do all this bragging, I do it as a fool and not for the Lord. 18Yet if others want to brag about what they have done, so will I. 19And since you are so smart, you will gladly put up with a fool. 20In fact, you let people make slaves of you and cheat you and steal from you. Why, you even let them strut around and slap you in the face. 21I am ashamed to say that we are too weak to behave in such a way.

If they can brag, so can I, but it is a foolish thing to do. 22Are they Hebrews? So am I. Are they Jews? So am I. Are they from the family of Abraham? Well, so am I. 23Are they servants of Christ? I am a fool to talk this way, but I serve him better than they do. I have worked harder and have been put in jail more times. I have been beaten with whips more and have been in danger of death more often.

24Five times the Jews gave me thirty-nine lashes with a whip. 25Three times the Romans beat me with a big stick, and once my enemies stoned me. I have been shipwrecked three times, and I even had to spend a night and a day in the sea. 26During my many travels, I have been in danger from rivers, robbers, Jews, and foreigners. My life has been in danger in cities, in deserts, at sea, and with people who only pretended to be the Lord's followers.

27I have worked and struggled and spent many sleepless nights. I have gone hungry and thirsty and often had nothing to eat. I have been cold from not having enough clothes to keep me warm. 28Besides everything else, each day I am burdened down, worrying about all the churches. 29When others are weak, I am weak too. When others are tricked into sin, I get angry.[l]

30If I have to brag, I will brag about how weak I am. 31God, the Father of our Lord Jesus, knows I am not lying. And God is to be praised forever! 32The governor of Damascus at the time of King Aretas had the city gates guarded, so that he could capture me. 33But I escaped by being let down in a basket through a window in the city wall.

[l]When others are tricked into sin, I get angry: Or "When others stumble into sin, I hurt for them."

Visions from the Lord

12 I have to brag. There is nothing to be gained by it, but I must brag about the visions and other things that the Lord has shown me. 2I know about one of Christ's followers who was taken up into the third heaven fourteen years ago. I don't know if the man was still in his body when it happened, but God surely knows.

3As I said, only God really knows if this man was in his body at the time. 4But he was taken up into paradise,*m* where he heard things that are too wonderful to tell. 5I will brag about that man, but not about myself, except to say how weak I am.

6Yet even if I did brag, I would not be foolish. I would simply be speaking the truth. But I will try not to say too much. That way, none of you will think more highly of me than you should because of what you have seen me do and say. 7Of course, I am now referring to the wonderful things I saw. One of Satan's angels was sent to make me suffer terribly, so that I would not feel too proud.*n*

8Three times I begged the Lord to make this suffering go away. 9But he replied, "My kindness is all you need. My power is strongest when you are weak." So if Christ keeps giving me his power, I will gladly brag about how weak I am. 10Yes, I am glad to be weak or insulted or mistreated or to have troubles and sufferings, if it is for Christ. Because when I am weak, I am strong.

Paul's Concern for the Lord's Followers at Corinth

11I have been making a fool of myself. But you forced me to do it, when you should have been speaking up for me. I may be nothing at all, but I am as good as those super apostles. 12When I was with you, I was patient and worked all the powerful miracles and signs and wonders of a true apostle. 13You missed out on only one blessing that the other churches received. That is, you didn't have to support me. Forgive me for doing you wrong.

14I am planning to visit you for the third time. But I still won't make a burden of myself. What I really want is you, and not what you have. Children are not supposed to save up for their parents, but parents are supposed to take care of their children. 15So I will gladly give all that I have and all that I am. Will you love me less for loving you too much? 16You agree that I was not a burden to you. Maybe that's because I was trying to catch you off guard and trick you. 17Were you cheated by any of those I sent to you? 18I urged Titus to visit you, and I sent another follower with him. But Titus didn't cheat you, and we felt and behaved the same way he did.

19Have you been thinking all along that we have been defending ourselves to you? Actually, we have been speaking to God as followers of Christ. But, my friends, we did it all for your good.

20I am afraid that when I come, we won't be pleased with each other.

---

m paradise: In the Greek translation of the Old Testament, this word is used for the Garden of Eden. In New Testament times it was sometimes used for the place where God's people are happy and at rest, as they wait for the final judgment. *n Of course . . . too proud*: Or "Because of the wonderful things that I saw, one of Satan's angels was sent to make me suffer terribly, so that I would not feel too proud."

I fear that some of you may be arguing or jealous or angry or selfish or gossiping or insulting each other. I even fear that you may be proud and acting like a mob. 21I am afraid God will make me ashamed when I visit you again. I will feel like crying because many of you have never given up your old sins. You are still doing things that are immoral, indecent, and shameful.

Final Warnings and Greetings

13 I am on my way to visit you for the third time. And as the Scriptures say, "Any charges must be proved true by at least two or three witnesses." 2During my second visit I warned you that I would punish you and anyone else who doesn't stop sinning. I am far away from you now, but I give you the same warning. 3This should prove to you that I am speaking for Christ. When he corrects you, he won't be weak. He will be powerful! 4Although he was weak when he was nailed to the cross, he now lives by the power of God. We are weak, just as Christ was. But you will see that we will live by the power of God, just as Christ does.

5Test yourselves and find out if you really are true to your faith. If you pass the test, you will discover that Christ is living in you. But if Christ isn't living in you, you have failed. 6I hope you will discover that we have not failed. 7We pray that you will stop doing evil things. We don't pray like this to make ourselves look good, but to get you to do right, even if we are failures.

8All we can do is to follow the truth and not fight against it. 9Even though we are weak, we are glad that you are strong, and we pray that you will do even better. 10I am writing these things to you before I arrive. This way I won't have to be hard on you when I use the authority that the Lord has given me. I was given this authority, so that I could help you and not destroy you.

11Good-by, my friends. Do better and pay attention to what I have said. Try to get along and live peacefully with each other.

Now I pray that God, who gives love and peace, will be with you. 12Give each other a warm greeting. All of God's people send their greetings.

13I pray that the Lord Jesus Christ will bless you and be kind to you! May God bless you with his love, and may the Holy Spirit join all your hearts together.

Paul's Letter
to the Churches in Galatia

ABOUT THIS LETTER

From the very beginning of this letter to the churches in the region of Galatia (in central Asia Minor), Paul makes two things clear to his readers: he is a true apostle, and his message is the only true message (1.1–10). These statements were very important, because some people claimed that Paul was a false apostle with a false message.

Paul was indeed a true apostle, and his mission to the Gentiles was given to him by the Lord and approved by the apostles in Jerusalem (1.18—2.10). Paul had even corrected the apostle Peter, when he had stopped eating with Gentile followers who were not obeying the Law of Moses (2.1–18).

Faith is the only way to be saved. Paul insists that this was true already for Abraham, who had received God's promise by faith. And Paul leaves no doubt about what his own faith means to him:

> I have been nailed to the cross with Christ. I have died, but Christ lives in me. And I now live by faith in the Son of God, who loved me and gave his life for me.
>
> (2.19b, 20)

A QUICK LOOK AT THIS LETTER

- A True Apostle and the True Message (1.1–10)
- God Chose Paul To Be an Apostle (1.11–24)
- Paul Defends His Message (2.1–21)
- Faith Is the Only Way To Be Saved (3.1—4.31)
- Guided by the Spirit and Love (5.1—6.10)
- Final Warnings (6.11–18)

---

1 **1-2**From the apostle Paul and from all the Lord's followers with me.

I was chosen to be an apostle by Jesus Christ and by God the Father, who raised him from death. No mere human chose or appointed me to this work.

To the churches in Galatia.

3I pray that God the Father and our Lord Jesus Christ will be kind to you and will bless you with peace! **4**Christ obeyed God our Father and gave himself as a sacrifice for our sins to rescue us from this evil world. **5**God will be given glory forever and ever. Amen.

The Only True Message

6I am shocked that you have so quickly turned from God, who chose you because of his kindness.ᵃ You have believed another message, 7when there is really only one true message. But some people are causing you trouble and want to make you turn away from the good news about Christ. 8I pray that God will punish anyone who preaches anything different from our message to you! It doesn't matter if that person is one of us or an angel from heaven. 9I have said it before, and I will say it again. I hope God will punish anyone who preaches anything different from what you have already believed.

10I am not trying to please people. I want to please God. Do you think I am trying to please people? If I were doing that, I would not be a servant of Christ.

How Paul Became an Apostle

11My friends, I want you to know that no one made up the message I preach. 12It was not given or taught to me by some mere human. My message came directly from Jesus Christ when he appeared to me.

13You know how I used to live as a Jew. I was cruel to God's church and even tried to destroy it. 14I was a much better Jew than anyone else my own age, and I obeyed every law that our ancestors had given us. 15But even before I was born, God had chosen me. He was kind and had decided 16to show me his Son, so that I would announce

his message to the Gentiles. I didn't talk this over with anyone. 17I didn't say a word, not even to the men in Jerusalem who were apostles before I was. Instead, I went at once to Arabia, and afterwards I returned to Damascus.

18Three years later I went to visit Peterᵇ in Jerusalem and stayed with him for fifteen days. 19The only other apostle I saw was James, the Lord's brother. 20And in the presence of God I swear I am telling the truth.

21Later, I went to the regions of Syria and Cilicia. 22But no one who belonged to Christ's churches in Judea had ever seen me in person. 23They had only heard that the one who had been cruel to them was now preaching the message that he had once tried to destroy. 24And because of me, they praised God.

2 Fourteen years later I went to Jerusalem with Barnabas. I also took along Titus. 2But I went there because God had told me to go, and I explained the good news that I had been preaching to the Gentiles. Then I met privately with the ones who seemed to be the most important leaders. I wanted to make sure that all my work in the past and my future work would not be for nothing.

3Titus went to Jerusalem with me. He was a Greek, but still he was not forced to be circumcised. 4We went there because of those who pretended to be followers and had sneaked in among us as spies. They had come to take away the freedom that Christ Jesus had given us, and they were

---

ᵃhis kindness: Some manuscripts have "the kindness of Christ." ᵇPeter: The Greek text has "Cephas," which is an Aramaic name meaning "rock." Peter is the Greek name with the same meaning.

trying to make us their slaves. 5But we wanted you to have the true message. That's why we didn't give in to them, not even for a second.

6Some of them were supposed to be important leaders, but I didn't care who they were. God doesn't have any favorites! None of these so-called special leaders added anything to my message. 7They realized that God had sent me with the good news for Gentiles, and that he had sent Peter with the same message for Jews. 8God, who had sent Peter on a mission to the Jews, was now using me to preach to the Gentiles.

9James, Peter,*c* and John realized that God had given me the message about his kindness. And these men are supposed to be the pillars of the church. They even gave Barnabas and me a friendly handshake. This was to show that we would work with Gentiles and that they would work with Jews. 10They only asked us to remember the poor, and that was something I had always been eager to do.

Paul Corrects Peter at Antioch

11When Peter came to Antioch, I told him face-to-face that he was wrong. 12He used to eat with Gentile followers of the Lord, until James sent some Jewish followers. Peter was afraid of the Jews and soon stopped eating with Gentiles. 13He and the other Jews hid their true feelings so well that even Barnabas was fooled. 14But when I saw that they were not really obeying the truth that is in the good news, I corrected Peter and said:

Peter, you are a Jew, but you live like a Gentile. So how can you force Gentiles to live like Jews?

15We are Jews by birth and are not sinners like Gentiles. 16But we know that God accepts only those who have faith in Jesus Christ. No one can please God by simply obeying the Law. So we put our faith in Christ Jesus, and God accepted us because of our faith.

17When we Jews started looking for a way to please God, we discovered that we are sinners too. Does this mean that Christ is the one who makes us sinners? No, it doesn't! 18But if I tear down something and then build it again, I prove that I was wrong at first. 19It was the Law itself that killed me and freed me from its power, so that I could live for God.

I have been nailed to the cross with Christ. 20I have died, but Christ lives in me. And I now live by faith in the Son of God, who loved me and gave his life for me. 21I don't turn my back on God's kindness. If we can be acceptable to God by obeying the Law, it was useless for Christ to die.

Faith Is the Only Way

3 You stupid Galatians! I told you exactly how Jesus Christ was nailed to a cross. Has someone now put an evil spell on you? 2I want to know only one thing. How were you given God's

---

*c*Peter: The Greek text has "Cephas," which is an Aramaic name meaning "rock." Peter is the Greek name with the same meaning.

Spirit? Was it by obeying the Law of Moses or by hearing about Christ and having faith in him? 3How can you be so stupid? Do you think that by yourself you can complete what God's Spirit started in you? 4Have you gone through all of this for nothing? Is it all really for nothing? 5God gives you his Spirit and works miracles in you. But does he do this because you obey the Law of Moses or because you have heard about Christ and have faith in him?

6The Scriptures say that God accepted Abraham because Abraham had faith. 7And so, you should understand that everyone who has faith is a child of Abraham.*d* 8Long ago the Scriptures said that God would accept the Gentiles because of their faith. That's why God told Abraham the good news that all nations would be blessed because of him. 9This means that everyone who has faith will share in the blessings that were given to Abraham because of his faith.

10Anyone who tries to please God by obeying the Law is under a curse. The Scriptures say, "Everyone who doesn't obey everything in the Law is under a curse." 11No one can please God by obeying the Law. The Scriptures also say, "The people God accepts because of their faith will live."*e* 12The Law is not based on faith. It promises life only to people who obey its commands. 13But Christ rescued us from the Law's curse, when he became a curse in our place. This is because the Scriptures say that anyone who is nailed to a tree is under a curse. 14And because of what Jesus Christ has done, the blessing that was promised to Abraham was taken to the Gentiles. This happened so that by faith we would be given the promised Holy Spirit.

The Law and the Promise

15My friends, I will use an everyday example to explain what I mean. Once someone agrees to something, no one else can change or cancel the agreement.*f* 16That is how it is with the promises that God made to Abraham and his descendant.*g* The promises were not made to many descendants, but only to one, and that one is Christ. 17What I am saying is that the Law cannot change or cancel God's promise that was made 430 years before the Law was given. 18If we have to obey the Law in order to receive God's blessings, those blessings don't really come to us because of God's promise. But God was kind to Abraham and made him a promise.

19What is the use of the Law? It was given later to show that we sin. But it was only supposed to last until the coming of that descendant*h* who was given the promise. In fact, angels gave the Law to Moses, and he gave it to the people. 20There is only one God, and the Law did not come directly from him.

---

d a child of Abraham: God chose Abraham, and so it was believed that anyone who was a child of Abraham was also a child of God. See the note at 3.29.   *e The people God accepts because of their faith will live*: Or "The people God accepts will live because of their faith."   *f Once someone . . . cancel the agreement*: Or "Once a person makes out a will, no one can change or cancel it."   *g descendant*: The Greek text has "seed," which may mean one or many descendants. In this verse Paul says it means Christ.   *h that descendant*: Jesus.

Slaves and Children

21Does the Law disagree with God's promises? No, it doesn't! If any law could give life to us, we could become acceptable to God by obeying that law. 22But the Scriptures say that sin controls everyone, so that God's promises will be for anyone who has faith in Jesus Christ.

23The Law controlled us and kept us under its power until the time came when we would have faith. 24In fact, the Law was our teacher. It was supposed to teach us until we had faith and were acceptable to God. 25But once a person has learned to have faith, there is no more need to have the Law as a teacher.

26All of you are God's children because of your faith in Christ Jesus. 27And when you were baptized, it was as though you had put on Christ in the same way you put on new clothes. 28Faith in Christ Jesus is what makes each of you equal with each other, whether you are a Jew or a Greek, a slave or a free person, a man or a woman. 29So if you belong to Christ, you are now part of Abraham's family,*i* and you will be given what God has promised. 1Children who are under age are no better off than slaves, even though everything their parents own will someday be theirs. 2This is because children are placed in the care of guardians and teachers until the time their parents have set. 3That is how it was with us. We were like children ruled by the powers of this world.

4But when the time was right, God sent his Son, and a woman gave birth to him. His Son obeyed the Law, 5so he could set us free from the Law, and we could become God's children. 6Now that we are his children, God has sent the Spirit of his Son into our hearts. And his Spirit tells us that God is our Father. 7You are no longer slaves. You are God's children, and you will be given what he has promised.

Paul's Concern for the Galatians

8Before you knew God, you were slaves of gods that are not real. 9But now you know God, or better still, God knows you. How can you turn back and become the slaves of those weak and pitiful powers?*j* 10You even celebrate certain days, months, seasons, and years. 11I am afraid I have wasted my time working with you.

12My friends, I beg you to be like me, just as I once tried to be like you. You didn't mistreat me 13when I first preached to you. No you didn't, even though you knew I had come there because I was sick. 14My illness must have caused you some trouble, but you didn't hate me or turn me away because of it. You welcomed me as though I were one of God's angels or even Christ Jesus himself. 15Where is that good feeling now? I am sure that if it had been possible, you would have taken out your own eyes and given them to me. 16Am I now your enemy, just because I told you the truth?

17Those people may be paying you a lot of attention, but it isn't for your

---

i you are now part of Abraham's family: Paul tells the Galatians that faith in Jesus Christ is what makes someone a true child of Abraham and of God. See the note at 3.7.   *j powers*: Spirits were thought to control human lives and were believed to be connected with the movements of the stars.

good. They only want to keep you away from me, so you will pay them a lot of attention. 18It is always good to give your attention to something worthwhile, even when I am not with you. 19My children, I am in terrible pain until Christ may be seen living in you. 20I wish I were with you now. Then I would not have to talk this way. You really have me puzzled.

Hagar and Sarah

21Some of you would like to be under the rule of the Law of Moses. But do you know what the Law says? 22In the Scriptures we learn that Abraham had two sons. The mother of one of them was a slave, while the mother of the other one had always been free. 23The son of the slave woman was born in the usual way. But the son of the free woman was born because of God's promise.

24All of this has another meaning as well. Each of the two women stands for one of the agreements God made with his people. Hagar, the slave woman, stands for the agreement that was made at Mount Sinai. Everyone born into her family is a slave. 25Hagar also stands for Mount Sinai in Arabia*k* and for the present city of Jerusalem. She*l* and her children are slaves.

26But our mother is the city of Jerusalem in heaven above, and she isn't a slave. 27The Scriptures say about her,

"You have never had children,
    but now you can be glad.
You have never given birth,
    but now you can shout.

Once you had no children,
    but now you will have
more children than a woman
who has been married
    for a long time."

28My friends, you were born because of this promise, just as Isaac was. 29But the child who was born in the natural way made trouble for the child who was born because of the Spirit. The same thing is happening today. 30The Scriptures say, "Get rid of the slave woman and her son! He won't be given anything. The son of the free woman will receive everything." 31My friends, we are children of the free woman and not of the slave.

Christ Gives Freedom

5 Christ has set us free! This means we are really free. Now hold on to your freedom and don't ever become slaves of the Law again.

2I, Paul, promise you that Christ won't do you any good if you get circumcised. 3If you do, you must obey the whole Law. 4And if you try to please God by obeying the Law, you have cut yourself off from Christ and his kindness. 5But the Spirit makes us sure that God will accept us because of our faith in Christ. 6If you are a follower of Christ Jesus, it makes no difference whether you are circumcised or not. All that matters is your faith that makes you love others.

7You were doing so well until someone made you turn from the truth. 8And that person was certainly not sent by the one who chose you. 9A little

---

*k*Hagar also stands for Mount Sinai in Arabia: Some manuscripts have "Sinai is a mountain in Arabia." This sentence would then be translated: "Sinai is a mountain in Arabia, and Hagar stands for the present city of Jerusalem." *l*She: "Hagar" or "Jerusalem."

yeast can change a whole batch of dough, 10but you belong to the Lord. That makes me certain that you will do what I say, instead of what someone else tells you to do. Whoever is causing trouble for you will be punished.

11My friends, if I still preach that people need to be circumcised, why am I in so much trouble? The message about the cross would no longer be a problem, if I told people to be circumcised. 12I wish that everyone who is upsetting you would not only get circumcised, but would cut off much more!

13My friends, you were chosen to be free. So don't use your freedom as an excuse to do anything you want. Use it as an opportunity to serve each other with love. 14All that the Law says can be summed up in the command to love others as much as you love yourself. 15But if you keep attacking each other like wild animals, you had better watch out or you will destroy yourselves.

God's Spirit and Our Own Desires

16If you are guided by the Spirit, you won't obey your selfish desires. 17The Spirit and your desires are enemies of each other. They are always fighting each other and keeping you from doing what you feel you should. 18But if you obey the Spirit, the Law of Moses has no control over you.

19People's desires make them give in to immoral ways, filthy thoughts, and shameful deeds. 20They worship idols, practice witchcraft, hate others, and are hard to get along with. People become jealous, angry, and selfish. They not only argue and cause trouble, but they are 21envious. They get drunk, carry on at wild parties, and do other evil things as well. I told you before, and I am telling you again: No one who does these things will share in the blessings of God's kingdom.

22God's Spirit makes us loving, happy, peaceful, patient, kind, good, faithful, 23gentle, and self-controlled. There is no law against behaving in any of these ways. 24And because we belong to Christ, we have killed our selfish feelings and desires. 25God's Spirit has given us life, and so we should follow the Spirit. 26But don't be conceited or make others jealous by claiming to be better than they are.

Help Each Other

6 My friends, you are spiritual. So if someone is trapped in sin, you should gently lead that person back to the right path. But watch out, and don't be tempted yourself. 2You obey the law of Christ when you offer each other a helping hand.

3If you think you are better than others, when you really aren't, you are wrong. 4Do your own work well, and then you will have something to be proud of. But don't compare yourself with others. 5We each must carry our own load.

6Share every good thing you have with anyone who teaches you what God has said.

7You cannot fool God, so don't make a fool of yourself! You will harvest what you plant. 8If you follow your selfish desires, you will harvest destruction, but if you follow the Spirit, you will harvest eternal life. 9Don't get tired of helping others. You will be rewarded when the time is right, if you don't give up. 10We should help people whenever we can, especially if they are followers of the Lord.

Final Warnings

11You can see what big letters I make when I write with my own hand.

12Those people who are telling you to get circumcised are only trying to show how important they are. And they don't want to get into trouble for preaching about the cross of Christ. 13They are circumcised, but they don't obey the Law of Moses. All they want is to brag about having you circumcised. 14But I will never brag about anything except the cross of our Lord Jesus Christ. Because of his cross, the world is dead as far as I am concerned, and I am dead as far as the world is concerned.

15It doesn't matter if you are circumcised or not. All that matters is that you are a new person.

16If you follow this rule, you will belong to God's true people. God will treat you with kindness and will bless you with peace.

17On my own body are scars that prove I belong to Christ Jesus. So I don't want anyone to bother me anymore.

18My friends, I pray that the Lord Jesus Christ will be kind to you! Amen.

Paul's Letter to the Church in Ephesus

ABOUT THIS LETTER

"**P**raise the God and Father of our Lord Jesus Christ for the spiritual blessings that Christ has brought us from heaven!" (1.3). Paul begins his letter to the Christians in Ephesus with a powerful reminder of the main theme of his message. Christ died on the cross to set us free (1.7,8). But God raised Christ from death, and he now sits at God's right side in heaven, where he rules over this world. And he will rule over the future world as well (1.20, 21).

Christ brought Jews and Gentiles together by "breaking down the wall of hatred" that separated them (2.14) and he united them all as part of that holy temple where God's Spirit lives (2.22). This was according to God's eternal plan (3.11).

There is only one Lord, one Spirit of God, and one God, who is the Father of all people (4.4, 5). This means that Christians must let the Spirit keep their hearts united, so they can live at peace with each other (4.3). The idea of all Christians being one with Christ is so central to this letter that it occurs twenty times. There is one faith and one baptism by which believers become one body.

Ephesus was a port city on the western shore of Asia Minor (modern-day Turkey). In Paul's time this was the fourth largest city in the Roman empire. It was also an ancient center of nature religion where the goddess Artemis was widely worshiped (Acts 19).

Paul lets the Ephesians know that much is expected of people who are called to a new life (4.17—5.20). Followers of the Lord are God's dear children, and they must do as God does (5.1). They used to live in the dark, but they must now live in the light and make their light shine (5.8, 9).

Paul then teaches husbands and wives, children and parents, and slaves and masters how to live as Christians (5.21—6.9).

Paul never forgets how kind God is:

God was merciful! We were dead because of our sins, but God loved us so much that he made us alive with Christ, and God's kindness is what saves you.   *(2.4-5)*

You were saved by faith in God, who treats us much better than we deserve. This is God's gift to you, and not anything you have done on your own. *(2.8)*

A QUICK LOOK AT THIS LETTER

- Greetings (1.1, 2)
- Christ Brings Spiritual Blessings (1.3—3.21)
- A New Life in Unity with Christ (4.1—6.20)
- Final Greetings (6.21–24)

---

1 From Paul, chosen by God to be an apostle of Christ Jesus.

To God's people who live in Ephesus and[a] are faithful followers of Christ Jesus.

²I pray that God our Father and our Lord Jesus Christ will be kind to you and will bless you with peace!

Christ Brings Spiritual Blessings

³Praise the God and Father of our Lord Jesus Christ for the spiritual blessings that Christ has brought us from heaven! ⁴Before the world was created, God had Christ choose us to live with him and to be his holy and innocent and loving people. ⁵God was kind[b] and decided that Christ would choose us to be God's own adopted children. ⁶God was very kind to us because of the Son he dearly loves, and so we should praise God.

⁷-⁸Christ sacrificed his life's blood to set us free, which means that our sins are now forgiven. Christ did this because God was so kind to us. God has great wisdom and understanding, ⁹and by what Christ has done, God has shown us his own mysterious ways. ¹⁰Then when the time is right, God will do all that he has planned, and Christ will bring together everything in heaven and on earth.

¹¹God always does what he plans, and that's why he had Christ choose us. ¹²He did this so that we Jews would bring honor to him and be the first ones

---

[a]*live in Ephesus and*: Some manuscripts do not have these words.   [b]*holy and innocent and loving people.* ⁵*God was kind*: Or "holy and innocent people. God was loving ⁵and kind."

to have hope because of him. [13]Christ also brought you the truth, which is the good news about how you can be saved. You put your faith in Christ and were given the promised Holy Spirit to show that you belong to God. [14]The Spirit also makes us sure that we will be given what God has stored up for his people. Then we will be set free, and God will be honored and praised.

Paul's Prayer

[15]I have heard about your faith in the Lord Jesus and your love for all of God's people. [16]So I never stop being grateful for you, as I mention you in my prayers. [17]I ask the glorious Father and God of our Lord Jesus Christ to give you his Spirit. The Spirit will make you wise and let you understand what it means to know God. [18]My prayer is that light will flood your hearts and that you will understand the hope that was given to you when God chose you. Then you will discover the glorious blessings that will be yours together with all of God's people.

[19]I want you to know about the great and mighty power that God has for us followers. It is the same wonderful power he used [20]when he raised Christ from death and let him sit at his right side[c] in heaven. [21]There Christ rules over all forces, authorities, powers, and rulers. He rules over all beings in this world and will rule in the future world as well. [22]God has put all things under the power of Christ,

and for the good of the church he has made him the head of everything. [23]The church is Christ's body and is filled with Christ who completely fills everything.[d]

From Death to Life

2 In the past you were dead because you sinned and fought against God. [2]You followed the ways of this world and obeyed the devil. He rules the world, and his spirit has power over everyone who does not obey God. [3]Once we were also ruled by the selfish desires of our bodies and minds. We had made God angry, and we were going to be punished.

[4-5]But God was merciful! We were dead because of our sins, but God loved us so much that he made us alive with Christ, and God's kindness is what saves you. [6]God raised us from death to life with Christ Jesus, and he has given us a place beside Christ in heaven above. [7]God did this so that in the future world he could show how truly good and kind he is to us because of what Christ Jesus has done. [8]You were saved by faith in God, who treats us much better than we deserve.[e] This is God's gift to you, and not anything you have done on your own. [9]It isn't something you have earned, so there is nothing you can brag about. [10]God planned for us to do good things and to live as he has always wanted us to live. That's why he sent Christ to make us what we are.

[c]*right side*: The place of power and honor. [d]*and is filled with Christ who completely fills everything*: Or "which completely fills Christ and fully completes his work." [e]*treats us much better than we deserve*: The Greek word *charis*, traditionally rendered "grace," is translated here and other places in the CEV to express the overwhelming kindness of God.

United by Christ

11Don't forget that you are Gentiles. In fact, you used to be called "uncircumcised" by Jews, who take pride in being circumcised. 12At that time you did not know about Christ. You were foreigners to the people of Israel, and you had no part in the promises that God had made to them. You were living in this world without hope and without God, 13and you were far from God. But Christ offered his life's blood as a sacrifice and brought you near to God.

14Christ has made peace between Jews and Gentiles, and he has united us by breaking down the wall of hatred that separated us. Christ gave his own body 15to destroy the Law of Moses with all its rules and commands. He even brought Jews and Gentiles together as though we were only one person, when he united us in peace. 16On the cross Christ did away with our hatred for each other. He also made peace*f* between us and God by uniting Jews and Gentiles in one body. 17Christ came and preached peace to you Gentiles, who were far from God, and peace to us Jews, who were near to God. 18And because of Christ, all of us can come to the Father by the same Spirit.

19You Gentiles are no longer strangers and foreigners. You are citizens with everyone else who belongs to the family of God. 20You are like a building with the apostles and prophets as the foundation and with Christ as the most important stone. 21Christ is the one who holds the building together and makes it grow into a holy temple for the Lord. 22And you are part of that building Christ has built as a place for God's own Spirit to live.

Paul's Mission to the Gentiles

3 Christ Jesus made me his prisoner, so that I could help you Gentiles. 2You have surely heard about God's kindness in choosing me to help you. 3In fact, this letter tells you a little about how God has shown me his mysterious ways. 4As you read the letter, you will also find out how well I really do understand the mystery about Christ. 5No one knew about this mystery until God's Spirit told it to his holy apostles and prophets. 6And the mystery is this: Because of Christ Jesus, the good news has given the Gentiles a share in the promises that God gave to the Jews. God has also let the Gentiles be part of the same body.

7God treated me with kindness. His power worked in me, and it became my job to spread the good news. 8I am the least important of all God's people. But God was kind and chose me to tell the Gentiles that because of Christ there are blessings that cannot be measured. 9God, who created everything, wanted me to help everyone understand the mysterious plan that had always been hidden in his mind. 10Then God would use the church to show the powers and authorities above that he has many different kinds of wisdom.

11God did this according to his eternal plan. And he was able to do what he had planned because of all that Christ Jesus our Lord had done. 12Christ now gives us courage and confidence, so that we can come to God

---

fHe also made peace: Or "The cross also made peace."

by faith. 13That's why you should not be discouraged when I suffer for you. After all, it will bring honor to you.

Christ's Love for Us

14I kneel in prayer to the Father. 15All beings in heaven and on earth receive their life from him.*g* 16God is wonderful and glorious. I pray that his Spirit will make you become strong followers 17and that Christ will live in your hearts because of your faith. Stand firm and be deeply rooted in his love. 18I pray that you and all of God's people will understand what is called wide or long or high or deep.*h* 19I want you to know all about Christ's love, although it is too wonderful to be measured. Then your lives will be filled with all that God is.

20-21I pray that Christ Jesus and the church will forever bring praise to God. His power at work in us can do far more than we dare ask or imagine. Amen.

Unity with Christ

4 As a prisoner of the Lord, I beg you to live in a way that is worthy of the people God has chosen to be his own. 2Always be humble and gentle. Patiently put up with each other and love each other. 3Try your best to let God's Spirit keep your hearts united. Do this by living at peace. 4All of you are part of the same body. There is only one Spirit of God, just as you were given one hope when you were chosen to be God's people. 5We have only one

Lord, one faith, and one baptism. 6There is one God who is the Father of all people. Not only is God above all others, but he works by using all of us, and he lives in all of us.

7Christ has generously divided out his gifts to us. 8As the Scriptures say,

"When he went up
to the highest place,
he led away many prisoners
and gave gifts
to people."

9When it says, "he went up," it means that Christ had been deep in the earth. 10This also means that the one who went deep into the earth is the same one who went into the highest heaven, so that he would fill the whole universe.

11Christ chose some of us to be apostles, prophets, missionaries, pastors, and teachers, 12so that his people would learn to serve and his body would grow strong. 13This will continue until we are united by our faith and by our understanding of the Son of God. Then we will be mature, just as Christ is, and we will be completely like him.*i*

14We must stop acting like children. We must not let deceitful people trick us by their false teachings, which are like winds that toss us around from place to place. 15Love should always make us tell the truth. Then we will grow in every way and be more like Christ, the head 16of the body. Christ holds it together and makes all of its parts work perfectly, as it grows and becomes strong because of love.

---

g receive their life from him: Or "know who they really are because of him."   *h what is called wide or long or high or deep*: This may refer to the heavenly Jerusalem or to God's love or wisdom or to the meaning of the cross.   *i and we will be completely like him*: Or "and he is completely perfect."

The Old Life and the New Life

17As a follower of the Lord, I order you to stop living like stupid, godless people. **18**Their minds are in the dark, and they are stubborn and ignorant and have missed out on the life that comes from God. They no longer have any feelings about what is right, **19**and they are so greedy that they do all kinds of indecent things.

20-21 But that isn't what you were taught about Jesus Christ. He is the truth, and you heard about him and learned about him. **22**You were told that your foolish desires will destroy you and that you must give up your old way of life with all its bad habits. **23**Let the Spirit change your way of thinking **24**and make you into a new person. You were created to be like God, and so you must please him and be truly holy.

Rules for the New Life

25We are part of the same body. Stop lying and start telling each other the truth. **26**Don't get so angry that you sin. Don't go to bed angry **27**and don't give the devil a chance.

28If you are a thief, quit stealing. Be honest and work hard, so you will have something to give to people in need.

29Stop all your dirty talk. Say the right thing at the right time and help others by what you say.

30Don't make God's Spirit sad. The Spirit makes you sure that someday you will be free from your sins.

31Stop being bitter and angry and mad at others. Don't yell at one another or curse each other or ever be rude. **32**Instead, be kind and merciful, and forgive others, just as God forgave you because of Christ.

5 Do as God does. After all, you are his dear children. **2**Let love be your guide. Christ loved us*j* and offered his life for us as a sacrifice that pleases God.

3You are God's people, so don't let it be said that any of you are immoral or indecent or greedy. **4**Don't use dirty or foolish or filthy words. Instead, say how thankful you are. **5**Being greedy, indecent, or immoral is just another way of worshiping idols. You can be sure that people who behave in this way will never be part of the kingdom that belongs to Christ and to God.

Living as People of Light

6Don't let anyone trick you with foolish talk. God punishes everyone who disobeys him and says*k* foolish things. **7**So don't have anything to do with anyone like that.

8You used to be like people living in the dark, but now you are people of the light because you belong to the Lord. So act like people of the light **9**and make your light shine. Be good and honest and truthful, **10**as you try to please the Lord. **11**Don't take part in doing those worthless things that are done in the dark. Instead, show how wrong they are. **12**It is disgusting even to talk about what is done in the dark. **13**But the light will show what these things are really like. **14**Light shows up everything,*l* just as the Scriptures say,

---

*j*us: Some manuscripts have "you." *k*says: Or "does." *l*Light shows up everything: Or "Everything that is seen in the light becomes light itself."

"Wake up from your sleep
and rise from death.
Then Christ will shine
on you."

15Act like people with good sense and not like fools. 16These are evil times, so make every minute count. 17Don't be stupid. Instead, find out what the Lord wants you to do. 18Don't destroy yourself by getting drunk, but let the Spirit fill your life. 19When you meet together, sing psalms, hymns, and spiritual songs, as you praise the Lord with all your heart. 20Always use the name of the Lord Jesus Christ to thank God the Father for everything.

Wives and Husbands

21Honor Christ and put others first. 22A wife should put her husband first, as she does the Lord. 23A husband is the head of his wife, as Christ is the head and the Savior of the church, which is his own body. 24Wives should always put their husbands first, as the church puts Christ first.

25A husband should love his wife as much as Christ loved the church and gave his life for it. 26He made the church holy by the power of his word, and he made it pure by washing it with water. 27Christ did this, so that he would have a glorious and holy church, without faults or spots or wrinkles or any other flaws.

28In the same way, a husband should love his wife as much as he loves himself. A husband who loves his wife shows that he loves himself. 29None of us hate our own bodies. We provide for them and take good care of them, just as Christ does for the church, 30because we are each part of his body. 31As the Scriptures say, "A man leaves his father and mother to get married, and he becomes like one person with his wife." 32This is a great mystery, but I understand it to mean Christ and his church. 33So each husband should love his wife as much as he loves himself, and each wife should respect her husband.

Children and Parents

6 Children, you belong to the Lord, and you do the right thing when you obey your parents. The first commandment with a promise says, 2"Obey your father and your mother, 3and you will have a long and happy life."

4Parents, don't be hard on your children. Raise them properly. Teach them and instruct them about the Lord.

Slaves and Masters

5Slaves, you must obey your earthly masters. Show them great respect and be as loyal to them as you are to Christ. 6Try to please them at all times, and not just when you think they are watching. You are slaves of Christ, so with your whole heart you must do what God wants you to do. 7Gladly serve your masters, as though they were the Lord himself, and not simply people. 8You know that you will be rewarded for any good things you do, whether you are slaves or free.

9Slave owners, you must treat your slaves with this same respect. Don't threaten them. They have the same Master in heaven that you do, and he doesn't have any favorites.

The Fight against Evil

10Finally, let the mighty strength of the Lord make you strong. 11Put on all the armor that God gives, so you can defend yourself against the devil's tricks. [12]We are not fighting against humans. We are fighting against forces and authorities and against rulers of darkness and spiritual powers in the heavens above. [13]So put on all the armor that God gives. Then when that evil day[m] comes, you will be able to defend yourself. And when the battle is over, you will still be standing firm.

[14]Be ready! Let the truth be like a belt around your waist, and let God's justice protect you like armor. [15]Your desire to tell the good news about peace should be like shoes on your feet. [16]Let your faith be like a shield, and you will be able to stop all the flaming arrows of the evil one. [17]Let God's saving power be like a helmet, and for a sword use God's message that comes from the Spirit.

[18]Never stop praying, especially for others. Always pray by the power of the Spirit. Stay alert and keep praying for God's people. [19]Pray that I will be given the message to speak and that I may fearlessly explain the mystery about the good news. [20]I was sent to do this work, and that's the reason I am in jail. So pray that I will be brave and will speak as I should.

Final Greetings

[21-22]I want you to know how I am getting along and what I am doing. That's why I am sending Tychicus to you. He is a dear friend, as well as a faithful servant of the Lord. He will tell you how I am doing, and he will cheer you up.

[23]I pray that God the Father and the Lord Jesus Christ will give peace, love, and faith to every follower! [24]May God be kind to everyone who keeps on loving our Lord Jesus Christ.

---

[m]*that evil day*: Either the present (see 5.16) or "the day of death" or "the day of judgment."

Paul's Letter
to the Church in Philippi

ABOUT THIS LETTER

Paul wrote this letter from jail (1.7) to thank the Lord's followers at Philippi for helping him with their gifts and prayers (1.5; 4.10–19). He hopes to be set free, so that he can continue preaching the good news (3.17–19). But he knows that he might be put to death (1.21; 2.17; 3.10).

The city of Philippi is in the part of northern Greece known as Macedonia. It was at Philippi that Paul had entered Europe for the first time, and there he preached the good news and began a church (Acts 16). He now warns the Christians at Philippi that they may have to suffer, just as Christ suffered and Paul is now suffering. If this happens, the Philippians should count it a blessing that comes from having faith in Christ (1.28–30).

There were problems in the church at Philippi, because some of the members claimed that people must obey the law of Moses, or they could not be saved. But Paul has no patience with such members and warns the church, "Watch out for those people who behave like dogs!" (3.2–11). This letter is also filled with joy. Even in jail, Paul is happy because he has discovered how to make the best of a bad situation and because he remembers all the kindness shown to him by the people in the church at Philippi.

Paul reminds them that God's people are to live in harmony (2.2; 4.2, 3) and to think the same way that Christ Jesus did:

> Christ was truly God.
> But he did not try to remain
>   equal with God.
> He gave up everything
>   and became a slave,
> when he became
>   like one of us.   (2.6, 7)

A QUICK LOOK AT THIS LETTER

- Greetings and a Prayer (1.1–11)
- What Life Means to Paul (1.12–30)
- Christ's Example of True Humility (2.1–18)
- News about Paul's Friends (2.19–30)
- Being Acceptable to God (3.1—4.9)
- Paul Thanks the Philippians (4.10–20)
- Final Greetings (4.21–23)

1 From Paul and Timothy, servants of Christ Jesus.

To all of God's people who belong to Christ Jesus at Philippi and to all of your church officials and officers.[a]

2I pray that God our Father and the Lord Jesus Christ will be kind to you and will bless you with peace!

Paul's Prayer for the Church in Philippi

3Every time I think of you, I thank my God. **4**And whenever I mention you in my prayers, it makes me happy. **5**This is because you have taken part with me in spreading the good news from the first day you heard about it. **6**God is the one who began this good work in you, and I am certain that he won't stop before it is complete on the day that Christ Jesus returns.

7You have a special place in my heart. So it is only natural for me to feel the way I do. All of you have helped in the work that God has given me, as I defend the good news and tell about it here in jail. **8**God himself knows how much I want to see you. He knows that I care for you in the same way that Christ Jesus does.

9I pray that your love will keep on growing and that you will fully know and understand **10**how to make the right choices. Then you will still be pure and innocent when Christ returns. And until that day, **11**Jesus Christ will keep you busy doing good deeds that bring glory and praise to God.

What Life Means to Paul

12My dear friends, I want you to know that what has happened to me has helped to spread the good news. **13**The Roman guards and all the others know that I am here in jail because I serve Christ. **14**Now most of the Lord's followers have become brave and are fearlessly telling the message.[b]

15Some are preaching about Christ because they are jealous and envious of us. Others are preaching because they want to help. **16**They love Christ and know that I am here to defend the good news about him. **17**But the ones who are jealous of us are not sincere. They just want to cause trouble for me while I am in jail. **18**But that doesn't matter. All that matters is that people are telling about Christ, whether they are sincere or not. That is what makes me glad.

I will keep on being glad, **19**because I know that your prayers and the help that comes from the Spirit of Christ Jesus will keep me safe. **20**I honestly expect and hope that I will never do anything to be ashamed of. Whether I live or die, I always want to be as brave as I am now and bring honor to Christ.

21If I live, it will be for Christ, and if I die, I will gain even more. **22**I don't know what to choose. I could keep on living and doing something useful. **23**It is a hard choice to make. I want to die and be with Christ, because that would be much better. **24-25**But I know that all of you still need me. That's why I am sure I will stay on to help you grow

---

[a]*church officials and officers*: Or "bishops and deacons."   [b]*the message*: Some manuscripts have "the Lord's message," and others have "God's message."

and be happy in your faith. 26Then, when I visit you again, you will have good reason to take great pride in Christ Jesus because of me.[c]

27Above all else, you must live in a way that brings honor to the good news about Christ. Then, whether I visit you or not, I will hear that all of you think alike. I will know that you are working together and that you are struggling side by side to get others to believe the good news.

28Be brave when you face your enemies. Your courage will show them that they are going to be destroyed, and it will show you that you will be saved. God will make all of this happen, 29and he has blessed you. Not only do you have faith in Christ, but you suffer for him. 30You saw me suffer, and you still hear about my troubles. Now you must suffer in the same way.

True Humility

2 Christ encourages you, and his love comforts you. God's Spirit unites you, and you are concerned for others. 2Now make me completely happy! Live in harmony by showing love for each other. Be united in what you think, as if you were only one person. 3Don't be jealous or proud, but be humble and consider others more important than yourselves. 4Care about them as much as you care about yourselves 5and think the same way that Christ Jesus did:[d]

6Christ was truly God.
But he did not try to remain[e]
equal with God.

7He gave up everything[f]
and became a slave,
when he became
like one of us.

8Christ was humble.
He obeyed God and even died
on a cross.
9Then God gave Christ
the highest place
and honored his name
above all others.

10So at the name of Jesus
everyone will bow down,
those in heaven, on earth,
and under the earth.
11And to the glory
of God the Father
everyone will openly agree,
"Jesus Christ is Lord!"

Lights in the World

12My dear friends, you always obeyed when I was with you. Now that I am away, you should obey even more. So work with fear and trembling to discover what it really means to be saved. 13God is working in you to make you willing to obey him.

14Do everything without grumbling or arguing. 15Then you will be the pure and innocent children of God. You live among people who are crooked and evil, but you must not do anything that they can say is wrong. Try to shine as lights among the people of this world, 16as you hold firmly to[g] the message that gives life. Then on the day when Christ returns, I can take pride

---

[c]take great pride in Christ Jesus because of me: Or "take great pride in me because of Christ Jesus." [d]think the same way that Christ Jesus did: Or "think the way you should because you belong to Christ Jesus." [e]remain: Or "become." [f]He gave up everything: Greek, "He emptied himself." [g]hold firmly to: Or "offer them."

in you. I can also know that my work and efforts were not useless.

17Your faith in the Lord and your service are like a sacrifice offered to him. And my own blood may have to be poured out with the sacrifice.[h] If this happens, I will be glad and rejoice with you. 18In the same way, you should be glad and rejoice with me.

Timothy and Epaphroditus

19I want to be encouraged by news about you. So I hope the Lord Jesus will soon let me send Timothy to you. 20I don't have anyone else who cares about you as much as he does. 21The others think only about what interests them and not about what concerns Christ Jesus. 22But you know what kind of person Timothy is. He has worked with me like a son in spreading the good news. 23I hope to send him to you, as soon as I find out what is going to happen to me. 24I feel sure that the Lord will also let me come soon.

25I think I ought to send my dear friend Epaphroditus back to you. He is a follower and a worker and a soldier of the Lord, just as I am. You sent him to look after me, 26but now he is eager to see you. He is worried, because you heard he was sick. 27In fact, he was very sick and almost died. But God was kind to him, and also to me, and he kept me from being burdened down with sorrow.

28Now I am more eager than ever to send Epaphroditus back again. You will be glad to see him, and I won't have to worry any longer. 29Be sure to give him a cheerful welcome, just as people who serve the Lord deserve. 30He almost died working for Christ, and he risked his own life to do for me what you could not.

Being Acceptable to God

3 Finally, my dear friends, be glad that you belong to the Lord. It doesn't bother me to write the same things to you that I have written before. In fact, it is for your own good.

2Watch out for those people who behave like dogs! They are evil and want to do more than just circumcise you. 3But we are the ones who are truly circumcised, because we worship by the power of God's Spirit[i] and take pride in Christ Jesus. We don't brag about what we have done, 4although I could. Others may brag about themselves, but I have more reason to brag than anyone else. 5I was circumcised when I was eight days old,[j] and I am from the nation of Israel and the tribe of Benjamin. I am a true Hebrew. As a Pharisee, I strictly obeyed the Law of Moses. 6And I was so eager that I even made trouble for the church. I did everything the Law demands in order to please God.

7But Christ has shown me that what I once thought was valuable is worthless. 8Nothing is as wonderful as knowing Christ Jesus my Lord. I have given up everything else and count it all as garbage. All I want is Christ 9and to know that I belong to him. I could not make myself acceptable to God by obeying the Law of Moses. God ac-

---

[h]*my own blood may have to be poured out with the sacrifice*: Offerings of water or wine were sometimes poured out when animals were sacrificed on the altar. [i]*by the power of God's Spirit*: Or "sincerely." [j]*when I was eight days old*: Jewish boys are circumcised eight days after birth.

cepted me simply because of my faith in Christ. 10All I want is to know Christ and the power that raised him to life. I want to suffer and die as he did, 11so that somehow I also may be raised to life.

Running toward the Goal

12I have not yet reached my goal, and I am not perfect. But Christ has taken hold of me. So I keep on running and struggling to take hold of the prize. 13My friends, I don't feel that I have already arrived. But I forget what is behind, and I struggle for what is ahead. 14I run toward the goal, so that I can win the prize of being called to heaven. This is the prize that God offers because of what Christ Jesus has done. 15All of us who are mature should think in this same way. And if any of you think differently, God will make it clear to you. 16But we must keep going in the direction that we are now headed.

17My friends, I want you to follow my example and learn from others who closely follow the example we set for you. 18I often warned you that many people are living as enemies of the cross of Christ. And now with tears in my eyes, I warn you again 19that they are headed for hell! They worship their stomachs and brag about the disgusting things they do. All they can think about are the things of this world.

20But we are citizens of heaven and are eagerly waiting for our Savior to come from there. Our Lord Jesus Christ 21has power over everything, and he will make these poor bodies of ours like his own glorious body.

4 Dear friends, I love you and long to see you. Please keep on being faithful to the Lord. You are my pride and joy.

Paul Encourages the Lord's Followers

2Euodia and Syntyche, you belong to the Lord, so I beg you to stop arguing with each other. 3And, my true partner,*k* I ask you to help them. These women have worked together with me and with Clement and with the others in spreading the good news. Their names are now written in the book of life.*l*

4Always be glad because of the Lord! I will say it again: Be glad. 5Always be gentle with others. The Lord will soon be here. 6Don't worry about anything, but pray about everything. With thankful hearts offer up your prayers and requests to God. 7Then, because you belong to Christ Jesus, God will bless you with peace that no one can completely understand. And this peace will control the way you think and feel.

8Finally, my friends, keep your minds on whatever is true, pure, right, holy, friendly, and proper. Don't ever stop thinking about what is truly worthwhile and worthy of praise. 9You know the teachings I gave you, and you know what you heard me say and saw me do. So follow my example. And God, who gives peace, will be with you.

Paul Gives Thanks for the Gifts He Was Given

10The Lord has made me very grateful that at last you have thought

---

kpartner: Or "Syzygus," a person's name.   *lthe book of life*: A book in which the names of God's people are written.

about me once again. Actually, you were thinking about me all along, but you didn't have any chance to show it. [11]I am not complaining about having too little. I have learned to be satisfied with[m] whatever I have. [12]I know what it is to be poor or to have plenty, and I have lived under all kinds of conditions. I know what it means to be full or to be hungry, to have too much or too little. [13]Christ gives me the strength to face anything.

[14]It was good of you to help me when I was having such a hard time. [15]My friends at Philippi, you remember what it was like when I started preaching the good news in Macedonia.[n] After I left there, you were the only church that became my partner by giving blessings and by receiving them in return. [16]Even when I was in Thessalonica, you helped me more than once. [17]I am not trying to get something from you, but I want you to receive the blessings that come from giving.

[18]I have been paid back everything, and with interest. I am completely satisfied with the gifts that you had Epaphroditus bring me. They are like a sweet-smelling offering or like the right kind of sacrifice that pleases God. [19]I pray that God will take care of all your needs with the wonderful blessings that come from Christ Jesus! [20]May God our Father be praised forever and ever. Amen.

Final Greetings

[21]Give my greetings to all who are God's people because of Christ Jesus.

The Lord's followers here with me send you their greetings.

[22]All of God's people send their greetings, especially those in the service of the Emperor.

[23]I pray that our Lord Jesus Christ will be kind to you and will bless your life!

---

[m]*be satisfied with*: Or "get by on."   [n]*when I started preaching the good news in Macedonia*: Paul is talking about his first visit to Philippi. See Acts 16.12-40.

Paul's Letter
to the Church in Colossae

ABOUT THIS LETTER

Colossae was an important city in western Asia Minor, about 100 miles east of the port city of Ephesus. Paul had never been to Colossae, but he was pleased to learn that the Christians there were strong in their faith (1.3–7; 2.6, 7). They had heard the good news from a man named Epaphras who had lived there (1.7; 4.12,13), but was in jail with Paul (Philemon 23) at the time that Paul wrote this letter (1.14; 4.3, 10,18).

Many of the church members in Colossae were Gentiles (1.27), and some of them were influenced by strange religious ideas and practices (2.16–23). They thought that to obey God fully they must give up certain physical desires and worship angels and other spiritual powers. But Paul wanted them to know that Christ was with God in heaven, ruling over all powers in the universe (3.1). And so, their worship should be directed to Christ.

Paul quotes a beautiful hymn that explains who Christ is:

> Christ is exactly like God,
> who cannot be seen.
> He is the first-born Son,
> superior to all creation.
>
> God himself was pleased
> to live fully in his Son.
> And God was pleased
> for him to make peace
> by sacrificing his blood
> on the cross.
> (1.15, 19, 20a)

A QUICK LOOK AT THIS LETTER

- Greetings (1.1,2)
- A Prayer of Thanks (1.3–8)
- The Person and Work of Christ (1.9—2.19)
- New Life with Christ (2.20—4.6)
- Final Greetings (4.7–18)

1 From Paul, chosen by God to be an apostle of Christ Jesus, and from Timothy, who is also a follower.

2To God's people who live in Colossae and are faithful followers of Christ.

I pray that God our Father will be kind to you and will bless you with peace!

A Prayer of Thanks

3Each time we pray for you, we thank God, the Father of our Lord Jesus Christ. 4We have heard of your faith in Christ and of your love for all of God's people, 5because what you hope for is kept safe for you in heaven. You first heard about this hope when you believed the true message, which is the good news.

6The good news is spreading all over the world with great success. It has spread in that same way among you, ever since the first day you learned the truth about God's kindness 7from our good friend Epaphras. He works together with us for Christ and is a faithful worker for you.[a] 8He is also the one who told us about the love that God's Spirit has given you.

The Person and Work of Christ

9We have not stopped praying for you since the first day we heard about you. In fact, we always pray that God will show you everything he wants you to do and that you may have all the wisdom and understanding that his Spirit gives. 10Then you will live a life that honors the Lord, and you will always please him by doing good deeds. You will come to know God even better. 11His glorious power will make you pa-

tient and strong enough to endure anything, and you will be truly happy.

12I pray that you will be grateful to God for letting you[a] have part in what he has promised his people in the kingdom of light. 13God rescued us from the dark power of Satan and brought us into the kingdom of his dear Son, 14who forgives our sins and sets us free.

15Christ is exactly like God,
   who cannot be seen.
He is the first-born Son,
   superior to all creation.
16Everything was created
   by him,
everything in heaven
   and on earth,
everything seen and unseen,
including all forces
   and powers,
and all rulers
   and authorities.
All things were created
   by God's Son,
and everything was made
   for him.

17God's Son was before all else,
   and by him everything
   is held together.
18He is the head of his body,
   which is the church.
He is the very beginning,
   the first to be raised
   from death,
so that he would be
   above all others.

19God himself was pleased
   to live fully in his Son.
20And God was pleased
   for him to make peace
by sacrificing his blood
   on the cross,

---

[a]*you*: Some manuscripts have "us."

so that all beings in heaven
and on earth
would be brought back
to God.

21You used to be far from God.
Your thoughts made you his enemies,
and you did evil things. 22But his Son
became a human and died. So God
made peace with you, and now he lets
you stand in his presence as people
who are holy and faultless and innocent. 23But you must stay deeply rooted
and firm in your faith. You must not
give up the hope you received when
you heard the good news. It was
preached to everyone on earth, and I
myself have become a servant of this
message.

Paul's Service to the Church

24I am glad that I can suffer for
you. I am pleased also that in my own
body I can continue[b] the suffering of
Christ for his body, the church. 25God's
plan was to make me a servant of his
church and to send me to preach his
complete message to you. 26For ages
and ages this message was kept secret
from everyone, but now it has been explained to God's people. 27God did this
because he wanted you Gentiles to understand his wonderful and glorious
mystery. And the mystery is that Christ
lives in you, and he is your hope of
sharing in God's glory.

28We announce the message about
Christ, and we use all our wisdom to
warn and teach everyone, so that all
of Christ's followers will grow and become mature. 29That's why I work so
hard and use all the mighty power he
gives me.

2 I want you to know what a struggle
I am going through for you, for
God's people at Laodicea, and for all
of those followers who have never met
me. 2I do it to encourage them. Then
as their hearts are joined together in
love, they will be wonderfully blessed
with complete understanding. And
they will truly know Christ. Not only
is he the key to God's mystery, 3but
all wisdom and knowledge are hidden
away in him. 4I tell you these things
to keep you from being fooled by fancy
talk. 5Even though I am not with you,
I keep thinking about you. I am glad
to know that you are living as you
should and that your faith in Christ is
strong.

Christ Brings Real Life

6You have accepted Christ Jesus
as your Lord. Now keep on following
him. 7Plant your roots in Christ and
let him be the foundation for your life.
Be strong in your faith, just as you were
taught. And be grateful.

8Don't let anyone fool you by using
senseless arguments. These arguments may sound wise, but they are
only human teachings. They come
from the powers of this world[c] and not
from Christ.

9God lives fully in Christ. 10And
you are fully grown because you belong
to Christ, who is over every power and
authority. 11Christ has also taken away
your selfish desires, just as circumcision removes flesh from the body.
12And when you were baptized, it was
the same as being buried with Christ.
Then you were raised to life because
you had faith in the power of God, who

---

[b]continue: Or "complete." [c]powers of this world: Spirits and unseen forces were thought to
control human lives and were believed to be connected with the movements of the stars.

raised Christ from death. 13You were dead, because you were sinful and were not God's people. But God let Christ make you*d* alive, when he forgave all our sins.

14God wiped out all the charges that were against us for disobeying the Law of Moses. He took them away and nailed them to the cross. 15There Christ defeated all powers and forces. He let the whole world see them being led away as prisoners when he celebrated his victory.

16Don't let anyone tell you what you must eat or drink. Don't let them say that you must celebrate the New Moon festival, the Sabbath, or any other festival. 17These things are only a shadow of what was to come. But Christ is real!

18Don't be cheated by people who make a show of acting humble and who worship angels.*e* They brag about seeing visions. But it is all nonsense, because their minds are filled with selfish desires. 19They are no longer part of Christ, who is the head of the whole body. Christ gives the body its strength, and he uses its joints and muscles to hold it together, as it grows by the power of God.

Christ Brings New Life

20You died with Christ. Now the forces of the universe*f* don't have any power over you. Why do you live as if you had to obey such rules as, 21"Don't handle this. Don't taste that. Don't touch this."? 22After these things are used, they are no longer good for any-

thing. So why be bothered with all the rules that humans have made up? 23Obeying these rules may seem to be the smart thing to do. They appear to make you love God more and to be very humble and to have control over your body. But they don't really have any power over our desires.

3 You have been raised to life with Christ. Now set your heart on what is in heaven, where Christ rules at God's right side.*g* 2Think about what is up there, not about what is here on earth. 3You died, which means that your life is hidden with Christ, who sits beside God. 4Christ gives meaning to your*h* life, and when he appears, you will also appear with him in glory.

5Don't be controlled by your body. Kill every desire for the wrong kind of sex. Don't be immoral or indecent or have evil thoughts. Don't be greedy, which is the same as worshiping idols. 6God is angry with people who disobey him by doing these things.*i* 7And that is exactly what you did, when you lived among people who behaved in this way. 8But now you must stop doing such things. You must quit being angry, hateful, and evil. You must no longer say insulting or cruel things about others. 9And stop lying to each other. You have given up your old way of life with all its habits.

10Each of you is now a new person. You are becoming more and more like your Creator, and you will understand him better. 11It doesn't matter if you are a Greek or a Jew, or if you are circumcised or not. You may even be a

---

*d*you: Some manuscripts have "us."   *e*worship angels: Or "worship with angels (in visions of heaven)."   *f*forces of the universe: See the note at 2.8.   *g*right side: The place of power and honor.   *h*your: Some manuscripts have "our."   *i*with people who disobey him by doing these things: Some manuscripts do not have these words.

barbarian or a Scythian,[j] and you may be a slave or a free person. Yet Christ is all that matters, and he lives in all of us.

12God loves you and has chosen you as his own special people. So be gentle, kind, humble, meek, and patient. **13**Put up with each other, and forgive anyone who does you wrong, just as Christ has forgiven you. **14**Love is more important than anything else. It is what ties everything completely together.

15Each one of you is part of the body of Christ, and you were chosen to live together in peace. So let the peace that comes from Christ control your thoughts. And be grateful. **16**Let the message about Christ completely fill your lives, while you use all your wisdom to teach and instruct each other. With thankful hearts, sing psalms, hymns, and spiritual songs to God. **17**Whatever you say or do should be done in the name of the Lord Jesus, as you give thanks to God the Father because of him.

Some Rules for Christian Living

18A wife must put her husband first. This is her duty as a follower of the Lord.

19A husband must love his wife and not abuse her.

20Children must always obey their parents. This pleases the Lord.

21Parents, don't be hard on your children. If you are, they might give up.

22Slaves, you must always obey your earthly masters. Try to please them at all times, and not just when you think they are watching. Honor the Lord and serve your masters with your whole heart. **23**Do your work willingly, as though you were serving the Lord himself, and not just your earthly master. **24**In fact, the Lord Christ is the one you are really serving, and you know that he will reward you. **25**But Christ has no favorites! He will punish evil people, just as they deserve.

4 Slave owners, be fair and honest with your slaves. Don't forget that you have a Master in heaven.

2Never give up praying. And when you pray, keep alert and be thankful. **3**Be sure to pray that God will make a way for us to spread his message and explain the mystery about Christ, even though I am in jail for doing this. **4**Please pray that I will make the message as clear as possible.

5When you are with unbelievers, always make good use of the time. **6**Be pleasant and hold their interest when you speak the message. Choose your words carefully and be ready to give answers to anyone who asks questions.

Final Greetings

7Tychicus is the dear friend, who faithfully works and serves the Lord with us, and he will give you the news about me. **8**I am sending him to cheer you up by telling you how we are getting along. **9**Onesimus, that dear and faithful follower from your own group, is coming with him. The two of them will tell you everything that has happened here.

10Aristarchus is in jail with me. He sends greetings to you, and so does Mark, the cousin of Barnabas. You

---

[j] *a barbarian or a Scythian*: Barbarians were people who could not speak Greek and would be in the lower class of society. Scythians were people who were known for their cruelty.

have already been told to welcome Mark, if he visits you. 11Jesus, who is known as Justus, sends his greetings. These three men are the only Jewish followers who have worked with me for the kingdom of God. They have given me much comfort.

12Your own Epaphras, who serves Christ Jesus, sends his greetings. He always prays hard that you may fully know what the Lord wants you to do and that you may do it completely. 13I have seen how much trouble he has gone through for you and for the followers in Laodicea and Hierapolis.

14Our dear doctor Luke sends you his greetings, and so does Demas.

15Give my greetings to the followers at Laodicea, especially to Nympha and the church that meets in her home.

16After this letter has been read to your people, be sure to have it read in the church at Laodicea. And you should read the letter that I have sent to them.[k]

17Remind Archippus to do the work that the Lord has given him to do.

18I am signing this letter myself: PAUL.

Don't forget that I am in jail.

I pray that God will be kind to you.

[k]*the letter that I have sent to them*: This is the only mention of the letter to the church at Laodicea.

Paul's First Letter to the Church in Thessalonica

ABOUT THIS LETTER

Paul started the church in Thessalonica (2.13,14), while working hard to support himself (2.9). In this important city of northern Greece, many of the followers had worshiped idols before becoming Christians (1.9). But they were faithful to the Lord, and because of them the Lord's message had spread everywhere in that region (1.8). This letter may have been the first one that Paul wrote, and maybe even the first of all the New Testament writings.

Some people in Thessalonica began to oppose Paul, and he had to escape to Athens. But he sent his young friend Timothy to find out how the Christians were doing (3.1–5). When Timothy returned, he gave Paul good reports of their faith and love (3.6–10).

The church itself had problems. Some of its members had quit working, since they thought that the Lord would soon return (4.11,12). Others were worried because relatives and friends had already died before Christ's return. So Paul tried to explain to them more clearly what would happen when the Lord returns (4.13–15), and then told them how they should live in the meanwhile (5.1–11).

Paul's final instructions are well worth remembering:

Always be joyful and never stop praying. Whatever happens, keep thanking God because of Jesus Christ. This is what God wants you to do. (5.16–18)

A QUICK LOOK AT THIS LETTER

- Greetings (1.1–3)
- The Thessalonians' Faith and Example (1.4—3.13)
- A Life That Pleases God (4.1–12)
- What to Expect When the Lord Returns (4.13—5.11)
- Final Instructions and Greetings (5.12–28)

1 From Paul, Silas,*a* and Timothy. To the church in Thessalonica, the people of God the Father and of the Lord Jesus Christ.

I pray that God will be kind to you and will bless you with peace!

2We thank God for you and always mention you in our prayers. Each time we pray, 3we tell God our Father about your faith and loving work and about your firm hope in our Lord Jesus Christ.

The Thessalonians' Faith and Example

4My dear friends, God loves you, and we know he has chosen you to be his people. 5When we told you the good news, it was with the power and assurance that come from the Holy Spirit, and not simply with words. You knew what kind of people we were and how we helped you. 6So, when you accepted the message, you followed our example and the example of the Lord. You suf-

fered, but the Holy Spirit made you glad.

7You became an example for all the Lord's followers in Macedonia and Achaia. 8And because of you, the Lord's message has spread everywhere in those regions. Now the news of your faith in God is known all over the world, and we don't have to say a thing about it. 9Everyone is talking about how you welcomed us and how you turned away from idols to serve the true and living God. 10They also tell how you are waiting for his Son Jesus to come from heaven. God raised him from death, and on the day of judgment Jesus will save us from God's anger.

Paul's Work in Thessalonica

2 My friends, you know that our time with you was not wasted. 2As you remember, we had been mistreated and insulted at Philippi. But God gave us the courage to tell you the good news about him, even though many

---

aSilas: The Greek text has "Silvanus," which is another form of the name Silas.

people caused us trouble. 3We didn't have any hidden motives when we won you over, and we didn't try to fool or trick anyone. 4God was pleased to trust us with his message. We didn't speak to please people, but to please God who knows our motives.

5You also know that we didn't try to flatter anyone. God himself knows that what we did was not a cover-up for greed. 6We were not trying to get you or anyone else to praise us. 7But as apostles, we could have demanded help from you. After all, Christ is the one who sent us. We chose to be like children or like a mother*b* nursing her baby. 8We cared so much for you, and you became so dear to us, that we were willing to give our lives for you when we gave you God's message.

9My dear friends, you surely haven't forgotten our hard work and hardships. You remember how night and day we struggled to make a living, so that we could tell you God's message without being a burden to anyone. 10Both you and God are witnesses that we were pure and honest and innocent in our dealings with you followers of the Lord. 11You also know we did everything for you that parents would do for their own children. 12We begged, encouraged, and urged each of you to live in a way that would honor God. He is the one who chose you to share in his own kingdom and glory.

13We always thank God that you believed the message we preached. It came from him, and it is not something made up by humans. You accepted it as God's message, and now he is working in you. 14My friends, you did just like God's churches in Judea and like the other followers of Christ Jesus

there. And so, you were mistreated by your own people, in the same way they were mistreated by the Jewish people.

15Those Jews killed the Lord Jesus and the prophets, and they even chased us away. God doesn't like what they do and neither does anyone else. 16They keep us from speaking his message to the Gentiles and from leading them to be saved. The Jews have always gone too far with their sins. Now God has finally become angry and will punish them.

Paul Wants to Visit the Church Again

17My friends, we were kept from coming to you for a while, but we never stopped thinking about you. We were eager to see you and tried our best to visit you in person. 18We really wanted to come. I myself tried several times, but Satan always stopped us. 19After all, when the Lord Jesus appears, who else but you will give us hope and joy and be like a glorious crown for us? 20You alone are our glory and joy!

3 Finally, we couldn't stand it any longer. We decided to stay in Athens by ourselves 2and send our friend Timothy to you. He works with us as God's servant and preaches the good news about Christ. We wanted him to make you strong in your faith and to encourage you. 3We didn't want any of you to be discouraged by all these troubles. You knew we would have to suffer, 4because when we were with you, we told you this would happen. And we did suffer, as you well know. 5At last, when I could not wait any

---

blike children or like a mother: Some manuscripts have "as gentle as a mother."

longer, I sent Timothy to find out about your faith. I hoped that Satan had not tempted you and made all our work useless.

6Timothy has come back from his visit with you and has told us about your faith and love. He also said that you always have happy memories of us and that you want to see us as much as we want to see you.

7My friends, even though we have a lot of trouble and suffering, your faith makes us feel better about you. 8Your strong faith in the Lord is like a breath of new life. 9How can we possibly thank God enough for all the happiness you have brought us? 10Day and night we sincerely pray that we will see you again and help you to have an even stronger faith.

11We pray that God the Father and our Lord Jesus Christ will let us visit you. 12May the Lord make your love for each other and for everyone else grow by leaps and bounds. That's how our love for you has grown. 13And when our Lord comes with all of his people, I pray that he will make your hearts pure and innocent in the sight of God the Father.

A Life That Pleases God

4 Finally, my dear friends, since you belong to the Lord Jesus, we beg and urge you to live as we taught you. Then you will please God. You are already living that way, but try even harder. 2Remember the instructions we gave you as followers of the Lord Jesus. 3God wants you to be holy, so don't be immoral in matters of sex. 4Respect and honor your wife.*c* 5Don't

be a slave of your desires or live like people who don't know God. 6You must not cheat any of the Lord's followers in matters of sex.*d* Remember, we warned you that he punishes everyone who does such things. 7God didn't choose you to be filthy, but to be pure. 8So if you don't obey these rules, you are not really disobeying us. You are disobeying God, who gives you his Holy Spirit.

9We don't have to write you about the need to love each other. God has taught you to do this, 10and you already have shown your love for all of his people in Macedonia. But, my dear friends, we ask you to do even more. 11Try your best to live quietly, to mind your own business, and to work hard, just as we taught you to do. 12Then you will be respected by people who are not followers of the Lord, and you won't have to depend on anyone.

The Lord's Coming

13My friends, we want you to understand how it will be for those followers who have already died. Then you won't grieve over them and be like people who don't have any hope. 14We believe that Jesus died and was raised to life. We also believe that when God brings Jesus back again, he will bring with him all who had faith in Jesus before they died. 15Our Lord Jesus told us that when he comes, we won't go up to meet him ahead of his followers who have already died.

16With a loud command and with the shout of the chief angel and a blast of God's trumpet, the Lord will return

---

c your wife: Or "your body."   *d in matters of sex*: Or "in business."

from heaven. Then those who had faith in Christ before they died will be raised to life. 17Next, all of us who are still alive will be taken up into the clouds together with them to meet the Lord in the sky. From that time on we will all be with the Lord forever. 18Encourage each other with these words.

5 I don't need to write you about the time or date when all this will happen. 2You surely know that the Lord's return*e* will be as a thief coming at night. 3People will think they are safe and secure. But destruction will suddenly strike them like the pains of a woman about to give birth. And they won't escape.

4My dear friends, you don't live in darkness, and so that day won't surprise you like a thief. 5All of you belong to the light and live in the day. We don't live in the night or belong to the dark. 6Others may sleep, but we should stay awake and be alert. 7People sleep during the night, and some even get drunk. 8But we belong to the day. So we must stay sober and let our faith and love be like a suit of armor. Our firm hope that we will be saved is our helmet.

9God does not intend to punish us, but to have our Lord Jesus Christ save us. 10Christ died for us, so that we could live with him, whether we are alive or dead when he comes. 11That's why you must encourage and help each other, just as you are already doing.

Final Instructions and Greetings

12My friends, we ask you to be thoughtful of your leaders who work hard and tell you how to live for the Lord. 13Show them great respect and love because of their work. Try to get along with each other. 14My friends, we beg you to warn anyone who is not living right. Encourage anyone who feels left out, help all who are weak, and be patient with everyone. 15Don't be hateful to people, just because they are hateful to you. Rather, be good to each other and to everyone else.

16Always be joyful 17and never stop praying. 18Whatever happens, keep thanking God because of Jesus Christ. This is what God wants you to do.

19Don't turn away God's Spirit 20or ignore prophecies. 21Put everything to the test. Accept what is good 22and don't have anything to do with evil.

23I pray that God, who gives peace, will make you completely holy. And may your spirit, soul, and body be kept healthy and faultless until our Lord Jesus Christ returns. 24The one who chose you can be trusted, and he will do this.

25Friends, please pray for us.

26Give all the Lord's followers a warm greeting.

27In the name of the Lord I beg you to read this letter to all his followers.

28I pray that our Lord Jesus Christ will be kind to you!

---

e the Lord's return: The Greek text has "the day of the Lord."

Paul's Second Letter to the Church in Thessalonica

ABOUT THIS LETTER

I n this letter to the believers in Thessalonica, Paul begins by thanking God that their faith and love keep growing all the time (1.3). They were going through a lot of troubles, but Paul insists that this is God's way of testing their faith, not a way of punishing them (1.4, 5).

Someone in Thessalonica claimed to have a letter from Paul, saying that the Lord had already returned (2.2). But Paul warns the church not to be fooled! The Lord will not return until after the "wicked one" has appeared (2.3).

Paul also warns against laziness (3.6–10), and he tells the church to guard against any followers who refuse to obey what he has written in this letter.

The letter closes with a prayer:

I pray that the Lord, who gives peace, will keep blessing you with peace no matter where you are. May the Lord be with all of you. (3.16)

A QUICK LOOK AT THIS LETTER

- Greetings (1.1, 2)
- The Lord's Return Will Bring Justice (1.3–12)
- The Lord Has Not Returned Yet (2.1–12)
- Be Faithful (2.13–17)
- Pray and Work (3.1–15)
- A Final Prayer (3.16–18)

---

1 From Paul, Silas,[a] and Timothy. To the church in Thessalonica, the people of God our Father and of the Lord Jesus Christ.

²I pray that God our Father and the Lord Jesus Christ will be kind to you and will bless you with peace!

When Christ Returns

³My dear friends, we always have good reason to thank God for you, because your faith in God and your love for each other keep growing all the time. ⁴That's why we brag about you to all of God's churches. We tell them how patient you are and how you keep on having faith, even though you are going through a lot of trouble and suffering.

⁵All of this shows that God judges fairly and that he is making you fit to share in his kingdom for which you are suffering. ⁶It is only right for God to

---

[a]*Silas*: The Greek text has "Silvanus," which is another form of the name Silas.

punish everyone who is causing you trouble, 7but he will give you relief from your troubles. He will do the same for us, when the Lord Jesus comes from heaven with his powerful angels 8and with a flaming fire.

Our Lord Jesus will punish anyone who doesn't know God and won't obey his message. 9Their punishment will be eternal destruction, and they will be kept far from the presence of our Lord and his glorious strength. 10This will happen on that day when the Lord returns to be praised and honored by all who have faith in him and belong to him. This includes you, because you believed what we said.

11God chose you, and we keep praying that God will make you worthy of being his people. We pray for God's power to help you do all the good things that you hope to do and that your faith makes you want to do. 12Then, because God and our Lord Jesus Christ are so kind, you will bring honor to the name of our Lord Jesus, and he will bring honor to you.

The Lord's Return

2 When our Lord Jesus returns, we will be gathered up to meet him. So I ask you, my friends, 2not to be easily upset or disturbed by people who claim that the Lord*b* has already come. They may say that they heard this directly from the Holy Spirit, or from someone else, or even that they read it in one of our letters. 3But don't be fooled! People will rebel against God. Then before the Lord returns, the

wicked*c* one who is doomed to be destroyed will appear. 4He will brag and oppose everything that is holy or sacred. He will even sit in God's temple and claim to be God. 5Don't you remember that I told you this while I was still with you?

6You already know what is holding this wicked one back until it is time for him to come. 7His mysterious power is already at work, but someone is holding him back. And the wicked one won't appear until that someone is out of the way. 8Then he will appear, but the Lord Jesus will kill him simply by breathing on him. He will be completely destroyed by the Lord's glorious return.

9When the wicked one appears, Satan will pretend to work all kinds of miracles, wonders, and signs. 10Lost people will be fooled by his evil deeds. They could be saved, but they will refuse to love the truth and accept it. 11So God will make sure that they are fooled into believing a lie. 12All of them will be punished, because they would rather do evil than believe the truth.

Be Faithful

13My friends, the Lord loves you, and it is only natural for us to thank God for you. God chose you to be the first ones to be saved.*d* His Spirit made you holy, and you put your faith in the truth. 14God used our preaching as his way of inviting you to share in the glory of our Lord Jesus Christ. 15My friends, that's why you must remain faithful

---

*b*Lord: The Greek text has "day of the Lord." *c*wicked: Some manuscripts have "sinful."
*d*God chose you to be the first ones to be saved: Some manuscripts have "From the beginning God chose you to be saved."

and follow closely what we taught you in person and by our letters.

16God our Father loves us. He is kind and has given us eternal comfort and a wonderful hope. We pray that our Lord Jesus Christ and God our Father 17will encourage you and help you always to do and say the right thing.

Pray for Us

3 Finally, our friends, please pray for us. This will help the message about the Lord to spread quickly, and others will respect it, just as you do. 2Pray that we may be kept safe from worthless and evil people. After all, not everyone has faith. 3But the Lord can be trusted to make you strong and protect you from harm. 4He has made us sure that you are obeying what we taught you and that you will keep on obeying. 5I pray that the Lord will guide you to be as loving as God and as patient as Christ.

Warnings against Laziness

6My dear friends, in the name of*e* the Lord Jesus, I beg you not to have anything to do with any of your people who loaf around and refuse to obey the instructions we gave you. 7You surely know that you should follow our example. We didn't waste our time loafing,

e in the name of: Or "as a follower of."

8and we didn't accept food from anyone without paying for it. We didn't want to be a burden to any of you, so night and day we worked as hard as we could.

9We had the right not to work, but we wanted to set an example for you. 10We also gave you the rule that if you don't work, you don't eat. 11Now we learn that some of you just loaf around and won't do any work, except the work of a busybody. 12So, for the sake of our Lord Jesus Christ, we ask and beg these people to settle down and start working for a living. 13Dear friends, you must never become tired of doing right.

14Be on your guard against any followers who refuse to obey what we have written in this letter. Put them to shame by not having anything to do with them. 15Don't consider them your enemies, but speak kindly to them as you would to any other follower.

Final Prayer

16I pray that the Lord, who gives peace, will keep blessing you with peace no matter where you are. May the Lord be with all of you.

17I always sign my letters as I am now doing: PAUL.

18I pray that our Lord Jesus Christ will be kind to all of you.

Paul's First Letter to Timothy

ABOUT THIS LETTER

Timothy traveled and worked with Paul (Romans 16.21; 1 Corinthians 16.10; Philippians 2.19), and because of their shared faith, Timothy was like a son to Paul (1.2). Timothy became one of Paul's most faithful co-workers, and Paul mentions Timothy in five of his letters.

Although this letter is addressed to Timothy personally, it actually addresses many of the concerns Paul had with the life of the entire church. Guidelines are given for choosing church officials (3.1–7), officers (3.8–13), and leaders (5.17–20).

Christians are to pray for everyone and to remember:

There is only one God,
and Christ Jesus
is the only one
who can bring us
to God.

(2.5)

A QUICK LOOK AT THIS LETTER

- Greetings (1.1, 2)
- Instructions for Church Life (1.3—3.13)
- The Mystery of Our Religion (3.14—4.5)
- Paul's Advice to Timothy (4.6—6.21)

---

1 From Paul. God our Savior and Christ Jesus commanded me to be an apostle of Christ Jesus, who gives us hope.

²Timothy, because of our faith, you are like a son to me. I pray that God our Father and our Lord Jesus Christ will be kind and merciful to you. May they bless you with peace!

Warning against False Teaching

³When I was leaving for Macedonia, I asked you to stay on in Ephesus and warn certain people there to stop spreading their false teachings. ⁴You needed to warn them to stop wasting their time on senseless stories and endless lists of ancestors. Such things only cause arguments. They don't help anyone to do God's work that can only be done by faith.

⁵You must teach people to have genuine love, as well as a good conscience and true faith. ⁶There are some who have given up these for nothing but empty talk. ⁷They want to be teachers of the Law of Moses. But they don't know what they are talking about, even though they think they do.

8We know that the Law is good, if it is used in the right way. 9We also understand that it was not given to control people who please God, but to control lawbreakers, criminals, godless people, and sinners. It is for wicked and evil people, and for murderers, who would even kill their own parents. 10The Law was written for people who are sexual perverts or who live as homosexuals or are kidnappers or liars or won't tell the truth in court. It is for anything else that opposes the correct teaching 11of the good news that the glorious and wonderful God has given me.

Being Thankful for God's Kindness

12I thank Christ Jesus our Lord. He gives me the strength for my work because he knew that he could trust me. 13I used to say terrible and insulting things about him, and I was cruel. But he had mercy on me because I didn't know what I was doing, and I had not yet put my faith in him. 14Christ Jesus our Lord was very kind to me. He has greatly blessed my life with faith and love just like his own.

15"Christ Jesus came into the world to save sinners." This saying is true, and it can be trusted. I was the worst sinner of all! 16But since I was worse than anyone else, God had mercy on me and let me be an example of the endless patience of Christ Jesus. He did this so that others would put their faith in Christ and have eternal life. 17I pray that honor and glory will always be given to the only God, who lives forever and is the invisible and eternal King! Amen.

18Timothy, my son, the instructions I am giving you are based on what some prophets*a* once said about you. If you follow these instructions, you will fight like a good soldier. 19You will be faithful and have a clear conscience. Some people have made a mess of their faith because they didn't listen to their consciences. 20Two of them are Hymenaeus and Alexander. I have given these men over to the power of Satan, so they will learn not to oppose God.

How to Pray

2 First of all, I ask you to pray for everyone. Ask God to help and bless them all, and tell God how thankful you are for each of them. 2Pray for kings and others in power, so that we may live quiet and peaceful lives as we worship and honor God. 3This kind of prayer is good, and it pleases God our Savior. 4God wants everyone to be saved and to know the whole truth, which is,

5There is only one God,
and Christ Jesus
is the only one
who can bring us
to God.
Jesus was truly human,
and he gave himself
to rescue all of us.
6God showed us this
at the right time.

7This is why God chose me to be a preacher and an apostle of the good news. I am telling the truth. I am not lying. God sent me to teach the Gentiles about faith and truth.

8I want everyone everywhere to lift innocent hands toward heaven and pray, without being angry or arguing with each other.

---

*a*prophets: Probably the Christian prophets referred to in 4.14.

9I would like for women to wear modest and sensible clothes. They should not have fancy hairdos, or wear expensive clothes, or put on jewelry made of gold or pearls. 10Women who claim to love God should do helpful things for others, 11and they should learn by being quiet and paying attention. 12They should be silent and not be allowed to teach or to tell men what to do. 13After all, Adam was created before Eve, 14and the man Adam was not the one who was fooled. It was the woman Eve who was completely fooled and sinned. 15But women will be saved by having children,[b] if they stay faithful, loving, holy, and modest.

Church Officials

3 It is true that[c] anyone who desires to be a church official[d] wants to be something worthwhile. 2That's why officials must have a good reputation and be married only once.[e] They must be self-controlled, sensible, well-behaved, friendly to strangers, and able to teach. 3They must not be heavy drinkers or troublemakers. Instead, they must be kind and gentle and not love money.

4Church officials must be in control of their own families, and they must see that their children are obedient and always respectful. 5If they don't know how to control their own families, how can they look after God's people?

6They must not be new followers of the Lord. If they are, they might become proud and be doomed along with the devil. 7Finally, they must be well-respected by people who are not followers. Then they won't be trapped and disgraced by the devil.

Church Officers

8Church officers[f] should be serious. They must not be liars, heavy drinkers, or greedy for money. 9And they must have a clear conscience and hold firmly to what God has shown us about our faith. 10They must first prove themselves. Then if no one has anything against them, they can serve as officers.

11Women[g] must also be serious. They must not gossip or be heavy drinkers, and they must be faithful in everything they do.

12Church officers must be married only once.[h] They must be in full control of their children and everyone else in their home. 13Those who serve well as officers will earn a good reputation and will be highly respected for their faith in Christ Jesus.

The Mystery of Our Religion

14I hope to visit you soon. But I am writing these instructions, 15so that if I am delayed, you will know how everyone who belongs to God's family ought to behave. After all, the church

---

[b]saved by having children: Or "brought safely through childbirth" or "saved by the birth of a child" (that is, by the birth of Jesus) or "saved by being good mothers." [c]It is true that: These words may be taken with 2.15. If so, that verse would be translated: "It is true that women will be saved . . . holy, and modest." And 3.1 would be translated, "Anyone who desires . . . something worthwhile." [d]church official: Or "bishop." [e]married only once: Or "the husbands of only one wife" or "faithful in marriage." [f]Church officers: Or "Deacons." [g]Women: Either church officers or the wives of church officers. [h]married only once: See the note at 3.2.

of the living God is the strong foundation of truth.

16Here is the great mystery of our religion:

Christ*ⁱ* came as a human.
The Spirit proved
that he pleased God,
and he was seen by angels.

Christ was preached
to the nations.
People in this world
put their faith in him,
and he was taken up to glory.

People Will Turn from Their Faith

4 God's Spirit clearly says that in the last days many people will turn from their faith. They will be fooled by evil spirits and by teachings that come from demons. 2They will also be fooled by the false claims of liars whose consciences have lost all feeling. These liars 3will forbid people to marry or to eat certain foods. But God created these foods to be eaten with thankful hearts by his followers who know the truth. 4Everything God created is good. And if you give thanks, you may eat anything. 5What God has said and your prayer will make it fit to eat.

Paul's Advice to Timothy

6If you teach these things to other followers, you will be a good servant of Christ Jesus. You will show that you have grown up on the teachings about our faith and on the good instructions you have obeyed. 7Don't have anything

to do with worthless, senseless stories. Work hard to be truly religious. 8-9As the saying goes,

"Exercise is good
for your body,
but religion helps you
in every way.
It promises life
now and forever."

These words are worthwhile and should not be forgotten. 10We have put our hope in the living God, who is the Savior of everyone, but especially of those who have faith. That's why we work and struggle so hard.*ʲ*

11Teach these things and tell everyone to do what you say. 12Don't let anyone make fun of you, just because you are young. Set an example for other followers by what you say and do, as well as by your love, faith, and purity.

13Until I arrive, be sure to keep on reading the Scriptures in worship, and don't stop preaching and teaching. 14Use the gift you were given when the prophets spoke and the group of church leaders*ᵏ* blessed you by placing their hands on you. 15Remember these things and think about them, so everyone can see how well you are doing. 16Be careful about the way you live and about what you teach. Keep on doing this, and you will save not only yourself, but the people who hear you.

How to Act toward Others

5 Don't correct an older man. Encourage him, as you would your own father. Treat younger men as you would your own brother, 2and treat

---

ⁱChrist: The Greek text has "he," probably meaning "Christ." Some manuscripts have "God."
ʲstruggle so hard: Some manuscripts have "are treated so badly." *ᵏgroup of church leaders*:
Or "group of elders" or "group of presbyters" or "group of priests." This translates one Greek word, and it is related to the one used in 5.17, 19.

older women as you would your own mother. Show the same respect to younger women that you would to your sister.

3Take care of any widow who is really in need. 4But if a widow has children or grandchildren, they should learn to serve God by taking care of her, as she once took care of them. This is what God wants them to do. 5A widow who is really in need is one who does not have any relatives. She has faith in God, and she keeps praying to him night and day, asking for his help.

6A widow who thinks only about having a good time is already dead, even though she is still alive.

7Tell all of this to everyone, so they will do the right thing. 8People who don't take care of their relatives, and especially their own families, have given up their faith. They are worse than someone who doesn't have faith in the Lord.

9For a widow to be put on the list of widows, she must be at least sixty years old, and she must have been married only once.*l* 10She must also be well-known for doing all sorts of good things, such as raising children, giving food to strangers, welcoming God's people into her home,*m* helping people in need, and always making herself useful.

11Don't put young widows on the list. They may later have a strong desire to get married. Then they will turn away from Christ 12and become guilty of breaking their promise to him. 13Besides, they will become lazy and get into the habit of going from house to house. Next, they will start gossiping and become busybodies, talking about things that are none of their business.

14I would prefer that young widows get married, have children, and look after their families. Then the enemy won't have any reason to say insulting things about us. 15Look what's already happened to some of the young widows! They have turned away to follow Satan.

16If a woman who is a follower has any widows in her family, she*n* should help them. This will keep the church from having that burden, and then the church can help widows who are really in need.

Church Leaders

17Church leaders*o* who do their job well deserve to be paid*p* twice as much, especially if they work hard at preaching and teaching. 18It is just as the Scriptures say, "Don't muzzle an ox when you are using it to grind grain." You also know the saying, "Workers are worth their pay."

19Don't listen to any charge against a church leader, unless at least two or three people bring the same charges. 20But if any of the leaders should keep on sinning, they must be corrected in front of the whole group, as a warning to everyone else.

21In the presence of God and Christ Jesus and their chosen angels, I order you to follow my instructions!

---

*l*married only once: Or "the wife of only one husband" or "faithful in marriage."   *m*welcoming God's people into her home: The Greek text has "washing the feet of God's people." In New Testament times most people either went barefoot or wore sandals, and a host would often wash the feet of special guests.   *n*woman . . . she: Some manuscripts have "man . . . he," and others have "man or woman . . . that person."   *o*leaders: Or "elders" or "presbyters" or "priests."   *p*paid: Or "honored" or "respected."

Be fair with everyone, and don't have any favorites.

22Don't be too quick to accept people into the service of the Lord^q by placing your hands on them.

Don't sin because others do, but stay close to God.

23Stop drinking only water. Take a little wine to help your stomach trouble and the other illnesses you always have.

24Some people get caught in their sins right away, even before the time of judgment. But other people's sins don't show up until later. 25It is the same with good deeds. Some are easily seen, but none of them can be hidden.

6 If you are a slave, you should respect and honor your owner. This will keep people from saying bad things about God and about our teaching. 2If any of you slaves have owners who are followers, you should show them respect. After all, they are also followers of Christ, and he loves them. So you should serve and help them the best you can.

False Teaching and True Wealth

These are the things you must teach and tell the people to do. 3Anyone who teaches something different disagrees with the correct and godly teaching of our Lord Jesus Christ. 4Those people who disagree are proud of themselves, but they don't really know a thing. Their minds are sick, and they like to argue over words. They cause jealousy, disagreements, unkind words, evil suspicions, 5and nasty quarrels. They have wicked minds

and have missed out on the truth.

These people think religion is supposed to make you rich. 6And religion does make your life rich, by making you content with what you have. 7We didn't bring anything into this world, and we won't^r take anything with us when we leave. 8So we should be satisfied just to have food and clothes. 9People who want to be rich fall into all sorts of temptations and traps. They are caught by foolish and harmful desires that drag them down and destroy them. 10The love of money causes all kinds of trouble. Some people want money so much that they have given up their faith and caused themselves a lot of pain.

Fighting a Good Fight for the Faith

11Timothy, you belong to God, so keep away from all these evil things. Try your best to please God and to be like him. Be faithful, loving, dependable, and gentle. 12Fight a good fight for the faith and claim eternal life. God offered it to you when you clearly told about your faith, while so many people listened. 13Now I ask you to make a promise. Make it in the presence of God, who gives life to all, and in the presence of Jesus Christ, who openly told Pontius Pilate about his faith. 14Promise to obey completely and fully all that you have been told until our Lord Jesus Christ returns.

15The glorious God
is the only Ruler,
the King of kings
and Lord of lords.
At the time that God
has already decided,

---

^q*to accept people into the service of the Lord*: Or "to forgive people." ^r*we won't*: Some manuscripts have "we surely won't."

he will send Jesus Christ
back again.

16Only God lives forever!
And he lives in light
that no one can come near.
No human has ever seen God
or ever can see him.
God will be honored,
and his power
will last forever. Amen.

17Warn the rich people of this
world not to be proud or to trust in
wealth that is easily lost. Tell them to
have faith in God, who is rich and
blesses us with everything we need to
enjoy life. 18Instruct them to do as
many good deeds as they can and to
help everyone. Remind the rich to be
generous and share what they have.
19This will lay a solid foundation for
the future, so that they will know what
true life is like.

20Timothy, guard what God has
placed in your care! Don't pay any attention to that godless and stupid talk
that sounds smart but really isn't.
21Some people have even lost their
faith by believing this talk.

I pray that the Lord will be kind
to all of you!

Paul's Second Letter to Timothy

ABOUT THIS LETTER

In his second letter to Timothy Paul is more personal than in his first one. Timothy is like a "dear child" to Paul, and Paul always mentions him in his prayers (1.2, 3) because he wants Timothy to be a "good soldier" of Christ Jesus and to learn to endure suffering (2.1, 3). Paul mentions Timothy's mother and grandmother by name in this letter and reminds Timothy how he had placed his hands on him as a special sign that the Spirit was guiding his work.

Some who claimed to be followers of the Lord had already been trapped by the devil, and Paul warns Timothy to run from those temptations that often catch young people (2.20–26; 3.1–9). He tells Timothy to keep preaching God's message, even if it is not the popular thing to do (4.2). He should also beware of false teachers.

Paul knows that he will soon die for his faith, but he will be rewarded for his faithfulness (4.6–8), and he reminds Timothy of the true message:

If we died with Christ,
we will live with him.
If we don't give up,
we will rule with him.
(2.11, 12a)

A QUICK LOOK AT THIS LETTER

- Greetings and Prayer for Timothy (1.1, 2)
- Do Not Be Ashamed of the Lord (1.3–18)
- How To Be a Good Soldier of Christ (2.1–26)
- What People Will Be Like in the Last Days (3.1–9)
- Keep Being Faithful (3.10—4.8)
- Personal Instructions and Final Greetings (4.9–22)

1 From Paul, an apostle of Christ Jesus. God himself chose me to be an apostle, and he gave me the promised life that Jesus Christ makes possible.

²Timothy, you are like a dear child to me. I pray that God our Father and our Lord Christ Jesus will be kind and merciful to you and will bless you with peace!

Do Not Be Ashamed of the Lord

³Night and day I mention you in my prayers. I am always grateful for you, as I pray to the God my ancestors and I have served with a clear conscience. ⁴I remember how you cried, and I want to see you, because that will make me truly happy. ⁵I also remember the genuine faith of your mother Eunice. Your grandmother Lois had the same sort of faith, and I am sure that you have it as well. ⁶So I ask you to make full use of the gift that God gave you when I placed my hands on you.ᵃ Use it well. ⁷God's Spiritᵇ does not make cowards out of us. The Spirit gives us power, love, and self-control.

⁸Don't be ashamed to speak for our Lord. And don't be ashamed of me, just because I am in jail for serving him.

Use the power that comes from God and join with me in suffering for telling the good news.

⁹God saved us and chose us
to be his holy people.
We did nothing
to deserve this,
but God planned it
because he is so kind.
Even before time began
God planned for Christ Jesus
to show kindness to us.

¹⁰Now Christ Jesus has come
to show us the kindness
of God.
Christ our Savior
defeated death
and brought us
the good news.
It shines like a light
and offers life
that never ends.

¹¹My work is to be a preacher, an apostle, and a teacher.ᶜ ¹²That's why I suffer. But I am not ashamed! I know the one I have faith in, and I am sure that he can guard until the last day what he has trusted me with.ᵈ ¹³Now follow the example of the correct teaching I gave you, and let the faith and love of Christ Jesus be your model.

ᵃwhen I placed my hands on you: Church leaders placed their hands on people who were being appointed to preach or teach. See 1 Timothy 4.14. ᵇGod's Spirit: Or "God." ᶜteacher: Some manuscripts add "of the Gentiles." ᵈwhat he has trusted me with: Or "what I have trusted him with."

14You have been trusted with a wonderful treasure. Guard it with the help of the Holy Spirit, who lives within you.

15You know that everyone in Asia has turned against me, especially Phygelus and Hermogenes.

16I pray that the Lord will be kind to the family of Onesiphorus. He often cheered me up and was not ashamed of me when I was put in jail. 17Then after he arrived in Rome, he searched everywhere until he found me. 18I pray that the Lord Jesus will ask God to show mercy to Onesiphorus on the day of judgment. You know how much he helped me in Ephesus.

A Good Soldier of Christ Jesus

2 Timothy, my child, Christ Jesus is kind, and you must let him make you strong. 2You have often heard me teach. Now I want you to tell these same things to followers who can be trusted to tell others.

3As a good soldier of Christ Jesus you must endure your share of suffering. 4Soldiers on duty don't work at outside jobs. They try only to please their commanding officer. 5No one wins an athletic contest without obeying the rules. 6And farmers who work hard are the first to eat what grows in their field. 7If you keep in mind what I have told you, the Lord will help you understand completely.

8Keep your mind on Jesus Christ! He was from the family of David and was raised from death, just as my good news says. 9And because of this message, I am locked up in jail and treated like a criminal. But God's good news isn't locked in jail, 10and so I am willing to put up with anything. Then God's special people will be saved. They will be given eternal glory because they belong to Christ Jesus. 11Here is a true message:

"If we died with Christ,
we will live with him.
12If we don't give up,
we will rule with him.
If we deny
that we know him,
he will deny
that he knows us.
13If we are not faithful,
he will still be faithful.
Christ cannot deny
who he is."

An Approved Worker

14Don't let anyone forget these things. And with God*e* as your witness, you must warn them not to argue about words. These arguments don't help anyone. In fact, they ruin everyone who listens to them. 15Do your best to win God's approval as a worker who does not need to be ashamed and who teaches only the true message.

16Keep away from worthless and useless talk. It only leads people farther away from God. 17That sort of talk is like a sore that won't heal. And Hymenaeus and Philetus have been talking this way 18by teaching that the dead have already been raised to life. This is far from the truth, and it is destroying the faith of some people.

19But the foundation that God has laid is solid. On it is written, "The Lord knows who his people are. So everyone who worships the Lord must turn away from evil."

20In a large house some dishes are made of gold or silver, while others are

---

e God: Some manuscripts have "the Lord," and others have "Christ."

made of wood or clay. Some of these are special, and others are not. 21That's also how it is with people. The ones who stop doing evil and make themselves pure will become special. Their lives will be holy and pleasing to their Master, and they will be able to do all kinds of good deeds.

22Run from temptations that capture young people. Always do the right thing. Be faithful, loving, and easy to get along with. Worship with people whose hearts are pure. 23Stay away from stupid and senseless arguments. These only lead to trouble, 24and God's servants must not be troublemakers. They must be kind to everyone, and they must be good teachers and very patient.

25Be humble when you correct people who oppose you. Maybe God will lead them to turn to him and learn the truth. 26They have been trapped by the devil, and he makes them obey him, but God may help them escape.

What People Will Be Like in the Last Days

3 You can be certain that in the last days there will be some very hard times. 2People will love only themselves and money. They will be proud, stuck-up, rude, and disobedient to their parents. They will also be ungrateful, godless, 3heartless, and hateful. Their words will be cruel, and they will have no self-control or pity. These people will hate everything that is good. 4They will be sneaky, reckless, and puffed up with pride. Instead of loving God, they will love pleasure. 5Even though they will make a show of being reli-

gious, their religion won't be real. Don't have anything to do with such people.

6Some men fool whole families, just to get power over those women, who are slaves of sin and are controlled by all sorts of desires. 7These women always want to learn something new, but they never can discover the truth. 8Just as Jannes and Jambres^f opposed Moses, these people are enemies of the truth. Their minds are sick, and their faith isn't real. 9But they won't get very far with their foolishness. Soon everyone will know the truth about them, just as Jannes and Jambres were found out.

Paul's Last Instructions to Timothy

10Timothy, you know what I teach and how I live. You know what I want to do and what I believe. You have seen how patient and loving I am, and how in the past I put up with 11trouble and suffering in the cities of Antioch, Iconium, and Lystra. Yet the Lord rescued me from all those terrible troubles. 12Anyone who belongs to Christ Jesus and wants to live right will have trouble from others. 13But evil people who pretend to be what they are not will become worse than ever, as they fool others and are fooled themselves.

14Keep on being faithful to what you were taught and to what you believed. After all, you know who taught you these things. 15Since childhood, you have known the Holy Scriptures that are able to make you wise enough to have faith in Christ Jesus and be saved. 16Everything in the Scriptures is God's Word. All of it is useful for teach-

---

^{f}*Jannes and Jambres*: These names are not found in the Old Testament. But many believe these were the names of the two Egyptian magicians who opposed Moses when he wanted to lead the people of Israel out of Egypt. See Exodus 7.11, 22.

ing and helping people and for correct-
ing them and showing them how to
live. 17The Scriptures train God's
servants to do all kinds of good deeds.

4 When Christ Jesus comes as king,
he will be the judge of everyone,
whether they are living or dead. So
with God and Christ as witnesses, I
command you 2to preach God's message. Do it willingly, even if it is not
the popular thing to do. You must correct people and point out their sins. But
also cheer them up, and when you instruct them, always be patient. 3The
time is coming when people won't listen to good teaching. Instead, they will
look for teachers who will please them
by telling them only what they are itch-
ing to hear. 4They will turn from the
truth and eagerly listen to senseless
stories. 5But you must stay calm and
be willing to suffer. You must work
hard to tell the good news and to do
your job well.

6Now the time has come for me
to die. My life is like a drink offering*g*
being poured out on the altar. 7I have
fought well. I have finished the race,
and I have been faithful. 8So a crown
will be given to me for pleasing the
Lord. He judges fairly, and on the day
of judgment he will give a crown to
me and to everyone else who wants
him to appear with power.

Personal Instructions

9Come to see me as soon as you
can. 10Demas loves the things of this
world so much that he left me and
went to Thessalonica. Crescens has
gone to Galatia, and Titus has gone to
Dalmatia. 11Only Luke has stayed
with me.

Mark can be very helpful to me,
so please find him and bring him with
you. 12I sent Tychicus to Ephesus.

13When you come, bring the coat
I left at Troas with Carpus. Don't forget
to bring the scrolls, especially the ones
made of leather.*h*

14Alexander, the metalworker, has
hurt me in many ways. But the Lord
will pay him back for what he has done.
15Alexander opposes what we preach.
You had better watch out for him.

16When I was first put on trial, no
one helped me. In fact, everyone deserted me. I hope it won't be held
against them. 17But the Lord stood beside me. He gave me the strength to
tell his full message, so that all Gentiles would hear it. And I was kept safe
from hungry lions. 18The Lord will always keep me from being harmed by
evil, and he will bring me safely into
his heavenly kingdom. Praise him forever and ever! Amen.

Final Greetings

19Give my greetings to Priscilla
and Aquila and to the family of Onesiphorus.

20Erastus stayed at Corinth.
Trophimus was sick, when I left
him at Miletus.

21Do your best to come before
winter.

Eubulus, Pudens, Linus, and Clau-
dia send you their greetings, and so do
the rest of the Lord's followers.

22I pray that the Lord will bless
your life and will be kind to you.

---

g drink offering: Water or wine was sometimes poured out as an offering when an animal
sacrifice was made. *h the ones made of leather*: A scroll was a kind of rolled up book, and it
could be made out of paper (called "papyrus") or leather (that is, animal skin) or even copper.

Paul's Letter to Titus

ABOUT THIS LETTER

Paul mentions Titus several times in his letters as someone who worked with him in Asia Minor and Greece (2 Corinthians 2.13; 7.6,13; 8.6,16,23; 12.18; Galatians 2.3). He is told by Paul to appoint church leaders and officials in Crete.

Paul instructs Titus to make sure that church leaders and officials have good reputations (1.5–9) and that all of the Lord's followers keep themselves pure and avoid arguments (1.10—2.9).

Paul includes special instructions for the different groups within the church in Crete. He reminds Titus that a new way of life is possible because of what God has done by sending Jesus Christ: God has saved them, washed them by the power of the Holy Spirit, and given them a fresh start and the hope of eternal life.

Paul also tells how we are saved:

*God our Savior showed us
    how good and kind he is.
He saved us because
    of his mercy,
and not because
    of any good things
    that we have done.*

(3. 4, 5)

A QUICK LOOK AT THIS LETTER

- Greetings and a Prayer for Titus (1.1–4)
- Instructions for Church Officials (1.5–16)
- Instructions for Church People (2.1—3.11)
- Personal Advice and Final Greetings (3.12–15)

---

1 From Paul, a servant of God and an apostle of Jesus Christ.

I encourage God's own people to have more faith and to understand the truth about religion. ²Then they will have the hope of eternal life that God promised long ago. And God never tells a lie! ³So, at the proper time, God our Savior gave this message and told me to announce what he had said.

⁴Titus, because of our faith, you are like a son to me. I pray that God our Father and Christ Jesus our Savior

will be kind to you and will bless you with peace!

What Titus Was to Do in Crete

⁵I left you in Crete to do what had been left undone and to appoint leaders*a* for the churches in each town. As I told you, ⁶they must have a good reputation and be married only once.*b* Their children must be followers of the Lord and not have a reputation for being wild and disobedient.

⁷Church officials*c* are in charge of God's work, and so they must also have a good reputation. They must not be bossy, quick-tempered, heavy drinkers, bullies, or dishonest in business. ⁸Instead, they must be friendly to strangers and enjoy doing good things. They must also be sensible, fair, pure, and self-controlled. ⁹They must stick to the true message they were taught, so that their good teaching can help others and correct everyone who opposes it.

¹⁰There are many who don't respect authority, and they fool others by talking nonsense. This is especially true of some Jewish followers. ¹¹But you must make them be quiet. They are after money, and they upset whole families by teaching what they should not. ¹²It is like one of their own prophets once said,

"The people of Crete
always tell lies.
They are greedy and lazy
like wild animals."

¹³That surely is a true saying. And you should be hard on such people, so you can help them grow stronger in their faith. ¹⁴Don't pay any attention to any of those senseless Jewish stories and human commands. These are made up by people who won't obey the truth.

¹⁵Everything is pure for someone whose heart is pure. But nothing is pure for an unbeliever with a dirty mind. That person's mind and conscience are destroyed. ¹⁶Such people claim to know God, but their actions prove that they really don't. They are disgusting. They won't obey God, and they are too worthless to do anything good.

Instructions for Different Groups of People

2 Titus, you must teach only what is correct. ²Tell the older men to have self-control and to be serious and sensible. Their faith, love, and patience must never fail.

³Tell the older women to behave as those who love the Lord should. They must not gossip about others or be slaves of wine. They must teach what is proper, ⁴so the younger women will be loving wives and mothers. ⁵Each of the younger women must be sensible and kind, as well as a good homemaker, who puts her own husband first. Then no one can say insulting things about God's message.

⁶Tell the young men to have self-control in everything.

⁷Always set a good example for others. Be sincere and serious when you teach. ⁸Use clean language that no one can criticize. Do this, and your enemies will be too ashamed to say anything against you.

---

aleaders: Or "elders" or "presbyters" or "priests."   *bmarried only once*: Or "the husbands of only one wife" or "faithful in marriage."   *cChurch officials*: Or "Bishops."

9Tell slaves always to please their owners by obeying them in everything. Slaves must not talk back to their owners 10or steal from them. They must be completely honest and trustworthy. Then everyone will show great respect for what is taught about God our Savior.

God's Kindness and the New Life

11God has shown us how kind he is by coming to save all people. 12He taught us to give up our wicked ways and our worldly desires and to live decent and honest lives in this world. 13We are filled with hope, as we wait for the glorious return of our great God and Savior Jesus Christ.*d* 14He gave himself to rescue us from everything that is evil and to make our hearts pure. He wanted us to be his own people and to be eager to do right.

15Teach these things, as you use your full authority to encourage and correct people. Make sure you earn everyone's respect.

Doing Helpful Things

3 Remind your people to obey the rulers and authorities and not to be rebellious. They must always be ready to do something helpful 2and not say cruel things or argue. They should be gentle and kind to everyone. 3We used to be stupid, disobedient, and foolish, as well as slaves of all sorts of desires and pleasures. We were evil and jealous. Everyone hated us, and we hated everyone.

4God our Savior showed us
how good and kind he is.

5He saved us because
of his mercy,
and not because
of any good things
that we have done.

God washed us by the power
of the Holy Spirit.
He gave us new birth
and a fresh beginning.
6God sent Jesus Christ
our Savior
to give us his Spirit.

7Jesus treated us much better
than we deserve.
He made us acceptable to God
and gave us the hope
of eternal life.
8This message is certainly true.

These teachings are useful and helpful for everyone. I want you to insist that the people follow them, so that all who have faith in God will be sure to do good deeds. 9But don't have anything to do with stupid arguments about ancestors. And stay away from disagreements and quarrels about the Jewish Law. Such arguments are useless and senseless.

10Warn troublemakers once or twice. Then don't have anything else to do with them. 11You know that their minds are twisted, and their own sins show how guilty they are.

Personal Instructions and Greetings

12I plan to send Artemas or Tychicus to you. After they arrive, please try

---

d the glorious return of our great God and Savior Jesus Christ: Or "the glorious return of our great God and our Savior Jesus Christ" or "the return of Jesus Christ, who is the glory of our great God and Savior."

your best to meet me at Nicopolis. I have decided to spend the winter there.

¹³When Zenas the lawyer and Apollos get ready to leave, help them as much as you can, so they won't have need of anything.

¹⁴Our people should learn to spend their time doing something useful and worthwhile.

¹⁵Greetings to you from everyone here. Greet all of our friends who share in our faith.

I pray that the Lord will be kind to all of you!

Paul's Letter to Philemon

ABOUT THIS LETTER

Philemon was a wealthy man who owned slaves and who used his large house for church meetings (2). He probably lived in Colossae, since Paul's letter to the Colossians mentions Onesimus, a slave of Philemon, and Archippus (Colossians 4.9,17).

Paul is writing from jail on behalf of Onesimus, a run-away slave owned by Philemon. Onesimus had become a follower of the Lord and a valuable friend to Paul, and Paul is writing to encourage Philemon to accept Onesimus also as a friend and follower of the Lord.

This letter is an excellent example of the art of letter-writing in the Roman world, and it is the most personal of all Paul's letters. The way the letter is written suggests that Paul and Philemon were close friends.

A QUICK LOOK AT THIS LETTER

- Greetings to Philemon (1–3)
- Paul Speaks to Philemon about Onesimus (4–22)
- Final Greetings and a Prayer (23–25)

¹From Paul, who is in jail for serving Christ Jesus, and from Timothy, who is like a brother because of our faith.

Philemon, you have worked with us and are very dear to us. This letter is to you ²and to the church that meets in your home. It is also to our dear friend Apphia and to Archippus, who serves the Lord as we do.

³I pray that God our Father and our Lord Jesus Christ will be kind to you and will bless you with peace!

Philemon's Love and Faith

⁴Philemon, each time I mention you in my prayers, I thank God. ⁵I hear about your faith in our Lord Jesus and about your love for all of God's people. ⁶As you share your faith with others, I pray that they may come to know all

the blessings Christ has given us. 7My friend, your love has made me happy and has greatly encouraged me. It has also cheered the hearts of God's people.

Paul Speaks to Philemon about Onesimus

8Christ gives me the courage to tell you what to do. 9But I would rather ask you to do it because of love, since I am a messenger*a* in jail for Christ. 10So I beg you to help Onesimus,*b* who has been like a son to me here in jail. 11Before this, he was useless to you, but now he is useful to you and me.

12Sending Onesimus to you has made me very sad. 13I would like to keep him here with me, where he could take your place in helping me spread the good news while I am a prisoner. 14But I won't do anything unless you agree to it first. I want your act of kindness to come from your heart, and not be something you feel forced to do.

15Perhaps Onesimus was taken from you for a little while so that you could have him back for good, 16but not as a slave. Onesimus is much more than a slave. To me he is a dear friend, but to you he is even more, both as a person and as a follower of the Lord.

17If you consider me a friend because of Christ, then welcome Onesimus as you would welcome me. 18If he has cheated you or owes you anything, charge it to my account. 19With my own hand I write: I, PAUL, WILL PAY YOU BACK. But don't forget that you owe me your life. 20My dear friend, I pray that the Lord will make you useful to me and that, as a follower of Christ, you will cheer me up.

21I am sure you will do all I have asked, and even more. 22Please get a room ready for me. I hope your prayers will be answered, and I can visit you.

23Epaphras is also here in jail for being a follower of Christ Jesus. He sends his greetings, 24and so do Mark, Aristarchus, Demas, and Luke, who work together with me.

25I pray that the Lord Jesus Christ will be with you!

---

a a messenger: Or "an old man." *bOnesimus*: In Greek this name means "useful."

The Letter to the Hebrews

ABOUT THIS LETTER

Many religious people in the first century after Jesus' birth, both Jews and Gentiles, had questions about the religion of the early Christians. They were looking for evidence that this new faith was genuine. Jews had the miracle of crossing the Red Sea and the agreement made with God at Mount Sinai to support their faith. But what miracles did Christians have? Jews had beautiful worship ceremonies and a high priest who offered sacrifices in the temple so that the people would be forgiven. But what did Christians have? How could this new Christian faith, centered in Jesus, offer forgiveness of sins and friendship with God?

The letter to the Hebrews was written to answer exactly these kinds of questions. In it the author tells the readers how important Jesus really is. He is greater than any of God's angels (1.5–14), greater than any prophet, and greater even than Moses and Joshua (2.1—4.14). Jesus is the perfect high priest because he never sinned, and by offering his own life he has made the perfect sacrifice for sin once for all time (9.23—10.18). By his death and return from death he has opened the way for all people to come to God (4.14—5.10; 7.1—8.13).

This letter has much to say about the importance of faith. The writer points out that what Jesus offers comes only by faith. And this faith makes his followers sure of what they hope for and gives them proof of things that cannot be seen. The writer praises God's faithful people of the past (11.1–40) and encourages those who follow Jesus now to keep their eyes on him as they run the race (12.1–3).

What does it mean to have a high priest like Jesus?

Jesus understands every weakness of ours, because he was tempted in every way that we are. But he did not sin! So whenever we are in need, we should come bravely before the throne of our merciful God. There we will be treated with undeserved kindness, and we will find help.

(4.15, 16)

A QUICK LOOK AT THIS LETTER

- The Greatness of God's Son (1.1–4)
- Jesus Is Greater than Angels (1.5—2.18)
- Jesus Is Greater than Moses and Joshua (3.1—4.13)
- Jesus Is the Great High Priest (4.14—7.28)
- Jesus Brings a Better Agreement (8.1—9.22)
- Jesus' Sacrifice Is Once and for All (9.23—10.31)
- Some of God's People Who Had Great Faith (11.1–40)
- Follow the Example of Jesus (12.1—13.19)
- Final Prayers and Greetings (13.20–25)

1 Long ago in many ways and at many times God's prophets spoke his message to our ancestors. 2But now at last God sent his Son to bring his message to us. God created the universe by his Son, and everything will someday belong to the Son. 3God's Son has all the brightness of God's own glory and is like him in every way. By his own mighty word he holds the universe together.

After the Son had washed away our sins, he sat down at the right side[a] of the glorious God in heaven. 4He had become much greater than the angels, and the name he was given is far greater than any of theirs.

God's Son Is Greater than Angels

5God has never said
to any of the angels,
"You are my Son, because today
I have become
your Father!"
Neither has God said
to any of them,
"I will be his Father,
and he will be my Son!"
6When God brings his first-born
Son[b] into the world, he commands all of his angels to worship him.
7And when God speaks about the angels, he says,
"I change my angels into wind
and my servants
into flaming fire."

8But God says about his Son,
"You are God,
and you will rule
as King forever!

Your[c] royal power
brings about justice.
9You loved justice
and hated evil,
and so I, your God,
have chosen you.
I appointed you
and made you happier
than any of your friends."

10The Scriptures also say,
"Lord, in the beginning
you were the one
who laid the foundation
of the earth
and created the heavens.
11They will all disappear
and wear out like clothes,
but you will last forever.
12You will roll them up
like a robe
and change them
like a garment.
But you are always the same,
and you will live forever."
13God never said to any
of the angels,
"Sit at my right side
until I make your enemies
into a footstool for you!"
14Angels are merely spirits sent to serve people who are going to be saved.

This Great Way of Being Saved

2 We must give our full attention to what we were told, so that we won't drift away. 2The message spoken by angels proved to be true, and all who disobeyed or rejected it were punished as they deserved. 3So if we refuse this great way of being saved, how can we

---

[a]*right side*: The place of honor and power. [b]*first-born Son*: The first son born into a family had certain privileges that the other children did not have. In 12.23 "first-born" refers to God's special people. [c]*Your*: Some manuscripts have "His."

hope to escape? The Lord himself was the first to tell about it, and people who heard the message proved to us that it was true. 4God himself showed that his message was true by working all kinds of powerful miracles and wonders. He also gave his Holy Spirit to anyone he chose to.

The One Who Leads Us To Be Saved

5We know that God did not put the future world under the power of angels. 6Somewhere in the Scriptures someone says to God,

"What makes you care
about us humans?
Why are you concerned
for weaklings such as we?
7You made us lower
than the angels
for a while.
Yet you have crowned us
with glory and honor.*d*
8And you have put everything
under our power!"

God has put everything under our power and has not left anything out of our power. But we still don't see it all under our power. 9What we do see is Jesus, who for a little while was made lower than the angels. Because of God's kindness, Jesus died for everyone. And now that Jesus has suffered and died, he is crowned with glory and honor!

10Everything belongs to God, and all things were created by his power. So God did the right thing when he made Jesus perfect by suffering, as Jesus led many of God's children to be saved and to share in his glory. 11Jesus

and the people he makes holy all belong to the same family. That is why he is not ashamed to call them his brothers and sisters. 12He even said to God,

"I will tell them your name
and sing your praises
when they come together
to worship."
13He also said,
"I will trust God."
Then he said,
"Here I am with the children
God has given me."
14We are people of flesh and blood. That is why Jesus became one of us. He died to destroy the devil, who had power over death. 15But he also died to rescue all of us who live each day in fear of dying. 16Jesus clearly did not come to help angels, but he did come to help Abraham's descendants. 17He had to be one of us, so that he could serve God as our merciful and faithful high priest and sacrifice himself for the forgiveness of our sins. 18And now that Jesus has suffered and was tempted, he can help anyone else who is tempted.

Jesus Is Greater than Moses

3 My friends, God has chosen you to be his holy people. So think about Jesus, the one we call our apostle and high priest! 2Jesus was faithful to God, who appointed him, just as Moses was faithful in serving all of*e* God's people. 3But Jesus deserves more honor than Moses, just as the builder of a house deserves more honor than the house. 4Of course, every house is built by someone, and God is really the one who built everything.

---

dand honor: Some manuscripts add "and you have placed us in charge of all you created."
eall of: Some manuscripts do not have these words.

5Moses was a faithful servant and told all of God's people what would be said in the future. 6But Christ is the Son in charge of God's people. And we are those people, if we keep on being brave and don't lose hope.

A Rest for God's People

7It is just as the Holy Spirit says,
"If you hear God's voice today,
8   don't be stubborn!
Don't rebel like those people
    who were tested
        in the desert.
9-10For forty years your ancestors
    tested God and saw
        the things he did.

"Then God got tired of them
    and said,
'You people never
    show good sense,
and you don't understand
    what I want you to do.'
11God became angry
    and told the people,
'You will never enter
    my place of rest!' "

12My friends, watch out! Don't let evil thoughts or doubts make any of you turn from the living God. 13You must encourage one another each day. And you must keep on while there is still a time that can be called "today." If you don't, then sin may fool some of you and make you stubborn. 14We were sure about Christ when we first became his people. So let's hold tightly to our faith until the end. 15The Scriptures say,

"If you hear his voice today,
    don't be stubborn
        like those who rebelled."

16Who were those people that heard God's voice and rebelled? Weren't they the same ones that came out of Egypt with Moses? 17Who were the people that made God angry for forty years? Weren't they the ones that sinned and died in the desert? 18And who did God say would never enter his place of rest? Weren't they the ones that disobeyed him? 19We see that those people did not enter the place of rest because they did not have faith.

4 The promise to enter the place of rest is still good, and we must take care that none of you miss out. 2We have heard the message, just as they did. But they failed to believe what they heard, and the message did not do them any good. 3Only people who have faith will enter the place of rest. It is just as the Scriptures say,

"God became angry
    and told the people,
'You will never enter
    my place of rest!' "

God said this, even though everything has been ready from the time of creation. 4In fact, somewhere the Scriptures say that God rested on the Sabbath. 5We also read that he later said, "You people will never enter my place of rest!" 6This means that the promise to enter is still good, because those who first heard about it disobeyed and did not enter. 7Much later God told David to make the promise again, just as I have already said,

"If you hear his voice today,
    don't be stubborn!"

8If Joshua had really given the people rest, there would not be any need for God to talk about another day of rest. 9But God has promised us a Sabbath when we will rest, even though it has not yet come. 10On that day God's people will rest from their work, just as God rested from his work.

11We should do our best to enter

that place of rest, so that none of us will disobey and miss going there, as they did. 12What God has said is not only alive and active! It is sharper than any double-edged sword. His word can cut through our spirits and souls and through our joints and marrow, until it discovers the desires and thoughts of our hearts. 13Nothing is hidden from God! He sees through everything, and we will have to tell him the truth.

Jesus Is the Great High Priest

14We have a great high priest, who has gone into heaven, and he is Jesus the Son of God. That is why we must hold on to what we have said about him. 15Jesus understands every weakness of ours, because he was tempted in every way that we are. But he did not sin! 16So whenever we are in need, we should come bravely before the throne of our merciful God. There we will be treated with undeserved kindness, and we will find help.

5 Every high priest is appointed to help others by offering gifts and sacrifices to God because of their sins. 2A high priest has weaknesses of his own, and he feels sorry for foolish and sinful people. 3That is why he must offer sacrifices for his own sins and for the sins of others. 4But no one can have the honor of being a high priest simply by wanting to be one. Only God can choose a priest, and God is the one who chose Aaron.

5That is how it was with Christ. He became a high priest, but not just because he wanted the honor of being one. It was God who told him,

"You are my Son, because today
I have become
your Father!"

6In another place, God says,

"You are a priest forever
just like Melchizedek."f

7God had the power to save Jesus from death. And while Jesus was on earth, he begged God with loud crying and tears to save him. He truly worshiped God, and God listened to his prayers. 8Jesus is God's own Son, but still he had to suffer before he could learn what it really means to obey God. 9Suffering made Jesus perfect, and now he can save forever all who obey him. 10This is because God chose him to be a high priest like Melchizedek.

Warning against Turning Away

11Much more could be said about this subject. But it is hard to explain, and all of you are slow to understand. 12By now you should have been teachers, but once again you need to be taught the simplest things about what God has said. You need milk instead of solid food. 13People who live on milk are like babies who don't really know what is right. 14Solid food is for mature people who have been trained to know right from wrong.

6 We must try to become mature and start thinking about more than just the basic things we were taught about Christ. We shouldn't need to keep talking about why we ought to turn from deeds that bring death and why we

---

fMelchizedek: When Melchizedek is mentioned in the Old Testament, he is described as a priest who lived before Aaron. Nothing is said about his ancestors or his death (see 7.3 and Genesis 14.17-20).

ought to have faith in God. [2]And we shouldn't need to keep teaching about baptisms[g] or about the laying on of hands[h] or about people being raised from death and the future judgment. [3]Let's grow up, if God is willing.

[4-6]But what about people who turn away after they have already seen the light and have received the gift from heaven and have shared in the Holy Spirit? What about those who turn away after they have received the good message of God and the powers of the future world? There is no way to bring them back. What they are doing is the same as nailing the Son of God to a cross and insulting him in public!

[7]A field is useful to farmers, if there is enough rain to make good crops grow. In fact, God will bless that field. [8]But land that produces only thorn bushes is worthless. It is likely to fall under God's curse, and in the end it will be set on fire.

[9]My friends, we are talking this way. But we are sure that you are doing those really good things that people do when they are being saved. [10]God is always fair. He will remember how you helped his people in the past and how you are still helping them. You belong to God, and he won't forget the love you have shown his people. [11]We wish that each of you would always be eager to show how strong and lasting your hope really is. [12]Then you would never be lazy. You would be following the example of those who had faith and were patient until God kept his promise to them.

God's Promise Is Sure

[13]No one is greater than God. So he made a promise in his own name when he said to Abraham, [14]"I, the Lord, will bless you with many descendants!" [15]Then after Abraham had been very patient, he was given what God had promised. [16]When anyone wants to settle an argument, they make a vow by using the name of someone or something greater than themselves. [17]So when God wanted to prove for certain that his promise to his people could not be broken, he made a vow. [18]God cannot tell lies! And so his promises and vows are two things that can never be changed.

We have run to God for safety. Now his promises should greatly encourage us to take hold of the hope that is right in front of us. [19]This hope is like a firm and steady anchor for our souls. In fact, hope reaches behind the curtain[i] and into the most holy place. [20]Jesus has gone there ahead of us, and he is our high priest forever, just like Melchizedek.[j]

The Priestly Family of Melchizedek

7 Melchizedek was both king of Salem and priest of God Most High. He was the one who went out and gave Abraham his blessing, when Abraham returned from killing the kings. [2]Then Abraham gave him a tenth of everything he had.

The meaning of the name

---

[g]baptisms: Or "ceremonies of washing." [h]laying on of hands: This was a ceremony in which church leaders and others put their hands on people to show that those people were chosen to do some special kind of work. [i]behind the curtain: In the tent that was used for worship, a curtain separated the "holy place" from the "most holy place," which only the high priest could enter. [j]Melchizedek: See the note at 5.6.

Melchizedek is "King Who Brings Justice." But since Salem means "peace," he is also "King Who Brings Peace." ³We are not told that he had a father or mother or ancestors or beginning or end. He is like the Son of God and will be a priest forever.ᵏ

⁴Notice how great Melchizedek is! Our famous ancestor Abraham gave him a tenth of what he had taken from his enemies. ⁵The Law teaches that even Abraham's descendants must give a tenth of what they possess. And they are to give this to their own relatives, who are the descendants of Levi and are priests. ⁶Although Melchizedek was not a descendant of Levi, Abraham gave him a tenth of what he had. Then Melchizedek blessed Abraham, who had been given God's promise. ⁷Everyone agrees that a person who gives a blessing is greater than the one who receives the blessing.

⁸Priests are given a tenth of what people earn. But all priests die, except Melchizedek, and the Scriptures teach that he is alive. ⁹Levi's descendants are now the ones who receive a tenth from people. We could even say that when Abraham gave Melchizedek a tenth, Levi also gave him a tenth. ¹⁰This is because Levi was born later into the family of Abraham, who gave a tenth to Melchizedek.

¹¹Even though the Law of Moses says that the priests must be descendants of Levi, those priests cannot make anyone perfect. So there needs to be a priest like Melchizedek, rather than one from the priestly family of Aaron.ˡ ¹²And when the rules for selecting a priest are changed, the Law must also be changed.

¹³The person we are talking about is our Lord, who came from a tribe that had never had anyone to serve as a priest at the altar. ¹⁴Everyone knows he came from the tribe of Judah, and Moses never said that priests would come from that tribe.

¹⁵All of this becomes clearer, when someone who is like Melchizedek is appointed to be a priest. ¹⁶That person was not appointed because of his ancestors, but because his life can never end. ¹⁷The Scriptures say about him,

"You are a priest forever,
    just like Melchizedek."

¹⁸In this way a weak and useless command was put aside, ¹⁹because the Law cannot make anything perfect. At the same time, we are given a much better hope, and it can bring us close to God.

²⁰⁻²¹God himself made a promise when this priest was appointed. But he did not make a promise like this when the other priests were appointed. The promise he made is,

"I, the Lord, promise that you
    will be a priest forever!
And I will never
    change my mind!"

²²This means that Jesus guarantees us a better agreement with God. ²³There have been a lot of other priests, and all of them have died. ²⁴But Jesus will never die, and so he will be a priest forever! ²⁵He is forever able to saveᵐ the people he leads to God, because he always lives to speak to God for them.

ᵏwill be a priest forever: See the note at 5.6. ˡdescendants of Levi . . . from the priestly family of Aaron: Levi was the ancestor of the tribe from which priests and their helpers (called "Levites") were chosen. Aaron was the first high priest. ᵐforever able to save: Or "able to save forever."

26Jesus is the high priest we need. He is holy and innocent and faultless, and not at all like us sinners. Jesus is honored above all beings in heaven, 27and he is better than any other high priest. Jesus does not need to offer sacrifices each day for his own sins and then for the sins of the people. He offered a sacrifice once for all, when he gave himself. 28The Law appoints priests who have weaknesses. But God's promise, which came later than the Law, appoints his Son. And he is the perfect high priest forever.

A Better Promise

8 What I mean is that we have a high priest who sits at the right side[n] of God's great throne in heaven. 2He also serves as the priest in the most holy place[o] inside the real tent there in heaven. This tent of worship was set up by the Lord, not by humans.

3Since all priests must offer gifts and sacrifices, Christ also needed to have something to offer. 4If he were here on earth, he would not be a priest at all, because here the Law appoints other priests to offer sacrifices. 5But the tent where they serve is just a copy and a shadow of the real one in heaven. Before Moses made the tent, he was told, "Be sure to make it exactly like the pattern you were shown on the mountain!" 6Now Christ has been appointed to serve as a priest in a much better way, and he has given us much assurance of a better agreement.

7If the first agreement with God had been all right, there would not have been any need for another one. 8But the Lord found fault with it and said,

> "I tell you the time will come,
>   when I will make
>   a new agreement
> with the people of Israel
>   and the people of Judah.
> 9It won't be like the agreement
> that I made
>   with their ancestors,
> when I took them by the hand
>   and led them out of Egypt.
> They broke their agreement
>   with me,
> and I stopped caring
>   about them!

> 10"But now I tell the people
> of Israel
>   this is my new agreement:
> 'The time will come
>   when I, the Lord,
> will write my laws
>   on their minds and hearts.
> I will be their God,
> and they will be
>   my people.
> 11Not one of them
> will have to teach another
>   to know me, their Lord.'

> "All of them will know me,
>   no matter who they are.
> 12I will treat them
>   with kindness,
> even though they
>   are wicked.
> I will surely forget
>   their sins."

13When the Lord talks about a new agreement, he means that the first one is out of date. And anything that is old and useless will soon disappear.

---

[n] right side: See the note at 1.3.   [o] most holy place: See the note at 6.19.

The Tent in Heaven

9 The first promise that was made included rules for worship and a tent for worship here on earth. 2The first part of the tent was called the holy place, and a lampstand, a table, and the sacred loaves of bread were kept there.

3Behind the curtain was the most holy place. 4The gold altar that was used for burning incense was in this holy place. The gold-covered sacred chest was also there, and inside it were three things. First, there was a gold jar filled with manna.p Then there was Aaron's walking stick that sprouted.q Finally, there were the flat stones with the Ten Commandments written on them. 5On top of the chest were the glorious creatures with wingsr opened out above the place of mercy.s

Now is not the time to go into detail about these things. 6But this is how everything was when the priests went each day into the first part of the tent to do their duties. 7However, only the high priest could go into the second part of the tent, and he went in only once a year. Each time he carried blood to offer for his sins and for any sins that the people had committed without meaning to.

8All of this is the Holy Spirit's way of saying that no one could enter the most holy place while the tent was still the place of worship. 9This also has a meaning for today. It shows that we cannot make our consciences clear by offering gifts and sacrifices. 10These rules are merely about such things as eating and drinking and ceremonies for washing ourselves. And rules about physical things will last only until the time comes to change them for something better.

11Christ came as the high priest of the good things that are now here.t He also went into a much better tent that was not made by humans and that does not belong to this world. 12Then Christ went once for all into the most holy place and freed us from sin forever. He did this by offering his own blood instead of the blood of goats and bulls.

13According to the Jewish religion, those people who become unclean are not fit to worship God. Yet they will be considered clean, if they are sprinkled with the blood of goats and bulls and with the ashes of a sacrificed calf. 14But Christ was sinless, and he offered himself as an eternal and spiritual sacrifice to God. That's why his blood is much more powerful and makes ouru consciences clear. Now we can serve the living God and no longer do things that lead to death.

15Christ died to rescue those who had sinned and broken the old agreement. Now he brings his chosen ones a new agreement with its guarantee of God's eternal blessings! 16In fact, mak-

---

pmanna: When the people of Israel were wandering through the desert, the Lord provided them with food that could be made into thin wafers. This food was called manna, which in Hebrew means "What is it?" qAaron's walking stick that sprouted: According to Numbers 17.1-11, Aaron's walking stick sprouted and produced almonds to show that the Lord was pleased with him and Moses. rglorious creatures with wings: Two of these creatures (called "cherubim" in Hebrew and Greek) with outspread wings were on top of the sacred chest and were symbols of God's throne. splace of mercy: The lid of the sacred chest, which was thought to be God's throne on earth. tthat are now here: Some manuscripts have "that were coming." uour: Some manuscripts have "your," and others have "their."

ing an agreement of this kind is like writing a will. This is because the one who makes the will must die before it is of any use. 17In other words, a will does not go into effect as long as the one who made it is still alive.

18Blood was also used[v] to put the first agreement into effect. 19Moses told the people all that the Law said they must do. Then he used red wool and a hyssop plant to sprinkle the people and the book of the Law with the blood of bulls and goats[w] and with water. 20He told the people, "With this blood God makes his agreement with you." 21Moses also sprinkled blood on the tent and on everything else that was used in worship. 22The Law says that almost everything must be sprinkled with blood, and no sins can be forgiven unless blood is offered.

Christ's Great Sacrifice

23These things are only copies of what is in heaven, and so they had to be made holy by these ceremonies. But the real things in heaven must be made holy by something better. 24This is why Christ did not go into a tent that had been made by humans and was only a copy of the real one. Instead, he went into heaven and is now there with God to help us.

25Christ did not have to offer himself many times. He was not like a high priest who goes into the most holy place each year to offer the blood of an animal. 26If he had offered himself every year, he would have suffered many times since the creation of the world. But instead, near the end of time he offered himself once and for all, so that he could be a sacrifice that does away with sin.

27We die only once, and then we are judged. 28So Christ died only once to take away the sins of many people. But when he comes again, it will not be to take away sin. He will come to save everyone who is waiting for him.

10 The Law of Moses is like a shadow of the good things to come. This shadow is not the good things themselves, because it cannot free people from sin by the sacrifices that are offered year after year. 2If there were worshipers who already have their sins washed away and their consciences made clear, there would not be any need to go on offering sacrifices. 3-4But the blood of bulls and goats cannot take away sins. It only reminds people of their sins from one year to the next.

5When Christ came into the world, he said to God,

"Sacrifices and offerings
     are not what you want,
but you have given me
     my body.
6No, you are not pleased
     with animal sacrifices
     and offerings for sin."

7Then Christ said,
"And so, my God,
     I have come to do
what you want,
     as the Scriptures say."

8The Law teaches that offerings and sacrifices must be made because of sin. But why did Christ mention these things and say that God did not want them? 9Well, it was to do away

---

[v]Blood was also used: Or "There also had to be a death."   [w]blood of bulls and goats: Some manuscripts do not have "and goats."

with offerings and sacrifices and to re-
place them. That is what he meant by
saying to God, "I have come to do what
you want." 10So we are made holy because Christ obeyed God and offered
himself once for all.

11The priests do their work each
day, and they keep on offering sacrifices that can never take away sins.
12But Christ offered himself as a sacrifice that is good forever. Now he is sitting at God's right side,^x 13and he will
stay there until his enemies are put
under his power. 14By his one sacrifice
he has forever set free from sin the people he brings to God.

15The Holy Spirit also speaks of
this by telling us that the Lord said,

16"When the time comes,
    I will make an agreement
        with them.
    I will write my laws
        on their minds and hearts.
17Then I will forget
        about their sins
    and no longer remember
        their evil deeds."

18When sins are forgiven, there is
no more need to offer sacrifices.

Encouragement and Warning

19My friends, the blood of Jesus
gives us courage to enter the most holy
place 20by a new way that leads to life!
And this way takes us through the curtain that is Christ himself.

21We have a great high priest who
is in charge of God's house. 22So let's
come near to God with pure hearts and
a confidence that comes from having
faith. Let's keep our hearts pure, our
consciences free from evil, and our
bodies washed with clean water. 23We

must hold tightly to the hope that we
say is ours. After all, we can trust the
one who made the agreement with us.
24We should keep on encouraging each
other to be thoughtful and to do helpful
things. 25Some people have gotten out
of the habit of meeting for worship, but
we must not do that. We should keep
on encouraging each other, especially
since you know that the day of the
Lord's coming is getting closer.

26No sacrifices can be made for
people who decide to sin after they find
out about the truth. 27They are God's
enemies, and all they can look forward
to is a terrible judgment and a furious
fire. 28If two or more witnesses accused
someone of breaking the Law of Moses,
that person could be put to death.
29But it is much worse to dishonor
God's Son and to disgrace the blood of
the promise that made us holy. And it
is just as bad to insult the Holy Spirit,
who shows us mercy. 30We know that
God has said he will punish and take
revenge. We also know that the Scriptures say the Lord will judge his people. 31It is a terrible thing to fall into
the hands of the living God!

32Don't forget all the hard times
you went through when you first received the light. 33Sometimes you were
abused and mistreated in public, and
at other times you shared in the sufferings of others. 34You were kind to people in jail. And you gladly let your possessions be taken away, because you
knew you had something better, something that would last forever.

35Keep on being brave! It will
bring you great rewards. 36Learn to be
patient, so that you will please God and
be given what he has promised. 37As
the Scriptures say,

---

^x right side: See the note at 1.3.

"God is coming soon!
It won't be very long.
38The people God accepts
will live because
of their faith.*y*
But he is not pleased
with anyone
who turns back."
39We are not like those people who turn back and get destroyed. We will keep on having faith until we are saved.

The Great Faith of God's People

11 Faith makes us sure of what we hope for and gives us proof of what we cannot see. 2It was their faith that made our ancestors pleasing to God.

3Because of our faith, we know that the world was made at God's command. We also know that what can be seen was made out of what cannot be seen.

4Because Abel had faith, he offered God a better sacrifice than Cain did. God was pleased with him and his gift, and even though Abel is now dead, his faith still speaks for him.

5Enoch had faith and did not die. He pleased God, and God took him up to heaven. That's why his body was never found. 6But without faith no one can please God. We must believe that God is real and that he rewards everyone who searches for him.

7Because Noah had faith, he was warned about something that had not yet happened. He obeyed and built a boat that saved him and his family. In this way the people of the world were judged, and Noah was given the blessings that come to everyone who pleases God.

8Abraham had faith and obeyed God. He was told to go to the land that God had said would be his, and he left for a country he had never seen. 9Because Abraham had faith, he lived as a stranger in the promised land. He lived there in a tent, and so did Isaac and Jacob, who were later given the same promise. 10Abraham did this, because he was waiting for the eternal city that God had planned and built.

11Even when Sarah was too old to have children, she had faith that God would do what he had promised, and she had a son. 12Her husband Abraham was almost dead, but he became the ancestor of many people. In fact, there are as many of them as there are stars in the sky or grains of sand along the beach.

13Every one of those people died. But they still had faith, even though they had not received what they had been promised. They were glad just to see these things from far away, and they agreed that they were only strangers and foreigners on this earth. 14When people talk this way, it is clear that they are looking for a place to call their own. 15If they had been talking about the land where they had once lived, they could have gone back at any time. 16But they were looking forward to a better home in heaven. That's why God was not ashamed for them to call him their God. He even built a city for them.

17-18Abraham had been promised

yThe people God accepts will live because of their faith: Or "The people God accepts because of their faith will live."

that Isaac, his only son,[z] would continue his family. But when Abraham was tested, he had faith and was willing to sacrifice Isaac, [19]because he was sure that God could raise people to life. This was just like getting Isaac back from death.

[20]Isaac had faith, and he promised blessings to Jacob and Esau. [21]Later, when Jacob was about to die, he leaned on his walking stick and worshiped. Then because of his faith he blessed each of Joseph's sons. [22]And right before Joseph died, he had faith that God would lead the people of Israel out of Egypt. So he told them to take his bones with them.

[23]Because Moses' parents had faith, they kept him hidden until he was three months old. They saw that he was a beautiful child, and they were not afraid to disobey the king's orders.[a] [24]Then after Moses grew up, his faith made him refuse to be called Pharaoh's grandson. [25]He chose to be mistreated with God's people instead of having the good time that sin could bring for a little while. [26]Moses knew that the treasures of Egypt were not as wonderful as what he would receive from suffering for the Messiah,[b] and he looked forward to his reward.

[27]Because of his faith, Moses left Egypt. Moses had seen the invisible God and was not afraid of the king's anger. [28]His faith also made him celebrate Passover. He sprinkled the blood of animals on the first-born sons of the people of Israel, so that they would not be killed by the destroying angel.

[29]Because of their faith, the people walked through the Red Sea on dry land. But when the Egyptians tried to do it, they were drowned.

[30]God's people had faith, and when they had walked around the city of Jericho for seven days, its walls fell down.

[31]Rahab had been an immoral woman, but she had faith and welcomed the spies. So she was not killed with the people who disobeyed.

[32]What else can I say? There is not enough time to tell about Gideon, Barak, Samson, Jephthah, David, Samuel, and the prophets. [33]Their faith helped them conquer kingdoms, and because they did right, God made promises to them. They closed the jaws of lions [34]and put out raging fires and escaped from the swords of their enemies. Although they were weak, they were given the strength and power to chase foreign armies away.

[35]Some women received their loved ones back from death. Many of these people were tortured, but they refused to be released. They were sure that they would get a better reward when the dead are raised to life. [36]Others were made fun of and beaten with whips, and some were chained in jail. [37]Still others were stoned to death or sawed in two[c] or killed with swords. Some had nothing but sheep skins or goat skins to wear. They were poor, mistreated, and tortured. [38]The world did not deserve these good people, who had to wander in deserts and on mountains and had to live in caves and holes in the ground.

[39]All of them pleased God because

---

[z]*his only son*: Although Abraham had a son by a slave woman, his son Isaac was considered his only son, because he was born as a result of God's promise to Abraham. [a]*the king's orders*: The king of Egypt ordered all Israelite baby boys to be left outside of their homes, so they would die or be killed. [b]*the Messiah*: Or "Christ." [c]*sawed in two*: Some manuscripts have "tested" or "tempted."

of their faith! But still they died without being given what had been promised. 40This was because God had something better in store for us. And he did not want them to reach the goal of their faith without us.

A Large Crowd of Witnesses

12 Such a large crowd of witnesses is all around us! So we must get rid of everything that slows us down, especially the sin that just won't let go. And we must be determined to run the race that is ahead of us. 2We must keep our eyes on Jesus, who leads us and makes our faith complete. He endured the shame of being nailed to a cross, because he knew that later on he would be glad he did. Now he is seated at the right side*d* of God's throne! 3So keep your mind on Jesus, who put up with many insults from sinners. Then you won't get discouraged and give up.

4None of you have yet been hurt*e* in your battle against sin. 5But you have forgotten that the Scriptures say to God's children,

"When the Lord punishes you,
    don't make light of it,
and when he corrects you,
    don't be discouraged.
6The Lord corrects the people
    he loves
and disciplines those
    he calls his own."

7Be patient when you are being corrected! This is how God treats his children. Don't all parents correct their children? 8God corrects all of his

children, and if he doesn't correct you, then you don't really belong to him. 9Our earthly fathers correct us, and we still respect them. Isn't it even better to be given true life by letting our spiritual Father correct us?

10Our human fathers correct us for a short time, and they do it as they think best. But God corrects us for our own good, because he wants us to be holy, as he is. 11It is never fun to be corrected. In fact, at the time it is always painful. But if we learn to obey by being corrected, we will do right and live at peace.

12Now stand up straight! Stop your knees from shaking 13and walk a straight path. Then lame people will be healed, instead of getting worse.

Warning against Turning from God

14Try to live at peace with everyone! Live a clean life. If you don't, you will never see the Lord. 15Make sure that no one misses out on God's kindness. Don't let anyone become bitter and cause trouble for the rest of you. 16Watch out for immoral and ungodly people like Esau, who sold his future blessing*f* for only one meal. 17You know how he later wanted it back. But there was nothing he could do to change things, even though he begged his father and cried.

18You have not come to a place like Mount Sinai*g* that can be seen and touched. There is no flaming fire or dark cloud or storm 19or trumpet sound. The people of Israel heard a

---

d right side: See the note at 1.3.   *e hurt*: Or "killed."   *f sold his future blessing*: As the firstborn son, Esau had certain privileges that were known as a "birthright."   *g a place like Mount Sinai*: The Greek text has "a place," but the writer is referring to the time that the Lord spoke to the people of Israel from Mount Sinai (Exodus 19.16-25).

voice speak. But they begged it to stop, 20because they could not obey its commands. They were even told to kill any animal that touched the mountain. 21The sight was so frightening that Moses said he shook with fear.

22You have now come to Mount Zion and to the heavenly Jerusalem. This is the city of the living God, where thousands and thousands of angels have come to celebrate. 23Here you will find all of God's dearest children,[h] whose names are written in heaven. And you will find God himself, who judges everyone. Here also are the spirits of those good people who have been made perfect. 24And Jesus is here! He is the one who makes God's new agreement with us, and his sprinkled blood says much better things than the blood of Abel.[i]

25Make sure that you obey the one who speaks to you. The people of Israel did not escape, when they refused to obey the one who spoke to them at Mount Sinai. Do you think you can possibly escape, if you refuse to obey the one who speaks to you from heaven? 26When God spoke the first time, his voice shook only the earth. This time he has promised to shake the earth once again, and heaven too. 27The words "once again" mean that these created things will someday be shaken and removed. Then what cannot be shaken will last. 28We should be grateful that we were given a kingdom that cannot be shaken. And in this kingdom we please God by worshiping him and by showing him great honor and respect. 29Our God is like a destructive fire!

Service That Pleases God

13 Keep being concerned about each other as the Lord's followers should.

2Be sure to welcome strangers into your home. By doing this, some people have welcomed angels as guests, without even knowing it.

3Remember the Lord's people who are in jail and be concerned for them. Don't forget those who are suffering, but imagine that you are there with them.

4Have respect for marriage. Always be faithful to your partner, because God will punish anyone who is immoral or unfaithful in marriage.

5Don't fall in love with money. Be satisfied with what you have. The Lord has promised that he will not leave us or desert us. 6That should make you feel like saying,

"The Lord helps me!
    Why should I be afraid
of what people can do
    to me?"

7Don't forget about your leaders who taught you God's message. Remember what kind of lives they lived and try to have faith like theirs.

8Jesus Christ never changes! He is the same yesterday, today, and forever. 9Don't be fooled by any kind of strange teachings. It is better to receive strength from God's kindness than to depend on certain foods. After all, these foods don't really help the people who eat them. 10But we have an altar where even the priests who serve in the place of worship have no right to eat.

---

[h]all of God's dearest children: The Greek text has "the gathering of the first-born children." See the note at 1.6. [i]blood of Abel: Cain and Abel were the two sons of Adam and Eve. Cain murdered Abel (Genesis 4.1-16).

11After the high priest offers the blood of animals as a sin offering, the bodies of those animals are burned outside the camp. 12Jesus himself suffered outside the city gate, so that his blood would make people holy. 13That's why we should go outside the camp to Jesus and share in his disgrace. 14On this earth we don't have a city that lasts forever, but we are waiting for such a city.

15Our sacrifice is to keep offering praise to God in the name of Jesus. 16But don't forget to help others and to share your possessions with them. This too is like offering a sacrifice that pleases God.

17Obey your leaders and do what they say. They are watching over you, and they must answer to God. So don't make them sad as they do their work. Make them happy. Otherwise, they won't be able to help you at all.

18Pray for us. Our consciences are clear, and we always try to live right. 19I especially want you to pray that I can visit you again soon.

Final Prayers and Greetings

20God gives peace, and he raised our Lord Jesus Christ from death. Now Jesus is like a Great Shepherd whose blood was used to make God's eternal agreement with his flock.^{j} 21I pray that God will make you ready to obey him and that you will always be eager to do right. May Jesus help you do what pleases God. To Jesus Christ be glory forever and ever! Amen.

22My friends, I have written only a short letter to encourage you, and I beg you to pay close attention to what I have said.

23By now you surely must know that our friend Timothy is out of jail. If he gets here in time, I will bring him with me when I come to visit you.

24Please give my greetings to your leaders and to the rest of the Lord's people.

His followers from Italy send you their greetings.

25I pray that God will be kind to all of you!^{k}

---

^{j}whose blood was used to make God's eternal agreement with his flock: See 9.18-22. ^{k}to all of you!: Some manuscripts add "Amen."

A Letter from James

ABOUT THIS LETTER

This is a good example of a general letter, because it is addressed to Christians scattered throughout the Roman empire. Though written as a letter, it is more like a short book of instructions for daily living.

For James faith means action! In fact, the entire book is a series of examples that show faith in action in wise and practical ways.

His advice was clear and to the point: If you are poor, don't despair! Don't give up when your faith is being tested. Don't get angry quickly. Don't favor the rich over the poor. Do good things for others. Control your tongue and desires. Surrender to God and rely on his wisdom. Resist the devil. Don't brag about what you are going to do. If you are rich, use your money to help the poor. Be patient and kind, and pray for those who need God's help.

A QUICK LOOK AT THIS LETTER

- Greetings (1.1)
- A Life of Faith and Wisdom (1.2–18)
- Hearing and Obeying God's Message (1.19–27)
- Don't Favor the Rich and Powerful (2.1–13)
- Faith and Works (2.14–26)
- Wisdom and Words (3.1–18)
- Warning against Friendship with the World (4.1—5.6)
- Patience, Kindness, and Prayer (5.7–20)

---

1 From James, a servant of God and of our Lord Jesus Christ.

Greetings to the twelve tribes scattered all over the world.[a]

Faith and Wisdom

2My friends, be glad, even if you have a lot of trouble. 3You know that you learn to endure by having your faith tested. 4But you must learn to endure everything, so that you will be completely mature and not lacking in anything.

5If any of you need wisdom, you should ask God, and it will be given to you. God is generous and won't correct you for asking. 6But when you ask for something, you must have faith and not doubt. Anyone who doubts is like an ocean wave tossed around in a storm. 7-8If you are that kind of person,

---

[a]twelve tribes scattered all over the world: James is saying that the Lord's followers are like the tribes of Israel that were scattered everywhere by their enemies.

you can't make up your mind, and you surely can't be trusted. So don't expect the Lord to give you anything at all.

Poor People and Rich People

9Any of God's people who are poor should be glad that he thinks so highly of them. **10**But any who are rich should be glad when God makes them humble. Rich people will disappear like wild flowers **11**scorched by the burning heat of the sun. The flowers lose their blossoms, and their beauty is destroyed. That is how the rich will disappear, as they go about their business.

Trials and Temptations

12God will bless you, if you don't give up when your faith is being tested. He will reward you with a glorious life,*b* just as he rewards everyone who loves him.

13Don't blame God when you are tempted! God cannot be tempted by evil, and he doesn't use evil to tempt others. **14**We are tempted by our own desires that drag us off and trap us. **15**Our desires make us sin, and when sin is finished with us, it leaves us dead.

16Don't be fooled, my dear friends. **17**Every good and perfect gift comes down from the Father who created all the lights in the heavens. He is always the same and never makes dark shadows by changing. **18**He wanted us to be his own special people,*c* and so he sent the true message to give us new birth.

Hearing and Obeying

19My dear friends, you should be quick to listen and slow to speak or to get angry. **20**If you are angry, you cannot do any of the good things that God wants done. **21**You must stop doing anything immoral or evil. Instead be humble and accept the message that is planted in you to save you.

22Obey God's message! Don't fool yourselves by just listening to it. **23**If you hear the message and don't obey it, you are like people who stare at themselves in a mirror **24**and forget what they look like as soon as they leave. **25**But you must never stop looking at the perfect law that sets you free. God will bless you in everything you do, if you listen and obey, and don't just hear and forget.

26If you think you are being religious, but can't control your tongue, you are fooling yourself, and everything you do is useless. **27**Religion that pleases God the Father must be pure and spotless. You must help needy orphans and widows and not let this world make you evil.

Warning against Having Favorites

2 My friends, if you have faith in our glorious Lord Jesus Christ, you won't treat some people better than others. **2**Suppose a rich person wearing fancy clothes and a gold ring comes to one of your meetings. And suppose a poor person dressed in worn-out clothes also comes. **3**You must not give

---

b a glorious life: The Greek text has "the crown of life." In ancient times an athlete who had won a contest was rewarded with a crown of flowers as a sign of victory. *c his own special people*: The Greek text has "the first of his creatures." The Law of Moses taught that the first-born of all animals and the first part of the harvest were special and belonged to the Lord.

the best seat to the one in fancy clothes and tell the one who is poor to stand at the side or sit on the floor. 4That is the same as saying that some people are better than others, and you would be acting like a crooked judge.

5My dear friends, pay attention. God has given a lot of faith to the poor people in this world. He has also promised them a share in his kingdom that he will give to everyone who loves him. 6You mistreat the poor. But isn't it the rich who boss you around and drag you off to court? 7Aren't they the ones who make fun of your Lord?

8You will do all right, if you obey the most important law*d* in the Scriptures. It is the law that commands us to love others as much as we love ourselves. 9But if you treat some people better than others, you have done wrong, and the Scriptures teach that you have sinned.

10If you obey every law except one, you are still guilty of breaking them all. 11The same God who told us to be faithful in marriage also told us not to murder. So even if you are faithful in marriage, but murder someone, you still have broken God's Law.

12Speak and act like people who will be judged by the law that sets us free. 13Do this, because on the day of judgment there will be no pity for those who have not had pity on others. But even in judgment, God is merciful!*e*

Faith and Works

14My friends, what good is it to say you have faith, when you don't do any-thing to show that you really do have faith? Can that kind of faith save you? 15If you know someone who doesn't have any clothes or food, 16you shouldn't just say, "I hope all goes well for you. I hope you will be warm and have plenty to eat." What good is it to say this, unless you do something to help? 17Faith that doesn't lead us to do good deeds is all alone and dead!

18Suppose someone disagrees and says, "It is possible to have faith without doing kind deeds."

I would answer, "Prove that you have faith without doing kind deeds, and I will prove that I have faith by doing them." 19You surely believe there is only one God. That's fine. Even demons believe this, and it makes them shake with fear.

20Does some stupid person want proof that faith without deeds is useless? 21Well, our ancestor Abraham pleased God by putting his son Isaac on the altar to sacrifice him. 22Now you see how Abraham's faith and deeds worked together. He proved that his faith was real by what he did. 23This is what the Scriptures mean by saying, "Abraham had faith in God, and God was pleased with him." That's how Abraham became God's friend.

24You can now see that we please God by what we do and not only by what we believe. 25For example, Rahab had been an immoral woman. But she pleased God when she welcomed the spies and sent them home by another way.

26Anyone who doesn't breathe is dead, and faith that doesn't do any-thing is just as dead!

---

*d*most important law: The Greek text has "royal law," meaning the one given by the king (that is, God).   *e*But even in judgment, God is merciful!: Or "So be merciful, and you will be shown mercy on the day of judgment."

The Tongue

3 My friends, we should not all try to become teachers. In fact, teachers will be judged more strictly than others. 2All of us do many wrong things. But if you can control your tongue, you are mature and able to control your whole body.

3By putting a bit into the mouth of a horse, we can turn the horse in different directions. 4It takes strong winds to move a large sailing ship, but the captain uses only a small rudder to make it go in any direction. 5Our tongues are small too, and yet they brag about big things.

It takes only a spark to start a forest fire! 6The tongue is like a spark. It is an evil power that dirties the rest of the body and sets a person's entire life on fire with flames that come from hell itself. 7All kinds of animals, birds, reptiles, and sea creatures can be tamed and have been tamed. 8But our tongues get out of control. They are restless and evil, and always spreading deadly poison.

9-10My dear friends, with our tongues we speak both praises and curses. We praise our Lord and Father, and we curse people who were created to be like God, and this is not right. 11Can clean water and dirty water both flow from the same spring? 12Can a fig tree produce olives or a grapevine produce figs? Does fresh water come from a well full of salt water?

Wisdom from Above

13Are any of you wise or sensible? Then show it by living right and by being humble and wise in everything you do. 14But if your heart is full of bitter jealousy and selfishness, don't brag or lie to cover up the truth. 15That kind of wisdom doesn't come from above. It is earthly and selfish and comes from the devil himself. 16Whenever people are jealous or selfish, they cause trouble and do all sorts of cruel things. 17But the wisdom that comes from above leads us to be pure, friendly, gentle, sensible, kind, helpful, genuine, and sincere. 18When peacemakers plant seeds of peace, they will harvest justice.

Friendship with the World

4 Why do you fight and argue with each other? Isn't it because you are full of selfish desires that fight to control your body? 2You want something you don't have, and you will do anything to get it. You will even kill! But you still cannot get what you want, and you won't get it by fighting and arguing. You should pray for it. 3Yet even when you do pray, your prayers are not answered, because you pray just for selfish reasons.

4You people aren't faithful to God! Don't you know that if you love the world, you are God's enemies? And if you decide to be a friend of the world, you make yourself an enemy of God. 5Do you doubt the Scriptures that say, "God truly cares about the Spirit he has put in us"?*f* 6In fact, God treats us with even greater kindness, just as the Scriptures say,

"God opposes everyone
who is proud,
but he is kind to everyone
who is humble."

---

*f*God truly cares about the Spirit he has put in us: The meaning of the Greek text is unclear, and other translations are possible, such as, "The Spirit that God put in us truly cares."

7Surrender to God! Resist the devil, and he will run from you. 8Come near to God, and he will come near to you. Clean up your lives, you sinners. Purify your hearts, you people who can't make up your mind. 9Be sad and sorry and weep. Stop laughing and start crying. Be gloomy instead of glad. 10Be humble in the Lord's presence, and he will honor you.

Saying Cruel Things about Others

11My friends, don't say cruel things about others! If you do, or if you condemn others, you are condemning God's Law. And if you condemn the Law, you put yourself above the Law and refuse to obey either it 12or God who gave it. God is our judge, and he can save or destroy us. What right do you have to condemn anyone?

Warning against Bragging

13You should know better than to say, "Today or tomorrow we'll go to the city. We'll do business there for a year and make a lot of money!" 14What do you know about tomorrow? How can you be so sure about your life? It is nothing more than mist that appears for only a little while before it disappears. 15You should say, "If the Lord lets us live, we will do these things." 16Yet you are stupid enough to brag, and it is wrong to be so proud. 17If you don't do what you know is right, you have sinned.

Warning to the Rich

5 You rich people should cry and weep! Terrible things are going to happen to you. 2Your treasures have already rotted, and moths have eaten

your clothes. 3Your money has rusted, and the rust will be evidence against you, as it burns your body like fire. Yet you keep on storing up wealth in these last days. 4You refused to pay the people who worked in your fields, and now their unpaid wages are shouting out against you. The Lord All-Powerful has surely heard the cries of the workers who harvested your crops.

5While here on earth, you have thought only of filling your own stomachs and having a good time. But now you are like fat cattle on their way to be butchered. 6You have condemned and murdered innocent people, who couldn't even fight back.

Be Patient and Kind

7My friends, be patient until the Lord returns. Think of farmers who wait patiently for the spring and summer rains to make their valuable crops grow. 8Be patient like those farmers and don't give up. The Lord will soon be here! 9Don't grumble about each other or you will be judged, and the judge is right outside the door.

10My friends, follow the example of the prophets who spoke for the Lord. They were patient, even when they had to suffer. 11In fact, we praise the ones who endured the most. You remember how patient Job was and how the Lord finally helped him. The Lord did this because he is so merciful and kind.

12My friends, above all else, don't take an oath. You must not swear by heaven or by earth or by anything else. "Yes" or "No" is all you need to say. If you say anything more, you will be condemned.

13If you are having trouble, you should pray. And if you are feeling good, you should sing praises. 14If you are sick, ask the church leaders[g] to come and pray for you. Ask them to put olive oil[h] on you in the name of the Lord. [15]If you have faith when you pray for sick people, they will get well. The Lord will heal them, and if they have sinned, he will forgive them.

[16]If you have sinned, you should tell each other what you have done. Then you can pray for one another and be healed. The prayer of an innocent person is powerful, and it can help a lot. [17]Elijah was just as human as we are, and for three and a half years his prayers kept the rain from falling. [18]But when he did pray for rain, it fell from the skies and made the crops grow.

[19]My friends, if any followers have wandered away from the truth, you should try to lead them back. [20]If you turn sinners from the wrong way, you will save them from death, and many of their sins will be forgiven.

---

[g]*church leaders*: Or "elders" or "presbyters" or "priests."   [h]*olive oil*: The Jewish people used olive oil for healing.

Peter's First Letter

ABOUT THIS LETTER

In this letter Peter has much to say about suffering. He shows how it can be a way of serving the Lord, of sharing the faith, and of being tested. The letter was written to Christians scattered all over the northern part of Asia Minor. In this part of the Roman empire many Christians had already suffered unfair treatment from people who did not believe in Jesus. And they could expect to suffer even more.

Peter was quick to offer encouragement. His letter reminds the readers that some of the Lord's followers may have to go through times of hard testing. But this should make them glad, Peter declares, because it will strengthen their faith and bring them honor on the day when Jesus Christ returns (1.6, 7).

Peter reminds them that Christ suffered here on earth, and when his followers suffer for doing right they are sharing his sufferings (2.18–25; 4.12–17). In fact, Christians should expect to suffer for their faith (3.8—4.19).

But because of who God is and because of what God has done by raising Jesus Christ from death, Christians can have hope in the future. Just as Christ suffered before he received honor from God, so will Christians be tested by suffering before they receive honor when the Lord returns. Peter uses poetic language to remind his readers of what Christ has done:

> Christ died once for our sins.   when his body
>   An innocent person died   was put to death
>   for those who are guilty.   and his spirit
>   Christ did this   was made alive.
>   to bring you to God,   (3.18)

A QUICK LOOK AT THIS LETTER

- Greetings and Prayer (1.1, 2)
- A Real Reason for Hope (1.3–12)
- Living as God's Holy People (1.13—2.17)
- The Example of Christ's Suffering (2.18–25)
- Being a Christian and Suffering (3.1—4.19)
- Advice for Church Leaders (5.1–11)
- Final Greetings (5.12–14)

1 From Peter, an apostle of Jesus Christ.

To God's people who are scattered like foreigners in Pontus, Galatia, Cappadocia, Asia, and Bithynia.

2God the Father decided to choose you as his people, and his Spirit has made you holy. You have obeyed Jesus Christ and are sprinkled with his blood.[a]

I pray that God will be kind to you and will keep on giving you peace!

A Real Reason for Hope

3Praise God, the Father of our Lord Jesus Christ. God is so good, and by raising Jesus from death, he has given us new life and a hope that lives on. 4God has something stored up for you in heaven, where it will never decay or be ruined or disappear.

5You have faith in God, whose power will protect you until the last day.[b] Then he will save you, just as he has always planned to do. 6On that day you will be glad, even if you have

to go through many hard trials for a while. 7Your faith will be like gold that has been tested in a fire. And these trials will prove that your faith is worth much more than gold that can be destroyed. They will show that you will be given praise and honor and glory when Jesus Christ returns.

8You have never seen Jesus, and you don't see him now. But still you love him and have faith in him, and no words can tell how glad and happy 9you are to be saved. That's why you have faith.

10Some prophets told how kind God would be to you, and they searched hard to find out more about the way you would be saved. 11The Spirit of Christ was in them and was telling them how Christ would suffer and would then be given great honor. So they searched to find out exactly who Christ would be and when this would happen. 12But they were told that they were serving you and not themselves. They preached to you by the power of the Holy Spirit, who was sent from heaven. And their message was only for you, even though

---

[a]sprinkled with his blood: According to Exodus 24.3-8 the people of Israel were sprinkled with the blood of cows to show they would keep their agreement with God. Peter says that it is the blood of Jesus that seals the agreement between God and his people. See Hebrews 9.18-21. [b]the last day: When God will judge all people.

angels would like to know more about it.

Chosen to Live a Holy Life

13Be alert and think straight. Put all your hope in how kind God will be to you when Jesus Christ appears. 14Behave like obedient children. Don't let your lives be controlled by your desires, as they used to be. 15Always live as God's holy people should, because God is the one who chose you, and he is holy. 16That's why the Scriptures say, "I am the holy God, and you must be holy too."

17You say that God is your Father, but God does not have favorites! He judges all people by what they do. So you must honor God while you live as strangers here on earth. 18You were rescued[c] from the useless way of life that you learned from your ancestors. But you know that you were not rescued by such things as silver or gold that don't last forever. 19You were rescued by the precious blood of Christ, that spotless and innocent lamb. 20Christ was chosen even before the world was created, but because of you, he did not come until these last days. 21And when he did come, it was to lead you to have faith in God, who raised him from death and honored him in a glorious way. That's why you have put your faith and hope in God.

22You obeyed the truth,[d] and your souls were made pure. Now you sincerely love each other. But you must keep on loving with all your heart. 23Do this because God has given you new birth by his message that lives on forever. 24The Scriptures say,

"Humans wither like grass,
and their glory fades
like wild flowers.
Grass dries up,
and flowers fall
to the ground.
25But what the Lord has said
will stand forever."

Our good news to you is what the Lord has said.

A Living Stone and a Holy Nation

2 Stop being hateful! Quit trying to fool people, and start being sincere. Don't be jealous or say cruel things about others. 2Be like newborn babies who are thirsty for the pure spiritual milk that will help you grow and be saved. 3You have already found out how good the Lord really is.

4Come to Jesus Christ. He is the living stone that people have rejected, but which God has chosen and highly honored. 5And now you are living stones that are being used to build a spiritual house. You are also a group of holy priests, and with the help of Jesus Christ you will offer sacrifices that please God. 6It is just as God says in the Scriptures,

"Look! I am placing in Zion
a choice and precious
cornerstone.
No one who has faith

---

[c]rescued: The Greek word often, though not always, means payment of a price to free a slave or prisoner.   [d]You obeyed the truth: Some manuscripts add "by the power of the Spirit."

in that one
will be disappointed."

7You are followers of the Lord, and that stone is precious to you. But it isn't precious to those who refuse to follow him. They are the builders who tossed aside the stone that turned out to be the most important one of all. **8**They disobeyed the message and stumbled and fell over that stone, because they were doomed.

9But you are God's chosen and special people. You are a group of royal priests and a holy nation. God has brought you out of darkness into his marvelous light. Now you must tell all the wonderful things that he has done. The Scriptures say,

10"Once you were nobody.
   Now you are God's people.
At one time no one
   had pity on you.
Now God has treated you
   with kindness.

Live as God's Servants Should

11Dear friends, you are foreigners and strangers on this earth. So I beg you not to surrender to those desires that fight against you. **12**Always let others see you behaving properly, even though they may still accuse you of doing wrong. Then on the day of judgment they will honor God by telling the good things they saw you do.

13The Lord wants you to obey all human authorities, especially the Emperor, who rules over everyone. **14**You must also obey governors, because they are sent by the Emperor to punish criminals and to praise good citizens. **15**God wants you to silence stupid and ignorant people by doing right. **16**You are free, but still you are God's servants, and you must not use your freedom as an excuse for doing wrong. **17**Respect everyone and show special love for God's people. Honor God and respect the Emperor.

The Example of Christ's Suffering

18Servants, you must obey your masters and always show respect to them. Do this, not only to those who are kind and thoughtful, but also to those who are cruel. **19**God will bless you, even if others treat you unfairly for being loyal to him. **20**You don't gain anything by being punished for some wrong you have done. But God will bless you, if you have to suffer for doing something good. **21**After all, God chose you to suffer as you follow in the footsteps of Christ, who set an example by suffering for you.

22Christ did not sin
   or ever tell a lie.
23Although he was abused,
   he never tried to get even.
And when he suffered,
   he made no threats.
Instead, he had faith in God,
   who judges fairly.
24Christ carried the burden
   of our sins.
He was nailed to the cross,
   so that we would stop sinning
   and start living right.
By his cuts and bruises
   you are healed.
25You had wandered away
   like sheep.
Now you have returned
   to the one
who is your shepherd
   and protector.

Wives and Husbands

3 If you are a wife, you must put your husband first. Even if he opposes our message, you will win him over by what you do. No one else will have to say anything to him, 2because he will see how you honor God and live a pure life. 3Don't depend on things like fancy hairdos or gold jewelry or expensive clothes to make you look beautiful. 4Be beautiful in your heart by being gentle and quiet. This kind of beauty will last, and God considers it very special.

5Long ago those women who worshiped God and put their hope in him made themselves beautiful by putting their husbands first. 6For example, Sarah obeyed Abraham and called him her master. You are her true children, if you do right and don't let anything frighten you.

7If you are a husband, you should be thoughtful of your wife. Treat her with honor, because she is not as strong as you are, and she shares with you in the gift of life. Then nothing will stand in the way of your prayers.

Suffering for Doing Right

8Finally, all of you should agree and have concern and love for each other. You should also be kind and humble. 9Don't be hateful and insult people just because they are hateful and insult you. Instead, treat everyone with kindness. You are God's chosen ones, and he will bless you. The Scriptures say,

10"Do you really love life?
    Do you want to be happy?
Then stop saying cruel things
    and quit telling lies.
11Give up your evil ways
    and do right,

as you find and follow
the road that leads
    to peace.
12The Lord watches over
    everyone who obeys him,
and he listens
    to their prayers.
But he opposes everyone
    who does evil."

13Can anyone really harm you for being eager to do good deeds? 14Even if you have to suffer for doing good things, God will bless you. So stop being afraid and don't worry about what people might do. 15Honor Christ and let him be the Lord of your life.

Always be ready to give an answer when someone asks you about your hope. 16Give a kind and respectful answer and keep your conscience clear. This way you will make people ashamed for saying bad things about your good conduct as a follower of Christ. 17You are better off to obey God and to suffer for doing right than to suffer for doing wrong.

18Christ died once for our sins.
    An innocent person died
        for those who are guilty.
    Christ did this
        to bring you to God,
    when his body
        was put to death
    and his spirit
        was made alive.

19Christ then preached to the spirits that were being kept in prison. 20They had disobeyed God while Noah was building the boat, but God had been patient with them. Eight people went into that boat and were brought safely through the flood.

21Those flood waters were like baptism that now saves you. But baptism is more than just washing your body. It means turning to God with a clear conscience, because Jesus Christ was raised from death. 22Christ is now in heaven, where he sits at the right side*e* of God. All angels, authorities, and powers are under his control.

Being Faithful to God

4 Christ suffered here on earth. Now you must be ready to suffer as he did, because suffering shows that you have stopped sinning. 2It means you have turned from your own desires and want to obey God for the rest of your life. 3You have already lived long enough like people who don't know God. You were immoral and followed your evil desires. You went around drinking and partying and carrying on. In fact, you even worshiped disgusting idols. 4Now your former friends wonder why you have stopped running around with them, and they curse you for it. 5But they will have to answer to God, who judges the living and the dead. 6The good news has even been preached to the dead,*f* so that after they have been judged for what they have done in this life, their spirits will live with God.

7Everything will soon come to an end. So be serious and be sensible enough to pray.

8Most important of all, you must sincerely love each other, because love wipes away many sins.

9Welcome people into your home and don't grumble about it.

10Each of you has been blessed with one of God's many wonderful gifts to be used in the service of others. So use your gift well. 11If you have the gift of speaking, preach God's message. If you have the gift of helping others, do it with the strength that God supplies. Everything should be done in a way that will bring honor to God because of Jesus Christ, who is glorious and powerful forever. Amen.

Suffering for Being a Christian

12Dear friends, don't be surprised or shocked that you are going through testing that is like walking through fire. 13Be glad for the chance to suffer as Christ suffered. It will prepare you for even greater happiness when he makes his glorious return.

14Count it a blessing when you suffer for being a Christian. This shows that God's glorious Spirit is with you. 15But you deserve to suffer if you are a murderer, a thief, a crook, or a busybody. 16Don't be ashamed to suffer for being a Christian. Praise God that you belong to him. 17God has already begun judging his own people. And if his judgment begins with us, imagine how terrible it will be for those who refuse to obey his message. The Scriptures say,

18"If good people barely escape,
　　what will happen to sinners
　　and to others
　　　who don't respect God?"

19If you suffer for obeying God, you must have complete faith in your faithful Creator and keep on doing right.

Helping Christian Leaders

5 Church leaders,*g* I am writing to encourage you. I too am a leader,

---

e right side: The place of honor and power. *f the dead*: Either people who died after becoming followers of Christ or the people of Noah's day (3.19). *g Church leaders*: Or "Elders" or "Presbyters" or "Priests."

as well as a witness to Christ's suffering, and I will share in his glory when it is shown to us.

2Just as shepherds watch over their sheep, you must watch over everyone God has placed in your care. Do it willingly in order to please God, and not simply because you think you must. Let it be something you want to do, instead of something you do merely to make money. 3Don't be bossy to those people who are in your care, but set an example for them. 4Then when Christ the Chief Shepherd returns, you will be given a crown that will never lose its glory.

5All of you young people should obey your elders. In fact, everyone should be humble toward everyone else. The Scriptures say,

"God opposes proud people,
   but he helps everyone
      who is humble."

6Be humble in the presence of God's mighty power, and he will honor you when the time comes. 7God cares for you, so turn all your worries over to him.

8Be on your guard and stay awake. Your enemy, the devil, is like a roaring lion, sneaking around to find someone to attack. 9But you must resist the devil and stay strong in your faith. You know that all over the world the Lord's followers are suffering just as you are. 10But God shows kindness to everyone. That's why he had Christ Jesus choose you to share in his eternal glory. You will suffer for a while, but God will make you complete, steady, strong, and firm. 11God will be in control forever! Amen.

Final Greetings

12Silvanus helped me write this short letter, and I consider him a faithful follower of the Lord. I wanted to encourage you and tell you how kind God really is, so that you will keep on having faith in him.

13Greetings from the Lord's followers in Babylon.[h] They are God's chosen ones.

Mark, who is like a son to me, sends his greetings too.

14Give each other a warm greeting. I pray that God will give peace to everyone who belongs to Christ.[i]

hBabylon: This may be a secret name for the city of Rome.   iChrist: Some manuscripts add "Amen."

Peter's Second Letter

ABOUT THIS LETTER

The writer of this letter wants the readers to know that Christians must live in a way that pleases God (1.3) and hold firmly to the truth they were given (1.12).

He warns them that false prophets and teachers had entered the Christian community and were trying to lead the Lord's followers away from the truth. But they will be punished for their evil deeds (2.1–22). When false teachers are at work, Christians must stick to their faith and be examples for others of right living. They must have understanding, self-control and patience, and they should show love for God and all people.

The readers must never forget that the Lord's return is certain, no matter what others may say (3.1–18):

Don't forget that for the Lord one day is the same as a thousand years, and a thousand years is the same as one day. The Lord isn't slow about keeping his promises, as some people think he is. In fact, God is patient, because he wants everyone to turn from sin and no one to be lost.

(3.8, 9)

A QUICK LOOK AT THIS LETTER

- Greetings and Prayer (1.1, 2)
- How the Lord's Followers Should Live (1.3–15)
- The Glory of Christ (1.16–21)
- False Prophets and Teachers (2.1–22)
- The Lord's Return Is Certain (3.1–18)

---

1 From Simon Peter, a servant and an apostle of Jesus Christ.

To everyone who shares with us in the privilege of believing that our God and Savior Jesus Christ will do what is just and fair.[a]

²I pray that God will be kind to you and will let you live in perfect peace! May you keep learning more and more about God and our Lord Jesus.

Living as the Lord's Followers Should

³We have everything we need to live a life that pleases God. It was all given to us by God's own power, when we learned that he had invited us to share in his wonderful goodness. ⁴God made great and marvelous promises, so that his nature would become part

---

[a]*To everyone who . . . just and fair*: Or "To everyone whose faith in the justice and fairness of our God and Savior Jesus Christ is as precious as our own faith."

of us. Then we could escape our evil desires and the corrupt influences of this world.

5Do your best to improve your faith. You can do this by adding goodness, understanding, 6self-control, patience, devotion to God, 7concern for others, and love. 8If you keep growing in this way, it will show that what you know about our Lord Jesus Christ has made your lives useful and meaningful. 9But if you don't grow, you are like someone who is nearsighted or blind, and you have forgotten that your past sins are forgiven.

10My friends, you must do all you can to show that God has really chosen and selected you. If you keep on doing this, you won't stumble and fall. 11Then our Lord and Savior Jesus Christ will give you a glorious welcome into his kingdom that will last forever.

12You are holding firmly to the truth that you were given. But I am still going to remind you of these things. 13In fact, I think I should keep on reminding you until I leave this body. 14And our Lord Jesus Christ has already told me that I will soon leave it behind. 15That is why I am doing my best to make sure that each of you remembers all of this after I am gone.

The Message about the Glory of Christ

16When we told you about the power and the return of our Lord Jesus Christ, we were not telling clever stories that someone had made up. But with our own eyes we saw his true greatness. 17God, our great and won-derful Father, truly honored him by saying, "This is my own dear Son, and I am pleased with him." 18We were there with Jesus on the holy mountain and heard this voice speak from heaven.

19All of this makes us even more certain that what the prophets said is true. So you should pay close attention to their message, as you would to a lamp shining in some dark place. You must keep on paying attention until daylight comes and the morning star rises in your hearts. 20But you need to realize that no one alone can understand any of the prophecies in the Scriptures. 21The prophets did not think these things up on their own, but they were guided by the Spirit of God.

False Prophets and Teachers

2 Sometimes false prophets spoke to the people of Israel. False teachers will also sneak in and speak harmful lies to you. But these teachers don't really belong to the Master who paid a great price for them, and they will quickly destroy themselves. 2Many people will follow their evil ways and cause others to tell lies about the true way. 3They will be greedy and cheat you with smooth talk. But long ago God decided to punish them, and God does not sleep.

4God did not have pity on the angels that sinned. He had them tied up and thrown into the dark pits of hell until the time of judgment. 5And during Noah's time God did not have pity on the ungodly people of the world. He destroyed them with a flood, though he did save eight people, including Noah, who preached the truth.

⁶God punished the cities of Sodom and Gomorrah[b] by burning them to ashes, and this is a warning to anyone else who wants to sin.

⁷⁻⁸Lot lived right and was greatly troubled by the terrible way those wicked people were living. He was a good man, and day after day he suffered because of the evil things he saw and heard. So the Lord rescued him. ⁹This shows that the Lord knows how to rescue godly people from their sufferings and to punish evil people while they wait for the day of judgment.

¹⁰The Lord is especially hard on people who disobey him and don't think of anything except their own filthy desires. They are reckless and proud and are not afraid of cursing the glorious beings in heaven. ¹¹Although angels are more powerful than these evil beings,[c] even the angels don't dare to accuse them to the Lord.

¹²These people are no better than senseless animals that live by their feelings and are born to be caught and killed. They speak evil of things they don't know anything about. But their own corrupt deeds will destroy them. ¹³They have done evil, and they will be rewarded with evil.

They think it is fun to have wild parties during the day. They are immoral, and the meals they eat with you are spoiled by the shameful and selfish way they carry on.[d] ¹⁴All they think about is having sex with someone else's husband or wife. There is no end to their wicked deeds. They trick people who are easily fooled, and their minds are filled with greedy thoughts. But they are headed for trouble!

¹⁵They have left the true road and have gone down the wrong path by following the example of the prophet Balaam. He was the son of Beor and loved what he got from being a crook. ¹⁶But a donkey corrected him for this evil deed. It spoke to him with a human voice and made him stop his foolishness.

¹⁷These people are like dried up water holes and clouds blown by a windstorm. The darkest part of hell is waiting for them. ¹⁸They brag out loud about their stupid nonsense. And by being vulgar and crude, they trap people who have barely escaped from living the wrong kind of life. ¹⁹They promise freedom to everyone. But they are merely slaves of filthy living, because people are slaves of whatever controls them.

²⁰When they learned about our Lord and Savior Jesus Christ, they escaped from the filthy things of this world. But they are again caught up and controlled by these filthy things, and now they are in worse shape than they were at first. ²¹They would have been better off if they had never known about the right way. Even after they knew what was right, they turned their backs on the holy commandments that they were given. ²²What happened to them is just like the true saying,

"A dog will come back
    to lick up its own vomit.
A pig that has been washed
    will roll in the mud."

---

[b]*Sodom and Gomorrah*: During the time of Abraham the Lord destroyed these cities because the people there were so evil. See Genesis 19.24. [c]*evil beings*: or "evil teachers." [d]*and the meals they eat with you are spoiled by the shameful and selfish way they carry on*: Some manuscripts have "and the meals they eat with you are spoiled by the shameful way they carry on during your feasts of Christian love."

The Lord Will Return

3 My dear friends, this is the second letter I have written to encourage you to do some honest thinking. I don't want you to forget ²what God's prophets said would happen. You must never forget what the holy prophets taught in the past. And you must remember what the apostles told you our Lord and Savior has commanded us to do.

³But first you must realize that in the last days some people won't think about anything except their own selfish desires. They will make fun of you ⁴and say, "Didn't your Lord promise to come back? Yet the first leaders have already died, and the world hasn't changed a bit."

⁵They will say this because they want to forget that long ago the heavens and the earth were made by God's command. The earth came out of water and was made from water. ⁶Later it was destroyed by the waters of a mighty flood. ⁷But God has commanded the present heavens and earth to remain until the day of judgment. Then they will be set on fire, and ungodly people will be destroyed.

⁸Dear friends, don't forget that for the Lord one day is the same as a thousand years, and a thousand years is the same as one day. ⁹The Lord isn't slow about keeping his promises, as some people think he is. In fact, God is patient, because he wants everyone to turn from sin and no one to be lost.

¹⁰The day of the Lord's return will surprise us like a thief. The heavens will disappear with a loud noise, and the heat will melt the whole universe.ᵉ Then the earth and everything on it will be seen for what they are.ᶠ

¹¹Everything will be destroyed. So you should serve and honor God by the way you live. ¹²You should look forward to the day when God judges everyone, and you should try to make it come soon.ᵍ On that day the heavens will be destroyed by fire, and everything else will melt in the heat. ¹³But God has promised us a new heaven and a new earth, where justice will rule. We are really looking forward to that!

¹⁴My friends, while you are waiting, you should make certain that the Lord finds you pure, spotless, and living at peace. ¹⁵Don't forget that the Lord is patient because he wants people to be saved. This is also what our dear friend Paul said when he wrote you with the wisdom that God had given him. ¹⁶Paul talks about these same things in all his letters, but part of what he says is hard to understand. Some ignorant and unsteady people even destroy themselves by twisting what he said. They do the same thing with other Scriptures too.

¹⁷My dear friends, you have been warned ahead of time! So don't let the errors of evil people lead you down the wrong path and make you lose your balance. ¹⁸Let the kindness and the understanding that come from our Lord and Savior Jesus Christ help you to keep on growing. Praise Jesus now and forever! Amen.ʰ

ᵉ*the whole universe*: Probably the sun, moon, and stars, or the elements that everything in the universe is made of.   ᶠ*will be seen for what they are*: Some manuscripts have "will go up in flames."   ᵍ*and you should try to make it come soon*: Or "and you should eagerly desire for that day to come."   ʰ*Amen*: Some manuscripts do not have "Amen."

John's First Letter

ABOUT THIS LETTER

John wants Christian believers to know that when we tell God about our sins, God will forgive us and take them away (1.9).

The true test of faith is love for each other (3.11–24). Because God is love, his people must be like him (4.1–21). For a complete victory over sin, we must not only love others, but we must believe that Jesus, the Son of God, is truly Christ, and that his death for us was real (5.1–12).

Remember:

> The Word that gives life
> was from the beginning,
> and this is the one
> our message is about.
> *(1.1)*

A QUICK LOOK AT THIS LETTER

- The Word That Gives Life (1.1–4)
- God Is Light and Christ Is Our Example (1.5—2.6)
- The New Commandment (2.7–17)
- The Enemies of Christ and God's Children (2.18—3.10)
- God's Love and Our Love (3.11—4.21)
- Victory Over the World (5.1–21)

1

The Word that gives life
was from the beginning,
and this is the one
our message is about.

Our ears have heard,
our own eyes have seen,
and our hands touched
this Word.
²The one who gives life appeared! We saw it happen, and we are witnesses to what we have seen. Now we are telling you about this eternal life that was with the Father and appeared to us. ³We are telling you what we have seen and heard, so that you may share in this life with us. And we share in it with the Father and with his Son Jesus Christ. ⁴We are writing to tell you these things, because this makes us*ᵃ* truly happy.

God Is Light

⁵Jesus told us that God is light and doesn't have any darkness in him. Now we are telling you.

⁶If we say that we share in life with

ᵃus: Some manuscripts have "you."

God and keep on living in the dark, we are lying and are not living by the truth. 7But if we live in the light, as God does, we share in life with each other. And the blood of his Son Jesus washes all our sins away. 8If we say that we have not sinned, we are fooling ourselves, and the truth is not in our hearts. 9But if we confess our sins to God, he can always be trusted to forgive us and take our sins away.

10If we say that we have not sinned, we make God a liar, and his message is not in our hearts.*b*

Christ Helps Us

2 My children, I am writing this so that you will not sin. But if you do sin, Jesus Christ always does the right thing, and he will speak to the Father for us. 2Christ is the sacrifice that takes away our sins and the sins of all the world's people.

3When we obey God, we are sure that we know him. 4But if we claim to know him and don't obey him, we are lying and the truth is not in our hearts. 5We truly love God only when we obey him as we should, and then we know that we belong to him. 6If we say we are his, we must follow the example of Christ.

The New Commandment

7My dear friends, I am not writing to give you a new commandment. It is the same one you were first given, and it is the message you heard. 8But it really is a new commandment, and you know its true meaning, just as

Christ does. You can see the darkness fading away and the true light already shining.

9If we claim to be in the light and hate someone, we are still in the dark. 10But if we love others, we are in the light, and we don't cause problems for them.*c* 11If we hate others, we are living and walking in the dark. We don't know where we are going, because we can't see in the dark.

12Children, I am writing you,
   because your sins
have been forgiven
   in the name of Christ.
13Parents, I am writing you,
   because you have known
the one who was there
   from the beginning.
Young people, I am writing you,
because you have defeated
   the evil one.
14Children, I am writing you,
   because you have known
   the Father.
Parents, I am writing you,
   because you have known
the one who was there
   from the beginning.
Young people, I am writing you,
   because you are strong.
God's message is firm
   in your hearts,
and you have defeated
   the evil one.
15Don't love the world or anything that belongs to the world. If you love the world, you cannot love the Father. 16Our foolish pride comes from this world, and so do our selfish desires and our desire to have everything we see. None of this comes from the Father.

band his message is not in our hearts: Or "because we have not accepted his message." *cand we don't cause problems for them*: Or "and we can see anything that might make us fall."

17The world and the desires it causes are disappearing. But if we obey God, we will live forever.

The Enemy of Christ

18Children, this is the last hour. You heard that the enemy of Christ would appear at this time, and many of Christ's enemies have already appeared. So we know that the last hour is here. 19These people came from our own group, yet they were not part of us. If they had been part of us, they would have stayed with us. But they left, which proves that they did not belong to our group.

20Christ, the Holy One,[d] has blessed[e] you, and now all of you understand.[f] 21I did not need to write you about the truth, since you already know it. You also know that liars do not belong to the truth. 22And a liar is anyone who says that Jesus isn't truly Christ. Anyone who says this is an enemy of Christ and rejects both the Father and the Son. 23If we reject the Son, we reject the Father. But if we say that we accept the Son, we have the Father. 24Keep thinking about the message you first heard, and you will always be one in your heart with the Son and with the Father. 25The Son[g] has promised us[h] eternal life.

26I am writing to warn you about those people who are misleading you. 27But Christ has blessed you with the Holy Spirit.[i] Now the Spirit stays in you, and you don't need any teachers. The Spirit is truthful and teaches you everything. So stay one in your heart with Christ, just as the Spirit has taught you to do.

Children of God

28Children, stay one in your hearts with Christ. Then when he returns, we will have confidence and won't have to hide in shame. 29You know that Christ always does right and that everyone who does right is a child of God.

3 Think how much the Father loves us. He loves us so much that he lets us be called his children, as we truly are. But since the people of this world did not know who Christ[j] is, they don't know who we are. 2My dear friends, we are already God's children, though what we will be has not yet been seen. But we do know that when Christ returns, we will be like him, because we will see him as he truly is.

---

[d]*Christ, the Holy One*: The Greek text has "the Holy One" which may refer either to Christ or to God the Father. [e]*blessed*: This translates a word which means "to pour olive oil on (someone's head)." In Old Testament times it was the custom to pour olive oil on a person's head when that person was chosen to be a priest or a king. Here the meaning is not clear. It may refer to the ceremony of pouring olive oil on the followers of the Lord right before they were baptized or it may refer to the gift of the Holy Spirit which they were given at baptism (see verse 27). [f]*now all of you understand*: Some manuscripts have "you understand all things." [g]*The Son*: The Greek text has "he" and may refer to God the Father. [h]*us*: Some manuscripts have "you." [i]*Christ has blessed you with the Holy Spirit*: The Greek text has "You received a pouring on of olive oil from him" (see verse 20). The "pouring on of olive oil" is here taken to refer to the gift of the Holy Spirit, and "he" may refer either to Christ or to the Father. [j]*Christ*: The Greek text has "he" and may refer to God.

³This hope makes us keep ourselves holy, just as Christ*ᵏ* is holy.

⁴Everyone who sins breaks God's law, because sin is the same as breaking God's law. ⁵You know that Christ came to take away sins. He isn't sinful, ⁶and people who stay one in their hearts with him won't keep on sinning. If they do keep on sinning, they don't know Christ, and they have never seen him.

⁷Children, don't be fooled. Anyone who does right is good, just like Christ himself. ⁸Anyone who keeps on sinning belongs to the devil. He has sinned from the beginning, but the Son of God came to destroy all that he has done. ⁹God's children cannot keep on being sinful. His life-giving power*ˡ* lives in them and makes them his children, so that they cannot keep on sinning. ¹⁰You can tell God's children from the devil's children, because those who belong to the devil refuse to do right or to love each other.

Love Each Other

¹¹From the beginning you were told that we must love each other. ¹²Don't be like Cain, who belonged to the devil and murdered his own brother. Why did he murder him? He did it because his brother was good, and he was evil. ¹³My friends, don't be surprised if the people of this world hate you. ¹⁴Our love for each other proves that we have gone from death to life. But if you don't love each other, you are still under the power of death.

¹⁵If you hate each other, you are murderers, and we know that murderers do not have eternal life. ¹⁶We know what love is because Jesus gave his life for us. That's why we must give our lives for each other. ¹⁷If we have all we need and see one of our own people in need, we must have pity on that person, or else we cannot say we love God. ¹⁸Children, you show love for others by truly helping them, and not merely by talking about it.

¹⁹When we love others, we know that we belong to the truth, and we feel at ease in the presence of God. ²⁰But even if we don't feel at ease, God is greater than our feelings, and he knows everything. ²¹Dear friends, if we feel at ease in the presence of God, we will have the courage to come near to him. ²²He will give us whatever we ask, because we obey him and do what pleases him. ²³God wants us to have faith in his Son Jesus Christ and to love each other. This is also what Jesus taught us to do. ²⁴If we obey God's commandments, we will stay one in our hearts with him, and he will stay one with us. The Spirit that he has given us is proof that we are one with him.

God Is Love

4 Dear friends, don't believe everyone who claims to have the Spirit of God. Test them all to find out if they really do come from God. Many false prophets have already gone out into the world, ²and you can know which ones come from God. His Spirit says that Jesus Christ had a truly human body. ³But when someone does not say this about Jesus, you know that person has a spirit that does not come from God and is the enemy of Christ. You knew

---

ᵏChrist: The Greek text has "that one" and may refer to God.   *ˡHis life-giving power*: The Greek text has "his seed."

that this enemy was coming into the world and now is already here.

⁴Children, you belong to God, and you have defeated these enemies. God's Spirit*ᵐ* is in you and is more powerful than the one that is in the world. ⁵These enemies belong to this world, and the world listens to them, because they speak its language. ⁶We belong to God, and everyone who knows God will listen to us. But the people who don't know God won't listen to us. That is how we can tell the Spirit that speaks the truth from the one that tells lies.

⁷My dear friends, we must love each other. Love comes from God, and when we love each other, it shows that we have been given new life. We are now God's children, and we know him. ⁸God is love, and anyone who doesn't love others has never known him. ⁹God showed his love for us when he sent his only Son into the world to give us life. ¹⁰Real love is not our love for God, but his love for us. God sent his Son to be the sacrifice by which our sins are forgiven. ¹¹Dear friends, since God loved us this much, we must love each other.

¹²No one has ever seen God. But if we love each other, God lives in us, and his love is truly in our hearts.

¹³God has given us his Spirit. That is how we know that we are one with him, just as he is one with us. ¹⁴God sent his Son to be the Savior of the world. We saw his Son and are now telling others about him. ¹⁵God stays one with everyone who openly says that Jesus is the Son of God. That's how we stay one with God ¹⁶and are sure that God loves us.

God is love. If we keep on loving others, we will stay one in our hearts with God, and he will stay one with us. ¹⁷If we truly love others and live as Christ did in this world, we won't be worried about the day of judgment. ¹⁸A real love for others will chase those worries away. The thought of being punished is what makes us afraid. It shows that we have not really learned to love.

¹⁹We love because God loved us first. ²⁰But if we say we love God and don't love each other, we are liars. We cannot see God. So how can we love God, if we don't love the people we can see? ²¹The two commandments that God has given us are: "Love God and love each other!"

Victory Over the World

5 If we believe that Jesus is truly Christ, we are God's children. Everyone who loves the Father will also love his children. ²If we love and obey God, we know that we will love his children. ³We show our love for God by obeying his commandments, and they are not hard to follow.

⁴Every child of God can defeat the world, and our faith is what gives us this victory. ⁵No one can defeat the world without having faith in Jesus as the Son of God.

Who Jesus Is

⁶Water and blood came out from the side of Jesus Christ. It was not just

---

ᵐ God's Spirit: The Greek text has "he" and may refer to the Spirit or to God or to Jesus.

water, but water and blood."[n] The Spirit tells about this, because the Spirit is truthful. [7]In fact, there are three who tell about it. [8]They are the Spirit, the water, and the blood, and they all agree.

[9]We believe what people tell us. But we can trust what God says even more, and God is the one who has spoken about his Son. [10]If we have faith in God's Son, we have believed what God has said. But if we don't believe what God has said about his Son, it is the same as calling God a liar. [11]God has also said that he gave us eternal life and that this life comes to us from his Son. [12]And so, if we have God's Son, we have this life. But if we don't have the Son, we don't have this life.

Knowing about Eternal Life

[13]All of you have faith in the Son of God, and I have written to let you know that you have eternal life. [14]We are certain that God will hear our prayers when we ask for what pleases him. [15]And if we know that God listens when we pray, we are sure that our prayers have already been answered.

[16]Suppose you see one of our people commit a sin that is not a deadly sin. You can pray, and that person will be given eternal life. But the sin must not be one that is deadly. [17]Everything that is wrong is sin, but not all sins are deadly.

[18]We are sure that God's children do not keep on sinning. God's own Son protects them, and the devil cannot harm them.

[19]We are certain that we come from God and that the rest of the world is under the power of the devil.

[20]We know that Jesus Christ the Son of God has come and has shown us the true God. And because of Jesus, we now belong to the true God who gives eternal life.

[21]Children, you must stay away from idols.

---

[n]*Water and blood came out from the side of Jesus Christ. It was not just water, but water and blood*: See John 19.34. It is also possible to translate, "Jesus Christ came by the water of baptism and by the blood of his death! He was not only baptized, but he bled and died." The purpose of the verse is to tell that Jesus was truly human and that he really died.

John's Second Letter

ABOUT THIS LETTER

John writes again about the importance of love in a Christian's life. He points out that truth and love must go together. We must also believe that Christ was truly human, and we must love each other.

A QUICK LOOK AT THIS LETTER

- Greetings and Prayer (1–3)
- Truth and Love (4–11)
- Final Greetings (12, 13)

---

¹From the church leader.ᵃ

To a very special woman and her children.ᵇ I truly love all of you, and so does everyone else who knows the truth. ²We love you because the truth is now in our hearts, and it will be there forever.

³I pray that God the Father and Jesus Christ his Son will be kind and merciful to us! May they give us peace and truth and love.

Truth and Love

⁴I was very glad to learn that some of your children are obeying the truth, as the Father told us to do. ⁵Dear friend, I am not writing to tell you and your children to do something you have not done before. I am writing to tell you to love each other, which is the first thing you were told to do. ⁶Love means that we do what God tells us. And from the beginning, he told you to love him.

⁷Many liars have gone out into the world. These deceitful liars are saying that Jesus Christ did not have a truly human body. But they are liars and the enemies of Christ. ⁸So be sure not to lose what weᶜ have worked for. If you do, you won't be given your full reward. ⁹Don't keep changing what you were taught about Christ, or else God will no longer be with you. But if you hold firmly to what you were taught, both the Father and the Son will be with you. ¹⁰If people won't agree to this teaching, don't welcome them into your home or even greet them. ¹¹Greeting them is the same as taking part in their evil deeds.

ᵃ*church leader*: Or "elder" or "presbyter" or "priest." ᵇ*very special woman and her children*: A group of the Lord's followers who met together for worship. "The children of your . . . sister" (verse 13) is another group of followers. "Very special" (here and verse 13) probably means "chosen (by the Lord)." ᶜ*we*: Some manuscripts have "you."

Final Greetings

12I have much more to tell you, but I don't want to write it with pen and ink. I want to come and talk to you in person, because that will make us[d] really happy.

13Greetings from the children of your very special sister.[e]

---

[d]us: Some manuscripts have "you."   [e]sister: See the note at verse 1.

John's Third Letter

~≈~

ABOUT THIS LETTER

I n this letter the writer reminds Christian readers that they should help support those who go to other parts of the world to tell others about the Lord. The letter is written to an important church member named Gaius, who had been very helpful to Christians who traveled around and preached the good news.

A QUICK LOOK AT THIS LETTER

- Greetings to Gaius (1–4)
- The Importance of Working Together (5–12)
- Final Greetings (13–15)

1From the church leader.[a]
To my dear friend Gaius.

I love you because we follow the truth, 2dear friend, and I pray that all goes well for you. I hope that you are as strong in body, as I know you are in spirit. 3It makes me very happy when the Lord's followers come by and speak openly of how you obey the truth. 4Nothing brings me greater happiness than to hear that my children[b] are obeying the truth.

Working Together

5Dear friend, you have always been faithful in helping other followers of the Lord, even the ones you didn't know before. 6They have told the church about your love. They say you were good enough to welcome them and to send them on their mission in a way that God's servants deserve. 7When they left to tell others about the Lord, they decided not to accept help

---

[a]church leader: Or "elder" or "presbyter" or "priest."   [b]children: Probably persons that the leader had led to be followers of the Lord.

from anyone who was not a follower. ⁸We must support people like them, so that we can take part in what they are doing to spread the truth.

⁹I wrote to the church. But Diotrephes likes to be the number-one leader, and he won't pay any attention to us. ¹⁰So if I come, I will remind him of how he has been attacking us with gossip. Not only has he been doing this, but he refuses to welcome any of the Lord's followers who come by. And when other church members want to welcome them, he puts them out of the church.

¹¹Dear friend, don't copy the evil deeds of others! Follow the example of people who do kind deeds. They are God's children, but those who are always doing evil have never seen God.

¹²Everyone speaks well of Demetrius, and so does the true message that he teaches. I also speak well of him, and you know what I say is true.

Final Greetings

¹³I have much more to say to you, but I don't want to write it with pen and ink. ¹⁴I hope to see you soon, and then we can talk in person.

¹⁵I pray that God will bless you with peace!

Your friends send their greetings. Please give a personal greeting to each of our friends.

A Letter from Jude

ABOUT THIS LETTER

Jude has much to say about false teachers. They are evil! God will punish them, and Christians should not follow their teaching or imitate the way they live.

Jude ends with a beautiful prayer-like blessing:

Offer praise to God our Savior because of our Lord Jesus Christ! Only God can keep you from falling and make you pure and joyful in his glorious presence. Before time began and now and forevermore, God is worthy of glory, honor, power, and authority. Amen.

(24-25)

A QUICK LOOK AT THIS LETTER

- Greetings (1, 2)
- Defending the Faith against False Teachers (3–23)
- Final Prayer (24-25)

1From Jude, a servant of Jesus Christ and the brother of James.

To all who are chosen and loved by God the Father and are kept safe by Jesus Christ.

2I pray that God will greatly bless you with kindness, peace, and love!

False Teachers

3My dear friends, I really wanted to write you about God's saving power at work in our lives. But instead, I must write and ask you to defend the faith that God has once for all given to his people. **4**Some godless people have sneaked in among us and are saying, "God is kind, and so it is all right to be immoral." They even deny that we must obey Jesus Christ as our only Master and Lord. But long ago the Scriptures warned that these godless people were doomed.

5Don't forget what happened to those people the Lord rescued from Egypt. Some of them did not have faith, and he later destroyed them. **6**You also know about the angels*ᵃ* who didn't do their work and left their proper places. God chained them with everlasting chains and is now keeping them in dark pits until the great day of judgment. **7**We should also be warned by what happened to the cities of Sodom and Gomorrah*ᵇ* and the nearby towns.

Their people became immoral and did all sorts of sexual sins. Then God made an example of them and punished them with eternal fire.

8The people I am talking about are behaving just like those dreamers who destroyed their own bodies. They reject all authority and insult angels. **9**Even Michael, the chief angel, didn't dare to insult the devil, when the two of them were arguing about the body of Moses.*ᶜ* All Michael said was, "The Lord will punish you!"

10But these people insult powers they don't know anything about. They are like senseless animals that end up getting destroyed, because they live only by their feelings. **11**Now they are in for real trouble. They have followed Cain's example*ᵈ* and have made the same mistake that Balaam*ᵉ* did by caring only for money. They have also rebelled against God, just as Korah did.*ᶠ* Because of all this, they will be destroyed.

12These people are filthy minded, and because of their shameful and selfish actions they spoil the meals you eat together. They are like clouds blown along by the wind, but never bringing any rain. They are like leafless trees, uprooted and dead, and unable to produce fruit. **13**Their shameful deeds show up like foam on wild ocean waves. They are like wandering stars

---

ᵃangels: This may refer to the angels who liked the women on earth so much that they came down and married them (Genesis 6.2). *ᵇSodom and Gomorrah*: During the time of Abraham the Lord destroyed these cities because the people there were so evil. *ᶜMichael . . . the body of Moses*: This refers to what was said in an ancient Jewish book about Moses. *ᵈCain's example*: Cain murdered his brother Abel. *ᵉBalaam*: According to the biblical account, Balaam refused to curse the people of Israel for profit (Numbers 22.18; 24.13), though he led them to be unfaithful to the Lord (Numbers 25.1-3; 31.16). But by New Testament times, some Jewish teachers taught that Balaam was greedy and did accept money to curse them. *ᶠjust as Korah did*: Together with Dathan and Abiram, Korah led a rebellion against Moses and Aaron (Numbers 16.1-35; 26.9, 10).

forever doomed to the darkest pits of hell.

14Enoch was the seventh person after Adam, and he was talking about these people when he said:

Look! The Lord is coming with thousands and thousands of holy angels **15**to judge everyone. He will punish all those ungodly people for all the evil things they have done. The Lord will surely punish those ungodly sinners for every evil thing they have ever said about him.

16These people grumble and complain and live by their own selfish desires. They brag about themselves and flatter others to get what they want.

More Warnings

17My dear friends, remember the warning you were given by the apostles of our Lord Jesus Christ. **18**They told you that near the end of time, selfish and godless people would start making fun of God. **19**And now these people are already making you turn against each other. They think only about this life, and they don't have God's Spirit.

20Dear friends, keep building on the foundation of your most holy faith, as the Holy Spirit helps you to pray. **21**And keep in step with God's love, as you wait for our Lord Jesus Christ to show how kind he is by giving you eternal life. **22**Be helpful to*g* all who may have doubts. **23**Rescue any who need to be saved, as you would rescue someone from a fire. Then with fear in your own hearts, have mercy on everyone who needs it. But hate even the clothes of those who have been made dirty by their filthy deeds.

Final Prayer

24-25 Offer praise to God our Savior because of our Lord Jesus Christ! Only God can keep you from falling and make you pure and joyful in his glorious presence. Before time began and now and forevermore, God is worthy of glory, honor, power, and authority. Amen.

g Be helpful to: Some manuscripts have "Correct."

Revelation

ABOUT THIS BOOK

This book tells what John had seen in a vision about God's message and about what Jesus Christ had said and done (1.2). The message has three main parts: (1) There are evil forces at work in the world, and Christians may have to suffer and die; (2) Jesus is Lord, and he will conquer all people and powers who oppose God; and (3) God has wonderful rewards in store for his faithful people, who remain faithful to him, especially for those who lose their lives in his service.

This was a powerful message of hope for those early Christians who had to suffer or die for their faith. In this book they learned that, in spite of the cruel power of the Roman empire, the Lamb of God would win the final victory. And this gave them the courage to be faithful.

Because this book is so full of visions that use ideas and word pictures from the Old Testament, it was like a book with secret messages for the early Christians. The book could be passed around and be understood by Christians, but an official of the Roman empire would not be able to understand it. For example, when the fall of Babylon is described (chapter 18), the early Christians knew that this pointed to the fall of the Roman empire. This knowledge gave them hope.

At the beginning of this book there are seven letters to seven churches. These letters show what different groups of the Lord's followers will do in times of persecution (2.1—3.22).

The author uses many powerful images to describe God's power and judgment. The vision of God's throne (4.1–11) and of the scroll and the Lamb (5.1–14) show that God and Christ are in control of all human and supernatural events. Opening seven seals (6.1—8.5), blowing the seven trumpets (8.6—11.19), and emptying the seven bowls (16.1–21) are among the visions that show God's fierce judgment on the world.

After the suffering has ended, God's faithful people will receive the greatest blessing of all:

> God's home is now with his people. He will live with them, and they will be his own. Yes, God will make his home among his people. He will wipe all tears from their eyes, and there will be no more death, suffering, crying, or pain. These things of the past are gone forever.
>
> (21.3, 4)

A QUICK LOOK AT THIS BOOK

- A Prophecy from John (1.1–8)
- A Vision of the Living Lord (1.9–20)
- Letters to the Seven Churches (2.1—3.22)
- A Vision of Worship in Heaven (4.1–11)
- A Scroll with Seven Seals (5.1—6.17)

- Worship in Front of God's Throne (7.1–17)
- Seven Trumpets (8.1—11.19)
- A Dragon and Two Beasts (12.1—13.18)
- Visions of God's Judgment and Protection (14.1—15.8)
- Seven Bowls of God's Anger (16.1–21)
- God's Enemies Are Defeated (17.1—20.10)
- The Final Judgment (20.11–15)
- A New Heaven and a New Earth (21.1–8)
- New Jerusalem (21.9—22.5)
- Christ Will Soon Return (22.6–21)

1 This is what God showed to Jesus Christ, so that he could tell his servants what must happen soon. Christ then sent his angel with the message to his servant John. ²And John told everything that he had seen about God's message and about what Jesus Christ had said and done.

³God will bless everyone who reads this prophecy to others,*a* and he will bless everyone who hears and obeys it. The time is almost here.

⁴From John to the seven churches in Asia.*b*

I pray that you
will be blessed
with kindness and peace
from God, who is and was
and is coming.
May you receive
kindness and peace
from the seven spirits
before the throne of God.
⁵May kindness and peace
be yours
from Jesus Christ,
the faithful witness.

Jesus was the first
to conquer death,
and he is the ruler
of all earthly kings.
Christ loves us,
and by his blood
he set us free
from our sins.
⁶He lets us rule as kings
and serve God his Father
as priests.
To him be glory and power
forever and ever! Amen.
⁷Look! He is coming with
the clouds.
Everyone will see him,
even the ones who stuck
a sword through him.
All people on earth
will weep because of him.
Yes, it will happen! Amen.

⁸The Lord God says, "I am Alpha and Omega,*c* the one who is and was and is coming. I am God All-Powerful!"

A Vision of the Risen Lord

⁹I am John, a follower together with all of you. We all suffer because Jesus is our king, but he gives us the strength to endure. I was sent to Patmos Island,*d* because I had preached

---

awho reads this prophecy to others: A public reading, in a worship service. *bAsia*: The section 1.4—3.22 is in the form of a letter. Asia was in the eastern part of the Roman empire and is present day Turkey. *cAlpha and Omega*: The first and last letters of the Greek alphabet, which sometimes mean "first" and "last." *dPatmos Island*: A small island where prisoners were sometimes kept by the Romans.

God's message and had told about Jesus. 10On the Lord's day*e* the Spirit took control of me, and behind me I heard a loud voice that sounded like a trumpet. 11The voice said, "Write in a book what you see. Then send it to the seven churches in Ephesus, Smyrna, Pergamum, Thyatira, Sardis, Philadelphia, and Laodicea."*f*

12When I turned to see who was speaking to me, I saw seven gold lampstands. 13There with the lampstands was someone who seemed to be the Son of Man.*g* He was wearing a robe that reached down to his feet, and a gold cloth was wrapped around his chest. 14His head and his hair were white as wool or snow, and his eyes looked like flames of fire. 15His feet were glowing like bronze being heated in a furnace, and his voice sounded like the roar of a waterfall. 16He held seven stars in his right hand, and a sharp double-edged sword was coming from his mouth. His face was shining as bright as the sun at noon.

17When I saw him, I fell at his feet like a dead person. But he put his right hand on me and said:

Don't be afraid! I am the first, the last, 18and the living one. I died, but now I am alive forevermore, and I have the keys to death and the world of the dead.*h* 19Write what you have seen and what is and what will happen after these things. 20I will explain the mystery of the seven stars that you saw at my right side and the seven gold lampstands. The seven stars are the angels *i* of the seven churches, and the lampstands are the seven churches.

The Letter to Ephesus

2 This is what you must write to the angel of the church in Ephesus:

I am the one who holds the seven stars in my right hand, and I walk among the seven gold lampstands. Listen to what I say.

2I know everything you have done, including your hard work and how you have endured. I know you won't put up with anyone who is evil. When some people pretended to be apostles, you tested them and found out that they were liars. 3You have endured and gone through hard times because of me, and you have not given up.

4But I do have something against you! And it is this: You don't have as much love as you used to. 5Think about where you have fallen from, and then turn back and do as you did at first. If you don't turn back, I will come and take away your lampstand. 6But there is one thing you are doing right. You hate what the Nicolaitans*j* are doing, and so do I.

7If you have ears, listen to

---

e Lord's day: Sunday, the day when Jesus was raised from death, and when many Christians worship. *f Ephesus . . . Laodicea*: Ephesus was in the center with the six other cities forming a half-circle around it. *g Son of Man*: That is, Jesus. *h keys to death and the world of the dead*: That is, power over death and the world of the dead. *i angels*: Perhaps guardian angels that represent the churches, or they may be church leaders or messengers sent to the churches. *j Nicolaitans*: Nothing else is known about these people, though it is possible that they claimed to be followers of Nicolaus from Antioch (Acts 6.5).

what the Spirit says to the churches. I will let everyone who wins the victory eat from the life-giving tree in God's wonderful garden.

The Letter to Smyrna

8This is what you must write to the angel of the church in Smyrna:

I am the first and the last. I died, but now I am alive! Listen to what I say.

9I know how much you suffer and how poor you are, but you are rich. I also know the cruel things being said about you by people who claim to be Jews. But they are not really Jews. They are a group that belongs to Satan.

10Don't worry about what you will suffer. The devil will throw some of you into jail, and you will be tested and made to suffer for ten days. But if you are faithful until you die, I will reward you with a glorious life.k

11If you have ears, listen to what the Spirit says to the churches. Whoever wins the victory will not be hurt by the second death.l

The Letter to Pergamum

12This is what you must write to the angel of the church in Pergamum:

I am the one who has the sharp double-edged sword! Listen to what I say.

13I know that you live where Satan has his throne.m But you have kept true to my name. Right there where Satan lives, my faithful witness Antipasn was taken from you and put to death. Even then you did not give up your faith in me.

14I do have a few things against you. Some of you are following the teaching of Balaam.o Long ago he told Balak to teach the people of Israel to eat food that had been offered to idols and to be immoral. 15Now some of you are following the teaching of the Nicolaitans.p 16Turn back! If you don't, I will come quickly and fight against these people. And my words will cut like a sword.

17If you have ears, listen to what the Spirit says to the churches. To everyone who wins the victory, I will give some of the hidden food.q I will also give each

---

ka glorious life: The Greek text has "a crown of life." In ancient times an athlete who had won a contest was rewarded with a crown of flowers as a sign of victory. lsecond death: The first death is physical death, and the "second death" is eternal death. mwhere Satan has his throne: The meaning is uncertain, but it may refer to the city as a center of pagan worship or of Emperor worship. nAntipas: Nothing else is known about this man, who is mentioned only here in the New Testament. oBalaam: According to Numbers 22—24, Balaam refused to disobey the Lord. But in other books of the Old Testament, he is spoken of as evil (Deuteronomy 23.4,5; Joshua 13.22; 24.9,10; Nehemiah 13.2). pNicolaitans: See the note at verse 6. qhidden food: When the people of Israel were going through the desert, the Lord provided a special food for them. Some of this was placed in a jar and stored in the sacred chest (Exodus 16). According to later Jewish teaching, the prophet Jeremiah rescued the sacred chest when the temple was destroyed by the Babylonians. He hid the chest in a cave, where it would stay until God came to save his people.

one a white stone[r] with a new name[s] written on it. No one will know that name except the one who is given the stone.

The Letter to Thyatira

18This is what you must write to the angel of the church in Thyatira:

I am the Son of God! My eyes are like flames of fire, and my feet are like bronze. Listen to what I say.

19I know everything about you, including your love, your faith, your service, and how you have endured. I know that you are doing more now than you have ever done before. **20**But I still have something against you because of that woman Jezebel.[t] She calls herself a prophet, and you let her teach and mislead my servants to do immoral things and to eat food offered to idols. **21**I gave her a chance to turn from her sins, but she did not want to stop doing these immoral things. **22**I am going to strike down Jezebel. Everyone who does these immoral things with her will also be punished, if they don't stop. **23**I will even kill her followers.[u] Then all the churches will see that I know everyone's thoughts and feelings. I will treat each of you as you deserve. **24**Some of you in Thyatira

don't follow Jezebel's teaching. You don't know anything about what her followers call the "deep secrets of Satan." So I won't burden you down with any other commands. **25**But until I come, you must hold firmly to the teaching you have.

26I will give power over the nations to everyone who wins the victory and keeps on obeying me until the end. **27-28**I will give each of them the same power that my Father has given me. They will rule the nations with an iron rod and smash those nations to pieces like clay pots. I will also give them the morning star.[v]

29If you have ears, listen to what the Spirit says to the churches.

The Letter to Sardis

3 This is what you must write to the angel of the church in Sardis:

I have the seven spirits of God and the seven stars. Listen to what I say.

I know what you are doing. Everyone may think you are alive, but you are dead. **2**Wake up! You have only a little strength left, and it is almost gone. So try to become stronger. I have found that you are not completely obeying God. **3**Remember the teaching that you

---

[r]*white stone*: The meaning of this is uncertain, though it may be the same as a ticket that lets a person into God's banquet where the "hidden food" is eaten. Or it may be a symbol of victory. [s]*a new name*: Either the name of Christ or God or the name of the follower who is given the stone. [t]*Jezebel*: Nothing else is known about her. This may have been her real name or a name that was given to her because she was like Queen Jezebel, who opposed the Lord (1 Kings 19.1,2; 21.1-26). [u]*her followers*: Or "her children." [v]*the morning star*: Probably thought of as the star that signals the end of night and the beginning of day. In 22.16 Christ is called the "morning star."

were given and that you heard. Hold firmly to it and turn from your sins. If you don't wake up, I will come when you least expect it, just as a thief does.

⁴A few of you in Sardis have not dirtied your clothes with sin. You will walk with me in white clothes, because you are worthy. ⁵Everyone who wins the victory will wear white clothes. Their names will not be erased from the book of life,ʷ and I will tell my Father and his angels that they are my followers.

⁶If you have ears, listen to what the Spirit says to the churches.

The Letter to Philadelphia

⁷This is what you must write to the angel of the church in Philadelphia:

I am the one who is holy and true, and I have the keys that belonged to David.ˣ When I open a door, no one can close it. And when I close a door, no one can open it. Listen to what I say.

⁸I know everything you have done. And I have placed before you an open door that no one can close. You were not very strong, but you obeyed my message and did not deny that you are my followers.ʸ ⁹Now you will see what I will do with those people who belong to Satan's group. They claim to be Jews, but they are liars. I will make them come and kneel down at your feet.

Then they will know that I love you.

¹⁰You obeyed my message and endured. So I will protect you from the time of testing that everyone in all the world must go through. ¹¹I am coming soon. So hold firmly to what you have, and no one will take away the crown that you will be given as your reward.

¹²Everyone who wins the victory will be made into a pillar in the temple of my God, and they will stay there forever. I will write on each of them the name of my God and the name of his city. It is the new Jerusalem that my God will send down from heaven. I will also write on them my own new name.

¹³If you have ears, listen to what the Spirit says to the churches.

The Letter to Laodicea

¹⁴This is what you must write to the angel of the church in Laodicea:

I am the one called Amen!ᶻ I am the faithful and true witness and the sourceᵃ of God's creation. Listen to what I say.

¹⁵I know everything you have done, and you are not cold or hot. I wish you were either one or the other. ¹⁶But since you are lukewarm and neither cold nor hot, I will spit you out of my mouth. ¹⁷You claim to be rich and successful and to have everything you need. But you don't know

---

ʷ*book of life*: The book in which the names of God's people are written. ˣ*the keys that belonged to David*: The keys stand for authority over David's kingdom. ʸ*did not deny that you are my followers*: Or "did not say evil things about me." ᶻ*Amen*: Meaning "Trustworthy." ᵃ*source*: Or "beginning."

how bad off you are. You are pitiful, poor, blind, and naked.

18Buy your gold from me. It has been refined in a fire, and it will make you rich. Buy white clothes from me. Wear them and you can cover up your shameful nakedness. Buy medicine for your eyes, so that you will be able to see.

19I correct and punish everyone I love. So make up your minds to turn away from your sins. 20Listen! I am standing and knocking at your door. If you hear my voice and open the door, I will come in and we will eat together. 21Everyone who wins the victory will sit with me on my throne, just as I won the victory and sat with my Father on his throne.

22If you have ears, listen to what the Spirit says to the churches.

Worship in Heaven

4 After this, I looked and saw a door that opened into heaven. Then the voice that had spoken to me at first and that sounded like a trumpet said, "Come up here! I will show you what must happen next." 2Right then the Spirit took control of me, and there in heaven I saw a throne and someone sitting on it. 3The one who was sitting there sparkled like precious stones of jasper*b* and carnelian.*c* A rainbow that looked like an emerald*d* surrounded the throne.

4Twenty-four other thrones were in a circle around that throne. And on each of these thrones there was an elder dressed in white clothes and wearing a gold crown. 5Flashes of lightning and roars of thunder came out from the throne in the center of the circle. Seven torches, which are the seven spirits of God, were burning in front of the throne. 6Also in front of the throne was something that looked like a glass sea, clear as crystal.

Around the throne in the center were four living creatures covered front and back with eyes. 7The first creature was like a lion, the second one was like a bull, the third one had the face of a human, and the fourth was like a flying eagle. 8Each of the four living creatures had six wings, and their bodies were covered with eyes. Day and night they never stopped singing,

"Holy, holy, holy is the Lord,
the all-powerful God,
who was and is
and is coming!"

9The living creatures kept praising, honoring, and thanking the one who sits on the throne and who lives forever and ever. 10At the same time the twenty-four elders kneeled down before the one sitting on the throne. And as they worshiped the one who lives forever, they placed their crowns in front of the throne and said,

11"Our Lord and God,
you are worthy
to receive glory,
honor, and power.
You created all things,
and by your decision they are
and were created."

The Scroll and the Lamb

5 In the right hand of the one sitting on the throne I saw a scroll*e* that

---

bjasper: Usually green or clear.　*ccarnelian*: Usually deep-red or reddish-white.　*demerald*: A precious stone, usually green.　*escroll*: A roll of paper or special leather used for writing on. Sometimes a scroll would be sealed on the outside with one or more pieces of wax.

had writing on the inside and on the outside. And it was sealed in seven places. ²I saw a mighty angel ask with a loud voice, "Who is worthy to open the scroll and break its seals?" ³No one in heaven or on earth or under the earth was able to open the scroll or see inside it.

⁴I cried hard because no one was found worthy to open the book or see inside it. ⁵Then one of the elders said to me, "Stop crying and look! The one who is called both the 'Lion from the Tribe of Judah'*f* and 'King David's Great Descendant'*g* has won the victory. He will open the book and its seven seals."

⁶Then I looked and saw a Lamb standing in the center of the throne that was surrounded by the four living creatures and the elders. The Lamb looked as if it had once been killed. It had seven horns and seven eyes, which are the seven spirits*h* of God, sent out to all the earth.

⁷The Lamb went over and took the scroll from the right hand of the one who sat on the throne. ⁸After he had taken it, the four living creatures and the twenty-four elders kneeled down before him. Each of them had a harp and a gold bowl full of incense,*i* which are the prayers of God's people. ⁹Then they sang a new song,

"You are worthy
     to receive the scroll
and open its seals,
     because you were killed.
And with your own blood
     you bought for God

people from every tribe,
     language, nation, and race.
¹⁰You let them become kings
     and serve God as priests,
     and they will rule on earth."

¹¹As I looked, I heard the voices of a lot of angels around the throne and the voices of the living creatures and of the elders. There were millions and millions of them, ¹²and they were saying in a loud voice,

"The Lamb who was killed
     is worthy to receive power,
riches, wisdom, strength,
     honor, glory, and praise."

¹³Then I heard all beings in heaven and on the earth and under the earth and in the sea offer praise. Together, all of them were saying,

"Praise, honor, glory,
and strength
     forever and ever
to the one who sits
on the throne
     and to the Lamb!"

¹⁴The four living creatures said "Amen," while the elders kneeled down and worshiped.

Opening the Seven Seals

6 At the same time that I saw the Lamb open the first of the seven seals, I heard one of the four living creatures shout with a voice like thunder. It said, "Come out!" ²Then I saw a white horse. Its rider carried a bow and was given a crown. He had already won some victories, and he went out to win more.

---

f'Lion from the Tribe of Judah': In Genesis 49.9 the tribe of Judah is called a young lion, and King David was from Judah. *g'King David's Great Descendant'*: The Greek text has "the root of David" which is a title for the Messiah based on Isaiah 11.1,10. *h the seven spirits*: Some manuscripts have "the spirits." *i incense*: A material that produces a sweet smell when burned. Sometimes it is a symbol for the prayers of God's people.

3When the Lamb opened the second seal, I heard the second living creature say, "Come out!" 4Then another horse came out. It was fiery red. And its rider was given the power to take away all peace from the earth, so that people would slaughter one another. He was also given a big sword.

5When the Lamb opened the third seal, I heard the third living creature say, "Come out!" Then I saw a black horse, and its rider had a balance scale in one hand. 6I heard what sounded like a voice from somewhere among the four living creatures. It said, "A quart of wheat will cost you a whole day's wages! Three quarts of barley will cost you a day's wages too. But don't ruin the olive oil or the wine."

7When the Lamb opened the fourth seal, I heard the voice of the fourth living creature say, "Come out!" 8Then I saw a pale green horse. Its rider was named Death, and Death's Kingdom followed behind. They were given power over one fourth of the earth, and they could kill its people with swords, famines, diseases, and wild animals.

9When the Lamb opened the fifth seal, I saw under the altar the souls of everyone who had been killed for speaking God's message and telling about their faith. 10They shouted, "Master, you are holy and faithful! How long will it be before you judge and punish the people of this earth who killed us?"

11Then each of those who had been killed was given a white robe and told to rest for a little while. They had to wait until the complete number of the Lord's other servants and followers would be killed.

12When I saw the Lamb open the sixth seal, I looked and saw a great earthquake. The sun turned as dark as sackcloth,[j] and the moon became as red as blood. 13The stars in the sky fell to earth, just like figs shaken loose by a windstorm. 14Then the sky was rolled up like a scroll,[k] and all mountains and islands were moved from their places.

15The kings of the earth, its famous people, and its military leaders hid in caves or behind rocks on the mountains. They hid there together with the rich and the powerful and with all the slaves and free people. 16Then they shouted to the mountains and the rocks, "Fall on us! Hide us from the one who sits on the throne and from the anger of the Lamb. 17That terrible day has come! God and the Lamb will show their anger, and who can face it?"

The 144,000 Are Marked for God

7 1-2After this I saw four angels. Each one was standing on one of the earth's four corners. The angels held back the four winds, so that no wind would blow on the earth or on the sea or on any tree. These angels had also been given the power to harm the earth and the sea. Then I saw another angel come up from where the sun rises in the east, and he was ready to put the mark of the living God on people. He shouted to the four angels, 3"Don't harm the earth or the sea or any tree! Wait until I have marked the foreheads of the servants of our God." 4Then I heard how many people had been marked on the forehead.

---

[j]sackcloth: A rough, dark-colored cloth made from goat or camel hair and used to make grain sacks. It was worn in times of trouble or sorrow.   [k]scroll: See the note at 5.1.

There were one hundred forty-four thousand, and they came from every tribe of Israel:

⁵12,000 from the tribe
    of Judah,
12,000 from the tribe
    of Reuben,
12,000 from the tribe
    of Gad,
⁶12,000 from the tribe
    of Asher,
12,000 from the tribe
    of Naphtali,
12,000 from the tribe
    of Manasseh,
⁷12,000 from the tribe
    of Simeon,
12,000 from the tribe
    of Levi,
12,000 from the tribe
    of Issachar,
⁸12,000 from the tribe
    of Zebulun,
12,000 from the tribe
    of Joseph, and
12,000 from the tribe
    of Benjamin.

People from Every Nation

⁹After this, I saw a large crowd with more people than could be counted. They were from every race, tribe, nation, and language, and they stood before the throne and before the Lamb. They wore white robes and held palm branches in their hands, ¹⁰as they shouted,

"Our God, who sits
    upon the throne,
has the power
to save his people,
    and so does the Lamb."

¹¹The angels who stood around the throne kneeled in front of it with their faces to the ground. The elders and the four living creatures kneeled there with them. Then they all worshiped God ¹²and said,

"Amen! Praise, glory, wisdom,
    thanks, honor, power,
and strength belong to our God
    forever and ever! Amen!"

¹³One of the elders asked me, "Do you know who these people are that are dressed in white robes? Do you know where they come from?"

¹⁴"Sir," I answered, "you must know."

Then he told me:

"These are the ones
    who have gone through
    the great suffering.
They have washed their robes
    in the blood of the Lamb
    and have made them white.
¹⁵And so they stand
    before the throne of God
and worship him in his temple
    day and night.
The one who sits on the throne
    will spread his tent
    over them.
¹⁶They will never hunger
    or thirst again,
and they won't be troubled
by the sun
    or any scorching heat.
¹⁷The Lamb in the center
    of the throne
    will be their shepherd.
He will lead them to streams
    of life-giving water,
and God will wipe all tears
    from their eyes."

The Seventh Seal Is Opened

8 When the Lamb opened the seventh seal, there was silence in heaven for about half an hour. ²I noticed that the seven angels who stood

before God were each given a trumpet.

3Another angel, who had a gold container for incense,¹ came and stood at the altar. This one was given a lot of incense to offer with the prayers of God's people on the gold altar in front of the throne. 4Then the smoke of the incense, together with the prayers of God's people, went up to God from the hand of the angel.

5After this, the angel filled the incense container with fire from the altar and threw it on the earth. Thunder roared, lightning flashed, and the earth shook.

The Trumpets

6The seven angels now got ready to blow their trumpets.

7When the first angel blew his trumpet, hail and fire mixed with blood were thrown down on the earth. A third of the earth, a third of the trees, and a third of all green plants were burned.

8When the second angel blew his trumpet, something like a great fiery mountain was thrown into the sea. A third of the sea turned to blood, 9a third of the living creatures in the sea died, and a third of the ships was destroyed.

10When the third angel blew his trumpet, a great star fell from heaven. It was burning like a torch, and it fell on a third of the rivers and on a third of the springs of water. 11The name of the star was Bitter, and a third of the water turned bitter. Many people died because the water was so bitter.

12When the fourth angel blew his trumpet, a third of the sun, a third of the moon, and a third of the stars were struck. They each lost a third of their light. So during a third of the day there was no light, and a third of the night was also without light.

13Then I looked and saw a lone eagle flying across the sky. It was shouting, "Trouble, trouble, trouble to everyone who lives on earth! The other three angels are now going to blow their trumpets."

9 When the fifth angel blew his trumpet, I saw a starᵐ fall from the sky to earth. It was given the key to the tunnel that leads down to the deep pit. 2As it opened the tunnel, smoke poured out like the smoke of a great furnace. The sun and the air turned dark because of the smoke. 3Locusts came out of the smoke and covered the earth. They were given the same power that scorpions have.

4The locusts were told not to harm the grass on the earth or any plant or any tree. They were to punish only those people who did not have God's mark on their foreheads. 5The locusts were allowed to make them suffer for five months, but not to kill them. The suffering they caused was like the sting of a scorpion. 6In those days people will want to die, but they will not be able to. They will hope for death, but it will escape from them.

7These locusts looked like horses ready for battle. On their heads they wore something like gold crowns, and they had human faces. 8Their hair was like a woman's long hair, and their teeth were like those of a lion. 9On their chests they wore armor made of iron. Their wings roared like an army of horse-drawn chariots rushing into battle. 10Their tails were like a scorpion's tail with a stinger that had the

---

¹incense: See the note at 5.8. ᵐstar: In the ancient world, stars were often thought of as living beings, such as angels.

power to hurt someone for five months. [11]Their king was the angel in charge of the deep pit. In Hebrew his name was Abaddon, and in Greek it was Apollyon.[n]

[12]The first horrible thing has now happened! But wait. Two more horrible things will happen soon.

[13]Then the sixth angel blew his trumpet. I heard a voice speak from the four corners of the gold altar that stands in the presence of God. [14]The voice spoke to this angel and said, "Release the four angels who are tied up beside the great Euphrates River." [15]The four angels had been prepared for this very hour and day and month and year. Now they were set free to kill a third of all people.

[16]By listening, I could tell there were more than two hundred million of these war horses. [17]In my vision their riders wore fiery-red, dark-blue, and yellow armor on their chests. The heads of the horses looked like lions, with fire and smoke and sulphur coming out of their mouths. [18]One third of all people were killed by the three terrible troubles caused by the fire, the smoke, and the sulphur. [19]The horses had powerful mouths, and their tails were like poisonous snakes that bite and hurt.

[20]The people who lived through these terrible troubles did not turn away from the idols they had made, and they did not stop worshiping demons. They kept on worshiping idols that were made of gold, silver, bronze, stone, and wood. Not one of these idols could see, hear, or walk. [21]No one stopped murdering or practicing witchcraft or being immoral or stealing.

The Angel and the Little Scroll

10 I saw another powerful angel come down from heaven. This one was covered with a cloud, and a rainbow was over his head. His face was like the sun, his legs were like columns of fire, [2]and with his hand he held a little scroll[o] that had been unrolled. He stood there with his right foot on the sea and his left foot on the land. [3]Then he shouted with a voice that sounded like a growling lion. Thunder roared seven times.

[4]After the thunder stopped, I was about to write what it had said. But a voice from heaven shouted, "Keep it secret! Don't write these things."

[5]The angel I had seen standing on the sea and the land then held his right hand up toward heaven. [6]He made a promise in the name of God who lives forever and who created heaven, earth, the sea, and every living creature. The angel said, "You won't have to wait any longer. [7]God told his secret plans to his servants the prophets, and it will all happen by the time the seventh angel sounds his trumpet."

[8]Once again the voice from heaven spoke to me. It said, "Go and take the open scroll from the hand of the angel standing on the sea and the land."

[9]When I went over to ask the angel for the little scroll, the angel said, "Take the scroll and eat it! Your stomach will turn sour, but the taste in your mouth will be as sweet as honey." [10]I took the little scroll from the hand of the angel and ate it. The taste was as sweet as honey, but my stomach turned sour.

[11]Then some voices said, "Keep on

---

[n]*Abaddon . . . Apollyon*: The Hebrew word "Abaddon" and the Greek word "Apollyon" each mean "destruction." [o]*scroll*: See the note at 5.1.

telling what will happen to the people of many nations, races, and languages, and also to kings."

The Two Witnesses

11 An angel gave me a measuring stick and said:

Measure around God's temple. Be sure to include the altar and everyone worshiping there. 2But don't measure the courtyard outside the temple building. Leave it out. It has been given to those people who don't know God, and they will trample all over the holy city for forty-two months. 3My two witnesses will wear sackcloth,*p* while I let them preach for one thousand two hundred sixty days.

4These two witnesses are the two olive trees and the two lampstands that stand in the presence of the Lord who rules the earth. 5Any enemy who tries to harm them will be destroyed by the fire that comes out of their mouths. 6They have the power to lock up the sky and to keep rain from falling while they are prophesying. And whenever they want to, they can turn water to blood and cause all kinds of terrible troubles on earth.

7After the two witnesses have finished preaching God's message, the beast that lives in the deep pit will come up and fight against them. It will win the battle and kill them. 8Their bodies will be left lying in the streets of the same great city where their Lord was nailed to a cross. And that city is spiritually like the city of Sodom or the country of Egypt.

9For three and a half days the people of every nation, tribe, language, and race will stare at the bodies of these two witnesses and refuse to let them be buried. 10Everyone on earth will celebrate and be happy. They will give gifts to each other, because of what happened to the two prophets who caused them so much trouble. 11But three and a half days later, God will breathe life into their bodies. They will stand up, and everyone who sees them will be terrified.

12The witnesses then heard a loud voice from heaven, saying, "Come up here." And while their enemies were watching, they were taken up to heaven in a cloud. 13At that same moment there was a terrible earthquake that destroyed a tenth of the city. Seven thousand people were killed, and the rest were frightened and praised the God who rules in heaven.

14The second horrible thing has now happened! But the third one will be here soon.

The Seventh Trumpet

15At the sound of the seventh trumpet, loud voices were heard in heaven. They said,

"Now the kingdoms
of this world
belong to our Lord
and to his Chosen One!
And he will rule
forever and ever!"

16Then the twenty-four elders, who were seated on thrones in God's presence, kneeled down and worshiped him. 17They said,

"Lord God All-Powerful,
you are and you were,
and we thank you.

Psackcloth: See the note at 6.12.

You used your great power
and started ruling.
18When the nations got angry,
you became angry too!
Now the time has come
for the dead
to be judged.
It is time for you to reward
your servants the prophets
and all of your people
who honor your name,
no matter who they are.
It is time to destroy everyone
who has destroyed
the earth."

19The door to God's temple in heaven was then opened, and the sacred chest^q could be seen inside the temple. I saw lightning and heard roars of thunder. The earth trembled and huge hailstones fell to the ground.

The Woman and the Dragon

12 Something important appeared in the sky. It was a woman whose clothes were the sun. The moon was under her feet, and a crown made of twelve stars was on her head. 2She was about to give birth, and she was crying because of the great pain.

3Something else appeared in the sky. It was a huge red dragon with seven heads and ten horns, and a crown on each of its seven heads. 4With its tail, it dragged a third of the stars from the sky and threw them down to the earth. Then the dragon turned toward the woman, because it wanted to eat her child as soon as it was born.

5The woman gave birth to a son, who would rule all nations with an iron rod. The boy was snatched away. He was taken to God and placed on his throne. 6The woman ran into the desert to a place that God had prepared for her. There she would be taken care of for one thousand two hundred sixty days.

Michael Fights the Dragon

7A war broke out in heaven. Michael and his angels were fighting against the dragon and its angels. 8But the dragon lost the battle. It and its angels were forced out of their places in heaven 9and were thrown down to the earth. Yes, that old snake and his angels were thrown out of heaven! That snake, who fools everyone on earth, is known as the devil and Satan. 10Then I heard a voice from heaven shout,

"Our God has shown
his saving power,
and his kingdom has come!
God's own Chosen One
has shown his authority.
Satan accused our people
in the presence of God
day and night.
Now he has been thrown out!

11Our people defeated Satan
because of the blood^r
of the Lamb
and the message of God.
They were willing
to give up their lives.

12The heavens should rejoice,
together with everyone
who lives there.

---

^q*sacred chest*: In Old Testament times the sacred chest was kept in the tent used for worship. It was the symbol of God's presence with his people and also of his agreement with them.
^r*blood*: Or "death."

But pity the earth
and the sea,
because the devil
was thrown down
to the earth.
He knows his time is short,
and he is very angry."

13When the dragon realized that it had been thrown down to the earth, it tried to make trouble for the woman who had given birth to a son. 14But the woman was given two wings like those of a huge eagle, so that she could fly into the desert. There she would escape from the snake and be taken care of for a time, two times, and half a time.

15The snake then spit out water like a river to sweep the woman away. 16But the earth helped her and swallowed the water that had come from the dragon's mouth. 17This made the dragon terribly angry with the woman. So it started a war against the rest of her children. They are the people who obey God and are faithful to what Jesus did and taught. 18The dragon[s] stood on the beach beside the sea.

The Two Beasts

13 I looked and saw a beast coming up from the sea. This one had ten horns and seven heads, and a crown was on each of its ten horns. On each of its heads were names that were an insult to God. 2The beast that I saw had the body of a leopard, the feet of a bear, and the mouth of a lion. The dragon handed over its own power and throne and great authority to this beast. 3One of its heads seemed to have been fatally wounded, but now it was well. Everyone on earth marveled at

this beast, 4and they worshiped the dragon who had given its authority to the beast. They also worshiped the beast and said, "No one is like this beast! No one can fight against it."

5The beast was allowed to brag and claim to be God, and for forty-two months it was allowed to rule. 6The beast cursed God, and it cursed the name of God. It even cursed the place where God lives, as well as everyone who lives in heaven with God. 7It was allowed to fight against God's people and defeat them. It was also given authority over the people of every tribe, nation, language, and race. 8The beast was worshiped by everyone whose name was not written before the time of creation in the book of the Lamb who was killed.[t]

9If you have ears,
then listen!
10If you are doomed
to be captured,
you will be captured.
If you are doomed
to be killed by a sword,
you will be killed
by a sword.
This means that God's people must learn to endure and be faithful!

11I now saw another beast. This one came out of the ground. It had two horns like a lamb, but spoke like a dragon. 12It worked for the beast whose fatal wound had been healed. And it used all its authority to force the earth and all its people to worship that beast. 13It worked mighty miracles, and while people watched, it even made fire come down from the sky.

14This second beast fooled people on earth by working miracles for the first one. Then it talked them into making an idol in the form of the beast that did not die after being wounded by a sword. 15It was allowed to put breath into the idol, so that it could speak. Everyone who refused to worship the idol of the beast was put to death. 16All people were forced to put a mark on their right hand or forehead. Whether they were powerful or weak, rich or poor, free people or slaves, 17they all had to have this mark, or else they could not buy or sell anything. This mark stood for the name of the beast and for the number of its name.

18You need wisdom to understand the number of the beast! But if you are smart enough, you can figure this out. Its number is six hundred sixty-six, and it stands for a person.

The Lamb and His 144,000 Followers

14 I looked and saw the Lamb standing on Mount Zion![u] With him were a hundred forty-four thousand, who had his name and his Father's name written on their foreheads. 2Then I heard a sound from heaven that was like a roaring flood or loud thunder or even like the music of harps. 3And a new song was being sung in front of God's throne and in front of the four living creatures and the elders. No one could learn that song, except the one hundred forty-four thousand who had been rescued from the earth. 4All of these are pure virgins, and they follow the Lamb wherever he leads. They have been rescued to be presented to God and the Lamb as the most precious people[v] on earth. 5They never tell lies, and they are innocent.

The Messages of the Three Angels

6I saw another angel. This one was flying across the sky and had the eternal good news to announce to the people of every race, tribe, language, and nation on earth. 7The angel shouted, "Worship and honor God! The time has come for him to judge everyone. Kneel down before the one who created heaven and earth, the oceans, and every stream."

8A second angel followed and said, "The great city of Babylon has fallen! This is the city that made all nations drunk and immoral. Now God is angry, and Babylon has fallen."

9Finally, a third angel came and shouted:

Here is what will happen if you worship the beast and the idol and have the mark of the beast on your hand or forehead. 10You will have to drink the wine that God gives to everyone who makes him angry. You will feel his mighty anger, and you will be tortured with fire and burning sulphur, while the holy angels and the Lamb look on.

11If you worship the beast and the idol and accept the mark of its name, you will be tortured day and night. The smoke from your torture will go up forever and ever, and you will never be able to rest.

---

[u]Mount Zion: Another name for Jerusalem.   [v]the most precious people: The Greek text has "the first people." The Law of Moses taught that the first-born of all animals and the first part of the harvest were special and belonged to the Lord.

12God's people must learn to endure. They must also obey his commands and have faith in Jesus.

13Then I heard a voice from heaven say, "Put this in writing. From now on, the Lord will bless everyone who has faith in him when they die."

The Spirit answered, "Yes, they will rest from their hard work, and they will be rewarded for what they have done."

The Earth Is Harvested

14I looked and saw a bright cloud, and someone who seemed to be the Son of Man[w] was sitting on the cloud. He wore a gold crown on his head and held a sharp sickle[x] in his hand. 15An angel came out of the temple and shouted, "Start cutting with your sickle! Harvest season is here, and all crops on earth are ripe." 16The one on the cloud swung his sickle and harvested the crops.

17Another angel with a sharp sickle then came out of the temple. 18After this, an angel with power over fire came from the altar and shouted to the angel who had the sickle. He said, "All grapes on earth are ripe! Harvest them with your sharp sickle." 19The angel swung his sickle on earth and cut off its grapes. He threw them into a pit[y] where they were stomped on as a sign of God's anger. 20The pit was outside the city, and when the grapes were mashed, blood flowed out. The blood turned into a river that was about two hundred miles long and almost deep enough to cover a horse.

The Last of the Terrible Troubles

15 After this, I looked at the sky and saw something else that was strange and important. Seven angels were bringing the last seven terrible troubles. When these are ended, God will no longer be angry.

2Then I saw something that looked like a glass sea mixed with fire, and people were standing on it. They were the ones who had defeated the beast and the idol and the number that tells the name of the beast. God had given them harps, 3and they were singing the song that his servant Moses and the Lamb had sung. They were singing,

"Lord God All-Powerful,
  you have done great
    and marvelous things.
You are the ruler
  of all nations,
and you do what is
  right and fair.
4Lord, who does not honor
    and praise your name?
You alone are holy,
  and all nations will come
    and worship you,
  because you have shown
    that you judge
      with fairness."

5After this, I noticed something else in heaven. The sacred tent used for a temple was open. 6And the seven angels who were bringing the terrible troubles were coming out of it. They were dressed in robes of pure white linen and wore belts made of pure gold. 7One of the four living creatures gave each of the seven angels a bowl made of gold. These bowls were filled with the

---

[w]Son of Man: See the note at 1.13. [x]sickle: A knife with a long curved blade, used to cut grain and other crops. [y]pit: It was the custom to put grapes in a pit (called a wine press) and stomp on them to make juice that would later turn to wine.

anger of God who lives forever and ever. 8The temple quickly filled with smoke from the glory and power of God. No one could enter it until the seven angels had finished pouring out the seven last troubles.

The Bowls of God's Anger

16 From the temple I heard a voice shout to the seven angels, "Go and empty the seven bowls of God's anger on the earth."

2The first angel emptied his bowl on the earth. At once ugly and painful sores broke out on everyone who had the mark of the beast and worshiped the idol.

3The second angel emptied his bowl on the sea. Right away the sea turned into blood like that of a dead person, and every living thing in the sea died.

4The third angel emptied his bowl into the rivers and streams. At once they turned to blood. 5Then I heard the angel, who has power over water, say,

"You have always been,
  and you always will be
    the holy God.
You had the right
    to judge in this way.
6They poured out the blood[z]
  of your people
    and your prophets.
So you gave them blood
    to drink, as they deserve!"
7After this, I heard
    the altar shout,
"Yes, Lord God All-Powerful,
  your judgments are honest
    and fair."

8The fourth angel emptied his bowl on the sun, and it began to scorch people like fire. 9Everyone was scorched by its great heat, and all of them cursed the name of God who had power over these terrible troubles. But no one turned to God and praised him.

10The fifth angel emptied his bowl on the throne of the beast. At once darkness covered its kingdom, and its people began biting their tongues in pain. 11And because of their painful sores, they cursed the God who rules in heaven. But still they did not stop doing evil things.

12The sixth angel emptied his bowl on the great Euphrates River, and it completely dried up to make a road for the kings from the east. 13An evil spirit that looked like a frog came out of the mouth of the dragon. One also came out of the mouth of the beast, and another out of the mouth of the false prophet. 14These evil spirits had the power to work miracles. They went to every king on earth, to bring them together for a war against God All-Powerful. But that will be the day of God's great victory.

15Remember that Christ says, "When I come, it will surprise you like a thief! But God will bless you, if you are awake and ready. Then you won't have to walk around naked and be ashamed."

16Those armies came together in a place that in Hebrew is called Armagedon.[a]

17As soon as the seventh angel emptied his bowl in the air, a loud voice from the throne in the temple shouted, "It's done!" 18There were flashes of lightning, roars of thunder, and the worst earthquake in all history.

---

[z]*They poured out the blood*: A way of saying, "They murdered." [a]*Armagedon*: The Hebrew form of the name would be "Har Megeddo," meaning "Hill of Megeddo," where many battles were fought in ancient times (see Judges 5.19; 2 Kings 23.29,30).

19The great city of Babylon split into three parts, and the cities of other nations fell. So God made Babylon drink from the wine cup that was filled with his anger. 20Every island ran away, and the mountains disappeared. 21Hailstones, weighing about a hundred pounds each, fell from the sky on people. Finally, the people cursed God, because the hail was so terrible.

The Immoral Woman and the Beast

17 One of the seven angels who had emptied the bowls came over and said to me, "Come on! I will show you how God will punish that shameless and immoral woman who sits on many oceans. 2Every king on earth has slept with her, and her shameless ways are like wine that has made everyone on earth drunk."

3With the help of the Spirit, the angel took me into the desert, where I saw a woman sitting on a red beast. The beast was covered with names that were an insult to God, and it had seven heads and ten horns. 4The woman was dressed in purple and scarlet robes, and she wore jewelry made of gold, precious stones, and pearls. In her hand she held a gold cup filled with the filthy and nasty things she had done. 5On her forehead a mysterious name was written:

I AM THE GREAT CITY
OF BABYLON,
THE MOTHER
OF EVERY IMMORAL
AND FILTHY THING
ON EARTH.

6I could tell that the woman was drunk on the blood of God's people who had given their lives for Jesus. This surprising sight amazed me, 7and the angel said:

Why are you so amazed? I will explain the mystery about this woman and about the beast she is sitting on, with its seven heads and ten horns. 8The beast you saw is one that used to be and no longer is. It will come back from the deep pit, but only to be destroyed. Everyone on earth whose names were not written in the book of life[b] before the time of creation will be amazed. They will see this beast that used to be and no longer is, but will be once more.

9Anyone with wisdom can figure this out. The seven heads that the woman is sitting on stand for seven hills. These heads are also seven kings. 10Five of the kings are dead. One is ruling now, and the other one has not yet come. But when he does, he will rule for only a little while.

11You also saw a beast that used to be and no longer is. That beast is one of the seven kings who will return as the eighth king, but only to be destroyed.

12The ten horns that you saw are ten more kings, who have not yet come into power, and they will rule with the beast for only a short time. 13They all think alike and will give their power and authority to the beast. 14These kings will go to war against the Lamb. But he will defeat them, because he is Lord over all lords and King over all kings. His followers are chosen and special and faithful.

[b]book of life: See the note at 3.5.

15The oceans that you saw the immoral woman sitting on are crowds of people from all races and languages. 16The ten horns and the beast will start hating the shameless woman. They will strip off her clothes and leave her naked. Then they will eat her flesh and throw the rest of her body into a fire. 17God is the one who made these kings all think alike and decide to give their power to the beast. And they will do this until what God has said comes true.

18The woman you saw is the great city that rules over all kings on earth.

The Fall of Babylon

18 I saw another angel come from heaven. This one had great power, and the earth was bright because of his glory. 2The angel shouted,
"Fallen! Powerful Babylon
    has fallen
and is now the home
    of demons.
It is the den
    of every filthy spirit
and of all unclean birds,
    and every dirty
    and hated animal.
3Babylon's evil
    and immoral wine
        has made all nations drunk.
Every king on earth
    has slept with her,
and every merchant on earth
    is rich because of
        her evil desires."

4Then I heard another voice
    from heaven shout,
"My people, you must escape
    from Babylon.

Don't take part in her sins
    and share her punishment.
5Her sins are piled
    as high as heaven.
God has remembered the evil
    she has done.
6Treat her as she
    has treated others.
Make her pay double
    for what she has done.
Make her drink twice as much
of what she mixed
    for others.
7That woman honored herself
    with a life of luxury.
Reward her now
    with suffering and pain.

"Deep in her heart
Babylon said,
    'I am the queen!
Never will I be a widow
or know what it means
    to be sad.'
8And so, in a single day
she will suffer the pain
    of sorrow, hunger,
    and death.
Fire will destroy
    her dead body,
because her judge
    is the powerful Lord God."

9Every king on earth who slept with her and shared in her luxury will mourn. They will weep, when they see the smoke from that fire. 10Her sufferings will frighten them, and they will stand at a distance and say,

"Pity that great
    and powerful city!
Pity Babylon!
In a single hour
    her judgment has come."

11Every merchant on earth will mourn, because there is no one to buy their goods. 12There won't be anyone to buy their gold, silver, jewels, pearls, fine linen, purple cloth, silk, scarlet cloth, sweet-smelling wood, fancy carvings of ivory and wood, as well as things made of bronze, iron, or marble. 13No one will buy their cinnamon, spices, incense, myrrh, frankincense,*c* wine, olive oil, fine flour, wheat, cattle, sheep, horses, chariots, slaves, and other humans.

14Babylon, the things
        your heart desired
have all escaped
        from you.
Every luxury
and all your glory
        will be lost forever.
You will never
        get them back.

15The merchants had become rich because of her. But when they saw her sufferings, they were terrified. They stood at a distance, crying and mourning. 16Then they shouted,

"Pity the great city
        of Babylon!
She dressed in fine linen
and wore purple
        and scarlet cloth.
She had jewelry
        made of gold
and precious stones
        and pearls.
17Yet in a single hour
        her riches disappeared."

Every ship captain and passenger and sailor stood at a distance, together with everyone who does business by traveling on the sea. 18When they saw the smoke from her fire, they shouted, "This was the greatest city ever!"

19They cried loudly, and in their sorrow they threw dust on their heads, as they said,

"Pity the great city
        of Babylon!
Everyone who sailed the seas
became rich
        from her treasures.
But in a single hour
        the city was destroyed.
20The heavens should be happy
        with God's people
        and apostles and prophets.
God has punished her
        for them."

21A powerful angel then picked up a huge stone and threw it into the sea. The angel said,

"This is how the great city
        of Babylon
will be thrown down,
        never to rise again.
22The music of harps
        and singers
and of flutes and trumpets
        will no longer be heard.
No workers will ever
        set up shop in that city,
and the sound
of grinding grain
        will be silenced forever.
23Lamps will no longer shine
        anywhere in Babylon,
and couples will never again
        say wedding vows there.
Her merchants ruled
        the earth,
and by her witchcraft
        she fooled all nations.
24On the streets of Babylon
is found the blood
        of God's people
        and of his prophets,
        and everyone else."

---

cmyrrh, frankincense: Myrrh was a valuable sweet-smelling powder often used in perfume. Frankincense was a valuable powder that was burned to make a sweet smell.

19 After this, I heard what sounded like a lot of voices in heaven, and they were shouting,

"Praise the Lord!
To our God belongs
    the glorious power to save,
²because his judgments
    are honest and fair.
That filthy, immoral woman
ruined the earth
    with shameful deeds.
But God has judged her
    and made her pay
the price for murdering
    his servants."

³Then the crowd shouted,

"Praise the Lord!
Smoke will never stop rising
    from her burning body."

⁴After this, the twenty-four elders and the four living creatures all kneeled before the throne of God and worshiped him. They said, "Amen! Praise the Lord!

The Marriage Supper of the Lamb

⁵From the throne a voice said,

"If you worship
    and fear our God,
give praise to him,
    no matter who you are."

⁶Then I heard what seemed to be a large crowd that sounded like a roaring flood and loud thunder all mixed together. They were saying,

"Praise the Lord!
Our Lord God All-Powerful
    now rules as king.
⁷So we will be glad and happy
    and give him praise.
The wedding day of the Lamb
is here,
    and his bride is ready.
⁸She will be given
    a wedding dress
made of pure
    and shining linen.
This linen stands
for the good things
    God's people have done."

⁹Then the angel told me, "Put this in writing. God will bless everyone who is invited to the wedding feast of the Lamb." The angel also said, "These things that God has said are true."

¹⁰I kneeled at the feet of the angel and began to worship him. But the angel said, "Don't do that! I am a servant, just like you and everyone else who tells about Jesus. Don't worship anyone but God. Everyone who tells about Jesus does it by the power of the Spirit."

The Rider on the White Horse

¹¹I looked and saw that heaven was open, and a white horse was there. Its rider was called Faithful and True, and he is always fair when he judges or goes to war. ¹²He had eyes like flames of fire, and he was wearing a lot of crowns. His name was written on him, but he was the only one who knew what the name meant.

¹³The rider wore a robe that was covered with[d] blood, and he was known as "The Word of God." ¹⁴He was followed by armies from heaven, which rode on horses and were dressed in pure white linen. ¹⁵From his mouth a sharp sword went out to attack the nations. He will rule them with an iron rod and will show the fierce anger of God All-Powerful by stomping the grapes in the pit where wine is made. ¹⁶On the part of the robe that

---

[d]*covered with*: Some manuscripts have "sprinkled with."

covered his thigh was written, "KING OF KINGS AND LORD OF LORDS."

17I then saw an angel standing on the sun, and he shouted to all the birds flying in the sky, "Come and join in God's great feast! 18You can eat the flesh of kings, rulers, leaders, horses, riders, free people, slaves, important people, and everyone else."

19I also saw the beast and all kings of the earth come together. They fought against the rider on the white horse and against his army. 20But the beast was captured and so was the false prophet. This is the same prophet who had worked miracles for the beast, so that he could fool everyone who had the mark of the beast and worshiped the idol. The beast and the false prophet were thrown alive into a lake of burning sulphur. 21But the rest of their army was killed by the sword that came from the mouth of the rider on the horse. Then birds stuffed themselves on the dead bodies.

The Thousand Years

20 I saw an angel come down from heaven, carrying the key to the deep pit and a big chain. 2He chained the dragon for a thousand years. It is that old snake, who is also known as the devil and Satan. 3Then the angel threw the dragon into the pit. He locked and sealed it, so that a thousand years would go by before the dragon could fool the nations again. But after that, it would have to be set free for a little while.

4I saw thrones, and sitting on those thrones were the ones who had been given the right to judge. I also saw the souls of the people who had their heads cut off because they had told about Jesus and preached God's message. They were the same ones who had not worshiped the beast or the idol, and they had refused to let its mark be put on their hands or foreheads. They will come to life and rule with Christ for a thousand years.

5-6These people are the first to be raised to life, and they are especially blessed and holy. The second death*e* has no power over them. They will be priests for God and Christ and will rule with them for a thousand years.

No other dead people were raised to life until a thousand years later.

Satan Is Defeated

7At the end of the thousand years, Satan will be set free. 8He will fool the countries of Gog and Magog, which are at the far ends of the earth, and their people will follow him into battle. They will have as many followers as there are grains of sand along the beach, 9and they will march all the way across the earth. They will surround the camp of God's people and the city that his people love. But fire will come down from heaven and destroy the whole army. 10Then the devil who fooled them will be thrown into the lake of fire and burning sulphur. He will be there with the beast and the false prophet, and they will be in pain day and night forever and ever.

The Judgment at the Great White Throne

11I saw a great white throne with someone sitting on it. Earth and heaven tried to run away, but there was no place for them to go. 12I also saw

---

e second death: The first death is physical death, and the "second death" is eternal death.

all the dead people standing in front of that throne. Every one of them was there, no matter who they had once been. Several books were opened, and then the book of life*f* was opened. The dead were judged by what those books said they had done.

13The sea gave up the dead people who were in it, and death and its kingdom also gave up their dead. Then everyone was judged by what they had done. 14Afterwards, death and its kingdom were thrown into the lake of fire. This is the second death.*g* 15Anyone whose name was not written in the book of life was thrown into the lake of fire.

The New Heaven and the New Earth

21 I saw a new heaven and a new earth. The first heaven and the first earth had disappeared, and so had the sea. 2Then I saw New Jerusalem, that holy city, coming down from God in heaven. It was like a bride dressed in her wedding gown and ready to meet her husband.

3I heard a loud voice shout from the throne:

God's home is now with his people. He will live with them, and they will be his own. Yes, God will make his home among his people. 4He will wipe all tears from their eyes, and there will be no more death, suffering, crying, or pain. These things of the past are gone forever.

5Then the one sitting on the throne said:

I am making everything new. Write down what I have said. My words are true and can be trusted. 6Everything is finished! I am Alpha and Omega,*h* the beginning and the end. I will freely give water from the life-giving fountain to everyone who is thirsty. 7All who win the victory will be given these blessings. I will be their God, and they will be my people.

8But I will tell you what will happen to cowards and to everyone who is unfaithful or dirtyminded or who murders or is sexually immoral or uses witchcraft or worships idols or tells lies. They will be thrown into that lake of fire and burning sulphur. This is the second death.*i*

The New Jerusalem

9I saw one of the seven angels who had the bowls filled with the seven last terrible troubles. The angel came to me and said, "Come on! I will show you the one who will be the bride and wife of the Lamb." 10Then with the help of the Spirit, he took me to the top of a very high mountain. There he showed me the holy city of Jerusalem coming down from God in heaven.

11The glory of God made the city bright. It was dazzling and crystal clear like a precious jasper*j* stone. 12The city

---

f book of life: See the note at 3.5. *g second death*: See the note at verse 6. *h Alpha and Omega*: See the note at 1.8. *i second death*: See the note at 20.6. *j jasper*: The precious and semiprecious stones mentioned in verses 19,20 are of different colors. *Jasper* is usually green or clear; *sapphire* is blue; *agate* has circles of brown and white; *emerald* is green; *onyx* has different bands of color; *carnelian* is deep-red or reddish-white; *chrysolite* is olive-green; *beryl* is green or bluish-green; *topaz* is yellow; *chrysoprase* is apple-green; *jacinth* is reddish-orange; and *amethyst* is deep purple.

had a high and thick wall with twelve gates, and each one of them was guarded by an angel. On each of the gates was written the name of one of the twelve tribes of Israel. 13Three of these gates were on the east, three were on the north, three more were on the south, and the other three were on the west. 14The city was built on twelve foundation stones. On each of the stones was written the name of one of the Lamb's twelve apostles.

15The angel who spoke to me had a gold measuring stick to measure the city and its gates and its walls. 16The city was shaped like a cube, because it was just as high as it was wide. When the angel measured the city, it was about fifteen hundred miles high and fifteen hundred miles wide. 17Then the angel measured the wall, and by our measurements it was about two hundred sixteen feet high.

18The wall was built of jasper, and the city was made of pure gold, clear as crystal. 19Each of the twelve foundations was a precious stone. The first was jasper, the second was sapphire, the third was agate, the fourth was emerald, 20the fifth was onyx, the sixth was carnelian, the seventh was chrysolite, the eighth was beryl, the ninth was topaz, the tenth was chrysoprase, the eleventh was jacinth, and the twelfth was amethyst. 21Each of the twelve gates was a solid pearl. The streets of the city were made of pure gold, clear as crystal.

22I did not see a temple there. The Lord God All-Powerful and the Lamb were its temple. 23And the city did not need the sun or the moon. The glory of God was shining on it, and the Lamb was its light.

24Nations will walk by the light of that city, and kings will bring their riches there. 25Its gates are always open during the day, and night never comes. 26The glorious treasures of nations will be brought into the city. 27But nothing unworthy will be allowed to enter. No one who is dirty-minded or who tells lies will be there. Only those whose names are written in the Lamb's book of life[k] will be in the city.

22 The angel showed me a river that was crystal clear, and its waters gave life. The river came from the throne where God and the Lamb were seated. 2Then it flowed down the middle of the city's main street. On each side of the river are trees[l] that grow a different kind of fruit each month of the year. The fruit gives life, and the leaves are used as medicine to heal the nations.

3God's curse will no longer be on the people of that city. He and the Lamb will be seated there on their thrones, and its people will worship God 4and will see him face to face. God's name will be written on the foreheads of the people. 5Never again will night appear, and no one who lives there will ever need a lamp or the sun. The Lord God will be their light, and they will rule forever.

The Coming of Christ

6Then I was told:
These words are true and can be trusted. The Lord God controls

---

[k]*book of life*: See the note at 3.5.   [l]*trees*: The Greek has "tree," which is used in a collective sense of trees on both sides of the heavenly river.

the spirits of his prophets, and he is the one who sent his angel to show his servants what must happen right away. ⁷Remember, I am coming soon! God will bless everyone who pays attention to what this book tells about the future.

⁸My name is John, and I am the one who heard and saw these things. Then after I had heard and seen all this, I kneeled down and began to worship at the feet of the angel who had shown it to me.

⁹But the angel said,

Don't do that! I am a servant, just like you. I am the same as a follower or a prophet or anyone else who obeys what is written in this book. God is the one you should worship.

¹⁰Don't keep the prophecies in this book a secret. These things will happen soon.

¹¹Evil people will keep on being evil, and everyone who is dirty-minded will still be dirty-minded. But good people will keep on doing right, and God's people will always be holy.

¹²Then I was told:

I am coming soon! And when I come, I will reward everyone for what they have done. ¹³I am Alpha and Omega,ᵐ the first and the last, the beginning and the end.

¹⁴God will bless all who have washed their robes. They will each have the right to eat fruit from the tree that gives life, and they can enter the gates of the city. ¹⁵But outside the city will be dogs, witches, immoral people, murderers, idol worshipers, and everyone who loves to tell lies and do wrong.

¹⁶I am Jesus! And I am the one who sent my angel to tell all of you these things for the churches. I am David's Great Descendant,ⁿ and I am also the bright morning star.ᵒ

¹⁷The Spirit and the bride say, "Come!"

Everyone who hears thisᵖ should say, "Come!"

If you are thirsty, come! If you want life-giving water, come and take it. It's free!

¹⁸Here is my warning for everyone who hears the prophecies in this book:

If you add anything to them, God will make you suffer all the terrible troubles written in this book. ¹⁹If you take anything away from these prophecies, God will not let you have part in the life-giving tree and in the holy city described in this book.

²⁰The one who has spoken these things says, "I am coming soon!"

So, Lord Jesus, please come soon!

²¹I pray that the Lord Jesus will be kind to all of you.

ᵐ*Alpha and Omega*: See the note at 1.8.   ⁿ*David's Great Descendant*: See the note at 5.5.
ᵒ*the bright morning star*: Probably thought of as the brightest star. See 2.27,28.   ᵖ*who hears this*: The reading of the book of Revelation in a service of worship.

Word List

Maps

Word List

Aaron The brother of Moses. Only he and his descendants were to serve as priests and offer sacrifices for the people of Israel.

Abel The second son of Adam and Eve and the younger brother of Cain, who killed him, after God accepted Abel's offering and refused Cain's.

Abijah A descendant of Aaron. King David divided the priests into twenty-four groups, and Abijah was head of the eighth group.

Abimelech The Philistine king of Gath when David escaped from there by pretending to be crazy. See the title of Psalm 34. He is called Achish in 1 Samuel 21.10—22.1.

Abraham The first great ancestor of the people of Israel. He was the husband of Sarah and the father of Isaac. Abraham put his faith in God, and God promised to bless everyone on earth because of Abraham.

Adam The first man and the husband of Eve.

Agrippa (1) Herod Agrippa was king of Judea A.D. 41–44 and mistreated Christians (Acts 12.1–5). (2) Agrippa II was the son of Herod Agrippa and ruled Judea A.D. 44–53. He and his sister Bernice listened to Paul defend himself (Acts 25.13–26, 32).

Agur, Son of Jakeh A wise man, otherwise unknown. Agur wrote some of the proverbs. See Proberbs 30.1.

Ahimelech A priest at Nob who gave food and a sword to David when he fled from Saul. See the title of Psalm 52.

aloes A sweet-smelling spice that was mixed with myrrh and used as a perfume.

altar A raised structure where sacrifices and offerings were presented to God or gods. Altars could be made of rocks, packed earth, metal or pottery.

amen A Hebrew word used after a prayer or a blessing and meaning, "Let it be that way."

ancestor Someone born one or more generations earlier in a family line, such as a grandparent or great-grandparent.

angel A supernatural being who tells God's messages or protects God's people.

Antipas The father of Herod the Great and ruler of Judea 55–43 B.C. He was also known as Antipater.

apostle A person chosen by Christ to take his message to others.

Aram-naharaim A territory in northern Mesopotamia. The name means Arameans from the land of the Two Rivers. See the title of Psalm 60.

Aram-zobah An Aramean kingdom north of Damascus. See the title of Psalm 60 and 2 Samuel 8.3–13.

Aramaic A language closely related to Hebrew. It was spoken by many Jews including Jesus during New Testament times.

Asaph One of David's musicians. He wrote many psalms and also sang at the dedication of Solomon's temple. See the titles of Psalms 50 and 73–83.

Asia A Roman province in what is today modern Turkey.

Augustus This is the title meaning "honored" that the Romans gave to Octavian when he began ruling the Roman world in 27 B.C. He was Emperor when Jesus was born (Luke 2.1).

Babylon A large city in south-central Mesopotamia, the capital of the kingdom of Babylonia. The Babylonians defeated the southern kingdom of Judah in the sixth century B.C. and forced many of its people to live in Babylonia.

barley A grain something like wheat and used to make bread.

Bashan Flatlands and wooded hills in southern Syria, northeast of Lake Galilee. It was known for its fat cattle and fine grain. See Psalm 68.15, 16.

Benjamin One of the tribes of Israel. It occupied land between Bethel and Jerusalem. The people of this tribe descended from Benjamin, the younger of Jacob and

Rachel's two sons. When the ten northern tribes of Israel broke away following the death of Solomon, only the tribes of Benjamin and Judah were left to form the southern kingdom.

Cain   The first son of Adam and Eve and the brother of Abel.

Christ   A Greek word meaning "the Chosen One" and used to translate the Hebrew word "Messiah." It is used in the New Testament both as a title and a name for Jesus.

circumcise   To cut off the foreskin from the male organ. This is done for Jewish boys as part of a religious ceremony eight days after they are born to show that they belong to God's people. God's command to Abraham (Genesis 17.9–14) was to circumcise all males on the eighth day. Jesus' circumcision on the eighth day is reported in Luke 2.21.

citizen   A person who is given special rights and privileges by a nation or state. In return, a citizen was expected to be loyal to that nation or state.

commandments   God's rules for his people to live by.

council   A leading group of Jewish men who were allowed by the Roman government to meet and make certain decisions for their people.

cumin   A plant with small seeds used for seasoning food.

David   The most famous ancestor of the Jewish people and the most powerful king Israel ever had. They hoped that one of his descendants would always be their king.

Day of Atonement   The one day each year (the tenth day after the Jewish new year's day in the fall) when the high priest went into the most holy part of the temple and sprinkled some of the blood of a sacrificed bull on the sacred chest. This was done so that the people's sins would be forgiven. This holy day is called Yom Kippur in Hebrew.

demons and *evil spirits*   Supernatural beings that do harmful things to people and sometimes cause them to do bad things. In the New Testament they are sometimes called "unclean spirits," because people under their power were thought to be unclean and unfit to worship God.

descendant   Someone born one or more generations later in a family line, such as a grandchild or great-grandchild.

devil   The chief of the demons and evil spirits, also known as "Satan."

disciple   Someone who was a follower of Jesus and learned from him.

Doeg of Edom   An Edomite who worked for King Saul as the head of his shepherds. He was known to be ruthless and conniving. See the title of Psalm 52 and 1 Samuel 21–22.

Edom   A kingdom south of the Dead Sea as far as the Gulf of Aqaba. The Edomites descended from Esau, the twin brother of Jacob.

Elijah   A prophet who spoke for God in the ninth century B.C. Many Jews in later centuries thought Elijah would return to get things ready for the coming of the Lord.

elders   Men whose age and wisdom made them respected leaders.

Emperor   The ruler who lived in the city of Rome and governed all the land around the Mediterranean Sea.

Ephraim   One of the most important tribes of northern Israel. It occupied the land north of Benjamin and south of Manasseh. The people of this tribe descended from Ephraim, Joseph's second son.

Epicureans   People who followed the teachings of a man named Epicurus, who taught that happiness should be a person's main goal in life.

eternal life   Life that is the gift of God and never ends.

Ethan the Ezrahite   One of David's musicians. See the title of Psalm 89.

Ethiopia   The extensive territory south of Egypt called Cush in Hebrew, traditionally translated as Ethiopia. In Bible times it included within its borders most of modern Sudan and present day Ethiopia.

evil spirits   See "demons."

exile   The time in Jewish history (597–539 B.C.) when the Babylonians took away most of the people of Jerusalem and Judah as prisoners of war and made them live in Babylonia.

Feast of Thin Bread   The days after Passover when Jews eat a kind of thin, flat bread made without yeast to remember how God freed the people of Israel from slavery in Egypt and give them a fresh start.

Felix The Roman governor of Judea A.D. 52–60, who listened to Paul speak and kept him in jail.

Festival of Shelters This festival celebrates the period of forty years when the people of Israel walked through the desert and lived in small shelters. This happy celebration takes place each year in connection with the fall harvest season. Its name in Hebrew is Sukkoth.

Festus The Roman governor after Felix, who sent Paul to stand trial in Rome.

Gath One of the five major Philistine towns on the coastal plain of southern Palestine.

Generation One way of describing a group of people who live during the same period of time. The time of one generation is often understood to be about forty years. See Psalm 95.10.

Gentile Someone who is not a Jew.

Glory The magnificence of God's presence that inspires awe and worship.

God's kingdom God's rule over people, both in this life and in the next.

God's Law God's rules for his people to live by. They are found in the Old Testament, especially in the first five books.

God's Tent The tent where the people of Israel worshiped God before the temple was built.

Greek The language in which the New Testament was written.

Hagar A personal servant of Sarah, the wife of Abraham. When Sarah could not have any children, she followed the ancient custom of letting her husband have a child by Hagar, her servant woman. The boy's name was Ishmael.

Hebrew The language used by the people of Israel and for the writing of most of the Old Testament.

Heman the Ezrahite One of David's musicians. See the title of Psalm 88.

Hermes The Greek god of skillful speaking and the messenger of the other Greek gods.

Herod (1) Herod the Great was the king of all Palestine 37–4 B.C. He ruled Judea at the time Jesus was born. (2) Herod Antipas was the son of Herod the Great and the ruler of Galilee 4 B.C.–A.D. 39, during the time of John the Baptist and Jesus. (3) Herod Agrippa I, the grandson of Herod the Great, ruled Palestine A.D. 41–44.

Hezekiah King of Judah during the Assyrian attack on Jerusalem in 701 B.C., known for his loyalty to the LORD.

high priest See "priest."

Holy One A name for the Savior that God had promised to send. See "Savior."

hyssop A bush with bunches of small, white flowers. A bunch of hyssop was used for sprinkling blood and water in religious ceremonies. These ceremonies made people rightly prepared to worship God after having a bad skin disease. In a similar way, Psalm 51.7 mentions using hyssop in making a person rightly prepared to worship God by taking away sin.

incense A material that makes a sweet smell when burned and is used in the worship of God.

Isaac The second of the three great ancestors of the people of Israel. He was the son of Abraham and father of Jacob.

Isaiah A prophet from Jerusalem, who lived during the eighth century B.C. He served as a prophet during the rule of four different kings of Judah, between the years 740–700 B.C.

Israel See Jacob/Israel.

Jacob/Israel The third great ancestor of the people of Israel. He was the son of Isaac. His name was changed to Israel when he struggled with God at the Jabbok River.

Jeduthun One of David's musicians. See the titles of Psalms 39, 62, 77.

Joab The commander of David's army during most of his reign. See the title of Psalm 60.

Joseph The older son of Jacob and Rachel. He was the father of Ephraim and Manasseh, whose descendants formed two of the most important northern tribes.

Judah One of the tribes of Israel. It occupied the hill country between the Dead Sea and the coastal flatlands. The people of this tribe descended from Judah, the fourth son of Jacob and Leah. When the ten northern tribes of Israel broke away following the death of Solomon, only the tribes of Judah and Benjamin were left to form the southern kingdom.

judges   Leaders chosen by the Lord for the people of Israel after the time of Joshua and before the time of the kings.

Kadesh   A town in the desert of Paran southwest of the Dead Sea, also known as Kadesh-Barnea. It was near the southern border of Israel and the western border of Edom.

King Lemuel of Massa   King of Massa, a country possibly located in northern Arabia. King Lemuel wrote a few of the proverbs. See Proverbs 31.1.

Korah   A Levite family of the clan of Kohath whose people formed one of the major groups of temple singers. The Korahites were also known as temple gatekeepers (1 Chronicles 9.19) and temple bakers (1 Chronicles 9.31).

Law and the Prophets   The sacred writings of the Jews in Jesus' day (the first two of the three sections of the Old Testament).

Law of Moses and *Law of the Lord*   Usually refers to the first five books of the Old Testament, but sometimes to the entire Old Testament.

Leviathan   A legendary sea monster representing revolt and evil, also known from Canaanite writings. Psalm 74.14 celebrates its defeat by God.

Levite   A member of the tribe of Levi, from which priests were chosen. Men from this tribe who were not priests helped with the work in the temple.

Lord   The word "Lord" in capital letters stands for the Hebrew consonants *YHWH,* the personal names of God. The word "Lord" represents the Hebrew term *Adonai,* the general word for "Lord." By late Old Testament times Jews considered God's personal name too holy to be pronounced. So they said *Adonai,* "Lord," whenever they read the Hebrew consonants *YHWH.* When the Jewish scribes first translated the Hebrew Scriptures into ancient Greek, they translated the personal name of God as *Kurios,* "Lord." Since then most translations, including the *Contemporary English Version,* have followed the Jewish example and avoided using the personal name of God.

Manasseh   One of the most important tribes of northern Israel. It occupied two areas of land. One was east of the Jordan River, from the Jabbok River north to include all of Bashan. The other was on the west side of the Jordan River and went all the way to the Mediterranean Sea. Its northern boundary began a few miles south of Lake Galilee and went as far south as the border with Ephraim. The people of this tribe descended from Manasseh, Joseph's first son.

Messiah   A Hebrew word meaning "the Chosen One." See "Christ."

mint   A garden plant used for seasoning and medicine.

Moab   A country east of the Dead Sea. Its people descended from Moab, the son of Lot, who was Abraham's nephew.

Moses   The leader of the people of Israel when God rescued them from Egypt.

Mt. Hermon   One of the highest mountains in the Near East, with an elevation of 9,230 feet. Located about 45 miles north of Lake Galilee, its three peaks tower over the upper Jordan River valley. In Hebrew the name means "sacred" or "forbidden."

Mt. Lebanon   A mountain range that stretches about 100 miles north and south along the coast of Phoenicia. In Hebrew the name means "white," and it was known for its white peaks and cedar forests.

Mt. Mizar   Probably a name for one of the lesser peaks of Mt. Hermon. Possibly a way of referring to the small size of Mt. Zion. In Hebrew the name means "small." See Psalm 42.6.

myrrh   A valuable sweet-smelling powder used in perfume.

Naphtali   One of the tribes of Israel. Its people descended from Naphtali, the second son of Jacob and Bilhah. The tribe occupied land north and west of Lake Galilee.

Nazarenes   A name that was sometimes used for the followers of Jesus, who came from the small town of Nazareth.

Noah   When God destroyed the world by a flood, Noah and his family were kept safe in a big boat that God had told him to build.

paradise   The place where God's people go when they die, often understood as another name for heaven.

Passover   A day each year in the spring when Jews celebrate the time God rescued them from slavery in Egypt.

Pentecost   A Jewish festival fifty days

after Passover to celebrate the wheat harvest.

Pharisees A large group of Jews who thought they could best serve God by strictly obeying the laws of the Old Testament as well as their own teachings.

Philistia The fertile strip of land along the Mediterranean coast controlled by the Philistine people. This land began at the Brook of Egypt, below Gaza in the south, and ended at the town of Joppa in the north. Philistia was often at war with Israel.

Phoenicia The territory along the Mediterranean Sea controlled by the cities of Tyre, Sidon, Arvad and Byblos. The coast of modern Lebanon covers about the same area.

pit or **deep pit** The place of punishment for demons and evil spirits.

priest A man who led the worship in the temple and offered sacrifices. Some of the more important priests were called "chief priests," and the most important priest was called the "high priest."

Promised One A title for the Savior that God promised to send. See "Savior."

prophesy See "prophet."

Prophet A person who delivers a message from God to another person or to a group. Often a prophet's message tells what will happen in the future. To speak as a prophet is thus to "prophesy."

Proverb A wise saying that is short and easy to remember.

Psalm A Hebrew poem that could be used as a song or a prayer. Psalms could be prayed by individuals or sung by groups in worship of God. Some of the psalms thank and praise God. Others ask God to take away sins or to give protection, comfort, vengeance or mercy.

rue A garden plant used for seasoning and medicine.

Sabbath The seventh day of the week when Jews worship and do not work, in obedience to the commandment.

Sacrifice/Offering Gifts to God of certain animals, grains, fruits, and sweet-smelling spices. Israelites offered sacrifices to give thanks to God, to beg for forgiveness, to make a payment for a wrong, or to ask for God's blessing. Some sacrifices were completely burned on the altar. In other sacrifices, a portion was offered to the

LORD and the remaining portions were eaten by the priests or ordinary people.

Sadducees A small and powerful group of Jews who were closely connected with the high priests and who accepted only the first five books of the Old Testament as their Bible. They also did not believe in life after death.

Samaria A district between Judea and Galilee. The people of Samaria, called Samaritans, worshiped God differently from the Jews and did not get along with them.

Sarah The wife of Abraham and the mother of Isaac. When she was very old, God promised her that she would have a son.

Satan See "devil."

save To rescue people from the power of evil, to give them new life, and to place them under God's care. See "Savior."

Savior The one who rescues people from the power of evil, gives them new life, and places them under God's care. See "save."

Scriptures The sacred writings known as the Old Testament. These were first written in Hebrew and Aramaic, then translated into Greek about two centuries before the birth of Jesus. This Greek translation, known as the Septuagint, was used both by Jews and Christians in the first century.

Sin Turning away from God and disobeying the teachings of God.

Solomon One of King David's sons. After David's death, Solomon took his place as king and became widely known for his wisdom. He wrote many of the proverbs and two of the psalms. See Proverbs 10.1 and 25.1; Psalms 72 and 127.

Son of Man A name often used by Jesus to refer to himself. It is also found in the book of Daniel and refers to the one to whom God has given the power to rule.

Stoics Followers of a man named Zeno, who believed that nature was controlled by the gods and who taught that people should learn self-control.

taxes and **tax collectors** Special fees collected by rulers, usually part of the value of a citizen's crop, property, or income. There were also market taxes to be paid, and customs taxes were collected at ports and border crossings. The wealthy Zacchaeus (Luke 19.1–10) was a tax collector who collected taxes at a border crossing near Jericho. Jews hired by the Roman government to collect taxes from other Jews were hated by their own people.

temple   A building used as a place of worship. The Jewish temple was in Jerusalem.

Temple Festival   In 165 B.C. the Jewish people recaptured the Jerusalem temple from their enemies and made it fit for worship again. They celebrate this event in December of each year by a festival which they call "dedication" (Hanukkah). In the New Testament it is mentioned only in John 10.22.

Theophilus   The name means "someone God loves" and is found only in Luke 1.3 and Acts 1.1. Nothing else is known about him.

Way   In the book of Acts the Christian religion is sometimes called "the Way" or "the Way of the Lord" or "God's Way."

Wisdom   The cleverness, common sense, and practical skill needed to solve the everyday problems of life. Wisdom is sometimes pictured as a wise woman who invites people to use good judgment. In Proverbs 8, Wisdom is pictured as helping God plan and build the universe.

Zebulun   One of the tribes of Israel. It occupied land that was north of Manasseh and that stretched from the eastern end of Mt. Carmel to Mt. Tabor. The people of this tribe descended from Zebulun, the sixth son of Jacob and Leah.

Zeus   The chief god of the Greeks.

Zion   Another name for Jerusalem. It can also refer to the hill in Jerusalem where the temple was built.

Ziph   A town in the hill country of southern Judah where David hid while running away from King Saul. See the title of Psalm 54 and 1 Samuel 23.19; 26.1.

PALESTINE IN THE TIME OF JESUS

Miles 0 40
Kms 0 40

Sidon
Zarephath
Tyre
PHOENICIA
LEBANON MTS.
SYRIA
Abila
ABILENE
Damascus
MT. HERMON
Caesarea Philippi

MEDITERRANEAN
SEA
Ptolemais
MT. CARMEL
Caesarea

GALILEE
Chorazin
Capernaum
Bethsaida
Magadan
Lake
Cana
Tiberias
Galilee
Nazareth
MT. TABOR
Nain
Gadara
DECAPOLIS

Salim
SAMARIA
Aenon
Samaria
MT. EBAL
MT. GERIZIM
Sychar
Gerasa

Joppa
Jordan River
PEREA
Arimathea?
Ephraim
Jericho
Emmaus
Bethany
Azotus
Jerusalem
Qumran
Ascalon
JUDEA
Bethlehem
Gaza
Hebron
Dead
Sea
NABATEA
IDUMEA

© United Bible Societies, 1976

JERUSALEM IN THE TIME OF JESUS

| 0 | Yards | 400 |
| 0 | Meters | 400 |

Walls in the time of Jesus
Later walls built by Agrippa I
Present-day wall

Road to Caesarea

Early wall of unknown origin and date

Road to Joppa

Road to Jericho

Pool of Bethzatha

Antonia Fortress (Praetorium?)

Golgotha

Gethsemane

Sheep Gate

TEMPLE

Solomon's Porch

To Mount of Olives

Pool

Bridge

Portico

Tombs

Staircase

Royal Portico

Road to Bethany

Hasmonean Palace

Herod's Palace

Hippodrome

Street

Theater?

Herodian Street

Kidron Valley

Aqueduct

Gihon Spring

Tunnel

Pool

?

Pool of Siloam

Hinnom Valley

Enrogel Spring

Road to Bethlehem

Road to the Dead Sea

© United Bible Societies, 1976

Special Reader's Helps

Rejoice!

You have in your hands a message of hope and Good News. It is called the New Testament. It is made up of 27 different books. Each one tells of God's great love and how he has made it possible, through the death and resurrection of Jesus Christ, to unite every person to himself, so that anyone who desires it may discover spiritual guidance and joy.

You are invited to begin reading this Good News today. The section of special helps provided here will help you begin this rewarding journey of discovery.

- *What's in the New Testament* gives you a brief summary of every book in the New Testament along with a handy chart.
- *How to Read the New Testament* provides simple suggestions on how to read the New Testament devotionally and to keep notes on the many lessons you'll learn.
- *Read through the New Testament* is a reading plan that suggests a simple way to read everything the New Testament has to say about Jesus' life, death and resurrection and the spread of the new religion which became known as Christianity.
- *Famous Passages of the New Testament* helps you to quickly locate passages you've heard time and again, but may never have read for yourself.
- *Finding Help in the New Testament* leads you to those passages that can help you when you're facing a difficult problem or special challenge.
- *What the New Testament Says about God's Forgiveness* will lead you to places in the New Testament where you can learn how much God loves each one of us and what he has done to put us right with himself.

So begin your journey of discovery today! Use any one of these special reader's helps to get you started on a daily habit of Scripture reading. And when you finish the New Testament, read the Old Testament, which you will find in any edition of the Bible. Discover for yourself the joy and hope God's Holy Scriptures have to offer.

The Bible

The New Testament is part of a larger book called the Bible. The word "Bible" comes from the Greek word *biblia*, which means "books." So the Bible is really a collection or library of many books. These books are divided into two main parts, the Old Testament and the New Testament.

Old Testament

The Old Testament was written in Hebrew and tells the history of the people of Israel. This history is based on their faith in the God of Israel and on their religious life as the people of God. The authors of these books wrote about what God had done for them as a people and how they were to worship and obey God in return. Because most of the authors of the books of the New Testament were Jewish, they were very familiar with the Hebrew Scriptures. The following chart shows the different groups of books that make up the Old Testament. After reading the New Testament you may want to obtain a copy of the Bible so that you can also read these important books.

The Law
Genesis, Exodus, Leviticus, Numbers, Deuteronomy

History
Joshua, Judges, Ruth, 1 Samuel, 2 Samuel, 1 Kings, 2 Kings, 1 Chronicles, 2 Chronicles, Ezra, Nehemiah, Esther

Poetry and Wisdom
Job, Psalms, Proverbs, Ecclesiastes, Song of Songs

Major Prophets
Isaiah, Jeremiah, Lamentations, Ezekiel, Daniel

Minor Prophets
Hosea, Joel, Amos, Obadiah, Jonah, Micah, Nahum, Habakkuk, Zephaniah, Haggai, Zechariah, Malachi

New Testament

The books of the New Testament were written by the followers of Jesus Christ. These followers wanted others to know the Good News about Jesus Christ and the possibility of a "new" life available to them through his death and resurrection. The following chart shows the different groups of books that make up the New Testament. Although scholarly opinion has varied, Paul has traditionally been identified as the author of the letters indicated below.

The Gospels
Matthew, Mark, Luke, John

Paul's Letters
Romans, 1 Corinthians, 2 Corinthians, Galatians, Ephesians, Philippians, Colossians, 1 Thessalonians, 2 Thessalonians, 1 Timothy, 2 Timothy, Titus, Philemon

History
Acts

General Letters
Hebrews, James, 1 Peter, 2 Peter, 1 John, 2 John, 3 John, Jude

Prophecy
Revelation

What's in the New Testament

The following are summaries of each book of the New Testament. It will be obvious from how brief the descriptions are that they are not complete. They should, however, serve as a quick and handy guide to the content of the New Testament. The grouping of the books by sections follows the divisions of the books as they are organized in the English Bible.

The Gospels

MATTHEW: This Gospel includes many Old Testament quotations, thus appealing to a Jewish audience and presenting Jesus as the Messiah promised in the Hebrew Scriptures. Matthew told the story of Jesus from birth to resurrection and placed emphasis on his teaching.

MARK: Mark wrote a short, action-packed Gospel. He emphasized Jesus' miracles and his life of suffering. His aim was to deepen the faith and commitment of the believers in the community to which he wrote.

LUKE: In this Gospel, the availability of salvation for all people is emphasized. Luke proclaimed this message by showing Jesus' involvement with people who are poor, needy, and on the fringes of society.

JOHN: The Gospel of John stands apart from the others. John organized his message around seven signs that point to Jesus as the Son of God. His writing style is reflective and filled with striking images.

History

ACTS: When Jesus left his disciples, the Holy Spirit came to abide with them. Written by Luke as the sequel to his Gospel, Acts records key events in the history of the work of the early Christian Church to spread the Gospel throughout the Mediterranean world.

Paul's Letters

ROMANS: In this important letter, Paul wrote to the Romans about life in the Spirit, which is given to believers in Christ through faith. The apostle tells them about God's great kindness and declares that because of Jesus Christ, God accepts us and sets us free from our sins.

1 CORINTHIANS: This letter deals with the problems the church in Corinth was experiencing: dissension, immorality, public worship, and confusion about spiritual gifts.

1 CORINTHIANS: In this letter, Paul wrote about his relationship with the church of Corinth and the effects of certain false apostles on his ministry.

GALATIANS: This letter addresses freedom from the law through Christ. Paul declares that it is by faith that all who believe are put right with God.

EPHESIANS: A central theme to this letter is that God's eternal purpose is to bring together from many nations and peoples the universal Church of Jesus Christ.

PHILIPPIANS: This letter emphasizes the joy found in any situation when a person believes in Christ. Paul wrote it while in prison.

COLOSSIANS: In this letter Paul tells the people of Colossae to make Christ the center of their faith and to put aside their superstitions.

1 THESSALONIANS: In this letter Paul gives advice to the people of Thessalonica concerning Christ's return.

2 THESSALONIANS: This letter discusses the same topics as the first. Paul teaches the people a way to be ready for the Lord.

1 TIMOTHY: This letter served as a guide for Timothy, a young leader in the church. It contains advice about worship, ministry, and relationships within the church.

2 TIMOTHY: This is Paul's last letter. In it he offers a final challenge to his co-worker.

TITUS: Titus was ministering in Crete. In this letter, Paul gave him advice on how to help Christians follow Christ.

PHILEMON: In this letter, Philemon is urged to forgive his runaway slave, Onesimus, and accept him as a friend in Christ.

General Letters

HEBREWS: The letter to the Hebrews challenges new Christians to move beyond their traditional rituals and ceremonies and believe that Christ has fulfilled them all.

JAMES: James advises putting beliefs into practice and offers practical ways for Christians to live out their faith.

1 PETER: This letter was written to comfort early Christians who were being persecuted for their faith.

2 PETER: In this letter Peter warns against false teachers and urges Christians to stay loyal to God.

1 JOHN: This letter explains basic truths about the Christian life, with emphasis on the command to love one another.

2 JOHN: This letter, addressed to "the dear Lady and to her children," warns against false teachers.

3 JOHN: In contrast to 2 John, this letter states the need to welcome people who preach Christ.

JUDE: Jude warns against the influence of evil ones outside the fellowship of believers.

Prophecy

REVELATION: This book was written to encourage persecuted believers and affirm their faith that God will care for them. Using visions and symbols, the writer illustrates the triumph of good over evil and the creation of a new heaven and new earth.

How to Read the New Testament

Set aside time each day to read from your New Testament. Try to make it the same time each day. Be realistic. Commit yourself only to as much time as you honestly feel that you can stick to on an ongoing basis. Before you begin reading ask for God's guidance and blessing. Some people have found that keeping a daily notebook is helpful. Use the following steps to get the most out of your daily Scripture reading:

1. Select a passage of Scripture (perhaps one from the *Read through the New Testament* section that follows). It is probably best not to try to read more than one to three chapters at one sitting.

2. Examine its context:

   a. What kind of book is it drawn from? A biographical book such as one of the Gospel accounts of Jesus' life; a long historical book, such as *The Acts of the Apostles*; a brief letter to a person (*The Letters of Paul to Timothy*) or to a specific church (*The Letters of Paul to the Corinthians*).

   b. What is the overall purpose/intent of this book? (Do not do lengthy research, but feel free to read the opening and closing paragraphs as well as section headings.)

   c. What occurs or is discussed in the passages immediately preceding and following the passage you chose?

3. Read the passage quickly for sense.

4. Identify key words or phrases. Are there words or thoughts that are repeated throughout the passage? Are any cause and effect relationships established? (These are often signaled by words like *if* and *then, therefore, because, since,* and *so*.) Are any comparisons made or similarities pointed out? Are any two people, things or concepts contrasted?

5. Read the passage again and ask yourself what is the intent or purpose of the passage. Try to find out what the author is saying. Be honest; don't just look for what you want to hear. The New Testament has many strong messages that can change lives!

6. What do you learn about God from this passage? What do you learn about human nature? Ask yourself how this message applies to you. Is there anything you need to change in your life in order to be a more faithful child of God or more loving toward your neighbor? Ask for God's help in making this change.

7. Re-read the passage one more time. Is there one verse you would like to commit to memory? Why not write it on an index card and carry it with you throughout the day as a study aid?

8. Thank God for what he has shown you, and ask for his help as you seek to apply this lesson in your life.

9. Share what you have learned with someone else.

Read through the New Testament

The books of the New Testament were written by the followers of Jesus Christ. The reading plan given here will help you to learn more about Jesus' life and ministry and about what his death and resurrection means to his followers. This Good News was so important to Jesus' first followers that they traveled great distances and took great risks to share it with others. They also wrote many letters to encourage one another to hold fast to their faith in Jesus.

The Life of Jesus

The New Testament gives four accounts of Jesus' life. They are called Gospels, which means "good news." They tell of his birth, baptism, ministry of teaching and healing, death and resurrection. Although similar in many ways, these books offer four different looks at the life of Jesus. Choose one of the following reading plans to learn more about Jesus and then go on to read the rest of the New Testament.

Plan A
Read:
  Mark 1-16
  John 1-21
  Luke 1-24
  Matthew 1-28

Plan B
Read:
The birth of Jesus
  Matthew 1, 2; Luke 1, 2
The public ministry of Jesus
  Matthew 3-20; Mark 1-10; Luke 3.1-19.27; John 1-12
The last days of Jesus' life
  Matthew 21-27; Mark 11-15; Luke 19.28-23.56; John 13-19
The resurrection of Jesus
  Matthew 28; Mark 16; Luke 24; John 20-21

The Early Church

Jesus speaks to his followers and is taken up to heaven
  Acts 1.1-11
The beginning of the Christian movement in Jerusalem
  Acts 1.12-8.3
The spread of the Christian movement into Judea and Samaria
  Acts 8.4-12.25

The Ministry of Paul

Paul's first missionary journey
  Acts 13, 14
An important conference in Jerusalem
  Acts 15.1-35
  Also read what Paul had to say about the issues discussed at this conference: Galatians.

Paul's second missionary journey
Acts 15.36-18.22
- After Acts 16.5 read 1 Timothy and 2 Timothy to learn more about the young man Timothy who was to become an important assistant to Paul.
- After Acts 18.17 read 1 Thessalonians and 2 Thessalonians.

Paul's third missionary journey
Acts 18.23-21.16
- After Acts 19.41 read 1 Corinthians, Philippians and Philemon.
- After Acts 20.6 read 2 Corinthians and Titus.
- After Acts 20.38 read Romans.

Paul's imprisonments in Jerusalem, Caesarea and Rome
Acts 21.17-28.31
- After Acts 28.31 read Ephesians and Colossians.

The Spread of Christianity under Roman Persecution

Read:
Hebrews
James
1 Peter
2 Peter
Jude
1 John
2 John
3 John
Revelation

How to look up a New Testament reference.

Every verse in this New Testament is marked by its own *verse number*. To find any one of the passages listed in these reader's helps, you need to find the book, the chapter in the book, and the verse or verses within that chapter. The chapter number immediately follows the name of the book. This is followed by a period (.) which is followed by the number or range of numbers for the verses you seek. For example: 1 Corinthians 12.1-11 is the First Letter of Paul to the Corinthians, chapter twelve, verses one through eleven.

Famous Passages from the New Testament

THE LIFE OF JESUS

The Birth of Jesus
Matthew 1.18-2.15; Luke 2.1-20

Jesus Is Named and Presented
in the Temple
Luke 2.21-40

The Young Jesus
Luke 2.41-52

The Baptism of Jesus
Matthew 3; Mark 1.1-11; Luke 3.21, 22

The Temptation of Jesus
Matthew 4.1-11; Mark 1.12, 13;
Luke 4.1-13

Jesus Calls His First Disciples
Matthew 4.18-22; Mark 1.16-20;
Luke 5.1-11

Jesus Chooses Twelve Apostles
Matthew 10.1-4; Mark 3.13-19;
Luke 6.12-16

The Transfiguration of Jesus
Matthew 17.1-13; Mark 9.2-13

JESUS' DEATH AND RESURRECTION

Jesus' Entry into Jerusalem
Matthew 21.1-11; Mark 11.1-11;
Luke 19.29-44; John 12.12-19

The Last Supper of Jesus
Matthew 26.17-35; Mark 14.12-26;
Luke 22.1-38

Jesus Prays in Gethsemane
Matthew 26.36-46; Mark 14.32-42;
Luke 22.39-46

Jesus' Trial and Crucifixion
Matthew 26.47-27.66; Mark 14.43-15.47;
Luke 22.47-23.56; John 18; 19

The Resurrection of Jesus
Matthew 28.1-10; Mark 16;
Luke 24.1-12; John 20

The Great Commission
Matthew 28.16-20

The Ascension of Jesus
Luke 24.50-53; Acts 1.1-12

MIRACLES AND HEALINGS OF JESUS

Jesus Turns Water into Wine
John 2.1-11

Jesus Feeds Many People
Matthew 14.13-21; Mark 6.30-44;
Luke 9.10-17; John 6.1-15;
Matthew 15.32-39; Mark 8.1-10

Jesus Calms a Storm
Matthew 8.23-27; Mark 4.35-41;
Luke 8.22-25

The Great Catch of Fish
Luke 5.1-11

Jesus Walks on Water
Matthew 14.22-33; Mark 6.45-52;
John 6.16-21

Jesus Heals People with
Skin Diseases
Matthew 8.1-4; Mark 1.40-45;
Luke 5.12-16; Luke 17.11-19

Jesus Casts Out Demons
Matthew 8.28-34; Mark 5.1-20;
Luke 8.26-39; Matthew 12.22-37;
Mark 3.20-30; Luke 11.14-23;
Matthew 17.14-21; Mark 9.14-29;
Luke 9.37-43; Mark 1.21-28;
Luke 4.31-37

Jesus Heals the Blind
Matthew 9.27-31; Matthew 20.29-34;
Mark 10.46-52; Luke 18.35-43

Jesus Heals a Deaf Man
Mark 7.31-37

Jesus Heals the Paralyzed and Crippled
Matthew 12.9-14; Mark 3.1-6;
Luke 6.6-11; John 5.1-8;
Luke 14.1-6; Matthew 9.1-8;
Mark 2.1-12; Luke 5.17-26

Jesus Heals Many Women
Matthew 9.18-26; Mark 5.21-43;
Luke 8.1-3; Luke 8.40-56;
Luke 13.10-17; Matthew 15.21-28;
Mark 7.24-30

Jesus Heals the Centurion's Servant
Matthew 8.5-13; Luke 7.1-10

Jesus Heals Peter's Mother-in-law
Matthew 8.14, 15; Mark 1.29-31;
Luke 4.38, 39

Jesus Heals an Official's Son
John 4.46-54

Jesus Revives an Official's Daughter
Matthew 9.18,19,23-26;
Mark 5.21-24,35-42; Luke 8.40-42,49-56

Jesus Raises the Dead
Luke 7.11-17; John 11.1-44

THE TEACHINGS AND PARABLES OF JESUS

The Sermon on the Mount
Matthew 5-7; Luke 6.20-49

The Beatitudes
Matthew 5.3-11; Luke 6.20-26

The Great Commandment
Matthew 22.37-39; Mark 12.29-31;
Luke 10.27

The Golden Rule
Matthew 7.12; Luke 6.31

The Grain of Mustard Seed
Matthew 13.31, 32; Mark 4.30-32;
Luke 13.18, 19

The Parable of the Sower
Matthew 13.1-23; Mark 4.1-20;
Luke 8.4-15

The Parable of the Growing Seed
Mark 4.26-29

Some Parables About the
Kingdom of Heaven
Matthew 13.24-52

The Parable of the Unforgiving Servant
Matthew 18.23-35

The Parable of the Workers
in the Vineyard
Matthew 20.1-16

The Parable of the Tenants
in the Vineyard
Matthew 21.33-46; Mark 12.1-11;
Luke 20.9-18

The Parable of the Wedding Feast
Matthew 22.1-14; Luke 14.15-24

The Parable of the Ten
Young Women (Virgins)
Matthew 25.1-13

The Parable of the Three
Servants and Their Coins
Matthew 25.14-30; Luke 19.11-27

The Parable of the Sheep and the Goats
Matthew 25.31-46

The Parable of the Good Samaritan
Luke 10.25-37

The Parable of the Shepherd
John 10.1-21

The Parable of the Rich Fool
Luke 12.16-21

The Parable of the Watchful Servants
Luke 12.35-48

The Parable of the Barren Fig Tree
Luke 13.6-9

The Parable of the Lost Sheep
Matthew 18.12-14; Luke 15.3-7

The Parable of the Lost Coin
Luke 15.8-10

The Parable of the Lost Son
Luke 15.11-32

The Parable of the Shrewd Manager
Luke 16.1-13

The Rich Man and Lazarus
Luke 16.19-31

The Parable of the Widow and the Judge
Luke 18.1-8

The Parable of the Pharisee and
the Tax Collector
Luke 18.9-14

OTHER NEW TESTAMENT STORIES

The Birth of John the Baptist
Luke 1.57-66

John the Baptist Is Executed
Matthew 14.1-12; Mark 6.14-29

Peter Receives the Keys of the Kingdom
Matthew 16.13-20

The Holy Spirit Comes on Pentecost
Acts 2

Stephen, the First Martyr
Acts 6.5-15; 7.54-60

Philip Baptizes the Ethiopian Official
Acts 8.26-39

The Conversion of Paul
Acts 9.1-31

Peter and Cornelius
Acts 10

Peter in Prison
Acts 12.1-19

The Baptism of Lydia
Acts 16.11-15

Paul in Prison
Acts 16.16-40

The Riot at Ephesus
Acts 19.23-41

Paul's Voyage to Rome
Acts 27; 28

What is a parable?

Parables are stories that use typical, everyday situations in order to teach important truths. Jesus used many parables to teach his followers about the Kingdom of God.

NEW TESTAMENT PRAYERS

The Lord's Prayer
Matthew 6.9-13
Jesus' Prayer in Gethsemane
Matthew 26.36-44
Jesus' Prayer for His Disciples
John 17
The Disciples' Prayer
Acts 4.24-31
Paul's Prayer for Believers
Ephesians 3.14-21

SPECIAL BLESSINGS FROM THE NEW TESTAMENT

Invocations and Openings
1 Corinthians 1.3; 1 Timothy 1.2;
2 John 3; Revelation 1.4-6
Dismissals and Closings
Romans 15.5,6,13; Romans 16.25-27;
2 Corinthians 13.13; Ephesians 6.23,24;
Philippians 4.7; Hebrews 13.20,21;
Jude 24,25

How to look up a New Testament reference.

Every verse in this New Testament is marked by its own *verse number*. To find any one of the passages listed in these reader's helps, you need to find the book, the chapter in the book, and the verse or verses within that chapter. The chapter number immediately follows the name of the book. This is followed by a period (.) which is followed by the number or range of numbers for the verses you seek. For example: 1 Corinthians 12.1-11 is the First Letter of Paul to the Corinthians, chapter twelve, verses one through eleven.

Finding Help in the New Testament

Help in Special Circumstances

Being a friend
Luke 10.25-37; John 15.11-17; Romans 16.1-2

Being a leader
1 Timothy 3.1-7; 2 Timothy 2.14-26; Titus 1.5-9

Caring for the aged and widowed
1 Timothy 5.3-8

Celebrating the birth/adoption of a child
Luke 18.15-17; John 16.16-22

Celebrating a graduation
Galatians 5.16-26; Philippians 4.4-9

Celebrating a marriage
Ephesians 5.21-33; Colossians 2.6-7

Celebrating a wedding anniversary
1 Corinthians 13

Controlling your temper
Galatians 5.16-26

Controlling your tongue
2 Thessalonians 2.16-17; James 3.1-12

Discovering God's will
Matthew 5.14-16; Luke 9.21-27; Romans 13.8-14; 2 Peter 1.3-9; 1 John 4.7-21

Encountering a cult
Matthew 7.15-20; 2 Peter 2; 1 John 4.1-6; Jude

Encountering peer pressure
Romans 12.1-2; Galatians 6.1-5; Ephesians 5.1-20

Entering college
Romans 8.1-17; 1 Corinthians 1.18-31

Entering military service
Ephesians 6.10-20; 2 Timothy 2.1-13

Experiencing the death of a loved one
John 11.25-27; John 14.1-7; Romans 8.31-39; Romans 14.7-9; 1 Thessalonians 4.13-18

Experiencing illness
Mark 1.29-34; Mark 6.53-56; James 5.14-16

Experiencing suffering and persecution
Matthew 5.3-12; John 15.18-16.4; Romans 8.18-30; 2 Corinthians 4.1-15; Hebrews 12.1-11; 1 Peter 4.12-19

Facing a difficult decision
Colossians 3.12-17

Facing a divorce
Matthew 19.1-9; Philippians 3.1-11

Facing homelessness
Luke 9.57-62; Revelation 21.1-4

Facing imprisonment
Matthew 25.31-46; Luke 4.16-21

Facing life alone
1 Corinthians 7.25-38; 1 Corinthians 12.1-31

Facing a natural disaster
Romans 8.31-39; 1 Peter 1.3-12

Facing a trial or lawsuit
Matthew 5.25-26; Luke 18.1-8

Losing your job
Luke 16.1-13; Philippians 4.10-13

Losing your property and possessions
Romans 8.18-39

Managing your time
Mark 13.32-37; Luke 21.34-36; 1 Timothy 4.11-16; Titus 3.8-14

Moving into a new home
John 14.1-7; Ephesians 3.14-21; Revelation 3.20,21

Overcoming addiction
2 Corinthians 5.16-21; Ephesians 4.22-24

Overcoming a grudge
Matthew 5.23-26; Luke 6.27-36; Ephesians 4.25-32

Overcoming prejudice
Matthew 7.1-5; Acts 10.34-36; Galatians 3.26-29; Ephesians 2.11-22; Colossians 3.5-11; James 2.1-13

Overcoming pride
Mark 9.33-37; Luke 14.7-11; Luke 18.9-14; Luke 22.24-27; Romans 12.14-16; 1 Corinthians 1.18-31; 2 Corinthians 12.1-10

Overcoming procrastination
Matthew 22.1-14; Matthew 25.1-13; 2 Corinthians 6.1-2

Raising children
Ephesians 6.4; Colossians 3.21

Respecting civil authorities
Mark 12.13-17; Romans 13.1-7; Titus 3.1-2; 1 Peter 2.13-17

Respecting parents
Ephesians 6.1-3; Colossians 3.20

Retiring from your job
Matthew 25.31-46; Romans 12.1-2; Philippians 3.12-21; 2 Peter 1.2

Seeking forgiveness
Matthew 6.14-15; Luke 15; Philemon; Hebrews 4.14-16; 1 John 1.5-10

Seeking God's help
Matthew 7.7-12

Seeking salvation
John 3.1-21; Romans 1.16-17; Romans 3.21-31; Romans 5.1-11; Romans 10.5-13; Ephesians 1.3-14; Ephesians 2.1-10

Seeking strength
Ephesians 6.10-20; 2 Thessalonians 2.16-17

Seeking truth
John 8.31-47; John 14.6-14; John 16.4b-15;
1 Timothy 2.1-7

Sharing your gifts
Luke 21.1-4; Acts 2.43-47; Acts 4.32-37;
Romans 12.9-13; 1 Corinthians 16.1-4;
2 Corinthians 8.1-15; 2 Corinthians 9.6-15

Starting a new job
Romans 12.3-11; 1 Thessalonians 5.12-18;
2 Thessalonians 3.6-13; 1 Peter 4.7-11

Understanding your relationship with God
John 15.1-17; Romans 5.1-11; Romans 8.1-17

Understanding your relationship with others
Matthew 18.15-17; Matthew 18.21-35;
Romans 14.13-23; Romans 15.1-16;
Galatians 6.1-10; Colossians 3.12-17;
1 John 4.7-12

Worrying about the future
1 Peter 1.3-5; Revelation 21.1-8

Worrying about money
Matthew 6.24-34; Luke 12.13-21;
1 Timothy 6.6-10

Experiencing Troublesome Feelings

Afraid?
Mark 4.35-41; Hebrews 13.5-6; 1 John 4.13-18

Afraid of death?
John 6.35-40; Romans 8.18-39;
1 Corinthians 15.35-57; 2 Corinthians 5.1-10;
2 Timothy 1.8-10

Angry?
Matthew 5.21-24; Romans 12.17-21;
Ephesians 4.26-32; James 1.19-21

Anxious? Worried?
Matthew 6.24-34; Matthew 10.26-31;
1 Peter 1.3-5; 1 Peter 5.7

Depressed?
John 3.14-17; Ephesians 3.14-21

Discouraged?
Romans 15.13; 2 Corinthians 4.16-18;
Philippians 4.10-13; Colossians 1.9-14;
Hebrews 6.9-12

Doubting your faith in God?
Matthew 7.7-12; Luke 17.5-6; John 20.24-31;
Romans 4.13-25; Hebrews 11; 1 John 5.13-15

Frustrated?
Matthew 7.13-14

Impatient?
Hebrews 6.13-20; James 5.7-11

Insecure? Lacking confidence?
Philippians 4.10-20; 1 John 3.19-24

Jealous?
James 3.13-18

Lonely?
John 14.15-31a

Overwhelmed? Experiencing stress?
Matthew 11.25-30; John 4.1-30;
2 Corinthians 6.3-10; Revelation 22.17

Rejected?
Matthew 9.9-13; Luke 4.16-30; John 15.18-16.4;
Ephesians 1.3-14; 1 Peter 2.1-10

Tempted?
Luke 4.1-13; Hebrews 2.11-18;
Hebrews 4.14-16; James 1.12-18

Tempted by sex?
1 Corinthians 6.12-20; Galatians 5.16-26

Tired? Weary?
Matthew 11.25-30; 2 Thessalonians 3.16;
Hebrews 4.1-11

Feeling useless? Inferior?
Galatians 1.11-24; Ephesians 4.1-16;
1 Peter 2.4-10

Vengeful?
Matthew 5.38-42; Romans 12.17-21

How to look up a New Testament reference.

Every verse in this New Testament is marked by its own *verse number*. To find any one of the passages listed in these reader's helps, you need to find the book, the chapter in the book, and the verse or verses within that chapter. The chapter number immediately follows the name of the book. This is followed by a period (.) which is followed by the number or range of numbers for the verses you seek. For example: 1 Corinthians 12.1-11 is the First Letter of Paul to the Corinthians, chapter twelve, verses one through eleven.

What the New Testament Says
about God's Forgiveness

Every person is separated from God because of sin.
> Romans 3.9-20
> Romans 5.12-21
> Romans 7.14-25

God has always sought to form a close relationship with people.
> Ephesians 1.3-14
> 1 Peter 1.1-10
> 1 John 3.1-10

God has reached out to people in a personal way by sending Jesus Christ.
> Colossians 1.15-23
> Romans 5.1-11
> 1 Peter 2.10-25
> John 3.1-21
> 2 Timothy 1.3-10
> Ephesians 2.1-10

God's forgiveness through Jesus Christ is available to every person.
> 1 John 1.5-10
> Romans 10.5-13
> Romans 8.31-39
> Romans 3.21-26

New life in Christ calls a person to live in a Christ-like way.
> Romans 6.1-14
> Matthew 20.20-28
> Ephesians 4.17-32
> Galatians 5.16-26
> 1 John 4.7-21
> Romans 12.1-21